Global Urban Heat Island Mitigation

Global Urban Heat Island Mitigation

Edited by

Ansar Khan

Department of Geography, Lalbaba College, University of Calcutta, India

Hashem Akbari

Department of Building, Civil, and Environmental Engineering,
Concordia University, Montreal, Quebec, Canada

Francesco Fiorito

Department of Civil, Environmental, Land, Building Engineering and Chemistry,
Polytechnic University of Bari, Italy;
Senior Visiting Fellow, University of New South Wales, Australia

Sk Mithun

Department of Geography, Haldia Government College, Vidyasagar University, India

Dev Niyogi

Department of Geological Sciences, Jackson School of Geosciences and
Department of Civil, Architectural, and Environmental Engineering,
The University of Texas at Austin, Texas, USA

ELSEVIER

Elsevier
Radarweg 29, PO Box 211, 1000 AE Amsterdam, Netherlands
The Boulevard, Langford Lane, Kidlington, Oxford OX5 1GB, United Kingdom
50 Hampshire Street, 5th Floor, Cambridge, MA 02139, United States

Notices
Knowledge and best practice in this field are constantly changing. As new research and experience broaden our understanding, changes in research methods, professional practices, or medical treatment may become necessary.

Practitioners and researchers must always rely on their own experience and knowledge in evaluating and using any information, methods, compounds, or experiments described herein. In using such information or methods they should be mindful of their own safety and the safety of others, including parties for whom they have a professional responsibility.

To the fullest extent of the law, neither the Publisher nor the authors, contributors, or editors, assume any liability for any injury and/or damage to persons or property as a matter of products liability, negligence or otherwise, or from any use or operation of any methods, products, instructions, or ideas contained in the material herein.

ISBN: 978-0-323-85539-6

For information on all Elsevier publications visit our website at
https://www.elsevier.com/books-and-journals

Publisher: Joseph P. Hayton
Acquisitions Editor: Kathryn Eryilmaz
Editorial Project Manager: Mica Ella Ortega
Production Project Manager: Swapna Srinivasan
Cover Designer: Vicky Pearson

Typeset by TNQ Technologies

Working together
to grow libraries in
developing countries

www.elsevier.com • www.bookaid.org

Contents

CHAPTER 10   StEMAIRF-BGI as a tool for UHI mitigation using land use planning and designing **177**

Mahua Mukherjee, Arjun Satheesh and Atul Kumar

CHAPTER 11   Urban heat island effect in India: assessment, impacts, and mitigation **199**

Manju Mohan, Shweta Bhati and Ankur Prabhat Sati

List of contributors

Luc Adolphe
LRA, Université de Toulouse, ENSA, Toulouse, France

Or Aleksandrowicz
Faculty of Architecture and Town Planning, Technion — Israel Institute of Technology, Technion City, Haifa, Israel

Lilly Rose Amirtham
Department of Architecture, School of Planning and Architecture, Vijayawada, India

Umberto Berardi
Faculty of Engineering and Architectural Science, Ryerson University, Toronto, ON, Canada

Saioa Etxebarria Berrizbeitia
Faculty of Mechanical Engineering, University of the Basque Country, Vitoria-Gasteiz, Spain

H.A. Bharath
Ranbir and Chitra Gupta School of Infrastructure Design and Management, Indian Institute of Technology Kharagpur, Kharagpur, West Bengal, India

Shweta Bhati
Centre for Atmospheric Sciences, Indian Institute of Technology Delhi, New Delhi, India

Meng Cai
School of Architecture, The Chinese University of Hong Kong, Hong Kong, PR China

Claudio Carrasco
Universidad de Valparaíso, Facultad de Ingeniería, Escuela de Ingeniería en Construcción, Valparaíso, Región de Valparaíso, Chile

C. Cartalis
Department of Environmental Physics — Meteorology, Department of Physics, National and Kapodistrian University of Athens, Panepistiopolis Zografou, Athens, Greece

Chiara Chiatti
CIRIAF — Interuniversity Research Center, University of Perugia, Perugia, Italy

Mohamed Dardir
Faculty of Engineering and Architectural Science, Ryerson University, Toronto, ON, Canada

Claudia Fabiani
CIRIAF — Interuniversity Research Center, University of Perugia, Perugia, Italy; Department of Engineering, University of Perugia, Perugia, Italy

Jeff Fahed
LMDC, Université de Toulouse, INSA, UPS, Toulouse, France

Zhiyu Fan
School of Urban Design, Wuhan University, Wuhan, China

Eulalia Jadraque Gago
Engineering Construction and Project Management, School of Civil Engineering, University of Granada, Granada, Spain

Sihang Gao
School of Urban Design, Wuhan University, Wuhan, China

Andrea Gatto
Wenzhou-Kean University, Wenzhou, Zhejiang, China; Natural Resources Institute, University of Greenwich, Chatham Maritime, United Kingdom

Stephane Ginestet
LMDC, Université de Toulouse, INSA, UPS, Toulouse, France

José Julio Guerra Macho
Grupo Termotecnia, Escuela Técnica Superior de Ingeniería, Universidad de Sevilla, Camino de los Descubrimientos S/N, Seville, Spain

Bo Huang
Institute of Space and Earth Information Science, The Chinese University of Hong Kong, Shatin, NT, China; Department of Geography and Resource Management, The Chinese University of Hong Kong, Shatin, NT, China

Elias Kinab
Lebanese University, Beirut, Lebanon

D. Kolokotsa
Chemical and Environmental Engineering School, Technical University of Crete, Kounoupidiana, Crete, Greece

Ioannis Kousis
CIRIAF — Interuniversity Research Center, University of Perugia, Perugia, Italy

Atul Kumar
Indian Institute of Technology Roorkee, Roorkee, Uttarakhand, India

Huimin Liu
School of Urban Design, Wuhan University, Wuhan, China

Manju Mohan
Centre for Atmospheric Sciences, Indian Institute of Technology Delhi, New Delhi, India

Mahua Mukherjee
Indian Institute of Technology Roorkee, Roorkee, Uttarakhand, India

Edward Ng
School of Architecture, The Chinese University of Hong Kong, Hong Kong, PR China

G. Nimish
Ranbir and Chitra Gupta School of Infrastructure Design and Management, Indian Institute of Technology Kharagpur, Kharagpur, West Bengal, India

T. Orlando Peralta
Department of Geography, University of Chile, Center for Climate and Resilience Research (CR)^2, Santiago, Chile

E. Pablo Sarricolea
Department of Geography, University of Chile, Center for Climate and Resilience Research (CR)^2, Santiago, Chile

Massimo Palme
Universidad Católica del Norte, Escuela de Arquitectura, Antofagasta, Región de Antofagasta, Chile; Universidad Católica del Norte, Centro de Investigación Tecnológica del Agua en el Desierto, Antofagasta, Región de Antofagasta, Chile

G. Pamela Smith
Department of Geography, University of Chile, Center for Climate and Resilience Research (CR)^2, Santiago, Chile

Anna Laura Pisello
CIRIAF — Interuniversity Research Center, University of Perugia, Perugia, Italy; Department of Engineering, University of Perugia, Perugia, Italy

A. Polydoros
Department of Environmental Physics, University of Athens, University Campus, Build PHYS-V, Athens, Greece

T.V. Ramachandra
Centre for Ecological Science, Indian Institute of Science, Bangalore, Karnataka, India

Chao Ren
Division of Landscape Architecture, Department of Architecture, Faculty of Architecture, The University of Hong Kong, Pokfulam, Hong Kong, PR China

Elkhan Richard Sadik-Zada
Institute of Development Research and Development Policy, Ruhr-University Bochum, Bochum, Germany

M. Santamouris
School of Built Environment, University of New South Wales (UNSW), Sydney, Australia

Arjun Satheesh
Indian Institute of Technology Roorkee, Roorkee, Uttarakhand, India

Ankur Prabhat Sati
Centre for Atmospheric Sciences, Indian Institute of Technology Delhi, New Delhi, India

A.N.V. Satyanarayana
Centre for Oceans, Rivers, Atmosphere and Land Sciences, Indian Institute of Technology Kharagpur, Kharagpur, West Bengal, India

Shanmuga Priya Gnanasekaran
Department of Architecture, School of Planning and Architecture, Vijayawada, India

José Sánchez Ramos
Grupo Termotecnia, Escuela Técnica Superior de Ingeniería, Universidad de Sevilla, Camino de los Descubrimientos S/N, Seville, Spain

Sabiha Sultana
Centre for Oceans, Rivers, Atmosphere and Land Sciences, Indian Institute of Technology Kharagpur, Kharagpur, West Bengal, India

Servando Álvarez Domínguez
Grupo Termotecnia, Escuela Técnica Superior de Ingeniería, Universidad de Sevilla, Camino de los Descubrimientos S/N, Seville, Spain

Catalina Toro
Department of Geography, University of Chile, Center for Climate and Resilience Research (CR)^2, Santiago, Chile

Ran Wang
College of Economic and Social Development, Nankai University, Tianjin, PR China

Qingming Zhan
School of Urban Design, Wuhan University, Wuhan, China

Mapping and management of urban shade assets: a novel approach for promoting climatic urban action

Or Aleksandrowicz

Faculty of Architecture and Town Planning, Technion — Israel Institute of Technology, Technion City, Haifa, Israel

1. Urban planning and urban microclimate: a challenge of knowledge communication

The term "Urban Heat Island" (UHI) describes microclimatic conditions in cities that are warmer than in surrounding rural areas (Arnfield, 2003; Landsberg, 1981; Oke, 1982, 1987; Stewart, 2019; Voogt, 2002). UHIs form because of the physical configuration of cities (including their topography, spatial morphology, and building density), the materials used for the construction of buildings, pavements, and roads, the flow of air through the street network, and heat-producing human activities such as transportation and industry (Akbari et al., 2001; Erell et al., 2011; Gartland, 2008; Grimmond, 2007; Santamouris, 2001; Taha, 1997; Unger, 2004). The most common indicator of urban overheating is higher air temperatures, usually recorded at street level. An increase in air temperatures can have diverse negative effects, including exacerbated outdoor heat stress (during daytime and nighttime alike), deteriorated air quality, increased energy consumption on indoor cooling, and even increase in mortality rates (Arnfield, 2003; Johansson and Emmanuel, 2014; Kleerekoper et al., 2012; Nikolopoulou et al., 2001; Oke, 1981).

Despite the solid scientific understanding of the relation between the physical composition of cities and urban climates, climatic factors are rarely considered in the common practice of urban planners and designers and, therefore, still have a relatively small impact on cities (Erell, 2008; Hebbert and Mackillop, 2013; Mills, 2014; Parsaee et al., 2019). This may be partly attributed to knowledge gaps among planning professionals that limit their ability to collect, comprehend, and analyze quantitative microclimatic data. As a result, planners and designers are usually unable to project and simulate the effects of certain design strategies on micro-level and local-level climatic conditions in cities (Heaphy, 2017; Hebbert, 2014; Mills, 2006, 2014; Oke, 2006). Even in cities that already promote climatic policies (Brandenburg et al., 2018; Francis et al., 2014; Osmond and Sharifi, 2017; Ruefenacht and Acero, 2017; Shorris, 2017), actions mainly focus on setting generalized guidelines and not on detailed planning of their concrete implementation. Detailed and site-specific climatic planning is still required for enhancing outdoor conditions because of the local climatic variance resulting from the inherent morphological, physical, and land-use diversity of streets and neighborhoods in every city.

The persisting failures in integrating scientifically sound and detailed climatic considerations into urban planning and design are becoming a major impediment to genuinely addressing the challenges of climate change, and, therefore, urgently call for new methods of translating scientific knowledge into terminologies, methodologies, and toolkits commonly understood and used by planners (Heaphy, 2017; Mauser et al., 2013; Mills et al., 2010). The main point of concern in this respect may lie in the inherently complex nature of urban climates and the diversity of factors affecting it, including air temperature, relative humidity, wind speed, incoming solar radiation, surface albedo and thermal absorption of materials, heat-generating human activities, air pollution levels, and the climatic performance of trees and vegetation (Erell et al., 2011; Mills, 2014). The main challenge is, therefore, to find ways for simplifying the transfer of climatic knowledge to planning professionals without compromising the quality, accuracy, and effectiveness of the decision-making process.

This chapter outlines a novel, quantitative approach to the evaluation of certain climatic properties of urban environments that could more easily be adopted in urban planning and design processes. It first examines the problematic nature of our current ways of evaluating urban overheating and the challenges of elucidating the outcomes of evaluation in directing concrete and effective planning and design actions. It then considers the applicability of a variety of common heat mitigation tools in real-life situations, acknowledging the limitations of municipal action. Based on this analysis, we then argue for a greater emphasis on outdoor shade provision in the adoption of climate-responsive urban policies and suggest a set of quantitative indicators that can support such policies. The chapter concludes with a demonstration of the applicability of the suggested indicators in actual situations, using Tel Aviv-Yafo, a city of hot summer Mediterranean climate, as a case study.

2. Correlating the language of urban morphology with its climatic outcomes

Until recent years, the quantification of urban overheating was usually done using the simple indicator of "urban heat island intensity" (Oke, 1987, p. 289), reflecting the maximum daily air temperature difference between air temperatures measured at a "representative" urban location and in a city's rural periphery. Evidently, this single indicator cannot capture the intricate variance in microclimatic conditions between different city parts, neighborhoods, and streets. It also ignores the effect of radiation fluxes on outdoor thermal comfort (Erell, 2017; Martilli et al., 2020). Therefore, additional and more precise indicators for describing urban climate should be developed and adopted for climatic urban planning and design.

One of the most promising approaches for enhancing the integration of scientific understanding of microclimatic effects in cities into urban planning and design is through the identification of statistically significant relations between certain morphological aspects of urban environments and the climatic properties of the same areas. Since planners regularly engage themselves in morphological questions by determining the spatial configuration and material properties of buildings, streets, neighborhoods, and cities, the language and terminologies of urban morphology are well understood by them. Thus, the identification of strong correlations between specific urban morphological properties and climatic conditions in cities can greatly enhance the capacity of planners to direct design decisions and actions in a way that will consciously and intentionally induce specific microclimatic conditions.

A recent comprehensive attempt to relate urban morphologies to climatic conditions was the development of the Local Climate Zone (LCZ) classification scheme by Stewart and Oke (2012). The system was initially conceived to address the ill-defined urban–rural dichotomy prevalent in many UHI studies, which is open to a variety of interpretations and does not describe well major differences in basic physical characteristics of cities and their environs (including building heights and densities, surface materials, and patterns of vegetative infrastructure). To resolve this problem, Stewart and Oke proposed a classification scheme that could be used to objectively define an environment based on several quantifiable morphological properties, as well as on its material characteristics.

Stewart and Oke's underlying assumption was that each LCZ, which can be defined as a region "of uniform surface cover, structure, material, and human activity that span[s] hundreds of meters to several kilometers in horizontal scale" (Stewart and Oke, 2012, p. 1884), produces distinctively different patterns of air temperature fluctuations at screen height (usually 1.2 m above ground) precisely because of the uniformity of its main physical features. While several comprehensive studies during the last decade have supported this assumption (Beck et al., 2018; Fenner et al., 2017; Kotharkar and Bagade, 2018; Leconte et al., 2015, 2018, 2021; Mandelmilch et al., 2020; Middel et al., 2014; Ren et al., 2019; Shi et al., 2018; Skarbit et al., 2017; Stewart and Oke, 2010), the climatic "footprint" of an LCZ changes from one city to another because of differences induced by their geographic location and overall composition and should, therefore, be mapped in each city separately (Stewart and Oke, 2015).

The LCZ classification scheme consists of 17 morphologically homogeneous urban formations, divided into 10 built types (compact high-rise, compact mid-rise, compact low-rise, open high-rise, open mid-rise, open low-rise, lightweight low-rise, large low-rise, sparsely built, and heavy industry) and seven land cover (or unbuilt) types (dense trees, scattered trees, bush/scrub, low plants, bare rock or paved, bare soil or sand, and water) (Stewart and Oke, 2012, 2015). Differentiation between the built types is almost entirely based on building morphology: three levels of average building height (above 25 m, 10–25 m, and 3–10 m) and several levels of building surface fraction (ratio of building plan area to total plan area). By definition, the "open" built types, as well as the sparsely built type, consist of substantial quantities of trees and vegetation interwoven into the built fabric (Stewart and Oke, 2012). It is true that other combinations between building heights, built densities, surface cover, and vegetation types may exist in the real world, but the LZC classification scheme is intentionally meant to cover only the most common and familiar situations. This is done to prevent overclassification that would reduce the system's capability to standardize communication and reporting on urban climatic conditions, including intercity comparisons (Stewart and Oke, 2012, 2015).

While the definition of each of the LCZs is primarily given in verbally descriptive terms, the classification scheme also relates LCZ types to value ranges of several morphological properties of the urban environment, thus ensuring that the classification process is based not strictly on subjective impressions but also on objective and quantifiable factors. These morphological properties include sky view factor (SVF, the ratio of the part of sky hemisphere visible from ground level to that of an unobstructed hemisphere), street aspect ratio (mean height-to-width ratio of street canyons), building surface fraction, impervious and pervious surface fraction, and height of "roughness elements" (mainly buildings) (Stewart and Oke, 2012). While the urban environment can be described by using other morphological metrics and definitions (Dibble et al., 2019; Serra et al., 2018; Taleghani et al.,

2015; Venerandi et al., 2017), it seems that Stewart and Oke chose the main properties that they perceived as contributing the most to the creation of local climatic conditions in cities.

According to Stewart and Oke, the way the classification scheme correlates urban morphology and urban climate "offers a basic package of urban climate principles for architects, planners, ecologists, and engineers" (Stewart and Oke, 2012, p. 1894) and can, therefore, be helpful in integrating urban climatic knowledge into city planning (Perera and Emmanuel, 2018). While the question whether these expectations for integration has been met is still open, it can be argued that the LCZ system already created a promising path for such an integration by correlating urban morphology with at least one important climatic factor (air temperature distribution across urban environments).

Notwithstanding its apparent merits, the LCZ system still suffers from two major drawbacks that limit its application in urban planning and design. The first is that of scale: LCZs are inherently defined as representing morphological homogeneity at the local level (from hundreds of meters to several kilometers) and are, therefore, not intended to capture micro-scale climatic differences at street level (Stewart and Oke, 2015). The second drawback of the LCZ system is its usability for outdoor thermal comfort evaluation; the system was originally developed to reflect intraurban differences in air temperatures and not in thermal comfort conditions. Although several studies have recently attempted to correlate LCZs to outdoor thermal comfort according to common comfort indices (Lau et al., 2019; Unger et al., 2018; Verdonck et al., 2018), they are, in a way, ignoring the fact that outdoor thermal comfort levels can show significant variance at street level (Quanz et al., 2018) because of micro-scale physical differences (such as street orientation, tree canopy cover, etc.) that are not considered in the LCZ classification scheme.

While the morphological approach to climatic urban design can become effective at certain scales, there is still a need for additional tools that would help planners and designers to effectively control the negative microclimatic effects of urban environments, focusing not only on air temperature levels but also on outdoor thermal comfort. Yet, such a morphological approach also lacks in a more fundamental sense, namely its applicability to mitigating heat stress in older city parts. While new developments can easily follow certain morphological guidelines to secure better climatic performance, a comprehensive morphological transformation of existing neighborhoods and city parts is in many times impractical. These older areas, typically located at a city's core, are also the same areas in which urban overheating is usually more profound. For these situations, evaluation of the applicability and effectiveness of available heat mitigation measures is, therefore, required.

3. Urban heat island mitigation measures: the limits of intervention

The concept of UHI mitigation describes strategies, measures, or actions that are meant to ameliorate the negative effects of urban overheating through modifications of the physical environments of cities (Aleksandrowicz et al., 2017; Gago et al., 2013; Solecki et al., 2005). Its origins probably date back to the pioneering work of Hashem Akbari, Arthur Rosenfeld, and Haider Taha at the Lawrence Berkeley National Laboratory. In 1985, they founded the Heat Island Research Project and in 1989, organized a first workshop that focused not only on the phenomenon of UHI itself, but also on the ways to mitigate it (Huang et al., 1990; Rosenfeld, 1999). Since then, research on the possible strategies to mitigate UHI intensity has significantly expanded and developed, creating a solid and rigorous body of knowledge that could potentially benefit urban planners and designers.

Contemporary scientific literature documents multiple mitigation measures that may be applied to combat urban overheating, with diverse perspectives or classification systems suggested by different authors (Gago et al., 2013; Gartland, 2008; Giguère, 2009; Jamei et al., 2016; Kleerekoper et al., 2012; Nuruzzaman, 2015; Wong and Jusuf, 2013). Following a previous work by Aleksandrowicz et al. (2017), this section classifies the central mitigation measures according to the *physical domain of intervention*: building envelopes; pavements and roads; urban landscape elements; and the geometric and morphological aspects of streets. This type of categorization reflects a practical approach toward UHI mitigation, focusing on concrete actions that can be realized as part of climatic urban policy.

3.1 Building envelopes

Cool roofs: The term "cool roof" describes roofs whose finishing material is relatively reflective. The high reflectance of the roof surface results in lower absorption of heat in the roof surface itself and in the building's envelope, as long as the solar radiation is reflected to the sky and not toward adjacent building parts. The application of "cool" surface finishes (for example, white paint) can thus reduce the heat emitted by the building envelope at night, as well as the heat emitted by air conditioning units because of indoor overheating.

Cool walls: "Cool" (i.e., relatively reflective) surface finishes can also be applied to exterior walls. The result of using cool finishing materials for exterior walls is similar to applying the same materials to roofs, although the degree of relative improvement expected from their application is smaller compared to roofs, due to the significant difference in sun incidence angle (walls absorb less solar radiation compared to roofs, assuming the application of similar finishing materials). In addition, the efficacy of solar reflectance from walls in terms of urban overheating reduction can be significantly reduced in densely built areas, since the solar radiation reflected from the walls is usually absorbed by adjacent surfaces of neighboring buildings.

Green roofs: Green roofs are roofs covered with vegetation. Green roofs are expected to significantly reduce the heat load on indoor spaces below the roof, due to their thermal insulation properties and the absorption of solar radiation in the vegetated layer on the roof. They can also locally cool the air around them because of evapotranspiration from the vegetative layer. Compared to cool roofs, the main downside of green roofs is their additional maintenance and irrigation requirements.

Green walls: Green walls are vertical building parts whose external surface is covered with an expansive layer of vegetation. Like green roofs, green walls block the incidence of solar radiation on parts of the building envelope and can thus help in reducing the building's heat load and the heat a building emits to its surroundings. In addition, evapotranspiration from the vegetative vertical layer is expected to reduce air temperature in close vicinity to the green wall itself.

3.2 Pavements and roads

Cool pavements: Like cool roofs, the application of reflective materials to sidewalks and roads is expected to reduce their heat absorption and their resulting heat release. However, and unlike the application of cool materials to roofs, the use of highly reflective materials at street level may cause undesirable levels of glare and heat stress through the increased exposure of road users to reflected shortwave radiation. This may limit the use of highly reflective paving materials and, as a result, the practical cooling capacity cool pavements.

Water-retentive pavements: In climates where the hot season is also characterized by frequent rainfall, pervious paving materials that are applied above a water-retentive sublayer can help in reducing air temperatures in their vicinity through evaporation. The pavement's exposure to direct solar radiation causes its upper layer to heat during daytime, which, in turn, leads to the evaporation of the water stored in the sublayer and the cooling of the upper layer. The cooler the pavement, the cooler is the ambient air near it.

3.3 Urban landscaping elements

Shade trees: Shade-giving trees (as opposed to trees with underdeveloped tree canopies) can play an important role in reducing urban heat, especially by shading streets in a way that absorbs solar radiation before it affects sidewalks, roads, and building facades. Shading can also play an important role in relieving heat stress in urban spaces during the hot season since they block solar radiation that affects the human body. In addition, evapotranspiration from trees exposed to solar radiation can help in reducing air temperatures in their immediate vicinity.

Ground cover through vegetation: Unlike synthetic flooring materials, vegetation (grass, shrubs) absorbs solar radiation in a way that does not release heat into the air but rather cools the air around it through evapotranspiration. Nevertheless, this immediate cooling effect depends on the water content of the soil and, therefore, may be less effective in plants that require small amounts of irrigation.

Lakes, streams, and ponds: Water sources may lower air temperature mainly through water evaporation. Streams or canals that pass through the heart of a city may also help in transporting heat away from within the city center due to water movement, while large water reservoirs may help in reducing air temperature in their vicinity because of the heat capacity of the water.

3.4 Street geometry

Sky view factor: The geometric proportion between the height of buildings along a street and its width (the "height-to-width ratio") can have the positive effect of reducing air temperatures at street level depending on a street's degree of "openness" to the sky or its "sky view factor". Streets of lower sky view factor, in which the street section is deep and narrow, may become cooler during the day, because they are less exposed to incoming solar radiation. However, extremely deep and narrow street sections may become too dark for long periods, creating gloomy indoors (infringing the residents' "solar rights") and undesirably dark outdoors during the cold season. Another possible downside of deep and narrow street sections is the lower heat release capacity of street surfaces to the sky precisely because of relatively low proportion of their exposure to the sky.

Wind corridors: Winds entering the urban area from contiguous open spaces tend to carry cooler air with them, and winds passing through the city may thus remove hot air from it. To secure effective passage of wind through a city, care must be taken to the way the street network is laid out. Main streets should, therefore, be oriented toward the prevailing wind directions, in a way that maintains effective "corridors" through which wind can penetrate the city core.

Solar orientation of streets: In subtropical latitudes, streets oriented along a north-south axis will usually provide significant shading from buildings at street level during the hot season, thus reducing street-level air temperature and pedestrian thermal discomfort during daytime. On the other hand, streets oriented along an east-west axis will be almost fully unshaded without the use of additional shading elements (trees, arcades, pergolas). Therefore, clever design of a street network that is based on street-level shading through the orientation and massing of the built volumes can generate cooler urban environments with lesser reliance on additional mitigation measures.

The broad range of tools for mitigating the negative effects of urban heat may create the false impression that an urban planner enjoys great flexibility in formulating an effective climatic action strategy. Yet, the applicability of each of the measures described above varies from one location to another in a way that may leave a planner with less than a handful of tools for facing the challenge of overheating urban environments. As the above description may suggest, the four different domains of intervention call for different scales of application and direction, as follows:

- Actions directed to building envelopes can bring about genuine urban change only when applied on a large scale and, therefore, seem to be less effective without the cooperation of numerous property owners. In real-life situations, while municipal planners can regulate and direct the application of cool or "green" materials to building envelopes, they may not have the means for supporting their comprehensive application by the private sector.
- Applying reflective materials to pavements and roads can be effectively directed as a "top-down" solution but may introduce only local and minor reduction in air temperatures since the reflectivity of the applied materials should be kept low to prevent glare. The reflectivity of pavements can also cause undesirable heat stress for pedestrians since it may significantly increase the overall radiation flux on the human body during daytime. Water-retentive pavements, on the other hand, can be effective only in nonarid locations, where frequent rainfall is typical to the hot season.
- Using landscaping elements for UHI mitigation is probably the most effective mitigation strategy in many urban locations. Landscaping elements can be comprehensively introduced into public spaces and can induce change at different scales, from the very local to the urban. This is especially true in respect to trees, which can be planted in a variety of locations, including streets, plazas, gardens, and parks. While trees may have a negative effect on the cooling capacity of streets at night because their canopies may reduce the flow of wind and heat released to the sky from street surfaces, it seems that their overall positive effect of daytime shading and evapotranspiration is in many times much more significant. Proper pruning of tree canopies may improve wind flow, as long as the trees are allowed to grow their canopies high enough. Additionally, desealing of paved surfaces and their replacement with vegetated landcover are another action that can be easily applied to existing cities in a comprehensive way and as a "top-down" policy directed by municipalities.
- As for street geometry, its modification to improve climatic conditions is almost impossible to realize in older city parts. While municipal planners have a decisive control over the regulation of street geometry, in cities where the rate of urban transformation and rebuilding is low or where new construction concentrates in the outskirts of cities, this control cannot be translated into effective mitigation of urban overheating.

It can, therefore, be concluded that the most climatically effective domain of intervention for urban planners and designers attempting to combat the climatic challenge of urban overheating is that of urban landscaping. More specifically, the green infrastructure of a city, and especially the clever use of trees, is essential to the success of an urban overheating mitigation strategy (Bowler et al., 2010; de la Barrera and Reyes-Paecke, 2021; Hiemstra et al., 2017; Saaroni et al., 2018). Yet trees can be regarded as an almost ideal design element for urban cooling not only because of their effect on air temperatures. While air temperatures are commonly used as an indicator of urban overheating intensity, in many cases the effect of a slight increase of air temperature is not the decisive factor generating outdoor thermal stress, especially during daytime. In that respect, the benefits of trees as shade providers at street level may be more important for improving the climatic conditions in cities than their direct air cooling effects (Jamei et al., 2016; Rahman et al., 2020; Sanusi et al., 2017; Taleghani, 2018).

4. Shade's pivotal effect on outdoor thermal comfort and its urban-scale mapping

Outdoor thermal comfort can be evaluated using comfort indices that correlate objectively quantifiable climatic variables with thermal stress. Two of the most prevalent indices in current scientific literature are the Physiologically Equivalent Temperature (PET) and the Universal Thermal Climate Index (UTCI), which follow an almost similar approach, calculating an "equivalent temperature" based on climatic variables and providing an estimated thermal comfort or discomfort levels for a range of equivalent temperatures. Both indices use air temperature, mean radiant temperature (MRT), relative humidity, wind speed, clothing level, and metabolic rate for calculating the equivalent temperature. UTCI index is simpler to calculate since it presupposes clothing and metabolic rate values (Bröde et al., 2013; Höppe, 1999; Matzarakis et al., 1999, 2015).

Recent studies have consistently demonstrated that in multiple geographic locations, during the hot season, direct and diffuse solar radiation largely contributes to excessive daytime heat stress, making shade provision a viable tool for heat stress mitigation (Balslev et al., 2015; Chen and Ng, 2012; Colter et al., 2019; Coutts et al., 2015; de Abreu-Harbich et al., 2015; Du et al., 2020; Hiemstra et al., 2017; Huang et al., 2020; Lee et al., 2013, 2018; Middel et al., 2021, 2016; Shashua-Bar et al., 2010, 2011). Shade has also the potential to reduce street-level air temperatures and cooling loads in buildings because it decreases irradiation of surfaces in cities (roads, pavements, building facades), thereby reducing the amount of heat absorbed and released by man-made elements in the built environment (Erell et al., 2011, pp. 48–54).

The potential of shade provision to substantially reduce heat stress is implicit in the PET and UTCI indices. Both indices consider the effect of exposure to shortwave and longwave radiation through inputs such as the mean radiant flux intensity or its derivative, MRT, which can be defined as "the uniform temperature of an imaginary enclosure in which radiant energy exchange with the body equals the radiant exchange in the actual non-uniform enclosure" (Erell et al., 2011, p. 119). Exposure to direct and diffuse solar radiation significantly increases MRT values and, thus, also the perceived heat stress according to each of the two indices. Shade quantification can, thus, enable us to give a good description of outdoor thermal comfort during the hot season in many geographic locations (Aleksandrowicz et al., 2020).

In practice, the capacity of urban design to control other factors considered by the PET and UTCI comfort indices, such as air temperature, relative humidity, and wind speed, is rather limited (Aleksandrowicz et al., 2017). Shade, on the other hand, is almost entirely determined by how urban streets and open spaces are designed and maintained, even at a rather local level. Therefore, in many locations, one can argue that tackling inadequate outdoor shading may be the single most important climatic task an urban planner can engage in for reducing urban heat stress.

Despite the acknowledged importance of shade provision at street level, until recently attempts to quantitatively analyze solar exposure levels on an urban scale were rare. This can be attributed to the computational power required for high-resolution shade quantification, but also to limitation in obtaining high-resolution 3D geographic mapping of urban areas. One of the early demonstrations of the potential of using 3D mapping for urban shade calculations appeared a decade ago in Yu et al. (2009), who based their study on LIDAR mapping and infrared aerial photography of downtown Houston. By improving an algorithm by Kumar et al. (1997), Yu et al. produced 1 m-per-pixel maps showing shading pattern in the city by calculating cumulative values of solar radiation exposure for each month and each season. These calculations enabled them to assess the effect of urban morphology on solar exposure patterns as well as the potential exposure of vegetation to solar radiation.

During the last decade, algorithms for calculating the exposure of horizontal surfaces in digital Geographic Information System (GIS) platforms were developed by Lindberg and Grimmond (2011) as part of the SOLWEIG/UMEP microclimatic calculation model (Lindberg et al., 2008, 2018) and by Hammerberg (2014). A simpler tool that facilitates the calculation of street irradiance values (area solar radiation function) is embedded in the ArcGIS platform (ESRI, 2020), based on a method developed by Rich et al. (1994) and Fu and Rich (2002). Unlike the other two computational tools, the ArcMap function is not capable of calculating irradiance values below tree canopies. All these tools use raster digital surface models (DSMs) for calculation. By using each of these tools it is, therefore, possible to create street-level maps in which a single irradiance value (given in Wh/m^2) is calculated for each pixel of the original DSM.

5. Quantifying shade levels and tree planting: suggested indicators

The new computational tools hold a genuine potential for high-resolution mapping of shade in large urban areas. Nevertheless, there is still a need for a comprehensive framework or methodology for translating the raw calculation results into indicators and benchmarks that could be applied for directing municipal action toward the conservation or improvement of the "shade assets" of a city: the integrative configuration of buildings, trees, arcades, pergolas, or any other devices that affect shading in public spaces. These indicators should enable us to direct efficient and effective actions to the locations where intervention is needed the most in terms of street-level shade provision. In the following sections, several of these indicators are discussed, most of which were developed by the author, as well as their application in analysing outdoor shade in Tel Aviv-Yafo (Aleksandrowicz et al., 2019, 2020), a Mediterranean coastal city exposed to relatively high levels of solar radiation (about 3300 annual sun hours, average daily global radiation of $5.33\ kWh/m^2$ throughout the year or $7.03\ kWh/m^2$ between the end of March and the end of September).

5.1 Shade index

The first and most basic shade indicator is that of a shade index (SI), which describes, on a scale of 0−1, the ratio between the blocked insolation at ground level at a certain location and the maximum insolation of an unobstructed horizontal surface at the same time and location. The higher the value, the higher the shading. This indicator considers shade produced by all elements in an urban environment: buildings, trees, and other shade-giving elements. It can be formulated as follows:

$$SI_p = 1 - \left(\frac{\text{Insolation}_p}{\text{Insolation}_r}\right)$$

where SI_p is the SI at a certain point, Insolation$_p$ is the insolation at that point, and Insolation$_r$ is the insolation at an unobstructed reference point.

The SI depends on the date of calculation: different dates will produce different SI values for the same location and urban morphology. While it is better to calculate SI values for mid-summer, when daily air temperatures are at their peak, it is possible to use other dates as reference dates for shade evaluation. Using the GIS calculation tools described above, it is possible to calculate SI values for each pixel of a DSM for an hour or a day (based on the cumulative daily insolation at that point) and then to calculate *spatial* SI values of street segments or neighborhoods by averaging the SI values for all the pixels contained within each spatial unit, as follows:

$$SI_a = \frac{\sum_{i=1}^{n} SI_n}{n}$$

where SI_a is the average SI value of an area, and n is the number of pixels contained within that area. If calculated for an entire neighborhood, the averaged SI value calculation should exclude pixels contained within building footprints, since they do not represent street-level shade.

When calculated for a relatively large number of street segments and neighborhoods, the SI can reveal the variance in street-level insolation across an entire urban area and, therefore, can be used by planners and designers for prioritizing interventions focusing on outdoor shade provision. Through shade mapping, a municipality may decide to designate certain streets for "shade intensification" (in streets of low shade values) or "shade conservation" (in streets of exceptional levels of shade). The prioritization can integrate additional quantifiable factors, such as the likelihood of a street to attract pedestrians or the socioeconomic condition of a neighborhood. For example, streets prioritized for "shade intensification" can be defined as only the streets with low SI values *and* high likelihood to become pedestrian attractors.

5.2 Tree canopy cover

The second suggested indicator is that of tree canopy cover (TCC) for street-level outdoor space. It describes, on a scale of 0−1, the ratio between the horizontal projection of all tree canopies located within a certain space and the total area of the same space. Thus, TCC equals $\frac{T_p}{A_p}$ where Tp is the number of tree-canopy pixels within a specific area, and Ap is the total number of pixels of that area. The higher the value, the higher is the TCC of the area. TCC values can give an indication for the likelihood of street segments or neighborhoods to enjoy high levels of street-level shading cast by wide-canopied trees. Nevertheless, since street-level shade depends also on the shade cast by buildings, TCC alone may not describe well the overall shade conditions in a certain street or neighborhood, especially where TCC values are low.

5.3 Tree shade efficacy index

The calculation of both SI and TCC values for a specific spatial unit can also help in evaluating the relative contribution of shading from trees to the overall shading at street level. For this purpose, we suggest a third indicator of tree shade efficacy index (TSEI), calculated by raising the power of the SI by the TCC value for the same spatial unit (SI^{TCC}). TSEI describes the efficacy of using trees for urban shading: the higher the value, the lower the dependency of the built environment on shade provided by trees for achieving higher SI values. Since the cost of tree planting and maintenance is not negligible, it is important to minimize the reliance on trees for street shading and to design streets that receive shading also from buildings.

5.4 Street tree density

The fourth indicator suggested here is that of street tree density (STD), which describes the number of street trees per street area (here, per 1000 m^2 of street area, which includes pavement and road space). STD value is independent of tree canopy area, since it only counts the number of trees (or tree trunks) in a certain street segment and, therefore, may not directly reflect shading conditions. Nevertheless, it can be used for setting benchmarks for street tree intensification when combined with the SI value of the same street segment. The integrative analysis of the two indicators may show, for example, that the STD of streets with relatively high SI values is usually higher than a certain number; this number can then be used as a benchmark for future improvements in relatively unshaded streets. An analysis of all the streets in the city can, therefore, reveal not only the number of poorly shaded streets, but also the rough number of trees required to significantly improve their shading conditions.

6. Case study: using the indicators for urban shade analysis in Tel Aviv-Yafo

The four indicators described above were used by the author in a recent study conducted in Tel Aviv-Yafo, partially reported on in Aleksandrowicz et al. (2020). Central to the study was the generation of shade maps and tree maps that were used for graphically presenting the spatial distribution of shade and trees across the entire city. Results showed that the city's historic core (referred to sometimes as the "White City of Tel Aviv") has relatively high levels of outdoor shade and a unique combination (compared with other parts of the city) between a relatively dense built morphology, which provides shading from buildings, and a comprehensive infrastructure of wide-canopied trees that is an essential component of its urban design. Analysis also showed strong correlation between a dense urban fabric (reflected in a street height-to-width ratio above 1) and high summer shading of streets and public spaces. Nevertheless, besides some exceptional neighborhoods, these high shade levels also rely on intensive planting of wide-canopied and street-lined trees or trees growing in front yards.

One of the city-scale maps we produced using the SI calculation procedure was a map showing average SI values for every street segment in the city during summer (specifically, in the month of August, Fig. 1.1). The map highlighted the climatic advantages of north-south oriented streets over east-west oriented streets in terms of summer shade. This is a result of the local characteristics of the sun path: in east-west oriented streets, buildings' effect on street shading is minor (since the summer southern sun appears high in the sky), and, therefore, reasonable SI values cannot be achieved without the application of a substantial and continuous layer of wide tree canopies (or similar artificial shading elements). In Tel Aviv-Yafo, the effect of street orientation on shading is highly evident in a series of

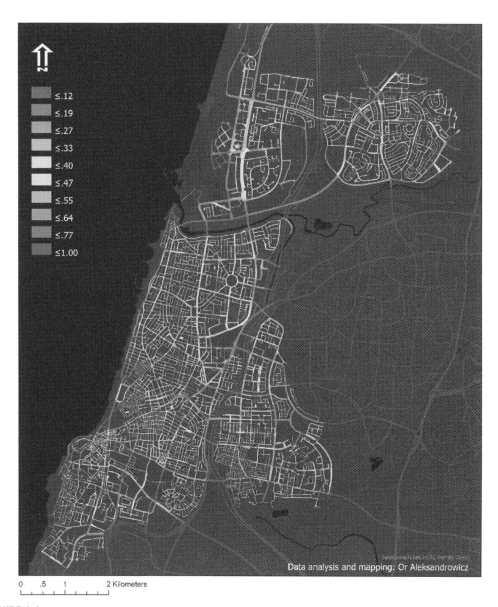

Legend:
≤.12
≤.19
≤.27
≤.33
≤.40
≤.47
≤.55
≤.64
≤.77
≤1.00

Data analysis and mapping: Or Aleksandrowicz

0   .5   1   2 Kilometers

FIGURE 1.1

Summer shade index values per street segment in Tel Aviv-Yafo (2017 data).

Credit: The author.

central east-west streets that have exceptionally low summer SI values (below 0.1). The effect of orientation is further exacerbated in these streets because of relatively high street width (above 30 m); their exposed asphalt surfaces may also become a major source of nocturnal heating of air temperatures, by releasing at night the heat absorbed in them during daytime.

Tel Aviv-Yafo also has several exceptionally shaded "boulevards" (as they are officially called) or avenues. These streets (whatever their orientation is) generally show high levels of summer shade resulting from the use of two to four rows of wide-canopied trees planted in a central esplanade, resulting in street TCC values above 0.6 (Fig. 1.2). While these boulevards are relatively wide (30 m or more), they provide SI values above 0.6 and sometimes even above 0.8. Trees also play a major role in adding significant shade to several segments of central east-west oriented streets, resulting in SI values above 0.7 despite the street orientation. This is achieved while maintaining a continuous tree canopy that extends from one tree to another along the street's pavements.

Street tree density analysis for the entire city enabled us to highlight street segments of relatively low SI values (below 0.5) in which STD values are also low (Fig. 1.3). This type of analysis can help in roughly estimating the quantities of street trees required for bringing these multiple street segments to a desirable STD level of at least 10 trees per 1000 m^2: around 38,000 trees (Figs. 1.4 and 1.5). While the calculation does not consider objective difficulties as above and below ground technical infrastructures that may limit street tree planting, it still provides good indication for the magnitude of additional tree planting requirements for the entire city. In Tel Aviv-Yafo, where the number of street trees is currently estimated to be around 42,000, the price of doubling it for significantly improving summer shading conditions across the entire city can, thus, be regarded as reasonable and achievable. This number is much lower than the number of new 100,000 trees the city's mayor recently pledged to plant in the city until 2030 (Huldai, 2019).

At the neighborhood level, SI results showed a high level of spatial variance (Fig. 1.6): relatively high levels of shading in Tel Aviv-Yafo's northern neighborhoods (0.53–0.67) and in the city's historic center (0.52–0.64), and relatively low levels of shading in its southern neighborhoods (0.3–0.48). In the city's eastern neighborhoods, shading values (0.46–0.55) were lower than in the city's central and northern parts, while higher than those in the southern parts. Exceptionally low shading values (0.13–0.28) were calculated in the major urban parks, which reflect their design as large open stretches of grass lawns with a relatively low number of trees.

Neighborhood TCC analysis (Fig. 1.7) showed that Tel Aviv-Yafo's northern neighborhoods are those with the highest TCC values (0.21–0.41 in most of them), while TCC values in the southern neighborhoods are much lower (0.03–0.19). Comparing neighborhood SI value with neighborhood TCC values showed that shade differences between the northern and southern parts of Tel Aviv-Yafo primarily result from the fundamental differences in the magnitude and quality of the green infrastructure in both parts of the city. The calculation of the complementary TSEI values (Fig. 1.8) reflected the high efficacy of tree shade application in the city's historic core, while revealing that the northern neighborhoods of the city heavily rely on intensive use of trees for street shading because of their low building density. This combined analysis also showed that TCC quantification alone may not provide an accurate indication for urban shade since it does not consider the central role of street-level shading generated by buildings.

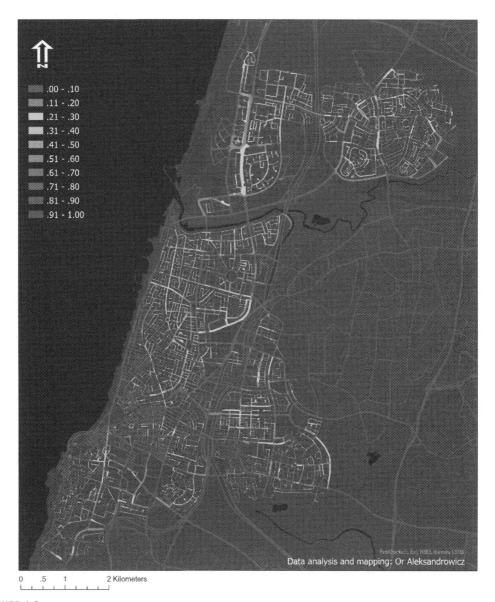

FIGURE 1.2

Tree canopy cover per street segment in Tel Aviv-Yafo (2017 data).

Credit: The author.

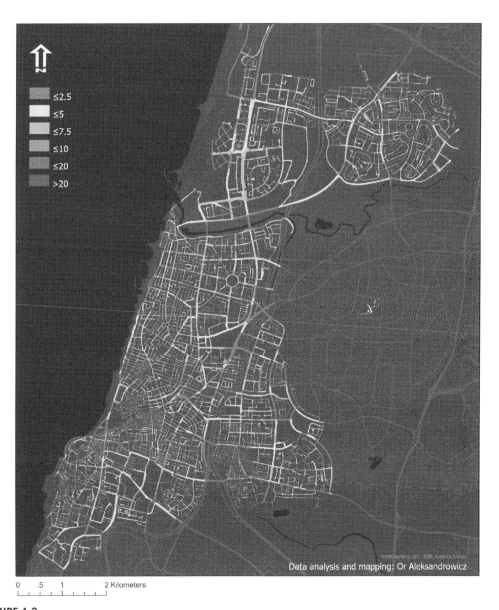

FIGURE 1.3

Street tree density in Tel Aviv-Yafo (2019 data).

Credit: The author.

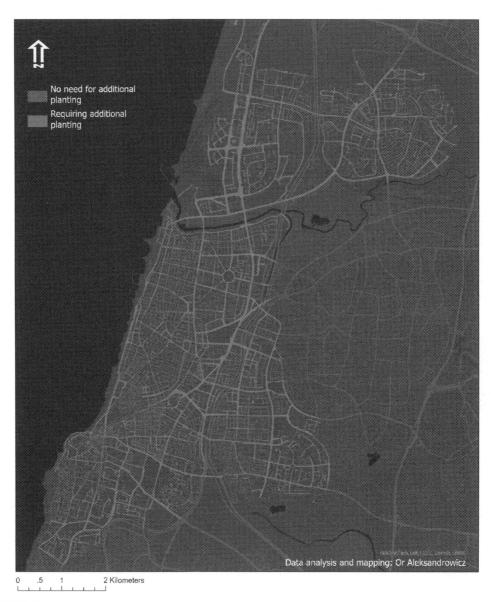

No need for additional planting

Requiring additional planting

0   .5   1   2 Kilometers

Data analysis and mapping: Or Aleksandrowicz

FIGURE 1.4

Streets requiring additional tree planting for improving street-level shade, Tel Aviv-Yafo (2019 data).

Credit: The author.

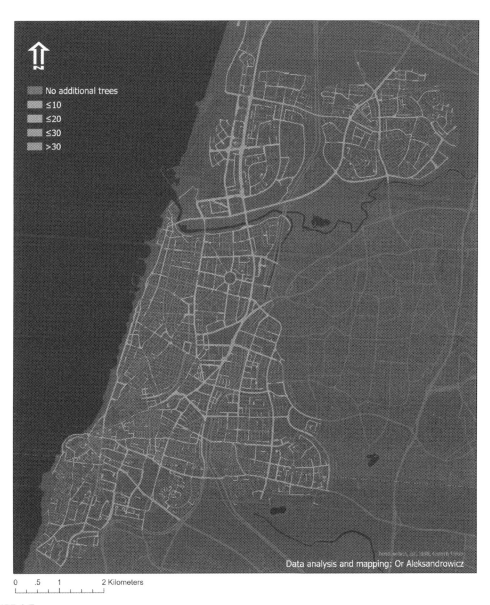

No additional trees
≤10
≤20
≤30
>30

Data analysis and mapping: Or Aleksandrowicz

0   .5   1   2 Kilometers

FIGURE 1.5

Absolute number of required additional street trees in Tel Aviv-Yafo (2019 data).

Credit: The author.

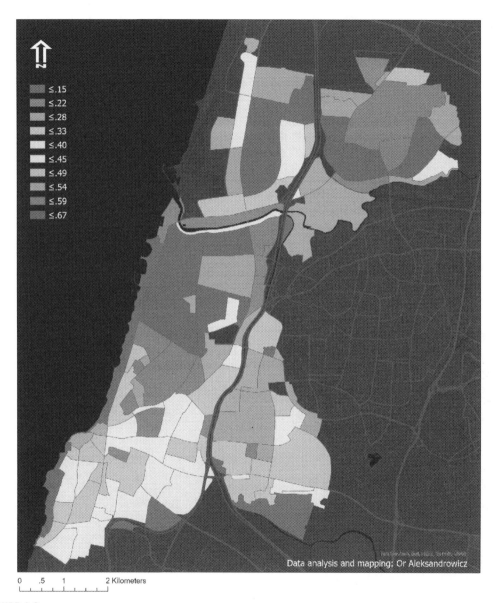

Legend:
≤.15
≤.22
≤.28
≤.33
≤.40
≤.45
≤.49
≤.54
≤.59
≤.67

Data analysis and mapping: Or Aleksandrowicz

0   .5   1   2 Kilometers

FIGURE 1.6

Summer shade index per neighborhood in Tel Aviv-Yafo (2017 data).

Credit: The author.

Legend:
≤.04
≤.07
≤.10
≤.14
≤.18
≤.24
≤.32
≤.41

Data analysis and mapping: Or Aleksandrowicz

0   .5   1   2 Kilometers

FIGURE 1.7

Tree canopy cover per neighborhood in Tel Aviv-Yafo (2017 data).

Credit: The author.

Legend:
≤.82
≤.85
≤.87
≤.88
≤.90
≤.93
≤.95
≤.99

Data analysis and mapping: Or Aleksandrowicz

0 .5 1 2 Kilometers

FIGURE 1.8

Summer tree shade efficacy values per neighborhood in Tel Aviv-Yafo (2017 data).

Credit: The author.

7. Conclusion

The results of the analysis in Tel Aviv-Yafo demonstrate the effectiveness of the suggested indicators in directing urban planning toward concrete climatic actions and locations that are expected to improve outdoor thermal comfort at street level around the entire city. The indicators help in revealing substantial differences in shade provision between streets and neighborhoods and enable us to conclude that these differences are the result of different urban morphologies (typical height—to-width ratio of streets, building densities, street orientation) and the characteristics of the city's urban forest (number and density of street trees, their canopy area, the continuity of canopy cover). Municipal planning and administration authorities can control these parameters and can, therefore, induce major improvements to the quality of urban shade.

The effectiveness of urban action on microclimatic issues largely depends on the large-scale collection of high-resolution physical, climatic, geographic, and functional data and on the development of quantitative indicators that can support a concise yet effective understanding of the climatic variance in streets and neighborhoods. A concerted municipal effort that consists of systematic data collection followed by data processing in the form of quantitative indicators is, therefore, required to significantly improve the evaluation of local microclimatic conditions and the direction of municipal actions for improving it.

The indicators used in the presented analysis were developed as tools that could significantly advance an evidence-based framework for the design of climate-responsive outdoor urban environments. Acknowledging the importance of shade for maintaining street-level comfort during summer in many geographic locations worldwide enables us to focus planning and design efforts on shade provision, which in many times can be significantly enhanced through the adoption of top-down municipal policies. The suggested indicators directly relate to this domain of intervention and can, therefore, be used for evaluating existing conditions as well as future modifications in multiple locations and settings that are currently struggling to mitigate the negative effects of urban overheating or are expected to do so in the foreseeable future because of global warming.

Acknowledgment

The author would like to thank Rinat Millo-Steinlauf, Uriel Babczik, Boaz Kedar, Qasem Salalha, Avital Marmelstein-Fox, and Idan Hauz of the Tel Aviv-Yafo Municipality for their help and support.

Funding

Parts of the study presented in this chapter were funded by the Conservation Department at the Tel Aviv-Yafo Municipality.

References

Akbari, H., Pomerantz, M., Taha, H., 2001. Cool surfaces and shade trees to reduce energy use and improve air quality in urban areas. Sol. Energy 70 (3), 295—310. https://doi.org/10.1016/S0038-092X(00)00089-X.

Aleksandrowicz, O., Vuckovic, M., Kiesel, K., Mahdavi, A., 2017. Current trends in urban heat island mitigation research: observations based on a comprehensive research repository. Urban Clim. 21, 1—26. https://doi.org/10.1016/j.uclim.2017.04.002.

Aleksandrowicz, O., Zur, S., Lebendiger, Y., Lerman, Y., 2019. Shade Maps and Their Application for Shade Conservation and Intensification in Tel Aviv-Yafo (in Hebrew). Tel Aviv-Yafo Municipality.

Aleksandrowicz, O., Zur, S., Lebendiger, Y., Lerman, Y., 2020. Shade maps for prioritizing municipal micro-climatic action in hot climates: learning from Tel Aviv-Yafo. Sustain. Cities Soc. 53, 101931. https://doi.org/10.1016/j.scs.2019.101931.

Arnfield, A.J., 2003. Two decades of urban climate research: a review of turbulence, exchanges of energy and water, and the urban heat island. Int. J. Climatol. 23 (1), 1−26. https://doi.org/10.1002/joc.859.

Balslev, Y.J., Potchter, O., Matzarakis, A., 2015. Climatic and thermal comfort analysis of the Tel-Aviv Geddes Plan: a historical perspective. Build. Environ. 93 (P2), 302−318. https://doi.org/10.1016/j.buildenv.2015.07.005.

Beck, C., Straub, A., Breitner, S., Cyrys, J., Philipp, A., Rathmann, J., Schneider, A., Wolf, K., Jacobeit, J., 2018. Air temperature characteristics of local climate zones in the Augsburg urban area (Bavaria, southern Germany) under varying synoptic conditions. Urban Clim. 25, 152−166. https://doi.org/10.1016/j.uclim.2018.04.007.

Bowler, D.E., Buyung-Ali, L., Knight, T.M., Pullin, A.S., 2010. Urban greening to cool towns and cities: a systematic review of the empirical evidence. Landsc. Urban Plann. 97 (3), 147−155. https://doi.org/10.1016/j.landurbplan.2010.05.006.

Brandenburg, C., Damyanovic, D., Reinwald, F., Allex, B., Gantner, B., Czachs, C., 2018. Urban Heat Island Strategy: City of Vienna. Vienna Environmental Protection Department (MA22).

Bröde, P., Błazejczyk, K., Fiala, D., Havenith, G., Holmér, I., Jendritzky, G., Kuklane, K., Kampmann, B., 2013. The universal thermal climate index UTCI compared to ergonomics standards for assessing the thermal environment. Ind. Health 51 (1), 16−24. https://doi.org/10.2486/indhealth.2012-0098.

Chen, L., Ng, E., 2012. Outdoor thermal comfort and outdoor activities: a review of research in the past decade. Cities 29 (2), 118−125. https://doi.org/10.1016/j.cities.2011.08.006.

Colter, K.R., Middel, A., Martin, C.A., 2019. Effects of natural and artificial shade on human thermal comfort in residential neighborhood parks of Phoenix, Arizona, USA. Urban For. Urban Green. 44, 126429. https://doi.org/10.1016/j.ufug.2019.126429.

Coutts, A.M., White, E.C., Tapper, N.J., Beringer, J., Livesley, S.J., 2015. Temperature and human thermal comfort effects of street trees across three contrasting street canyon environments. Theor. Appl. Climatol. 124 (1−2), 55−68. https://doi.org/10.1007/s00704-015-1409-y.

de Abreu-Harbich, L.V., Labaki, L.C., Matzarakis, A., 2015. Effect of tree planting design and tree species on human thermal comfort in the tropics. Landsc. Urban Plann. 138, 99−109. https://doi.org/10.1016/j.landurbplan.2015.02.008.

de la Barrera, F., Reyes-Paecke, S., 2021. Green infrastructure to mitigate extreme temperatures in cities. In: Palme, M., Salvati, A. (Eds.), Urban Microclimate Modelling for Comfort and Energy Studies. Springer, pp. 403−417. https://doi.org/10.1007/978-3-030-65421-4.

Dibble, J., Prelorendjos, A., Romice, O., Zanella, M., Strano, E., Pagel, M., Porta, S., 2019. On the origin of spaces: morphometric foundations of urban form evolution. Environ. Plann. 46 (4), 707−730. https://doi.org/10.1177/2399808317725075.

Du, J., Liu, L., Chen, X., Liu, J., 2020. Field assessment of neighboring building and tree shading effects on the 3D radiant environment and human thermal comfort in summer within urban settlements in northeast China. Adv. Meteorol. https://doi.org/10.1155/2020/8843676.

Erell, E., 2008. The application of urban climate research in the design of cities. Adv. Build. Energy Res. 2 (1), 95−121. https://doi.org/10.3763/aber.2008.0204.

Erell, E., 2017. Is urban heat island mitigation necessarily a worthy objective?. In: Proceedings of 33rd PLEA International Conference: Design to Thrive, PLEA 2017, vol. 2, pp. 1693−1700.

Erell, E., Pearlmutter, D., Williamson, T.J., 2011. Urban Microclimate: Designing the Spaces between Buildings, first ed. Earthscan.

ESRI, 2020. ArcGIS Pro V. 2.6.3. ESRI.

Fenner, D., Meier, F., Bechtel, B., Otto, M., Scherer, D., 2017. Intra and inter 'local climate zone' variability of air temperature as observed by crowdsourced citizen weather stations in Berlin, Germany. Meteorol. Z. 26 (5), 525−547. https://doi.org/10.1127/metz/2017/0861.

Francis, J., Hall, G., Murphy, S., Rayner, J., 2014. Growing Green Guide: A Guide to Green Roofs, Walls and Facades in Melbourne and Victoria, Australia. Department of Environment and Primary Industries, State of Victoria.

Fu, P., Rich, P.M., 2002. A geometric solar radiation model with applications in agriculture and forestry. Comput. Electron. Agric. 37 (1−3), 25−35. https://doi.org/10.1016/S0168-1699(02)00115-1.

Gago, E.J., Roldan, J., Pacheco-Torres, R., Ordóñez, J., 2013. The city and urban heat islands: a review of strategies to mitigate adverse effects. In: Renewable and Sustainable Energy Reviews, vol. 25, pp. 749−758. https://doi.org/10.1016/j.rser.2013.05.057.

Gartland, L., 2008. Heat islands: understanding and mitigating heat in urban areas. Earthscan.

Giguère, M., 2009. Literature Review of Urban Heat Island Mitigation Strategies. Institut national de santé publique Québec.

Grimmond, S., 2007. Urbanization and global environmental change: local effects of urban warming. Geogr. J. 173 (1), 83−88. https://doi.org/10.1111/j.1475-4959.2007.232_3.x.

Hammerberg, K., 2014. Accounting for the Role of Trees in Urban Energy Balance Modeling Using GIS Techniques (Master's thesis). TU Wien.

Heaphy, L.J., 2017. The challenges of aligning the scales of urban climate science and climate policy in London and Manchester. Environ. Plan. C 36 (4), 609−628. https://doi.org/10.1177/2399654417723342.

Hebbert, M., 2014. Climatology for city planning in historical perspective. Urban Clim. 10 (P2), 204−215. https://doi.org/10.1016/j.uclim.2014.07.001.

Hebbert, M., Mackillop, F., 2013. Urban climatology applied to urban planning: a postwar knowledge circulation failure. Int. J. Urban Reg. Res. 37 (5), 1542−1558. https://doi.org/10.1111/1468-2427.12046.

Hiemstra, J.A., Saaroni, H., Amorim, J.H., 2017. The urban heat island: thermal comfort and the role of urban greening. In: Pearlmutter, D., Calfapietra, C., Samson, R., O'Brien, L., Ostoić, S.K., Sanesi, G., del del Amo, R.A. (Eds.), The Urban Forest: Cultivating Green Infrastructure for People and the Environment. Springer, pp. 7−19. https://doi.org/10.1007/978-3-319-50280-9_2.

Höppe, P., 1999. The physiological equivalent temperature - a universal index for the biometeorological assessment of the thermal environment. Int. J. Biometeorol. 43 (2), 71−75. https://doi.org/10.1007/s004840050118.

Huang, J., Davis, S., Akbari, H., 1990. A Guidebook for the Control of Summer Heat Islands. Lawrence Berkeley Laboratory.

Huang, Z., Wu, C., Teng, M., Lin, Y., 2020. Impacts of tree canopy cover on microclimate and human thermal comfort in a shallow street canyon in Wuhan, China. Atmosphere 11 (6). https://doi.org/10.3390/atmos11060588.

Huldai, R., 2019. Address to the 4th Israeli Climate Conference, Tel Aviv (in Hebrew). https://youtu.be/swVHG6QOek4.

Jamei, E., Rajagopalan, P., Seyedmahmoudian, M., Jamei, Y., 2016. Review on the impact of urban geometry and pedestrian level greening on outdoor thermal comfort. Renew. Sustain. Energy Rev. 54, 1002−1017. https://doi.org/10.1016/j.rser.2015.10.104.

Johansson, E., Emmanuel, R., 2014. The influence of urban design on outdoor thermal comfort in the hot, humid city of Colombo, Sri Lanka. Int. J. Biometeorol. 51 (2), 119−133. https://doi.org/10.1007/s00484-006-0047-6.

Kleerekoper, L., van Esch, M., Salcedo, T.B., 2012. How to make a city climate-proof, addressing the urban heat island effect. Resour. Conserv. Recycl. 64, 30−38. https://doi.org/10.1016/j.resconrec.2011.06.004.

Kotharkar, R., Bagade, A., 2018. Local Climate Zone classification for Indian cities: a case study of Nagpur. Urban Clim. 24, 369−392. https://doi.org/10.1016/j.uclim.2017.03.003.

Kumar, L., Skidmore, A.K., Knowles, E., 1997. Modelling topographic variation in solar radiation in a GIS environment. Int. J. Geogr. Inf. Sci. 11 (5), 475−497. https://doi.org/10.1080/136588197242266.

Landsberg, H.E., 1981. The Urban Climate. Academic Press.

Lau, K.K.L., Chung, S.C., Ren, C., 2019. Outdoor thermal comfort in different urban settings of sub-tropical high-density cities: an approach of adopting local climate zone (LCZ) classification. Build. Environ. 154, 227−238. https://doi.org/10.1016/j.buildenv.2019.03.005.

Leconte, F., Bouyer, J., Claverie, R., Pétrissans, M., 2015. Using Local Climate Zone scheme for UHI assessment: evaluation of the method using mobile measurements. Build. Environ. 83, 39−49. https://doi.org/10.1016/j.buildenv.2014.05.005.

Lee, H., Holst, J., Mayer, H., 2013. Modification of human-biometeorologically significant radiant flux densities by shading as local method to mitigate heat stress in summer within urban street canyons. Adv. Meteorol. 1−13. https://doi.org/10.1155/2013/312572.

Lee, I., Voogt, J.A., Gillespie, T., 2018. Analysis and comparison of shading strategies to increase human thermal comfort in urban areas. Atmosphere 9 (3), 91. https://doi.org/10.3390/atmos9030091.

Lehnert, M., Geletič, J., Dobrovolný, P., Jurek, M., 2018. Temperature differences among local climate zones established by mobile measurements in two central European cities. Clim. Res. 75 (1), 53−64. https://doi.org/10.3354/cr01508.

Lehnert, M., Savić, S., Milošević, D., Dunjić, J., Geletič, J., 2021. Mapping local climate zones and their applications in European urban environments: a systematic literature review and future development trends. ISPRS Int. J. Geo-Inf. 10 (4), 260. https://doi.org/10.3390/ijgi10040260.

Lindberg, F., Grimmond, C.S.B., 2011. The influence of vegetation and building morphology on shadow patterns and mean radiant temperatures in urban areas: model development and evaluation. Theor. Appl. Climatol. 105 (3−4), 311−323. https://doi.org/10.1007/s00704-010-0382-8.

Lindberg, F., Grimmond, C.S.B., Gabey, A., Huang, B., Kent, C.W., Sun, T., Theeuwes, N.E., Järvi, L., Ward, H.C., Capel-Timms, I., Chang, Y., Jonsson, P., Krave, N., Liu, D., Meyer, D., Olofson, K.F.G., Tan, J., Wästberg, D., Xue, L., Zhang, Z., 2018. Urban Multi-scale Environmental Predictor (UMEP): an integrated tool for city-based climate services. Environ. Model. Software 99, 70−87. https://doi.org/10.1016/j.envsoft.2017.09.020.

Lindberg, F., Holmer, B., Thorsson, S., 2008. SOLWEIG 1.0 − modelling spatial variations of 3D radiant fluxes and mean radiant temperature in complex urban settings. Int. J. Biometeorol. 52 (7), 697−713. https://doi.org/10.1007/s00484-008-0162-7.

Mandelmilch, M., Ferenz, M., Mandelmilch, N., Potchter, O., 2020. Urban spatial patterns and heat exposure in the Mediterranean city of Tel Aviv. Atmosphere 11 (9), 963. https://doi.org/10.3390/atmos11090963.

Martilli, A., Krayenhoff, E.S., Nazarian, N., 2020. Is the Urban Heat Island intensity relevant for heat mitigation studies? Urban Clim. 31, 100541. https://doi.org/10.1016/j.uclim.2019.100541.

Matzarakis, A., Mayer, H., Iziomon, M.G., 1999. Applications of a universal thermal index: physiological equivalent temperature. Int. J. Biometeorol. 43 (2), 76−84. https://doi.org/10.1007/s004840050119.

Matzarakis, A., Muthers, S., Rutz, F., 2015. Application and comparison of UTCI and PET in temperate climate conditions. Finisterra 49 (98). https://doi.org/10.18055/Finis6453.

Mauser, W., Klepper, G., Rice, M., Schmalzbauer, B.S., Hackmann, H., Leemans, R., Moore, H., 2013. Transdisciplinary global change research: the co-creation of knowledge for sustainability. Curr. Opin. Environ. Sustain. 5 (3−4), 420−431. https://doi.org/10.1016/j.cosust.2013.07.001.

Middel, A., AlKhaled, S., Schneider, F.A., Hagen, B., Coseo, P., 2021. 50 Grades of shade. Bull. Am. Meteorol. Soc. 102 (9), 1−35. https://doi.org/10.1175/BAMS-D-20-0193.1.

Middel, A., Häb, K., Brazel, A.J., Martin, C.A., Guhathakurta, S., 2014. Impact of urban form and design on mid-afternoon microclimate in Phoenix Local Climate Zones. Landsc. Urban Plann. 122, 16−28. https://doi.org/10.1016/j.landurbplan.2013.11.004.

Middel, A., Selover, N., Hagen, B., Chhetri, N., 2016. Impact of shade on outdoor thermal comfort—a seasonal field study in Tempe, Arizona. Int. J. Biometeorol. 60 (12), 1849−1861. https://doi.org/10.1007/s00484-016-1172-5.

Mills, G., 2006. Progress toward sustainable settlements: a role for urban climatology. Theor. Appl. Climatol. 84 (1−3), 69−76. https://doi.org/10.1007/s00704-005-0145-0.

Mills, G., 2014. Urban climatology: history, status and prospects. Urban Clim. 10, 479−489. https://doi.org/10.1016/j.uclim.2014.06.004.

Mills, G., Cleugh, H., Emmanuel, R., Endlicher, W., Erell, E., McGranahan, G., Ng, E., Nickson, A., Rosenthal, J., Steemer, K., 2010. Climate information for improved planning and management of mega cities (needs perspective). Proc. Environ. Sci. 1, 228−246. https://doi.org/10.1016/j.proenv.2010.09.015.

Nikolopoulou, M., Baker, N., Steemers, K., 2001. Thermal comfort in outdoor urban spaces: understanding the Human parameter. Sol. Energy 70 (3), 227−235. https://doi.org/10.1016/S0038-092X(00)00093-1.

Nuruzzaman, M., 2015. Urban heat island: causes, effects and mitigation measures - a review. Int. J. Environ. Monit. Anal. 3 (2), 67. https://doi.org/10.11648/j.ijema.20150302.15.

Oke, T.R., 1981. Canyon geometry and the nocturnal urban heat island: comparison of scale model and field observations. J. Climatol. 1 (3), 237−254. https://doi.org/10.1002/joc.3370010304.

Oke, T.R., 1982. The energetic basis of the urban heat island. Quarter. J. Meteorol. Soc. 108 (455), 1−24. https://doi.org/10.1002/qj.49710845502.

Oke, T.R., 1987. Boundary Layer Climates, second ed. Routledge.

Oke, T.R., 2006. Towards better scientific communication in urban climate. Theor. Appl. Climatol. 84 (1−3), 179−190. https://doi.org/10.1007/s00704-005-0153-0.

Osmond, P., Sharifi, E., 2017. Guide to Urban Cooling Strategies. Low Carbon Living CRC.

Parsaee, M., Joybari, M.M., Mirzaei, P.A., Haghighat, F., 2019. Urban heat island, urban climate maps and urban development policies and action plans. Environ. Technol. Innovat. 14 (August), 100341. https://doi.org/10.1016/j.eti.2019.100341.

Perera, N.G.R., Emmanuel, R., 2018. A "Local Climate Zone" based approach to urban planning in Colombo, Sri Lanka. Urban Clim. 23, 188−203. https://doi.org/10.1016/j.uclim.2016.11.006.

Quanz, J.A., Ulrich, S., Fenner, D., Holtmann, A., Eimermacher, J., 2018. Micro-scale variability of air temperature within a local climate zone in Berlin, Germany, during summer. Climate 6 (1), 5. https://doi.org/10.3390/cli6010005.

Rahman, M.A., Hartmann, C., Moser-Reischl, A., von Strachwitz, M.F., Paeth, H., Pretzsch, H., Pauleit, S., Rötzer, T., 2020. Tree cooling effects and human thermal comfort under contrasting species and sites. Agric. For. Meteorol. 287 (August 2019), 107947. https://doi.org/10.1016/j.agrformet.2020.107947.

Ren, C., Cai, M., Li, X., Zhang, L., Wang, R., Xu, Y., Ng, E., 2019. Assessment of local climate zone classification maps of cities in China and feasible refinements. Sci. Rep. 9 (1), 1−11. https://doi.org/10.1038/s41598-019-55444-9.

Rich, P.M., Hetrick, W.A., Saving, S.C., 1994. Using Viewshed models to calculate intercepted solar radiation: applications in ecology. In: American Society for Photogrammetry and Remote Sensing Technical Papers. American Society for Photogrammetry and Remote Sensing, pp. 524−529.

Rosenfeld, A.H., 1999. The art of energy efficiency: protecting the environment with better technology. Annu. Rev. Energy Environ. 24 (1), 33−82. https://doi.org/10.1146/annurev.energy.24.1.33.

Ruefenacht, L., Acero, J.A., 2017. Strategies for Cooling Singapore. Singapore ETH Centre. https://doi.org/10.3929/ethz-b-000258216.

Saaroni, H., Amorim, J.H., Hiemstra, J.A., Pearlmutter, D., 2018. Urban Green Infrastructure as a tool for urban heat mitigation: survey of research methodologies and findings across different climatic regions. Urban Clim. 24, 94–110. https://doi.org/10.1016/j.uclim.2018.02.001.

Santamouris, M., 2001. On the built environment - the urban influence. In: Santamouris, M. (Ed.), Energy and Climate in the Urban Built Environment. Routledge, pp. 3–18.

Sanusi, R., Johnstone, D., May, P., Livesley, S.J., 2017. Microclimate benefits that different street tree species provide to sidewalk pedestrians relate to differences in Plant Area Index. Landsc. Urban Plann. 157, 502–511. https://doi.org/10.1016/j.landurbplan.2016.08.010.

Serra, M., Psarra, S., O'Brien, J., 2018. Social and physical characterization of urban contexts: techniques and methods for quantification, classification and purposive sampling. Urban Plann. 3 (1), 58–74. https://doi.org/10.17645/up.v3i1.1269.

Shashua-Bar, L., Pearlmutter, D., Erell, E., 2011. The influence of trees and grass on outdoor thermal comfort in a hot-arid environment. Int. J. Climatol. 31 (10), 1498–1506. https://doi.org/10.1002/joc.2177.

Shashua-Bar, L., Potchter, O., Bitan, A., Boltansky, D., Yaakov, Y., 2010. Microclimate modelling of street tree species effects within the varied urban morphology in the Mediterranean city of Tel Aviv, Israel. Int. J. Climatol. 30 (1), 44–57. https://doi.org/10.1002/joc.1869.

Shi, Y., Lau, K.K.-L., Ren, C., Ng, E., 2018. Evaluating the local climate zone classification in high-density heterogeneous urban environment using mobile measurement. Urban Clim. 25, 167–186. https://doi.org/10.1016/j.uclim.2018.07.001.

Shorris, A., 2017. Cool Neighborhoods NYC: A Comprehensive Approach to Keep Communities Safe in Extreme Heat. New Yotk City's Mayor's Office of Recovery and Resiliency.

Skarbit, N., Stewart, I.D., Unger, J., Gál, T., 2017. Employing an urban meteorological network to monitor air temperature conditions in the 'local climate zones' of Szeged, Hungary. Int. J. Climatol. 37, 582–596. https://doi.org/10.1002/joc.5023.

Solecki, W.D., Rosenzweig, C., Parshall, L., Pope, G., Clark, M., Cox, J., Wiencke, M., 2005. Mitigation of the heat island effect in urban New Jersey. Environ. Hazards 6 (1), 39–49. https://doi.org/10.1016/j.hazards.2004.12.002.

Stewart, I.D., 2019. Why should urban heat island researchers study history? Urban Clim. 30, 100484. https://doi.org/10.1016/j.uclim.2019.100484.

Stewart, I.D., Oke, T.R., 2010. Thermal Differentiation of local climate zones using temperature observations from urban and rural field sites. In: Ninth Symposium on the Urban Environment.

Stewart, I.D., Oke, T.R., 2012. Local climate zones for urban temperature studies. Bull. Am. Meteorol. Soc. 93 (12), 1879–1900. https://doi.org/10.1175/BAMS-D-11-00019.1.

Stewart, I.D., Oke, T.R., 2015. Local climate zones and urban climatic mapping. In: Ng, E., Ren, C. (Eds.), The Urban Climatic Map: A Methodology for Sustainable Urban Planning. Routledge, pp. 397–401. https://doi.org/10.4324/9781315717616.

Taha, H., 1997. Urban climates and heat islands: albedo, evapotranspiration, and anthropogenic heat. Energy Build. 25 (2), 99–103. https://doi.org/10.1016/s0378-7788(96)00999-1.

Taleghani, M., 2018. Outdoor thermal comfort by different heat mitigation strategies- A review. Renew. Sustain. Energy Rev. 81, 2011–2018. https://doi.org/10.1016/j.rser.2017.06.010.

Taleghani, M., Kleerekoper, L., Tenpierik, M., van den Dobbelsteen, A., 2015. Outdoor thermal comfort within five different urban forms in The Netherlands. Build. Environ. 83, 65–78. https://doi.org/10.1016/j.buildenv.2014.03.014.

Unger, J., 2004. Intra-urban relationship between surface geometry and urban heat island: review and new approach. Clim. Res. 27 (3), 253–264. https://doi.org/10.3354/cr027253.

Unger, J., Skarbit, N., Gál, T., 2018. Evaluation of outdoor human thermal sensation of local climate zones based on long-term database. Int. J. Biometeorol. 62 (2), 183–193. https://doi.org/10.1007/s00484-017-1440-z.

Venerandi, A., Zanella, M., Romice, O., Dibble, J., Porta, S., 2017. Form and urban change - an urban morphometric study of five gentrified neighbourhoods in London. Environ. Plann. B 44 (6), 1056–1076. https://doi.org/10.1177/0265813516658031.

Verdonck, M.L., Demuzere, M., Hooyberghs, H., Beck, C., Cyrys, J., Schneider, A., Dewulf, R., Van Coillie, F., 2018. The potential of local climate zones maps as a heat stress assessment tool, supported by simulated air temperature data. Landsc. Urban Plann. 178, 183–197. https://doi.org/10.1016/j.landurbplan.2018.06.004.

Voogt, J.A., 2002. Urban heat island. In: Munn, R.E. (Ed.), Encyclopedia of Global Environmental Change. Wiley, pp. 660–666.

Wong, N.H., Jusuf, S.K., 2013. Urban heat island and mitigation strategies at city and building level. In: Advances in the Development of Cool Materials for the Built Environment, pp. 3–32. https://doi.org/10.2174/9781608054718113010004.

Yu, B., Liu, H., Wu, J., Lin, W.-M., 2009. Investigating impacts of urban morphology on spatio-temporal variations of solar radiation with airborne LIDAR data and a solar flux model: a case study of downtown Houston. Int. J. Rem. Sens. 30 (17), 4359–4385. https://doi.org/10.1080/01431160802555846.

Vulnerability to the urban heat islands effect in the Global North and the Global South: assessment of the drivers and mitigation strategies

Elkhan Richard Sadik-Zada[1] and Andrea Gatto[2,3]

[1]*Institute of Development Research and Development Policy, Ruhr-University Bochum, Bochum, Germany;* [2]*Wenzhou-Kean University, Wenzhou, Zhejiang, China;* [3]*Natural Resources Institute, University of Greenwich, Chatham Maritime, United Kingdom*

1. Introduction

The replacement of natural landscapes with anthropogenic landscapes and relatively high intensity of human activity in the urban or metropolitan areas implies notably high temperatures in these spatial locations with respect to the surrounding rural areas (Mitchell, 1961; Oke, 1982; Chakraborty et al., 2019). Following, principal causes of the urban−rural temperature differential are the lack of evapotranspiration via the lack of vegetation and higher emission of infrared radiation (Oke, 1982; Rojagopalan et al., 2014; Kumar et al., 2017; Synnefa et al., 2007; Akbari and Kolokosta, 2016). Importantly, less greenery contributes to the storage of additional heat in the ground layer and impervious anthropogenic landscapes. This leads to the alterations of the microclimate of urban areas epitomized by higher air and surface temperatures (Li et al., 2014; Fallmann et al., 2016; Rajagopalan et al., 2014). The primary cause of the temperature differential is the daytime absorption and the subsequent reradiation of the solar radiation during the night by mass building structures, roads, and other hard surfaces (Landsberg, 1981, Wong, 2005). UHI is also connected to urban rainfall modification. In fact, urban areas are shown to affect regional climate (Liu and Niyogi, 2020).

UHI is closely related to climate change. Estrada et al. (2017) found that urban heat islands (UHIs) significantly increase the health and climate risks of global climate change. Combined with the negative health risks rendered by global climate change and heatwaves, the UHI effects can have grave repercussions on the environmental and public health status of urban residents (Tewari et al., 2019). There is broad empirical evidence that UHIs cause heat stroke, dehydration, and exacerbate the health conditions of persons with cardiovascular diseases, diabetes, respiratory diseases, asthma, and further chronic diseases (Tan et al., 2010; Heaviside et al., 2017; Shahmohamadi et al., 2011a;

Chakraborty et al., 2019). Furthermore, UHI intensity is positively correlated with an increased level of physical and mental stress and increased predisposition to infectious diseases (Shahmohamadi et al., 2011b).

Besides its negative effects on the health status of urban dwellers, UHIs also exacerbate global climate change by increasing energy consumption and increased exposure to energy vulnerability. UHIs lead to greater energy demand for cooling and less energy demand for heating of urban agglomerations. Li et al. (2019) find that UHIs lead to a median of 19% increase in building cooling energy consumption and a median of 18,7% decrease in building heating energy consumption in a number of the large cities of Western Europe, North America, Japan, and Australia. However, the effects of the UHI on the cities with less than 1 million population and urban areas of the developing and transition economies have not been studied yet.

The global demographic trends and the rural—urban interplays are quite influential for analyzing the sketched dynamics and outline climate change and sustainable development aspects (Seto and Shepherd, 2009). In 1950, there were only 26 countries worldwide, where the share of the urban population was over 50%. These were mostly economically advanced economies in Western Europe (15), North America (2), Latin America (6), Australia, and New Zealand (UN, 2018). Since then, durable economic modernization of developing countries and countries within the orbit of the former USSR—now transition economies—led to an inexorable growth of the share of the urban population. In the overwhelming majority of worldwide countries, the share of the urban population is above 50%. Since 2009, China is also part of this group of countries.

The overwhelming majority of the countries with a predominantly rural population today belong to the least developed countries, which pertain to the Global South (Gatto et al., 2016). These two major vulnerable socioeconomic groups are often exposed to energy insecurity and lack of proper access to electricity (Gatto and Drago, 2021; Sadik-Zada et al., 2022). Hence, urbanization and the emergence of the heat islands are concomitant with social, environmental, and economic development. Today, 54% of the world population lives in urban areas and it is expected that by the year 2030, 60% and by the year 2050, more than 70% of the global population will live in the urban areas (Gerland et al., 2014; Tzavai et al., 2015; Rajagopalan et al., 2014). As illustrated in Fig. 2.1, the global growth of the urban population in the coming three decades will be mostly driven by the countries in the Global South. Futhermore, Chakraborty et al. (2019) find that the poor urban neighborhoods are disproportionately exposed to the urban heat waves than the neighborhoods inhabited by the middle and high incomes.

There is a wealth of empirical literature on the drivers of the UHI effects in individual, and mostly large urban areas, cities and countries (Tomlinson et al., 2011; Lee et al., 2020). Despite data availability and the development of the sophisticated Urban Heat Island Intensity Indexes for most countries worldwide, there is no investigation, which accounts for the systematic differences between individual large country groups (Sangiorgio et al., 2020). By accounting for the systematic differences between Global South and Global South on the one hand, and individual countries, on the other hand, this study yields statistically more robust results. This is due to the identification of the essential drivers and assessment of the intensity of the individual drivers of the UHI effects. This book chapter makes the first step to differentiating two large groups of countries vulnerable to the phenomenon and provides a bird's eye perspective on the urban heat adaptation and mitigation strategies by revealing the systematic differences between the Global North and the Global South. Nevertheless, the practical value of the inferences of this inquiry comes to its own only in combination with the city- or commune-level data.

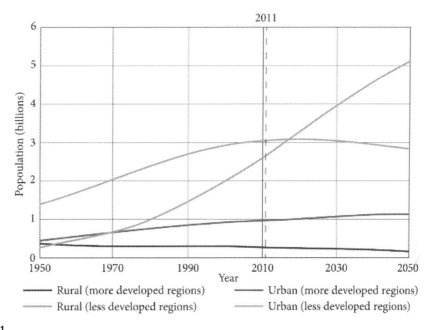

FIGURE 2.1

World population in urban and rural areas. The *dashed line* denotes the year 2011.

Based on United Nations, 2014. World Urbanization Prospects: The 2014 Revision, United Nations: New York. Toparar, Y. 2018.
A Multiscale Analysis of the Urban Heat Island Effect: From City Averaged Temperatures to the Energy Demand of Individual
Buildings. Technishe Universiteit Eindhoven. https://pure.tue.nl/ws/files/95411608/20180425_Toparlar.pdf.

The work proceeds as follows: Section 2 reviews the existing publication on the drivers and consequences of the UHI. Following, Section 3 deals with the statistical and econometrics techniques employed to run this exercise, including the ordinary least squares (OLS) and the multilevel multivariate regression analysis. Section 4 provides insights on the results from the descriptive statistics and econometrics analyses. Lastly, Section 5 wraps up this research's conclusion, whereas the results are commented in light of policy countermeasures.

2. Drivers and consequences of the UHI: a brief literature review

The Father of modern meteorology, Luke Howard, was the first scholar who observed this phenomenon for London and its suburbs and addressed this in the first edition of his book dealing with the climatology of the city (Howard, 1818, 1833). Howard attributed the temperature differential to the extensive use of fuel in urban London. This phenomenon has been redetected and extensively documented in 1927 by Wilhelm Schmidt for Vienna. Since the early 1930s, the UHI effect could be documented for a large number of cities around the world. The first scholarly use of the term UHI took place in a study by Gordon Manley in 1958 in his study on snowfall in metropolitan England in the Quarterly Journal of Meteorological Society (Manley, 1958). This work opened the attention of the scholarly community to anthropogenically induced microclimate changes. There is now a sizable empirical literature, which indicates that UHI is not only confined to large cities (Landsberg, 1981). Nevertheless, the UHI effect is more pronounced in the most densely built-up city districts (Alcoforado and Andrade, 2006).

The determinants of the UHI effect can be divided into two broad categories—meteorological and urban design parameters (Che-Ani et al., 2009). Meteorological determinants are air temperature, wind, humidity, and cloud cover. Urban density determinants are: density of urban areas, build-up ratios in percentage, used construction materials, aspect ratio of urban canyons. Crutzen (2004) finds that UHIs lead to greater energy consumption, the surge of atmospheric pollution deterioration of indoor and outdoor thermal comfort, and deterioration of health conditions as well as increased mortality (Akbari and Kolokosta, 2016; Santamouris and Kolokosta, 2016). Sarrat et al. (2006) analyzed the impact of UHI on summertime pollution in Paris. The authors find that urban islands are a significant driver of harmful atmospheric pollution, especially in the summer months. Furthermore, UHIs have a detrimental effect on the level of tropospheric ozone and nitrogen oxides. Stathopoulou et al. (2006) find similar results for Athens. Drafting a systematic literature review of determinants and climatic effects of the UHI, Santamouris (2011) finds similar results for all large urban areas in Europe.

Despite a positive relationship between the city size and the UHI effects, smaller settlements are also vulnerable to the urban heat effects (Chandler, 1964; Oke, 1973). The overwhelming majority of the studies on the drivers and repercussions of UHI focuses on the mid-latitudes (Eliasson, 1996; Tzavali et al., 2015). de Shiller and Evans (1998) and Baker (2002) show that, especially in winter months, in mid- and high-latitudes, UHI could be deemed to be a blessing due to their role in the reduction of energy needs of the urban areas. Taesler et al. (2006) show that this effect especially strings in the countries of the Nordic-Baltic Sea region.

However, in the tropical regions, the negative effects on the coefficient of the performance of the energy systems and the substantial increase of energy efficiency of buildings over the increased use of air conditioners are more pronounced than in the moderate latitudes (Akbari et al., 2005; Santamouris, 2011, 2014; Chatterjee et al., 2019). Air conditioners lead not only to an increased energy demand but also to a direct increase of temperatures in densely populated urban areas (Rajagopalan et al., 2014). Despite the more severe repercussions of the UHI on the economies and microclimate of the tropical countries, the number of studies on the UHI in the tropical latitudes is rather scarce (Sham, 1973, 1986; Padmanabhamurty, 1979; Chow and Roth, 2006). The existing studies indicate that the level of UHI exposure in the tropical environment is much greater than in the temperate environments (Amorim and Dubreuil, 2017). If we consider that the world's fastest-growing cities are in the tropics, the issue of the urban heat islands in the context of tropic latitudes or their comparison with the urban areas of the Global North is a pivotal research direction in the context of adaptation and mitigation to the climate change vulnerability on the one hand. Secondly, research in this field is particularly important in the context of development economics (Lewis, 1954; Gatto and Busato, 2020).

3. Methodology and data issues

This work exploited the CIESIN's Satellite-Derived Environmental Indicators on Global Urban Heat Island issued by the Columbia University and NASA's Earth Observing System Data and Information System (EOSDIS) (CIESIN, 2016b). From this database, a large dataset covering both Global North and Global South countries is constructed, making use of different econometrics techniques. To address the sketched research question, this study employs linear OLS and multilevel mixed linear regression approaches. The estimators are based on a comprehensive literature review on the major determinants of the UHI in Toparar (2018) and on the data on the UHI effects in more than 30,000 urban regions. Due to the fact that belonging to the Global South/North or a specific country could have an impact on the intensity of the UHI effect, the employment of these variables as a dummy variable in the OLS estimation or the second-level variables within the multilevel analyses is necessary. A multilevel approach may make sense if the observations within Global South/North or countries would correlate. The underlying dataset has been described in the following Table 2.1. This dataset encompasses the data for more than 25,599 urban areas in 88 countries. Data availability served both as a trigger and a serious limitation of the present study. Global Urban Heat Island Data Set, 2013, is the major source of the empirical data of this study and is predicated on two datasets. These are:

- The Global Summer Land Surface Temperature (LST) Grids, 2013: daytime maximum temperature and nighttime minimum temperature grids (CIESIN, 2016).
- SEDAC's Global Rural-Urban Mapping Project, Version 1 (GRUMPv1): Urban Extent Polygons (internal working version) (CIESIN, 2015).

Table 2.1 Description of data.

Variable name	Description	Source
ES00POP	Estimated population for 2000.	Global Urban Heat Island (UHI) Data Set, 2013. Palisades, NY: NASA Socioeconomic Data and Applications Center (SEDAC). https://doi.org/10.7927/H4H70CRF.
SQKM_FINAL	Area of urban extent in square kilometers.	Global Urban Heat Island (UHI) Data Set, 2013. Palisades, NY: NASA Socioeconomic Data and Applications Center (SEDAC). https://doi.org/10.7927/H4H70CRF.
N_T_DIFF	The difference (in degrees Celsius) in average nighttime minimum land surface temperature between the urban area and buffer area (URB_N_MEAN minus BUF_N_MEAN).	Global Urban Heat Island (UHI) Data Set, 2013. Palisades, NY: NASA Socioeconomic Data and Applications Center (SEDAC). https://doi.org/10.7927/H4H70CRF.
LATITUDE	Latitude of centroid of urban extent in decimal degrees.	Global Urban Heat Island (UHI) Data Set, 2013. Palisades, NY: NASA Socioeconomic Data and Applications Center (SEDAC). https://doi.org/10.7927/H4H70CRF.
PCI	Per capita income PPP USD in 2013.	World Bank, World Development Indicators, 2021.
Urbanization	Share of urban population in total population.	World Bank, World Development Indicators, 2021.
Slums	Share of urban population, which lives in slums.	World Bank, World Development Indicators, 2021.
Wind	Wind m/s in 10% windiest area of the urban area.	World Wind Atlas, 2021.

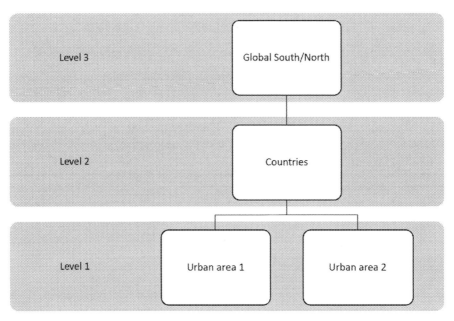

FIGURE 2.2

Hierarchies of data.

Source: Authors' elaborations.

The simple OLS estimator assumes uncorrelated residuals. In the case of the hierarchically oriented datasets, this is nevertheless, not the case. Hence, the employment of the ordinary linear least squares estimators could lead to flawed results (Lois, 2015; Searle, 1997; Wooldridge, 2016) (Fig. 2.2).

4. Empirical analysis
4.1 Descriptive statistics

Our assessment of the UHI dataset shows that, in 2013, among 25,500 inquired urban areas, only 242 revealed temperature differences (in Celsius degrees). On average, the nighttime minimum land surface temperature between the urban area and buffer area was more than 5 Celsius degrees. Except for just three cities, all of those cities were situated in the Global South. China, Colombia, Ethiopia, and India are the countries with the greatest number of cities that are exposed to these temperature extremes. This evidence clearly shows that the UHI problem is more pronounced in the Global South than in the mid-latitudes. As illustrated in the box plots in Fig. 2.3, in 50% of the inspected urban areas in the Global North, the daytime temperature difference between urban areas and suburbs varies between 2.00 and 3.75 Celsius degrees.

Within the Global North, the respective numbers vary between 1.00 and 3.80°. The overall dispersion of the diurnal UHI is substantially greater in the Global South and ranges between 0 and 6 Celsius degrees. Within the Global North countries, the temperature differential ranges between 0.4 and 5.5 Celsius degrees.

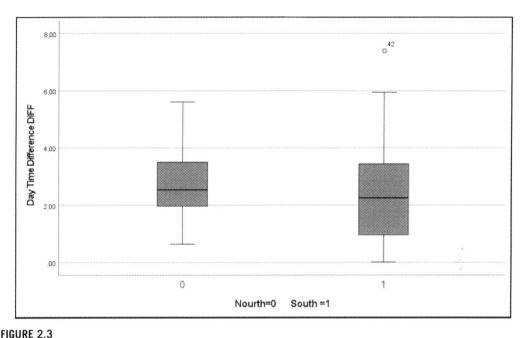

FIGURE 2.3

Diurnal urban heat island effect in Global South and Global North.

Source: Authors' elaborations.

With regard to nocturnal temperature dispersion—presented in Fig. 2.4—the countries of the Global South and Global North show similar performances. The overall dispersion of the nocturnal UHI in the Global South ranges between 0 and 2.1 Celsius degrees. For the Global North, the UHI ranges between 0.00 and 1.60 Celsius degrees.

The comparison of the diurnal and nocturnal UHI effects in the Global South and Global North indicates that, in tendency, the areas with extreme UHI effects are concentrated in the Global South.

Furthermore, we find a slightly positive association between the level of per capita income and the strength of the UHI effect. Based on Fig. 2.5, a slightly positive impact between the level of per-capita income and UHI effects can be concluded.

Wind intensity is an additional inspected variable. The assessment of the association between wind statistics for 10% windiest area in the respective urban area and the diurnal UHI effect is positive and exhibits a positive impact on the UHI effect. Interestingly, this finding is not in line with the existing literature, which suggests a negative nexus between wind intensity and the strength of the UHI effect (Rajagopalan et al., 2014) (Fig. 2.6).

4.2 Multilevel multivariate regression analysis

To account for the fact that more than 25,599 urban areas in the dataset belong to two large groups and 88 different countries, the study employs a multilevel mixed-effects linear regression with potential

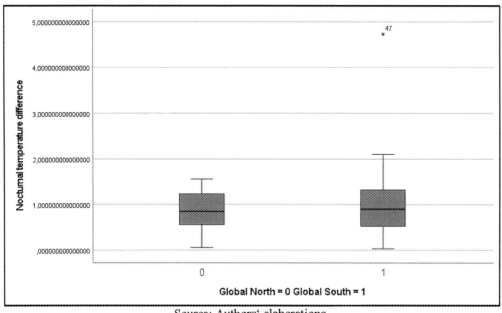

FIGURE 2.4

Nocturnal urban heat island effect in Global South and Global North.

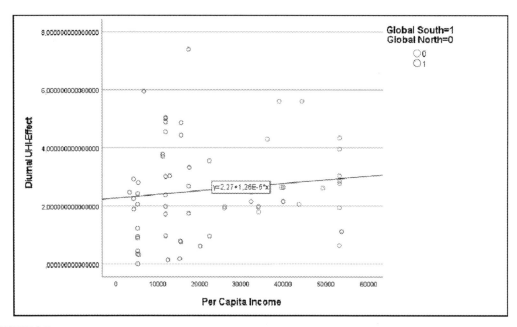

FIGURE 2.5

Per capita income and diurnal UHI effect.

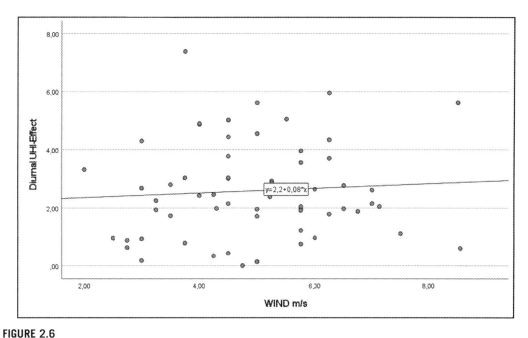

FIGURE 2.6

Wind intensity and diurnal UHI effect.

Source: Authors' elaborations.

drivers of urban heating. As reported in Table 2.2, residual interclass correlations indicate that belonging to different a specific country is a valid and statistically significant random determinant of the UHI effect.

Multilevel estimators indicate a statistically significant negative impact of latitude on the intensity of the UHI effect: 1% increase of latitude corresponds with a 3.32% additional temperature differential between urban and suburban areas. One percentage increase of population corresponds with a 0.039 percentage increase of the respective temperature differential. Furthermore, the estimator reveals that larger urban areas in terms of square kilometers suffer more under the UHI effect: 1% greater urban area corresponds with a 0.00,578 percentage increase of the UHI effect. Another interesting result is related to per-capita income levels. The study finds that per capita income has no statistically significant impact on the respective temperature differential.

The outcomes emerging from a development economics perspective returns important research and policy implications. However, despite the relevance of the differentiation between the Global North and the Global South, which has been illustrated in the previous subsection, it is rather difficult to draw a clear line between these two groups of countries. Hence, one can conclude that the mitigation and adaptation strategies to counteract the vulnerability to the UHI effects must be formulated primarily at the national level. Hence, in the following section, the study presents the results of a two-level mixed-effects linear estimator without taking into account the Global South/North as the highest data level. The findings sketched in Table 2.3 indicate that belonging to the Global South corresponds to a 201%

Table 2.2 Three-level mixed-effects maximum-likelihood regression.

```
. mixed lnUNI_NIGHT LATITUDE  lnPCI  lnPOPULTION  SQKM_FINAL  || SouthNourth:

Performing EM optimization:

Performing gradient-based optimization:

Iteration 0:   log likelihood = -30525.844
Iteration 1:   log likelihood = -30525.807
Iteration 2:   log likelihood = -30525.805

Computing standard errors:

Mixed-effects ML regression                  Number of obs    =     18,679
```

Group Variable	No. of Groups	Observations per Group Minimum	Average	Maximum
SouthNourth	2	3,838	9,339.5	14,841
COUNTRY_ID	88	1	212.3	6,486

```
                                             Wald chi2(4)     =      51.12
Log likelihood = -30525.805                  Prob > chi2      =     0.0000
```

lnUNI_NIGHT	Coef.	Std. Err.	z	P>|z|	[95% Conf. Interval]	
LATITUDE	-.0033234	.001557	-2.13	0.033	-.006375	-.0002717
lnPCI	-.0109657	.0422464	-0.26	0.795	-.093767	.0718357
lnPOPULTION	.0394226	.0087416	4.51	0.000	.0222893	.0565559
SQKM_FINAL	.0000578	.0000206	2.80	0.005	.0000173	.0000982
_cons	-.977818	.3878124	-2.52	0.012	-1.737916	-.2177195

Random-effects Parameters	Estimate	Std. Err.	[95% Conf. Interval]	
SouthNourth: Identity				
var(_cons)	8.54e-11	3.16e-09	2.72e-42	2.68e+21
COUNTRY_ID: Identity				
var(_cons)	.1229644	.0257359	.081588	.1853242
var(Residual)	1.525838	.0158226	1.49514	1.557167

```
LR test vs. linear model: chi2(2) = 538.26            Prob > chi2 = 0.0000

Note: LR test is conservative and provided only for reference.

. estat icc

Residual intraclass correlation
```

Level	ICC	Std. Err.	[95% Conf. Interval]	
SouthNourth	5.18e-11	0	5.18e-11	5.18e-11
COUNTRY_ID|SouthNourth	.074578	.0144739	.0507171	.1083831

Source: Authors' calculations.

Table 2.3 Two-level mixed-effects maximum-likelihood regression.

```
Performing EM optimization:

Performing gradient-based optimization:

Iteration 0:   log likelihood = -30529.406
Iteration 1:   log likelihood = -30529.406

Computing standard errors:

Mixed-effects ML regression              Number of obs     =     18,678
Group variable: COUNTRY_ID               Number of groups  =         87

                                         Obs per group:
                                                    min =          1
                                                    avg =      214.7
                                                    max =      6,486

                                         Wald chi2(4)      =      41.50
Log likelihood = -30529.406              Prob > chi2       =     0.0000
```

lnUNI_NIGHT	Coef.	Std. Err.	z	P>|z|	[95% Conf. Interval]	
lnPCI	.0099101	.0510834	0.19	0.846	-.0902115	.1100317
lnPOPULTION	.0464416	.014494	3.20	0.001	.0180339	.0748493
lnAREA	.0037942	.0174187	0.22	0.828	-.0303458	.0379342
SouthNourth	.201939	.126121	1.60	0.109	-.0452537	.4491316
_cons	-1.475949	.543064	-2.72	0.007	-2.540335	-.4115632

Random-effects Parameters	Estimate	Std. Err.	[95% Conf. Interval]	
COUNTRY_ID: Identity				
var(_cons)	.1241972	.0257414	.0827351	.1864376
var(Residual)	1.526652	.0158308	1.495937	1.557997

```
LR test vs. linear model: chibar2(01) = 575.93       Prob >= chibar2 = 0.0000
```

greater UHI effect. The effect is statistically significant at a 10% level. The number of inhabitants is another statistically significant determinant of the UHI effect: a 1% additional population corresponds with a 0.04% additional temperature differential.

5. Conclusion and policy discussion

The UHI effect is a detrimental phenomenon for climate change and environmental and public health. However, to date, this topic has not been sufficiently disentangled in either climate change mitigation and adaptation or development economics and sustainability terms. On top of that, UHI calls for additional studies based on vulnerability, resilience, adaptation, and mitigation perspectives. Furthermore, looking at the past scholarship on this issue, a call for quantitative inquiries emerges. To address this research question, this book chapter made the first step toward portraying the contours of the systematic difference between the vulnerability and magnitude to the UHI effect of countries of the Global South and Global North. To this scope, the work exploited the CIESIN's Satellite-Derived Environmental Indicators on Global Urban Heat Island provided by a joint effort of the Columbia University and NASA. A worldwide extensive dataset is built for this purpose, and a number of econometrics tools are employed.

The study finds that being a country of the Global South corresponds with a 201 percentage greater exposure to the risks related to the UHI. Global climate change exacerbates these risks in tropical regions. Hence, international action on climate change must focus both on the prevention of the local UHI effects and global climate change. Solar radiation management (SRM), which is expressed in the whitening of the cities and other kinds of reflectivity, is an appropriate strategy to counteract both phenomena.

Addressing the issue of global UHI mitigation will signify marking a noteworthy step toward climate change adaptation. This pathway will be of primary importance to shape resilience policy where environmental and climate justice is ensured to all, firstly to the vulnerable socioeconomic groups (Leal Filho et al., 2018, Mitchell and Chakraborty, 2014; Cisco and Gatto, 2021; Gatto and Drago, 2020). Key strategies will take into account cleaner energy transition pathways, capable of smoothing energy insecurity and vulnerability (Santamouris, 2020; Sadik-Zada and Gatto, 2021a,b; Aldieri et al., 2021).

Possible policy actions arise. The SRM is underpinned by the goal to "make the planet a little more reflective," which, in turn, will "partially and imperfectly compensate for the buildup of greenhouse gases like carbon dioxide, which are tending to trap heat and make the earth warmer" (Keith, 2015). SRM technologies would place reflective material in space or in Earth's atmosphere to scatter or reflect sunlight (for example, by injecting sulfate aerosols into the stratosphere to scatter incoming solar radiation or brightening clouds). Alternatively, it would increase the planet's reflectivity (for example, by painting roofs and pavements in light colors). The central advantage of SRM is that it is cheap and affordable for most developing and even least developed countries (Eddebbar et al., 2015; Lawrence et al., 2018; Marzeion et al., 2018; Rogelj et al., 2019).

UHI countermeasures include three major mitigation measures to combat negative UHI effects. These include: i) designing cool pavements by installing reflective surfaces; ii) increasing green spaces; and iii) making use of the cooling effects of wind and water (Sanchez and Reames, 2019; Gorsevski et al., 1998; Mohajerani et al., 2017; Santamouris et al., 2018). Cool pavements come to their own over increased use of the construction materials with a high degree of solar reflectance and emit absorbed energy fast (Akbari and Kolokosta, 2016). Such surfaces transmit less heat into the buildings. In general, "cool" materials are those with high solar reflectance and high thermal transmittance.

The second strategy in the mitigation of UHI is planting trees and extension of vegetation. Trees and vegetation counteract UHI by providing shade and increasing water evaporation and transpiration to the atmosphere, i.e., evapotranspiration. Shading and evapotranspiration have the potential of reducing summer peak temperatures by 5 Celsius degrees (Huang et al., 1990; Kurn et al., 1994). Trees and vegetation yield the greatest counter UHI effects if planted around buildings and alongside streets to shade pavements. Planting trees, extending park spaces contribute also to the attractiveness of the urban areas for living and bring additional taxes for the local community budgets. Indeed, McPherson et al. (2005) show that the costs of planting trees and the follow-up costs of forestry are 30%−50% less than the benefits for the urban communities.

References

Akbari, H., Kolokosta, D., 2016. Three decades of urban heat islands and mitigation technologies research. Energy Build. 133, 834−842. https://doi.org/10.1016/j.enbuild.2016.09.067.

Akbari, H., Levinson, R., Miller, W., Berdahl, P., 2005. Cool colored roofs to save energy and improve air quality. In: Proceedings of International Conference on Passive and Low Energy Cooling for the Built Environment, Santorini, Greece.

Alcoforado, M.J., Andrade, H., 2006. Nocturnal urban heat island in Lisbon (Portugal): main features and modelling attempts. Theor. Appl. Climatol. 84, 151−159.

Aldieri, L., Gatto, A., Vinci, C.P., 2021. Evaluation of energy resilience and adaptation policies: an energy efficiency analysis. Energy Pol. 157, 112505.

Amorim, M., Dubreuil, V., 2017. Intensity of urban heat islands in tropical and temperate climates. Climate 5 (4), 91. https://doi.org/10.3390/cli5040091.

Baker, L.A., Brazel, A.J., Selover, N., Martin, C., McIntyre, N., Steiner, F.R., Nelson, A., Musacchio, L., 2002. Urbanization and warming of Phoenix (Arizona, USA): impacts, feedbacks and mitigation. Urban Ecosyst. 6 (3), 183−203.

Center for International Earth Science Information Network - CIESIN - Columbia University, 2016. Global Summer Land Surface Temperature (LST) Grids, 2016. NASA Socioeconomic Data and Applications Center (SEDAC), Palisades, NY. https://doi.org/10.7927/H408638T (Accessed 8 March 2021).

Center for International Earth Science Information Network - CIESIN - Columbia University, CUNY Institute for Demographic Research - CIDR - City University of New York, International Food Policy Research Institute - IFPRI, The World Bank, and Centro Internacional de Agricultura Tropical - CIAT, 2015. Global Rural-Urban Mapping Project, Version 1 (GRUMPv1): Urban Extent Polygons, Revision 02. NASA Socioeconomic Data and Applications Center (SEDAC), Palisades, NY. https://doi.org/10.7927/np6p-qe61 (Accessed 8 March 2021).

Center for International Earth Science Information Network (CIESIN), Columbia University, 2016. Global Urban Heat Island (UHI) Data Set, 2013. NASA Socioeconomic Data and Applications Center (SEDAC), Palisades, NY. https://doi.org/10.7927/H4H70CRF (Accessed 8 March 2021).

Chakraborty, T., Hsu, A., Manya, D., Sheriff, G., 2019. Disproportionately higher exposure to urban heat in lower-income neighborhoods: a multi-city perspective. Environ. Res. Lett. 14 (10), 105003. https://iopscience.iop.org/article/10.1088/1748-9326/ab3b99.

Chandler, T.J., 1964. City growth and urban climates. Weather 19, 170−171.

Chatterjee, S., Khan, A., Dinda, A., Mithun, S., Khatun, R., Akbari, H., Kusaka, H., Mitra, C., Bhatti, S.S., Van Doan, Q., Wang, Y., 2019. Simulating micro-scale thermal interactions in different building environments for mitigating urban heat islands. Sci. Total Environ. 663, 610−631.

Che-Ani, A.I., Shahmohamadi, P., Sairi, A., Mohd-Nor, M.F.I., Zain, M.F.M., Surat, M., 2009. Mitigating the urban heat island effect: some points without altering existing city planning. Eur. J. Sci. Res. 35 (2), 204−216.

Chow, W.T.L., Roth, M., 2006. Temporal dynamics of the urban heat island of Singapore. Int. J. Climatol. 26 (15), 2243−2260.

Cisco, G., Gatto, A., 2021. Climate justice in an intergenerational sustainability framework: a stochastic OLG model. Economies. https://www.preprints.org/manuscript/202011.0664/v1.

Crutzen, P.J., 2004. New directions: the growing urban heat and pollution island effect-impact on chemistry and climate. Atmos. Environ. 38, 3539−3540. https://doi.org/10.1016/j.atmosenv.2004.03.032.

de Schiller, S., Martin Evans, J., 1998. Sustainable urban development: design guidelines for warm humid cities. Urban Des. Int. 3, 165−184. https://doi.org/10.1057/udi.1998.23.

Eddebbar, Y.A., Gallo, N.D., Linsmayer, L.B., 2015. The Ocean and the UN Framework Convention on Climate Change. Association for the Sciences in Limnology and Oceanography. ASLO. https://doi.org/10.1002/lob.10059.

Eliasson, I., 1996. Urban nocturnal temperatures, street geometry and land use. Environment 30, 379−392.

Estrada, F., Tol, R.S.J., Botzen, W.J.W., 2017. Global economic impacts of climate variability and change during the 20th century. PLoS One 12 (2). https://doi.org/10.1371/journal.pone.0172201 e0172201.

Fallmann, J., Forkel, R., Emeis, S., 2016. Secondary effects of urban heat island mitigation measures on air quality. Atmos. Environ. 125, 199−211.

Gatto, A., Busato, F., 2020. Energy vulnerability around the world: the global energy vulnerability index (GEVI). J. Clean. Prod. 253, 118691.

Gatto, A., Drago, C., 2021. When renewable energy, empowerment, and entrepreneurship connect: measuring energy policy effectiveness in 230 countries. Energy Res. Social Sci. 78, 101977.

Gatto, A., Drago, C., 2020. Measuring and modeling energy resilience. Ecol. Econ. 172, 106527.

Gatto, A., Polselli, N., Bloom, G., 2016. Empowering Gender Equality through Rural Development: Rural Markets and Micro-finance in Kyrgyzstan. L'Europa e la Comunità Internazionale Difronte alle Sfide dello Sviluppo, pp. 65−89.

Gerland, P., Raftery, A., Ševčíková, H., Li, H., Gu, D., Spoorenberg, T., Alkema, L., Fosdick, B.K., Chunn, J., Lalic, N., n Bay, G., Buettner, T., Heilig, G.K., Wilmoth, J., 2014. World population stabilization unlikely this century. Science 346 (6206), 234−237. https://doi.org/10.1126/science.1257469.

Gorsevski, V., Taha, H., Quattrochi, D., Luvall, J., 1998. Air pollution prevention through urban heat island mitigation: an update on the Urban Heat Island Pilot Project. In: Proceedings of the ACEEE Summer Study, Asilomar, CA, 9, pp. 23−32.

Heaviside, C., Macintyre, H., Vardoulakis, S., 2017. The Urban Heat Island: implications for health in a changing environment. Curr. Environ. Health Rep. 4, 296−305.

Howard, L., 1833. The Climate of London, vols. I−III (London).

Howard, L., 1818. The Climate of London, Deduced from Meteorological Observations, Made at Different Places in the Neighbourhood of the Metropolis, vol. 2 (London).

Huang, J., Akbari, H., Taha, H., 1990. The wind-shielding and shading effects of trees on residential heating and cooling requirements. In: ASHRAE Winter Meeting, American Society of Heating, Refrigerating and Air-Conditioning Engineers. Atlanta, Georgia.

Kumar, R., Mishra, V., Buzan, J., Kumar, R., Shindell, D., Huber, M., 2017. Dominant control of agriculture and irrigation on urban heat island in India. Sci. Rep. 7 (1), 14054. https://doi.org/10.1038/s41598-017-14213-2.

Kurn, D., Bretz, S., Huang, B., Akbari, H., 1994. The potential for reducing urban air temperatures and energy consumption through vegetative cooling (PDF). In: ACEEE Summer Study on Energy Efficiency in Buildings, American Council for an Energy Efficient Economy. Pacific Grove, California, p. 31.

Landsberg, H.E., 1981. In: The Urban Climate, vol. 28. Academic Press.

Lawrence, M.G., Schäfer, S., Muri, H., et al., 2018. Evaluating climate geoengineering proposals in the context of the Paris Agreement temperature goals. Nat. Commun. 9, 3734.

Leal Filho, W., Icaza, L.E., Neht, A., Klavins, M., Morgan, E.A., 2018. Coping with the impacts of urban heat islands. A literature based study on understanding urban heat vulnerability and the need for resilience in cities in a global climate change context. J. Clean. Prod. 171, 1140−1149.

Lee, K., Kim, Y., Sung, H.C., Ryu, J., Jeon, S.W., 2020. Trend analysis of urban heat island intensity according to urban area change in Asian mega cities. Sustainability 12 (1), 112. https://doi.org/10.3390/su12010112.

Lewis, A., 1954. Economic development with unlimited supplies of labour. Manch. Sch. 22 (2), 139—191. https://doi.org/10.1111/j.1467-9957.1954.tb00021.x.

Li, D., Bou-Zeid, E., Oppenheimer, M., 2014. The effectiveness of cool and green roofs as urban heat island mitigation strategies. Environ. Res. Lett. 9 (5), 055002.

Li, X., Zhou, Y., Yu, S., Jia, G., Li, H., Li, W., 2019. Urban heat island impacts on building energy consumption: a review of approaches and findings. Energy 174, 407—419. https://doi.org/10.1016/j.energy.2019.02.183.

Liu, J., Niyogi, D., 2020. Identification of linkages between urban heat Island magnitude and urban rainfall modification by use of causal discovery algorithms. Urban Clim. 33, 100659.

Lois, D., 2015. Mehrabenenanalyse mit STATA: Grundlagen und Erweiterungen. Fakultät für Human-wissenschaften Sozialwissenschaftliche Methodenlehre. Universität München.

Manley, G., 1958. On the frequency of snowfall in metropolitan England. Q. J. R. Meteorol. Soc. 84, 70—72.

Marzeion, B., Kaser, G., Maussion, F., et al., 2018. Limited influence of climate change mitigation on short-term glacier mass loss. Nat. Clim. Change 8, 305—308. https://doi.org/10.1038/s41558-018-0093-1.

McPherson, E.G., Simpson, J.R., Peper, P.J., Maco, S.E., Xiao, Q., 2005. Municipal forest benefits and costs in five US cities (PDF) (6 pp, 267K). J. For. 103 (8), 411—416.

Mitchell, J.M., 1961. A preliminary evaluation of atmospheric pollution as a cause of the global temperature fluctuation of the past century. In: Singer, S.F. (Ed.), Global Effects of Environmental Pollution. Springer, Dordrecht. https://doi.org/10.1007/978-94-010-3290-2_15.

Mitchell, B.C., Chakraborty, J., 2014. Urban heat and climate justice: a landscape of thermal inequity in Pinellas County, Florida. Geogr. Rev. 104 (4), 459—480.

Mojajerani, A., Bakaric, J., Jeffrey-Bailey, T., 2017. The urban heat island effect, its causes, and mitigation, with reference to the thermal properties of asphalt concrete. J. Environ. Manag. 197, 522—538. https://doi.org/10.1016/j.jenvman.2017.03.095.

Oke, T.R., 1982. The energetic basis of the urban heat island. Q. J. R. Meteorol. Soc. 108, 1—24.

Oke, T.R., 1973. City size and urban heat island. Atmos. Environ. 7, 769—779.

Padmanabhamurty, B., 1979. Isotherms and isohumes in Pune on clear winter nights: a Mesometeorological study. Mausam 30, 134—138.

Rajagopalan, P., Lim, K.C., Jamei, E., 2014. Urban heat island and wind flow characteristics of a tropical city. Sol. Energy 107, 159—170. https://doi.org/10.1016/j.solener.2014.05.042.

Rogelj, J., Forster, P.M., Kriegler, E., et al., 2019. Estimating and tracking the remaining carbon budget for stringent climate targets. Nature 571, 335—342. https://doi.org/10.1038/s41586-019-1368-z.

Sadik-Zada, E.R., Gatto, A., 2021a. The Puzzle of Greenhouse Gas Footprints of Oil Abundance. Socio-Economic Planning Sciences, p. 100936.

Sadik-Zada, E.R., Gatto, A., 2021b. Energy security pathways in South East Europe: diversification of the natural gas supplies, energy transition, and energy futures. In: From Economic to Energy Transition. Palgrave Macmillan, Cham, pp. 491—514.

Sadik-Zada, E.R., Gatto, A., Blick, N., 2022. Rural electrification and transition to clean cooking: the case study of kanyegaramire and kyamugarura solar mini-grid energy cooperatives in the Kyenjojo District of Uganda. In: Sustainable Policies and Practices in Energy, Environment and Health Research. Springer, Cham, pp. 547—562.

Sanchez, L., Reames, T.G., 2019. Cooling Detroit: a socio-spatial analysis of equity in green roofs as an urban heat island mitigation strategy. Urban For. Urban Green. 44, 126331.

Sangiorgio, V., Fiorito, F., Santamouris, M., 2020. Development of a holistic urban heat island evaluation methodology. Sci. Rep. 10, 17913. https://doi.org/10.1038/s41598-020-75018-4.

Santamouris, M., 2020. Recent progress on urban overheating and heat island research. Integrated assessment of the energy, environmental, vulnerability and health impact. Synergies with the global climate change. Energy Build. 207, 109482.

Santamouris, M., Haddad, S., Saliari, M., Vasilakopoulou, K., Synnefa, A., Paolini, R., Ulpiani, G., Garshasbi, S., Fiorito, F., 2018. On the energy impact of urban heat island in Sydney: climate and energy potential of mitigation technologies. Energy Build. 166, 154–164.

Santamouris, M., 2011. Heat island research in Europe: the state of the art. Adv. Build. Energy Res. 1 (1), 123–150. https://doi.org/10.1080/17512549.2007.9687272.

Santamouris, M., Kolokotsa, D., 2016. Urban Climate Mitigation Techniques. Taylor & Francis Group Ltd, 2 Park Square, Milton Park, Abingdon, Oxford, OX14 4RN, UK. https://doi.org/10.4324/9781315765839.

Santamouris, M., Adnot, J., Alvarez, S., Klitsikas, N., Orphelin, M., Lopes, C., Sanchez, F., 2004. Cooling the Cities. Eyrolles, Paris.

Sarrat, C., Lemonsu, A., Masson, V., Guédalia, D., 2006. Impact of urban heat island on regional atmospheric pollution. Atmos. Environ. 40, 1743–1758.

Searle, S.R., 1997. Linear Models for Unbalanced Data. Wiley, New York.

Seto, K.C., Shepherd, J.M., 2009. Global urban land-use trends and climate impacts. Curr. Opin. Environ. Sustain. 1 (1), 89–95.

Shahmohamadi, P., Che-Ani, A.I., Etessam, I., Maulud, K.,N.A., Tawil, N.M., 2011a. Healthy environment: the need to mitigate urban heat island effects on human health. Procedia Eng. 20, 61–70. https://doi.org/10.1016/j.proeng.2011.11.139.

Shahmohamadi, P., Che-Ani, A.I., Maulud, K.N.A., Tawil, N.M., Abdullah, N.A.G., 2011b. The impact of anthropogenic heat on formation of urban heat island and energy consumption balance. Urban Stud. Res. 2011 (9). https://doi.org/10.1155/2011/497524. Article ID 497524.

Sham, S., 1973. The urban heat island: its concept and application to Kuala Lumpur. Sains Malays. 2 (1), 53–64.

Sham, S., 1986. Temperatures in Kuala Lumpur and the Merging Klang Valley Conurbation. Institute of Advanced Studies, University of Malaya, Malaysia (Kuala Lumpur, Report prepared for UNESCO under the Ecoville Project).

Stathopoulou, E., Mihalakakou, G., Santamouris, M., 2008. On the impact of temperature on tropospheric ozone concentration levels in urban environments. J. Earth Syst. Sci. 117, 227–236. https://doi.org/10.1007/s12040-008-0027-9.

Synnefa, A., Santamouris, M., Apostolakis, K., 2007. On the development, optical properties and thermal performance of cool colored coatings for the urban environment. Sol. Energy 81 (4), 488–497.

Taesler, R., Andersson, C., Nord, M., Gollvik, L., 2006. Analyses of impacts of weather and climate on building energy performance with special regard to urban climate characteristics. In: Proceedings of Sixth International Conference on Urban Climate, Gothenburg, Sweden.

Tan, J., Zheng, Y., Tang, X., Guo, C., Li, L., Song, G., Chen, H., 2010. The urban heat island and ist impact on heat waves and human health in Shanghai. Int. J. Biometereol. 54, 75–84.

Tomlinson, C.J., Chapman, L., Thornes, J.E., 2011. Including the urban heat island in spatial heat health risk assessment strategies: a case study for Birmingham, UK. Int. J. Health Geogr. 10 (42), 1–14. https://doi.org/10.1186/1476-072X-10-42.

Toparar, Y., 2018. A Multiscale Analysis of the Urban Heat Island Effect: From City Averaged Temperatures to the Energy Demand of Individual Buildings. Technishe Universiteit Eindhoven. https://pure.tue.nl/ws/files/95411608/20180425_Toparlar.pdf.

Tewari, M., Yang, J., Kusaka, H., Palou, F.S., Watson, C., Treinish, L., 2019. Interaction of urban heat islands and heat waves under current and future climate conditions and their mitigation using green and cool roofs in New York City and Phoenix. Arizona Environ. Res. Lett. 14, 034002.

Tzavali, A., Paravantis, J.P., Mihalakokou, G., Fotiadi, A., Stigka, E., 2015. Urban heat island intensity: a literature review. Fresenius Environ. Bull. 24 (12b), 4537–4554.

United Nations, 2018. World Urbanization Prospects. United Nations, New York.

United Nations, 2014. World Urbanization Prospects: The 2014 Revision. United Nations, New York.

Wong, N.H., 2005. Study of green areas and urban heat island in a tropical city. Habitat Int. 29 (3), 547−558. https://doi.org/10.1016/j.habitatint.2004.04.008.

Wooldridge, J.M., 2016. Introductory Econometrics: A Modern Approach. Nelson Education.

Luminescence for the built environment: from lighting to urban heat island mitigation purposes

Chiara Chiatti[1], Ioannis Kousis[1], Claudia Fabiani[1,2] and Anna Laura Pisello[1,2]

[1]*CIRIAF — Interuniversity Research Center, University of Perugia, Perugia, Italy;* [2]*Department of Engineering, University of Perugia, Perugia, Italy*

1. Introduction

Because of the rapid evolution of urbanization and the consequent increase in anthropogenic emissions, climate change has become one of the most pressing problems of the 21st century. Accordingly, the urban heat island (UHI) phenomenon, resulting in higher surface and air temperatures within cities compared to their rural surroundings, has been recognized as responsible for negative environmental impacts, such as health issues for people, increased greenhouse gases (GHG) emission, and higher energy consumption (Harlan and Ruddell, 2011; Mushtaha et al., 2021). In particular, the role played by building constructions as both natural resources consumers and GHGs generators is exacerbated because of the increased cooling energy demand they need to face, especially during the summer months (de Wilde and Coley, 2012; Zinzi et al., 2018; Dino and Meral Akgül, 2019).

In this context, several passive strategies have been investigated by the research community with the aim of mitigating UHI (Kousis and Pisello, 2020). A special focus has been dedicated to the implementation of cool materials in cities, i.e., materials characterized by high solar reflectance (SR) and thermal emittance (ε) values, whose ability to reject and reemit the incident and absorbed radiation helps in maintaining urban surfaces cooler (Santamouris and Yun, 2020; Bartesaghi-Koc et al., 2021). According to their peculiar behavior, cool materials can be divided into different subcategories:

- Reflective materials, both natural and artificial, with the ability to highly reject the incident radiation, especially in the visible (VIS) and near infrared (NIR) spectrum. They can be white (Alghamdy et al., 2021; Rosso et al., 2017a) or colored (Lv et al., 2021; Synnefa et al., 2007), depending on the architectural needs to be met, and suitable for a wide range of applications (roofs, pavements, facades, etc.).
- Retroreflective materials, which reject the incoming solar radiation in the same direction of incidence (Castellani, 2021). They are particularly suitable for applications on vertical surfaces, because they partially avoid neighboring buildings and pavements from being reached by reflected energy (Hernández-Pérez et al., 2017; Rossi et al., 2014).

— Thermochromics materials, characterized by a color transition behavior due to a temperature change in their transition range, which influences the crystalline phase and structure of the material (Fabiani et al., 2020). They are generally implemented in advanced coatings for roof applications, showing an adaptable reflectance that helps in reducing buildings energy consumptions in summer and winter by preserving the positive passive heating phenomenon in the colder season (Mann et al., 2020; Nguyen et al., 2021).

Recently, materials with luminescent properties have thrusted into prominence among the new generation of cool materials. Indeed, their ability to emit light may be seen as a further contribution to the release of the absorbed solar radiation (Garshasbi et al., 2020a). The parameter quantifying the fraction of incident solar energy rejected by both reflection (at the same wavelength) and light emission (at longer wavelength) has been defined as effective solar reflectance (Levinson et al., 2017). Given that luminescence can be activated by different types of sources (Capelletti, 2017), the main focus of this chapter is photoluminescence, i.e., the emission of light caused by the energy absorption of a material when exposed to UV or visible (VIS) radiation. If the emission stops at the end of the excitation, the phenomenon is referred to as fluorescence, while a longer light emission is referred to as phosphorescence.

Photoluminescence has been known for many centuries: the first observation dates back to the 17th century, when a barite stone was found to glow in the dark after a calcination process (Lastusaari et al., 2012). Almost 200 years after that, other luminescent products made of copper- and cobalt-doped ZnS were discovered by T. Sidot (Kolar & den Hollander, 2003) and chemically identified by Lenard et al. (Lenard et al., 1928), together with other compounds. However, their luminous intensity and duration were not satisfactory to think about possible applications and, the subsequent addition of radioactive elements to improve their performance, led to environmental and health concerns. These concerns together with the contemporaneous need for innovative materials for more efficient lighting products gave the inputs for searching new nonradioactive phosphors. Starting from the work of Matsuzawa et al. (1996) on $SrAl_2O_4$:Eu^{2+}, Dy^{3+}, and its potential for different civil applications (e.g., safety signs, toys, watch dials, etc.), a huge number of photoluminescent compounds has been discovered and optimized through the last 20 years (Smet et al., 2015).

As previously mentioned, the search for new photoluminescent materials has been mainly driven by their potential to provide free and rechargeable lighting. Many research studies concerning the chemical characterization of phosphors have acknowledged their potential in terms of luminous lifetime and quality. As a consequence, promising innovative applications for lighting have been suggested, coming from the fact that, at present days, public lighting service accounts for almost 50% of the electricity consumption in cities (European Commission, 2012). In particular, the research community has been focused on lighting systems' optimization strategies because of the scarcity of traditional energy sources. This is why lighting devices that usually require a huge amount of energy in exchange for poor performance tend to be removed (Mizon, 2012): for instance, incandescent and fluorescent lamps are increasingly being replaced by solid-state lighting, which uses the LED (light emitting diode) technology. Among LEDs solutions to obtain efficient white light, phosphor conversion's strategies make use of photoluminescence to turn the blue LED light emission into longer wavelengths (Azarifar et al., 2021; Xia and Liu, 2016). However, the need for further investigations on the physics behind the luminescent mechanism and on compounds optimization processes has always hindered the implementation of the pure photoluminescent material in the built environment and the upscaling at higher technology readiness levels (Chiatti et al., 2021a). As a result, despite luminescent building materials being already commercially available (e.g., glass, ceramics, paints, etc.), their use is currently limited to decorative and ornamental purposes (e.g., toys, gadgets and furnishing elements) (Rojas-Hernandez et al., 2018).

At the same time, the cooling potential of photoluminescence is even less investigated. Recent studies have demonstrated the additional heat rejection contribution of the photoluminescent effect to the normal ability of traditional cool materials to reflect and release the absorbed energy, according to the following equation (Garshasbi et al., 2020a; Kousis et al., 2021):

$$R_n = SW_\downarrow + LW_\downarrow - SW_\uparrow - LW_\uparrow =$$
$$= SW_\downarrow + LW_\downarrow - \left(\rho_{SW} \cdot SW_\downarrow + \varepsilon_{SW}\sigma T^4\right) - \left(\rho_{LW} \cdot LW_\downarrow + (\varepsilon + \varepsilon_{LW})\sigma T^4\right)$$

where R_n is the net radiation gain of the material, while SW and LW are the short- and long-wave radiation components that hit ($\downarrow$) or are rejected ($\uparrow$) by the surface. In particular, the latter can be seen as functions of the reflectance (ρ) and thermal emittance (ε) of the material, as well as the temperature (T) of the surface. The cooling capability through photoluminescence is given by the extra factors of emissivity in both short (ε_{SW}) and near-infrared (ε_{LW}) wave range. Up to now, techniques for the evaluation of the photoluminescent cooling are based on empirical methods aimed at comparing the surface temperature of the luminescent sample to that of the corresponding nonluminescent one, characterized by the same optical properties.

In general, photoluminescent materials can be divided into bulk photoluminescent prototypes, such as Ruby and Egyptian blue, and nanoscale photoluminescent materials, such as quantum dots (QDs) and perovskite nanocrystals. The former are characterized by fixed optical properties, while the performance of the latter can be tuned by modifying their characteristics (e.g., size, shape, distance between nanoparticles, etc.) (Jana et al., 2016). Both scales have been experimentally and numerically tested with promising outcomes in terms of cooling potential. For instance, Ruby crystals were utilized for fabricating cool fluorescent coatings, while doped strontium aluminates were investigated as cool components for paving applications (Kousis et al., 2020). At the same time, photoluminescent QDs were tested and optimized for their cooling potential (Garshasbi et al., 2020a,b), while perovskite nanocrystals were studied as possible candidates for the upper layer of colored radiative coolers, i.e., supercooling structures that can achieve subambient surface temperatures (Son et al., 2021). However, in most cases, the making of the most suitable reference sample results in being too time-consuming and laborious for the procedure to be effectively applied. This is why further investigations on the radiative photoluminescence properties are needed on both theoretical and practical level, toward the optimization of luminescent materials for real-life applications.

Under this framework, the present chapter is intended to introduce the reader to the topic of photoluminescent materials and their potential for different environmental purposes. More in detail, after a presentation of the basic physics behind the phenomenon and the main discovered phosphors, the state of the art on their current applications is investigated, to finally land on the illustration of possible engineering urban-scale exploitation strategies. In addition to applications in the lighting sector, special attention is given to those solutions aimed at the mitigation of the UHI phenomenon, through both surfaces' temperature reduction and energy saving in the built environment.

2. Materials

According to the nature of the excitation source, different types of luminescence can be distinguished (Fig. 3.1). As introduced in Section 1, the present chapter is focused on the photoluminescent phenomenon concerning solid-state compounds, caused by UV or visible irradiation. Luminescent materials are also known as "light carriers." Indeed, the emission of light is the main luminescence effect and depends on the energy storage capacity of the phosphor itself: if the emission stops as the excitation ends, the phenomenon is addressed as fluorescence, while a longer exhibition of light deals with phosphorescence.

According to the latter distinction, the following sections introduce the main discoveries about fluorescent and phosphorescent materials, respectively. After a brief description of the specific luminescent mechanism, well-known compounds are introduced, highlighting their most interesting properties coming from recent research studies.

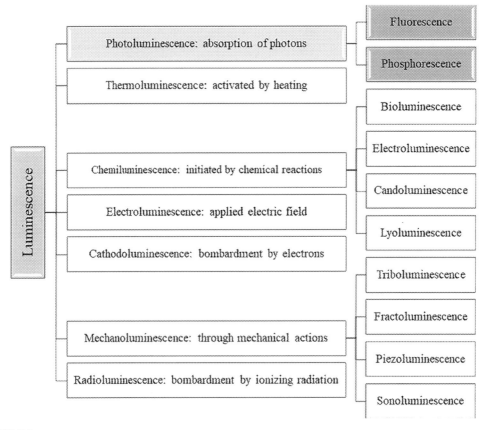

FIGURE 3.1

Types of luminescence and their excitation sources.

2.1 Fluorescent materials

Fluorescence is a light-emission mechanism that occurs due to the relaxation of photochemically excited electrons from their lowest excited to the ground state. The emitted photon is typically of lower energy, i.e., longer wavelength, than the absorbed one, since a part of the energy due to excitation is dissipated through vibrational relaxation. Fluorescent materials can be categorized into: (i) conventional bulk fluorescent and (ii) nanoscale materials. Examples of bulk fluorescent materials include ruby (Al_2O_3:Cr), Egyptian blue ($CaCuSi_4O_{10}$), and Han blue ($BaCuSi_4O_{10}$). Ruby's emission takes place in the deep red (~ 694 nm) and near infrared (700−800 nm). Similarly, Egyptian blue and Han blue emit at around 950 nm (Pozza et al., 2000). Recently, several fluorescent nanoscale materials have been fabricated and experimentally tested for various applications. For instance, Das et al. (2015) designed iron(III)phthalocyanine-based nanomaterials making use of pH responsive-magnetic-fluorescent nanoparticles with an absorbance and an emission peak around 260 and 460 nm, respectively. Wang et al. (2014) prepared a stable, red-emitting copper nanocluster (CuNCs) with peak emission near 620 nm and a quantum yield (QY) of 4.1%, by utilizing bovine serum albumin (BSA) as a template and hydrazine hydrate as reducing agent, under alkaline conditions at room temperature. Moreover, the same authors (Wang et al., 2014) developed a straightforward one-pot method to prepare very bright CuNCs with a QY as high as 14.1% in water using D-penicillamine. Similarly, Zhang et al. (Wang et al., 2015) have established a one-pot sonochemical route to GSH-stabilized CuNCs, which fluoresces at 608 nm with a QY of 5.6%.

Even though advanced and highly fluorescent structures are already developed, one of the main barriers for their scalable application is the deterioration of their properties when integrated into real-life components. Under this scenario, Benson et al. (2020) introduced small-molecule ionic isolation lattices (SMILES) that undergo the highest known brightness per volume. They reported that SMILES perfectly transfer the optical properties of dyes to solids, they are simple to make by mixing cationic dyes with anion-binding cyanostar macrocycles and work with major classes of commercial dyes, including xanthenes, oxazines, styryls, cyanines, and trianguleniums. Another nanoscale material that performs substantial fluorescence is the QD, i.e., light-emitting inorganic particles composing of groups II−VI (e.g., CdSe and CdTe) or III−V (e.g., InP) (Garshasbi and Santamouris, 2019). Unlike many fluorescent materials, their optical properties can be easily tuned while they can also exhibit thermochromism, adapting their optical performance with respect to temperature. Therefore, they are considered as promising candidates for cooling applications into the built environment.

2.2 Phosphorescent materials

The process of phosphorescence occurs in a manner similar to fluorescence, but with a much longer excited state lifetime. Phosphorescent materials are a subcategory of photoluminescent materials that emit light due to a precedent absorbance of photons. In this case, the emitted light is the result of a spin-forbidden process, through which the radiative decay of the excited electrons takes place within different spin multiplicity states (Mukherjee and Thilagar, 2015). Therefore, the emitted radiation in the form of light can persist for a long period, from seconds up to a couple of days. Generally speaking, phosphors with a VIS afterglow are useful when large visibility in the dark is of practical importance, such as luminous signage or lighting sources, while luminescence in the NIR range has proven to be promising for biomedical analyses.

Classic phosphorescent materials typically emit due to photoluminescence within the visible region. They are made with inorganic components, such as oxide, silicate, selenide, nitride, oxynitride and sulfide, and are generally doped with transition metal ions, such as Eu^{3+}, Eu^{2+}, Gd^{3+}, Tb^{3+}, Sm^{3+}, Pr^{3+}, Ho^{3+}, and Yb^{3+}, and rare-earth ions, such as Cr^{3+} and Mn^{2+} (Huang et al., 2019). A widely investigated persistent green phosphor is $SrAl_2O_4$:Eu^{2+}, Dy^{3+}, as well as other green Eu^{2+}-doped compounds. Tb^{3+}, Ce^{3+}, and Mn^{2+} also play as activators for a green phosphorescence. Other green-emitting artificial silicate phosphors are reported by doping Zn_2SiO_4 with Mn^{2+}, whose cations partly replace the positions of the Zn^{2+} cations, resulting in a broad emission band (Wang et al., 2008). Green emission activators may also be combined with blue phosphors, such as $BaMgAl_{10}O_{17}$:Eu^{2+} and $CaAl_2O_4$:Eu^{2+}, Dy^{3+}. Blue-emitting phosphors, such as $CsBaYB_6O_{12}$:Ce^{3+}, with high color purity of about 97% are also reported (Ntarisa et al., 2021). A cost-effective alternative to Eu is Ce^{3+} that can activate blue phosphorescence as well. Cerium and europium are also appropriate doping ions for yellow emitting phosphors. A yellow-emitting phosphor $Li_2CaSi_2N_4$:Ce^{3+} was designed by Wei et al. (2020) and reported with tunable photoluminescence and excellent thermal stability. Overall, blue and yellow emitting phosphors are the most commercially exploitable ones. A smaller number of studies investigated the development of phosphors that emit within the NIR range mainly due to the need for improved optical imaging techniques. For instance, Kamimura et al. (Kamimura et al., 2014) discovered that Sr_2SnO_4:Nd^{3+} phosphor exhibits NIR luminescence ranging from 850 to 1400 nm, while Caratto et al. (2014) found that introducing the Yb^{3+} dopant in Gd-oxycarbonate compounds, their NIR luminescence was increased to more than 144 h. Under the same framework, Pan et al. (2012) studied a series of Cr^{3+}- doped zinc gallogermanates that could be useful not only for bioimaging tools, but also for different outdoor environments. Indeed, such compounds showed the ability to be activated by only 1 min of sunlight exposure in different outdoor conditions, paving the way for promising applications in night-vision surveillance and solar energy exploitation.

3. Characterizing photoluminescent materials for building applications

In this section, several experimental procedures and standards for the characterization of photo-luminescent materials at different scales are introduced. First, a focus on the main techniques for the study of their composition is provided, highlighting the structural (Section 3.1) and thermo-optical (Section 3.2) procedures that are generally performed at a chemical scale of investigation. At a later stage, traditional methods to study the main properties of photoluminescent materials as cool materials based on acknowledged standards elaborated during the last years are also described (Section 3.3).

3.1 Structural characterization techniques

Knowing the crystalline structure of a sample is fundamental, as well as having information about the doping elements responsible for the luminescent effect. To these aims, X-ray diffraction (XRD) is usually performed as a primary method of investigation (Fig. 3.2A and B). It is based on the diffraction of an X-ray beam inside a crystal, according to the Bragg's law: by detecting the directions and intensities of the diffracted beam, a 3d model of the electrons' density can be obtained and, subsequently, the position of the atoms in the crystal. The model is then compared to standard

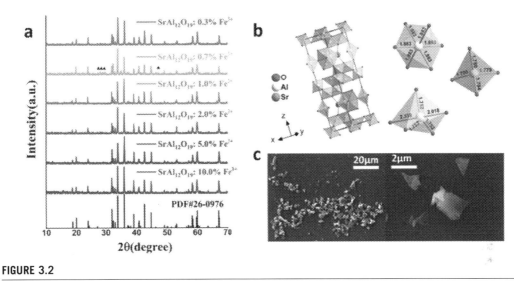

FIGURE 3.2

(A) XRD patterns of $SrAl_{12}O_{19}$ phosphors with different concentration of Fe^{3+}; (B) Structure diagram of $SrAl_{12}O_{19}$; (C) SEM images of $SrAl_{12}O_{19}:Fe^{3+}$ sample.

Reproduced from Zeng, J., Peng, G., Zhang, S., Krishnan, R.G, Ju, G., Li Y., et al., 2021. In-situ Insights into trap attributions in Fe^{3+}-activated long persistent phosphors. J. Lumin. 232, 117810. https://doi.org/10.1016/j.jlumin.2020.117810.

reference patterns to identify its specific nature. Another procedure to study the chemical composition of a sample makes use of a scanning electron microscope (SEM) that produces a focused beam of electrons hitting the material (Fig. 3.2C). Through the scanning process, the interaction between electrons and atoms in the sample causes different signals to be interpreted, containing information about the sample's topography and composition. Further microstructure investigations can be carried out through energy-dispersive X-ray analysis (EDX) and elemental mapping by time-of-flight secondary ion mass spectroscopy (TOF-SIMS). X-ray absorption spectroscopy (XAS) is another common technique used to identify the geometry of the lattice and its electronic structure: XAS profiles are obtained by means of an X-ray beam exciting the electrons, in order to detect the material absorption coefficient versus energy.

As introduced in Section 2, the photoluminescent performance of a material mainly depends on traps' nature, especially in terms of intensity and decay time. For this reason, dedicated procedures for the characterization of traps' concentration and depth may be useful for the correct evaluation of phosphors' behavior. For instance, electron spin resonance (ESR) has proven to be an effective technique for the detection of traps' structure and doping ions in materials with unpaired electrons, i.e., with characteristic magnetic properties. Indeed, an ESR spectrum is obtained by varying the magnetic field and recording the microwave absorption. Thermoluminescence (TL) techniques, instead, are usually applied to evaluate traps' depth. They consist of the emission of light during the sample heating, performed to help the material in releasing the stored energy, after the excitation: changing both the excitation time and temperature, traps' depth and their distribution can be estimated.

3.2 Thermo-optical characterization techniques

The complete thermooptical characterization of a material can be obtained by the combination of different investigation techniques. Spectrophotometric analyses are commonly performed to collect the reflectance spectrum of the sample, representative of the ability to reject incident frequencies in the visible range of the electromagnetic field. Focusing on the luminous performance of phosphors, their specific excitation and emission spectra can be collected through the use of a spectrofluorometer. In particular, the emission intensity corresponding to a singular wavelength (λ_{em}) depends on the number of emitted photons per unit time. The emission wavelength (λ_{em}), instead, is determined by the number of absorbed photons per unit time, at a given excitation wavelength (λ_{exc}). Keeping the latter fixed, the emission intensity is detected as a function of λ_{em} (Fig. 3.3B). Conversely, at fixed λ_{em}, the excitation intensity can be obtained as a function of λ_{exc} (Fig. 3.3A). Following this procedure, the excitation spectrum can be compared to the absorption one: if the two coincide, then the emission is due to the presence of an impurity characterized by that specific absorption profile. In solids, luminescence excitation spectrum may present multiple peaks because of multiple centers: in this case, multiple emission measurements should be performed, one for each excitation peak. Results of spectrofluorometric analyses are usually combined into excitation/emission maps (EEMs), considered as useful representations of the luminescent behavior of a sample.

Moving to a wider wavelength range of investigation, other spectroscopy techniques are usually adopted. For instance, Fourier-transform infrared (FTIR) spectroscopy is a procedure that allows detecting the absorption, emission, or reflection behavior of a material at each wavelength. While fluorometric measurements make use of a monochromatic beam of light hitting the sample, for FTIR one different combination of multiple-frequency beams is used to detect the amount that is absorbed,

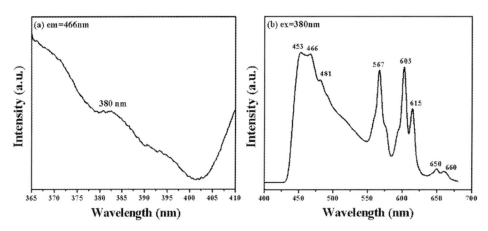

FIGURE 3.3

(A) Excitation and (B) emission spectrum of $ZrSiO_4{:}Sm^{3+}$ phosphor.

Reproduced with permission from Wu, M., Liu, S., Sun, Y., Chen, W., Huang, L., Chen, G., et al., 2020. Energy transfer of wide band long persistent phosphors of Sm^{3+}-Doped $ZrSiO_4$. Mater. Chem. Phys. 251, 123086. https://doi.org/10.1016/j. matchemphys.2020.123086.

emitted, or reflected by the compound. IR spectroscopy is successfully exploited in both organic and inorganic chemistry not only for the chemical identification of a compound, but also to make considerations about the thermal performance of a material.

3.3 Cool photoluminescent materials characterization techniques

As introduced in Section 1, the main features to look at when working with cool materials are high values of both solar reflectance (SR) and infrared emissivity (ε), and of course, these properties also need to be evaluated for cool photoluminescent materials. Solar reflectance estimates the ability of a surface to reflect the incident solar radiation, while infrared emissivity measures the capability of a material to release the absorbed heat. Both are defined on a scale from 0 to 1 and are generally combined in a secondary indicator widely used for building materials, i.e., the solar reflectance index (SRI) (ASTM International, 2019a).

According to the sample size and to the type of experimental campaign, solar reflectance measurements can be performed using different instruments:

— A spectrophotometer with an integrating sphere (Fig. 3.4A), according to the ASTM E903-12: 2012 standard (ASTM International, 2012) and suitable for 0.1 m^2 samples. The sphere allows for the detection of the material's spectral hemispherical reflectance between 250 and 2500 nm, taking a standard white of known reflectance as reference specimen. The weighted average value, with respect to the standard solar spectral irradiance provided by ASTM G173-03:2020 (ASTM International, 2020), gives the final SR result.
— A reflectometer, according to the ASTM C1549-16:2016 (ASTM International, 2016a), and suitable for in-field campaigns. It measures the reflectance by varying the air mass setup, after a calibration procedure based on a null reflectance sample (blackbody cavity) and on a known reflectance sample.

(a)   (b)   (c)

FIGURE 3.4

(A) Spectrophotometer with an integrating sphere, (B) albedometer made of two pyranometers, (C) portable emissometer.

- A pyranometer, following the ASTM E1918-16:2016 standard (ASTM International, 2016b). The instrument can be used to detect the global solar reflectance of a horizontal or low-sloped surface under clear sky conditions and during the central hours of the day. In order to optimize the precision of the measurement, an albedometer is usually installed (Fig. 3.4B), with the upward oriented pyranometer detecting the incident solar radiation and the downward oriented one collecting the reflected component. The albedo of the investigated surface is then obtained as the ratio between the two measured quantities. The standard requires a minimum sample size of 4 m^2, but a similar characterization procedure has been developed by Akbari et al. for samples of about 1 m^2 (Akbari et al., 2008).

Also the thermal emittance of a surface can be derived using different investigating approaches. Among the following procedures, the first is usually preferred because of its higher reliability. ε measurement can be carried out by means of:

- A portable differential thermopile emissometer (Fig. 3.4C), according to the ASTM C1371-15: 2015 standard (ASTM International, n.d). The instrument must be calibrated using a known high-emissivity and low-emissivity reference sample, alternatively. The sample should have a minimum area of 15 cm^2, and it should be placed on a heat sink to avoid the excessive temperature increase during the test.
- Inspection meter techniques, following the ASTM E408-13:2019 standard (ASTM International, 2019b). The procedure consists of two methods (A and B), both based on thermal reflectance measurements: the emittance value is just calculated, often leading to erroneous estimations.

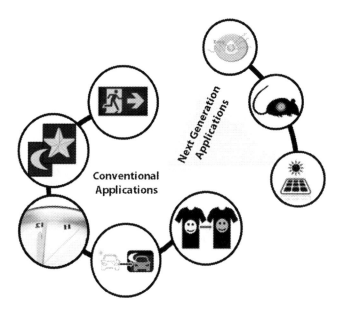

FIGURE 3.5

Conventional applications versus the new-generation solutions implementing persistent phosphors.

Reproduced with permission from Rojas-Hernandez, R.E., Rubio-Marcos, F., Rodriguez, M.Á., Fernandez, J.F., 2018. Long lasting phosphors: SrAl$_2$O$_4$:Eu, Dy as the most studied material. Renew. Sustain. Energy Rev. 81, 2759–2770. https://doi.org/10.1016/ j.rser.2017.06.081.

4. Fields of application

Photoluminescence has found application in many disciplines over the years (Fig. 3.5). Still its main exploitation involves simple commercial and decorative purposes, such as gadgets, furnishing elements, toys, and so on. This section focuses on more scientific and technological uses of phosphors, highlighting their potential for the built environment with special focus on passive cooling applications (Section 4.1). At a later stage, some of the most interesting applications of photoluminescent components in building-related applications are presented (Section 4.2).

4.1 Potential for cool photoluminescent applications

Materials used in the envelope of buildings or as outdoor pavements play a crucial role in the thermal energy balance of the urban surface, as well as in the local microclimate (Santamouris et al., 2017). As previously stated, a shared characteristic among cool materials is the high reflectance value, which passively helps in reducing both surface and air temperatures in cities through the rejection of part of the incident solar radiation (Rosso et al., 2017b). In this framework, the implementation of photo-luminescent elements in traditional construction materials may be seen as a further improvement of their cooling potential, thanks to the active release of the stored energy as visible light (Berdahl et al., 2016). Photoluminescent components significantly reduce light-to-heat conversion phenomena of the absorbed short-wave radiation, replacing it with a characteristic light-to-photon conversion. Indeed, unlike conventional materials, they reemit the absorbed short-wave radiation, and the magnitude of the emittance is given by photoluminescence quantum yield. This twofold rejection mechanism of absorbed radiation with reflection and emission is defined as the effective solar reflectance and makes photoluminescent materials good candidates for colored passive (reflectance) and simultaneously active (photoluminescence) cooling applications (Chiatti et al., 2021b).

The first evaluation of the cooling effect of photoluminescent components was performed by, Berdahl et al. (Berdahl et al., 2016), who investigated the cooling potential of ruby, Al_2O_3:Cr, char-acterized by efficient emission in the deep red (~ 694 nm) and near infrared (700−800 nm) wave range. Utilizing a transparent acrylic overcoat, they attached a layer comprising an array of square pyramidal synthetic fluorescent ruby crystals on a TiO_2 pigmented substrate (coating) using a trans-parent acrylic overcoat. The developed photoluminescent sample was exposed to full sunlight on a clear day and was found to maintain up to 6.5°C cooler than an off-white sample. Under the same scenario, Kousis et al. (2020) integrated photoluminescent strontium aluminate with dysprosium and europium dopants within paving fields. They performed an extensive monitoring campaign with respect to the thermooptical properties of five fields made with (i) yellow phosphorescent grits, (ii) blue phosphorescent grits, (iii) blue and yellow phosphorescent grains, (iv) phosphorescent fine-grain glaze, and (v) phosphorescent coarse-grain glaze. The base material of all fields was commer-cially available concrete that is used in real-life application. The authors showed that the addition of the phosphorescent components did not compromise that intrinsic albedo the surface. Instead, due to the effective solar reflectance, the phosphorescent pavements were found to maintain an up to 3.3°C lower surface temperature than a conventional concrete pavement. In addition, they significantly delayed within the daytime their peak surface temperature, leading to lower early afternoon surface temperatures. Rosso et al. (2019) performed both in-lab characterization and numerical investigation of phosphorescent paints and evaluated them for building application. They developed 10×10 cm samples by applying a phosphorescent coating on a white substrate. The paint was composed of a primer, i.e., 75% of the total weight, and a hardener, i.e., 25% of the total weight. The solar reflectance of each sample was measured by means of a spectrophotometer, and the results were used as inputs for the numerical investigation in which the paints were applied as an external finishing in a case-study building in Italy. The dynamic thermal-energy simulation showed a temperature reduction up to 6°C in the indoor environment during summer, which produced significant cooling energy saving, ranging from 30 to 200 kWh/yr, depending on the window area. Another simulation study performed by Kousis et al. (2021) showed that by appropriately tuning the QY of photoluminescent coatings surface temperature reductions up to 17°C as compared with nonphotoluminescent colored counterparts could be reached.

Nanoscale photoluminescent components are also regarded as promising cool candidates, due to their tunable optical properties. Factors such as the size, surface chemistry, and specific optical properties of nanoscale components can be tailored according the need of the user (Garshasbi and Santamouris, 2019). Moreover, unlike the corresponding bulk matter, the properties of materials of $2-10$ nm scale size originate from the molecular rearrangements and therefore are not prone to photodegradation issues. Under this framework, Garshasbi and Santamouris (2019) suggested that the integration of QDs into the built environment could yield breakthroughs in terms of cooling potential not only because of their intrinsic fluorescence mechanism but also thanks to their adaptability to external stimuli, such as temperature. In fact, Garshasbi et al. (2020b) fabricated CIS/ZnS QD samples and tested them both experimentally and numerically. The QD samples maintained a 2°C lower surface temperature than their nonfluorescent counterpart, while rejecting up to 54.2 W/m^2 of the absorbed short-wave radiation through photoluminescence. In addition, due to their high near-infrared penetrability, QDs layers backed by near-infrared reflective layers, such as silver-coated PET films, were found to decrease their surface temperature up to 8°C (Fig. 3.6).

Similarly, perovskite nanocrystals are tested as components of daytime radiative coolers, due to their high photoluminescent quantum yield. Daytime radiative coolers are sophisticated structures that: (i) highly reflect incident shortwave radiation, and (ii) highly absorb (and then emit) radiation within the atmospheric window range, i.e., $8-13$ μm. As a result, they can achieve subambient surface temperature. Yet, to ensure high reflectance within the short-wave spectrum, their surface color is typically confined to whitish or silver one. The application of perovskite nanocrystal on the external layer of the radiative cooler, however, allows not only to equip the surface with the desired color, but also to contribute toward subambient temperatures due to the intrinsic mechanism of light-to-photon conversion. In this context, Son et al. (2021) synthesized two types of perovskite nanocrystals, i.e., $CsPbBr_3$ and $CsPbBr_xI_{3-x}$, and embedded them in a $SiO_2@CPB_3$ and $SiO_2 @CPB_xI_{3-x}$ shells, respectively, creating green and red colors. They utilized these layers as the upper/external layers of a radiative cooler structure comprising a silver solar-reflective layer (bottom layer), and a PMMA+ZnO was coated onto a PET substrate. The results showed that the green and red radiative coolers were able to maintain up to 3.6 and 1.7°C subambient temperature, respectively, opening new horizons on the real-life application of photoluminescent radiative coolers into the built environment.

Yet, despite these promising results, full-scale implementations and investigations are still needed for further pushing the optimization process of luminescent materials' integration within traditional

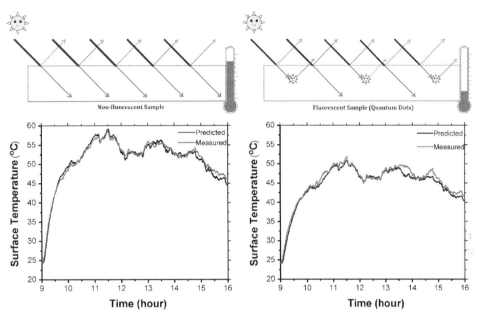

FIGURE 3.6

Predicted and experimental surface temperatures guaranteed by a nonluminescent (on the left) and a luminescent (on the right) sample.

Modified with permission from Garshasbi, S., Huang, S., Valenta, J., Santamouris, M., 2020a. Can quantum dots help to mitigate urban overheating? An experimental and modelling study. Sol. Energy 206, 308–316. https://doi.org/10.1016/j.solener.2020. 06.010.

building components. A big challenge that needs to be overcome is the quantitative evaluation of effective solar reflectance (Levinson et al., 2017). Traditional experimental methodologies with respect to the optical characterization of materials that comprise solar spectrometers or solar reflectometers fail to accurately capture the magnitude of the effective solar reflectance. This is because the detectors of the apparatus misinterpret the detected light due to photoluminescence as reflected light, since photoluminescence occurs within the short-wave spectrum, resulting in biased outcomes. In addition, a wide scalability of sophisticated photoluminescent applications toward cooling application is still impeded due to high costs associated with the raw material itself, including rare-earth elements and chemical synthesis methods. Dedicated and optimized production processes should be developed for obtaining highly efficient and easily accessible commercial products for large scale implementation.

4.2 Additional benefits of photoluminescent materials in building-related applications

4.2.1 Toward the implementation in solar cells

Photovoltaic (PV) technology is based on the conversion of solar energy to electricity, by means of solar cells. These cells are made of semiconductor materials, mostly silicon (Si), which can absorb the energy of photons in the visible range: longer-wavelength radiation is rejected, while shorter-wavelength radiation is partly wasted. Considering this, the theoretical limit of PV efficiency is about 33% (Hashmi et al., 2011). Therefore, one of the main research targets concerns the study of alternatives to the classical silicon solar cell. Among them, dye-sensitized solar cells (DSSC) were found to be more convenient solutions in terms of both fabrication procedure and installation restrictions. They are made of five main components: (i) a glass or plastic support, coated with a transparent conductive oxide (TCO); (ii) a layer of wide-bandgap semiconductor material, mostly TiO_2; (iii) a dye-sensitizer that is connected to the previous layer surface; (iv) an electrolyte, typically an organic solvent, as redox mediator; (v) a transparent conductive support with a thin layer of catalyst.

The main advantage of this system is the separation between charge generation and charge transfer: the first occurs between the semiconductor and the dye sensitizer, thanks to the absorption of sunlight; the second happens within the electrolyte and the semiconductor, after the electrons transfer through an external circuit (Lau and Soroush, 2019). Such separation allows for a more flexible design to better optimize configuration, paving the way for novel investigations toward maximizing the solar spectrum absorption of solar cells. To this aim, long persistent phosphors have been proposed as converters of the UV part of solar radiation toward longer wavelengths, so as to match the absorption range of common cells and improve their photoelectric conversion efficiency (PCE) (Chen et al., 2020). In this view, B.S. Richards reported that the implementation of inorganic phosphors in a silicon solar cell can theoretically boost its PCE up to 38.6%, against the 30.9% registered in the same solar cell without phosphors (Richards, 2006). Similar investigations concerned dye-sensitized devices (Puntambekar and Chakrapani, 2016; He et al., 2014): He et al. described DSSCs with $SrAl2O_4:Eu^{2+}$, Dy^{3+} particles, finding a 13% improvement in their performance due to different effects played by the phosphor (He et al., 2013). In fact, beyond the aforementioned downconversion function, the blue-green afterglow, together with the VIS light scattering helped by particles, contributes to the dye's energy collection. Moreover, the open-circuit voltage was found to be higher in the luminescent DSSC.

4.2.2 Toward the implementation for photocatalysis

Another process exploiting solar energy for environmental remediation is photocatalysis. The main feature of photocatalysis is the acceleration of a chemical reaction due to the absorption of light from the sun. Higher ambient temperatures, caused, for instance, by the UHI effect, lead to an increase in energy consumption for cooling and, thus, to higher emissions that contribute for the overall air quality degradation. Among the countermeasures aimed at the improvement of urban air quality, photocatalytic materials have proven to efficiently purify both air and water from contamination (Malato et al., 2009). They use solar radiation to activate the chemical conversion of pollutants to innocuous elements (Lewis, 2001; Desario and Gray, 2012): photogenerated electrons and holes produce free radicals interacting with molecular oxygen and water, which are responsible for the decomposition of organic and inorganic pollutants also found in urban areas. Different compounds can be used as catalysts for this kind of applications (Mills and Le Hunte, 1997), but the most convenient and practicably feasible performance is usually attributed to TiO_2 molecules, thanks to their stability, low toxicity, and minor cost (Gaya and Abdullah, 2008). Given the possibility to combine TiO_2 with traditional building materials, such as cementitious products, different in-lab investigations have been carried out to evaluate their possible effect in outdoor environments in terms of both self-cleaning and air pollution reducing (D'Alessandro et al., 2016).

In this context, persistent phosphors have been proposed as extra excitation sources for the photocatalytic process, whose normal activity mainly occurs under solar UV irradiation: indeed, the proper implementation of UV-emitting phosphors in TiO_2 would extend their operation during the night. In this context, $CaAl_2O_4$:Eu,Nd afterglow was found to be a good phosphor to be coupled with TiO_2, because of its emission peak at 440 nm and 10-hour-lasting afterglow (Li et al., 2012). In addition, nanoparticles with self-activated luminescence were directly proposed as photocatalysts, with the purpose of reducing the material cost, avoiding the doping with rare earth elements (Wang et al., 2013). Investigations have also been carried out aiming at modify TiO_2 band gap, toward the absorption of both UV and VIS light: a higher reactivity of the material can lead to the exploitation of the main part of the solar spectrum. Results on this direction identify nitrogen as the most promising doping element to introduce visible-light activity in TiO_2 (Asahi, 2001; Wang et al., 2003; Sakthivel et al., 2004).

4.2.3 Toward the implementation in lighting systems

Considering strategies to reduce energy consumption in the built environment, the public lighting sector cannot be ignored. A significant percentage of the world's existing systems still use technologies from the 1960s, so retrofitting actions have proved to be necessary not only in terms of energy savings, but also for a better visual comfort and safety for citizens (Lobão et al., 2015; Ferrari and Beccali, 2017). For instance, the replacement of traditional lighting devices with LED technology has led to advantages in terms of lower consumptions and environmental impacts, a longer life, and less maintenance costs (Campisi et al., 2018; Li et al., 2015). LEDs' further improvements, toward a higher light emission quality, have led to the implementation of downconverting inorganic phosphors to the system: their absorption at a certain wavelength and the reemission at a longer wavelength help in the reproduction of different colors in the visible spectrum (Nair et al., 2020). In this framework, rare-earth-doped inorganic phosphors are the most significant class of dopants used for phosphor-converted light-emitting diodes (pc-LEDs), because of their capability of being excited by UV or near-UV light. White-light LEDs (WLEDs) are probably the most promising option for the next generation of lighting and energy saving (George et al., 2013). However, efficiency reductions may be caused by phosphors' unequal distribution or reabsorption effects, and for this reason, spectral tuning strategies are implemented. The latter consist of local structural variations of the phosphor lattice, which allow for the correction of the luminescent emission spectrum, i.e., for the complete control of lighting parameters such as color rendering index (CRI), correlated color temperature (CCT), luminous efficacy, etc (Lin and Liu, 2011).

A more direct role is played by photoluminescent compounds in some applications involving the replacement of existing lighting devices. For example, in safety signage, their main goal is to mark indoor emergency routes or guidelines in case of electricity failure: luminescent paints or plastic strips are usually applied as door or path markings, for obstructions identification, directional signage, and so on (Proulx et al., 1999; Aizlewood and Webber, 1995), as suggested also by some standard recommendations (IBC, 2014; Photoluminescent Safety Products Association, 1997). Currently, materials for safety signage mostly consist of strontium aluminate green-emitting phosphors, since they are safer and chemically stable. Because of their decorative aspect, they have been also implemented in traditional building materials, such as glass bricks, paints, and ceramics. However, the most promising known compounds in terms of afterglow intensity and decay time are still not commercially exploited.

For instance, Gao et al. (2009) investigated the behavior of $Sr_4Al_{14}O_{25}$:Eu^{2+}, Dy^{3+} coating on a ceramic surface, finding an afterglow duration longer than 20 h: if similar performances could actually be implemented in available building materials, their impact would be truly significant.

Focusing more on the outdoor environment, luminescent components have demonstrated to be a valid option for road lighting (Fabiani et al., 2021). Since the traditionally used reflective materials are visible only when directly hit by an approaching light, and thus at a limited distance, alternative solutions have been investigated by researchers, including glow-in-the-dark materials. Their implementation would improve road safety, while limiting the installation, maintenance, and electricity costs linked to traditional road lighting systems.

However, only few phosphors are suitable for a night-lasting performance: well-known candidates are strontium aluminate compounds, which are appreciated for their long lifetimes, brightness, and stability (Rojas-Hernandez et al., 2018). Bacero et al. (2015) evaluated the effect of $SrAl_2O_4$:Eu in paint pavement markings, highlighting their positive impact in users' perception, especially in low-illuminated roads. A similar application was proposed for the Scottish Road Research Board, in 2014, aiming at the provision of luminous information for drivers in those areas where electric power is unavailable (Turnpenny and Crawford, 2014). Wiese et al. (2015), instead, developed a luminescent sealant to be applied on concrete surfaces, with the aim of supplementing or even replacing streetlights and increasing public safety at night.

Speaking of outdoor application, the interaction between luminescent surfaces and weathering should be taken into account. Indeed, an efficient combination of phosphors and traditional building materials can lead to mutual benefits while the firsts provide for free-cost lighting, the seconds may play a protective role. A possible solution may concern the development of coatings to keep water from penetrating to the photoluminescent surface below, avoiding the material's degradation in case of rainfall (Nance and Sparks, 2020; Kasson et al., 2008).

5. Conclusions and future developments

Cool materials are an environmentally friendly and relatively cost-effective solution developed for reducing building cooling energy needs and improving local environmental conditions. Recent research advances showed the importance of developing even more effective technologies capable of adapting their behavior to local environmental stimuli for tackling the most common drawbacks of the established cool solutions. In this context, photoluminescent materials represent a crucial step forward in cool materials developments.

In the last decades, many luminescent compounds have been discovered and characterized. However, only a few of them currently find a practical application in the market. In particular, visible light-emitting phosphors are usually employed for improving human visibility in dark environments, while near-infrared emitting phosphors are mainly used for biomedical purposes. Some applications also make use of photoluminescence for improving the efficiency of photovoltaics and photocatalytic surfaces. Further, during recent years, photoluminescent materials are gaining increasing attention within the scientific community as possible passive cooling solutions for the built environment. Indeed, their capability to reemit visible rather than thermal radiation when exposed to a certain excitation source, besides being convenient in terms of lighting energy-saving applications, also has great potential for UHI mitigation purposes. Recent research findings showed that the integration of new photoluminescent components in the built environment could significantly reduce the intrinsic phonon-assisted thermal relation of urban surfaces, drastically decreasing the amount of heat released in the neighboring air domain.

Future research trends will focus on the integration of photoluminescent materials within advanced, radiative coolers capable of effectively coupling the astonishing cooling performance of these radiators with the light-emitting capability of additional photoluminescent layers. Additionally, the well-known winter penalty affecting common cool materials should be evaluated in both persistent and nonpersistent phosphors and eventually optimized by developing advanced nanoscale thermo-chromics based on QDs, plasmonic or photonic structures, among others. Finally, the aging and long-term durability of photoluminescent applications should also be evaluated trying to verify their performance throughout the life span of a building or a pavement, particularly focusing on their exposure to ambient and adverse weather conditions.

Acknowledgments

Authors acknowledgments are due to the European Union's Horizon Europe within the HELIOS ERC StG project, under Grant Agreement No. 101041255.

References

Aizlewood, C.E., Webber, G.M.B., 1995. Escape route lighting: comparison of human performance with traditional lighting and wayfinding systems. Light. Res. Technol. 27, 133−143. https://doi.org/10.1177/14771535950270030101.

Akbari, H., Levinson, R., Stern, S., 2008. Procedure for measuring the solar reflectance of flat or curved roofing assemblies. Sol. Energy 82, 648−655. https://doi.org/10.1016/j.solener.2008.01.001.

Alghamdy, S., Alleman, J.E., Alowaibdi, T., 2021. Cool white marble pavement thermophysical assessment at Al Masjid Al-Haram, Makkah City, Saudi Arabia. Construct. Build. Mater. 285, 122831. https://doi.org/10.1016/j.conbuildmat.2021.122831.

Asahi, R., 2001. Visible-light photocatalysis in nitrogen-doped titanium oxides. Science (80) 293, 269−271. https://doi.org/10.1126/science.1061051.

ASTM International, 2012. ASTM E903-12, Standard Test Method for Solar Absorptance, Reflectance, and Transmittance of Materials Using Integrating Spheres. West Conshohocken, PA. https://doi.org/10.1520/E0903-12.

ASTM International, 2016a. ASTM C1549-16, Standard Test Method for Determination of Solar Reflectance Near Ambient Temperature Using a Portable Solar Reflectometer. West Conshohocken, PA. https://doi.org/10.1520/C1549-16.

ASTM International, 2016b. ASTM E1918-16, Standard Test Method for Measuring Solar Reflectance of Horizontal and Low-Sloped Surfaces in the Field. West Conshohocken, PA. https://doi.org/10.1520/E1918-16.

ASTM International, 2019a. ASTM E1980-11, Standard Practice for Calculating Solar Reflectance Index of Horizontal and Low-Sloped Opaque Surfaces. West Conshohocken, PA. https://doi.org/10.1520/E1980-11R19.

ASTM International, 2019b. ASTM E408-13, Standard Test Methods for Total Normal Emittance of Surfaces Using Inspection-Meter Techniques. West Conshohocken, PA. https://doi.org/10.1520/E0408-13R19.

ASTM International, 2020. ASTM G173-03, Standard Tables for Reference Solar Spectral Irradiances: Direct Normal and Hemispherical on 37° Tilted Surface. West Conshohocken, PA. https://doi.org/10.1520/G0173-03R20.

ASTM International, n.d. ASTM C1371-15, Standard Test Method for Determination of Emittance of Materials Near Room Temperature Using Portable Emissometers. West Conshohocken, PA. https://doi.org/10.1520/C1371-15.

Azarifar, M., Cengiz, C., Arik, M., 2021. Particle based investigation of self-heating effect of phosphor particles in phosphor converted light emitting diodes. J. Lumin. 231, 117782. https://doi.org/10.1016/j.jlumin.2020.117782.

Bacero, R., To, D., Arista, J.P., Dela Cruz, M.K., Villaneva, J.P., Uy, F.A., 2015. Evaluation of strontium aluminate in traffic paint pavement markings for rural and unilluminated roads. J. East Asia Soc. Transp. Stud. 11, 1726–1744. https://doi.org/10.11175/easts.11.1726.

Bartesaghi-Koc, C., Haddad, S., Pignatta, G., Paolini, R., Prasad, D., Santamouris, M., 2021. Can urban heat be mitigated in a single urban street? Monitoring, strategies, and performance results from a real scale redevelopment project. Sol. Energy 216, 564–588. https://doi.org/10.1016/j.solener.2020.12.043.

Benson, C.R., Kacenauskaite, L., VanDenburgh, K.L., Zhao, W., Qiao, B., Sadhukhan, T., et al., 2020. Plug-and-Play optical materials from fluorescent dyes and macrocycles. Inside Chem. 6, 1978–1997. https://doi.org/10.1016/j.chempr.2020.06.029.

Berdahl, P., Chen, S.S., Destaillats, H., Kirchstetter, T.W., Levinson, R.M., Zalich, M.A., 2016. Fluorescent cooling of objects exposed to sunlight – the ruby example. Sol. Energy Mater. Sol. Cells 157, 312–317. https://doi.org/10.1016/j.solmat.2016.05.058.

Campisi, D., Gitto, S., Morea, D., 2018. Economic feasibility of energy efficiency improvements in street lighting systems in Rome. J. Clean. Prod. 175, 190–198. https://doi.org/10.1016/j.jclepro.2017.12.063.

Capelletti, R., 2017. Luminescence ☆. Ref. Modul. Mater. Sci. Mater. Eng. Elsevier. https://doi.org/10.1016/B978-0-12-803581-8.01247-9.

Caratto, V., Locardi, F., Costa, G.A., Masini, R., Fasoli, M., Panzeri, L., et al., 2014. NIR persistent luminescence of lanthanide ion-doped rare-earth oxycarbonates: the effect of dopants. ACS Appl. Mater. Interfaces 6, 17346–17351. https://doi.org/10.1021/am504523s.

Castellani, B., 2021. Application of retro-reflective materials in urban canyon at different geographical locations. Build. Environ. 193, 107676. https://doi.org/10.1016/j.buildenv.2021.107676.

Chen, E.Z., Gu, X.Y., Wei, K., Cheng, Y., Chen, Z.L., Tan, J.R., et al., 2020. Role of long persistence phosphors on their enhancement in performances of photoelectric devices: in case of dye-sensitized solar cells. Appl. Surf. Sci. 507, 145098. https://doi.org/10.1016/j.apsusc.2019.145098.

Chiatti, C., Fabiani, C., Pisello, A.L., 2021a. Long persistent luminescence: a road map toward promising future developments in energy and environmental science. Annu. Rev. Mater. Res. 51, 409–433. https://doi.org/10.1146/annurev-matsci-091520-011838.

Chiatti, C., Fabiani, C., Cotana, F., Pisello, A.L., 2021b. Exploring the potential of photoluminescence for urban passive cooling and lighting applications: a new approach towards materials' optimization. Energy 231, 120815. https://doi.org/10.1016/j.energy.2021.120815.

D'Alessandro, A., Fabiani, C., Pisello, A.L., Ubertini, F., Materazzi, A.L., Cotana, F., 2016. Innovative concretes for low-carbon constructions: a review. Int. J. Low Carbon Technol. https://doi.org/10.1093/ijlct/ctw013.

Das, S., Magut, P.K.S., Zhao, L., Hasan, F., Karki, A.B., Jin, R., et al., 2015. Multimodal theranostic nanomaterials derived from phthalocyanine-based organic salt. RSC Adv. 5, 30227–30233. https://doi.org/10.1039/C5RA00872G.

de Wilde, P., Coley, D., 2012. The implications of a changing climate for buildings. Build. Environ. 55, 1–7. https://doi.org/10.1016/j.buildenv.2012.03.014.

Desario, P.A., Gray, K.A., 2012. Passive Systems to Improve Air Quality and Reduce Heat Retention in the Urban Environment. Metrop. Sustain., Elsevier, pp. 292−316. https://doi.org/10.1533/9780857096463.3.292.

Dino, I.G., Meral Akgül, C., 2019. Impact of climate change on the existing residential building stock in Turkey: an analysis on energy use, greenhouse gas emissions and occupant comfort. Renew. Energy 141, 828−846. https://doi.org/10.1016/j.renene.2019.03.150.

European Commission, 2012. Lighting the Cities − Accelerating the Deployment of Innovative Lighting in European Cities. Luxembourg. https://doi.org/10.2759/96173.

Fabiani, C., Castaldo, V.L., Pisello, A.L., 2020. Thermochromic materials for indoor thermal comfort improvement: finite difference modeling and validation in a real case-study building. Appl. Energy 262, 114147. https://doi.org/10.1016/j.apenergy.2019.114147.

Fabiani, C., Chiatti, C., Pisello, A.L., 2021. Development of photoluminescent composites for energy efficiency in smart outdoor lighting applications: an experimental and numerical investigation. Renew. Energy 172, 1−15. https://doi.org/10.1016/j.renene.2021.02.071.

Ferrari, S., Beccali, M., 2017. Energy-environmental and cost assessment of a set of strategies for retrofitting a public building toward nearly zero-energy building target. Sustain. Cities Soc. 32, 226−234. https://doi.org/10.1016/j.scs.2017.03.010.

Gao, F., Xiong, Z., Xue, H., Liu, Y., 2009. Improved performance of strontium aluminate luminous coating on the ceramic surface. J. Phys. Conf. Ser. 152, 012082. https://doi.org/10.1088/1742-6596/152/1/012082.

Garshasbi, S., Santamouris, M., 2019. Using advanced thermochromic technologies in the built environment: recent development and potential to decrease the energy consumption and fight urban overheating. Sol. Energy Mater. Sol. Cells 191, 21−32. https://doi.org/10.1016/j.solmat.2018.10.023.

Garshasbi, S., Huang, S., Valenta, J., Santamouris, M., 2020a. Can quantum dots help to mitigate urban overheating? An experimental and modelling study. Sol. Energy 206, 308−316. https://doi.org/10.1016/j.solener.2020.06.010.

Garshasbi, S., Huang, S., Valenta, J., Santamouris, M., 2020b. On the combination of quantum dots with near-infrared reflective base coats to maximize their urban overheating mitigation potential. Sol. Energy 211, 111−116. https://doi.org/10.1016/j.solener.2020.09.069.

Gaya, U.I., Abdullah, A.H., 2008. Heterogeneous photocatalytic degradation of organic contaminants over titanium dioxide: a review of fundamentals, progress and problems. J. Photochem. Photobiol. C Photochem. Rev. 9, 1−12. https://doi.org/10.1016/j.jphotochemrev.2007.12.003.

George, N.C., Denault, K.A., Seshadri, R., 2013. Phosphors for solid-state white lighting. Annu. Rev. Mater. Res. 43, 481−501. https://doi.org/10.1146/annurev-matsci-073012-125702.

Harlan, S.L., Ruddell, D.M., 2011. Climate change and health in cities: impacts of heat and air pollution and potential co-benefits from mitigation and adaptation. Curr. Opin. Environ. Sustain. 3, 126−134. https://doi.org/10.1016/j.cosust.2011.01.001.

Hashmi, G., Miettunen, K., Peltola, T., Halme, J., Asghar, I., Aitola, K., et al., 2011. Review of materials and manufacturing options for large area flexible dye solar cells. Renew. Sustain. Energy Rev. 15, 3717−3732. https://doi.org/10.1016/j.rser.2011.06.004.

He, W., Atabaev, T.S., Kim, H.K., Hwang, Y.-H., 2013. Enhanced sunlight harvesting of dye-sensitized solar cells assisted with long persistent phosphor materials. J. Phys. Chem. C 117, 17894−17900. https://doi.org/10.1021/jp307954n.

He, W., Timur, A.S., Kim, H.-K., Hwang, Y.-H., 2014. Energy harvesting of dye-sensitized solar cells assisted with Ti-mesh and phosphor materials. IOP Conf. Ser. Mater. Sci. Eng. 54, 012025. https://doi.org/10.1088/1757-899X/54/1/012025.

Hernández-Pérez, I., Xamán, J., Macías-Melo, E.V., Aguilar-Castro, K.M., 2017. Reflective Materials for Cost-Effective Energy-Efficient Retrofitting of Roofs. Cost-Effective Energy Effic. Build. Retrofit. Elsevier, pp. 119−139. https://doi.org/10.1016/B978-0-08-101128-7.00004-6.

Huang, P., Zheng, W., Gong, Z., You, W., Wei, J., Chen, X., 2019. Rare earth ion− and transition metal ion−doped inorganic luminescent nanocrystals: from fundamentals to biodetection. Mater. Today Nano 5, 100031. https://doi.org/10.1016/j.mtnano.2019.100031.

IBC, 2014. New York City Building Code - Photoluminescent Exit Path Markings. NYC.

Jana, J., Ganguly, M., Pal, T., 2016. Enlightening surface plasmon resonance effect of metal nanoparticles for practical spectroscopic application. RSC Adv. 6, 86174−86211. https://doi.org/10.1039/C6RA14173K.

Kamimura, S., Xu, C.-N., Yamada, H., Terasaki, N., Fujihala, M., 2014. Long-persistent luminescence in the near-infrared from Nd^{3+} -doped Sr_2SnO_4 for in vivo optical imaging. Jpn. J. Appl. Phys. 53, 092403. https://doi.org/10.7567/JJAP.53.092403.

Kasson, O.P., Martuch, R.A., Ilori, C.O., Miller, G.A., Gerow, D.M., 2008. Method for Incorporating Water Soluble, Reactive, Phosphorescent Pigments into a Stable Waterborne Coating through pH Buffering. US8298441B1.

Kolar, Z.I., den Hollander, W., 2004. A centennial of spinthariscope and scintillation counting. Appl. Radiat. Isot. 61, 261−266. https://doi.org/10.1016/j.apradiso.2004.03.056.

Kousis, I., Pisello, A.L., 2020. For the mitigation of urban heat island and urban noise island: two simultaneous sides of urban discomfort. Environ. Res. Lett. 15, 103004. https://doi.org/10.1088/1748-9326/abaa0d.

Kousis, I., Fabiani, C., Gobbi, L., Pisello, A.L., 2020. Phosphorescent-based pavements for counteracting urban overheating − a proof of concept. Sol. Energy 202, 540−552. https://doi.org/10.1016/j.solener.2020.03.092.

Kousis, I., Fabiani, C., Pisello, A.L., 2021. A study on the thermo-optical behaviour of phosphorescent coatings for passive cooling applications. E3S Web Conf. 238, 06002. https://doi.org/10.1051/e3sconf/202123806002.

Lastusaari, M., Laamanen, T., Malkamäki, M., Eskola, K.O., Kotlov, A., Carlson, S., et al., 2012. The Bologna Stone: history's first persistent luminescent material. Eur. J. Mineral 24, 885−890. https://doi.org/10.1127/0935-1221/2012/0024-2224.

Lau, K.K.S., Soroush, M., 2019. Overview of dye-sensitized solar cells. Dye. Sol. Cells 1−49. https://doi.org/10.1016/B978-0-12-814541-8.00001-X.

Lenard, P., Harms, F., Schmidt, F., Tomaschek, R., Wien, W., 1928. Phosphorescence and Fluorescence, Part 2. Acad. Verlag-Ges.

Levinson, R., Chen, S., Ferrari, C., Berdahl, P., Slack, J., 2017. Methods and instrumentation to measure the effective solar reflectance of fluorescent cool surfaces. Energy Build. 152, 752−765. https://doi.org/10.1016/j.enbuild.2016.11.007.

Lewis, N.S., 2001. Light work with water. Nature 414, 589−590. https://doi.org/10.1038/414589a.

Li, H., Yin, S., Wang, Y., Sato, T., 2012. Effect of phase structures of TiO_2-xN_y on the photocatalytic activity of $CaAl_2O_4$:(Eu, Nd)-coupled TiO_2-xN_y. J. Catal. 286, 273−278. https://doi.org/10.1016/j.jcat.2011.11.013.

Li, G., Tian, Y., Zhao, Y., Lin, J., 2015. Recent progress in luminescence tuning of Ce^{3+} and Eu^{2+} -activated phosphors for pc-WLEDs. Chem. Soc. Rev. 44, 8688−8713. https://doi.org/10.1039/C4CS00446A.

Lin, C.C., Liu, R.-S., 2011. Advances in phosphors for light-emitting diodes. J. Phys. Chem. Lett. 2, 1268−1277. https://doi.org/10.1021/jz2002452.

Lobão, J.A., Devezas, T., Catalão, J.P.S., 2015. Energy efficiency of lighting installations: software application and experimental validation. Energy Rep. 1, 110−115. https://doi.org/10.1016/j.egyr.2015.04.001.

Lv, C., Zu, M., Xie, D., Liu, D., Cheng, H., 2021. Ellipsoid ultramarine blue pigment with high near-infrared reflectance. Mater. Today Commun. 27, 102267. https://doi.org/10.1016/j.mtcomm.2021.102267.

Malato, S., Fernández-Ibáñez, P., Maldonado, M.I., Blanco, J., Gernjak, W., 2009. Decontamination and disinfection of water by solar photocatalysis: recent overview and trends. Catal. Today 147, 1−59. https://doi.org/10.1016/j.cattod.2009.06.018.

Mann, D., Yeung, C., Habets, R., Vroon, Z., Buskens, P., 2020. Comparative building energy simulation study of static and thermochromically adaptive energy-efficient glazing in various climate regions. Energies 13, 2842. https://doi.org/10.3390/en13112842.

Matsuzawa, T., Aoki, Y., Takeuchi, N., Murayama, Y., 1996. A new long phosphorescent phosphor with high brightness, $SrAl_2O_4$: Eu^{2+}, Dy^{3+}. J. Electrochem. Soc. 143, 2670−2673. https://doi.org/10.1149/1.1837067.

Mills, A., Le Hunte, S., 1997. An overview of semiconductor photocatalysis. J. Photochem. Photobiol. Chem. 108, 1−35. https://doi.org/10.1016/S1010-6030(97)00118-4.

Mizon, B., 2012. Light Pollution. Springer New York, New York, NY. https://doi.org/10.1007/978-1-4614-3822-9.

Mukherjee, S., Thilagar, P., 2015. Recent advances in purely organic phosphorescent materials. Chem. Commun. 51, 10988−11003. https://doi.org/10.1039/C5CC03114A.

Mushtaha, E., Shareef, S., Alsyouf, I., Mori, T., Kayed, A., Abdelrahim, M., et al., 2021. A study of the impact of major Urban Heat Island factors in a hot climate courtyard: the case of the University of Sharjah. UAE. Sustain Cities Soc. 69, 102844. https://doi.org/10.1016/j.scs.2021.102844.

Nair, G.B., Swart, H.C., Dhoble, S.J., 2020. A review on the advancements in phosphor-converted light emitting diodes (pc-LEDs): phosphor synthesis, device fabrication and characterization. Prog. Mater. Sci. 109, 100622. https://doi.org/10.1016/j.pmatsci.2019.100622.

Nance, J., Sparks, T.D., 2020. Comparison of coatings for $SrAl_2O_4$:Eu^{2+},Dy^{3+} powder in waterborne road striping paint under wet conditions. Prog. Org. Coating 144, 105637. https://doi.org/10.1016/j.porgcoat.2020.105637.

Nguyen, V.-L., Chen, C.-R., Chung, C.-Y., Chen, K.-W., Lai, R.-B., 2021. Research on Performance of Color Reversible Coatings for Exterior Wall of Buildings, pp. 453−465. https://doi.org/10.1007/978-3-030-62324-1_39.

Ntarisa, A.V., Daniel, D.J., Balaji, D., Raja, A., Kim, H.J., Quang, N.D., 2021. A novel blue-emitting phosphors $(CsBaYB_6O_{12}:Ce^{3+})$: potential applications in w-LEDs and X-ray phosphors. J. Alloys Compd. 159676. https://doi.org/10.1016/j.jallcom.2021.159676.

Pan, Z., Lu, Y.-Y., Liu, F., 2012. Sunlight-activated long-persistent luminescence in the near-infrared from Cr^{3+}-doped zinc gallogermanates. Nat. Mater. 11, 58−63. https://doi.org/10.1038/nmat3173.

Photoluminescent Safety Products Association, 1997. Standard 002 Emergency Way-Finding Guidance Systems, Part 1 Code of Practice for the Installation of Emergency Way-Finding Guidance (LLL) Systems Produced from Photoluminescence for Use in Public, Industrial and Commercial Buildings. UK.

Pozza, G., Ajò, D., Chiari, G., De Zuane, F., Favaro, M., 2000. Photoluminescence of the inorganic pigments Egyptian blue, Han blue and Han purple. J. Cult. Herit. 1, 393−398. https://doi.org/10.1016/S1296-2074(00)01095-5.

Proulx, G., Tiller, D., Kyle, B.R., Creak, J., 1999. Assessment of Photoluminescent Material during Office Occupant Evacuation. https://doi.org/10.4224/20331274.

Puntambekar, A., Chakrapani, V., 2016. Excitation energy transfer from long-persistent phosphors for enhancing power conversion of dye-sensitized solar cells. Phys. Rev. B 93, 245301. https://doi.org/10.1103/PhysRevB.93.245301.

Richards, B.S., 2006. Luminescent layers for enhanced silicon solar cell performance: down-conversion. Sol. Energy Mater. Sol. Cells 90, 1189−1207. https://doi.org/10.1016/j.solmat.2005.07.001.

Rojas-Hernandez, R.E., Rubio-Marcos, F., Rodriguez, M.Á., Fernandez, J.F., 2018. Long lasting phosphors: $SrAl_2O_4$:Eu, Dy as the most studied material. Renew. Sustain. Energy Rev. 81, 2759−2770. https://doi.org/10.1016/j.rser.2017.06.081.

Rossi, F., Pisello, A.L., Nicolini, A., Filipponi, M., Palombo, M., 2014. Analysis of retro-reflective surfaces for urban heat island mitigation: a new analytical model. Appl. Energy 114, 621−631. https://doi.org/10.1016/j.apenergy.2013.10.038.

Rosso, F., Pisello, A., Castaldo, V., Ferrero, M., Cotana, F., 2017a. On innovative cool-colored materials for building envelopes: balancing the architectural appearance and the thermal-energy performance in historical districts. Sustainability 9, 2319. https://doi.org/10.3390/su9122319.

Rosso, F., Pisello, A.L., Cotana, F., Ferrero, M., 2017b. Cool, translucent natural envelope: thermal-optics characteristics experimental assessment and thermal-energy and day lighting analysis. Energy Proc. 111, 578−587. https://doi.org/10.1016/j.egypro.2017.03.220.

Rosso, F., Fabiani, C., Chiatti, C., Pisello, A.L., 2019. Cool, photoluminescent paints towards energy consumption reductions in the built environment. J. Phys. Conf. Ser. 1343. https://doi.org/10.1088/1742-6596/1343/1/012198.

Sakthivel, S., Janczarek, M., Kisch, H., 2004. Visible light activity and photoelectrochemical properties of nitrogen-doped TiO$_2$. J. Phys. Chem. B 108, 19384−19387. https://doi.org/10.1021/jp046857q.

Santamouris, M., Yun, G.Y., 2020. Recent development and research priorities on cool and super cool materials to mitigate urban heat island. Renew. Energy 161, 792−807. https://doi.org/10.1016/j.renene.2020.07.109.

Santamouris, M., Ding, L., Fiorito, F., Oldfield, P., Osmond, P., Paolini, R., et al., 2017. Passive and active cooling for the outdoor built environment − analysis and assessment of the cooling potential of mitigation technologies using performance data from 220 large scale projects. Sol. Energy 154, 14−33. https://doi.org/10.1016/j.solener.2016.12.006.

Smet, P.F., Van den Eeckhout, K., De Clercq, O.Q., Poelman, D., 2015. Persistent Phosphors, pp. 1−108. https://doi.org/10.1016/B978-0-444-63483-2.00001-6.

Son, S., Jeon, S., Chae, D., Lee, S.Y., Liu, Y., Lim, H., et al., 2021. Colored emitters with silica-embedded perovskite nanocrystals for efficient daytime radiative cooling. Nano Energy 79, 105461. https://doi.org/10.1016/j.nanoen.2020.105461.

Synnefa, A., Santamouris, M., Apostolakis, K., 2007. On the development, optical properties and thermal performance of cool colored coatings for the urban environment. Sol. Energy 81, 488−497. https://doi.org/10.1016/j.solener.2006.08.005.

Turnpenny, K., Crawford, E., 2014. Investigating the Potential for Reactive "Glowing" Roads as an Initiative on the Scottish Road Network. Glasgow, GB.

Wang, J., Yin, S., Zhang, Q., Saito, F., Sato, T., 2003. Mechanochemical synthesis of SrTiO$_{3-x}$ F$_x$ with high visible light photocatalytic activities for nitrogen monoxide destruction. J. Mater. Chem. 13, 2348−2352. https://doi.org/10.1039/B303420H.

Wang, L., Liu, X., Hou, Z., Li, C., Yang, P., Cheng, Z., et al., 2008. Electrospinning synthesis and luminescence properties of one-dimensional Zn$_2$ SiO$_4$:Mn^{2+} microfibers and microbelts. J. Phys. Chem. C 112, 18882−18888. https://doi.org/10.1021/jp806392a.

Wang, Z., Zhang, J., Zheng, G., Peng, X., Dai, H., 2013. Violet-blue afterglow luminescence properties of non-doped SrZrO$_3$ material. J. Lumin. 144, 30−33. https://doi.org/10.1016/j.jlumin.2013.06.033.

Wang, C., Wang, C., Xu, L., Cheng, H., Lin, Q., Zhang, C., 2014. Protein-directed synthesis of pH-responsive red fluorescent copper nanoclusters and their applications in cellular imaging and catalysis. Nanoscale 6, 1775−1781. https://doi.org/10.1039/C3NR04835G.

Wang, C., Cheng, H., Sun, Y., Lin, Q., Zhang, C., 2015. Rapid sonochemical synthesis of luminescent and paramagnetic copper nanoclusters for bimodal bioimaging. ChemNanoMat 1, 27−31. https://doi.org/10.1002/cnma.201500004.

Wei, Q., Ding, J., Wang, Y., 2020. A novel tunable extra-broad yellow-emitting nitride phosphor with zero-thermal-quenching property. Chem. Eng. J. 386, 124004. https://doi.org/10.1016/j.cej.2019.124004.

Wiese, A., Washington, T., Tao, B., Weiss, W.J., 2015. Assessing performance of glow-in-the-dark concrete. Transp. Res. Rec. J. Transp. Res. Board 2508, 31−38. https://doi.org/10.3141/2508-04.

Wu, M., Liu, S., Sun, Y., Chen, W., Huang, L., Chen, G., et al., 2020. Energy transfer of wide band long persistent phosphors of Sm^{3+}-Doped ZrSiO$_4$. Mater. Chem. Phys. 251, 123086. https://doi.org/10.1016/j.matchemphys.2020.123086.

Xia, Z., Liu, Q., 2016. Progress in discovery and structural design of color conversion phosphors for LEDs. Prog. Mater. Sci. 84, 59−117. https://doi.org/10.1016/j.pmatsci.2016.09.007.

Zeng, J., Peng, G., Zhang, S., Krishnan, R.G., Ju, G., Li, Y., et al., 2021. In-situ Insights into trap attributions in Fe^{3+}-activated long persistent phosphors. J. Lumin. 232, 117810. https://doi.org/10.1016/j.jlumin.2020.117810.

Zinzi, M., Carnielo, E., Mattoni, B., 2018. On the relation between urban climate and energy performance of buildings. A three-years experience in Rome, Italy. Appl. Energy 221, 148−160. https://doi.org/10.1016/j.apenergy.2018.03.192.

Urban heat island: land cover changes, management, and mitigation strategies

4

Sabiha Sultana and A.N.V. Satyanarayana

Centre for Oceans, Rivers, Atmosphere and Land Sciences, Indian Institute of Technology Kharagpur, Kharagpur, West Bengal, India

1. Introduction

Cities provide improved lifestyle with advanced infrastructure, job opportunities, and economic development that lead to accumulation of earth's population in major global cities. Global cities occupy only 3% of the area of the Earth's land (Roth, 2013), but about half of the global population lives in cities (World Urbanization Prospectus, 2014) and utilizes about 60%−80% of the total energy consumption and also responsible for 70% of the carbon emission. The global cities are thus abruptly growing in both horizontal and vertical directions to meet the socioeconomic demand and encountering the urban heating phenomena, urban heat island (UHI). The rapid and random developments of infrastructure make the urban heating threat more critical by increasing the energy consumption for air conditioning, anthropogenic heating, greenhouse gas (GHG) emission, and air pollution (Ramanathan and Feng, 2009). In addition to that, the urban climate suffers frequent heat waves, altered precipitation patterns, storms, water stress, and high risk of flash flooding or drought (Trenberth, 2008). Furthermore, the public health is compromised due to reduced thermal comfort levels, heat stress, and respiratory problems. Therefore, in today's scenario, it is essential to convert the present cities into and develop new cities as sustainable cities. A sustainable city can be defined as a habitat having social, economic, and environmental sustainability and resilience with minimum requirement of food, water, and energy inputs and significant reduction in waste, heat output, air pollution, and water pollution.

2. Urban heat island (UHI)

The phenomenon of UHI can be defined as the warmer city core in comparison to the surrounding undeveloped natural environment (Voogt and Oke, 2003), caused mainly by excessive surface heating and heat storage, pollution emission, anthropogenic heating, hindrance to wind circulation, and lower evapotranspiration. The UHI can be categorized into surface UHI, canopy-layer UHI and boundary-layer UHI based on the vertical height it is measured. The UHI is driven by the surface dynamics, and hence, analysis of the surface UHI plays a vital role in understanding the whole concept.

Causes: Urban surfaces (walls, roofs, roads, and canyons) are comprised of impermeable, heat-retaining, and low-albedo materials, and lack of vegetation and water surfaces induces heating within the city core. High-density built-up areas with tall buildings and narrow urban street canyons result in reduced outgoing long-wave radiation and lower urban wind speed. In addition to that, anthropogenic heating, high energy consumption, greenhouse gas emission, and air pollution make UHI worse. The industrial smoke and burning of biomass modify the atmospheric acrosol concentrations, which in the absence of urban wind get trapped in lower atmosphere, creating smog, and hence affect the global solar radiation intensity and daytime surface temperature. Release of CO_2 into atmosphere due to transportation, fossil fuel combustion, and industrial emissions remains persistent and accelerates the greenhouse gas concentration causing more heating. Moreover, poor city planning, maintenance, and public unawareness can also be included in causes of excessive urban heating.

Effects: The impact of UHI has two domains: the city residents and the environment. Urban heating diminishes the thermal comfort, withers public health, and raises heat mortality. The senior citizens, physically weak, homeless, poor, and low-incoming peoples suffer mostly from the heat stress and the after effects. According to Reserve Bank of India (2013), more than 21% of Indians live below poverty line and are highly vulnerable to different health hazards. Mortality due to heat wave and heat stress over many locations of India has been increased in past couple of decades. Increase in concentration of ground-level ozone due to photochemical oxidation of volatile organic compounds leads to smog formation and hence increasing many cardiorespiratory diseases. On the other hand, raised air temperature affects the regional climatic conditions such as frequent storms, flash floods, heat waves, and altered urban wind circulation and precipitation patterns. The variation in the climatic conditions due to UHI further affects agriculture, public health, and risks of property loss and life, thus raised as extensive interest of researchers.

3. Land use land cover (LULC)

The land cover can be defined as "the Earth's land surface and the immediate sub-surface above it," and the land cover change is either replacing a certain land cover type by another or intensification of the existing one (Luyssaert et al., 2014). Therefore, land cover changes occur when urban areas extend or intensify, agricultural lands expand, or deforestation happens. The land cover changes occur naturally, or it can be human-driven. The term land use is "the purpose for which the land cover is modified by human," i.e., urban setup, agricultural field, pavements, etc. The land use pattern for an urban setup depends completely on technology and economic advancement and the degree of civilization of the residents.

Due to urbanization, the natural surfaces are replaced by the artificial surfaces of less permeability, less reflectivity, high thermal conductivity, and high heat capacity. The altered properties of the urban surfaces lead to high heat storage, less evaporation, and reduced outgoing long-wave radiation, which result in increasing temperature. Due to spreading of urban surfaces, drastic vegetation loss occurs in the form of deforestation, and loss of agricultural field results in further decrease in evapotranspiration and the cooling due to it. In developing countries, the rate of population growth, demand of food and fuel, and industrial activities are essentially high, and hence, the LULC changes happen in brisk rate and abrupt way. Therefore, it is essential to obtain exact estimation about the rate and kind of LULC changes for proper management planning and regulated use of the resources.

Obtaining accurate and up-to-date information regarding the LULC changes is quite challenging except for the remote-sensing-based change detection, which provides recent information with good spatial resolution. The satellite data can be processed in many ways to obtain the land cover maps. The land cover maps can be obtained through manual interpretation of these satellite images, which is a lengthy and boring process and completely subjective to the analyst doing it, or the digital process, which is controlled by computer programming, is much quicker and with less human interference. In the digital process, many algorithms are proposed by the researchers and the scientists to classify or divide the satellite images into different land cover types termed as "classes." The most common and basic classification methods are: unsupervised classification and supervised classification. Apart from these two methods, many machine-learning classifiers are available for more accurate classification. Remote sensing indices are also very useful tool for identifying different LULC classes where different indices are devised for the purpose of identifying a specific class or classes. There are many indices that are used for identifying built-up areas and are discussed in Section 4.

3.1 Impact of LULC changes on land surface temperature

The pressure of growing population, industrial extension, and technological improvement has forced natural surfaces to modify into artificial urban surfaces (Fig. 4.1). The artificial surfaces are in general impermeable, less reflective, lack in moisture, heat-capturing and heat retaining-surfaces in contrast to moist, porous, less heat-capturing and -retaining natural surfaces, thus affect the surface dynamics. Due to these altered properties, the "land surface temperature" (LST) of the urban surface is higher than that of the natural surface and thus generates the phenomena of UHI. Many research studies explored the interrelation of LST with LULC changes worldwide and concluded that LULC variation

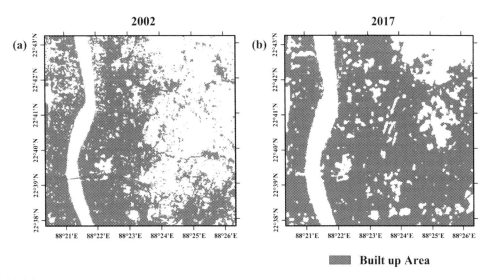

FIGURE 4.1

Built-up area over a section of Kolkata city during (A) 2002 and (B) 2017, indicating expansion.

has significant impact on LST and hence atmospheric temperature (Coseo and Larsen, 2014; Estoque et al., 2017; Sultana and Satyanarayana, 2018, 2019, 2020). The studies indicated that the LST is generally highest over the dense built-up regions, industrial areas, pavements, parking lots, barren lands, fallow lands, rocky and sandy surfaces, whereas the vegetated areas and water surfaces are comparatively cooler (Fig. 4.2). Fig. 4.2 depicts the spatial distribution of LST over a part of Kolkata city where the LST over the water body is in the range of 20.3−22.8°C, over the vegetation in the range of 22.9−27.6°C, and over urban settlement and barren lands in the range of 25.5−34.5°C. Fig. 4.3 shows the variation in the LST due to the changes in the LULC. As the built-up areas expanded (Fig. 4.1), the LST is noticed to increase (Fig. 4.3).

3.2 Impact of LULC on climate system

The modified land cover leads to change in LST, which can influence atmospheric temperature, humidity level, precipitation pattern (Lin et al., 2011), wind circulation (Rajagopalan et al., 2014), and other climatic activities on a regional scale. The regional change in the climate can affect the nearby climatic conditions, and thus, the local and regional climate can have the influence on the global climate (Mahmood et al., 2014). Studies indicated that urban setup can modify the structure and intensity of thunderstorms as Niyogi et al. (2011) found that about 60% of thunderstorms over urban areas of Indianapolis, Indiana, have modified structure in comparison to only 25% over the rural area. The study also indicated splitting of storms close to the urban area and merging again near downwind. Meir and Orton (2013) found the enhancing effect of UHI on heat wave over the New York City, which also influenced the sea breeze during the heat wave events.

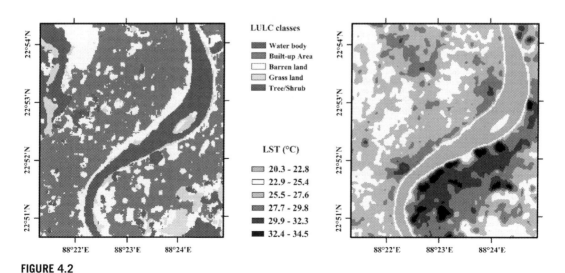

FIGURE 4.2

Delineating the land surface temperature (LST) with different land use land cover (LULC) over a section of Kolkata city during January 24, 2017.

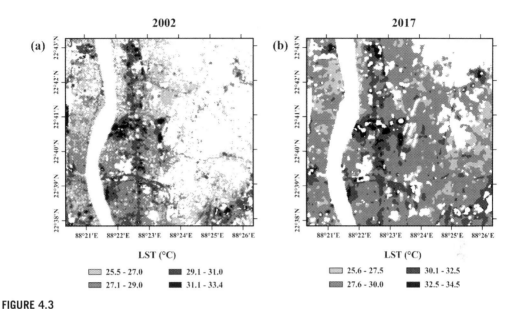

FIGURE 4.3

Change in land surface temperature (LST) with respect to the changes in built-up area during (A) 2002 and (B) 2017.

4. Remote sensing indices

Modification in the land use land cover associated with urban expansion is most abrupt, frequent, and rapid in comparison to any other land use land cover variations. Urban areas where the natural surfaces are replaced with the impervious surfaces significantly influence the surface−atmosphere interaction, hydrologic system, biodiversity and regional climatic conditions, and hence demands effective estimation and monitoring of the land cover changes. These changes can be most accurately tracked in the form of land cover maps from aerial or remotely sensed data, which provides relatively up-to-date, broad-ranged images with different spatial and spectral resolutions. The most efficient way of mapping land covers is utilizing the remote sensing indices. The remote sensing indices are generally in the form of ratios of the radiance of the spectral bands of the satellite images. The most common indices are the Normalized Difference Vegetation Index (NDVI), which is used to map the vegetation abundance, and the Normalized Difference Built-up Index (NDBI), which identifies the built-up areas. In addition to these, many remote sensing indices are devised and are used for different purposes. For differentiating built-up areas, a number of indices are proposed, and few of the mostly mentioned are discussed below along with other significant indices.

4.1 Normalized difference vegetation index (NDVI)

The NDVI is one of the most common and significant index used in remote sensing. In simplified way, the NDVI can be defined as the measure of greenness in a section of land. In addition to mapping the greenery, it is also employed to monitor droughts, forest fires, assessing agricultural lands and many more. NDVI is also a good indicator of plant health.

NDVI can be calculated with the formula (Carlson and Ripley, 1997),

$$NDVI = \frac{NIR - Red}{NIR + Red} \qquad (4.1)$$

NIR—reflected near infrared range of the spectrum.
Red—reflected red range of the visible spectrum.

The value of NDVI ranges from -1 to 1, where negative values indicate clouds and water, values close to zero are rocks, sand, or bare soil. Moderate values around $0.2-0.3$ indicate shrubs, grass lands, or crop fields, and higher values around $0.6-0.8$ represent larger vegetation canopies such as forests. The chlorophylls in the leaves strongly absorb the visible spectra of light, whereas the near-infrared spectra are strongly reflected, hence higher the value of NDVI, higher is the greenness.

4.2 Normalized difference built-up index (NDBI)

NDBI is essentially used to extract built-up features over a section of land. The built-up areas mostly characterized by the impervious surfaces of negligible moisture content and the bare soil possess low moisture content, hence both respond similarly to radiation spectrum. Therefore, in addition to the built-up areas, the NDBI also characterizes the bare soil, fallow lands, rock, and sand in the same category.

NDBI can be estimated by (Zha et al., 2003),

$$NDBI = \frac{SWIR1 - NIR}{SWIR1 + NIR} \qquad (4.2)$$

SWIR1—reflected short-wave near-infrared range of the spectrum.

NDBI value also lies between -1 and 1, the negative values indicate water bodies, and the higher positive values points to built-up areas and bare soil. Because the built-up areas and the bare soil reflect the SWIR spectrum more than the NIR spectrum, water rarely reflects the infrared spectrum. In case of vegetation, NIR is more reflected than the SWIR, and hence, NDBI value is noticed to be lower.

Build-up Index (BUI)

It is the index that identifies the urban areas using the NDBI and NDVI. The BUI is a binary image where positive value is only attributed to the built-up areas and barren lands and thus maps the built-up areas automatically.

The NDBI and the NDVI images are recoded to obtain binary images, positive values are reassigned as a higher positive value (254), and the negative values are reassigned as 0. Then the BUI can be calculated by subtracting NDVI from NDBI (Zha et al., 2003),

$$BUI = NDBI - NDVI \qquad (4.3)$$

The resultant BUI is a binary image with positive value only for built-up areas and barren lands, and all other land covers have either zero or negative value.

4.3 Normalized difference bareness index (NDBaI)

This index is used to differentiate different classes of urban areas and identifies urban areas as secondary bare land. NDBaI can be estimated as (Zhao and Chen, 2005),

$$NDBaI = \frac{SWIR1 - TIR}{SWIR1 + TIR} \qquad (4.4)$$

TIR—reflected thermal infrared range of the spectrum.

The value of NDBaI less than 0.2 is attributed to the built-up area (Chen et al., 2006).

4.4 Enhanced built-up and bareness index (EBBI)

In order to overcome the complexity in the pixel combinations for identifying both built-up and barren lands, As-syakur et al. (2012) devised EBBI. This index effectively distinguishes built-up areas and bare land and maps them separately. It utilizes the near-infrared, short-wave near-infrared and thermal infrared spectra to enhance the built-up area and the bare land pixels.

The EBBI can be calculated from (As-syakur et al., 2012),

$$EBBI = \frac{SWIR1 - NIR}{10\sqrt{SWIR1 + TIR}} \tag{4.5}$$

The value of EBBI varies from -1 to 1, positive for built-up areas and bare land, negative for the vegetation, and very negligible for water bodies. The value of EBBI is between 0.1 and 0.35 for urban areas and higher than 0.35 for bare lands.

4.5 Dry built-up index (DBI) and dry bareness index (DBSI)

These indices are proposed by Rasul et al. (2018) for separately mapping built-up areas and bare lands in the dry climate using Landsat 8. DBI is estimated using the blue and the thermal infrared spectra, and DBSI is estimated using green and short-wave near-infrared spectra from the following relations,

$$DBI = \frac{Blue - TIR}{Blue + TIR} - NDVI \tag{4.6}$$

$$DBSI = \frac{SWIR1 - Green}{SWIR1 + Green} - NDVI \tag{4.7}$$

Blue—reflected blue range of the spectrum.

Green—reflected green range of the spectrum.

The indices are subtracted by NDVI to enhance the value of indices for built-up areas and bare lands. The DBI value for vegetation is decreased and the higher DBI over built-up areas with lower NDVI values will further enhanced. Similarly, DBSI is enhanced over the bare lands and decreased for vegetation and water.

The DBI and the DBSI values range between -2 and 2, and the higher values represent more built-up areas and bare lands, respectively. For DBI, a value of 0.72 or higher is assigned as built-up area, and lower values are for nonurban areas. Similarly for DBSI, a value of 0.26 or higher is assigned as bare soil, and values less than that are identified as other classes.

4.6 Urban heat island index (UHI index)

The UHI intensity over a particular location varies significantly during different period, and meaningful comparison is not possible. Again it is difficult to estimate the overall UHI effect over the location using LST data for a longer period. In 2016, Mathews et al. proposed UHI_{index} to obtain such calculations. These can be estimated by following relation,

$$UHIindex = \frac{LSTi - LSTmin}{LSTmax - LSTmin} \tag{4.8}$$

where LST_i is spatial distribution of LST of the particular image, LST_{max} and LST_{min} are respectively the maximum and the minimum value of the LST for the image.

Through this index, the LST values are normalized between 0 and 1. Higher values of the index indicate higher LST. Over the built-up area and the bare soil, the index value is more than 0.6, for vegetation the value ranges between $0.3 - 0.6$, and for water bodies it is 0.3 or less than that.

4.7 Urban index (UI)

This index utilizes near-infrared (NIR) and short-wave infrared (SWIR2) spectra to estimate urban density (Kawamura et al., 1996). The UI value increases with increasing density.

$$UI = \frac{SWIR2 - NIR}{SWIR2 + NIR} \tag{4.9}$$

SWIR2—reflected short-wave infrared range of the spectrum.

4.8 Index-based built-up index (IBI)

It is calculated to enhance built-up area using the NDBI, Soil Adjusted Vegetation Index (SAVI), and Modified Normalized Difference Water Index (MNDWI).

The IBI can be calculated by using the relation (Xu, 2008),

$$IBI = \frac{\left[NDBI - \frac{(SAVI + MNDWI)}{2} \right]}{\left[NDBI + \frac{(SAVI + MNDWI)}{2} \right]} \tag{4.10}$$

$$SAVI = \frac{(NIR - Red)(1 + L)}{(NIR + Red + L)} \tag{4.10a}$$

where L is soil brightness correction factor

$$MNDWI = \frac{Green - SWIR1}{Green + SWIR1} \tag{4.10b}$$

4.9 Normalized difference water index (NDWI)

NDWI is very useful in identifying water sources over a section of land (McFeeters, 1996), but most significantly it is utilized for detecting water stress over the drought-affected areas and areas where meeting the need for water is difficult. NDWI is really useful in improving irrigation and hence, agriculture.

NDWI indicates the moisture content in the plants and the soil and is estimated by,

$$NDWI = \frac{NIR - SWIR1}{NIR + SWIR1} \qquad (4.11)$$

NIR—reflected near infrared range of the spectrum (0.841—0.876 nm).

SWIR1—reflected short-wave near-infrared range of the spectrum (1.628—1.652 nm).

The NDWI value varies from −1 to 1, higher values correspond to higher possibility of water and vice versa. NDWI is also sensitive to the variation in the liquid water in the vegetation canopy, hence, can also identify vegetation complementary to NDVI (Gao, 1996).

4.10 Normalized difference snow index (NDSI)

Snow is a common global climatological phenomenon in the higher latitudes and considered as a destructive natural hazard. Therefore, identifying snow cover is essential for weather forecasting and hazard mitigation.

NDSI can be calculated from the formula (Sidjak and Wheate, 1999),

$$NDSI = \frac{Green - SWIR}{Green + SWIR} \qquad (4.12)$$

Green—reflected green range of the spectrum (0.53—0.61 nm).

SWIR—reflected short-wave infrared range of the spectrum (1.55—1.75 nm).

5. Land cover management strategies for heat and temperature management

The land management is "the way the land cover is treated for a specific purpose without resulting in any land cover changes." Use of fertilizers or pesticides in crop fields, irrigation mechanism for agriculture purpose, planting different plant species in reforestation are examples of land management. The land cover changes may cause modification in the surface properties, but land management does not introduce any such changes (Luyssaert et al., 2014).

Many land cover management strategies are considered for diminishing the UHI effects. The most common strategies are vegetation, green roofing, cool roofing, etc. The most effective strategies are discussed in detail in the following (U.S. Environmental Protection Agency, 2008).

5.1 Trees and vegetations

Trees and other smaller plants provide cooler environment and low surface and atmospheric temperatures through shading and evapotranspiration. Planting right type of tree at appropriate locations such as around the building or to shade parking lots or roads can serve as a useful mitigation strategy. Researchers indicated that planting deciduous trees and vines in the west side of buildings offer effective cooling. Depending on building height, distance between the trees and building and the species of tree and energy-efficient strategy must be adapted. For shading the parking lots and streets, trees can be planted around and medians of the parking lots and along the sides of the streets. Large trees can also be placed in playground, schoolyards, and other open spaces. Shade trees grow slow and take enough space, but vines take less space and need less soil and grow comparatively faster can sometimes be replacement for shade trees (U.S. Environmental Protection Agency − Ch. 2, 2008).

The solar radiations get blocked by the leaves and the branches of the trees, and the amount of radiation that transmits through depends on the plant species. About 10%−30% of sun light reaches below the canopy during summer time in comparison to 10%−80% in winter due to greater foliage during summer (Huang et al., 1990). Shading reduces the surface temperature below the canopy, thus reduces heat transfer to the building or pavements it shading. Presence of larger trees enhances the evapotranspiration, which cools the nearby air. In combination with the tree shading, the evapo-transpiration can reduce air temperature by a considerable amount. Trees and vegetations often act as wind shields, which prevents ventilation around the buildings, which significantly saves energy during the winter seasons.

5.1.1 Benefits

Storm-water management and water quality: Shade trees and vegetation provide storm-water management, runoff, and pavement maintenance. Rain water gets better infiltration due to tree roots and gets restored at groundwater reservoirs.

Reduced energy use: The energy consumption for cooling the building is considerably reduced due to shading effect of trees. The benefit depends on size and orientation of trees and their distance from the building.

Reduced air pollution and GHG emission: The tree leaves remove pollution particles from air as dry deposition. Vegetations also provide quality air by removing industrial and residential GHG, evaporative emission of volatile organic compounds (VOC) from parked vehicles and ground-level ozone.

Carbon storage and sequestration: Trees help in carbon sequestration as they take carbon from the atmosphere and store it as they grow up and later either release it to atmosphere or transfer it to soil during depositing litter or debris or when they die. This is an important stage of the carbon cycle.

Improved human health: Trees help in improving air quality by reducing pollutants and GHG, which reduces respiratory illness. Cooling effect of shade trees reduces heat stress and thermal discomfort during summer. It also protects us from direct exposure to UV rays, which causes skin and eyes irritation.

Enhanced quality of life: Trees and vegetations help in reducing noise pollution and also act as home for many birds and other living beings.

5.1.2 Negative impacts

Rise in humidity level: Evapotranspiration cools the atmosphere as well as releases moisture to it, which raises the humidity level. This increase might be a trouble for an already humid climate as thermal discomfort.

Biogenic emission: Few trees emit VOCs as biogenic emission, which can counteract the quality air benefits from the trees. However, the emission depends on temperature, and cooling effect of trees may end up as reduction in the emission.

Maintenance and solid waste: Shading trees demand proper maintenance and watering. Solid waste increases due to falling leaves and branches, pruning, or tree removal.

Possible damage to infrastructure: The sidewalks or the power lines may get damaged, or other infrastructural damage may occur due to the roots and falling branches.

It is really necessary to chose most beneficial plants for placing them in the right location to maximize the purpose and avoid the ones causing problems. Proper and in time maintenance and wise placement can minimize the possible damages.

5.2 Greenery in buildings

The buildings are the heat sink as the roofs and façades are exposed to the direct solar radiation, and the heat is absorbed by the roofs and walls in day time and retained till night to be emitted. By modifying these surfaces, the heating caused can be controlled. Growing plants over the roofs, balcony, or on the building façades not only provides desired solution but also adds beauty to the structure too.

5.2.1 Green roofs

A green roof is simply modifying the existing roof for growing flora by installing water proofing, root repellent, drainage, and irrigation system keeping the structure safe and undamaged. The green roofs are also termed as "vegetative roofs" or "eco-roofs." Green roofs simply provide vegetation over a neglected space and making it useful without interfering urban infrastructure. Green roofs are noticed to be more durable than the conventional roofs with greater benefit of reducing UHI effect over cities. The vegetation of the green roof and the growing medium together block the solar heat to reach the roof surface, thus keep the roof cool and reduce temperature (U.S. Environmental Protection Agency − Ch. 3, 2008).

Green roofing is primarily of two forms: intensive and extensive based on the vegetation it supports and amount of maintenance required. The extensive green roofs can support up to 15−50 pound (7−23 Kg) per square foot of vegetation with yearly maintenance, and the intensive green roofs can hold 80−150 pounds (36−68 Kg) per square foot and require more maintenance (https://science. howstuffworks.com/environmental/green-science/green-rooftop.htm). Extensive green roof usually has shallow growing medium, less than 6 inches, whereas intensive green roofs have deeper growing medium of several feet. Sometimes a form of semiintensive green roof is also noticed with features of both the above forms.

5.2.2 Green wall

A green wall is a vertical wall with growing medium intentionally covered with flora. Green walls are also termed as "living walls" or "vertical gardens," have a vertical growth medium and integrated hydration system. The green walls or the vertical gardens should not be confused with the "green facades" or "vertical farming," which are two different concepts. The green walls have most of the same functionality as green roofs and hence can be considered as complementary to the green roofs. The green walls are constructed of modular panels holding different type of growth media and thus categorized accordingly. The green walls can be installed indoors as well as outdoors with different benefits. The indoor green walls cleanse the air from the volatile organic compounds that get released from the paints, furniture, and adhesives causing headache, asthma, eye irritation, etc.

5.2.3 Green façades

Green façades are simply growing climbing plants vertically up and across a building façade with growth medium at the base from the garden bed or in a container installed at different levels across the building. It takes very little space in a dense built-up area and provides a large area of greenery and provides indoor cooling and reduces energy consumption. The green façades can have following forms of vegetation; (a) self-climbing plants that use tendrils and twining stems or suckers, (b) climbing plants that require structural support placed in front of the wall, (c) hanging plant growing from pots on the roof or the balcony, and (d) green façade garden, where plants grow upward from the container fastened to the façades.

5.2.3.1 Benefits

Reduced energy use: The insulation and shading effect offered by the green roof/wall/façade reduce the heat conduction through roof/wall, and the amount of energy required for heating/cooling is also decreased. Hence, the life span of household products such as HVAC system improves through decreased use. Converting hottest surfaces (black rooftops) of urban domain into green roofs helps in decreasing air temperature and mitigating UHI.

Reduced temperature through evapotranspiration: Daily evapotranspiration cycle cools the ambient air and reduces the UHI effect.

Reduced air pollution and GHG emissions: The green roof/wall/façade plays significant role in reducing greenhouse gas emission, dust, and pollution particles and production of smog in the city. They slow down ground-level ozone formation and lower air temperature.

Reduced wastage: It reduces amount of waste generated by the house as green roofs utilize waste products.

Improved storm water management: Green roofs also improve the storm water management, act as natural filters for runoff water, and delay the runoff time to reduce stress on local sewer system.

Enhanced quality of life: The roof-top vegetations reduce noise pollution and also act as home for many living creatures and birds.

Protect buildings: Evergreen plants protect the building from heavy precipitation and keep the façade dry.

5.2.3.2 Negative impacts

Damage to buildings: Plants may damage the building if roots grow into the cracks, or weight of the green roof may cause sagging if the setup is not installed properly.

Costly process: The green roofs should be insured as the potential damage due to drought or sudden storm may come expensive.

5.3 Cool roofs

Cool roofs are made up of materials of high reflectivity and emissivity that are observed to be about 28−33°C cooler than the traditional material during hottest summer times. Cool roofs can reduce UHI effect generated due to combined heat of number of individual hot roofs in an urban setup. The incoming solar radiation has UV rays (5%) responsible for sunburn, visible spectrum (43%), and infrared rays (52%) responsible for heating effect. The traditional materials used in the roofs have low reflectance or albedo (0.05−0.15), hence absorb most of the solar radiation. The cool roof materials have albedo as high as 0.65 and thus reduce the fraction of absorbed radiation. The materials are also highly emissive that means readily radiate back and do not retain the heat. Both of these features in combination reduce the heat retaining in the roof surface and thus reduce the temperature. The reduced roof temperature decreases air temperature and thus decreases UHI effect.

Cool roof coatings are thick paints applied that increase the adhesion, durability, relief from algae and fungal growth, and self-wash ability. The cool roof coating can be of two types: cementitious and elastomeric. As the name suggests, the cementitious coating contains cement particles, whereas the elastomeric coating has polymers for better adhesion and low brittleness. Both the coatings have reflectance 65% and emittance 80%−90%. Elastomeric coatings have a waterproofing membrane, while a cementitious coating does not provide that (U.S. Environmental Protection Agency − Ch. 4, 2008).

5.3.1 Benefits

Reduced energy use: Roofs made of cooling materials retain less heat and thus transfer less heat. The building below remains cooler and comfortable, and energy uses are cut off. The benefits depend on the local climate, insulation level, attic configuration, and duct placement. The cooling effect also reduces the electricity demands.

Improves human health and comfort: Cool roofs reduce temperature inside buildings, hence reduce heat stress, and thermal comfort is improved.

Reduced air pollution and GHG emissions: The cool roofs reduce building temperature and the use of air conditioning. Therefore, the emission of anthropogenic heat and GHG is reduced, and air pollution is reduced.

5.3.2 Negative impacts

Heat loss in winter: Cool roofs eradicate the solar heating during winter, which could help warming the buildings. Though, the useful energy lost in winter is less than the unwanted energy reflected in summer.

Glaring: Sloped reflecting roofs close to streets could have glaring effect that might affect the drivers' vision and cause accidents.

Maintenance: Reflectivity reduces with time and soot deposition; hence, the cool roofs are required to be clean and maintained regularly.

5.4 Cool pavements

Conventional pavements are generally made of impervious concrete or asphalt, which get as hot as 50−60°C in summer and retain the heat to release at night. Hotter pavement can also warm the storm water running over it and degrade water quality. Cool pavements can be use a range of latest technology materials that can lower the surface temperature of pavements. Cool pavements are still an evolving technology; hence, a lot of is unknown about them. Ongoing research is expected to improve existing technologies, and new approaches can be implemented for achieving cool pavements.

Solar radiation consists of UV rays, visible lights, and IR rays, and all of these three components contribute to UHI formation. To cool the pavements, it is essential to use materials of high albedo or reflectivity, so that most of the solar radiation could be reflected back and lesser fraction is retained as stored heat. The conventional pavement materials have 5%−40% reflectivity depending on the material properties, sky-view factor (SVF), etc. The thermal emittance of the material for cool pavement should be high so that it can readily emit back the heat transferred and retain very small amount of heat as storage. Permeable pavements are also serve good as potential cool pavements, sometimes include grasses or low-lying vegetation to keep cooler temperature. Cool pavement technology also needs to consider the convection, thermal conductivity, heat capacity, urban geometry, and thickness of the pavement for better output (U.S. Environmental Protection Agency − Ch. 5, 2012).

5.4.1 Benefits

Reduced energy use: Increasing the reflectance of the pavements by 10%—35% reduces the air temperature by 0.6°C. Evaporation by permeable pavements contributes to lower air temperatures and better storm water management. Hence, it reduces energy consumptions.

Air quality and GHG emission: By decreasing the energy consumption, the cool pavements indirectly reduce air pollution and GHG emission and thus improve the air quality. Cooler air slows down the ground-level ozone formation and evaporative emission from the vehicles.

Water quality and storm water runoff: lower surface temperature of the pavements reduces temperature of the runoff water and thus reduces thermal shock to the aquatic life. Permeable pavements reduce storm water runoff and improve water quality by filtering pollution particles.

Increased pavement life: Lower surface temperature increases the durability of the pavements and reduces damage due to temperature-related stress.

Quality of life: Cool pavements provide nighttime illumination, thermal comfort, and safety. Reflective pavements increase visibility and reduce energy for lighting requirements.

5.4.2 Negative impacts

Glaring: Cool pavements have high reflectivity that causes glare and risk of trouble for driver increases.

Maintenance: The reflectivity of the cool pavements decreases with time and hence requires regular maintenance and cleaning.

5.5 Smart growth

Dense and compact urban structure play significant role in UHI formation, and thus, practice of proper development strategies keeping the urban structure in mind to protect the natural environment is essential. The decisions taken for development of an area have maximum impact on the lives of the residents. Smart growth includes the creative use of technologies for development that preserves the natural lands, projects air and water quality, and reuses the developed land. The smart growth process has few basic principles, such as mixing land use, a range of housing opportunity, walkable neighborhood, preserves natural land, variety of transport choices, cost-effective development decisions, and involvement of the community. The UHI cooling strategies can involve these principles in the implementation for better output.

6. Mitigation strategies

The UHI effects can be mitigated by: (1) increasing the evapotranspiration, (2) increasing albedo of the urban surface, (3) reducing the concentration of greenhouse gases and pollution particles, and (4) improving urban wind circulation. In order to achieve these mitigation conditions, the following components are analyzed:

- Effect of vegetation on atmosphere
- Presence of water bodies in urban set up
- Use of high albedo and pervious materials
- Well-designed urban geometry
- Careful mitigation policies and public awareness

6.1 Green vegetation

Green leaves absorb the greenhouse gases such as SO_2, NO_2, O_3 and CO_2 from the atmosphere along with filtering the suspended air pollutants such as soot, coal ash, fuel oil particles, soil dust, etc. Trees are also useful in decreasing noise pollution and endorsing passive environmental cooling. Vegetation can serve as cooling element through green roofs/walls, green façades, and vegetation patches in appropriate places.

6.1.1 Green roofs

A green roof can simply be defined as a vegetative layer grown over rooftops with no damage to the structure. Like any other vegetation, the green roof vegetation provides cooling effect through shading and evapotranspiration. The surface of the green roof is often $15-45°C$ cooler than the conventional roof top surface, whereas the nearby air is cooled by $2-5°C$. Green roofing can be done to all types of building and hence can be installed in industrial and commercial properties, offices and government facilities, residential and educational buildings, etc.

6.1.2 Green wall

Green walls can be installed in any vertical façade both indoors and outdoors depending on the demand and climatic conditions. The plant species varies for the indoor and outdoor setups, hence should be chosen wisely. The indoor green walls cleanse the air from volatile organic compound, and the outdoor green wall filters the pollution particles and reduces the GHG concentration. Green walls provide significant cooling by evapotranspiration and hence reduce the UHI effect.

6.1.3 Green façades

Green façade captures fine particulate and improves the air quality. It lowers urban temperature through cooling effect of evapotranspiration and absorption of significant greenhouse gases. Green façades protect walls from direct solar radiation and thus reduce heat absorption in day time as well as heat emission at the night. It protects building from solar heating in summer, keeping it cooler, and in winter, the vegetation protects the building from wind and reduces heat loss through convection and the energy consumption for air conditioning. Evergreen plants protect the building from heavy precipitation and keep the façade dry.

6.1.4 Parks and roadside plantation

Apart from green roofing and vertical vegetation, the roadside plantation and parks are of equal importance for serving as cooling element in urban setup. It is necessary to convert the available vacant and barren areas into well-planned parks with native, drought-tolerant shade trees, shrubs, grasses, and bushes to enhance the cooling effect. Planting appropriate plants in and around the street side should be done to boost roadside cooling and shading. The roadside plantations also absorb the greenhouse gases from the transportation and the industrial emissions and filter the released pollution particle. It is important to choose appropriate plant species for roadside plantation as trees block natural flow of the air within the urban areas, and hence, cooling breeze might get affected due to it.

6.1.5 Shade trees

Trees with large canopy that protects houses and pedestrians from direct sun light are the shade trees. It reduces the air temperature by the process of evapotranspiration and shading effect, keeps the buildings comparatively cool, which reduces the energy consumption and helps in mitigating heat island effect. The shade trees also improve air quality by filtering the pollution particles and absorbing the greenhouse gases. Shade trees are vulnerable to extreme storms and can be threat to living beings. The roots of these can affect the nearby building foundations and roads, therefore are not suitable for dense urban sectors.

6.1.6 Green pavements
Replacing footpaths of artificial material with natural soil elements with grass can reduce heating of pavement. Apart from grass, the permeable and pervious concrete or permeable pavers can also be considered for this purpose. Green pavements increase evaporation and decrease heat trapping due to the impervious surfaces, therefore reduce air temperature.

6.1.7 Green parking lot
Green parking lots decrease the use of artificial material instead natural soil, and grass is used which have cooling effect on the atmosphere in contrast to the conventional impervious dark asphalt surfaces. By decreasing the heat accumulation by the parking lot surface, the heating of the vehicles can be reduced.

6.1.8 Urban farming
It involves growing food within the urban area in less utilized spaces such as roofs, vacant plots, or abandoned building structure. The urban farms not only provide locally produced food but also provide shade and increased evapotranspiration for cooling effect. It also reduces transport expenses and air pollution due to transportation (cuts off GHG emissions). Urban farming lowers the UHI effect and also building energy consumption.

6.2 Water cover
The surface temperature of water does not increase much in comparison to the rest of urban areas, and the water surfaces provide huge amount of evaporation and thus increase humidity and can increase the wind circulation. Hence, large amount of evaporation and high wind speed due to presence of water bodies may reduce air temperature within the urban setup. High heat absorption capacity of water can further reduce the urban temperature. For mitigation purpose, we can consider two categories: water bodies and water features. Water bodies represent mitigation measures using large water areas, which are natural elements, whereas water features are artificial elements using water that can provide thermal comfort (Ruefenacht and Acero, 2017).

6.2.1 Water bodies
Natural surface water: The rivers, lakes, ponds, or wetlands present within urban area can serve as natural cool sink for reducing urban heat. The cooling effect is subjected to the size and distribution of the water bodies. A bigger water body such as lake can have better cooling effect than the smaller ones, but a collection of equally distribution smaller lakes can have significant result (Theeuwes et al., 2013).

Blue and green space: Vegetation within the city can provide significant cooling, but the combined effect of greenery and water can bring distinct benefits for UHI mitigation. Studies indicated that the green space is more receptive to the blue space cooling when within the range of 200 m (Wu and Zhang, 2019). The blue space has nocturnal warming effect, thus the fact needs to be considered before implementing the mitigation strategy.

Wetlands: The wetlands are usually cooler than the surrounding land cover, and the location and the shape are of significance for mitigation purpose. Wetlands are also considered for runoff regulation improvement, pollutant removal, and reducing GHG emission. Studies indicate that wetland cooling is more significant for downtown region and more effective when a larger unit is substituted by several smaller units within the same area. Thus it is essential for bigger cities to install evenly distributed regular-shaped water areas in dense built-up areas.

Water catchment area: A water catchment area is an integrated land that collects the rain water into a bigger reservoir. A collection of water catchment areas can reduce the overheating in the urban surface.

6.2.2 Water features

Ponds: A pond is a water-filled depressed area smaller than a lake; emerges by filling of rain water, runoff water, or groundwater. Ponds either natural or artificial can provide cooling effect in the neighborhood. The artificial ponds either present in the ground or installed on the roof of the building can be a significant cooling agent for nearby locality.

Water misting and spray: The water misting and spray are not just suitable for fire extinguishing, but the technology can also be implemented for diminishing the heat stress. The water misting method produces droplets of small diameter, which maximize heat absorption and evaporation and increase cooling effect and humidity. Water misting and spraying combined with fan can reduce heat stress and thermal discomfort.

Fountains: The artificial fountains installed in parks, lounges, and porticos for beautification increase humidity and decrease thermal discomfort. Placing better designed fountains that recycle water in different locations can provide thermal comfort with low budget.

The UHI mitigation with water bodies is generally based on the evaporative cooling during daytime that enhances the humidity level. This mitigation strategy works better for dry climate, but it causes thermal discomfort for humid climate and thus may not be considered as a mitigation option. Additionally, the high heat capacity of water prevents nighttime cooling, and it may increase the urban heating. Moreover, the nocturnal stable condition reduces the wind speed, which might further affect the urban temperature. Therefore, it is essential to plan the mitigation wisely.

6.3 Modified building materials

A high albedo material reflects most of the incoming radiation and absorbs a smaller amount of heat, results in less heat storage and reduced urban temperature. Use of such materials in building roofing and pavements reduces the temperature. The photocatalytic surfaces and retroreflective materials are very useful for this purpose. The permeable materials allow water to infiltrate and arises the scope of cooling through evaporation.

6.3.1 High albedo roofing

The hottest surface in an urban region is the dark roof, which absorbs heat from sun and causes heating effect, whereas light-colored roofs or cool roofs have no such heating effect as solar radiation gets reflected significantly. White materials, which have higher albedo (0.6), can be used in place of dark material having lower albedo (0.05−0.1). The reflection capability of reflective roofs reduces with time due to soot deposition; hence, the roofs demand periodic cleaning. Additionally, a sloped reflecting roof may create glares that affect the drivers' vision and cause accidents.

6.3.2 Cool façades
Painting the building façades with materials less absorptive and more reflective to solar radiation reduces the heat storage and thus decreases the temperature of the façades and the air nearby. It also reduces the multiple reflection heat gain within the urban canyon. The cool façades can be more beneficial if designed to avoid visual discomfort or glaring. Combining cool façades with cool roofs can significantly increase the indoor cooling.

6.3.3 High albedo pavements
Use of high albedo materials in road and highway pavements results in reflecting more solar radiation and reduction of UHI effect. However, high albedo materials for roads and highways do not appear much effective as the reflected radiation from the roads may get trapped by tall buildings. In addition to that, most of the portions of roads remain covered by vehicles, and risk of glaring is very high. Though reflective or cool pavements might increase nighttime visibility and reduce requirement of light, the reflectivity reduces quickly due to vehicular movements and hence demands regular maintenance.

6.3.4 Pervious pavements
Impervious surfaces resist water infiltration, and hence, evapotranspiration process is negligible in this case. Replacing impermeable pavements with pervious surfaces allows water infiltration, and the temperature is expected to reduce significantly through the process of evaporation. The infiltrated water keeps the pavement cool and directly affects the temperature. In addition, the permeable surface decreases the runoff water loss, and the infiltrated water can be collected as storage or recycled to the underground reservoirs.

6.3.5 Hi-tech materials
The retroreflective or the directionally reflective materials have high albedo that can reflect back solar energy. The phase-change materials can stabilize indoor temperature by storing and releasing latent heat during phase changes. The nanotechnology-based thermochromic materials can change color from darker shades to lighter shade with increasing temperature and also reversibly can regulate temperature passively.

6.3.6 Water cooling and desiccant systems
Water cooling and desiccant systems use evaporation and latent cooling respectively to maintain moisture concentration for a comfortable and indoor environment. Water cooling systems can also be installed in the pedestrian level for providing thermal comfort. The desiccant systems are ideal for hot and humid climates.

6.3.7 Dynamic and active roofs/façades
These are the building façades and roofs that dynamically alter their configuration according to the weather conditions. This strategy focuses on reducing the heat piling up specifically during intense solar radiation. The strategy is applicable to all climates but more effective for temperate climate than tropical climate as the variability of weather condition is high over temperate zones.

6.4 Urban geometry

The geometry of the urban structures can affect the process of urban heating and thus is of importance for the mitigation strategies. Modifying or improving the crucial features can provide opportunities of more effective UHI mitigation and promote thermal comfort. The urban planning should be according to the regional climatic conditions that the shading effect and wind circulation should be more effective. Few important strategies are discussed below (Ruefenacht and Acero, 2017).

6.4.1 Sky-view factor and aspect ratio

Both the SVF and the aspect ratio are the characteristics of urban geometry that checks the incoming and outgoing radiation. The SVF at a point can be defined as the ratio of visible sky and the hemisphere centered at that point (Oke, 1982), and the aspect ratio is the ration of the average building height to the urban canyon width. The values of SVF and aspect ratio should be chosen such that the shading effect of buildings and heat trapping of the canyons are in balance. The SVF is lower and aspect ratio is high, that is, we have taller buildings and narrow canyons. the shading effect of buildings is high, but also outgoing radiation trapping is high, making the day time cooler and nighttime uncomfortable. On the other hand, high SVF and low aspect ratio due to broader streets can increase day time heating but increase wind ventilation also. Hence, the urban planning should be in such a way that maximum benefits can be taken by enhancing building shading and air circulation and lowering the heat trapping.

6.4.2 Building form

Building form is the way in which multiple buildings are arranged, that is, in linear or blocked form. The building form can influence the wind circulation and the shading effect. Combining suitable building arrangements with urban vegetation can increase the mitigation benefits. The building form should be planned to minimize the direct solar radiation and increase the shading of the façades to ensure high thermal comfort indoors and outdoors as well. Cheng et al. (2006) analyzed different combinations and suggested the best option is horizontal layout with different building heights and low site coverage.

6.4.3 Building heights

Compact buildings with equal height can block the wind ventilation through the buildings, and the urban canyons raises thermal discomfort. Constructing buildings in ascending heights in the direction of wind flow can improve wind circulation and thus enhance the thermal comfort. The asymmetric canyons, use of galleries and terrace podium can also enhance wind speed and thermal comfort.

6.4.4 Avoid obstruction

Presence of building or any other urban structure in the way of wind can obstruct the wind and decrease the thermal comfort as well as air quality for pedestrians. Similarly, dense construction in seashore can block the sea breeze and affect the thermal comfort. On the contrary, the open spaces at road junctions can increase the wind ventilation significantly for the pedestrians.

6.4.5 Building porosity

Including horizontal or vertical gaps and opening in the building structure is termed as building porosity. Porous buildings increase the air permeability in the building areas, which otherwise lack air flow and hence are high in thermal discomfort. Similarly, ventilated walkways can be provided by constructing them parallel to the direction of wind flow.

6.4.6 Passive design for thermal comfort

In order to keep a comfortable and constant indoor temperature, the architects and the designers use passive design strategy to achieve complete thermal control and continuous air-tight environment. If we can put these two together, the temperature in indoors is maintained no matter what happens outside. Continuous insulation and triple-glazed windows are few of the building features that keep building temperature maintained. Installing solar array on rooftop that also provides shades, underground parking and planting big shade trees are few other measures that help in minimizing urban temperature.

6.5 Policies and awareness

Construction and implementation of urban mitigation policies in the individual cities are really essential for diminishing the UHI effect. The authorities should remain responsible for bringing out appropriate policies and strategies as per the demand of the city, and the general public should be made aware of the fact of the UHI effects and the mitigation methods (Imam and Banerjee, 2016).

Renewable energy: The government buildings, offices, educational institutes should use renewable energy for consumption purpose and should promote the idea among the public by setting examples. More renewable energy programs should be initiated by the authorities.

Energy efficient systems: The use of energy efficient air conditioners, household appliances, and office equipment should be encouraged. The energy-efficient industries can decrease the heat losses and overall energy consumption. This strategy is also useful in reducing GHG emission. Coupling it with the heat recovery systems can decrease the thermal pollution.

Green corridors: Dense road traffic is one of the major air pollution sources. The initiatives such as green corridors, grassed foot-path green parking lots can replace the conventional structures to help in reducing the air pollution and have cooling effect.

Transportation rules: CNG-based vehicles, public transport, and car-pooling should be encouraged. The older commercial vehicles should be banned based on vehicle regulation rules. Electric private and public transports should be more encouraged.

Plantation programs: Youth should be encouraged to learn and get involved in plantation and gardening activities. Extensive green cover should be installed around the industrial areas and transport corridors. Large-scale industries can utilize the carbon-credit projects. Implementing the policy of "right place, right tree" in urban area can lead toward smart green cities.

Preserving existing greenery: The concept of tree census based on species variety, richness, health, and age should be initiated. The trees with ecological significance termed as "champion trees" should be identified and preserved. Increasing property value due to the presence of vegetation will encourage plantation and preservation among the residents.

Performance-based incentive program: The programs such as gardening competition, plantation activities based on performance incentives should be encouraged.

Neighborhood solutions: A neighborhood-level focus on the solution to UHI effect is most critical as the community has the most experience of the struggle they are having and solutions they are already practicing. The group of the community members along with export can further identify the mitigation strategies that are essential and ideal for the locality.

7. Summary

The improved lifestyle the city residents availed has in turn paid the prize by different health hazards, risk of life and property, and modified climate behavior. Urbanization brings change in land cover and thus surface properties that influence the atmosphere by altering temperature, humidity, aerosol, pollutant, and GHG concentrations. As a result of urbanization, the quality of air and water is degraded, heat stress and thermal discomfort are enhanced, and surface and air temperature is increased over the urban domain, generating UHI phenomena. In order to control the impact of UHI, the changes occurring to the LULC have to be monitored through efficient methodology. Many remote sensing indices that are devised for the purpose can be utilized depending upon the requirement and the effectiveness of the index. The land cover has to be essentially managed to minimize the impact toward the enhancement of urban heating. The strategies such as urban plantation, green roofing, cool roofing, cool pavements, smart growth, etc., are noticed to be resulting effectively and need to be implemented in global scale. Different mitigation strategies depending upon the requirement of the individual cities should be applied to make the city more comfortable and more sustainable. The industrial sector can minimize the huge anthropogenic heating and excess emission of GHG and pollutants by promoting green belts, vast plantation programs, and utilizing carbon-credit projects. Proper implementation of the policies and strategies along with the individual involvement is really necessary for UHI mitigation.

References

As-syakur, A.R., Adnyana, I.W.S., Arthana, I.W., Nuarsa, I.W., 2012. Enhanced built-up and bareness index (EBBI) for mapping built-up and bare land in an urban area. Rem. Sens. 4, 2957–2970.

Carlson, T.N., Ripley, D.A., 1997. On the relation between NDVI, fractional vegetation cover, and leaf area index. Sens. Environ. 62 (3), 241–252. http://www.sciencedirect.com/science/journal/00344257.

Chen, H., Zhao, M., Li, P.X., Yin, Z.Y., 2006. Remote sensing image-based analysis of the relationship between urban heat island and land use/cover changes. Remote Sens. Environ. 104 (2), 133–146.

Cheng, V., Steemers, K., Montavon, M., Compagnon, R., 2006. Urban form, density and solar potential. In: Presented at PLEA2006 - the 23rd Conference on Passive and Low Energy Architecture, Geneva.

Coseo, P., Larsen, L., 2014. How factors of land use/land cover, building configuration, and adjacent heat sources and sinks explain Urban Heat Islands in Chicago. Landsc. Urban Plann. 125, 117–129.

Estoque, R.C., Murayama, Y., Myint, S.W., 2017. Effects of landscape composition and pattern on land surface temperature: an urban heat island study in the megacities of Southeast Asia. Sci. Total Environ. 577, 349–359.

Gao, B.C., 1996. NDWI—a normalized difference water index for remote sensing of vegetation liquid water from space. Remote Sens. Environ. 58, 257–266.

Huang, J., Akbari, H., Taha, H., 1990. The wind-shielding and shading effects of trees on residential heating and cooling requirements. In: ASHRAE Winter Meeting. American Society of Heating, Refrigerating and Air-Conditioning Engineers, Atlanta, Georgia.

Imam, A.U.K., Banerjee, U.K., 2016. Urbanisation and greening of Indian cities: problems, practices, and policies. Ambio 45, 442–457. https://doi.org/10.1007/s13280-015-0763-4.

Kawamura, M., Jayamanna, S., Tsujiko, Y., 1996. Relation between social and environmental conditions in Colombo Sri Lanka and the urban index estimated by satellite remote sensing data. Int. Arch. Photogra. Rem. Sen. 31 (B7), 321–326.

Lin, C., Chen, W., Chang, P., Sheng, Y., 2011. Impact of the urban heat island effect on precipitation over a complex geographic environment in North Taiwan. J. Appl. Meteorol. Climatol. 50 (2), 339–353. https://doi.org/10.1175/2010JAMC2504.1.

Luyssaert, S., Jammet, M., Stoy, P., et al., 2014. Land management and land-cover change have impacts of similar magnitude on surface temperature. Nat. Clim. Change 4, 389–393. https://doi.org/10.1038/nclimate2196.

Mahmood, R., Pielke Sr., R.A., Hubbard, K.G., Niyogi, D., et al., 2014. Land cover changes and their bio-geophysical effects on climate. Int. J. Climatol. 34, 929–953. https://doi.org/10.1002/joc.3736.

Mathew, A., Khandelwal, S., Kaul, N., 2016. Spatial and temporal variations of urban heat island effect and the effect of percentage impervious surface area and elevation on landsurface temperature: study of Chandigarh city, India. Sustain. Cities Soc. 26, 264–277. https://doi.org/10.1016/j.scs.2016.06.018.

McFeeters, S.K., 1996. The use of the Normalized Difference Water Index (NDWI) in the delineation of open water features. Int. J. Rem. Sens. 17, 1425–1432.

Meir, T., Orton, P.,M., et al., 2013. Forecasting the New York city urban heat island and sea breeze during extreme heat events. Weather Forecast. 28 (6), 1460–1477. https://doi.org/10.1175/WAF-D-13-00012.1.

Niyogi, D., Pyle, P., Lei, M., Arya, S.P., Kishtawal, C.M., Shepherd, M., Chen, F., Wolfe, B., 2011. Urban modification of thunderstorms: an observational storm climatology and model case study for the Indianapolis urban region. J. Appl. Meteorol. Climatol. 50, 1129–1144.

Oke, T.R., 1982. The energetic basis of the urban heat island. Q. J. R. Meteorol. Soc. 108 (455), 1–24. https://doi.org/10.1002/qj.49710845502.

Rajagopalan, P., Lim, K.C., Jamei, E., 2014. Urban heat island and wind flow characteristics of a tropical city. Sol. Energy 107, 159–170. https://doi.org/10.2016/j.solener.2014.05.042.

Ramanathan, V., Feng, Y., 2009. Air pollution, greenhouse gases and climate change: global and regional perspectives. Atmos. Environ. 43 (1), 37–50.

Rasul, A., Balzter, H., Ibrahim, G.R.F., Hameed, H.M., Wheeler, J., Adamu, B., et al., 2018. Applying built-up and bare-soil indices from landsat 8 to cities in dry climates. Land 7 (3), 81. https://doi.org/10.3390/land7030081.

Reserve Bank of India, Government of India, 2013. Number & Percentage of People below Poverty Line. Retrieved on 28 January 2021, from. https://www.rbi.org.in/scripts/PublicationsView.aspx?id=19887.

Roth, M., 2013. In: Handbook of Environmental Fluid Dynamics, Vol. 2. Harindra Joseph Shermal Fernando, ISBN 978-1-4665-5601-0, pp. 143–159.

Ruefenacht, L., Acero, J.A., 2017. Strategies for Cooling Singapore: A Catalogue of 80+ Measures to Mitigate Urban Heat Island and Improve Outdoor Thermal Comfort. https://doi.org/10.3929/ethz-b-000258216. Available from: https://www.research-collection.ethz.ch/handle/20.500.11850/258216 (Accessed 27 January 2021).

Sidjak, R.W., Wheate, R.D., 1999. Glacier mapping of the Illecillewaet icefield, British Columbia, Canada, using Landsat TM and digital elevation data. Int. J. Rem. Sens. 20, 273–284.

Sultana, S., Satyanarayana, A.N.V., 2018. Urban heat island intensity during winter over metropolitan cities of India using remote-sensing techniques: impact of urbanization. Int. J. Rem. Sens. 39, 6692–6730. https://doi.org/10.1080/01431161.2018.1466072.

Sultana, S., Satyanarayana, A.N.V., 2019. Impact of urbanisation on urban heat island intensity during summer and winter over Indian metropolitan cities. Environ. Monit. Assess. 191 (Suppl. 3), 789. https://doi.org/10.1007/s10661-019-7692-9.

Sultana, S., Satyanarayana, A.N.V., 2020. Assessment of urbanisation and urban heat island intensities using Landsat imageries during 2000–2018 over a sub-tropical Indian City. Sustain. Cities Soc. 52, 101846. https://doi.org/10.1016/j.scs.2019.101846.

Trenberth, K.E., 2008. The impact of climate change and variability on heavy precipitation, floods, and droughts. In: Anderson, M.G., McDonnells, J.J. (Eds.), Encyclopedia of Hydrological Sciences. John Wiley and Sons, New York, NY, pp. 2–11. https://doi.org/10.1002/0470848944.hsa211.

Theeuwes, N.E., Solcerová, A., Steeneveld, G.J., 2013. Modeling the influence of open water surfaces on the summertime temperature and thermal comfort in the city. J. Geophys. Res. Atmos. 118 (6), 8881−8896. https://doi.org/10.1002/jgrd.50704.

U.S. Environmental Protection Agency, 2008. Reducing Urban Heat Islands: Compendium of Strategies. https://www.epa.gov/heat-islands/heat-island-compendium.

U.S. Environmental Protection Agency (Ch 2), 2008. Trees and vegetation. In: Reducing Urban Heat Islands: Compendium of Strategies. https://www.epa.gov/heat-islands/heat-island-compendium.

U.S. Environmental Protection Agency (Ch 3), 2008. Green roofs. In: Reducing Urban Heat Islands: Compendium of Strategies. https://www.epa.gov/heat-islands/heat-island-compendium.

U.S. Environmental Protection Agency (Ch 4), 2008. Cool roofs. In: Reducing Urban Heat Islands: Compendium of Strategies. https://www.epa.gov/heat-islands/heat-island-compendium.

U.S. Environmental Protection Agency (Ch 5), 2012. Cool pavements. In: Reducing Urban Heat Islands: Compendium of Strategies. https://www.epa.gov/heat-islands/heat-island-compendium.

Voogt, J.A., Oke, T.R., 2003. Thermal remote sensing of urban climates. Remote Sens. Environ. 86, 370−384.

World Urbanization Prospectus, 2014. Department of Economic and Social Affairs. http://esa.un.org/unpd/wup/highlights/wup2014-highlights.pdf.

Wu, Z., Zhang, Y., 2019. Water bodies' cooling effects on urban land daytime surface temperature: ecosystem service reducing heat island effect. Sustainability 11 (787), 1−11.

Xu, H., 2008. A new index for delineating built-up land features in satellite imagery. Int. J. Rem. Sens. 29 (14), 4269−4276.

Zha, Y., Gao, J., Ni, S., 2003. Use of normalized difference built-up index in automatically mapping urban areas from TM imagery. Int. J. Rem. Sens. 24 (3), 583−594. https://doi.org/10.1080/01431160304987.

Zhao, H.M., Chen, X.L., 2005. Use of normalized difference bareness index in quickly mapping bare areas from TM/ETM+. Geoscience and Remote Sensing Symposium Vol. 3(25−29), 1666−1668.

Use of landscape metrics for the mitigation of the surface urban heat island effect in Mediterranean cities

A. Polydoros[4], C. Cartalis[1], M. Santamouris[2] and D. Kolokotsa[3]

[1]*Department of Environmental Physics – Meteorology, Department of Physics, National and Kapodistrian University of Athens, Panepistiopolis Zografou, Athens, Greece;* [2]*School of Built Environment, University of New South Wales (UNSW), Sydney, Australia;* [3]*Chemical and Environmental Engineering School, Technical University of Crete, Kounoupidiana, Crete, Greece;* [4]*Department of Environmental Physics, University of Athens, University Campus, Build PHYS-V, Athens, Greece*

1. Introduction

Urbanization is among the most evident aspects of human impact on the earth system. In the process of urbanization, natural landscapes are transformed into buildings, roads, and other impervious surfaces, making urban landscapes fragmented and complex and affecting the sustainability of cities (Xian and Crane, 2006; Chrysoulakis et al., 2013; Alberti and Marzluff, 2004). The increasing urbanization rate of cities in the coming decades (IPCC, 2013) is an important concern as more than 66% of the world's population is expected to reside in cities by 2050 (Yuan and Bauer, 2007; Schwarz et al., 2012; United Nations, 2018), the total global urban land area is expected to increase by more than 1.5 million square kilometers by 2030 (Seto et al., 2011), and climate projections foresee an increase in the frequency and intensity of extreme events relevant to the vulnerability of urban areas such as heavy rain, storm events, and heat waves (IPCC, 2007, 2013; Santamouris et al., 2004). Urbanization affects human thermal comfort (Johansson and Emmanuel, 2006; Charalampopoulos et al., 2013), air quality (Santamouris, 2013; Duh et al., 2008; Han et al., 2014), storm water runoff (Bhaduri et al., 2001; Papagiannaki et al., 2015), and the thermal environment of cities (Cai et al., 2017; Shi et al., 2015).

Urban warming has a very important impact on the energy consumption of buildings (Santamouris, 2007). Increased urban temperatures exacerbate the cooling load of buildings, increase CO_2 emissions due to increased cooling demand, increase the peak electricity demand for cooling, and decrease the efficiency of air-conditioners (Santamouris et al., 2004; Asimakopoulos et al., 2012). According to a survey released in 2016 by the International Energy Agency (IEA), urban areas are responsible for the 70% of global energy-related carbon emissions, and this percentage will increase as the urbanization trend continues (International Energy Agency, 2016).

Satellite thermal infrared data can effectively depict the spatial patterns of the thermal environment of extensive urban areas on a repeated basis through the estimation of the land surface temperature

(LST). With the advantages of lower cost, spatial coverage, and temporal repetition, remote sensing technology has become a powerful tool for monitoring the dynamics of the thermal environment of cities in recent decades (Zhang et al., 2015; Zhou et al., 2016; Sun et al., 2018).

During the last decades, significant effort is performed to provide evidence of the climate projections in the Mediterranean region in terms of the increase of the mean and extreme temperatures. Based on MedECC (2020), the annual mean temperatures of the Mediterranean basin are now 1.5°C above the preindustrial level while the annual mean surface temperature is expected to increase by 2.7−3.8°C and 1.1−2.1°C in one century under the RCP8.5 and the RCP4.5 scenarios, respectively.

For example, Martinelli et al. (2020) performed a study for the coastal city of Bari showing high values of urban heat island intensity both during daytime (4.0°C) and nighttime (4.2°C). In this research, by analyzing current and future weather scenarios, up to additional 4°C of increase of urban air temperature is expected.

Same temperature rises are reported by Hertig and Jacobeit (2008) where the Mediterranean temperature changes in the 21st century are calculated using the ECHAM4/OPYC3 and HadCM3 global general circulation models. The temperature increase for the whole region during 2071−2100 is more than 4°C compared to the 20th-century recorded temperatures.

Coppola et al. (2021) analyzed regional climate models projections for whole Europe. For the Mediterranean region, an increase of heat extremes is revealed where for the summer period has its maximum increase in land regions that are 4°C, 4.5°C, and 6.5°C for RCM, CMIP5, and CMIP6 models, respectively.

In Polydoros et al. (2018), the estimation of the summer LST trends of the period 2000−17 in five major cities of the Mediterranean region provided a clear evidence of positive LST trends during nighttime in the urban areas of these cities. The LST change in the past 18 years was found to vary from +0.412°K in Marseille to +0.923°K in Cairo. Moreover, remote sensing data are used in various studies to estimate the spatial patterns of LST and to pinpoint the hot and cool spots in a city region (Lemus-Canovas et al., 2020; Benas et al., 2017).

To this end, the aim of the present paper is to analyze the surface urban heat island using landscape metrics for three cities in the Mediterranean region.

2. Landscape metrics and the urban heat island

The unique feature of the urban environment is its spatial−temporal variation, practically the urban landscape heterogeneity. Urban areas consist of different land cover types of constructed and open spaces such as roads, buildings, parking lots, green areas such as parks and gardens, bare soil fields, and water bodies (Vanderhaegen and Canters, 2017). In particular, central urban spaces are characterized by high degree of land-use mix, limited green spaces, or open public spaces and closed vents to the natural environment of the surrounding countryside leading to a deteriorated thermal environment (Santamouris, 2013; Duh et al., 2008; Oke et al., 2017).

Urban form and morphology are defined by the composition (e.g., diversity, dominance) and the spatial configuration (e.g., connectivity, spatial arrangement) of the above land cover types (Kowe et al., 2015). Previous studies have examined the relation between land use or land cover composition and configuration with LST (Stathopoulou and Cartalis, 2007; Zhou et al., 2011) to conclude on the importance of the combination of spatiotemporal satellite data and landscape metrics in terms of urban land cover change analyses and environmental impact assessment (Haas and Ban, 2014; Herold et al., 2003; Huang et al., 2007; Liu and Yang, 2015).

The Copernicus Land Monitoring Service (CLMS) provides geographical information on land cover, land use, land cover changes over the years, vegetation state, and water cycle. The pan-European component of the service provides high-resolution products describing land cover, land use, and their changes over the years, and the local component provides specific and detailed information on specific environmental challenges in Europe. The Copernicus data are distributed on a full, free, and open basis, and their usefulness relies on the use of high-resolution satellite data, which provide homogeneity, repetitiveness, and objectivity over the whole of Europe, whereas compiling available local and/or national datasets throughout Europe in order to compare cities would be difficult to achieve since the data would originate from different materials and methods (Lefebvre et al., 2016).

3. Material and methods
3.1 Study area

The study areas consist of the urban core areas (defined as an area of 314 km^2 delimited by a 10 km radius from the city center) of three major Mediterranean capital cities, namely Athens, Madrid, and Rome (Fig. 5.1).

3.2 Land use

Land use data from the Urban Atlas of the European Environmental Agency (European Union, 2018) were used in order to classify the study areas into eight major urban land use classes (UC) following the classification scheme in (Prastacos et al., 2017). For example, the six urban fabric classes were grouped to three built-up densities classes, namely "High built up density," "Medium built up density,"

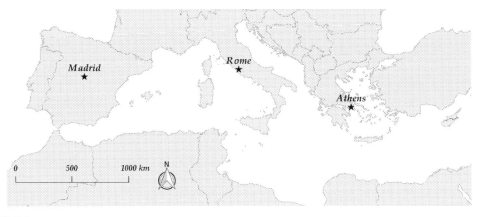

FIGURE 5.1

The three cities under study.

Table 5.1 Classification scheme for the eight urban classes.

Urban classes	Urban atlas classes
UC1: High built-up density	11100: Continuous urban fabric (S.L. > 80%)
UC2: Medium built-up density	11210: Discontinuous dense urban fabric (S.L.: 50%−80%)
UC3: Low built-up density	11220: Discontinuous medium density urban fabric (S.L.: 30%−50%) 11230: Discontinuous low density urban fabric (S.L.: 10%−30%) 11240: Discontinuous very low density urban fabric (S.L. < 10%) 11300: Isolated structures
UC4: Industrial	12100: Industrial, commercial, public, military, and private units
UC5: Transportation	12210: Fast transit roads and associated land 12220: Other roads and associated land 12230: Railways and associated land 12300: Port areas 12400: Airports
UC6: Construction sites	13100: Mineral extraction and dump sites 13300: Construction sites 13400: Land without current use
UC7: Urban green	14100: Green urban areas 14200: Sports and leisure facilities
UC8: Natural land	All other categories i.e., agricultural + water bodies + wetlands + forests

and "Low built up density." Roads, ports, railways, and airports were grouped in the "Transportation" class, and agricultural, seminatural, forests, and water bodies were aggregated into one class named "Natural land" (Table 5.1). The reason for this reclassification is that many of the land use classes of Urban Atlas account for a very small percentage of the urban area, and a detailed analysis would not provide a meaningful insight on the form of the city (Prastacos et al., 2017).

3.3 Landscape metrics

The landscape metrics used in this study are presented in Table 5.2. These metrics were chosen after a review of the most commonly used landscape metrics in urban studies. Five landscape metrics were chosen to quantify the urban form of the city in terms of spatial composition and another five in terms of spatial configuration. Landscape composition refers to properties concerning the presence and the proportion of land cover type without explicitly describing its spatial features. Landscape configuration, on the other hand, refers to the physical distribution and the spatial features of the patches present within the landscape (Vanderhaegen and Canters, 2010). Five of them are calculated at class level and five of them at landscape level. All metrics were generated using the Fragstats free software (McGarigal et al., 2012).

The area-weighted mean metrics are used instead of their mean equivalents because they provide a landscape-centric perspective of the landscape structure as they reflect the average conditions of a pixel chosen at random. This landscape-centric perspective is best suited for this study since different landscapes are studied and compared.

Table 5.2 Set of landscape metrics used.

Metric	Landscape characteristic	Level
Mean patch area (AREA_MN)	Composition	Class
Percentage of landscape (PLAND)	Composition	Class
Patch density (PD)	Composition	Class
Shannon's evenness index (SHEI)	Composition	Landscape
Simpson's evenness index (SIEI)	Composition	Landscape
Number of patches (NP)	Configuration	Landscape
Area-weighted mean patch shape index (SHAPE_AM)	Configuration	Class
Patch cohesion index (COHESION)	Configuration	Class
Contagion (CONTAG)	Configuration	Landscape
Area-weighted mean patch fractal dimension (FRAC_AM)	Configuration	Class

3.4 Land surface temperature

Land surface temperature products (at 30 m resolution) used in this study were made available from http://rslab.gr/downloads_LandsatLST.html. These LST products were created from Landsat 8 data using the NDVI-based emissivity method and the RMSE was found to be 1.31°C (Parastatidis et al., 2017). At least three summer days of each reference year (2006, 2012, and 2018) were selected for each city, and the mean LST was produced in order to reveal the spatial patterns of the thermal environment in these years. Data from 2018 correspond to the most current thermal state of the cities; the other 2 years were used in order to access the relation between land use changes and LST.

Due to the time difference for acquiring the remote sensing images and considering the heterogeneity of the climatic conditions prevailing in the examined cities, the retrieved LSTs from the remote sensing images could not be directly used to analyze the differentiations in temperature. In order to better understand and compare the effects of landscape patters to the thermal environment of these cities, the retrieved mean LSTs were normalized between 0 and 1 using the following equation:

$$T_i = \frac{T_{S_i} - T_{S_{min}}}{T_{S_{max}} - T_{S_{min}}}$$

where T_i is the normalized value of pixel i; T_{S_i} is the LST of pixel i; $T_{S_{max}}$ is the maximum LST; and $T_{S_{min}}$ is the minimum LST (Chen et al., 2016). The advantage of using normalized LST data is that the spatial differences of LST can be revealed regardless of the actual LST values, which vary between different cities or between different days.

4. Results and discussion

4.1 Urban composition

Fig. 5.2 depicts the classification of the three study areas in the eight urban classes. Each city has its own landscape composition characteristics as it is clearly observed in Fig. 5.2. Athens, Rome and Madrid consist of over 30% of UC7 and UC8 mainly at the periphery of their 10 km radius landscape an information easily retrieved by the PLAND metric (Fig. 5.3).

The PLAND metric gives a rough estimate about the distribution of the urban classes. A quantitative measure of the spatial distribution of the urban classes is given by evenness metrics such as Shannon's Evenness Index (SHEI), which describes the evenness degree of distribution of different urban classes of the landscape; higher values of SHEI indicate an even proportional distribution of areas within the urban classes. Simpson's Evenness Index (SIEI) gives the same information as SHEI, but it is less sensitive to the presence of rare class types and has an interpretation that is much more intuitive than SHEI. Madrid exhibits the most even distribution among the eight urban classes as Fig. 5.4 exhibits, whereas Athens has the most uneven distribution of urban classes between the three cities.

The mean patch size (AREA_MN) metric gives the average area of the patches of each class. It must be noted that it does not convey any information about how many patches are present and is usually best interpreted in conjunction with patch density (PD) metric. Table 5.3 presents the results of the application of these two metrics for the three study areas, where AREA_MN is given in hectares and PD in number of patches per 100 ha. A common point in all cities is that UC5 consists of many (over 45 patches per 100 ha) small patches (less than 0.25 ha), due to the fact that many small blocks exist in central urban areas. Natural land (UC8) areas are usually found in large patches, but only rarely and urban parks (UC7) are approximately found in two patches per 100 ha with the larger ones found in Madrid (>8 ha). In general, high built-up density urban areas (UC1) are found in larger size patches than the other built-up classes (UC2 and UC3).

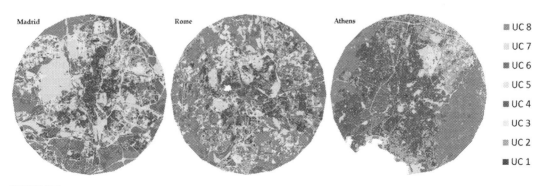

FIGURE 5.2

Urban classes of the three study areas.

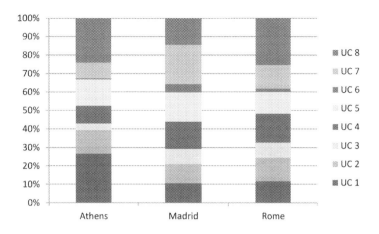

FIGURE 5.3

Percentage of landscape (PLAND) metric for the three cities.

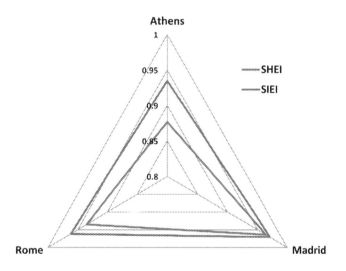

FIGURE 5.4

Shannon's evenness index (SHEI) and Simpson's evenness index (SIEI) for the three cities.

4.2 Urban configuration

Shape metrics measure the complexity of patch shape compared to a standard shape (square) of the same size; higher values of this metric indicate a more complex shape. The area weighted mean patch shape metric (SHAPE_AM) was used in this study because it is the simplest and perhaps most straightforward measure of overall shape complexity. The results revealed that the transportation class (UC5) and the high built-up density class (UC1) exhibit the larger SHAPE_AM values in all three cities (Fig. 5.5A).

The area-weighted mean patch fractal dimension metric (FRAC_AM) also characterizes the degree of complexity of the patches in the landscape. FRAC approaches 1 for shapes with very simple

Table 5.3 Area MN and PD metrics (areas in hectares).

	Metric	Athens	Madrid	Rome
UC 1	AREA_MN	10.50	5.29	6.19
	PD	1.86	1.56	1.47
UC 2	AREA_MN	2.45	3.12	4.57
	PD	3.83	2.54	2.14
UC 3	AREA_MN	1.81	4.71	3.04
	PD	1.43	1.37	2.07
UC 4	AREA_MN	2.86	3.87	3.86
	PD	2.46	2.89	3.11
UC 5	AREA_MN	0.14	0.25	0.18
	PD	73.90	49.66	50.19
UC 6	AREA_MN	1.14	4.80	1.75
	PD	0.48	0.76	0.82
UC 7	AREA_MN	3.25	8.33	5.83
	PD	1.88	1.97	1.69
UC 8	AREA_MN	67.00	18.12	35.56
	PD	0.26	0.61	0.55

perimeters such as squares, and approaches 2 for shapes with highly convoluted, plane-filling perimeters. Similarly to SHAPE_AM, the larger values of this index, which indicates larger shape complexity, were found for UC1 and UC5, and the smallest values indicate less complexity for UC4, UC6, and UC7 (Fig. 5.5B).

The COHESION metric measures the physical connectedness of the patch types of each class, and its value increases as a class becomes more aggregated (Fig. 5.5C). In general, UC1 and UC8 were found to be the most aggregated urban classes while UC6 was by far the most disaggregated one. Increasing urban built-up densities usually leads to less aggregation.

The number of patches (NP) metric is a measure of subdivision and fragmentation of the different patch types across a landscape. Athens has a larger NP than Rome and Madrid indicating that Athens' landscape is more fragmented (Fig. 5.6A). The Contagion metric describes the tendency of patch types to be spatially aggregated. Contagion approaches 0 when the patch types are maximally disaggregated and interspersed. In our study, Rome and Madrid have the most disaggregated landscapes (Fig. 5.6B).

The above metrics give a quantitative understanding of the urban configuration characteristics of major Mediterranean cities.

4.3 Urban thermal environment

The normalized LST distribution of the three cities is presented in Fig. 5.7; in addition, the values of the mean normalized LST of each urban class are provided in Table 5.4. With the help of Fig. 5.2, it is easily observed that the highest LSTs are usually found at the industrial areas of the cities (UC4) and at large transportation areas (UC5). On the other hand, the lower LSTs are related to vegetated areas (UC7 and UC8).

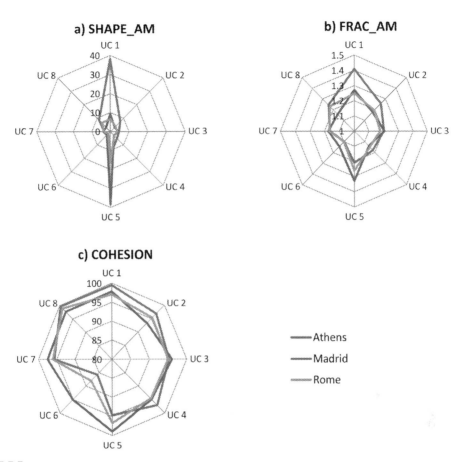

FIGURE 5.5

(A) Area-weighted mean patch shape (SHAPE_AM), (B) area-weighted mean patch fractal dimension (FRAC_AM), and (C) cohesion metrics of the three cities.

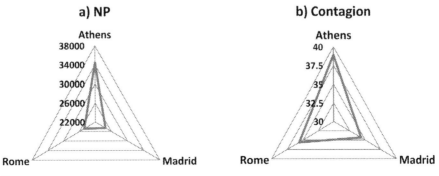

FIGURE 5.6

(A) Number of patches (NP) and (B) Contagion metrics of the three cities.

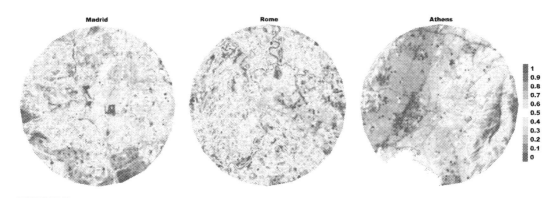

FIGURE 5.7

Normalized LST distribution of the three cities.

Table 5.4 Mean normalized LST of each urban class.			
	Madrid	**Rome**	**Athens**
UC1	0.47	0.59	0.67
UC2	0.41	0.55	0.61
UC3	0.34	0.45	0.54
UC4	0.53	0.63	0.76
UC5	0.51	0.58	0.67
UC6	0.61	0.57	0.70
UC7	0.40	0.45	0.64
UC8	0.65	0.50	0.49

To better understand the relationship between the LST and the urban class, the mean normalized LST of each urban class is calculated for all cities and is presented in Table 5.5. In general, UC3 (low built-up density), UC7 (urban green), and UC8 (natural land) exhibit the lowest LSTs contrary to UC1 (high built-up density), UC4 (industrial), UC5 (industrial), and UC6 (construction sites), which are dominated by higher LSTs.

Increasing built-up density (UC3->UC2->UC1) leads to increasing LSTs in all cities. This increase is 20% on the average between UC3 and UC2 and 10% on average between UC2 and UC1. Given that increasing built-up density means increasing spatial aggregation, it is deduced that spatial aggregation of built-up land uses leads to increased LSTs. UC4 usually exhibits the highest LST among the urban classes except some particular cases such as the city of Madrid where UC8 exhibits the highest LST due to the high percentage of dry barren land that composes this urban class.

The Pan-European High-Resolution Layers (HRL) of CLMS provide information on specific land cover characteristics, which are complementary to the land cover/land use mapping products. Using the imperviousness product, which captures the percentage of soil sealing, we can examine the relationship between impervious surfaces and LST. In all cities, increasing imperviousness leads to increasing LSTs as it can be seen in Fig. 5.8.

Table 5.5 Mean normalized LST of the total study area, of the street trees area, and the percentage of street trees in each city.

City	Total area	Tree area	Trees area percent
Athens	0.59	0.51	7.05
Madrid	0.48	0.31	7.93
Rome	0.51	0.37	8.1

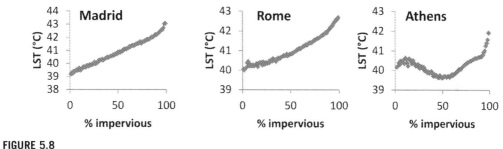

FIGURE 5.8

Relationship between impervious surface percentage and LST.

Another useful dataset provided by the CLMS is the Street Tree Layer (STL), which includes contiguous rows or patches of trees covering 500 m^2 or more with a minimum width of 10 m within the urban mask of the Urban Atlas 2012 dataset. The difference of the mean LST of the total area compared to the mean LST of the street trees (Table 5.5) highlights the cooling effect that trees have in the thermal state of the urban environment.

5. Conclusions

This study exploited the capacity of landscape metrics in combination to thermal remote sensing data to assess the state of the urban thermal environment for selected Mediterranean cities.

The harmonized information provided by the CLMS with the Urban Atlas product provides the opportunity to scientists, local authorities, and policymakers to monitor the spatial patterns of urban areas, to assess the effectiveness of urban policies, and to develop a comparative benchmarking between cities in different climatic zones. Given the above, the CLMS products provide a better insight into cities and their structure, thus facilitating evidence-based policymaking. This is critical for identifying and underpinning the most appropriate European policy initiatives in the urban domain.

Landscape metrics were proven to be a useful tool for quantifying the composition and the spatial configuration of the urban agglomeration of the cities under examination. The use of the Urban Atlas dataset provides the opportunity for an objective comparison of European cities in different climatic zones. Using a reclassification method to reduce the number of urban classes and a 10 km radius circular study area, the unique landscape composition and configuration pattern of each city were highlighted. Using the combination of the AREA_MN and PD metrics, the specific distribution characteristics of each urban class are possible, and common conclusions for some of them are derived. The use of spatial configuration metrics revealed the differences in the complexity of each urban class and more interestingly the relation between built-up aggregation and LST.

The relationship between the LST and the eight urban classes was examined with the use of thermal remote sensing data for each city, and the results revealed the urban classes associated with the highest LSTs. In all three cities under study, increasing built-up densities lead to increased LSTs while areas with industrial, transportation and constructional land uses have very high LSTs as well. These results were enhanced by the relation of impervious surfaces percentage with LST as increasing imperviousness leads to increased LSTs. Finally, the STL of the Copernicus Land Monitoring Service provided an insight of the cooling effects that trees have on the urban thermal environment and demonstrated the usefulness of the complementary datasets provided by the service.

References

Alberti, M., Marzluff, J.M., 2004. Ecological resilience in urban ecosystems: linking urban patterns to human and ecological functions. Urban Ecosystems 7 (3), 241−265.

Asimakopoulos, D.A., Santamouris, M., Farrou, I., Laskari, M., Saliari, M., Zanis, G., Giannakopoulos, C., 2012. Modelling the energy demand projection of the building sector in Greece in the 21st century. Energy Build. 49, 488−498.

Benas, N., Chrysoulakis, N., Cartalis, C., 2017. Trends of urban surface temperature and heat island characteristics in the Mediterranean. Theor. Appl. Climatol. 130 (3), 807−816.

Bhaduri, B., Minner, M., Tatalovich, S., Harbor, J., 2001. Long-term hydrologic impact of urbanization: a tale of two models. J. Water Resour. Plann. Manag. 127 (1), 13−19.

Cai, D., Fraedrich, K., Guan, Y., Guo, S., Zhang, C., 2017. Urbanization and the thermal environment of Chinese and US-American cities. Sci. Total Environ. 589, 200−211.

Charalampopoulos, I., Tsiros, I., Chronopoulou-Sereli, A., Matzarakis, A., 2013. Analysis of thermal bioclimate in various urban configurations in Athens, Greece. Urban Ecosyst. 16 (2), 217−233.

Chen, L., Jiang, R., Xiang, W.N., 2016. Surface heat island in Shanghai and its relationship with urban development from 1989 to 2013. Adv. Meteorol., 9782686, 2016.

Chrysoulakis, N., Mitraka, Z., Stathopoulou, M., Cartalis, C., 2013. A comparative analysis of the urban web of the greater Athens agglomeration for the last 20 years period on the basis of Landsat imagery. Fresenius Environ. Bull. 22, 2139−2144.

Coppola, E., Nogherotto, R., Ciarlò, J.M., Giorgi, F., van Meijgaard, E., Kadygrov, N., Wulfmeyer, V., 2021. Assessment of the European climate projections as simulated by the large EURO-CORDEX regional and global climate model ensemble. J. Geophys. Res. Atmos. e2019JD032356.

Duh, J.D., Shandas, V., Chang, H., George, L.A., 2008. Rates of urbanisation and the resiliency of air and water quality. Sci. Total Environ. 400 (1−3), 238−256.

European Union, 2018. Copernicus Land Monitoring Service. European Environment Agency (EEA), 4.4.2021. https://land.copernicus.eu/local/urban-atlas.

Haas, J., Ban, Y., 2014. Urban growth and environmental impacts in jing-jin-ji, the yangtze, river delta and the pearl river delta. Int. J. Appl. Earth Obs. Geoinf. 30, 42−55.

Han, L., Zhou, W., Li, W., Li, L., 2014. Impact of urbanization level on urban air quality: a case of fine particles (PM2. 5) in Chinese cities. Environ. Pollut. 194, 163−170.

Herold, M., Liu, X., Clarke, K.C., 2003. Spatial metrics and image texture for mapping urban land use. Photogramm. Eng. Rem. Sens. 69 (9), 991−1001.

Hertig, E., Jacobeit, J., 2008. Downscaling future climate change: temperature scenarios for the Mediterranean area. Global Planet. Change 63 (2–3), 127–131.

Huang, J., Lu, X.X., Sellers, J.M., 2007. A global comparative analysis of urban form: applying spatial metrics and remote sensing. Landsc. Urban Plann. 82 (4), 184–197.

International Energy Agency, 2016. Energy Technology Perspectives 2016.

IPCC, 2007. In: Metz, B., Davidson, O.R., Bosch, P.R., Dave, R., Meyer, L.A. (Eds.), Climate Change, 2007b. Mitigation. Contribution of Working Group III to the Fourth Assessment Report of the Intergovernmental Panel on Climate Change. Cambridge University Press, Cambridge, United Kingdom and New York, NY, USA, p. 852.

IPCC, 2013. Climate Change 2013: The Physical Science Basis, Contribution of Working Group I to the Fifth Assessment Report of the Intergovernmental Panel on Climate Change. Cambridge University Press, Cambridge, USA, 978-1107661820.

Johansson, E., Emmanuel, R., 2006. The influence of urban design on outdoor thermal comfort in the hot, humid city of Colombo, Sri Lanka. Int. J. Biometeorol. 51 (2), 119–133.

Kowe, P., Pedzisai, E., Gumindoga, W., Rwasoka, D.T., 2015. An analysis of changes in the urban landscape composition and configuration in the Sancaktepe District of Istanbul Metropolitan City, Turkey using landscape metrics and satellite data. Geocarto Int. 30 (5), 506–519.

Lefebvre, A., Sannier, C., Corpetti, T., 2016. Monitoring urban areas with Sentinel-2A data: application to the update of the Copernicus high resolution layer imperviousness degree. Rem. Sens. 8 (7), 606.

Lemus-Canovas, M., Martin-Vide, J., Moreno-Garcia, M.C., Lopez-Bustins, J.A., 2020. Estimating Barcelona's metropolitan daytime hot and cold poles using Landsat-8 Land Surface Temperature. Sci. Total Environ. 699, 134307.

Liu, T., Yang, X., 2015. Monitoring land changes in an urban area using satellite imagery, GIS and landscape metrics. Appl. Geogr. 56, 42–54.

Martinelli, A., Kolokotsa, D.D., Fiorito, F., 2020. Urban heat island in Mediterranean coastal cities: the case of Bari (Italy). Climate 8 (6), 79.

McGarigal, K., Cushman, S.A., Ene, E., 2012. Spatial Pattern Analysis Program for Categorical and Continuous Maps. Computer Software Program Produced by the Authors at the University of Massachusetts, Amherst. FRAGSTATS V4. See. http://wwwumassedu/landeco/research/fragstats/fragstatshtml.

MedECC, 2020. In: Cramer, W., Guiot, J., Marini, K. (Eds.), Climate and Environmental Change in the Mediterranean Basin − Current Situation and Risks for the Future. First Mediterranean Assessment Report. Union for the Mediterranean, Plan Bleu, UNEP/MAP, Marseille, France, p. 600pp (in press).

Oke, T.R., Mills, G., Christen, A., Voogt, J.A., 2017. Urban Climates. Cambridge University Press.

Papagiannaki, K., Lagouvardos, K., Kotroni, V., Bezes, A., 2015. Flash flood occurrence and relation to the rainfall hazard in a highly urbanized area. Nat. Hazards Earth Syst. Sci. 15 (8), 1859–1871.

Parastatidis, D., Mitraka, Z., Chrysoulakis, N., Abrams, M., 2017. Online global land surface temperature estimation from Landsat. Rem. Sens. 9 (12), 1208.

Polydoros, A., Mavrakou, T., Cartalis, C., 2018. Quantifying the trends in land surface temperature and surface urban heat island intensity in mediterranean cities in view of smart urbanization. Urban Sci. 2 (1), 16.

Prastacos, P., Lagarias, A., Chrysoulakis, N., 2017. Using the Urban Atlas Dataset for Estimating Spatial Metrics. Methodology and Application in Urban Areas of Greece. Cybergeo: European Journal of Geography.

Santamouris, M., Adnot, J., Alvarez, S., Klitsikas, N., Orphelin, M., Lopes, C., Sanchez, F., 2004. Cooling the Cities. Eyrolles, Paris.

Santamouris, M., 2007. Heat island research in Europe: the state of the art. Adv. Build. Energy Res. 1 (1), 123–150.

Santamouris, M. (Ed.), 2013. Energy and Climate in the Urban Built Environment. Routledge.

Schwarz, N., Schlink, U., Franck, U., Großmann, K., 2012. Relationship of land surface and air temperatures and its implications for quantifying urban heat island indicators—an application for the city of Leipzig (Germany). Ecol. Indicat. 18, 693—704.

Seto, K.C., Fragkias, M., Güneralp, B., Reilly, M.K., 2011. A meta-analysis of global urban land expansion. PLoS One 6 (8), e23777.

Shi, T., Huang, Y., Wang, H., Shi, C.E., Yang, Y.J., 2015. Influence of urbanization on the thermal environment of meteorological station: satellite-observed evidence. Adv. Clim. Change Res. 6 (1), 7—15.

Stathopoulou, M., Cartalis, C., 2007. Daytime urban heat islands from Landsat ETM+ and Corine land cover data: an application to major cities in Greece. Sol. Energy 81 (3), 358—368.

Sun, Y., Gao, C., Li, J., Li, W., Ma, R., 2018. Examining urban thermal environment dynamics and relations to biophysical composition and configuration and socio-economic factors: a case study of the Shanghai metropolitan region. Sustain. Cities Soc. 40, 284—295.

United Nations, 2018. World Urbanization Prospects: The 2018 Revision, Key Facts (Technical report).

Vanderhaegen, S., Canters, F., 2010. Developing urban metrics to describe the morphology of urban areas at block level. Int. Arch. Photogram. Rem. Sens. Spatial Inf. Sci. 36, 192—197.

Vanderhaegen, S., Canters, F., 2017. Mapping urban form and function at city block level using spatial metrics. Landsc. Urban Plann. 167, 399—409.

Xian, G., Crane, M., 2006. An analysis of urban thermal characteristics and associated land cover in Tampa Bay and Las Vegas using Landsat satellite data. Remote Sens. Environ. 104 (2), 147—156.

Yuan, F., Bauer, M.E., 2007. Comparison of impervious surface area and normalized difference vegetation index as indicators of surface urban heat island effects in Landsat imagery. Remote Sens. Environ. 106 (3), 375—386.

Zhang, Y., Balzter, H., Zou, C., Xu, H., Tang, F., 2015. Characterizing bi-temporal patterns of land surface temperature using landscape metrics based on sub-pixel classifications from Landsat TM/ETM+. Int. J. Appl. Earth Obs. Geoinf. 42, 87—96.

Zhou, W., Huang, G., Cadenasso, M.L., 2011. Does spatial configuration matter? Understanding the effects of land cover pattern on land surface temperature in urban landscapes. Landsc. Urban Plann. 102 (1), 54—63.

Zhou, D., Zhang, L., Hao, L., Sun, G., Liu, Y., Zhu, C., 2016. Spatiotemporal trends of urban heat island effect along the urban development intensity gradient in China. Sci. Total Environ. 544, 617—626.

Effects of land use composition and pattern on land surface temperature: an urban heat island study in the megacities of Scotland, UK, using time series of landsat TM/ETM + data

Eulalia Jadraque Gago[1] and Saioa Etxebarria Berrizbeitia[2]

[1]*Engineering Construction and Project Management, School of Civil Engineering, University of Granada, Granada, Spain;* [2]*Faculty of Mechanical Engineering, University of the Basque Country, Vitoria-Gasteiz, Spain*

1. Introduction

Climate change is the greatest environmental challenge facing humanity today, due to its global scale and profound social and economic implications. In 2015, during the United Nations Climate Change Conference in Paris, the first balanced global agreement was adopted to address global warming, and the objective of limiting temperature increase to 2°C by 2100 was agreed (Rhodes, 2016).

Cities only represent the 2% of the earth's surface (Grimm et al., 2000); however, the 60% of the word's energy consumption and more than the 70% of carbon dioxide emissions take place in cities (Grimm et al., 2000; Behera and Dash, 2017). Therefore, cities contribute significantly to climate change.

Furthermore, there is a global trend to migrate from rural to urban areas. This migratory flow, much more notorious in developed countries, represents a social, economic, and technical challenge. According the United Nations, by 2050, the population in the cities will increase by 2.5 billion (United Nations, 2014).

In recent decades, because of rapid urbanization, biodiversity, and several natural habitats (Carsjens and van Lier, 2002; Gibb and Hochuli, 2002), soils destined to agriculture and forests have been lost. There has also been an increase in the temperature in cities closely related to urban air quality, energy consumption, and the health of at-risk populations (Souch and Grimmond, 2006; Yow, 2007; Xu et al., 2009; Kolokotroni et al., 2006; Arnfield, 2003; Hattis et al., 2012; Johnson et al., 2012; Gartland, 2012). All this shows the conclusion of the important protagonist that human activities play in the alteration and modification of the climate system (Houšková and Montanarella, 2008; Prokop et al., 2011; Montanarella and Rusco, 2008; Jin et al., 2005; Oke, 1982; Stone et al., 2010; Mohajerani et al., 2017). In this situation, it is essential to know and understand the role and impact of different land uses on the environmental system (Trenberth et al., 2007; Gaur et al., 2018).

Urban heat island (UHI) is a thermal phenomenon in which temperature of urban spaces is higher than nearby rural zones (Arnfield, 2003; Oke, 1982; Mohajerani et al., 2017; Howard, 1818; Voogt, 2004; EPA US Environmental Protection Agency, 2008; Oke and Hannell, 1970; Voogt and Oke, 2003; Memon et al., 2009; Martin-Vide et al., 2015). In 1818, Luke Howard was the first researcher to discover London's thermal variation, pointing out that the temperature of the city center was 3.7°F higher than the surrounding fields (Howard, 1818). Subsequently, in 1958, Gordon Manley was the first to define this thermal variation as a UHI (Manley, 1958). The interest in the study of the UHI is well justified, since urban areas constitute unique sectors within the climate of the region where they are located. This interest responds not only to the need for knowledge to achieve a more pleasant environment for city dwellers, but also to the need to analyze and anticipate the changes these entail and the repercussions they may have on the climate.

There are two types of UHI; the first is based on the fact that air temperature is higher during the night, while the second is based on the fact that land surface temperature (LST) tends to be higher during the day due to solar radiation (EPA US Environmental Protection Agency, 2008).

The formation of a surface urban heat island (SUHI) is principally caused by changes in the landscape due to urban development, mainly in the reduction of vegetation in urban areas, the properties of urban materials used, urban geometry, anthropogenic heat and climate, and location, all of which generate an increase in LST (Voogt, 2004; Estoque et al., 2017; Ibrahim and Rasul, 2017; Yang et al., 2018; Zhang et al., 2017).

LST is a key variable in SUHI generation and constitutes a determining factor in surface radiation and energy exchange (Weng, 2009), as well as the control of heat distribution between the surface and atmosphere (Oke, 2006; Guillevic et al., 2012). Therefore, it is necessary to model and predict environmental changes, as well as to analyze and comprehend the dynamics of the LST and its connection with changes of anthropogenic origin (Tan et al., 2010).

The composition of land use/cover is one of the key factors influencing LST (Zhou et al., 2011; Bokaie et al., 2016; Huang and Wang, 2019). LST generally has a positive correlation with an impervious surface (IS) and a negative with areas of vegetation (Guillevic et al., 2012; Meng et al., 2009).

Currently, it is still difficult to identify the distribution and spatial pattern of SUHI with temperature data observed in situ because of the lack of total coverage of the studied zone and the limited spatial resolution of the data (Streutker, 2003; Li et al., 2012).

Remote sensing provides a very promising approach for the generalized study of LST, and therefore, it makes it possible to monitor the spatial outline of the SUHI. The high-spatial-resolution thermal satellite data obtained during the daytime have been extensively used to identify and evaluate SUHI at the mesoscale, i.e., in the space occupied by the entire city that usually extends between 10 and 200 km (Voogt and Oke, 2003; Rao, 1972; Roth et al., 1989; Carlson et al., 1981; Aniello et al., 1995; Dousset and Gourmelon, 2003; Gallo and Tarpley, 1996; Hung et al., 2006; Kato and Yamaguchi, 2005; Lo et al., 1997; Lo and Quattrochi, 2003; Ma et al., 2010; Pongrácz et al., 2010; Streutker, 2002; Snider and Wan, 1998; Weng, 2001; Li et al., 2013; Zhou et al., 2018; Shirani-bidabadi et al., 2019; Srivastava et al., 2009).

Among the available satellite data, Landsat data have been widely used in numerous SUHI case studies around the world thanks to their precision such as the detection capability in terms of the spatial and temporal resolutions with the uncertainties. And due to the fact that data acquisition is freely accessible with spatial and temporal coverage for most of the areas susceptible to develop SUHI (Streutker, 2002; Li et al., 2013; Stathopoulou and Cartalis, 2007; Xian and Crane, 2006). On the other hand, the integration of remote sensors and geographic information systems (GISs) has been recognized as a powerful and effective tool to detect the different uses of urban land and changes in its coverage, which are decisive in the understanding of the relationship between human activities and the SUHI (Wieslaw, 1993; Treitz et al., 1992; Harris and Ventura, 1995).

To establish the relationship between the composition and pattern of the urban landscape and the formation and evolution of the SUHI in the Edinburgh and Glasgow cities, various landscape variables are explored to analyze the spatial and temporal variations of the land surface temperature in the analyzed areas. The land cover groups considered in this analysis were: impervious surface (IS) (including surfaces found in urban and suburban landscapes such roads, parking lots drive ways, sidewalks, roofs, and industrial areas), green space (GS) (including land that is covered with grass, trees, shrubs, or other vegetation), water (W) (including all bodies of water), and other (IS2) (including all the not classified lands as GS, ISs, and water. This category includes bare soil and cultivated. Also included are those residential areas relatively far from the center. In these areas, residential housing alternates with green areas).

The methodology and the results obtained would constitute a powerful tool that will allow to know which zones and why are more vulnerable to the formation of the SUHI. It is essential to implement strategies in the design and initial phases of the engineering projects to improve the adaptation of cities to the climate change and to increase their resilience.

2. Methodology
2.1 Study area

Edinburgh and Glasgow cities have different climatic conditions, natural environments, and levels of urban and socioeconomic development.

Edinburgh is the capital city of Scotland and located between 55.953251 latitudes and −3.188267 longitudes, in Lothian on the shore of the Firth of Forth. Edinburgh has a population of 536,800, which makes it the second most populous city in Scotland and the seventh in the United Kingdom (UK). Edinburgh has a population density of 1830 people per square kilometer in the city proper. The total surface area in Edinburgh is 264 square kilometers (statista).

The average annual temperature is 9.3°C, with a minimum temperature of 4.2°C (December) and a maximum temperature of 15.3°C (July), based on average daily mean temperature of 2018 (Synop, 2018).

Glasgow with a city population of 1,680,669, is the most populous city in Scotland, the third most populous city in the United Kingdom, as well as the 56th largest city by population in Europe. Glasgow is located between 55.860916 latitudes and −4.251433 longitudes, situated on the River Clyde in the country's West Central Lowlands. Glasgow has a population density of 4023 people per square kilometer, and the total surface area in Glasgow is 175 square kilometers (statista).

Despite its northerly latitude, similar to that of Moscow, Glasgow's climate is classified as oceanic. Owing to its westerly position and proximity to the Atlantic Ocean, Glasgow is one of Scotland's milder areas. Winter temperatures are usually higher than in most places of equal latitude away from the United Kingdom, due to the warming influence of the Gulf Stream. However, this results in less distinct seasons as compared to continental Western Europe.

The average annual temperature is 9.6°C, with a minimum temperature of 4.3°C (December) and a maximum temperature of 15.9°C (July), based on average daily mean temperature of 2018 (Synop, 2018).

Glasgow is the economic powerhouse of Scotland and generates £19.3 billion GVA per annum—by far the largest of any Scottish city. It is the fastest growing major city economy in the United Kingdom with growth significantly outperforming all other core cities in recent years (Glasgow, 2018).

2.2 Satellite data used and preprocessing

In this chapter, Landsat satellite images captured in 1989; July 11; GMT 10:43:23 (Landsat 5 TM), 2000; July 17; GMT 11:07:22 (Landsat 7 ETM+) and 2018; June 25; GMT 11:14:55 (Landsat 8 OLI/ TIRS) have been used (http:/earthexplorer.usgs.gov/) (Table 6.1). For the selection of the satellite images; cloud-free ones or those with minimum cloud coverage (less than 10%) have been considered. The study area is contained entirely within path 205 and row 21. All images were acquired in the same month, during the dry season (Fig. 6.1).

In order to carry out land cover mapping, image classification, index derivation, and LST retrieval, all satellite images were subjected to two preprocessing procedures consisting of radiometric calibration and atmospheric correction using ArcMap software. The atmospheric correction was performed using the dark-object subtraction (DOS) model proposed by (Chávez, 1988). This model postulates that atmospheric mist increases the digital number (DN) value in areas of clean, deep, and calm water, where the physical characteristics must have zero reflectance. The representative value of that difference is subtracted, in each band, in all the pixels of the scene. To estimate LST, it is necessary to convert the DN from each of the thermal bands to radiance values as a measure of the amount of energy that reaches the satellite (Weng, 2009; Estoque and Murayama, 2017; Chander et al., 2009). These radiance values are then used to perform the conversion to surface brightness temperature (expressed in Kelvin degrees), considering emissivity, vegetation fraction, the normalized vegetation index, and calibration constants.

2.3 Land cover mapping

The maximum likelihood supervised classification method was used to classify the land cover maps of the study area in 1989, 2000, and 2018 from the Landsat imagery (Fig. 6.2) (Zhang et al., 2017; Haashemi et al., 2016). The following land cover groups were considered in this analysis:

Table 6.1 Descriptions of the Landsat images used.

Sensor	Scene ID	Time (GMT)	Season
Landsat 5 TM	LT05L1TP2050211989071112017020201T1	10:43:23	Dry
Landsat 7 ETM+	LE07L1TP2050212000071720170210 01T1	11:07:22	
Landsat 8 OLI/TIRS	LC08L1TP2050212018062520180704 01T1	11:14:55	

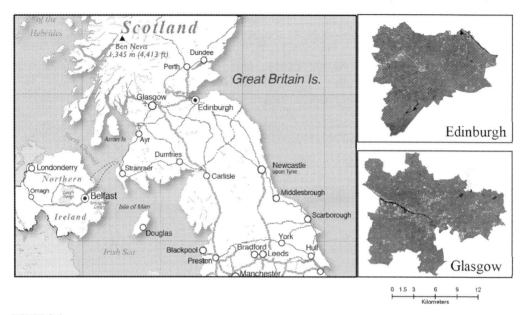

FIGURE 6.1

Map of United Kingdom showing the location of the study areas (Edinburg and Glasgow) (Map source: www. nationsonline.org); and Landsat-8 images of the study areas in 2018 displayed in false color composite (black − Band 5; white − Band 4, and gray − Band 3).

  i. IS. Including surfaces found in urban and suburban landscapes such roads, parking lots drive ways, sidewalks, roofs, and industrial areas.
  ii. GS. Including land that is covered with grass, trees, shrubs, or other vegetation.
 iii. Water (W). Including all bodies of water.
 iv. Other (IS2). Including all the not classified lands as GS, ISs, and water. This category includes bare soil and cultivated. Also included are those residential areas relatively far from the center. In these areas, residential housing alternates with green areas.

    The bodies of water and the ISs were extracted from the images using the modified normalized difference water index (MNDWI) (Eq. 6.1) and the visible red and NIR-based built-up index (VrNIR-BI) (Eq. 6.2), respectively (Xu, 2006; Ji et al., 2009; Li et al., 2013; Du et al., 2014; Estoque and Murayama, 2015).

    The GSs were extracted from the images via the normalized difference vegetation index (NDVI) (Eq. 6.3) (Rouse et al., 1974).

$$MNDWI = \frac{\rho_{Green} - \rho_{SWIR1}}{\rho_{Green} + \rho_{SWIR1}} \tag{6.1}$$

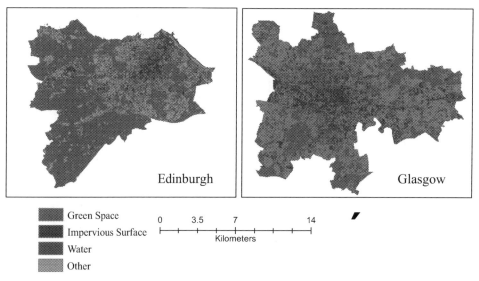

FIGURE 6.2

Land cover maps of Edinburgh and Glasgow cities and its immediate surrounding areas derived from Landsat imagery (2018. Landsat 8 OLI/TIRS).

$$VrNIR - BI = \frac{\rho_{Red} - \rho_{NIR}}{\rho_{Red} + \rho_{NIR}} \tag{6.2}$$

$$NDVI = \frac{\rho_{NIR} - \rho_{Red}}{\rho_{NIR} + \rho_{Red}} \tag{6.3}$$

where ρ_{Green}, ρ_{Red}, ρ_{NIR}, and ρ_{SWIR1} refer to the surface reflectance values of bands 2, 3, 4, and 5 for Landsat 5 TM and Landsat 7 ETM+ and bands 3, 4, 5, 6 for Landsat 8 OLI/TIRS.

In order to verify the accuracy obtained in the classification of each of the land uses and land cover, different bands were combined (Table 6.2) and the information obtained from the MNDWI, VrNIR-BI, and NDVI indices was used as a reference. A total of 1000 reference points generated by the stratified random sampling technique were used (Stehman, 2009). Finally, an overall accuracy of 86% was obtained.

Table 6.2 Composition of Bands for Landsat 8 OLI/TIRS satellites.

Composite bands	Landsat 5 TM	Landsat 7 ETM+	Landsat 8 OLI/TIRS
Vegetation	4, 3, 2	4, 3, 2	5, 4, 3
Urban areas	7, 5, 3	7, 5, 3	7, 6, 4
Agriculture	5, 4, 1	5, 4, 1	6, 5, 2
Water	4, 5, 3	4, 5, 3	5, 6, 4
Natural color	3, 2, 1	3, 2, 1	4, 3, 2

2.4 LST retrieval

To retrieve the LST from remote sensing satellite thermal bands, the NDVI was used to derive the emissivity of the land surface. Subsequently, using these values the at-satellite brightness temperature was scaled (Sobrino et al., 2004). The preprocessed thermal bands created in Section 2.2 were used as follows Eq. (6.4) (Artis and Carnahan, 1982; Weng et al., 2004):

$$LST = \frac{T_B}{1 + \left(\lambda \times \dfrac{T_B}{\rho}\right) \times \ln\varepsilon} \tag{6.4}$$

where T_B = at-satellite brightness temperature in degrees Kelvin; λ = wavelength of emitted radiance (λ = 11.5 μm for Landsat 5 TM band 6 and Landsat 7 ETM + band 6 (Artis and Carnahan, 1982; Markham and Barker, 1985), and 10.8 μm for Landsat 8 OLI/TIRS band 10 (Chávez, 1988); ρ = h × c/σ (1.438 × 10^{-2} mK), σ = Boltzmann constant (1.38 × 10^{-34} Js), and c = velocity of light (2.998 × 108 m/s); and ε is the land surface emissivity estimated using the NDVI method (Stehman, 2009). The resulting LST values were then changed from degrees Kelvin to degrees Celsius (°C).

2.5 Spatial analysis

2.5.1 Urban–rural gradient analysis

This analysis determines the spatial variability of LST, the spatial distribution of IS, GS, and other across the urban–rural gradient of the study area. Firstly, Edinburgh and Glasgow's city center was located and called kilometer 0. Multiple ring buffer zones were then created around the center of each study area defined by the time period analyzed, with an interval of 300 m distance. Mean LST and the density of IS, GS, other land were obtained for each of the rings. For each of the rings, the number of pixels of each of the land uses was counted; each pixel has dimensions of 30 × 30. Multiplying the number of pixels by the area of each pixel, we obtain the total area of each land uses in each of the rings. The fraction of each of the uses was obtained by establishing the relationship between the total area of each of the land uses in each ring and the total area of the ring. Finally, mean LST and the density of IS, GS, other land were obtained for each of the rings.

2.5.2 Multiresolution grid-based analysis

This study focuses on determining the effect of IS, GS, and other land on LST. For this purpose, a set of polygonal grids adjusted to LST raster maps was generated, considering Edinburgh and Glasgow's city center calculated in Section 2.5.1. The size of each grid was 210 × 210 m (Estoque et al., 2017; Chávez, 1988; Myint et al., 2010). Finally, the mean LST and the density of IS, GS, and other land were obtained for each of the grids.

3. Results

3.1 Impervious surface, green space, and other versus LST

Land cover classification maps indicate that in 2018 (Fig. 6.2) in the Edinburg city, IS area was 2403 ha. The GS area was 17,228 ha. For IS2, the area was 6503 ha. For the Glasgow city, IS area was 3715 ha. The GS area was 5561 ha. For IS2, the area was 8181 ha. The LST maps of the study areas for

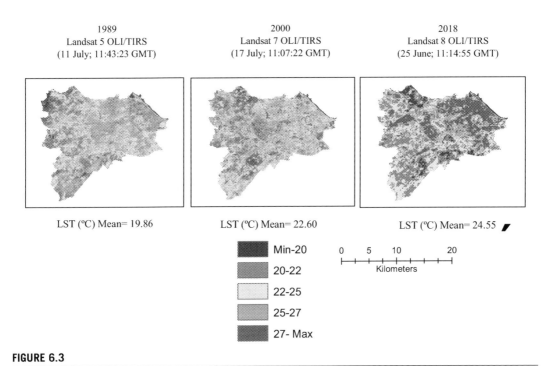

1989	2000	2018
Landsat 5 OLI/TIRS	Landsat 7 OLI/TIRS	Landsat 8 OLI/TIRS
(11 July; 11:43:23 GMT)	(17 July; 11:07:22 GMT)	(25 June; 11:14:55 GMT)

LST (°C) Mean= 19.86   LST (°C) Mean= 22.60   LST (°C) Mean= 24.55

Min-20
20-22
22-25
25-27
27- Max

0 5 10 20
Kilometers

FIGURE 6.3

LST maps; Edinburgh city and its immediate surrounding areas derived from Landsat imagery (1989, 2000, and 2018).

1989, 2000, and 2018 are shown in Fig. 6.3 for Edinburgh city and Fig. 6.4 for Glasgow city. In Edinburgh city, the average temperature for July 1989 was 19.86°C, rising to 22.60°C in 2000 and 24.55°C in 2018. It can be observed that from 1989 to 2018, the land surface temperature has increased by 4.69°C, the most notable increase being 2.74°C in the time interval between 1989 and 2018; whereas the increase for the interval between 2002 and 2018 was 1.95°C. In Glasgow city, the average temperature for July 1989 was 21.50°C, rising to 27.30°C in 2000 and decreased to 25.70°C in 2018. It can be observed that from 1989 to 2018, the land surface temperature has increase by 4.2°C. It is observed that the LST is higher in the city of Glasgow for the three periods analyzed: 1.64°C in 1989, 4.7°C in 2000, and 1.15 in 2018.

Fig. 6.5 shows mean LST of the LULC classes for 2018. In the year analyzed, the urban class (IS) together with other (IS2) had the highest mean LST for both cities. The temperature difference between both (IS and IS2) is 0.72°C for Glasgow and 1.37°C for Edinburgh.

As for GS, LST for Edinburgh is higher than that for Glasgow (0.3°C). Therefore, the results indicate that urban areas along with other land have influenced the spatial pattern of LST.

3.2 Impervious surface, green space, and other versus LST along urban–rural gradient

Regarding the urban–rural gradient, for both cities, mean LST is higher in the center than in the surrounding areas (Figs. 6.6 and 6.7). However, it is observed that in the case of Glasgow city, there is a greater temperature difference between the center and the surrounding areas, i.e., there is a greater

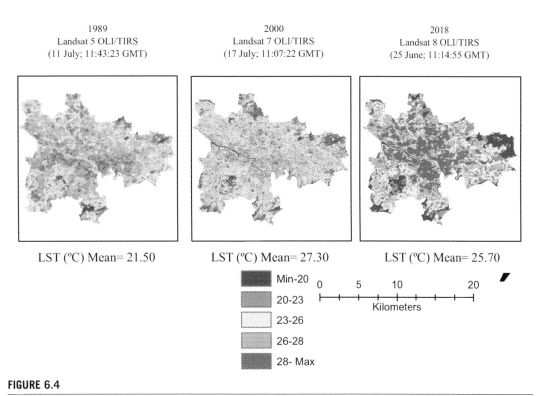

1989	2000	2018
Landsat 5 OLI/TIRS	Landsat 7 OLI/TIRS	Landsat 8 OLI/TIRS
(11 July; 11:43:23 GMT)	(17 July; 11:07:22 GMT)	(25 June; 11:14:55 GMT)

LST (°C) Mean= 21.50   LST (°C) Mean= 27.30   LST (°C) Mean= 25.70

Min-20
20-23
23-26
26-28
28- Max

FIGURE 6.4

LST maps; Glasgow city and its immediate surrounding areas derived from Landsat imagery (1989, 2000, and 2018).

temperature drop than in Edinburgh city. In the case of Edinburgh, the highest temperature (28.52°C) is reached 0.6 km from the city center. From about 8 km from the city center, mean LST remains around 23°C. In the case of Glasgow, the highest LST mean (28.94°C) is reached 1.8 km from the city center. From this point, it gradually decreases to a value of 19.43°C at 11.7 km from the city center.

For both cities, the IS fraction decreases from the city center along the urban gradient. The IS2 fraction is low in the city center in both cases. However, for Edinburgh from a point (approx. 8.4 km), this fraction decreases. This decrease does not occur in the same way for the city of Glasgow since the fraction IS2 remains high from 3.9 to 10 km and then decreases. The GS fraction is higher in Edinburgh than in Glasgow.

In the studied time, the linear correlation analysis presents a positive relationship of mean LST with fraction of IS and a negative correlation with the fraction of GS. In all cases, the correlation between mean LST and fraction of IS and GS is stronger (Fig. 6.8). The sample number varies according to the year and the land use/cover. Thus, for the year 2018 for the Edinburgh city, the sample size is 61.788, 41.277, and 90.903 for GS, IS, and BSC, respectively. For the year 2018 for the Glasgow city, the sample size is 191.423 for GS, 267.000 for IS, and 72.254 for BSC.

On the other hand, the linear regression analysis between mean LST and IS2 is shown in Fig. 6.9 where a positive relationship between them is observed with a weak correlation with mean LST.

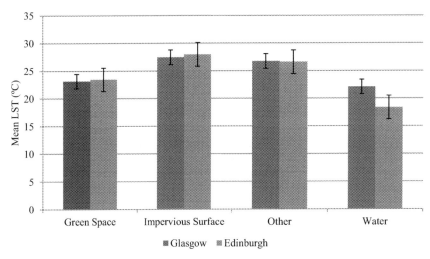

FIGURE 6.5

Mean LST of the LULC classes in Edinburgh and Glasgow cities (1989, 2000, and 2018).

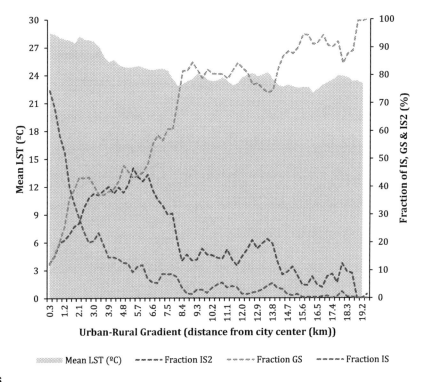

FIGURE 6.6

Mean LST and fractions of impervious surface (IS), green space (GS), and other (IS2) along the urban—rural gradient for the Edinburgh city.

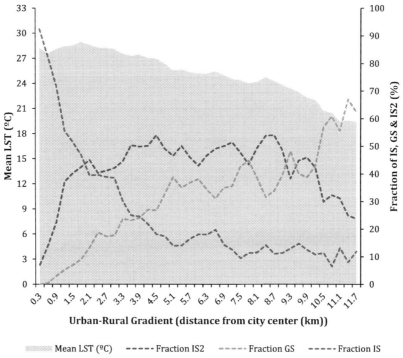

FIGURE 6.7

Mean LST and fractions of impervious surface (IS), green space (GS), and other (IS2) along the urban—rural gradient for the Glasgow city.

3.3 Impervious surface, green space, and bare soil and cultivated versus LST at multiple resolutions

Across grid sizes in Edinburgh and Glasgow cities, the correlation is stronger between mean LST and GS density than between mean LST, IS and 2 densities over the year (Figs. 6.10 and 6.11).

4. Discussion and conclusions

In this study, we used Landsat 5 TM, Landsat 7 ETM+, and Landsat 8 OLI/TIRS data to examine the relationship of the abundance and spatial pattern of impervious surface (IS and IS2) and GS with LST in the cities of Scotland. Our results show that the city of Glasgow has a higher percentage of IS and IS2 than Edinburgh with the percentage of GS being higher in the latter. On the other hand, Edinburgh was the cooler city. This may be due to the difference in the proportion of GS and ISs in the two cities. Edinburgh has 32% more GS than Glasgow. This implies that more GS coverage compared to IS is necessary to mitigate urban warming (Myint et al., 2010). Overall, our results show that the mean LST of SI and SI2 was 4.43°C and 3.39°C higher than the mean LST of GS, respectively. In Edinburgh, the mean LST for the three periods analyzed was always lower than the mean LST of Glasgow, coupled

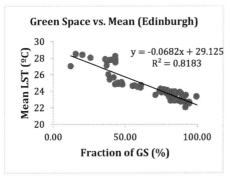

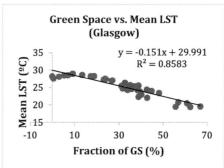

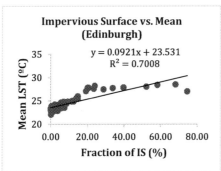

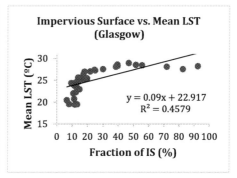

FIGURE 6.8

Scatter plots and statistical relationships (GS and IS).

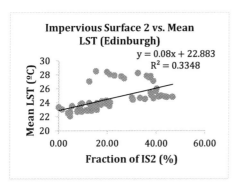

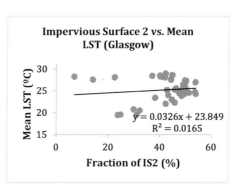

FIGURE 6.9

Scatter plots and statistical relationships (IS2).

with what has been said above about the higher percentage of GS in Edinburgh shows that GS plays an important role in mitigating UHI effects (Sun et al., 2012; Song et al., 2014; Weng et al., 2004; Bokaie et al., 2016; Weng, 2001).

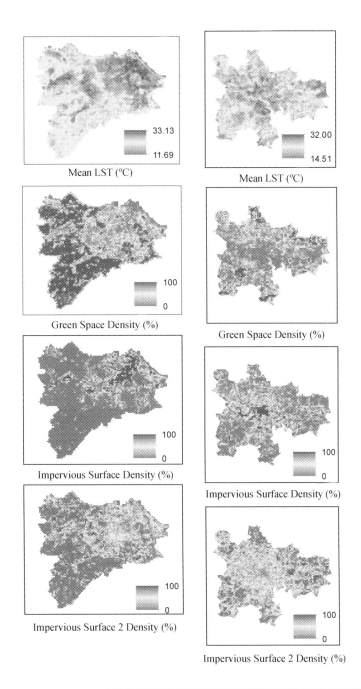

FIGURE 6.10

Graphical illustration of the polygon grid (210 × 210 m), showing the maps of mean LST, impervious surface density, green space density, and other.

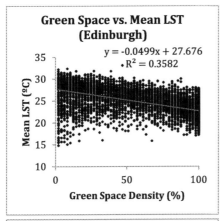

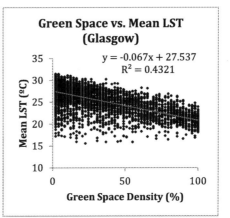

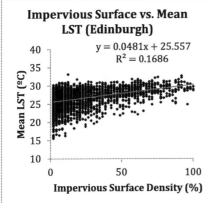

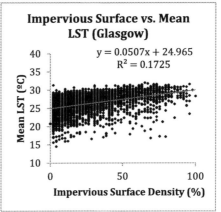

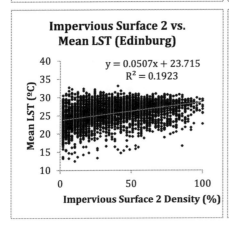

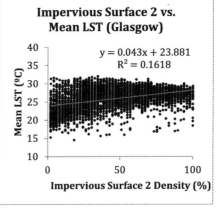

FIGURE 6.11

Scatter plots between impervious surface, green space, impervious surface 2 densities, and mean LST in Seville City.

Fig. 6.7 shows that in the city of Glasgow, the areas closest to the city center do not have the highest mean LST as is the case for the city of Edinburgh (Fig. 6.6). This can be explained through the IS, IS2, and GS fractions as these have a significant correlation with the mean LST (Nastran et al., 2019).

Mean LST in Glasgow peaked about 1.8 km away from the city center before gradually decreasing along the urban−rural gradient. This was not the case in Edinburgh where mean LST peaked in the city center. However, despite these differences in the spatial location of the peaks, the pattern of mean LST across the urban−rural gradients of the two cities generally reflects a typical profile of the UHI phenomenon, with LST gradually decreasing along the urban−rural gradient with some peaks, valleys, plateaus, and basins.

It is also observed that the decrease in mean LST coincides with an increase in GS fraction and a decrease in IS and IS2 fractions. As the distance to the city center increases, the IS fraction decreases and the IS2 fraction increases as a consequence of land use change. This is more pronounced in the city of Edinburgh and can be explained by the higher GS fraction, which causes the mean LST to decrease sharply, compensating for the increase in the IS and IS2 fractions.

Our results show that mean LST is correlated with IS density (positive) and GS density (negative). These results are consistent with other studies (Weng et al., 2004; Nastran et al., 2019).

From Figs. 6.10 and 6.11, it can be seen that IS had the greatest impact on the Glasgow mean LST (slope = 0.0507) while IS2 had the greatest impact on the Edinburgh mean LST with a slope value of 0.0481. From the same figure it can be seen that GS had the greatest impact on mean LST in Glasgow (slope = −0.067). This confirms that Glasgow is generally slightly warmer than Edinburgh. In general, the slope values of GS versus mean LST of the two cities are systematically lower than the slope values of IS and IS2 versus mean LST. This confirms that IS has a greater impact on LST than GS.

In conclusion, it can be said that, cities are adopting an urban disperse model in that they tend to occupy increasingly larger areas with the removal of certain sectors outside the city limits (office parks, industrial activities, low-density residences, university institutions, etc.) for the creation of dormitories, etc. This is partly motivated by the emergence of a series of factors such as the increase in land prices, changing perceptions on the quality of life that influence the construction of new housing (the building of closed residential complexes with private gardens and the high value of being in close contact with nature, among others), the dominance of the car over the city, and so on. This entirely means that cities need an ever-increasing consumption of energy and materials, therefore making them less sustainable.

The solution to this problem is closely linked to efficient urban planning, in which measures that are based on an exhaustive territorial, economic, and sociological analysis are adopted aimed at restoring the cities' environmental quality and reducing the effects generated by climate change.

In summary, it is vital to introduce an assessment planning culture in the framework of climate change (Nastran et al., 2019; Sun et al., 2019; Hyoungsub et al., 2018). The control of urban expansion, the increase of green areas (including roofs and building façades) as well as the percentage of permeable soil, the modification of the albedo of materials and pavements (increasing the degree of reflection of incoming solar radiation), the integration of artificial water bodies, the promotion of urban ventilation, the layout of buildings and, in general, the composition of urban morphology in order to facilitate air circulation, generate urban canyons and ease temperatures (Georgakis et al., 2014). These are all elements that must be included in the daily practices of urban and land planning (Szopińska et al., 2019).

It concludes that there is a need to implement UHI mitigation strategies during the design and initial phases of the engineering project, from where the origin of this problem can be acted upon, since the process of creating streets and public space offers a valuable opportunity to restore the environmental quality of our cities and diminish the effects generated by climate change.

References

Aniello, C., Morgan, K., Busbey, A., Newland, L., 1995. Mapping micro-urban heat islands using Landsat TM and a GIS. Comput. Geosci. 21, 965−969. https://doi.org/10.1016/0098-3004(95)00033-5.

Arnfield, A.J., 2003. Two decades of urban climate research: a review of turbulence, exchanges of energy and water, and the urban heat island. Int. J. Climatol. 23 (1), 1−26. https://doi.org/10.1002/joc.859.

Artis, D.A., Carnahan, W.H., 1982. Survey of emissivity variability in thermography of urban areas. Remote Sens. Environ. 12, 313−329. https://doi.org/10.1016/0034-4257(82)90043-8.

Behera, S.R., Dash, D.P., 2017. The effect of urbanization, energy consumption, and foreign direct investment on the carbon dioxide emission in the SSEA (South and Southeast Asian) region. Renew. Sustain. Energy Rev. 70, 96−106. https://doi.org/10.1016/j.rser.2016.11.201.

Bokaie, M., Zarkesh, M.K., Arasteh, P.D., Hosseini, A., 2016. Assessment of urban heat island based on the relationship between land surface temperature and land use/land cover in Tehran. Sustain. Cities Soc. 23, 94−104. https://doi.org/10.1016/j.scs.2016.03.009.

Carlson, T.N., Dodd, J.K., Benjamin, S.G., Cooper, J.M., 1981. Satellite estimation of surface energy balance, moisture availability and thermal inertia. J. Appl. Meteorol. 20 (1), 67−87. https://doi.org/10.1175/1520-0450(1981)020<0067:SEOTSE>2.0.CO;2.

Carsjens, G.J., van Lier, H.N., 2002. Fragmentation and land use planning: an introduction. Landsc. Urban Plann. 58, 79−82. https://doi.org/10.1016/S0169-2046(01)00210-9.

Chander, G., Markham, B.L., Helder, D.L., 2009. Summary of current radiometric calibration coefficients for Landsat MSS, TM, ETM+, and EO-1 ALI sensors. Remote Sens. Environ. 113, 893−903. https://doi.org/10.1016/j.rse.2009.01.007.

Chávez, P.S., 1988. An improved dark-object subtraction technique for atmospheric scattering correction of multispectral data. Remote Sens. Environ. 24, 459−479. https://doi.org/10.1016/0034-4257(88)90019-3.

Dousset, B., Gourmelon, F., 2003. Satellite multi-sensor data analysis of urban surface temperatures and landcover. ISPRS J. Photogramm. Remote Sens. 58, 43−54. https://doi.org/10.1016/S0924-2716(03)00016-9.

Du, Z., Li, W., Zhou, D., Tian, L., Ling, F., Wang, H., Gui, Y., Sun, B., 2014. Analysis of Landsat-8 OLI imagery for land surface water mapping. Remote Sens. Lett. 5, 672−681. https://doi.org/10.1080/2150704X.2014.960606.

EPA US Environmental Protection Agency, 2008. Reducing Urban Heat Islands: Compendium of Strategies. US Environmental Protection Agency, Washington, DC. https://www.epa.gov/sites/production/files/2014-06/documents/basicscompendium.pdf.

Estoque, R.C., Murayama, Y., 2015. Classification and change detection of built-up lands from Landsat-7 ETM+ and Landsat-8 OLI/TIRS imageries: a comparative assessment of various spectral indices. Ecol. Indicat. 56, 205−217. https://doi.org/10.1016/j.ecolind.2015.03.037.

Estoque, R.C., Murayama, Y., 2017. Monitoring surface urban heat island formation in a tropical mountain city using Landsat data (1987-2015). ISPRS J. Photogramm. Eng. Remote Sens. 133, 18−29. https://doi.org/10.1016/j.isprsjprs.2017.09.008.

Estoque, R.C., Murayama, Y., Myint, S.W., 2017. Effects of landscape composition and pattern on land surface temperature: an urban heat island study in the megacities of Southeast Asia. Sci. Total Environ. 577, 349−359. https://doi.org/10.1016/j.scitotenv.2016.10.195.

Gallo, K.P., Tarpley, J.D., 1996. The comparison of vegetation index and surface temperature composites of urban heat-island analysis. Int. J. Remote Sens. 17, 3071−3076. https://doi.org/10.1080/01431169608949128.

Gartland, L.M., 2012. Heat Islands: Understanding and Mitigating Heat in Urban Areas. Routledge. https://doi.org/10.4324/9781849771559.

Gaur, A., Eichenbaum, M.K., Simonovic, S.P., 2018. Analysis and modelling of surface Urban Heat Island in 20 Canadian cities under climate and land-cover change. J. Environ. Manag. 206, 145−157. https://doi.org/10.1016/j.jenvman.2017.10.002.

Georgakis, C., Zoras, S., Santamouris, M., 2014. Studying the effect of "cool" coatings in street urban canyons and its potential as a heat island mitigation technique. Sustain. Cities Soc. 13, 20−31. https://doi.org/10.1016/j.scs.2014.04.002.

Gibb, H., Hochuli, D.F., 2002. Habitat fragmentation in an urban environment: large and small fragments support different arthropod assemblages. Biol. Conserv. 106 (1), 91−100. https://doi.org/10.1016/S0006-3207(01)00232-4.

Glasgow, 2018. Glasgow economic strategy, 2016-23. https://www.glasgow.gov.uk/CHttpHandler.ashx?id=36137&p=0#:~:text=The%20new%20Glasgow%20Economic%20Strategy,wellbeing%20for%20all%20its%20citizens.

Grimm, N.B., Grove, J.G., Pickett, S.T., Redman, C.L., 2000. Integrated approaches to long-term studies of urban ecological systems: urban ecological systems present multiple challenges to ecologists—pervasive human impact and extreme heterogeneity of cities, and the need to integrate social and ecological approaches, concepts, and theory. Bioscience 50 (7), 571−584. https://doi.org/10.1641/0006-3568(2000)050[0571:IATLTO]2.0.CO;2.

Guillevic, P.C., Privette, J.L., Coudert, B., Palecki, M.A., Demarty, J., Ottle, C., Augustine, J.A., 2012. Land Surface Temperature product validation using NOAA's surface climate observation networks—scaling methodology for the Visible Infrared Imager Radiometer Suite (VIIRS). Remote Sens. Environ. 124, 282−298. https://doi.org/10.1016/j.rse.2012.05.004.

Haashemi, S., Weng, Q., Darvishi, A., Alavipanah, S.K., 2016. Seasonal variations of the surface urban heat island in a semi-arid city. Remote Sens. 8, 352. https://doi.org/10.3390/rs8040352.

Harris, P.M., Ventura, S.J., 1995. The integration of geographic data with remotely sensed imagery to improve classification in an urban area. Photogramm. Eng. Remote Sens. 61, 993−998. https://www.asprs.org/wp-content/uploads/pers/1995journal/aug/1995_aug_993-998.pdf.

Hattis, D., Ogneva-Himmelberger, Y., Ratick, S., 2012. The spatial variability of heat-related mortality in Massachusetts. Appl. Geogr. 33, 45−52. https://doi.org/10.1016/j.apgeog.2011.07.008.

Houšková, B., Montanarella, L., 2008. The natural susceptibility of European soils to compaction. In: Threats to Soil Quality in Europe EUR, 23438, pp. 23−35.

Howard, L., 1818. The Climate of London, vol. 2. London Harvey and Dorton, London, UK, pp. 1818−1820. https://www.urban-climate.org/documents/LukeHoward_Climate-of-London-V1.pdf.

Huang, X., Wang, Y., 2019. Investigating the effects of 3D urban morphology on the surface urban heat island effect in urban functional zones by using high-resolution remote sensing data: a case study of Wuhan, Central China. ISPRS J. Photogrammetry Remote Sens. 152, 119−131. https://doi.org/10.1016/j.isprsjprs.2019.04.010.

Hung, T., Uchihama, D., Ochi, S., Yasouka, Y., 2006. Assessment with satellite data of the urban heat island effects in Asian mega cities. Int. J. Appl. Earth Obs. Geoinf. 8, 34−48. https://doi.org/10.1016/j.jag.2005.05.003.

Hyoungsub, K., Donghwan, G., Hwan Yong, K., 2018. Effects of Urban Heat Island mitigation in various climate zones in the United States. Sustain. Cities Soc. 41, 841−852. https://doi.org/10.1016/j.scs.2018.06.021.

Ibrahim, F., Rasul, G., 2017. Urban land use land cover changes and their effect on land surface temperature: case study using Dohuk City in the Kurdistan Region of Iraq. Climate 5 (1), 13. https://doi.org/10.1016/j.scitotenv.2016.10.195.

Ji, L., Zhang, L., Wylie, B., 2009. Analysis of dynamic thresholds for the normalized difference water index. ISPRS J. Photogramm. Eng. Remote Sens. 75, 1307−1317. https://doi.org/10.14358/PERS.75.11.1307.

Jin, M., Dickinson, R.E., Zhang, D.A., 2005. The footprint of urban areas on global climate as characterized by MODIS. J. Clim. 18 (10), 1551−1565. https://doi.org/10.1175/JCLI3334.1.

Johnson, D.P., Stanforth, A., Lulla, V., Luber, G., 2012. Developing an applied extreme heat vulnerability index utilizing socioeconomic and environmental data. Appl. Geogr. 35 (1−2), 23−31. https://doi.org/10.1016/j.apgeog.2012.04.006.

Kato, S., Yamaguchi, Y., 2005. Analysis of urban heat-island effect using ASTER and ETM+ data: separation of anthropogenic heat discharge and natural heat radiation from sensible heat flux. Remote Sens. Environ. 99, 44−54. https://doi.org/10.1016/j.rse.2005.04.026.

Kolokotroni, M., Giannitsaris, I., Watkins, R., 2006. The effect of the London urban heat island on building summer cooling demand and night ventilation strategies. Sol. Energy 80 (4), 383−392. https://doi.org/10.1109/JSTARS.2009.2023088.

Li, Y.Y., Zhang, H., Kainz, W., 2012. Monitoring patterns of urban heat islands of the fast-growing Shanghai metropolis, China: using time-series of Landsat TM/ETM+ data. Int. J. Appl. Earth Obs. Geoinf. 19, 127−138. https://doi.org/10.1016/j.jag.2012.05.001.

Li, W., Du, Z., Ling, F., Zhou, D., Wang, H., Gui, Y., Sun, B., Zhang, X., 2013. A comparison of land surface water mapping using the normalized difference water index from TM, ETM+ and ALI. Remote Sens. 5, 5530−5549. https://doi.org/10.3390/rs5115530.

Li, Z.L., Tang, B.H., Wu, H., Ren, H., Yan, G., Wan, Z., Trigo, I.F., Sobrino, J.A., 2013. Satellite-derived land surface temperature: current status and perspectives. Remote Sens. Environ. 131, 14−37. https://doi.org/10.1016/j.rse.2012.12.008.

Lo, C.P., Quattrochi, D.A., 2003. Land-use and land-cover change, urban heat island phenomenon, and health implications: a remote sensing approach. Photogramm. Eng. Remote Sens. 69 (9), 1053−1063. https://www.ingentaconnect.com/contentone/asprs/pers/2003/00000069/00000009/art00011?crawler=true.

Lo, C.P., Quattrochi, D.A., Luvall, J.C., 1997. Application of high resolution thermal infrared remote sensing and GIS to assess the urban heat island effect. Int. J. Remote Sens. 18, 287−304. https://doi.org/10.1080/014311697219079.

Ma, Y., Kuang, Y., Huang, N., 2010. Coupling urbanization analyses for studying urban thermal environment and its interplay with biophysical parameters based on TM/ETM+ imagery. Int. J. Appl. Earth Obs. Geoinf. 12, 110−118. https://doi.org/10.1016/j.jag.2009.12.002.

Manley, G., 1958. On the frequency of snowfall in metropolitan England. Q. J. R. Meteorol. Soc. 84 (359), 70−72. https://doi.org/10.1002/qj.49708435910.

Markham, B.L., Barker, J.K., 1985. Spectral characteristics of the LANDSAT thematic mapper sensors. Int. J. Remote Sens. 6, 697−716. https://doi.org/10.1080/01431168508948492.

Martin-Vide, J., Sarricolea, P., Moreno-García, M.C., 2015. On the definition of urban heat island intensity: the "rural" reference. Front. Earth Sci. 3, 24. https://doi.org/10.3389/feart.2015.00024.

Memon, R.A., Leung, D.Y., Liu, C.H., 2009. An investigation of urban heat island intensity (UHII) as an indicator of urban heating. Atmos. Res. 94 (3), 491−500. https://doi.org/10.1016/j.atmosres.2009.07.006.

Meng, C.L., Li, Z.L., Zhan, X., Shi, J.C., Liu, C.Y., 2009. Land surface temperature data assimilation and its impact on evapotranspiration estimates from the Common Land Model. Water Resour. Res. 45, 1−14. https://agupubs.onlinelibrary.wiley.com/doi/pdf/10.1029/2008WR006971.

Mohajerani, A., Bakaric, J., Jeffrey-Bailey, T., 2017. The urban heat island effect, its causes, and mitigation, with reference to the thermal properties of asphalt concrete. J. Environ. Manag. 197, 522−538. https://doi.org/10.1016/j.jenvman.2017.03.095.

Montanarella, L., Rusco, E., 2008. Threats to soil quality in Europe. In: Tóth, G. (Ed.), Luxembourg: Office for Official Publications of the European Communities. http://publications.jrc.ec.europa.eu/repository/handle/JRC46574.

Myint, S.W., Brazel, A., Okin, G., Buyantuyev, A., 2010. Combined effects of impervious surface and vegetation cover on air temperature variations in a rapidly expanding desert city. GIScience Remote Sens. 47, 301−320. https://doi.org/10.2747/1548-1603.47.3.301.

Nastran, M., Kobal, M., Eler, K., 2019. Urban heat islands in relation to green land use in European cities. Urban For. Urban Green. 37, 33−41. https://doi.org/10.1016/j.ufug.2018.01.008.

Oke, T.R., Hannell, F.G., 1970. The Form of the Urban Heat Island in Hamilton, Canada, vol. 108. WMO Technical Note, pp. 113−126.

Oke, T.R., 1982. The energetic basis of the urban heat island. Q. J. R. Meteorol. Soc. 108 (455), 1−24. https://doi.org/10.1002/qj.49710845502.

Oke, T.R., 2006. Towards better scientific communication in urban climate. Theor. Appl. Climatol. 84 (1), 179−190. https://link.springer.com/content/pdf/10.1007%2Fs00704-005-0153-0.pdf.

Pongrácz, R., Bartholy, J., Dezso, Z., 2010. Application of remotely sensed thermal information to urban climatology of Central European cities. Phys. Chem. Earth 35, 95−99. https://doi.org/10.1016/j.pce.2010.03.004.

Prokop, J., Jobstmann, H., Schönbauer, A., 2011. Overview on Best Practices for Limiting Soil Sealing and Mitigating its Effects in EU-27. http://ec.europa.eu/environment/archives/soil/pdf/sealing/Soil%20sealing%20-%20Final%20Report.pdf.

Rao, P.K., 1972. Remote sensing of urban "heat islands" from an environmental satellite. Bull. Am. Meteorol. Soc. 53, 647−648.

Rhodes, C.J., 2016. The 2015 Paris climate change conference: COP21. Sci. Prog. 99 (1), 97−104. https://doi.org/10.3184/003685016X14528569315192.

Roth, M., Oke, T.R., Emery, W.J., 1989. Satellite-derived urban heat islands from 3 coastal cities and the utilization of such data in urban climatology. Int. J. Remote Sens. 10, 1699−1720. https://doi.org/10.1080/01431168908904002.

Rouse, Z.W., Haas, W.H., Schell, D.A., Deering, L.W., 1974. Monitoring vegetation systems in the great plains with ERTS. In: Freden, S.C., Mercanti, E.P., Becker, M. (Eds.), Third Earth Resources Technology Satellite-1 Symposium Technical Presentations, NASA SP-351 1. NASA, Washington, DC, pp. 309−317. https://ntrs.nasa.gov/archive/nasa/casi.ntrs.nasa.gov/19740022614.pdf.

Shirani-bidabadi, N., Nasrabadi, T., Faryadi, S., Larijani, A., Roodposhti, M.S., 2019. Evaluating the spatial distribution and the intensity of urban heat island using remote sensing, case study of Isfahan city in Iran. Sustain. Cities Soc. 45, 686−692. https://doi.org/10.1016/j.scs.2018.12.005.

Snider, W., Wan, Z., 1998. BRDF models to predict spectral reflectance and emissivity in the thermal infrared. IEEE Trans. Geosci. Remote Sens. 36 (1), 214−225. http://citeseerx.ist.psu.edu/viewdoc/download?doi=10.1.1.4.1493&rep=rep1&type=pdf.

Sobrino, J.A., Jiménez-Muñoz, J.C., Paolini, L., 2004. Land surface temperature retrieval from LANDSAT 5 TM. Remote Sens. Environ. 90, 434−440. https://doi.org/10.1016/j.rse.2004.02.003.

Song, J., Du, S., Feng, X., Guo, L., 2014. The relationships between landscape compositions and land surface temperature: quantifying their resolution sensitivity with spatial regression models. Landsc. Urban Plann. 123, 145−157.

Souch, C., Grimmond, S., 2006. Applied climatology: urban climate. Prog. Phys. Geogr. 30 (2), 270−279. https://doi.org/10.1191/0309133306pp484pr.

Srivastava, P.K., Majumbar, T.J., Bhattacharya, A.K., 2009. Surface temperature estimation in Singhbhum Shear Zone of India using Landsat-7 ETM+ thermal infrared data. Adv. Space Res. 43, 1563−1574. https://doi.org/10.1016/j.asr.2009.01.023.

Stathopoulou, M., Cartalis, C., 2007. Daytime urban heat islands from Landsat ETM+ and Corine land cover data: an application to major cities in Greece. Sol. Energy 81, 358−368. https://doi.org/10.1016/j.solener.2006.06.014.

https://www.statista.com/statistics/1101883/largest-european-cities/.

Stehman, A.V., 2009. Sampling designs for accuracy assessment of land cover. Int. J. Remote Sens. 30, 5243−5272. https://doi.org/10.1080/01431160903131000.

Stone, B., Hess, J.J., Frumkin, H., 2010. Urban form and extreme heat events: are sprawling cities more vulnerable to climate change than compact cities? Environ. Health Perspect. 118 (10), 1425−1428. https://doi.org/10.1289/ehp.0901879.

Streutker, D.R., 2002. A remote sensing study of the urban heat island of Houston, Texas. Int. J. Remote Sens. 23 (13), 2595−2608. https://doi.org/10.1080/01431160110115023.

Streutker, D.R., 2003. Satellite-measured growth of the urban heat island of Houston, Texas. Remote Sens. Environ. 85, 282−289. https://doi.org/10.1016/S0034-4257(03)00007-5.

Sun, Q., Wu, Z., Tan, J., 2012. The relationship between land surface temperature and land use/land cover in Guangzhou, China. Environ. Earth Sci. 65, 1687−1694.

Sun, R., Lü, Y., Yang, X., Chen, L., 2019. Understanding the variability of urban heat islands from local background climate and urbanization. J. Clean. Prod. 208, 743−752. https://doi.org/10.1016/j.jclepro.2018.10.178.

Synop, 2018. Synop report summary. www.ogimet.com.

Szopińska, R., Kazak, J., Kempa, O., Rubaszek, J., 2019. Spatial form of greenery in strategic environmental management in the context of urban adaptation to climate change. Pol. J. Environ. Stud. 28 (4), 2845−2856. https://doi.org/10.15244/pjoes/92244.

Tan, K.C., Lim, H.S., Matjafri, M.Z., Abdullah, K., 2010. Landsat data to evaluate urban expansion and determine land use/land cover changes in Penang Island, Malaysia. Environ. Earth Sci. 60 (7). https://doi.org/10.1007/s12665-009-0286-z.

Treitz, P.M., Howard, P.J., Gong, P., 1992. Application of satellite and GIS technologies for land-cover and land-use mapping at the rural-urban fringe: a case study. Photogramm. Eng. Remote Sens. 58, 439−448. https://www.asprs.org/wp-content/uploads/pers/1992journal/apr/1992_apr_439-448.pdf.

Trenberth, K.E., Jones, P.D., Ambenje, P., Bojariu, R., Easterling, D., Klein Tank, A., Parker, D., Rahimzadeh, F., Renwick, J.A., Rusticucci, M., Soden, B., Zhai, P., 2007. Observations. Surface and Atmospheric Climate Change (Chapter 3). United Kingdom: N. p. Web. https://wg1.ipcc.ch/publications/wg1-ar4/ar4-wg1-chapter3.pdf.

United Nations, 2014. United Nations, World Urbanization Prospects the 2014 Revision, United Nations, 2014.

Voogt, J.A., Oke, T.R., 2003. Thermal remote sensing of urban climates. Remote Sens. Environ. 86 (3), 370−384. https://doi.org/10.1016/S0034-4257(03)00079-8.

Voogt, J.A., 2004. Urban Heat Islands: Hotter Cities. America Institute of Biological Sciences. http://www.actionbioscience.org/environment/voogt.html.

Weng, Q., Lu, D., Schubring, J., 2004. Estimation of land surface temperature vegetation abundance relationship for urban heat island studies. Remote Sens. Environ. 89, 467−483. https://doi.org/10.1016/j.rse.2003.11.005.

Weng, Q., 2001. A remote sensing-GIS evaluation of urban expansion and its impact on surface temperature in the Zhujiang Delta, China. Int. J. Remote Sens. 22, 1999−2014. https://doi.org/10.1080/713860788.

Weng, Q., 2009. Thermal infrared remote sensing for urban climate and environmental studies: methods, applications, and trends. ISPRS J. Photogrammetry Remote Sens. 64 (4), 335−344. https://doi.org/10.1016/j.isprsjprs.2009.03.007.

Wieslaw, Z.M., 1993. GIS in land use change analysis: integration of remotely sensed data into GIS. Appl. Geogr. 13 (1), 28−44. https://doi.org/10.1016/0143-6228(93)90078-F.

Xian, G., Crane, M., 2006. An analysis of urban thermal characteristics and associated land cover in Tampa Bay and Las Vegas using Landsat satellite data. Remote Sens. Environ. 104, 147–156. https://doi.org/10.1016/j.rse.2005.09.023.

Xu, H., Ding, F., Wen, X., 2009. Urban expansion and heat island dynamics in the Quanzhou region, China. IEEE J. Sel. Top. Appl. Earth Obs. Remote Sens. 2 (2), 74–79. https://doi.org/10.1109/JSTARS.2009.2023088.

Xu, H., 2006. Modification of normalized difference water index (NDWI) to enhance open water features in remotely sensed imagery. Int. J. Remote Sens. 27, 3025–3033. https://doi.org/10.1080/01431160600589179.

Yang, K., Yu, Z., Luo, Y., Yang, Y., Zhao, L., Zhou, X., 2018. Spatial and temporal variations in the relationship between lake water surface temperatures and water quality-A case study of Dianchi Lake. Sci. Total Environ. 624, 859–871.

Yow, D.M., 2007. Urban heat islands: observations, impacts, and adaptation. Geogr. Compass 1 (6), 1227–1251. https://doi.org/10.1111/j.1749-8198.2007.00063.x.

Zhang, X., Estoque, R.C., Murayama, Y., 2017. An urban heat island study in Nanchang City, China based on land surface temperature and social-ecological variables. Sustain. Cities Soc. 32, 557–568. https://doi.org/10.1016/j.scs.2017.05.005.

Zhou, W., Huang, G., Cadenasso, M.L., 2011. Does spatial configuration matter? Understanding the effects of land cover pattern on land surface temperature in urban landscapes. Landsc. Urban Plann. 102 (1), 54–63. https://doi.org/10.1016/j.landurbplan.2011.03.009.

Zhou, D., Xiao, J., Bonafoni, S., Berger, C., Deilami, K., Zhou, Y., Frolking, S., Yao, R., Qiao, Z., Sobrino, J.A., 2018. Satellite remote sensing of surface urban heat islands: progress, challenges, and perspectives. Remote Sens. 11 (48). https://doi.org/10.3390/rs11010048.

Urban heat island mitigation and adaptation in China: policies and practices

Huimin Liu[1], Bo Huang[2,3], Qingming Zhan[1], Sihang Gao[1] and Zhiyu Fan[1]

[1]*School of Urban Design, Wuhan University, Wuhan, China;* [2]*Institute of Space and Earth Information Science, The Chinese University of Hong Kong, Shatin, NT, China;* [3]*Department of Geography and Resource Management, The Chinese University of Hong Kong, Shatin, NT, China*

1. Introduction

In face of rapid urbanization and global climate change, there is a growing need for policymaking to control the effects of urban heat islands (UHIs), which represents a phenomenon of elevated temperature in urban areas compared to their nonurban surroundings (Grimm et al., 2008; Zhao et al., 2014; Manoli et al., 2019). UHI is largely induced by land surface modification of natural land covers being replaced by artificial surfaces (Foley et al., 2005; Grimm et al., 2008; Oke et al., 2017). Its intensity can be further magnified by reduced overall wind ventilation and elevated anthropogenic heat release in urban areas (Li et al., 2020). The UHI effect is detrimental in many ways. For instance, it can result in increased energy consumption (Santamouris et al., 2015; Estrada et al., 2017), deteriorated air and water quality (Foley et al., 2005), and also enhanced risk of heat-related morbidity and mortality especially during heat wave events (Patz et al., 2005; He et al., 2021). These consequences can be even more severe in the context of global climate change and rapid urbanization (Zhou et al., 2019).

Policy intervention of UHI attenuation is especially urgent in China. China has experienced unprecedented urbanization since reform and "opening up". The proportion of urban population in China has dramatically increased from 18% in 1978 to about 60% in 2020. The landscape urbanization rate is even reported to have exceeded demographic urbanization over the last two decades (Zhang et al., 2018). The rapid urbanization has resulted in extensive local warming progressively threating the sustainable development in China. This kind of situation is expected to be increasingly severe given the further massive urbanization to take place over the coming decades (Chen et al., 2020). Therefore, UHI in China has gained considerable research interest, especially in the last decade. According to a recent review summarizing studies of surface UHI (SUHI) during the 1972–2018 period using satellite remotely sensed Land surface temperature (LST) data (Zhou et al., 2019), China dominated as the most actively studied country worldwide. The related studies have facilitated our understanding of the (S)UHI evolution in China and can be helpful in formulating effective strategies to control the effects of (S)UHI.

Nevertheless, it is challenging to achieve a nationwide effectiveness in China. First, existing literature of (S)UHI study in China is largely big-city-biased, either focuses on only a single big city (Li et al., 2011; Yang et al., 2016) or simultaneously covering dozens (Zhou et al., 2016; Yao et al., 2017), thus may have provided an incomplete picture of (S)UHI variation in China. In fact, the small and medium-sized cities in China have also experienced rapid urban expansion since the 1990s as a consequence of national policy incentive (Ye et al., 2006) and hence are nonnegligible in (S)UHI investigations. Besides, the urban heat problems and corresponding coping strategies can be different between large and small cities (Liu et al., 2021a). Second, as a vast country spanning a wide range of background climates from tropics to cold climate, the influencing effects of urbanization on (S)UHI vary across climate zones (Liu et al., 2021a; 2021b). Therefore, it would be ineffective to use a single set of technical standards to cope with the urban heat problems for cities located in different climate zones.

Given the above backgrounds, this chapter aims to summarize existing knowledge support for (S)UHI mitigation and adaptation in China and the corresponding policies and practices. In response to this aim, it specifically addresses the following aspects: (1) summarizes the spatial and temporal variations of (S)UHI in China; (2) evaluates the overall efficacy of historical and current efforts in controlling the effects of (S)UHI, and elaborates the successes and failures of Wuhan, the pioneer city in mainland China in (S)UHI attenuation; (3) concludes the existing challenges and future directions of UHI mitigation and adaptation in China.

2. Significant spatiotemporal variations of (S)UHI in China

The intensity of (S)UHI demonstrates significant spatial and temporal variations in China. Geographically, higher daytime SUHI intensity (SUHII) tends to occur in the hotter areas located in southeastern China, while higher nighttime SUHII is mainly observed in the northern regions characterized with lower levels of temperature and precipitation (Zhou et al., 2014). Such spatial patterns indicate that SUHII variations over large regions are highly determined by background climates (Manoli et al., 2019; Zhou et al., 2019). Therefore, it is crucial for decision-making to take such an external influence into consideration while grading and coping with the urban heat problems of cities located in different climate zones.

As for temporal variations, studies using (S)UHIs calculated based on different time granularities generate inconsistent conclusions. Specifically, Yao et al. (2017) uncovered significant rising trends of SUHII for half of the 31 major cities in China in summer days from 2001–15. Recently, they further revealed similar rising trends for the canopy layer urban heat island (CLUHI) (Yao et al., 2021). Nevertheless, studies exploring interannual variation patterns demonstrate overall insignificant increasing tendencies of SUHII for most cities in China (Zhou et al., 2016; Liu et al., 2020). Such inconsistent conclusions may be largely induced by the less rising, even declining trends of SUHII in other seasons, especially in winter and autumn (Yao et al., 2021). Overall, the general rising (S)UHII for half of cities in summer, when the negative effects of (S)UHI are the mostly pronounced, signifies an urgent need for decision-making to control (S)UHI.

3. Policies and practices of UHI mitigation in China
3.1 National policies: a focus from climate change to urban climate

Given the high expenses of resource consumption and environmental deterioration of traditional urbanization models, China has altered its way of development toward more sustainable in recent years.

In 2007, in the report of the 17th national congress of the communist party of China, it officially adopted Ecological Civilization as its national strategy toward a greener and more sustainable China (Fang et al., 2018). Thereafter, the central government has enacted multiple related policies to meet the needs of environmental protection in China. Those related to the mitigation and adaptation of climate change are summarized in Table 7.1. In 2007, the State Council published "China's National Climate Change Program," which is the first national program issued by developing countries (CSC, 2007). In the following year, the China Meteorological Administration issued the "Regulation of Climate Feasibility Demonstration" (CMA, 2008). This document highlights the necessity to assess the climatic suitability and risk of the planning and construction projects closely related to climatic conditions. Later in 2013, the National Development and Reform Commission published the "National Strategy on Climate Change" to coordinate efforts for adapting climate change nationwide (NDRC, 2013).

Nevertheless, in terms of addressing local warming, it is not until 2013 that a policy directly related to UHI was issued. It is the "Design Standard for Thermal Environment of Urban Residential Areas" published by the Ministry of Housing and Urban—Rural Development (MOHURD, 2013) to guide the detailed planning of new urban residential area into higher levels of thermal comfort. It was proposed to deal with the outdoor thermal discomfort and related morbidity and mortality induced by UHI in China, especially in the south. Later in 2014, policies related to urban climate were firstly mentioned in

Table 7.1 Policies related to climate change in China. Note: the policies targeted on local warming mitigation and adaptation are highlighted in bold, while those only mentioning local warming are underlined.

Year	Issuer	Policy
2007	State Council	China's National Climate Change Program
2008	China Meteorological Administration	Regulation of Climate Feasibility Demonstration
2013	National Development and Reform Commission	National Strategy on Climate Change
2013	Ministry of Housing and Urban-Rural Development	**Design Standard for Thermal Environment of Urban Residential Areas**
2014	National Development and Reform Commission	National Plan on Climate Change (2014—20)
2015	China Meteorological Administration	**Technical Specifications for Climatic Feasibility Demonstration in the Urban Master Plan**
2016	National Development and Reform Commission; Ministry of Housing and UrbanRural Development	Action Plan for Urban Adaptation to Climate Change
2017	National Development and Reform Commission; Ministry of Housing and UrbanRural Development	Pilots for Climate-adaptive City Construction
2018	China Meteorological Administration	**Specifications for climatic feasibility demonstration-Urban Ventilation Corridor**
2019	China Meteorological Administration	**Technical for Climatic Feasibility Demonstration in Master Planning**

the national plans centered on addressing global climate change. Specifically, in the "National Plan on Climate Change (2014−20)" (NDRC, 2014), it pointed out to actively respond to UHI and carry out pilot projects for prevention and control of urban climate disasters. In 2015, the "Technical Specifications for Climatic Feasibility Demonstration in the Urban Master Plan" drew up by the China Meteorological Administration back in 2009 was finally passed (BMO, 2015). Four years later, it was updated as the "Technical for Climatic Feasibility Demonstration in Master Planning" (BMO, 2019). These two documents reflect the initiative for the Chinese Government to steer cities into more climate-friendly based on climate and urban climatic knowledge (Ng and Ren, 2017). It specifically indicates the necessity to acquire multisource data to quantify the indexes related to urban climate evaluation. In 2018, another national technical guide, the "Specifications for climatic feasibility demonstration-Urban Ventilation Corridor" (CMA, 2018), was issued. It was aimed to provide a standard methodology to create urban ventilation corridors in the early stages of city master planning (Ren et al., 2018).

Overall, a series of recent policy documents reveals that, with a growing awareness of urban climate change, the Chinese government has attached an increasing importance to the mitigation and adaptation of UHI. The related policies demonstrate two typical features. First, the policies showed a growing tendency to cover UHI mitigation as a part of China's response to climate change. That is to say, they simultaneously considered the mitigation of UHI, the reduction of greenhouse gas emissions, and the adaptation to meteorological disasters. The comprehensive consideration of the multiple aspects can promote synergies among the different types of efforts. Second, the policies have highlighted the critical role of urban planning and design in proactively addressing urban heat problems, especially in new urban areas to be built. The technical supports are also constantly updated to ensure that the most recent knowledge of climate change can be effectively transferred to practical application.

Limitations also exist in existing policies. First, the policies, especially those related to master planning, generally arose from a local perspective and hence neglect the intrinsic variation of UHI on the regional scale. Specifically, the technical documents list a unified standard to classify UHII for cities across China. For instance, a city with a UHII value lower than 0.5°C is regarded to have no phenomenon of UHI (BMO, 2015, 2019). Such a unified classification standard may mislead decision-making that there is no need for urban heat mitigation for cities with a UHII lower than 0.5°C. Nevertheless, UHI is a comparative measurement largely affected by rural temperatures (Manoli et al., 2019). Hence, a lower or even negative UHII for arid cities such as Xining (Yao et al., 2017) does not necessarily indicate a better urban thermal environment, it may be just contributed by a hotter rural environment. These cities may still be confronted with significant urban heat problems, for instance, inhabitants may still suffer strong discomfort and even worse impacts during summer days (Martilli et al., 2020). Therefore, it is in great necessity to formulate discrepant classification standards for cities located in diversified climate zones. Second, there is a lacking of supervision and assessment mechanism to guarantee the implementation effect of urban planning and design (Liu et al., 2020). Given that a politician can only stay in the same position for a maximum of 10 years (Ng and Ren, 2017), such a supervision mechanism is particularly indispensable in China.

3.2 City practice: Wuhan, the pioneer in mainland China

Local governments in cities have also exerted multiple efforts in the mitigation and adaptation of UHI. Taking Wuhan as an example, as the pioneer for urban climatic application in mainland China, it started its ventilation corridor plan as early as in 2006 (Ng and Ren, 2017). Wuhan is a megacity located in central China, with a climate of humid subtropical. It was among the four hottest Chinese cities in summer known as "stoves" before 2017, imposing inhabitants with severe thermal discomfort. This threat to human health has impelled local governments to consider the increasing public demand for a cooler city into decision-making. Fortunately, the city is with sufficient "cold" land covers such as large parks and water bodies (Fig. 7.1A and C), enabling urban planner to create urban ventilation corridors to cool the city. Specifically, the first version of its ventilation corridor plan was started by the local planning and land resources bureau in 2006 as a conceptual design (Ng and Ren, 2017). Its

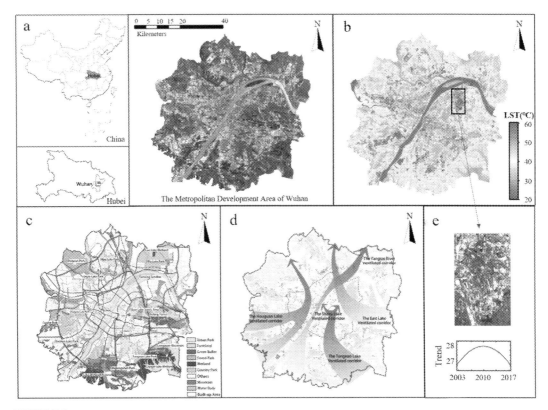

FIGURE 7.1

(A) The city of Wuhan represented by the Landsat 8 image (RGB) acquired on August 3, 2020; (B) the Land surface temperature (LST) of Wuhan at 10:56 a.m., August 3, 2020, acquired from the Landsat image; (C) the green space system planned for the metropolitan development area of Wuhan; (D) the urban ventilation corridors planned for Wuhan, drew by authors by referring to the figure provided in website of Wuhan natural resources and planning bureau (http://zrzyhgh.wuhan.gov.cn/zwdt/tpxw/202001/t20200107_613234. shtml); (E) the Qingshan industrial district represented by the Landsat 8 image (RGB) acquired on August 3, 2020 and its long-term trend of LST variation in the 2003–17 period (Liu et al., 2019).

(C) Source: http://gtghj.wuhan.gov.cn/pc-0-61109.html.

original intention is to designate six large green belts so that the fresh air and cool wind in suburban can be introduced into downtown to improve the thermal comfort in these areas. Such a conceptual design is emphasized in the "Comprehensive Planning of Wuhan (2010—20)" issued in 2009. Later in 2012, the local government commissioned urban climate researchers from Wuhan University and the Chinese University of Hong Kong to provide the second version of ventilation corridor planning with a stronger scientific-evidence-based support. In this version, the researchers identified the spatial structure and overall layout of the corridors. Then, in 2015, the local planning and land resources bureau invited Aria of France, an overseas institution, to work with city bureaus of meteorology and planning so as to verify the corridors identified in the second version and provide planning guidance and control measures for improving wind environment in Wuhan. The specific corridors they identified are presented in Fig. 7.1D. By far, the ventilation corridors have been recognized as a critical part ensuring the ecological security of Wuhan. Their importance has been further emphasized in strategic plans of Wuhan, including the "Wuhan 2049." In the latest version of comprehensive planning (2016—30), the corridors have been assigned with new functions for entertainment and leisure, so that the green parks and water bodies constituting the corridors can be maximally used by citizens.

In addition to the planning and creation of ventilation corridors, local governments in Wuhan have also exerted other efforts to create a cooler and more sustainable urban environment. For instance, the Qingshan industrial district has carried out lots of cooling efforts since 2007, which has successfully brought its surface temperature in 2017 back to the level of 2003 even in the context of global warming (Fig. 7.1E) (Liu et al., 2019). The Qingshan industrial district is generally the hottest area in Wuhan because of its massive emission of industrial heat. In 2007, the district was selected as one of the second batch of Pilot Demonstrations of Circular Economy in China. From then on, the local government has carried out many recycling measures, including the upgrading of hot stoves, the recycling of exhaust heat for electricity generation, etc. (http://www.qingshan.gov.cn/). Besides, the afforestation projects in areas such as the Liangzihu wetland nature reserve have also achieved sound cooling effect (Liu et al., 2019).

Overall, the conjoint efforts in Wuhan are effective in cooling the city. Hence, since 2017, the city has successfully dropped out of the "four stoves" in China. It was also examined to be outstanding in coordinating economic development with UHI mitigation among the cities with similar economic levels and consistent background climatic conditions (Liu et al., 2020). The success of Wuhan is largely contributed by its well-managed digital urban database, which enables the effective quantification of how urban form and land use intensity affect local climate (Ng and Ren, 2017). Nevertheless, the response to UHI in Wuhan still largely stays in the master planning level. The cooling effect is largely a consequence of city-level ecoenvironment management. In contrast, how to achieve cool communities with excellent arrangement of land use layout and construction intensity is seldom concerned. Besides, there is also a lack of supervision and assessment mechanism to guarantee the implementation effect of related urban planning and design (Liu et al., 2020).

4. Existing challenges and future directions

Given the massive urbanization expected in the near future and rising challenges associated with global climate change, it is urgent for China to adapt its cities to address urban climate change and steer them into long-term sustainability. The related national policies and city practice outlined above provide a glimpse into China's efforts in mitigating and adapting UHI. The experience also highlights certain existing challenges. First, data availability, which is the key contributing to the cooling success of Wuhan, is, however, a challenge for most cities in China. Although local governments, especially those of large cities, possess vast amounts of data acquired from multiple sources, only a small portion is publicly available. Such a limited access to urban datasets restricts the exploration of local warming, especially for the research institutions that share no cooperation with local governments. Second, environmental concern (Liu and Mu, 2016) is essential in creating cool cities and communities, yet it is still not strong enough among decision-makers and citizens in Chinese cities. Till 2016, only 36 cities in China have conducted studies related to urban climate (Ng and Ren, 2017). The concern of UHI is especially insufficient in western cities with lower levels of economy (Liu et al., 2020). Third, it is challenging to cool old urban centers, which are highly densified with limited heat-adaptive capacity (Liu et al., 2021a). It would be at a great cost to modify existing buildings to take on the new climatic challenges (Ng and Ren, 2017). Urban renewal with increasing vegetation cover (Wang and Shu, 2020) through flexible policies such as "Plant Where Possible" (Liu et al., 2021a) can be helpful, nevertheless, only to a limited extent. Local governments may draw the experiences from Phoenix, United States, and work with nongovernmental organizations to provide extra supports for the vulnerable poor residents living in these areas (Zhao et al., 2020). For instance, to provide extra financial assistance for electricity costs in hot summers.

In the future, a consistent and coherent policy framework across multiple administrative levels (Liu et al., 2020) is required to guarantee the overall efficacy of UHI attenuation efforts. On the national scale, it is urgent to outline an integrated policy framework combining the mitigation and adaptation of UHI with other sustainable development goals. Hence, we may maximize synergies, rather than trade-offs among the multiple efforts promoting urban sustainability. Besides, it is crucial to upgrade national technique guides with the regional differentiation of background climates taken into consideration, so that we may possibly achieve all-round effectiveness of UHI attenuation across China. For instance, to grade the severity of urban heat problems according to UHIIs of cities in same climate zones and recommend cooling vegetation according to their background climates. On the city scale, first, it is crucial to enhance the cooperation with research institutes or promote the availability of urban datasets to researchers, so that the specific urban heat problems and potential solutions can be possibly captured. Second, discrepant policies are demanded for old urban centers and new towns or industry zones yet to be built. For instance, to provide more financial support to assist vulnerable citizens in old urban centers to adapt to urban heat events, while to call upon newly expanded urban lands to pursue higher standards of UHI attenuation, such as the "zero UHI impact building" (He, 2019). On the community level, we may make full use of the environmental awareness among citizens and private sectors in climate adaptation. For instance, to encourage vertical planting in densely populated communities. Besides, we may use economic incentives to align citizens and private sectors' interests with UHI attenuation (Liu et al., 2020).

The recent actions of "One Map" for territorial spatial planning (CSC, 2019) and "Replace Multiple Plans with One Master Plan" in China further provide a valuable opportunity to effectively deliver the needs and requirements of UHI attenuation across multiple plans. It is also helpful for the supervision and assessment of the urban planning and design projects related to UHI attenuation.

5. Conclusion

China now stands at the crossroad of a future development alternative under considerable internal transition demand and intense international pressure. Among multiple efforts of transitional development, the mitigation and adaptation of local warming can significantly contribute to the sustainable development of Chinese cities. Hence, in this chapter, we summarize the policies and practices related to UHI attenuation in China and point out the existing challenges and future directions. To enhance the pursuit of more climate-friendly urban environments in the future, we further outline a nation—city—community policy skeleton. Overall, it is urgent for China to address (1) data availability, (2) regional differentiation of background climates, and (3) continuity and coherence across multiple administrative levels and various plans.

References

Beijing Meteorological Office (BMO), 2015. Technical Specifications for Climatic Feasibility Demonstration in Urban Master Plan (In Chinese). China Meteorological Administration. QX/T 242—2014. Available at: http://www.cma.gov.cn/root7/auto13139/201612/t20161213_350507.html.

Beijing Meteorological Office (BMO), 2019. Technical for Climatic Feasibility Demonstration in Master Planning (In Chinese). China Meteorological Administration. GB/T 37529-2019. Available at: http://zwgk.cma.gov.cn/zfxxgk/gknr/flfgbz/bz/202102/t20210210_2720358.html.

Chen, G., Li, X., Liu, X., Chen, Y., Liang, X., Leng, J., Xu, C., Liao, W., Qiu, Y., Wu, Q., Huang, K., 2020. Global projections of future urban land expansion under shared socioeconomic pathways. Nat. Commun. 11, 537. https://doi.org/10.1038/s41467-020-14386-x.

China Meteorological Administration (CMA), 2008. Regulation of Climate Feasibility Demonstration. Available at: http://www.cma.gov.cn/2011zwxx/2011zflfg/2011zbmgz/201110/t20111027_135194.html.

China Meteorological Administration (CMA), 2018. Specifications for Climatic Feasibility Demonstration-Urban Ventilation Corridor. Available at: https://max.book118.com/html/2018/1027/6222134130001224.shtm.

China State Council (CSC), 2007. China's National Climate Change Program (In Chinese). Available at: http://www.gov.cn/gzdt/2007-06/04/content_635590.htm.

China State Council (CSC), 2019. Guidelines on the Establishment of a Territorial Spatial Planning System and the Supervision of its Implementation (In Chinese). Available at: http://www.gov.cn/zhengce/2019-05/23/content_5394187.htm.

Estrada, F., Botzen, W.J.W., Tol, R.S.J., 2017. A global economic assessment of city policies to reduce climate change impacts. Nat. Clim. Change 7, 403—406. https://doi.org/10.1038/nclimate3301.

Fang, J., Yu, G., Liu, L., Hu, S., Chapin III, F.S., 2018. Climate change, human impacts, and carbon sequestration in China. Proc. Natl. Acad. Sci. U.S.A. 115, 4015—4020. www.pnas.org/cgi/doi/10.1073/pnas.1700304115.

Foley, J.A., Defries, R., Asner, G.P., Barford, C., Bonan, G., Carpenter, S.R., Stuart Chapin, F., Coe, M.T., Daily, G.C., Gibbs, H.K., Helkowski, J.H., Holloway, T., Howard, E.A., Kucharik, C.J., Monfreda, C., Patz, J.A., Colin Prentice, I., Ranmankutty, N., Snyder, P.K., 2005. Global consequences of land use. Science 309, 570—574. https://doi.org/10.1126/science.1111772.

Grimm, N.B., Faeth, S.H., Golubiewski, N.E., Redman, C.L., Wu, J., Bai, X., Briggs, J.M., 2008. Global change and the ecology of cities. Science 319, 756. https://doi.org/10.1126/science.1150195.

He, B.J., 2019. Towards the next generation of green building for urban heat island mitigation: zero UHI impact building. Sustain. Cities Soc. https://doi.org/10.1016/j.scs.2019.101647, 101647.

He, B., Wang, J., Liu, H., Ulpiani, G., 2021. Localized synergies between heat waves and urban heat islands: implications on human thermal comfort and urban heat management. Environ. Res. 193, 110584. https://doi.org/10.1016/j.envres.2020.110584.

Li, J., Song, C., Cao, L., Zhu, F., Meng, X., Wu, J., 2011. Impacts of landscape structure on surface urban heat islands: a case study of Shanghai, China. Remote Sens. Environ. 115, 3249−3263. https://doi.org/10.1016/j.rse.2011.07.008.

Li, Y., Schubert, S., Kropp, J.P., Rybski, D., 2020. On the influence of density and morphology on the Urban Heat Island intensity. Nat. Commun. 11, 2647. https://doi.org/10.1038/s41467-020-16461-9.

Liu, X., Mu, R., 2016. Public environmental concern in China: determinants and variations. Global Environ. Change 37, 116−127. https://doi.org/10.1016/j.gloenvcha.2016.01.008.

Liu, H., Zhan, Q., Yang, C., Wang, J., 2019. The multi-timescale temporal patterns and dynamics of land surface temperature using ensemble empirical mode decomposition. Sci. Total Environ. 652, 243−255. https://doi.org/10.1016/j.scitotenv.2018.10.252.

Liu, H., Huang, B., Yang, C., 2020. Assessing the coordination between economic growth and urban climate change in China from 2000 to 2015. Sci. Total Environ. 732, 139283. https://doi.org/10.1016/j.scitotenv.2020.139283.

Liu, H., Huang, B., Gao, S., Wang, J., Yang, C., Li, R., 2021a. Impacts of the evolving urban development on intra-urban surface thermal environment: evidence from 323 Chinese cities. Sci. Total Environ. 144810. https://doi.org/10.1016/j.scitotenv.2020.144810.

Liu, H., Huang, B., Zhan, Q., Gao, S., Li, R., Fan, Z., 2021b. The influence of urban form on surface urban heat island and its planning implications: evidence from 1288 urban clusters in China. Sustain. Cities Soc. 71, 102987. https://doi.org/10.1016/j.scs.2021.102987.

Manoli, G., Fatichi, S., Schläpfer, M., Yu, K., Crowther, T.W., Meili, N., Burlando, P., Katul, G.G., Bou-Zeid, E., 2019. Magnitude of urban heat islands largely explained by climate and population. Nature 573, 55−60. https://doi.org/10.1038/s41586-019-1512-9.

Martilli, A., Roth, M., Chow, W.T., Demuzere, M., Lipson, M., Krayenhoff, E.S., Sailor, D., Nazarian, N., Voogt, J., Wouters, H., Middel, A., Stewart, I.D., Bechtel, B., Christen, A., Hart, M.A., 2020. Summer Average Urban-Rural Surface Temperature Differences Do Not Indicate the Need for Urban Heat Reduction. https://doi.org/10.31219/osf.io/8gnbf.

Ministry of Housing and Urban-Rural Development (MOHURD), 2013. Design Standard for Thermal Environment of Urban Residential Areas, JGJ 286−2013 (In Chinese). Beijing. Available at: http://www.soujianzhu.cn/Norm/csgh38.htm.

National Development and Reform Commission (NDRC), 2013. National Strategy on Climate Change (In Chinese). Available at: http://www.gov.cn/gzdt/att/att/site1/20131209/001e3741a2cc140f6a8701.pdf.

National Development and Reform Commission (NDRC), 2014. National Plan on Climate Change 2014−2020 (In Chinese). Available at: http://www.scio.gov.cn/xwfbh/xwbfbh/wqfbh/35861/37265/xgzc37271/Document/1603660/1603660.htm.

Ng, E., Ren, C., 2017. China's adaptation to climate & urban climatic changes: a critical re-view. Urban Clim. 23, 352−372. https://doi.org/10.1016/j.uclim.2017.07.006.

Oke, T.R., Mills, G., Christen, A., Voogt, J.A., 2017. Urban Climates. Cambridge University Press, Cambridge, UK.

Patz, J.A., Campbell-Lendrum, D., Holloway, T., Foley, J.A., 2005. Impact of regional climate change on human health. Nature 438, 310−317. https://doi.org/10.1038/nature04188.

Ren, C., Yang, R., Cheng, C., Xing, P., Fang, X., Zhang, S., Wang, H., Shi, Y., Zhang, X., Kwork, Y.T., Ng, E., 2018. Creating breathing cities by adopting urban ventilation assessment and wind corridor plan-The implementation in Chinese cities. J. Wind Eng. Ind. Aerod. 182, 170−188. https://doi.org/10.1016/j.jweia.2018.09.023.

Santamouris, M., Cartalis, C., Synnefa, A., Kolokotsa, D., 2015. On the impact of urban heat island and global warming on the power demand and electricity consumption of buildings—a review. Energy Build. 98, 119—124. https://doi.org/10.1016/j.enbuild.2014.09.052, 2015.

Wang, W., Shu, J., 2020. Urban renewal can mitigate urban heat islands. Geophys. Res. Lett. 47, 6. https://doi.org/10.1029/2019GL085948.

Yang, L., Niyogi, D., Tewari, M., Aliaga, D., Chen, F., Tian, F., Ni, G., 2016. Contrasting impacts of urban forms on the future thermal environment: example of Beijing metropolitan area. Environ. Res. Lett. 11, 034018. https://doi.org/10.1088/1748-9326/11/3/034018.

Yao, R., Wang, L., Huang, X., Niu, Y., Liu, F., Wang, Q., 2017. Temporal trends of surface urban heat islands and associated determinants in major Chinese cities. Sci. Total Environ. 609, 742—754. https://doi.org/10.1016/j.scitotenv.2017.07.217.

Yao, R., Wang, L., Huang, X., Liu, Y., Niu, Z., Wang, S., Wang, L., 2021. Long-term trends of surface and canopy layer urban heat island intensity in 272 cities in the mainland of China. Sci. Total Environ. 772, 145607. https://doi.org/10.1016/j.scitotenv.2021.145607.

Ye, J.A., Xu, J., Yi, H., 2006. The fourth wave of urbanization in China. City Plan. Rev. 30, 13—18.

Zhang, C., Miao, C., Zhang, W., Chen, X., 2018. Spatiotemporal patterns of urban sprawl and its relationship with economic development in China during 1990—2010. Habitat Int. 79, 51—60. https://doi.org/10.1016/j.habitatint.2018.07.003.

Zhao, L., Lee, X., Smith, R.B., Oleson, K., 2014. Strong contributions of local background climate to urban heat islands. Nature 511, 216—219. https://doi.org/10.1038/nature13462.

Zhao, Q., Dickson, C., Thornton, J., Solis, P., Wentz, E.A., 2020. Articulating strategies to address heat resilience using spatial optimization and temporal analysis of utility assistance data of the Salvation Army Metro Phoenix. Appl. Geogr. 122, 102241. https://doi.org/10.1016/j.apgeog.2020.102241.

Zhou, D., Zhao, S., Liu, S., Zhang, L., Zhu, C., 2014. Surface urban heat island in China's 32major cities: spatial patterns and drivers. Remote Sens. Environ. 152, 51—61. https://doi.org/10.1016/j.rse.2014.05.017.

Zhou, D., Zhao, S., Zhang, L., Liu, S., 2016. Remotely sensed assessment of urbanization effects on vegetation phenology in China's 32 major cities. Remote Sens. Environ. 176, 272—281. https://doi.org/10.1016/j.rse.2016.02.010.

Zhou, D., Xiao, J., Bonafoni, S., Berger, C., Deilami, K., Zhou, Y., Frolking, S., Yao, R., Qiao, Z., Sobrino, J.A., 2019. Satellite remote sensing of surface urban heat islands: progress, challenges, and perspectives. Rem. Sens. 11, 48. https://doi.org/10.3390/Rs11010048.

Climatic control of outdoor spaces in the Universal Exposition 1992 (EXPO'92)

Servando Álvarez Domínguez, José Julio Guerra Macho and José Sánchez Ramos

Grupo Termotecnia, Escuela Técnica Superior de Ingeniería, Universidad de Sevilla, Camino de los Descubrimientos S/N, Seville, Spain

1. Side description

The Seville Universal Exposition took place between April 20th and October 12th, 1992. The 215 ha it was occupied are located on what is known as the Cartuja Island (Seville, Spain), a lowland surrounded by the two branches, which form the natural and artificial courses of the Guadalquivir River (see Fig. 8.1).

Five large avenues measuring 300×80 m make up the area reserved for the pavilions of the international participants. Perpendicular to these avenues there is a wide pedestrian way some 2 km in length, along which are strung the various theme pavilions. A 15 ha artificial lake, semicircular in shape, is bordered by the pavilions, which represent the different autonomous regions of Spain.

In all, the built-up area id 500,000 m^2. Scattered throughout 170 ha of open spaces in which restaurants, cafeterias, shops, bars, kiosks, and small show areas abounded. Over 350,000 trees and plants, 35 km of hedges, and 500,000 m^2 of parks and gardens alternate with avenues, promenades, and rest areas, forming in a certain sense one immense park. The attendance was of some 18 million visitors, who generated more than 40 million visits to the site.

Nowadays, the Cartuja Science and Technology Park (see Fig. 8.2) named STP Cartuja 93 is the first international example of the reuse of a world exhibition facility as a connection point between universities, science, and business. STP had an essential competitive advantage: there were 56 buildings inherited from the Universal Exposition and 35 new buildings within the STP. At present, it hosts 442 private companies, research, technology, and training entities.

2. Mitigation measure description

From the initial conception of the EXPO'92, it was intended that the open spaces were the component that gave unity to the site. The function of public space was therefore not limited to allowing the transition between the different pavilions, but they were spaces with their own personality that favored their use as places of leisure, with cafeterias and open-air restaurants, as well as squares where shows were held.

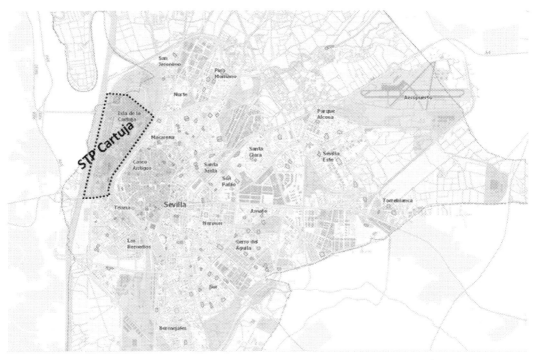

FIGURE 8.1

STP Cartuja (Science and Technology Park) in relation to the city center.

FIGURE 8.2

Recent aerial view of the STP Cartuja and part of the city in the background.

Among the last reasons that gave this prominence to the public space of the EXPO'92 is on the one hand the desire that this exhibition reflects the Mediterranean tradition in general and Sevillian in particular to live on the street and on the other the fact, not less important, that the number of visitors anticipated exceeded the capacity of the pavilions. Typically, half of the visitors were inside the pavilions and the other half outside.

The densely occupied public space was concentrated in the five large avenues that ordered the international pavilions, on the edge of the lake that ordered the national pavilions and in the Palenque.

The objective of the work of climate control of the open spaces in EXPO'92 was simply to allow visitors to stay in them and carry out the planned activities in a comfortable enough manner.

The central hours of the summer in Seville made the public space absolutely unbearable if the improving microclimate actions had not been implemented.

The interventions included a first level that sought to prevent the heat island effect in the enclosure and that was substantiated in two strategies:

- Eliminating anthropogenic heat by suppressing road traffic and preventing the air release of the condensation heat from the air-conditioning systems through the raw water ring.
- Include environmental heat sink heat constituted by water and vegetation in percentages far higher than conventional urban design in order to mitigate the overall warming of the outdoor spaces (see Table 8.1)

At a second level, the treatment of specific spaces within the public space was undertaken. The intensity of the treatment of each of them depended on the expected stay time of the visitors. The longer the stay, the greater the intensity of conditioning. In this second level, actions undertaken included confinement, solar control, surface cooling, and air cooling (Fig. 8.3).

Fig. 8.4 shows the condensation ring with a total length of more than 42 km. Cool water was taken from the upper branch of the river while the hot water was delivered to the lower branch. It provides the condensation water required to the air conditioning of 84 buildings.

Solar control was basically provided from the vegetation (trees and pergolas) due to its ideal properties, which allow achieving of low levels of solar transmissivity, while the radiation absorbed does not entail overheating since this is compensated by the plants' evapotranspiration.

Nevertheless, in order to ensure this good performance, the vegetation has to produce a continuous and uniform covering. The growth of the plants was assured by use of the so called "EXPO pergola," which incorporates plant containers situated in the shade structure itself, thus avoiding the need to have

Table 8.1 Fraction of land covered by vegetation o water.

Name	Percentage of surface covered by vegetation (%)	Percentage of surface covered by water ponds or fountains (%)
Avenue I	15	25
Avenue II	42	12
Avenue III	31	4
Avenue IV	19	5
Avenue V	35	4

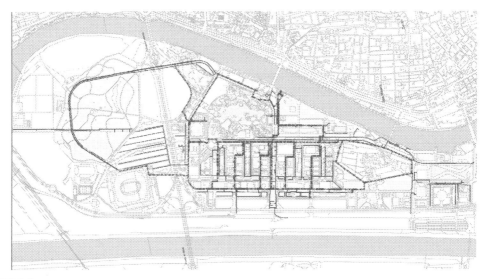

FIGURE 8.3

The condensation loop.

FIGURE 8.4

Vegetation pergolas while growing and aspect of one of them at the final destination.

the plants grow from ground level. In total, 50,000 m², in 6 × 6 and 12 × 12 m modules were developed for the open spaces and situated at different heights (see Fig. 8.4).

When shadow from vegetation was not suitable, two alternatives were the use of double coverings as in the case of the rail terminal or single PVC ones with controlled irrigation (see Fig. 8.5).

Cooling of vertical surfaces surrounding the occupied areas was guaranteed basically from water in the form of water walls or artificial cascades. By way of example, we would mention the cascade of over 400 m in length and 6 in height, which runs all the way along Avenue V (see Fig. 8.6).

FIGURE 8.5

Double PVC covering and single covering with heat dissipation on the top and surface cooling via irrigation.

FIGURE 8.6

Wall of water and cascade.

Micronizers are nozzles that create an artificial fog by injecting water at high pressure through minute orifices. The small droplets (volume median diameter around 20 μm) evaporate in contact with the surrounding hot air, which becomes cooler. As the cool air is heavier than the hot air, a continuous descending flow of cool air is obtained. It is worthwhile underlining the 12 cool towers, 30 m in height, in Avenue II, which contain wind catchers at their upper end and the so-called bioclimatic sphere in Avenue III (see Fig. 8.7).

3. Assessment method

The monitoring campaign took place from April to October 1992 to evaluate the impact of the mitigation measures on the microclimate of specific zones. The emphasis was paid on the five avenues and the Palenque (see Fig. 8.8).

Temperature and humidity sensors were installed as shown in Table 8.2:

FIGURE 8.7

A micronizer in a tree, cool tower, and the bioclimatic sphere.

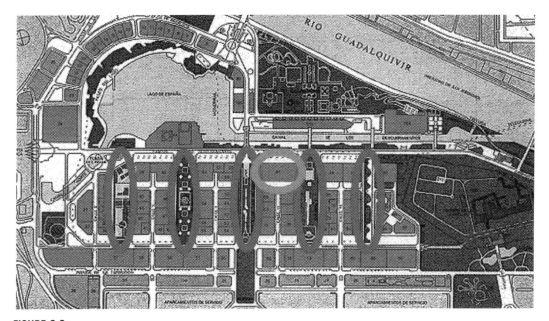

FIGURE 8.8

The avenues I—V from left to right (in white) and the Palenque (in green (gray in print)).

Table 8.2 List of sensors and localization.

Place	Air temperature (°C)	Relative humidity (%)	Surface temperature (°C)	Water temperature (°C)
Avenue 1	6	6	1	1
Avenue 2	2	2		
Avenue 3	7	7		
Avenue 4	3	3		
Avenue 5	3	3		
Palenque	20	20	2	10

Global and direct solar radiation on a horizontal surface, as well as wind velocity and direction data were collected from two meteorological stations (10 m height) placed in Avenue III and the Palenque, respectively.

However, the major indicator of the results achieved was a comfort assessment of the spaces in term of sweating rate (g/h). Sweating rate is calculated from a comfort model assuming one met of metabolic activity (ref) and 0.6 clo.

Without any treatment of the outdoor areas, during central hours of the Sevillian summer and in a sunny situation, a sweating of about 300 g/h was expected.

Three categories of spaces were identified:

- "Walkways" are used to refer to a space whose purpose is to serve as a thoroughfare for visitors; the main flow of people moving from one building to another will take place along such areas. These thoroughfares of varied architectural styles range from 3 to 8 m in width, and the length of stay in such areas was will not exceed 15 min. The conditioning intensity required for such areas was estimated to be a sweating rate of 90 g/h.
- The "Rest Zones" differ appreciably from the former. Their purpose is to offer places to rest, take light refreshment, watch a short informal show, etc. Accordingly, such areas had a maximum characteristic length ranging between 20 and 40 m, such that whatever the specific use of a given area, the visitor will engage in activities of a sedentary nature. The length of stay in such areas was less than 1 hour and the conditioning intensity required for them was estimated to be a sweating rate of 60 g/h.
- The third category was the space for shows of the Palenque with capacity for 1500 spectators. Typically, the length of stay in such space ranged between 1 and 2 h and the conditioning intensity required for it was estimated to be a sweating rate of 30 g/h.

4. Results

4.1 Description

An extensive monitoring campaign was performed during the entire summer period from April to October. The results can be divided in three groups:

- Those corresponding to the so-called representative days, which are a sequence of three actual days that represent the average conditions during the summer period: from June to September.

- Those corresponding to the so-called extreme days, which are a sequence of three actual days that represent the hottest climatic conditions recorded in the meteorological station during the summer period.
- Those representing the comfort assessment during the typical daily hot spell (from 3 to 7 p.m. local time), integrated during the summer period.

4.2 Climatically controlled zones in avenues

With some exceptions, in most walkways and rest zones of the avenues, the cooling strategy was based on evaporative cooling with micronizers planed in trees or under pergolas. The air temperature achieved was very dependent not only on the evaporative cooling potential but rather on the confinement degree of the space.

We will concentrate on three areas with very different degree of confinement. The degree of confinement of the space can be obtained as the average number of air changes per hour (ACH $[h^{-1}]$) of nonclimatically controlled outdoor air entering the zone during the daily hot spell. Figs. 8.9−8.11 show respectively:

- A highly confined rest zone in Avenue I (ZELO) used as an informal restaurant. The average ACH obtained was of 30 h^{-1}
- A moderately confined rest zone in Avenue III (ZEC2). The average ACH obtained was of 50 h^{-1}
- A poorly confined walkway between Avenue II and Avenue III (ZPLS). The average ACH obtained was of 200 h^{-1}

SO, comfort assessment of the three spaces can be seen in Figs. 8.9−8.11 (right). In this figure, dots represent sweating rate values for every combination of temperature and the relative humidity of the space (assuming average values for solar radiation and air velocity). The sweating rate is shown in relation with three lines of equal value corresponding to 90 g/h, 60 g/h and 30 g/h, respectively.

It can be seen how in the three zones, the comfort level achieved is very close to the expectations: around 60 g/h in ZELO, between 60 and 90 in ZEC2 and around 90 g/h in ZPLS. As the three areas as the same solar control strategy (vegetation in pergolas) and the density of micronizers is quite the same in the three areas, the difference in comfort is due to the confinement degree.

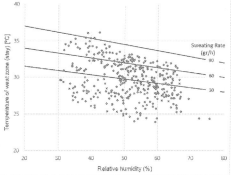

FIGURE 8.9

View of ZELO and comfort assessment (from June to September from 3 to 7 p.m.).

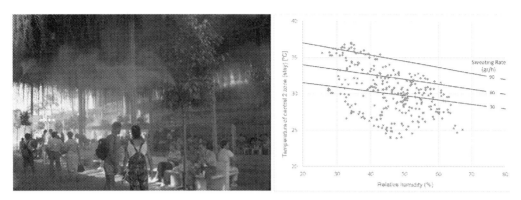

FIGURE 8.10

View of ZEC2 and comfort assessment (from June to September from 3 to 7 p.m.).

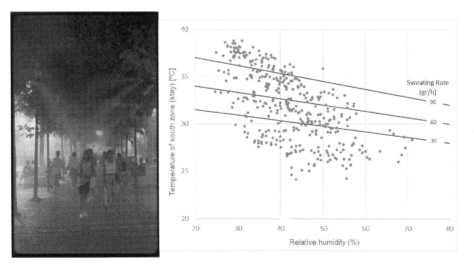

FIGURE 8.11

View of ZPLS and comfort assessment (from June to September from 3 to 7 p.m.).

4.3 Central space for shows at the Palenque

The Palenque had a surface of 8000 m^2 and was formed by two squares without solution of continuity and included a zone of shows surrounded in three of its sides by a grandstand for 1500 people seated (see Fig. 8.12).

Apart from solar control with white PVC covering with irrigation, the central space of the Palenque included cooling of the air based on four successive strategies (see Fig. 8.13):

FIGURE 8.12

View of the Palenque while it was being built and the central space for shows.

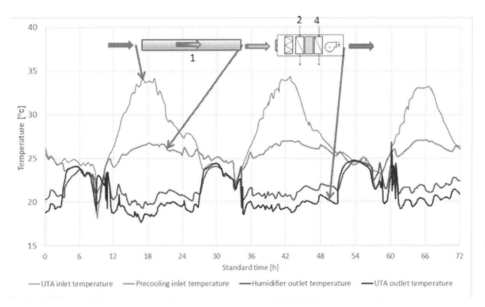

FIGURE 8.13

Air temperature at different points of the cooling strategy during the representative days.

- Ground heat exchangers 40 m long (1),
- Cooling coil (2) that used water stored in a pond (200 m³) surrounding the stage, which was cooled during the night with 2500 spray nozzles with a drop diameter of 1 mm.
- Direct evaporative cooling (3) when the air crossed wet cellulose pads.
- Cooling coil that used water from a conventional chiller (4).

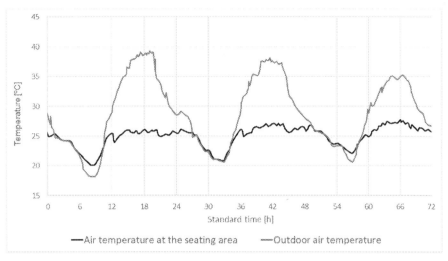

FIGURE 8.14

Outdoor air temperature and air temperature at the seating area (average of four sensors).

- It can be seen that the supply air temperature at the central space is around 20°C and how the majority of the air temperature drop is due to the ground heat exchanger and the cool water from the pond.

The resulting air temperature can be seen in Fig. 8.14 for the extreme days. It can be seen that the temperature ranges between 25 and 30°C.

The comfort assessment of the space can be seen in Fig. 8.15 with a comfort level around 10 g/h, which is equivalent to what can be expected in indoor comfort situations.

This very low level can be explained by the significant confinement of the space (sunken in relation to the adjacent spaces) with a14 h^{-1} and by the very low surface temperature of the irrigated covering (around 25°C).

The contribution of each cooling strategy to the total air cooling during the whole exhibition period is as follows:

- Ground heat exchangers: 22%
- Cooling coil that used water from the pond: 28%
- Direct evaporative cooling: 38%
- Conventional chiller: 12%.

It can be seen how 88% of the cooling required is provided by natural cooling techniques. In terms of energy split of the cooling produced.

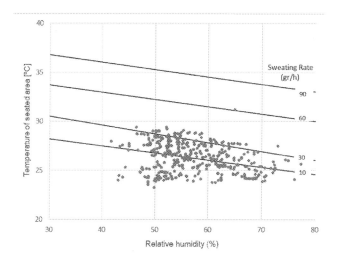

FIGURE 8.15

Comfort assessment of the seated area of central space of the Palenque.

5. Conclusions

From a conceptual and methodological point of view, the research has revealed that:

- There are considerable differences between the conventional conditioning of buildings and the treatment of outdoor spaces, and it should be underlined that there has to be a strong link in the latter case between Architecture and Engineering from the beginning of the design in order to achieve the objectives pursued.
- The use of a specific technique to condition an outdoor space should be adopted with the utmost care, in view of the fact that an apparently adequate concept may have a negligible effect if insufficient attention is paid to the design details.
- The actual capacity of each subsystem should always be evaluated in terms of the ultimate objective (to obtain a given level of comfort) and in comparison with other alternative subsystems.
- To determine in a consistent manner, the appropriateness of each specific measure in each specific situation, it is necessary to hove prior knowledge based on the modeling/experimentation/simulation process.

From the point of view of the experimental results, we have been able to confirm that it is possible to temper and soften the conditions of outdoor spaces by means of the use of soft and natural technologies at low cost. At the same time, we have established that such techniques are compatible with the aesthetic and functional aspects required by architecture and urban planning.

Further reading

Álvarez, S., Cejudo, J., Guerra, J., Molina, J., Rodríguez, E., Velázquez, R., 1992. In: Ciemat (Ed.), Control Climático en Espacios Abiertos: Proyecto EXPO 92 (Spain).

Guerra, J., Cejudo, J., Molina, J., Álvarez, S., Velázquez, R., 1994. In: Ciemat (Ed.), Control Climático en Espacios Abiertos: Evaluación del Proyecto EXPO 92 (Spain).

Velázquez, R., Álvarez, S., Guerra, J., 1991. Control Climático en Espacios Abiertos. In: Sociedad Estatal para la Exposición Universal Sevilla 92, S.A, Spain.

Open space and built form metrics: identification and implementation of strategies to mitigate UHI in tropical climates

Lilly Rose Amirtham and Shanmuga Priya Gnanasekaran

Department of Architecture, School of Planning and Architecture, Vijayawada, India

1. Introduction

Addressing issues related to Urban Heat Island (UHI) in cities is essential as the air temperature and humidity ranges are generally high in tropical regions causing thermal discomfort, and the UHI effect would be an additional burden increasing the discomfort levels significantly. Factors such as urban morphology, population density, land use, open space characteristics, street geometry, sky view factor (SVF), percentage of vegetation cover and impervious layers, traffic densities etc., influence the UHI in a built environment. Therefore, the relationship between these factors and UHI is explored by several researchers at varying scales (Harlan et al., 2006; Kruger et al., 2011; Stewart and Oke. 2012; Yang et al., 2013; Chen et al., 2014; Mathew et al., 2016; Cao et al., 2021; Rajan and Amirtham. 2021) Based on the knowledge gained, it is also crucial to develop tools and strategies for implementation in cities. Development Regulations (DRs) can be instrumental in mitigating the UHI as they dictate the built form in cities.

In India, urban form and built geometry in cities are governed by the DR, which are reviewed and modified regularly in view of accommodating higher densities in urban areas. Increased densities have created variation in thermal anomalies impacting UHI and affecting the outdoor thermal comfort, thereby influencing the outdoor activities and pedestrian movement in cities. However, open space and built form configuration metrics in the DR are considered only in terms of increased densities while ignoring their impacts on UHI and outdoor thermal comfort. Therefore, it is imperative to identify the most effective urban built characteristics and implement them through DR. This chapter shows the way toward cohesive understanding and optimization of open space and built form parameters and their implementation to mitigate UHI through analysis of neighborhoods in two tropical Indian cities.

The chapter first surveys various parameters related to open space and built form such as porosity, percentage of impervious surface area, aspect ratio of streets, edge density, patch density, Normalized Difference Vegetation Index (NDVI), plot coverage, Normalized Difference Built-up Index (NDBI) etc., and their relationship to UHI. Secondly, landscape metrics and UHI impacts are explored in two residential neighborhoods in Vijayawada, India, through simulations. Further, the impact of DR on

UHI is simulated and analyzed in a mixed residential neighborhood in Chennai, India. Analysis of various combinations of parameters in both cities was carried out using Envi-Met. Based on the analysis, the chapter concludes with recommendations on effective strategies combining open space and built form metrics at neighborhood level for implementation through DR.

2. Open space and built form metrics

Three scales of UHI studies are generally carried out, namely Atmospheric or Boundary layer UHI, Canyon Layer UHI, and Surface UHI. Open space studies mainly focus on Surface UHI integrating Land Surface Temperature (LST) and Landscape Metrics both Composition and Configuration metrics. Built form parameters such as density, orientation, building heights, aspect ratio (street geometry), vegetation, percentage of green cover, SVF, floor space index, plot coverage etc., at neighborhood level, are studied to understand Canyon Layer UHI. Open space and Built form metrics are defined by the DRs in urban areas. They can be used as an effective tool in defining the urban morphology, which can enhance the comfort conditions at neighborhood level. The studies pertaining to Open space and Built form parameters and UHI are reviewed below.

2.1 Open space metrics

Relationship between urban open spaces and UHI has been analyzed at various scales with LST and open space characteristics using multiple landscape metrics in the UHI literature. Positive correlation between LST and air temperature has been established (Cao et al., 2021; Good et al., 2017). The term "landscape metrics" commonly refers to numerical indices developed to quantify landscape patterns (McGarigal, 2015), and they effectively depict the characteristics of urban open spaces such as proportion, shape, spatial arrangement etc. FRAGSTAT software and the landscape metrics developed by McGarigal (2015) are commonly used landscape metrics, and they are defined at four levels, namely Cell, Patch, Class, and Landscape, and in two categories, i.e., Composition (patch types without reference to spatial attributes) and Configuration (spatial arrangement and distribution of patch types).

Studies that explore the relationship between the urban open spaces and UHI frequently employ landscape metrics such as Percentage of Landscape (PLAND), Total Edge (TE), Edge Density (ED), Patch Density (PD), Landscape Shape Index (LSI), Number of Patches (NP), Aggregation Index (AI), and Normalized Difference Vegetation Index e (NDVI), etc., and they have established the relationship between spatial composition and configuration of open spaces and UHI. A combination of one composition metric with a maximum of four configuration metrics for LST prediction is suggested by Chen et al. (2014).

More connected and less fragmented large patches of open spaces with simple shape are found to be effective in reducing the LST (Masoudi and Tan, 2019). Chen et al. (2014) attempted to identify the most effective Landscape metrics for LST studies and concluded that composition metric such as PLAND (e.g., percentage of impervious surface in a landscape) and a configuration metric such as LSI or Gyrate MN (Mean Gyration Index) significantly explain LST variations. The influence of patch-level metrics such as patch area (PA), patch perimeter (PERIM), perimeter–area ratio (PARA), and shape index (SHAPE) on UHI is found to be varied. In the study carried out by Yang et al. (2017), green space patch (PA) of area between 1.44 and 5.76 ha is effective in lowering the LST and other patch-level metrics PERIM, PARA, and SHAPE did not significantly influence LST. However, in large open spaces (PA> 15.2 ha), the patch-level metrics influenced LST. While establishing a positive correlation between LST and PD, Terfa et al. (2020) also highlighted the change in the intensity of correlation between LST and patch-level metrics, such as PD, ED, and Mean Nearest-Neighbor Distance (MNN), with the change in analysis scale. More recent analysis by Song et al. (2020) identified PLAND and largest patch index (LPI) as the two most significant metrics influencing UHI supporting the earlier studies.

While the significance of composition metrics such as PLAND on UHI is established in most of the studies, they are inconclusive about the configuration metrics at different spatial scales (Masoudi and Tan, 2019). Therefore, the growing body of literature on UHI will benefit from further studies on UHI and urban open spaces under varied spatial–temporal scales.

2.2 Built form parameters

Impact of building development regulations on canyon layer UHIs has been studied by various researchers (Harlan et al., 2006; Emmanuel and Fernando, 2007; Berardi and Wang, 2016; Jin et al., 2018; He, 2019; Rajan and Amirtham, 2021) Development policies framed with a specific focus on increasing the built form densities affect the canyon layer UHI significantly. High-density settlements in the neighborhood with sparse vegetation and absence of open space elevate the air temperatures by 1–6°C and increase the heat stress index (Harlan et al., 2006). In addition to higher built-up density, the intensity of UHI also increases with heavy traffic densities and reduces with dense vegetation (Devadas and Rose, 2009). Kotharkar and Surawar (2016) identified that the densely populated zones along with dense built-up urban areas in Nagpur, India, increased the intensity of night time canopy layer UHI. The existence of a strong correlation between urban built form and UHI intensity highlights the importance of framing appropriate built form guidelines to attain comfortable and sustainable urban environments (Amirtham, 2016). The proposed high-rise built form of Church-Yonge corridor reduced the daytime air temperatures and the average Mean Radiant Temperature (MRT) by more than 1°C due to mutual shading of buildings (Berardi and Wang, 2016). Appropriate planning of land use and urban form in Wuhan city reduced the intensity of UHI (Yin et al., 2018). The tall buildings in high-density urban areas reduced the MRT significantly (up to 15°C) when compared to air temperatures, due to increased shading thereby improving the thermal comfort (Heris et al., 2020).

The aspect ratio and the SVF in the street canyons define the urban geometry of a neighborhood, which in turn affects the comfort conditions outdoors. Kruger et al. (2011) found that canyons with higher SVF (Curitiba, Brazil) experienced greater discomfort due to the direct exposure to solar radiation. Wind speed modified by the urban morphology also influences the thermal sensation and the MRT values significantly resulting in lesser correlation between MRT and SVF. Surfaces with high albedo in the street canyons lowered the daytime air temperatures in Colombo and Phoenix (Emmanuel and Fernando, 2007). An increase of 26.94% of total built-up area in Noida (India) between 2000 and 2013 modified the albedo and NDBI, which in turn revealed a positive correlation with the UHI intensity and is attributed to the substantial increase in the impervious cover (Kikon et al., 2016). The increase in the percentage of impervious surface area (ISA) in the city core (Chandigarh, India) resulted in higher land surface temperatures with an average intensity varying from 3.84 to 6.16 K (Mathew et al., 2016). The core plot ratio can also act as a scientific measure to mitigate UHI through planning regulations (Huang et al., 2017). He (2019) proposed the Green Building–based UHI

Mitigation techniques through the analysis of various building components (site orientation, built form, building envelope, building materials, etc.) to arrive at Zero UHI impact buildings.

Orientation of the street geometry with regard to the wind speed and wind direction resulted in pollution-free comfortable city atmosphere (Deosthali, 2000). SVF, tree view factor (TVF), and green plot ratio (GPR), which represented the degree of enclosure in an urban neighborhood were found to have a significant correlation with pedestrian-level wind velocity ratio (WVR). The WVR increased up to 7%−8% with an increase of 10% SVF (Yang et al., 2013). Linear built forms in Bhubaneswar enhanced the wind movement by up to 1.5 m/s at pedestrian level in warm humid climate. Increased plot coverage and staggered built forms in the hot and dry climate of Jaipur created wind shadow regions and provided protection from dust storms (Dash and Chakraborty, 2018). The appropriate orientation of the layout design of multistoried apartments improved the outdoor natural ventilation (Dash and Chakraborty, 2020) and highlights the need for climate-centric development regulations.

Local climate zone (LCZ) classification is the representation of surface characteristics of various built parameters in urban areas in the UHI study, classified by Stewart and Oke (2012), and it is possible to understand the contribution of various combinations of built parameters in mitigating the UHI. In Kochi (India), the maximum UHI intensity was recorded in the compact mid-rise zones (LCZ 2) and intense cooling in open sparsely built zones (LCZ 9). Two parameters, namely Zone Boundary Distance (ZBD) and Nearest Adjacent Zone (NAZ), were proposed by Thomas et al. (2014) to comprehend the intrazone variation in the UHI intensity within the same LCZ classification with different coverage and varying adjacent zones. Perera and Emmanuel (2018) explored the LCZ-based approach toward climate-sensitive planning in Colombo, Sri Lanka, and identified the importance of customization of LCZ subclassifications in order to map the context-specific characteristics of a region and the corresponding microclimate modifications. Kotharkar and Bagade (2018) highlighted the need for assessing the inter-LCZ temperature variations in identifying the critical LCZs for suggesting UHI mitigation measures in the city of Nagpur. Kotharkar et al. (2020) examined the UHI mitigation strategies in critical LCZs in Nagpur, India, and identified the UHI mitigating effect of increased green area ratio in LCZ 9 and LCZ 3F(subclassification of compact low-rise with bare soil and sand) and the reduction of air temperature in LCZ 3 classifications through the implementation of cool roofs. Also, greening 100% of roofs and walls was found to be effective in mitigating the UHI in the open mid-rise (LCZ5) and compact low-rise (LCZ3) classifications in the English Bazaar Town at West Bengal (India), and greening 50% of roofs and walls with vegetation at suitable areas was effective in open low-rise classifications (Ziaul and Pal, 2020). As the DRs are context-specific, it is imperative to study the region-specific LCZ subclassification and its impact on UHI to understand the effect of various configurations of built form parameters on microclimate.

3. Open space metrics and UHI at Vijayawada

To analyze the varied configurations of open spaces in the built environment, two existing planned neighborhoods in the city of Vijayawada were selected. Vijayawada is located between 16°50′ N latitude and 80°64′ E longitude and is one of the largest cities in the state of Andhra Pradesh. The criteria for selecting the sites were planned development of the neighborhood, presence of open spaces such as parks or playgrounds, and more than 80% of occupancy of the plots to ensure that no large open pockets are left due to unbuilt land in the neighborhood.

The selected neighborhoods had grid-iron layout with varying numbers of open spaces, sizes, and distribution patterns. The selected neighborhoods have FSI between 0.50 and 0.56. The ground coverage varies from 38% to 40.7%, and the percentage of open space from 7.5 to 10. The built form and open space characteristics of the selected neighborhoods are listed in Table 9.1. Porosity of the open spaces is 0% in almost all the cases. It can be observed that all the selected neighborhoods have similar characteristics enabling a comparative study.

The effect of variation in built form and open space parameters was analyzed by varying the following five parameters and combination of parameters: Porosity; High LAD Trees, Porosity with High LAD Trees; Mean Patch Size; Distribution (NNR). First, variation and simulation were created by increasing the porosity of the open spaces. Porosity around open space is determined by the streets opening on to the open space, setbacks between the buildings, and empty plots surrounding the open spaces. In this study, porosity is determined by the ratio of total width of streets opening toward the open space to the perimeter of the open space. Porosity of the open spaces was increased by changing the orientation of the streets so that they lead to the open space. This change in the layout has increased the porosity by 5%–8% in the chosen neighborhoods. In the second variation, high leaf area density trees were added along the perimeter of the open spaces to increase the cooling effect of the open space through transpiration and shade. The third variation combines the first and second variations to increase the porosity of the open spaces with vegetation. The fourth variation analyzed the effect of a single large open space in LBS Nagar compared to the multiple smaller open space modifying the Mean Patch Size (MPS) metrics. The final variation analyzed the distribution of the open spaces in RRpet by increasing the distance between the open spaces (NNR) and changing the orientation of the open space without changing the dimension and area of the open spaces. Envi-met Simulation was carried out for a summer day (March 21, 2019) at 1:00 p.m. and 11:00 p.m. to understand the daytime and nighttime UHI. The variations in the layout and the simulation results for both the selected cases

Table 9.1 Built form and open space parameters of the selected neighborhoods.

	Parameters	**LbS Nagar**	**RR Pet (Rajarajeswari Pet)**
Built parameters	Area	62000 sq.m	44000 sq.m
	FSI	0.55	0.50
	Ground coverage	39.2%	40.7%
	Open space percentage	10.0%	8.2%
	Roads percentage	30.4%	34.3%
	Max. height of buildings	9 m	6 m
	Porosity around open space	0%	6%
Open space parameters	Patch density	4/62,000	2/44,000
	Edge density	0.12	0.10
	Mean patch size	1524 sq.m	1600 sq.m
	Nearest neighbor distance	42.0 m	12.0 m

are shown in Tables 9.2 and 9.3. For each case of simulation, average air temperature and % of area under different ranges of air temperatures were determined and tabulated in Tables 9.4 and 9.5.

In the base case, the maximum percentage of the plot was under the temperature range of 37.5—37.9°C. In the case of RR pet, as much as 50% of the area was under 37.90°C. In the third (Green) variation, a shift to the lower temperature was observed in both the cases. Particularly, 27.5% of LbS Nagar plot has shifted to lower temperature with a variation of 0.4°C. Porous variations did not show considerable change in air temperature. However, porous green variation showed an appreciable shift in the percentage of plot area to the lower-temperature categories in both cases with a reduction in air temperature by 0.4—0.54°C. Consolidated and scatter cases do not show reduction in temperature.

In the nighttime, Max percentage of the plot was under temp range of 32.0—32.3°C in the base cases. The green variation indicated a shift in the percentage of plot to the lower-temperature categories in both cases. Particularly, 22.0% of LBS Nagar plot has shifted to lower temperature with a difference of 0.2°C. In the porous green variation, 23% plot area has shifted to the lower temperature. Porous green variation was found to be the best case among all variations with a temperature reduction of 0.4°C in LBS Nagar and 0.5°C in RR pet.

In the above simulations, the landscape metrics, such as PD, ED, MPS, and NNR distance have been modified in two variations, namely consolidated LBS Nagar and scattered RR pet. In the consolidated LBS case, MPS has increased and all the other three metrics have decreased. This has not reduced the average temperature significantly from the base case. This could be due to lower values of PD, ED, and NNR distance. In the scattered RR pet case, ED and NNR distance have been increased keeping the other two metrics constant. This has resulted in % of plot areas shifting to lower temperature. This may be attributed to the ED and NNR distance as suggested in the literature. The study demonstrated that porous green variation with closely distributed scattered open spaces was the most effective variation in reducing the air temperature. during daytime.

4. Development regulations and UHI at Chennai

Improving the outdoor thermal comfort through appropriate development regulation measures is demonstrated through comparative analysis of 2013 and 2019 DR in the city of Chennai, India. Chennai is located between 12°50′—13°15′ N latitude and 80°0′—80°20′ E longitude and experiences a monsoon dry summer climate denoted as "As" according to Koppen's classification. Chennai's first Master plan 2001 that regulated its urban growth was approved in 1976. The "Second Master plan for Chennai Metropolitan Area 2026" approved in 2008 was subsequently revised with amendments in 2013 (CMDA, 2013). The present skyline and the growth of Chennai city are the result of the 2013 revision. In 2019, the regulations were further revised as "Tamil Nadu Combined Development and Building Rules, 2019" (TNCDBR, 2019), with an aim to use the available urban land efficiently by increasing the building density (Government of Tamil Nadu, 2019). The 2019 regulations vary in terms of Floor Space Index, plot coverage, and building heights. The variations in key parameters between 2013 and 2019 regulations are shown in Table 9.6.

In Chennai, Thyagaraya Nagar—a mixed residential neighborhood, was selected for the analysis of DR variations and its impact on UHI. Thyagaraya Nagar neighborhood has retail shopping activities on all its primary access roads and residential neighborhoods on the interior feeder roads. It was originally planned as a residential neighborhood and has transformed into one of the busiest shopping districts of

Table 9.2 LBS Nagar: layout variations and simulation results.

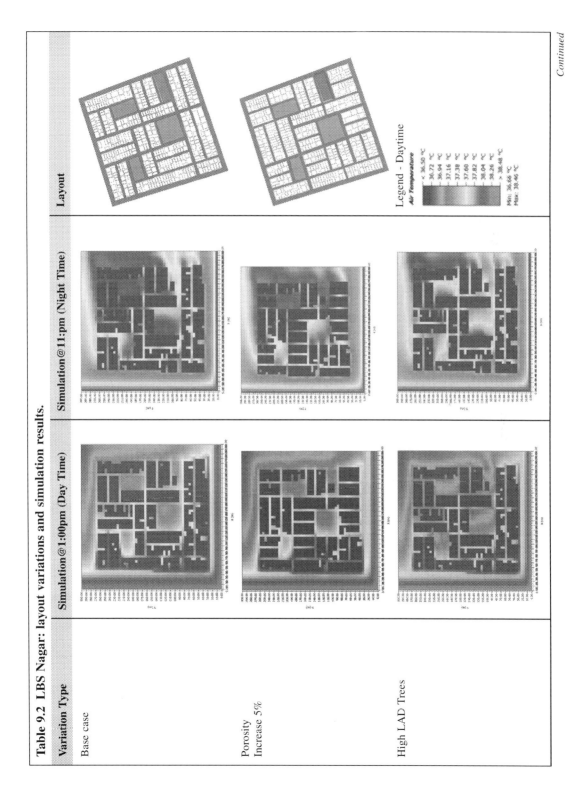

Continued

Table 9.2 LBS Nagar: layout variations and simulation results.—cont'd

Variation Type	Simulation@1:00pm (Day Time)	Simulation@11:pm (Night Time)	Layout
Porous + High LAD Trees			Legend - Night Time Air Temperature < 31.00 °C 31.18 °C 31.36 °C 31.54 °C 31.72 °C 31.90 °C 32.08 °C 32.26 °C 32.44 °C > 32.62 °C Min: 31.40 °C Max: 32.35 °C
Consolidated- Mean Patch Size increase			

Table 9.3 RR Pet: layout variations and simulation results.

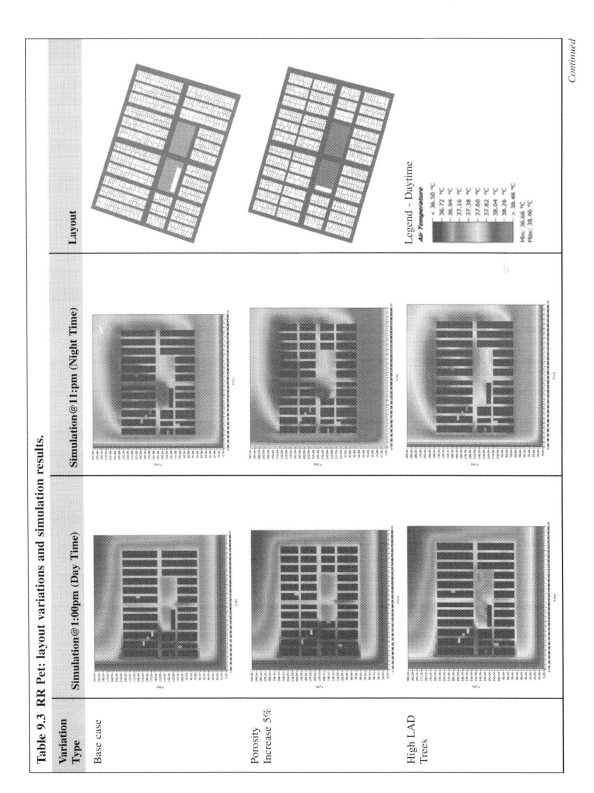

Variation Type	Simulation@1:00pm (Day Time)	Simulation@11:pm (Night Time)	Layout
Base case			
Porosity Increase 5%			
High LAD Trees			

Legend - Daytime
Air Temperature

< 36.50 °C
36.72 °C
36.94 °C
37.16 °C
37.38 °C
37.60 °C
37.82 °C
38.04 °C
38.26 °C
> 38.48 °C

Min: 36.66 °C
Max: 38.46 °C

Continued

Table 9.3 RR Pet: layout variations and simulation results.—cont'd

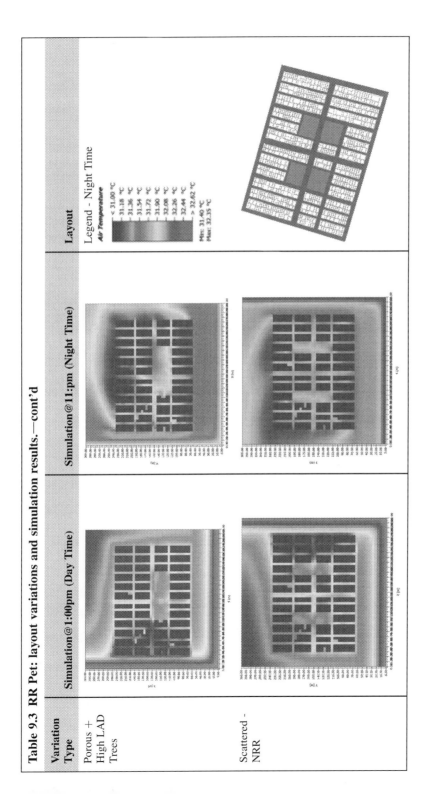

Variation Type	Simulation @ 1:00pm (Day Time)	Simulation @ 11:pm (Night Time)	Layout
Porous + High LAD Trees			Legend - Night Time
Scattered - NRR			

Table 9.4 Percentage of area under different ranges of air temperatures—daytime.

Air temp	LBS Nagar					Air temp	RR Pet				
	Base case	Green case	Porous case	Porous green case	Consolidated		Base case	Green case	Porous case	Porous green case	Scattered
<36.7	0.0	0.0	0.0	0.0	0.0	<36.7	0.0	0.0	0.0	0.0	0.0
36.83	0.0	9.0	0.0	13.5	9.0	36.83	0.0	2.0	0.0	0.0	1.0
37.05	9.5	27.5	5.5	24.0	14.5	37.05	1.5	13.0	2.0	7.0	9.0
37.27	24.0	25.0	21.0	20.0	21.0	37.27	10.0	14.5	13.0	18.5	19.5
37.49	27.5	10.0	31.0	20.0	13.5	37.49	17.5	21.0	25.5	24.0	22.5
37.71	21.5	15.0	24.0	12.5	12.5	37.71	50.5	30.0	32.5	30.0	34.0
37.93	14.0	9.0	17.0	8.5	9.5	37.93	11.0	13.0	17.5	11.5	11.0
38.04	3.5	4.5	1.5	1.5	20.0	38.04	7.5	6.5	8.5	8.5	3.0
38.26	0.0	0.0	0.0	0.0	0.0	38.26	0.0	0.0	0.0	0.5	0.0
>38.48	0.0	0.0	0.0	0.0	0.0	>38.48	0.0	0.0	0.0	0.0	0.0
Avg. air temp (°C)	37.62	37.15	37.54	37.08	37.5	Avg. air temp (°C)	37.82	37.55	37.69	37.42	37.51

Table 9.5 Percentage of area under different ranges of air temperatures—nighttime.

Air temp (°C)	LBS Nagar:					Air temp (°C)	RR Pet:				
	Base case	Green case	Porous case	Porous green case	Consolidated		Base case	Green case	Porous case	Porous green case	Scattered
<31.8	0.0	0.0	0.0	0.0	0.0	<31.8	0.0	0.0	0.0	0.0	0.0
31.27	0.0	0.0	0.0	0.0	0.0	31.27	0.0	0.0	0.0	0.0	0.0
31.45	4.5	8.0	1.5	4.5	3.5	31.45	1.5	0.0	0.0	1.5	1.0
31.63	3.5	11.5	2.0	9.5	17.0	31.63	1.5	19.0	8.5	17.0	12.0
31.81	10.0	21.0	11.0	26.5	21.0	31.81	20.5	41.0	14.5	34.0	24.0
32	38.0	40.5	39.0	44.0	35.5	32	37.5	30.5	44.0	32.5	62.0
32.17	30.5	19.0	37.5	15.5	18.0	32.17	35.5	9.5	29.0	14.5	1.0
32.35	13.5	0.0	9.0	0.0	5.0	32.35	3.5	0.0	4.0	0.0	0.0
32.53	0.0	0.0	0.0	0.0	0.0	32.53	0.0	0.0	0.0.	0.0	0.0
>32.62	0.0	0.0	0.0	0.0	0.0	>32.62	0.0	0.0	0.0.	00	0.0
Avg. air temp (°C)	32.21	31.92	32.04	31.62	31.82	Avg. air temp (°C)	32.18	31.81	32.0	31.68	31.88

Table 9.6 Key parameters in the development regulations with amendments specified by CMDA incorporated up to 2013 and Tamil Nadu Combined Development and Building Rules, 2019.

Category of buildings	Development regulations with amendments by CMDA up to 2013			Tamil Nadu Combined Development and Building Rules, 2019	
	Ordinary buildings	Special buildings	Multistoried buildings	Non-high-rise buildings	High-rise buildings
Road width	4.8−7.2 m	9.0−10.0 m	12.0 m and above	3.0 m and above	12.0−18.0 m
Floor space index (FSI)	1.5	1.5 for residential 2.0 for commercial	1.5−2.5 Premium FSI of an additional 0.5 to 1.0 depending on the width of road and premium fee.	2	2.0−3.5 Premium FSI of additional 0.6 to 1.75 depending on the width of road and premium fee
Plot coverage	75%	Not specified	30%−50%	Not specified	50%
Maximum height	9.0 m	15.25 m	Above 15.25−60.0 m. The 60.0 m height is for 18.0 m abutting road width.	12.0−18.3 m	30.0 m and above
Number of floors	G+1 or Stilt+2	G+3 or Stilt+4	Not specified	Not specified	Not specified
Front	1.5−6.0 m	1.5−6.0 m	7.0 m all around	1.5−6.0 m	7.0 m all around
Side	1.0 m on one side − 1.5 m on both sides	3.5−4.0 m		1.0 m on one side − 3.0 m on both sides	
Rear	1.5 m	1.5−4.0 m		1.5 m	
NOTE	The front setback value is governed by the abutting road width. The side setback value is governed by the plot width and height of the building. Rear setback value is governed by the depth of the plot.			The front setback value is governed by the abutting road width. The side and rear setback value are governed by the height of the building. The 18.3 m height limit is for 9.0 m and above abutting road width. For every 6.0 m increase in height above 30.0 m and part there off a 1.0 m additional setback should be added.	

Chennai. The shopping streets during festive seasons are pedestrianized for crowd management, which highlights the need to enhance the outdoor thermal comfort while providing quality urban spaces.

With the changes in the 2019 development regulations, the low-rise mixed residential neighborhood is gradually transforming into a mid-rise high-density neighborhood. Two locations A and B in the neighborhood (Fig. 9.1) with LCZ classifications (Stewart and Oke, 2012) as LCZ3 (compact low-rise) and LCZ6 (open low-rise) respectively were analyzed. The urban built form of the two locations A and B was analyzed for three different variations (Case-I to Case-III) based on 2013 and 2019 development regulations (Table 9.7). In Case-I, the existing built form, which is the resultant of the DRs with amendments incorporated up to 2013, was analyzed. In Case-II, the proposed built form as

STUDY AREA   COMMERCIAL ZONE   URBAN PARK   COMMERCIAL ROAD

FIGURE 9.1

The study area boundary and the measurement locations A and B.

Table 9.7 Study area characteristics and LCZ classification.

	Sky view factor	Aspect ratio	Building surface fraction	Impervious surface fraction	Pervious surface fraction	Height of roughness elements	LCZ classification
Case I							
LOCATION A	0.45	1	40.52	50.56	8.92	12.21	LCZ 3 Compact low-rise
LOCATION B	0.69	0.36	21.28	63.96	14.76	10.41	LCZ 6 Open low-rise
Case II							
LOCATION A	0.32	2	37.32	53.76	8.92	18.5	LCZ 2 Compact mid-rise
	0.444	0.65	17.16	68.08	14.76	19	LCZ 5 Open mid-rise

Continued

Table 9.7 Study area characteristics and LCZ classification.—cont'd

	Sky view factor	Aspect ratio	Building surface fraction	Impervious surface fraction	Pervious surface fraction	Height of roughness elements	LCZ classification
LOCATION B	0.211						
Case III							
LOCATION A		2	37.32	38.82	23.86	8.70	LCZ 2 Compact mid-rise
LOCATION B	0.363	0.65	17.16	51.64	31.2	8.15	LCZ 5 Open mid-rise

per the TNCDBR 2019 was analyzed, in which the plot coverage was arrived by utilizing the maximum permissible height and FSI, while considering the existing amount of on-site vegetation cover. The built characteristics in Case-II have changed the LCZ classifications of location A and B to LCZ2 (compact mid-rise) and LCZ5(open mid-rise), respectively. Case-III is a slight modification of Case-II, in which 50% of the building setbacks were considered as vegetation with trees planted at 6.0−9.0 m intervals.

The thermal comfort indices, namely mean radiant temperature (T_{mrt}) and physiological equivalent temperature (PET), were computed for May 30, 2018 through Envi-met (version v.4.4.4) simulations and Leonardo tool. The simulated data were compared with the measured data in locations A and B in Case-I for validation and were found to estimate the thermal comfort indices correctly as established by Tsoka et al. (2018). Further, the thermal comfort indices were simulated for case-II and case-III in the two locations to analyze the impact of varying DRs on the outdoor thermal comfort conditions.

The air temperature ($T_a°C$) variations in the three cases at the two chosen locations A and B are shown in Fig. 9.2. Location B recorded higher temperatures when compared to Location A due to the variations in the built-up parameters. A maximum temperature difference of 1.5°C was found between the three cases in the two locations around 14.00 h. The difference in the temperatures between the three cases is significant during the daytime (in the presence of solar radiation) when compared to night. This indicates that the impact of built form variations due to the 2019 regulations on air temperatures is minimum in the night but is significant during day influencing the outdoor thermal comfort at the canyon level. Case-I recorded the maximum temperatures in both the locations. However, the

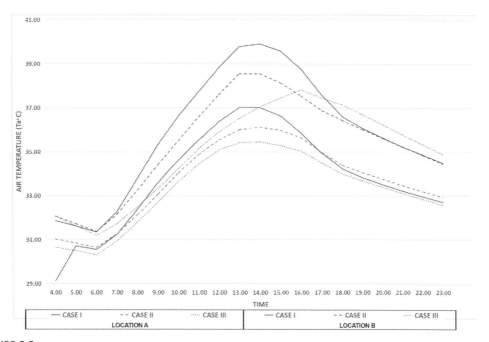

FIGURE 9.2

Air temperature variations at locations A and B for Case I, Case II, and Case III.

increased building height and FSI in the 2019 regulations in Case- II reduced the air temperatures due to mutual shading of taller buildings and reduced SVF. In Case-III, the increase of pervious layer through vegetation cover and trees with tall canopy further reduced the SVF, thus resulting in the reduction of air temperatures at the canyon level improving the outdoor comfort during daytime significantly.

The average SVF was significantly reduced from Case-I to Case-III at both the locations (location A—0.45 to 0.211 and location B—0.69 to 0.363) due to changes in the built-up characteristics with the 2019 DRs. Though the plot coverage in the homogeneous residential neighborhood at location A did not vary much between 2013 and 2019 regulations, the increased building heights and FSI reduced the SVF significantly, thus improving the canyon-level comfort outdoors. The wider roads at Location B enabled the increase in the building heights to above 20 m in the 2019 regulations (Table 9.6) resulting in the asymmetrical deeper canyons of the commercial buildings along the main roads.

Fig. 9.3 shows the spatial distribution of Mean Radiant Temperature (T_{mrt}) at Locations A and B for all three cases. The T_{mrt} values in Case-I were 65.84 and 73.88°C at locations A and B, respectively. The higher T_{mrt} value at location B is due to the wider roads with an aspect ratio of 0.36 and higher SVF value of 0.69. The reduction in the T_{mrt} values between case-I and case-III was highly significant in location B (with a difference of 22°C) when compared to location A (with a difference of 15°C), highlighting the role of SVF on T_{mrt} values.

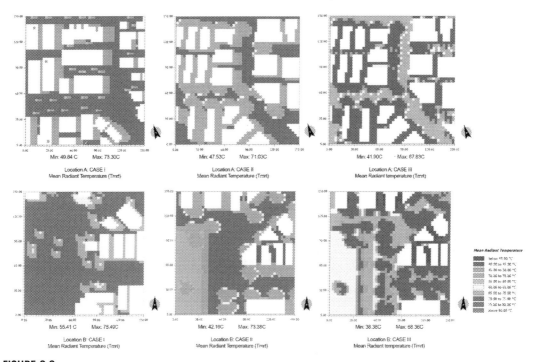

FIGURE 9.3

Spatial distribution of mean radiant temperature (T_{mrt}) at locations A and B for Case I, Case II, and Case III at 14:00 h.

The spatial distribution of Physiological Equivalent Temperature (PET) at locations A and B for Case I, Case II, and Case III is shown in Fig. 9.4. The increased pervious layer and the vegetation cover in Case-III at location A reduced the PET values by up to 7°C when compared to Case-I, improving the comfort levels throughout the day from very hot thermal sensation to warm and slightly warm sensation as classified by Matzarakis et al. (1999). Though the SVF at location B in case-III was higher than that at location A, the PET values at location B were lower than those at location A due to the presence of urban park with increased pervious layer, which reduced the thermal stress and increased comfort. This highlighted the strong correlation between the percentage of pervious layers and PET.

The impact of Tamil Nadu Combined Development and Building Rules (2019) was lesser in the air temperature variations. However, its impact on the T_{mrt} and PET values was highly significant. The difference between the mean radiant temperatures in Case-I and Case-III at the two locations A and B ranged from 15.29 to 22.13°C, respectively. Similarly, the difference between the PET of case I and Case III at the two locations A and B ranged from 5.58 to 8.49°C, respectively. Due to the increase in the pervious ground cover and tree canopy in 2019 regulations, the PET values significantly reduced from case-I to case-III, which in turn improved the comfort conditions outdoors by considerably reducing the duration of high thermal stress during the day.

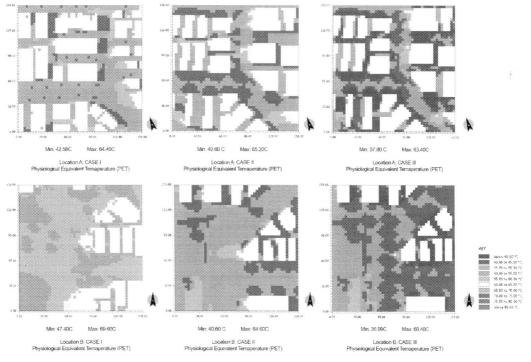

FIGURE 9.4

Spatial distribution of physiological equivalent temperature (PET) at locations A and B for Case I, Case II, and Case III at 14:00 h.

Though the 2019 regulations were focused on increasing the building density in the existing land parcels by increasing FSI and building height, it improved the outdoor thermal comfort considerably in the mixed residential neighborhood. However, the comfort levels could further be enhanced by regulating the ground cover of the setback areas with pervious ground cover and tall canopy trees. This would reduce the duration of high thermal stress sensation at a particular location, thereby increasing the outdoor comfort. The study demonstrated that it is possible to improve the outdoor pedestrian comfort during daytime in the cities by appropriate formulation of development regulations in cities.

5. Conclusion

This study attempted to identify the UHI mitigation strategies through analysis of neighborhoods in two tropical cities. Simulation of various open spaces and built form metrics in the selected neighborhoods enabled the understanding of urban morphology and its effect on UHI. Further it helped in identification of optimum configuration metrics and implementation of strategies to reduce UHI through DR and improve outdoor thermal comfort in tropical cities.

The study identified a few strategies that could be translated into development regulations. Open spaces should be evenly distributed rather than scattered in order to have an uniform effect of open spaces on UHI in the neighbourhood. This could be achieved by DR that promotes high density through high-rise buildings with reduced plot coverage at neighborhood level. To effectively reduce the UHI, these open spaces need to be located between built forms at plot level, and these open spaces can be used to increase the percentage of impervious layers, which can be implemented through DR. In tropical cities with high temperatures and humidity, appropriate orientation of streets at neighborhood level is necessary to enhance wind movement to provide thermal comfort and reduce stagnant air pollution. This can be realized by orienting major streets and open spaces in the predominant wind direction in the detailed development plans of neighborhoods. Suitable vegetation strategies at neighborhood levels can be further employed to mitigate UHI. Evergreen High LAD (Leaf Area Density) trees planted along the edge of the open spaces at 6.0—9.0 m intervals at plot and street level can reduce the SVF considerably and improve the pedestrian-level comfort at neighborhoods. It can be concluded based on the studies at Vijayawada and Chennai that in tropical cities, DR that integrates appropriate configuration of open space and built form metrics can effectively reduce the UHI and its impacts at neighborhood level.

Acknowledgment

The authors acknowledge Mr. G.Vamsikrishna, postgraduate student, School of Planning and Architecture Vijayawada, and Mr. Ebin Horrison, research scholar, Sathyabama Institute of Science and Technology, for their contribution in the data for case studies discussed.

References

Amirtham, L.R., 2016. Urbanization and its impact on urban heat island intensity in Chennai Metropolitan Area, India. Indian J. Sci. Technol. 9 (5), 1—8.

Berardi, U., Wang, Y., 2016. The effect of a denser city over the urban microclimate: the case of Toronto. Sustainability 8 (8), 822. https://doi.org/10.3390/su8080822.

Cao, J., Zhou, W., Zheng, Z., Ren, T., Wang, W., 2021. Within-city spatial and temporal heterogeneity of air temperature and its relationship with land surface temperature. Landsc. Urban Plann. 206, 103979.

Chen, A., Yao, L., Sun, R., Chen, L., 2014. How many metrics are required to identify the effects of the landscape pattern on land surface temperature? Ecol. Indicat. 45, 424–433.

CMDA, 2013. Second master plan for Chennai Metropolitan Area, 2026. In: Development Regulations, Amendments incorporated upto May, 2013. Volume II.

Dash, M., Chakraborty, M., 2018. Influence of climate on building codes: comparative analysis of indian cities. Environ. Prog. Sustain. Energy 37. https://doi.org/10.1002/ep.12875.

Dash, M., Chakraborty, M., 2020. Outdoor ventilation and ground coverage: exploring a climate centric approach to building byelaws for multi storied apartments in Bhubaneswar. J. Sustain. Architect. Civ. Eng. 27, 78–95.

Deosthali, V., 2000. Impact of rapid urban growth on heat and moisture islands in Pune City, India. Atmos. Environ. 34, 2745–2754.

Devadas, M.D., Rose, A.L., 2009. Urban factors and the intensity of heat island in the city of Chennai. In: The Seventh International Conference on Urban Climate. http://www.ide.titech.ac.jp/~icuc7/extended_abstracts/pdf/384826-1-090520120431-005.pdf.

Emmanuel, R., Fernando, H.J.S., 2007. Urban heat islands in humid and arid climates: role of urban form and thermal properties in Colombo, Sri Lanka and Phoenix, USA. Clim. Res. 34, 241–251.

Good, E.J., Ghent, D.J., Bulgin, C.E., Remedios, J.J., 2017. A spatiotemporal analysis of the relationship between near-surface air temperature and satellite land surface temperatures using 17 years of data from the ATSR series. J. Geophys. Res. Atmos. 122 (17), 9185–9210.

Government of Tamil Nadu, 2019. Tamil Nadu Combined Development and Building Rules, 2019.Tamil Nadu Government Gazette Extraordinary, G.O. Ms. No. 18. Municipal Administration and Water Supply (MA 1).

Harlan, S.L., Brazel, A.J., Prashad, L., Stefanov, W.L., Larsen, L., 2006. Neighborhood microclimates and vulnerability to heat stress. Soc. Sci. Med. 63 (11), 2847–2863.

He, B.-J., 2019. Towards the next generation of green building for urban heat island mitigation: Zero UHI impact building. Sustain. Cities Soc. 50. https://doi.org/10.1016/j.scs.2019.10164.

Heris, M., Middel, A., Muller, B., 2020. Impacts of form and design policies on urban microclimate: assessment of zoning and design guideline choices in urban redevelopment projects. Landsc. Urban Plann. 202, 103870. https://doi.org/10.1016/j.landurbplan.2020.103870.

Huang, H., Yun, Y., Xu, J., Huang, R., Fu, J., Huang, K., 2017. Scale response of summer urban heat island to building plot ratio and its warning parameter. Teh. Vjesn. 24 (3), 877–886.

Jin, H., Cui, P., Wong, N.H., Ignatius, M., 2018. Assessing the effects of urban morphology parameters on microclimate in Singapore to control the urban heat island effect. Sustainability 10. https://doi.org/10.3390/su10010206.

Kikon, N., Singh, P., Singh, S.K., Vyas, A., 2016. Assessment of urban heat islands (UHI) of Noida City, India using multi-temporal satellite data. Sustain. Cities Soc. 22, 19–28.

Kotharkar, R., Bagade, A., 2018. Evaluating urban heat island in the critical local climate zones of an Indian city. Landsc. Urban Plann. 169, 92–104.

Kotharkar, R., Surawar, M., 2016. Land use, Land cover, and population density impact on the formation of Canopy urban heat islands through traverse survey in the Nagpur urban Area, India. J. Urban Plann. Dev. 142 (1). https://doi.org/10.1061/(ASCE)UP.1943-5444.0000277.

Kotharkar, R., Bagade, A., Singh, P.R., 2020. A systematic approach for urban heat island mitigation strategies in critical local climate zones of an Indian city. Urban Clim. 34, 100701. https://doi.org/10.1016/j.uclim.2020.100701.

Kruger, E.L., Minella, F.O., Rasia, F., 2011. Impact of urban geometry on outdoor thermal comfort and air quality from field measurements in Curitiba. Brazil Buil. Environ. 46 (3), 621–634.

Masoudi, M., Tan, P.Y., 2019. Multi-year comparison of the effects of spatial pattern of urban green spaces on urban land surface temperature. Landsc. Urban Plann. 184, 44–58.

Mathew, A., Khandelwal, S., Kaul, N., 2016. Spatial and temporal variations of urban heat island effect and the effect of percentage impervious surface area and elevation on land surface temperature: study of Chandigarh city, India. Sustain. Cities Soc. 26, 264–277.

Matzarakis, A., Helmut, M., Moses, I.G., 1999. Applications of a universal thermal index: physiological equivalent temperature. Int. J. Biometeorol. 43 (2), 76–84.

McGarigal, K., 2015. FRAGSTATS Help. University of Massachusetts, Amherst, MA, USA, p. 182.

Perera, N.G.R., Emmanuel, R., 2018. A Local Climate Zone based approach to urban planning in Colombo, Sri Lanka. Urban Clim. 23, 188–203.

Rajan, E.H.S., Lilly Rose Amirtham, L.R., 2021. Impact of building regulations on the perceived outdoor thermal comfort in the mixed-use neighbourhood of Chennai. Front. Architect. Res. 10 (1), 148–163.

Song, Y., Song, X., Shao, G., 2020. Effects of green space patterns on urban thermal environment at multiple spatial–temporal scales. Sustainability 12 (17), 6850.

Stewart, I.D., Oke, T., 2012. Local climate zones for urban temperature studies. Bull. Am. Meteorol. Soc. 93, 1879–1900.

Terfa, B.K., Chen, N., Zhang, X., Niyogi, D., 2020. Spatial configuration and extent explains the urban heat mitigation potential due to green spaces: analysis over Addis Ababa, Ethiopia. Rem. Sens. 12 (18), 2876.

Thomas, A.P.G., Ansar, S.S., Zachariah, E.J., 2014. Analysis of urban heat island in Kochi, India, using a modified local climate zone classification. Proced. Environ. Sci. 21, 3–13.

Tsoka, S., Tsikaloudaki, A., Theodosiou, T., 2018. Analyzing the ENVI-met microclimate model's performance and assessing cool materials and urban vegetation applications—a review. Sustain. Cities Soc. 43, 55–76.

Yang, C., He, X., Wang, R., Yan, F., Yu, L., Bu, K.,,., Zhang, S., 2017. The effect of urban green spaces on the urban thermal environment and its seasonal variations. Forests 8 (5), 153.

Yang, F., Qian, F., Lau, S.Y.S., 2013. Urban form and density as indicators for summertime outdoor ventilation potential: a case study on high-rise housing in Shanghai. Build. Environ. 70, 122–137.

Yin, C., Yuan, M., Lu, Y., Huang, Y., Liu, Y., 2018. Effects of urban form on the urban heat island effect based on spatial regression model. Sci. Total Environ. 634, 696–704.

Ziaul, S.K., Pal, S., 2020. Modeling the effects of green alternatives on heat island mitigation of a meso level town, West Bengal, India. Adv. Space Res. 65 (7), 1789–1802.

StEMAIRF-BGI as a tool for UHI mitigation using land use planning and designing

10

Mahua Mukherjee, Arjun Satheesh and Atul Kumar

Indian Institute of Technology Roorkee, Roorkee, Uttarakhand, India

1. Introduction

An urban heat island (UHI) is defined as rise in temperature over an urban area with respect to surrounding area. A town or city has an ability to generate UHI (Oke and Fuggle, 1972). The boundary of UHI is defined by a sharp change in magnitude of the skin temperature or land surface temperature (LST) over the area. The concept of UHI can be well understood by studying the urban area and the thermal characteristics with its surrounding area (Howard, 1833; Shuzhen, 1994). The phenomenon was first observed in London and was named by Manley. UHI phenomenon is a result of the differences in the surface roughness, surface albedos, anthropogenic activities, and building densities between an urban center and its suburban surroundings, which cause differences in the local boundary layer characteristics and the underlying surface energy balance. Surface modification due to urbanization leads to increases the imperviousness of the urban surface and thereby making the urban climate warmer as compared to surrounding nonurbanized areas (Oke and Maxwell, 1975). Surveys have reported that 60% of the global population is concentrated in Asian countries among which India is the second most populated with 1.3 billion people (United Nations, 2015). In recent times, urban areas are growing population hubs with about 54% of the total world population living in urban areas. India being one of the fastest growing country in terms of population and economy has an urban population of 410 million in 2014 (International Organization for Migration (IOM), 2015). This remarkable population can be stated responsible for the formation and expansion of UHI. According to the statistics of the *World Migration Report*, 2015, the urban growth in India is showing a steady growth with an urban population of 410 million in 2014 and the estimated urban population by 2050 is 814 million. A tremendous growth in the number of cities with an average population of 1 million is seen from 3 in 1951 to 53 in 2014, respectively (International Organization for Migration (IOM), 2015).

The UHI can be studied by ground-based observation which involves collection of data from fixed automatic weather station or by collecting the data along a transverse with thermometers mounted on a vehicle (Voogt and Oke, 2003). Several statistical methods have been employed to understand the change in growth of the city or urban area (Weng et al., 2004). The size of the city plays an important role in determining the magnitude of the UHI (Oke and Fuggle, 1972). The study of UHI using thermal remote sensing becomes possible only because of advancement of sensor technology and the use of satellite, airborne, and aircraft platforms. The surface temperature calculated using thermal data contains the effects of surface radiative and thermodynamics properties that include surface emissivity, moisture, and surface albedo, and contain the effect of near surface atmosphere.

Urban climates are influences by a combination of process occurring at a variety of scales, which intern effects by the biophysical nature of cities and structure of the urban atmosphere. Urban scale is considered as one of the important parameters while characterizing UHI and modeling its different forms. Scale helps us to determine the size of the source area from where thermal influence originates and how it slowly changes the urban climate. Small-scale study of the UHI found inside the roughness layer (RSL) is known as microscale, where we study individual buildings, trees, and the intervening spaces between the buildings. Mesoscale study involves plumes from individual local scale system, which extends vertically above and produces urban boundary layer (UBL) over the entire city.

2. UHI as a disaster risk

It is a well-documented fact that air temperatures around the world are rising on average and the phenomenon of global warming is accelerating the pace of disasters including tropical storms caused by changing seasonal patterns and air circulation patterns. Global sea levels have been rising as more and more Artic Sea ice melts and the ice shelves disappear due to the increasing global temperatures (Bernstein et al., 2007). The global rise in temperatures is directly and indirectly caused by human activity. Heat produced by human activities include the heat produced from factories, industries, and other manufacturing activities, heat generated by internal combustion engines burning fossil fuels for transportation, heat that is conducted through building fabric, like walls and ceilings due to the internal heating, ventilation, and air conditioning systems, and even the heat produced from natural metabolic processes by humans beings can all combine to cause local air temperatures to rise in urban areas where human populations are the densest. All of this contributes to the phenomenon known as UHIs. UHIs alongside elevated air temperatures around the world can compound and create additional thermal stress. This clearly shows us that the effect of global warming will be increasingly felt within the densely populated urban areas of the world (Watkins et al., 2002).

2.1 UHI and urbanization

Research at the regional scale suggests that urban temperatures are correlated to the Land Use and Land Cover (LULC) patterns. The reason for LULC impacts on UHI has to do with the systematic replacement of vegetated regions by the urban cover. Vegetation provides natural shade, helps with rainwater runoff capture and harvesting, and reduces soil erosion which encourages further vegetative growth which compounds the benefits of vegetation. LULC changes from urbanization tend to replace green cover and vegetated surfaces with built surfaces and impervious ground cover (Whitford et al., 2001). As of 2018, 54% of the global population has been ascertained to live in urban areas (United Nations, 2018) and that alone makes it really important for researchers to understand the effects of UHI. The risks from UHI effects have been studied over the years especially with focus accelerating on the same recently. Urban area specific studies exist for multiple cities around the world, particularly with regard to LULC change impact on UHI. Traverse survey studies done in the city of Nagpur, India, to assess the LULC change effects on UHI showed that the mean UHI intensity within the city was

2.14°C (Kotharkar and Surawar, 2016). Another study conducted from 1994 to 2002 in the city of Bandung, Indonesia, discovered that areas with higher air temperatures in the range of 30−35°C expanded after the industrial and housing zones had increased to about 12,606 ha at the rate of 4.47% per year (Kuze et al., 2012).

2.2 UHI and air pollution

Intensive change in the land cover and emission of air pollutants can affect the energy balance and atmospheric heating rates and thus may influence the intensity of UHI. High temperature in urban area accelerate the formation of smog and polluted air (Yang et al., 2011). Radiative force of particulate matters is different in urban and suburban regions due to different load of concentration, causing difference in the surface temperature (Wu et al., 2017). The air pollutants such as particulate matter, water vapor, and carbon dioxide over a city absorb the thermal radiation emitted by the surface and reemitted to the atmosphere causing warming up of ambient air. Airborne pollutants intensify the UHI intensity and rise in temperature hinder the dispersion of the pollutants (Peterson, 1969). On the other hand concentration of particulate matter over the city causes more scattering of radiation that leads to the comparative cooling of the urban temperature (Zhong et al., 2019). Previous study showed that the UHI intensity lower down by 0.1−0.2 k in urban and suburban regions due to PM2.5 concentration load (Wu et al., 2017). A number of studies have discussed the impact of UHI on local air quality, considering the wind condition at mesoscale created by differential heating which circulates pollutants and moves upward leading to air pollution issues in urban area (Agarwal and Tandon, 2010). Thus, UHIs have significant effects on pollutant concentrations, due to their feedbacks on boundary layer stability, which decreases the intensity of vertical mixing.

2.3 Methods, tools, and techniques for UHI analysis

In the field of climatology of which UHI study is a part, the determination of the factors leading to UHI and working out systems on how to resolve, mitigate, and adapt to this urban climate risk is of particular interest. Researchers have adopted various methods to try and analyze the impact of UHI over the years. In fact, there is an ever-growing body of work that includes many studies that have been published on various aspects of UHI (Huang and Lu, 2018). A systematic review of and critique of the methodologies used in 190 empirical studies that covered both the ground-level and canopy layer of UHI from 1950 to 2007 concluded that about 75% of the studies failed to communicate metadata of the instrumentation used for on-ground studies. Another issue noticed was that at least half of the studies failed to account for general weather effects within the urban system (Stewart, 2011). Even with all these shortcomings observed in the methods of UHI study, the earlier and most widely adopted method was to take readings of ambient air temperature at different points of the day and night from different locations that are within the urban environment and then compare them with temperatures for the corresponding time periods in areas outside the identifiable urban region. In short, UHI and UHI intensity are measured by the temperature difference between urban and rural areas, and the research indicators include temperature, surface temperature, LST, and air temperature. UHI study methods other than field measurement and comparison include remote sensing, small-scale physical models, and modeling with the help of mathematical simulations and GPS system data imported into GIS. The modeling methods mentioned are geared toward forecasting and prediction while the other methods are observational (Ren et al., 2007; Miao et al., 2009; Yang et al., 2011; Adachi et al., 2012; Pal et al., 2012; Ching et al., 2018; Kotharkar and Bagade, 2018).

Traditional field measurements studies benefit from their long time series but they usually cover much smaller areas than satellite data can and have data inconsistencies arising from both human error and machine error. There is also the issue of the actual spatial distribution of the ground-level observation stations that may not be as thorough as the "tile" snaps of multispectral information that a satellite sensor can take (Sismanidis et al., 2015; Bechtel et al., 2019). On the other hand, in situ UHI measurement has shown to be more reliable as the comparison between day-time measurement of UHI via satellites, especially MODIS data, does not seem to accurately reflect skin temperature unlike in situ measurements (Mohan et al., 2009). Even so a few researchers have suggested that a majority of the UHI study can be successfully done with satellite observation based data (Hu and Brunsell, 2015).

3. Climate scenarios

3.1 Representative Concentration Pathways

The Earth's future climate depends strongly on the development of greenhouse gas emissions. Several scenarios describing future emissions consistent with various socioeconomic assumptions are available, describing a range of climate outcomes. Earlier scenarios were created by the Intergovernmental Panel on Climate Change (SA90, IS92, and SRES). A more recent scenario suggestion was the Representative Concentration Pathways (RCPs) (Moss, 2010; van Vuuren et al., 2011). The RCPs are simulations ranging from a global climate scenario known as RCP 2.6 (van Vuuren et al., 2011) where the average global radiative forcing increases by 2.6 W/m^2 toward the end of the century as there is an assumption of a consistently decreasing greenhouse gas emissions trend after 2020 (decisive climate action), to the worst-case scenario of RCP 8.5 (Riahi et al., 2011), in which GHGs are increasingly emitted by the nations of the world and we reach a radiative forcing level of 8.5 W/m^2 by the end of the century. Certain intermediate scenarios have also been proposed where a radiative forcing level of 6 W/m^2 can be expected by 2100 as the peak of GHG emissions globally may approach in 2070 only (Masui et al., 2011) and another where a more benign trend of GHG emissions peaking in 2030 leads to a global radiative forcing of 4.5 W/m^2 by the close of the 21st century (Thomson et al., 2011). These assumed climate scenarios form the basis of climate projections.

These scenarios which were developed by the researcher community noticeably lacked any social or economic dimensions. It has been noted that climate change is occurring due to human intervention and the same cannot be mitigated suitably without human intervention. The mitigation and adaptation part would definitely involve a socioeconomic component (IPCC, 2014). This eventually led to the creation of Shared Socioeconomic Pathways (SSPs).

3.2 Shared Socioeconomic pathways

SSPs are projected pathways for socioeconomic development through the remainder of the 21st century and these incorporate both quantitative aspects and a qualitative narrative as part of its projection. The numerically quantifiable aspects which include the direct causes of the climate change such as GHG emissions, air pollution, anthropogenic activity, heat from LULC change, etc., are considered part of the quantitative aspect. Macroeconomic trends and associated energy consumption trends reflected through the GDP growth along with the population trends reflecting the demographic scenario also constitute the quantitative aspect in SSPs. The narrative depends more on the attitudes of the people toward adopting climate friendly processes as a function of their education and economic prosperity. There are five such SSP scenarios that are discussed where the touch points include economic inequality, regional rivalry leading to fossil-fueled development, or maybe a compromised development. There is also a narrative with the possibility of achieving sustainable development but it is generally considered as something which most nations and regions should strive to aspire to, toward the end of the century. The scenarios with their inherent quantifications and narratives as portrayed in the SSPs from SSP 1 to SSP 5 can be considered as broadly representative of current literature. They also allow for further assessment and development in research projects (Riahi et al., 2017; Kebede et al., 2018). The SSP narratives were developed using expert teams that jointly designed the storylines which ensured that there are no inconsistencies in the stories. Three different economic perspectives (Cuaresma, 2017; Dellink et al., 2017; Leimbach et al., 2017), urbanization projections, (Jiang et al., 2017), population projections (Samir, 2017), and land use patterns (Popp et al., 2017) were developed for each SSP. Six integrated assessment models (IAMs) were used for the quantification of the SSP scenarios (Calvin et al., 2017; Fricko, 2017; Fujimori et al., 2017; Kriegler et al., 2017; van Vuuren et al., 2017). After the publication of the SSPs, there have been a wide range of applications from global human system to the nature and ecosystems assessment (Chaudhary et al., 2018; Kim et al., 2017; Rogelj et al., 2018). A newer framework combining the so-called SSPs and the RCPs (and other climate scenarios) in a Scenario Matrix Architecture has been proposed.

3.3 UHI and climate change

As climate scenarios are being used to project the future for Earth in the coming decades, global mean surface temperatures have been observed to increase; and for all scenarios. Furthermore global mean temperatures keep showing an upward trend and there appears to be no respite in sight (Working Group I - AR 5 IPCC, 2013). The studies show that from the middle of the 20th century, the LST average has been increasing and is further projected to increase globally. The global mean rise notwithstanding, the annual average LST mean for Europe is projected to rise more than the global mean (Collins et al., 2013).

Various international organizations have identified heat and specifically increase in ambient air temperatures within urban areas as a strategic risk to human well-being and also as a contributing factor to the acceleration of climate change. The increased energy costs and the reduction in human productivity especially due to night-time increase in ambient temperature leading to a lack of restful sleep are the immediate and noticeable impacts. Long-term impacts include increase in harm due to air pollution, increased drying of the atmosphere thereby making it difficult for vegetation to survive, and potential reduction of human lifespan from exposure to a hotter and more polluted environment. This makes the phenomenon of UHIs a slow onset disaster that is in one way a symptom of and further a causative event in rapidly accelerating the deteriorating impacts of climate change.

4. Mitigation and adaptation for UHI
4.1 Blue-Green Infrastructure

Blue-Green Infrastructure (BGI) systems can change our understanding and expectations of urban environments and their infrastructure services as a whole. The advantage of large-scale adoption of BGI is that it can reduce and even mitigate the effects of UHIs.

Open spaces may include a vast category of urban and urban fringe spaces which can come under many types. There may be protected areas, such as Ramsar sites, wildlife sanctuaries, and national parks; apart from that we may observe any of the following types of open spaces in the urban fringes or even in 'leftover' space within urban area.

The suitable types of BGI elements for such areas are usually the local flora, fauna, soil, and ambient environment. The best intervention for such spaces is, in fact, least intervention and ideally human intervention would only be to encourage nature is taking its course. Increase in such spaces can lead to reduction of energy consumption requirements for indoor climate control as a consequence of a reverse trend of rising numbers of hot days. Projections predicting the future of infrastructure systems show a radically changed system of generation and delivery of basic services like electricity as shown in figure. Smart grids are another form of infrastructure which is not considered as BGI but can be categorized as sustainable infrastructure. The evolution of infrastructure systems today leading to 'mixed' Gray to Green infrastructure systems may create a future scenario where decentralized and nonfossil fuel—based energy generation may become a considerable part of the electrical grid.

4.2 Policy and planning actions against UHI

Asmartgridwouldgenerateitselectricityinadecentralizedmannerfocusingonrenewableenergysourceswhich addstotheGreencomponentofaneventual'Green Economy' The economic benefits of having to produce lesser energy and being less dependent on large-scale mining and refining of fossil fuels can add to the per capita GDP spending power of any nation. BGI can smartly bring about multipole changes that we cannot foresee at this point, yet all the literature sources agree that these would be highly positive.

An electric grid, evolving from a relatively simple power delivery system drawing power from large central power plants to an internet of an energy system that manages, controls, conditions, buys, sells, and stores power in a dynamic marketplace involving millions of participants, might not be classified as a prime example of BGI, according to a few stricter definitions (United Nations, 2018). Even so, the combination of smart technologies with its decentralized, renewable energy source focus makes it a lot Greener infrastructure than Gray infrastructure in nature. The economic benefits of such a system would also be highly distributed, and larger benefits would accrue over a longer-term via the environmental and social benefits this would lead to.

As discussed previously the need of the hour is to identify the intensity of the issue and suggest potential solutions both via direct and immediate physical interventions apart from long-term policy structuring that oversees interim physical interventions that help cities and urban regions rid themselves of UHI generating microenvironments.

In order to achieve this objective, we are suggesting the creation and deployment of a framework that is nuanced enough to identify and highlight the urban hotspots and critical zones where immediate attention is required while is also capable of guiding the implementation process.

5. Strategic Ecosystem Monitoring, Assessment, and BGI Implementation-Based Resilience Framework

5.1 StEMAIR Framework concept

Resilience is defined as the function of resistivity and adaptation capacity of the system or community (Ribeiro and Pena Jardim Goncalves, 2019). The term introduces in scientific research in the year 1973 by Holling (ref); initially, resilience was majorly associated with the ecological system. In later years of research studies, it has been associated with multiple systems such as urban resilience. With the high rate of urbanization, cities are developing territories that are most at risk like urban flood, UHI deteriorating air quality. Urban resilience across multiple research publications and reports includes five broad dimensions: natural, economic, social, physical, and institutional (Ostadtaghizadeh et al., 2017).

The global experts' methodology follows the monitoring, management, assessment, and strategic implementation of mitigation measures (Pitman and Ely, 2013; Ghofrani et al., 2017).

The present publication discusses the '**Strategic Ecosystem Monitoring, Assessment, and BGI Implementation-based Resilience (StEMAIR) Framework**' as shown in Fig. 10.1. The framework helps in developing urban resiliency following the global process from monitoring to implementation. It has two sections: the first section of the framework discusses applying geospatial data and tools for monitoring and assessing multiple risks simultaneously. It is named as Geospatial Tools and Natural Solutions (GEOS-NAT) framework. The latter section of the StEMAIR framework discusses the strategic intervention of the optimum nature-based solution (BGI) considering solution basket and concerning the region's social, economic, and institutional body.

5.2 Features involved the StEMAIR Framework

The framework is an iterative loop of monitoring, assessment, and implementations. In this framework, geospatial images and advanced image processing are used to monitor the trend and availability

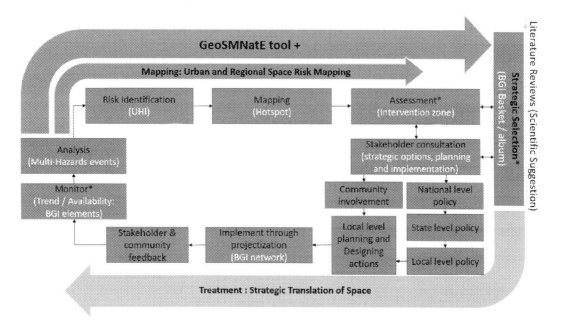

FIGURE 10.1

StEMAIR concept Framework.

of risk zone for a more extended period (a decade or more) in the region. Although the framework can analyze multiple hazards, in the present study, the focus is on the impact of UHI from the LST data. The knowledge of extreme historical events of the UHI intensities provides the potential risk of thermal stress in the region. The GIS platform used to map for assessing and identifying hotspots and implementation zone, which will later help the urban authorities discuss and draw concrete resilience planning and the suggested strategic BGI. The final action plan is prepared after consultation with stakeholders, which may be revised based on information gained from feedback and performance monitoring. A brief description of tasks and their consequent sequence involved in the **StEMAIR** Framework focusing UHI is as follows.

5.2.1 GeoSMNatE tool+

This section of the framework is the comprehensive framework of GEOS-NAT, which discusses the analysis tools and techniques on the GIS platform using the geospatial image. The process starts with demarcating the area of interest (AOI); the AOI scale can be neighborhood to city level. The +tool assesses the multiple risks of the region and suggested various BGI elements as solutions for the particular risk.

5.2.2 Monitoring and analyzing

Monitoring of the trend of UHI risk in the region is done by checking the trend of various urban feature classes like Urban (built-up region); Vegetation (depletion and health); Water (surface water, sub-surface water, quality); **Temperature (LST)**; Terrain features (slope, streams, etc.). Monitoring will identify a probable list of hazards that the region can face or going to face.

5.2.3 Risk identification and mapping

Risk identification of the region will help focus on multiple hazards at a time. Historical inventory of extreme events or disasters from various sources will scale down the concern or focus region of hazards spatially and temporally. Historical weather data collected from secondary sources like meteorological datasets and primary real-time traverse data surveys help create site climate profiles. Mapping is done to locate the potential high-risk zone that is the hotspot zone and the intervention zone. Mapping is done from a macroscale to a microscale to assess the risk profile and suggest mitigative measures.

5.2.4 Strategic transition of space

The framework advocates a comprehensive integration of BGI in the planning process. In this section of the strategic framework, selecting the mitigative measures is suggested to local authorities or stakeholders for implementation with various scientific literature and experiments. The process of assessment is the primary linkage between the first and second sections of the framework. Local authorities or organizations need to consult for the discussion of social, economic, and institutional suggestions. Policy level discussion finally, the selection of BGI elements for implementation.

5.2.5 Assessment and strategic selection

The assessment process has two levels of intervention. One will discuss the BGI elements that need to be intervene and later discuss the BGI elements' efficacy. Assessment of the BGI elements impact in the region can be done both spatially and temporally. Selection of the particular BGI elements itself has a critical task. It requires assessment and consultation with the local and regional level authority and stakeholders considering various scientific literature suggestions.

5.2.6 Implementation

Finally, implementations of the BGI will be done through projectization. Implemented BGI elements will be monitored for its efficacy and management and its impact on the risk.

6. StEMAIR framework application for UHI

The StEMAIR Framework as discussed in Section 5.2 involves different stages and also tools and techniques. So to make the explanation more simplified, the case for Gurugram City is presented here.

6.1 Study area of Gurugram, India—demarcation of area of interest

Gurgaon or Guru-gram (Fig. 10.1), the city is a glaring example of urban growth and emerges as a millennium city of the country. Witnessing modern reincarnation, the city has developed in both forms spatially and demographically. The state of Haryana was formulated in 1966 and Gurugram was named as one of its district. Earlier most of the land mass was devoted to agriculture; the district has an agro-based economy. After 1990s Gurugram becomes hub for numerous jobs options; this leads to the moving of huge number of population to the city. Right now the city has become a financial and industrial center and contributing third highest per capital income. Gurgaon District is at the southernmost region of Haryana. Latitudinal and longitudinal expansion for the city is 27° 27′ 20″ and 28° 32′ 25″ latitude, and 76° 39′ 39″ and 77° 20′ 50″ longitude. The spatial expansion of the city is the part of National Capital Region, which is situated to the north of the district. The district has 1254 sq. km area. It has 1,514,432 populations with population density 1241 persons per square kilometer as per census 2011.

This South-Asian city has been growing rapidly over the period of the last 20 years, and the disappearance of blue and green cover is very much the norm. The area is a recently developed urban center that has been planned in most parts except for a few urban villages within. The area has a huge concentration of Multinational Corporations (MNCs) operating out of the region and therefore, is a poster child of the development in the country. As a new urban region, the potential for intervention is expected to be higher. The urban authorities of the region are already working closely with private organizations and the local people to sort out liveability challenges. It makes the introduction of the BGI much more plausible as a proactive community of stakeholders may appreciate and integrate such initiatives.

6.2 Monitoring and analysis of study area

6.2.1 Base data (historical hazardous event and risk identification)

6.2.1.1 Demography

In 2005, Mewat district was created out of Gurugram district with a size of 1500 km. sq. The number in brackets, in Table 10.1, denotes the 2001 census population of the larger Gurugram district while the other number is the population of the current Gurugram district without the population of the new Mewat district. The population of the current Gurgaon district has gone up in leaps and bounds over the last 20 years with the average population growth rate of the last two decades being close to 60%.

Table 10.1 Population trend in the selected study area—Gurugram, Haryana.

Year	Population	Area (sq. km)	Density (per sq. km)	Growth rate
2011	1,514,085	1254	1241	73.93%
2001	870,539 (1,660,289)*	1254 (2754)*	694	44.16%
1991	603,900 (1,146,090)*	1254 (2754)*	482	—

As mentioned in the section '6.2.1.1 demography', a new district was created out in year 2005, the number in the bracket is the population figure of the current gurugram region.

6.2.2 Hazardous events in Gurugram: UHI

In India, all the metropolitan cities are victims of UHI effect and the severity of heat formation; the cities are becoming hotter day by day (Veena et al., 2020). Gurugram the Millennium City may soon become "a living hell" is an article published by *The Hindu* (Gurugram may soon be 'living hell'); the article discussed the worse environmental condition in the region due to rapid urbanization. The article focused on the burning issues of concern in the Gurugram including UHI, high pollution, depletion of ground water, etc., with the reference of the document published by Centre for Science and Environment (CSE) and Gurgaon First. Various scientific research also confirmed the high impact of UHI in the region; Kushwant et al. has discussed the temperature trend in the Gurugram from year 1990–2018 and suggest that there is rise in mean LST by 8°C and 6°C in minimum temperature of Gurugram (Kushwaha and Nithiyanandam, 2019). Other study by Mohan et al. showed the consistent warming trend in annual and seasonal mean temperature in their study (Mohan et al., 2011).

6.3 Mapping: process framework

6.3.1 Green Infrastructure (vegetation)

Two land cover types can broadly characterize urban ecosystems: impervious surface and Vegetation (Endsley et al., 2018). In this study, NDVI is used to quantify the density of Vegetation in the area of interest, and to check the trend of vegetation spatial extent. Vegetation (Green infrastructure) is an integral part of the urban ecosystem. Vegetation provides enriched biodiversity and is a significant driver of biophysical components. The composition of the urban landscape is a trade-off between built up and Vegetation while developing the land mass; their weightage is strongly negatively correlated (Endsley et al., 2018). It is easier to map vegetation cover as the bare soil and built up has similar spectral behavior. Map in the figure shows the vegetation cover of the Gurugram Master Plan boundary for the year 2013, 2017, and 2020.

6.3.2 Urbanization (built-up region)

The Normalized Difference Built-up Index (NDBI) is used to identify the built-up features and area. Numerically NDBI values correspond to the reflection in the short-wave infrared spectrum. It uses the SWIR and near-infrared spectral bands to define built-up features in any region. In this study, NDBI is used to check the changing trend of built-up spatial extent. The NDBI brings out the built-up area data with high accuracy in almost all cases. This index works on the principle that most built-up areas and barren land experience a drastic increment in their reflectance of SWIR (short-wave infrared/

reradiation) when compared to NIR (near-infrared) while Vegetation has a slightly larger or smaller reflectance of SWIR when compared to NIR. NDBI = (SWIR - NIR)/(SWIR + NIR) ... (3). Although NDBI provides built-up area with significant accuracy but in this particular study, limitations while mapping built-up area are differencing between expose rocky surface and actual built-up region is validated and corrected by comparing NDBI with Google Earth imagery.

The NDVI and NDBI for the Gurugram city over the study period are presented in Fig. 10.2.

6.3.3 Land surface temperature

LST is an important parameter to analyze skin temperature of urban landscape. The measurement of surface energy of physical components of urban ecosystem will help in study of thermal behavior of various components. The relative cooling and warming characteristics of various surface help in identification of heat sink zone. The LST can process using thermal band of satellite imagery on GIS platform using various model, the study used the radiative transfer equations model to delineate LST. To determine the effective radiometric temperature of the Earth's surface "skin" in the instrument field of view ("skin" refers to the top surface in bare soil conditions and top of the canopies in vegetative cover and built-up). This method assumes that there is linear relation between surface temperature and brightness. In Fig. 10.3 the LST Map for selected study period is presented.

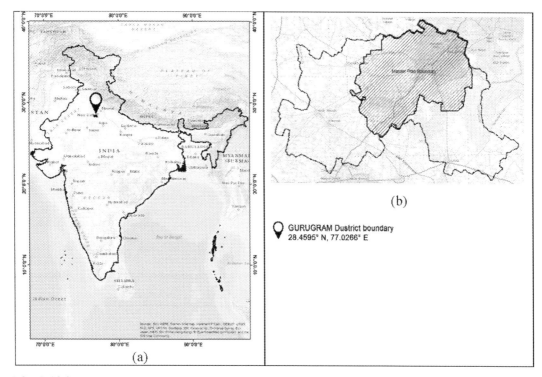

FIGURE 10.2

Study Area of (A) location map, (B) Gurugram District and AOI (Hatch part) Planning Boundary.

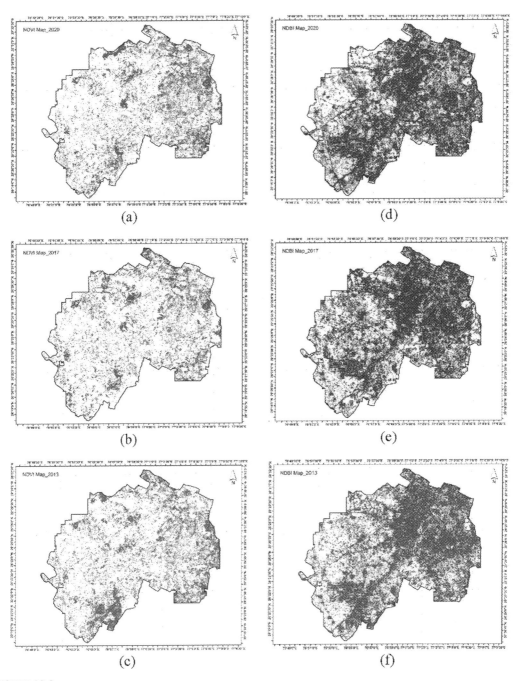

FIGURE 10.3

NDVI map: (A) Year 2020, (B) Year 2017, (C) Year 2013; and NDBI map (D) Year 2020, (E) Year 2017, (F) Year 2013.

Table 10.2 Trend of built-up, vegetation, and land surface temperature of gurugram master plan boundary area.

Feature class	2020	2019	2017	2013
Built-up (sq.km.)	237	237	234	227
Vegetation (sq.km.)	103	107	91	119
Land surface temp. (Mean)	46.00	49.00	49.00	46.00

6.4 Results and discussion

- Built up area was 227 sq.km in 2013; it has been increased by 10 sq. km by 2020 (Table 10.2 and Fig. 10.4).
- In the year 2013 vegetation in the urban boundary was 119 sq. km; it reduced to 91 sq.km in the year 2017. In later year 2020 vegetation increased to 103 sq. km.
- Maximum temperature trend is showing increasing trend from 2013 to 2019; in the year 2020 maximum temperature in LST calculation decreased to 46° centigrade, probably due to no anthropogenic activity, as there was complete lockdown period from March to May.
- In the year 2020, although the highest temperature in LST calculation is showing a bit lower degree than previous year, the spatial extent of the higher degree zone is increased.
- Most of the dense urban region are falling under high temperature zone of LST.
- Since the Landsat 8 provides day time data, so the LST map is showing high temperature zone in the area where major parcel of land are barren and expose to solar radiation.
- Built-up regions are showing comparatively low temperature zone due to mutual shading and urban shadow.
- Built-up area was 227 sq.km in 2013; it has been increased by 10 sq. km by 2020.

6.5 Analysis: hotspots and intervention zone

- Remote sensing imagery: The study was conducted using freely available images from the Landsat series of satellites under the USGS Earth Explorer project with Landsat 8 Data from 2013 to 2020.
- NDVI map is showing the area of vegetation and NDBI is showing the built up in the region.
- LST Map has been developed to check the potential zone of having high intensity of UHI. This clearly shows the difference of temperature gradient in the urban and suburban region.
- Overlay of the NDVI and LST Map of the year 2019 shows that the region with vegetation (Green Infrastructure) and water body (Blue Infrastructure) are having lower temperature gradient (Fig. 10.5).
- The barren land area and the built up region are showing high temperature region.
- The built-up region with matrix or patches of Green Infrastructure are showing comparatively lower temperature.

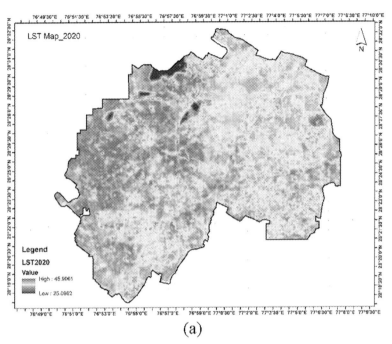

(a)

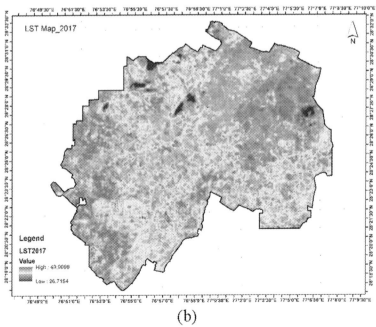

(b)

FIGURE 10.4

LST Map of the year: (A) 2020, (B) 2017, and (C) 2013.

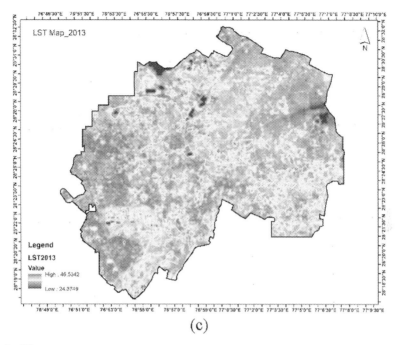

FIGURE 10.4 Cont'd

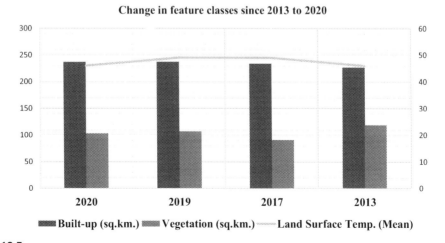

FIGURE 10.5

Graph representing change trend in feature class from 2013 to 2020.

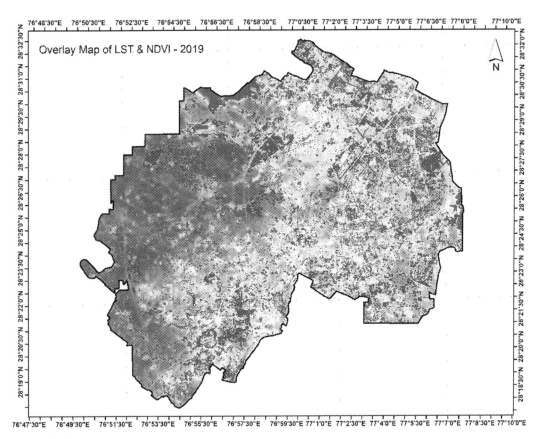

FIGURE 10.6

Overlay map of LST and NDVI, 2019.

- Identification of hotspots zone has been done with the conditional analysis, considering the condition of the region with minimum Green Infrastructure and high temperature zone and marked as a circle with cross-hatching.
- Hotspot zone of area ranging from 0.5 sq. km to 1 sq.km has been identified.
- The intervention zone in the critical hotspots is decided by the identification of opportunity of designing or proposing matrix or patches of Green Infrastructure in the dense built-up region with no or minimum vegetation (Figs. 10.6 and 10.7).

7. Conclusion

In this chapter we discuss multiple systems of UHI analysis and proceeded to analyze the example case through the framework titled as Strategic Ecosystem Monitoring, Assessment, and BGI Implementation-

FIGURE 10.7

Overlay map of LST, NDVI, and NDBI, 2020.

based Resilience (StEMAIR) Framework. StEMAIR framework can be an assistive tool to analyze multiple hazards simultaneously in any region.

The GeosMNate tool+ which forms the initial part of the analysis shows us clearly that there is an increasing trend in the LST and a decreasing trend in the vegetation cover along with a rise in impervious surface cover. This leads us to conclude that extensive urbanization happening over the last decade has converted open and vegetated lands into built space covered with urban materials that directly increases night-time ambient air temperature while also increasing LST during the day. The retaining of heat by the urban materials is a serious contributor to UHI and air pollution. This can only further complicate the urban issues that we face today. A concurrent increase in mortality rate has been observed world over due to the increase in UHI and air pollution and related other issues.

The present study analyzes the trend and impact of UHI in the Gurugram master plan boundary region. The temperature trend is monitored using LST map of the year 2013–2020; thermal band of Landsat 8 data has been used to develop the LST in the region. Built-up and vegetation index has been developed to check the spatial condition of built up and vegetation in the region. The mean, minimum, and maximum temperature in these two urban features has been checked to discuss the potential condition and intensity of UHI in the region. Finally the critical or hotspots zone has been identified considering the conditional analysis of high built-up, low vegetation, and high temperature zone. StEMAIR framework suggests the BGI solution basket based on various literature review to mitigate multiple hazards in the region, from the solution basket specific mitigative approach having high potential to combat UHI impact has been suggested. The BGI solution has been proved by checking the condition of zone having potential BGI network, patches, or matrix in the region.

Acknowledgment

We would like to acknowledge Department of Science and Technology Govt. of India for their financial and logistic support under the project "Translating urban spaces as strategic energy and water security measure (APD-1078)" and also Indian Institute of Technology, Roorkee, for supporting this research. We would also acknowledge Department of Architecture and Planning IIT Roorkee climatology lab for research support.

References

Adachi, S.A., et al., 2012. Comparison of the impact of global climate changes and urbanization on summertime future climate in the Tokyo metropolitan area. J. Appl. Meteorol. Climatol. 51 (8), 1441—1454. https://doi.org/10.1175/JAMC-D-11-0137.1.

Agarwal, M., Tandon, A., 2010. Modeling of the urban heat island in the form of mesoscale wind and of its effect on air pollution dispersal. Appl. Math. Model. 34 (9), 2520—2530. https://doi.org/10.1016/j.apm.2009.11.016.

Bechtel, B., et al., 2019. SUHI analysis using Local Climate Zones—a comparison of 50 cities. Urban Clim. 28, 100451. https://doi.org/10.1016/j.uclim.2019.01.005.

Bernstein, L., et al., 2007. Climate Change 2007 Synthesis Report. Geneva. Available at: https://www.ipcc.ch/report/ar4/syr/ (Accessed 8 February 2021).

Calvin, K., et al., 2017. The SSP4: A world of deepening inequality Katherine. Global Env. Change 42, 284—296. https://doi.org/10.1016/j.gloenvcha.2016.06.010.

Chaudhary, A., et al., 2018. Terrestrial vertebrate biodiversity loss under future global land use change scenarios. Sustainability 10 (2764). https://doi.org/10.3390/su10082764.

Ching, J., et al., 2018. WUDAPT: an urban weather, climate, and environmental modeling infrastructure for the anthropocene. Bull. Am. Meteorol. Soc. 99 (9), 1907—1924. https://doi.org/10.1175/BAMS-D-16-0236.1.

Collins, M., et al., 2013. Long-term Climate Change: Projections, Commitments and Irreversibility. Cambridge University Press, pp. 1029—1136. Available at: https://research.monash.edu/en/publications/long-term-climate-change-projections- commitments-and-irreversibil (Accessed 9 February 2021).

Cuaresma, J.C., 2017. Income projections for climate change research: A framework based on human capital dynamics. Global Env. Change 42, 226—236. https://doi.org/10.1016/j.gloenvcha.2015.02.012.

Dellink, R., et al., 2017. Long-term economic growth projections in the Shared Socioeconomic Pathways. Global Env. Change 42, 200—214. https://doi.org/10.1016/j.gloenvcha.2015.06.004.

Endsley, K.A., et al., 2018. Remote sensing of socio-ecological dynamics in urban neighborhoods. Comprehensive Remote Sensing. Elsevier.

Fricko, O., 2017. The marker quantification of the Shared Socioeconomic Pathway 2: A middle-of-the-road scenario for the 21st century. Global Env. Change J. 42, 251−267. https://doi.org/10.1016/j.gloenvcha.2016.06.004.

Fujimori, S., et al., 2017. SSP3: AIM implementation of shared socioeconomic pathways Shinichiro. Global Env. Change 42, 268−283. https://doi.org/10.1016/j.gloenvcha.2016.06.009.

Ghofrani, Z., Sposito, V., Faggian, R., 2017. A Comprehensive Review of Blue-Green Infrastructure Concepts, International Journal of Environment and Sustainability. Available at: www.sciencetarget.com (Accessed 10 February 2019).

https://www.thehindu.com/news/cities/Delhi/gurugram-may-soon-be-living-hell/article18702548.ece, 2017−. (Accessed 2 June 2017).

Howard, L., 1833. The Climate of London: Deduced from Meteorological Observations Made in the Metropolis and at Various Places Around it. Available at: https://books.google.co.in/books?hl=en&lr=&id=-yllMDVOz1IC&oi=fnd&pg=PA1&dq=Howard+1833&ots=4_A2kd5lxV&sig=x9c0GJjq3Qn q1JMQgPLWox9D9PE#v=onepage&q=Howard 1833&f=false (Accessed 8 February 2021).

Hu, L., Brunsell, N.A., 2015. A new perspective to assess the urban heat island through remotely sensed atmospheric profiles. Remote Sens. Environ. 158, 393−406. https://doi.org/10.1016/j.rse.2014.10.022.

Huang, Q., Lu, Y., 2018. Urban heat island research from 1991 to 2015: a bibliometric analysis. Theor. Appl. Climatol. 131 (3−4), 10551067. https://doi.org/10.1007/s00704-016-2025-1.

International Organization for Migration (IOM), 2015. World Migration Report Migrants and Cities: New Partnerships to Manage Mobility. Available at: www.iom.int (Accessed 8 February 2021).

IPCC, W.G.I., 2014. AR5 Climate Change 2014 - Impacts, Adaptation and Vulnerability: Part B: Regional Aspects, vol. 2. Cambridge University Press. Available at: https://www.google.co.in/books/edition/_/aJTBQAAQBAJ?hl=en&gbpv=0#pli=1 (Accessed 9 February 2021).

Jiang, L., et al., 2017. Global urbanization projections for the Shared Socioeconomic Pathways. Global Env. Change 42, 193−199. https://doi.org/10.1016/j.gloenvcha.2015.03.008.

Kebede, A.S., et al., 2018. Applying the global RCP-SSP-SPA scenario framework at subnational scale: a multiscale and participatory scenario approach. Sci. Total Environ. 635, 659−672. https://doi.org/10.1016/j.scitotenv.2018.03.368.

Kim, J.B., et al., 2017. Assessing climate change impacts, benefits of mitigation, and uncertainties on major global forest regions under multiple socioeconomic and emissions scenarios. Env. Res. Lett. 12. https://doi.org/10.1088/1748-9326/aa63fc.

Kotharkar, R., Bagade, A., 2018. Evaluating urban heat island in the critical local climate zones of an Indian city. Landsc. Urban Plann. 169, 92−104. https://doi.org/10.1016/J.LANDURBPLAN.2017.08.009.

Kotharkar, R., Surawar, M., 2016. Land use, land cover, and population density impact on the formation of canopy urban heat islands through traverse survey in the Nagpur urban area, India. J. Urban Plann. Dev. 142 (1), 04015003. https://doi.org/10.1061/(asce)up.1943-5444.0000277.

Kriegler, E., et al., 2017. Fossil-fueled development (SSP5): An energy and resource intensive scenario for the 21st century. Global Env. Change 42, 297−315. https://doi.org/10.1016/j.gloenvcha.2016.05.015.

Kushwaha, S., Nithiyanandam, Y., 2019. The study of heat island and its relation with urbanization in Gurugram, Delhi NCR for the period of 1990 to 2018. Int. Arch. Photogr. Remote Sens. Spatial Inf. Sci. ISPRS Arch. 42 (5/W3), 49−56. https://doi.org/10.5194/isprs-archives-XLII-5-W3-49-2019.

Kuze, H., et al., 2012. Surface energy balance method into remote sensing application and GIS for drought monitoring in Bandung, Indonesia. J. Emerg. Trends Eng. Appl. Sci. 3, 394−400. https://doi.org/10.10520/EJC137044.

Leimbach, M., et al., 2017. Future growth patterns of world regions − A GDP scenario approach. Global Env. Change J. 42, 215−225. https://doi.org/10.1016/j.gloenvcha.2015.02.005.

Masui, T., et al., 2011. An emission pathway for stabilization at 6 Wm-2 radiative forcing. Climatic Change 109 (1), 59−76. https://doi.org/10.1007/s10584-011-0150-5.

Miao, S., et al., 2009. An observational and modeling study of characteristics of urban heat island and boundary layer structures in Beijing. J. Appl. Meteorol. Climatol. 48 (3), 484−501. https://doi.org/10.1175/2008JAMC1909.1.

Mohan, M., et al., 2009. Assessment of urban heat islands intensities over Delhi. In: The Seventh International Conference on Urban Climate, 3, pp. 3−6.

Mohan, M., Kandya, A., Battiprolu, A., 2011. Urban heat island effect over national capital region of India: a study using the temperature trends. J. Environ. Protect. 02 (04), 465−472. https://doi.org/10.4236/jep.2011.24054.

Moss, R.H., et al., 2010. The next generation of scenarios for climate change research and assessment. Nature 463 (7282), 747−756. https://doi.org/10.1038/nature08823.

Oke, T.R., Fuggle, R.F., 1972. Comparison of urban/rural counter and net radiation at night. Boundary-Layer Meteorol. 2 (3), 290−308. https://doi.org/10.1007/BF02184771.

Oke, T.R., Maxwell, G.B., 1975. Urban heat island dynamics in Montreal and Vancouver. Atmos. Environ. 9 (2), 191−200. https://doi.org/10.1016/0004-6981(75)90067-0.

Ostadtaghizadeh, A., et al., 2017. Community disaster resilience: a systematic review on assessment models and tools. PLOS Curr. Disasters (August).

Pal, S., et al., 2012. Spatio-temporal variability of the atmospheric boundary layer depth over the Paris agglomeration: an assessment of the impact of the urban heat island intensity. Atmos. Environ. 63, 261−275. https://doi.org/10.1016/j.atmosenv.2012.09.046.

Peterson, J.T., 1969. Temerature. The Climate of Cities: A Survey of Recent Literature. U.S. Department of Health, Education and Welfare, pp. 7−15.

Pitman, S., Ely, M., 2013. 'From Grey to Green: Life Support for Human Habitats. The Evidence Base for Green Infrastructure', Greenhouse 2013: The Science of Climate Change, pp. 4−5 (December 2012).

Popp, A., et al., 2017. Land-use futures in the shared socio-economic pathways. Global Env. Change 42, 331−345. https://doi.org/10.1016/j.gloenvcha.2016.10.002.

Ren, G.Y., et al., 2007. Implications of temporal change in urban heat island intensity observed at Beijing and Wuhan stations. Geophys. Res. Lett. 34 (5). https://doi.org/10.1029/2006GL027927.

Riahi, K., et al., 2011. RCP 8.5-A scenario of comparatively high greenhouse gas emissions. Climatic Change 109 (1), 33−57. https://doi.org/10.1007/s10584-011-0149-y.

Riahi, K., et al., 2017. The Shared Socioeconomic Pathways and their energy, land use, and greenhouse gas emissions implications: an overview. Global Environ. Change 42, 153−168. https://doi.org/10.1016/j.gloenvcha.2016.05.009.

Ribeiro, P.J.G., Pena Jardim Goncalves, L.A., 2019. Urban resilience: a conceptual framework. Sustain. Cities Soc. 50 (November 2018). https://doi.org/10.1016/j.scs.2019.101625.

Rogelj, J., et al., 2018. Scenarios towards limiting global mean temperature increase below 1.5 °C. Nature Clim. Change (April). https://doi.org/10.1038/s41558-018-0091-3.

Samir, K.C., et al., 2017. The human core of the shared socioeconomic pathways: Population scenarios by age, sex and level of education for all countries to 2100. Global Env. Change 42, 181−192. https://doi.org/10.1016/j.gloenvcha.2014.06.004.

Shuzhen, Z., 1994. Discussion OF the urban-rural differences IN atmospheric humidity of Shanghai area. Trans. Oceanol. Limnol. Available at: https://en.cnki.com.cn/Article_en/CJFDTotal-HYFB199402001.htm (Accessed 8 February 2021).

Sismanidis, P., Keramitsoglou, I., Kiranoudis, C.T., 2015. A satellite-based system for continuous monitoring of Surface Urban Heat Islands. Urban Clim. 14, 141−153. https://doi.org/10.1016/j.uclim.2015.06.001.

Stewart, I.D., 2011. A systematic review and scientific critique of methodology in modern urban heat island literature. Int. J. Climatol. 31 (2), 200−217. https://doi.org/10.1002/joc.2141.

Thomson, A.M., et al., 2011. RCP4.5: a pathway for stabilization of radiative forcing by 2100. Climatic Change 109 (1), 77–94. https://doi.org/10.1007/s10584-011-0151-4.

United Nations, 2015. World Population Prospects the 2015 Revision. Available at: https://population.un.org/wpp/Publications/Files/Key_Findings_WPP_2015.pdf.

United Nations, 2018. World Urbanization Prospects. Department of Economic and Social Affairs, Population Division.

Veena, K., Parammasivam, K.M., Venkatesh, T.N., 2020. Urban heat island studies: current status in India and a comparison with the international studies. J. Earth Syst. Sci. 129 (1). https://doi.org/10.1007/s12040-020-1351-y.

Voogt, J.A., Oke, T.R., 2003. Thermal remote sensing of urban climates. Remote Sens. Environ. 86 (3), 370–384. https://doi.org/10.1016/S0034-4257(03)00079-8.

van Vuuren, D.P., et al., 2011. The representative concentration pathways: an overview. Climatic Change 109 (1), 5–31. https://doi.org/10.1007/s10584-011-0148-z.

van Vuuren, D.P., et al., 2017. Energy, land-use and greenhouse gas emissions trajectories under a green growth paradigm. Global Env. Change 42, 237–250. https://doi.org/10.1016/j.gloenvcha.2016.05.008.

Watkins, R., et al., 2002. The London Heat Island: results from summertime monitoring. Build. Serv. Eng. Technol. 23 (2), 97–106. https://doi.org/10.1191/0143624402bt031oa.

Weng, Q., Lu, D., Schubring, J., 2004. Estimation of land surface temperature-vegetation abundance relationship for urban heat island studies. Remote Sens. Environ. 89 (4), 467–483. https://doi.org/10.1016/j.rse.2003.11.005.

Whitford, V., Ennos, A.R., Handley, J.F., 2001. "City form and natural process" - indicators for the ecological performance of urban areas and their application to Merseyside, UK. Landsc. Urban Plann. 57 (2), 91–103. https://doi.org/10.1016/S0169-2046(01)00192-X.

Working Group I - AR 5 IPCC, 2013. In: Stocker, T.F., Qin, D. (Eds.), Climate Change 2013: The Physical Science Basis. Cambridge University Press. Available at: https://books.google.co.in/books?hl=en&lr=&id=o4gaBQAAQBAJ&oi=fnd&pg=PR1&dq=S tocker+et+al.+2013&ots=WhkveOHqOk&sig=XfEg PYcJPa28sfi9jPZG2TO0IGQ#v=onepag e&q=Stocker et al. 2013&f=false (Accessed 9 February 2021).

Wu, H., et al., 2017. Urban heat island impacted by fine particles in Nanjing, China. Sci. Rep. 7 (1), 1–11. https://doi.org/10.1038/s41598-017-11705-z.

Yang, X., Hou, Y., Chen, B., 2011. Observed surface warming induced by urbanization in east China. J. Geophys. Res. Atmos. 116 (14). https://doi.org/10.1029/2010JD015452.

Zhong, C., et al., 2019. A specific study on the impacts of PM2.5 on urban heat islands with detailed in situ data and satellite images. Sustainability 11 (24). https://doi.org/10.3390/su11247075.

Urban heat island effect in India: assessment, impacts, and mitigation

11

Manju Mohan, Shweta Bhati and Ankur Prabhat Sati

Centre for Atmospheric Sciences, Indian Institute of Technology Delhi, New Delhi, India

1. Introduction

Cities have existed in the world from as early as Neolithic age. The ancient cities such as Memphis (Egypt) and Uruk (Iraq) were housing several tens of thousands of inhabitants by 31st-century BCE (Chandler, 1987). The Indus valley civilization, which was prevalent from about 3000 to 1500 BCE, was one of the first civilizations in which a sophisticated and technologically advanced urban culture was discovered (Wright, 2009). The cities of the ancient world, however, were generally small, which were supported by relatively large rural populations. "Urbanized societies," in which a high proportion of the population lives in cities, developed only in the 19th and 20th centuries (Davis, 1955).

It has been more than 200 years since the first scientific study on urban climate was presented by Luke Howard, which was focused on London (Howard, 1818) and indicated that urban areas have a distinct meteorology as compared to the rural areas. Since that time, our knowledge about urban meteorology has increased systematically, particularly over the last three to four decades (Przybylak et al., 2015). Numerous studies have pointed out that as a city grows, the heat of the city builds, which makes it warmer than a rural area. This urban localized weather is a condition that is referred to as the urban heat island (UHI) effect. The urban—rural temperature contrast was termed the "urban heat island" by Manley (1958), and since then, the term has been widely used in the literature.

Parry (1950) summed up the basic causes of UHI as follows:

> By concentrating his buildings, by confronting the elements with surfaces of brick and concrete, paving and paint, and by the indirect results of his industrial activity, the townsman has created a distinctive local climate

The major causes of the heat island phenomena are alterations of land surface coverings and increased anthropogenic waste heat. As population centers grow from village to town to city, they tend to have a corresponding increase in average temperature. This consequently increases building energy demand for air-conditioning in warmer countries like that of tropical regions. This increase in energy demand could result in not only additional generation of anthropogenic heat but also further intensification of heat islands themselves (Kikegawa et al., 2003). UHI intensity estimations are therefore important in urban planning as well as emission reduction strategies. Changes in land use and land cover (LULC), due to increasing population and infrastructure pressures for rapidly growing megacities, play an important role in the development of UHIs.

A sharp rise in population vis-a-vis urbanization has been recorded in India in past five decades. Currently, the most populated nation in the world is China, and it is expected that India will surpass China by 2025 to become the most populated country in the world. With this continuous increase in population, cities have seen large-scale migration of the rural population to earn their livelihood, thereby leading to a steady increase in urban population in India. Consequently, a vast majority of population growth is around the economically strong cities, which expand into Megacities or urban agglomerates. For instance, in National Capital Region of Delhi, the urban and built-up areas recorded an almost 17-fold increase during the period from 1972 to 2014 (Sati and Mohan, 2018). Such rapidly increasing population in megacities is associated with somewhat similar growth rates in vehicular population, residential and commercial complexes, industries, and other infrastructure.

Such growth has resulted in significant changes in LULC and increase in anthropogenic heat emissions, which may consequently generate pockets of high UHI. While increasing temperatures can be a direct consequence of global warming or may be a local phenomenon because of LULC changes and anthropogenic heat, they necessitate study of effect of heat island phenomenon that is expected to be greater in megacities. With this background in consideration, the present work reviews research efforts undertaken in India for studying UHI in terms of assessment methodologies, its degree of prevalence, impacts, and mitigation strategies. Literature explored for this review has been extracted from major peer-reviewed literature research databases pertaining to UHI studies in India till March 31, 2021.

2. Growth of research in urban heat island in India

Some of the earliest studies pertaining to UHI effect in India were carried out in 1970s and early 1980s for cities such as Delhi (Bahl and Padmanabhmurthy, 1979; Padmanabhmurthy and Bahl, 1982, 1984), Mumbai (Mukherjee and Daniel, 1976), and Pune (Daniel and Krishnamurty, 1973; Maske et al., 1978; Padmanabhmurthy, 1979) based on measurements. Varying heat island intensities from different authors were studied and effects on mean mixing depths were estimated by Mohan (1985). All these studies have documented profound impact of urbanization on climate of tropical cities by identifying a strong heat island over the city region. However, there is not much literature on Indian UHI studies from late 1980 to 2000s except for Sundersingh (1990) for Chennai city (erstwhile Madras), Padmanabhamurty (1990) for Delhi, and few studies for Pune (Mukherjee et al., 1987; Gadgil and Deosthali, 1994; Deosthali, 2000). All these studies measured canopy layer heat island in their respective study areas. Sarkar et al. (1998) developed a two-dimensional numerical model to study the effect of the coastal UHI on the sea breeze front and the thermal internal boundary layer height.

While earlier studies on UHI in India focused on canopy layer heat island, post-2000 era saw the emergence of studies using satellite-derived data to study surface urban heat island (SUHI). As mentioned in Section 2.1, SUHI studies constitute the majority of UHI studies in India. Badrinath et al. (2005) analyzed day and night ENVISAT-AATSR satellite data for UHI zones in Hyderabad city. Other surface heat island studies include those by Ramachandra and Kumar (2009) for Bangalore, Faris and Sudhakar Reddy (2010) for Chennai, and Katpatal et al., (2008) for Nagpur.

Mohan et al. (2009) conducted an extensive field campaign to understand the prevalent (canopy layer) heat island phenomena in Delhi based on in situ measurement using multisite ground-based mini weather stations.

The decade of 2001–10 also saw emergence of UHI impact studies. Das and Padmanabhamurty (2007) discussed the small-scale spatial variations of thermal discomfort index associated with heat island intensity in Delhi. UHI impacts on precipitation were explored by Mohapatra et al. (2010). UHI influence on sea-breeze circulation was studied by Simpson et al. (2008) while Agarwal and Tandon (2010) formulated a steady state two-dimensional mathematical model to study the dispersion of air pollutants under the effect of UHI.

Study of various aspects of UHI phenomenon has taken prominence in India only in the past decade. Past decade has seen rise in studies exploring variation in magnitudes of UHI intensities, interrelationship of UHI and air pollution, impacts of UHI in terms of microclimate alteration as well as human health and UHI mitigation strategies. Fig. 11.1 presents the number of studies yielded by Scopus search for the keyword "urban heat island" and affiliation country as India in the search criteria. It can be seen that number of UHI studies have increased by leap and bounds especially in the latter half of the past decade.

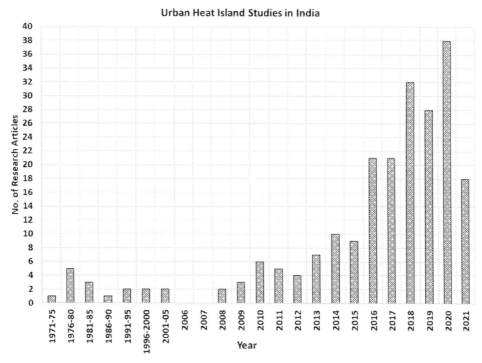

FIGURE 11.1

Literature available for urban heat island in India [SCOPUS Database till March 31, 2021].

3. Classification and assessment methodologies for UHI
3.1 Classification of UHI

The phenomenon of UHI was defined by Chandler (1962) as warm air, which characteristically rests within and above a city, and its effect is manifested in central districts having average temperatures greater than those of the suburbs and country areas outside the city. The measure of UHI effect, termed as urban heat island intensity (UHII), was standardized by Oke (1973) as difference between background rural and highest urban temperatures. Over the years, UHI effect has been observed for land surface and boundary layer temperatures as well as along with air temperatures. Overall, UHIs are classified into (i) atmospheric UHIs and (ii) SUHIs as show in Fig. 11.2 and represented diagrammatically in Fig. 11.3.

Canopy layer heat island is the relative warming of the urban canopy layer, which is the layer of air closest to the surface in the cities extending upward, approximately to the mean building height. For urban canopy heat island studies, air temperature measurements are done below the roof tops in the spaces between the buildings, i.e., within the urban canopy layer. Air temperatures are usually measured at about 1.5—2 m above the ground, where standard weather observations are taken. Studies related to canopy layer UHI in India are explored in Section 3.1.

Boundary layer heat island is the relative warming of the boundary layer, which is that part of the atmosphere that is in direct interaction with the Earth's surface and responds to surface forcing with a timescale of about an hour or less. Boundary layer depth is variable, typically between 100 and 3000 m. There are no studies reported that explored boundary layer heat island in India.

Surface UHIs refer to the relative warmth of urban surfaces and are based on Land Surface Temperatures (LST). Surface temperatures have an indirect but significant influence on air temperatures. For example, parks and vegetated areas, which typically have cooler surface temperatures, contribute to cooler air temperatures. Dense built-up areas, on the other hand, typically lead to warmer air temperatures. SUHIs have been studied the most in India. This could be due to the advantage of satellite data offering a spatial continuity and convenience of not carrying out instrument maintenance for field campaigns as in canopy layer heat island studies. In situ observations have a limitation of spatial continuity, which can be accounted for by satellite observations.

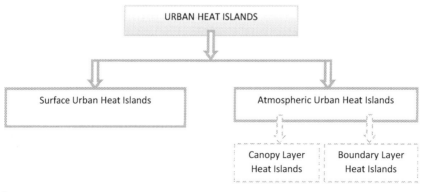

FIGURE 11.2

Classification of urban heat islands.

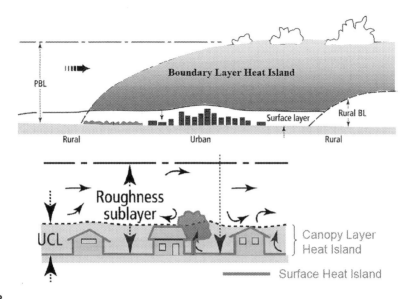

FIGURE 11.3

Types of urban heat islands (Voogt, 2004).

3.2 Methodologies for estimation of urban heat island intensity

(i) UHII with respect to rural reference station

The conventional method of determining UHII is the difference in ambient air surface temperature between the city center and a nearby rural area. The conventional method of determining UHII keeping rural areas as reference point is continuing to be used as per the data availability and cities in consideration (Mohammad and Goswami, 2019, 2021a; Nimish et al., 2020; Raj et al., 2020).

However, over the years, the urban geometry has become more complex, and we have multifaceted land use and cover in the cities with lots of commercial, industrial, residential, and green areas distributed. Therefore, one can also expect large spatial temperature gradients within the city that can be relevant in the context of cooling and/or heating energy demand. With growth of satellite towns, finding a rural site free from influence of urban canopies near the boundaries of urban areas is very difficult. Martin et al. (2015) remarked that while the classical UHI definition requires reference observations to be made before the human disturbance of the land, current rural areas are zones that may not be urbanized but in which the land has nevertheless been disturbed by humans. Hence, alternative methods for assessing UHI are being adopted as discussed in subsections (ii)−(v) below.

(ii) UHII with respect to peripheral areas

Another method is to keep peripheral areas as reference areas for determination of UHII with respect to main urban centers (Dutta and Das, 2020; Maral and Mukopadhyay 2015; Jain et al., 2019. While these areas are not rural areas, they present a case of zones least modified by human activity as compared to inner core urban zones.

(iii) Intracity temperature variation

The method of assessing UHI in terms of intracity temperature variation with respect to green areas such as large parks, urban forests, etc., is increasingly being followed (Mohan et al., 2012, 2013; Sharma and Joshi 2014), especially in SUHI studies. SUHI studies often analyze UHII as difference between land surface temperature of built-up (impervious) areas and green spaces within the city (Dutta et al., 2021b; Shukla and Jain, 2021; Mohammad and Goswami, 2021b).

To assess the applicability of intracity temperature variation for UHII, Mohan et al., 2013 estimated UHII from two different methods: (1) using difference between urban station temperature and the rural site temperature as a reference and (2) using difference between urban station temperature and the lowest temperature among all urban stations. Average UHII computed from both the methods was found to be quite close. Mohan et al., 2013 further suggested that in the absence of a reference rural site for UHI assessment, method (2) based on the lowest temperature within the city could be a good representation of UHII.

(iv) Inter-LULC temperature variation

Rather than reporting UHIIs by fixing one LULC as reference point, some SUHI studies prefer to explore temperature of built-up surfaces with respect to all relevant LULCs within the considered study area such as urban peripheral areas, forests patches within the city, barren soils, and water bodies (Pathak et al., 2021; Puppala and Singh, 2021; Mohan et al., 2020a; Neog et al., 2020; Pramanik and Punia, 2020). Martin et al. (2015) proposed the thermal reference of newly defined surface intraurban heat islands (SIUHIs), which is based on various temperature thresholds above the spatial average of LSTs within the city's administrative limits.

(v) WUDAPT-local climate zones−based UHI

UHI studies generally need to first identify the urban, rural, vegetated, or other land use land covers within the study area to determine the UHI intensity or inter-LULC temperature difference. Hence, these studies vary by opting for standard USGS/MODIS LULC classification or their own assigned classification relevant to their study area. This makes it difficult to compare different reported UHIIs on a same scale. Stewart and Oke (2012) suggested a uniform land classification system termed as "Local Climate Zone" (LCZ), which incorporates the physical and geometrical elements of the urban areas and introduces a logical approach in studying UHI effect in a city. This method has been suggested to maintain a uniformity in UHI studies for adopting classification of different land forms as it includes not only the different land covers but also different building forms, which is not present in standard USGS/MODIS LULC classification. Building further on LCZ classification, the World Urban Database and Access Portal Tools (WUDAPT) was initiated as an international community-generated urban canopy information and modeling infrastructure to facilitate urban-focused climate, weather, air quality, and energy-use modeling application studies. The base level of information (L0) consists of LCZ maps of cities; each LCZ category is associated with a range of values for model-relevant surface descriptors (roughness, impervious surface cover, roof area, building heights, etc.). Levels 1 (L1) and 2 (L2) will provide specific intraurban values for other relevant descriptors at greater precision, such as data morphological forms, material composition data, and energy usage (Ching et al., 2018). In India, there are now studies pertaining to LCZ delineation method incorporated by WUDAPT (Patel et al., 2020; Choudhary et al., 2021). This LCZ classification is being used now in recent studies for UHI assessment (Kotharkar and Bagade, 2018a, 2018b; Budhiraja et al., 2019; Kotharkar et al., 2019).

3.3 Assessment of heat islands

3.3.1 In situ measurements

Measurements for canopy layer heat islands are carried out through stationary weather station networks (Mohan et al., 2012, 2013; Roy et al., 2011). These weather stations can be administration's official automatic weather stations (AWS) or setup temporarily as part of field campaigns. Another method of carrying out measurements is through transect studies, which involve using handheld measurement devices or mounting measurement equipment on a moving vehicle (Borbora and Das, 2014; Jegananthan et al., 2016; Chakraborty et al., 2017; Kotharkar and Bagade, 2018a; Yadav and Sharma, 2018; Kotharkar et al., 2019).

The SUHI is generally estimated by satellite-based sensors, and there are very few in situ surface measurement-based studies of SUHI across the world. The in situ measurements of LST are mostly done for limited durations for specific campaigns. Mohan et al. (2013) measured the in situ LST using HOBO instruments (HOBO-U12-014 data logger with T type thermocouple) during the second week of March 2010 across few representative stations across Delhi. Similarly, Mallick et al. (2013) did field survey to measure LST using TELETEMP infrared thermometer. Mini infrared thermometer (make Fluke, model 59) was used for in situ measurements of LST by Mathew et al. (2018a). These in situ measurements at selected stations were mainly used to validate the satellite-based retrievals of the surface temperature toward assessing SUHI. However, Neog et al. (2020) studied SUHI pattern above Dibrugarh City through in situ observations only using noncontact infrared thermometer for a period of 4 months (from February to May 2019) over 16 locations.

3.3.2 Satellite-derived observations

All surfaces give off thermal energy that is emitted in wavelengths. Instruments on-board various satellites and other forms of remote sensing can identify and measure these wavelengths, providing an indication of temperature. (LST is an important factor in climate change, estimation of radiation budgets, and heat balance studies. LST is usually derived from thermal bands of remotely sensed data and is used to assess SUHI effect. LST-based SUHI obtained from various sensors, especially MODIS and Landsat, are also often used to validate the model simulated SUHI (Mohan et al., 2013, 2020b). A brief description of LST retrieval from various satellites and some studies over Indian cities is mentioned below:

- **ASTER:** Advanced Spaceborne Thermal Emission and Reflection Radiometer (ASTER) has 14 spectral bands, out of which five thermal bands (10−14) operate between 8 and 12 μm. Accurate estimation of LST requires atmospheric correction of the satellite data and the estimation of surface emissivity.
  The studies by Kant et al. (2009) and Mallick et al. (2013) over Delhi revealed a strong correlation between urbanization, LST increase, and strengthening of the heat island over the city using the LST retrieved from ASTER.
- **MODIS:** The moderate-resolution imaging spectroradiometer (MODIS) instruments on board the Terra and Aqua satellites have been functional since the years 2000 and 2002, respectively, providing day and night thermal observations of the Earth's surface. The MODIS Terra and Aqua LST product suite (MOD11 and MYD11) provides estimates of LST at 1 km spatial resolution. The MODIS LST product had been validated against in situ data and found to have an accuracy of about 1 K (Wan et al., 2004)

There are several studies utilizing MODIS LST toward UHI studies in various Indian cities, namely Chandigarh (Mathew et al., 2016c); Bhubaneshwar (Swain et al., 2017); Ahmedabad and Jaipur (Matthew et al., 2018a); five cities of Bihar (Barat et al., 2018); Bengaluru (Sussman et al., 2019). These studies indicate seasonal and interannual variabilities in UHII over the respective study regions. Furthermore, spatial distribution of UHI also indicated a strong urban core in the densely built-up area/city centers as compared to area within the suburban periphery.

- **Landsat:** Landsat mission, spanning over four decades, is the world's longest continuous program providing a huge collection of space-based moderate-resolution land remote sensing data. In 1972, with the launch of the Earth Resources Technology Satellite (ERTS-1), which was later renamed Landsat 1 this mission began, followed by Landsat 2, Landsat 3, and Landsat 4 in 1975, 1978, and 1982, respectively. The Landsat 5 launched in 1984 continued to deliver high-quality global data of Earth's land surfaces for almost 29 years. Landsat 7 was successfully launched in 1999 and, along with Landsat 8, which was launched in 2013, continues to provide daily global data.

Various studies have used the LST retrieval methods from the Landsat missions over Indian cities, namely Chennai (Faris et al., 2010); Ahmedabad (Joshi et al., 2015); Noida (Kikon et al., 2016); Lucknow (Singh et al., 2017a); Raipur (Guha et al., 2017); Nagpur (Surawar and Kotharakar 2017); Tirunelveli, Tamilnadu (Padmanabhan et al., 2019); Chandigarh (Sultana and Satyanarayana, 2020); Shantiniketan, West Bengal (Dutta and Das 2020); Vishakhapatnam (Puppala and Singh 2021).

Some of the major satellite-based surface heat island studies in India are listed in Table 11.2.

There exists a trade-off between the spatial and the temporal resolution of the satellite systems: they have either a higher spatial resolution with a lower temporal resolution or a lower spatial resolution with a higher temporal resolution. They do not fully capture radiant emissions from vertical surfaces, such as a building's wall, because the equipment mostly observes emissions from horizontal surfaces such as streets, rooftops, and treetops. Very few studies in India have analyzed and intercompared both canopy and surface heat islands for a given study area. Mohan et al. (2012, 2013) were some of the first studies to present analysis of both canopy layer and SUHI and an intercomparison of both for Delhi. Their studies revealed better comparison during nighttime as compared to daytime. Similar observations were noted in Mohan et al. (2020a) for industrial heat island case study.

3.3.3 Numerical modeling

Field observations and satellite measurements have limitation of continuity in spatial and temporal variation of UHI, which is accounted for by numerical methods. Numerical models can provide the spatial and temporal variation of UHIs, and several such modeling studies have been undertaken internationally. In India, however, numerical modeling for UHI has gained momentum only in the past half decade. Earlier attempts involving numerical models in India for UHI were aimed at studying impact of urban effects on sea breeze circulation (Sarkar et al., 1998; Simpson et al., 2008). In the past two decades, the Weather Research and Forecasting (WRF) Model has become one of the world's most widely used numerical weather prediction models, which offers a range of Earth system prediction applications, such as air chemistry, hydrology, wildland fires, hurricanes, and regional climate (Powers et al., 2017). In India also, WRF model has been used for both operational weather forecasting and weather and climate research (Pattnaik, 2019) including model evaluation and sensitivity analysis

(Gunwani et al., 2021; Gunwani and Mohan, 2017; Mohan and Sati, 2016; Mohan and Bhati, 2011), fog prediction (Payra and Mohan, 2014), and air quality (Mohan and Gupta, 2018; Gupta and Mohan, 2013, 2015), among others.

WRF model, however, being a mesoscale model, cannot incorporate energy exchanges that take place at urban scale. To better represent the physical processes involved in the exchange of heat, momentum, and water vapor in urban environment in mesoscale model, an urban canopy model (UCM) is coupled to the WRF model. The main purpose of the coupled model is to improve the description of lower boundary conditions and to provide more accurate forecasts for urban regions. The UCM is a single layer model, which has a simplified urban geometry. Some of the features of the UCM include shadowing from buildings, reflection of short and longwave radiation, wind profile in the canopy layer and multilayer heat transfer equation for roof, wall, and road surfaces (Tewari et al., 2007; Kusaka and Kimura, 2004). Some of the first attempts in India to use a UCM coupled with WRF regional numerical mesoscale weather prediction model to study urbanization impacts were by Shastri et al. (2015) for Mumbai and Bhati and Mohan (2016) for Delhi. Since then, there have been a few studies that use WRF-UCM coupled modeling system to study the UHI effect (Bhati and Mohan, 2018; Gupta et al., 2021; Kedia et al., 2021) and investigate urbanization impacts mainly on precipitation (Mohapatra et al., 2017; Paul et al., 2018; Shastri et al., 2019; Patel et al., 2019; Niyogi et al., 2020; Sahoo et al., 2020). All these studies have emphasized the importance of incorporating urban canopy parametrizations in mesoscale modeling through coupling with UCM. Internationally, WRF model coupled with single or multilayer UCMs consist of the most used method for simulation of UHI using the atmospheric numerical model (Kim and Brown, 2021). However, in India, more modeling-based research studies considering numerical weather prediction models and urban canopies are needed and may be addressed as a prevailing research gap in the Indian context.

Some studies have attempted to study and model UHI effect through statistical techniques. In these studies, statistical approaches and regression methods are implemented to correlate the UHI to the complex and large-scale characteristic of a city such as population, or height/width ratio of street canyons, land use, weather variables, etc (Singh et al., 2017b; Gopinath and Thippesh, 2018; Kotharkar et al., 2019; Mehrotra et al., 2020b).

Table 11.1 lists the salient features of major canopy layer UHI studies in India, which are based on in situ measurements and numerical models.

3.3.4 Diurnal temperature range (DTR) as a proxy to urbanization and heat island
Diurnal temperature range is an important index of climate change (Karl et al., 1984) and is susceptible to urban effects (IPCC, 2001). Urbanization-induced UHI effect prominently takes place at night when buildings and streets release the solar heat absorbed during the day and lower sky-view factor (SVF) trapping that heat within the urban canopies, thereby increasing the nighttime temperatures. Further, a slight cooling happens in the daytime owing to the shading effect, presence of aerosols, etc. A combined effect of these two causes lowering of DTR with increase in urbanization. As more and more areas are getting urbanized, a downward trend of local DTR has been observed. Mohan et al. (2011a) analyzed annual and seasonal temperature trends and anomalies for maximum, minimum, and mean temperatures of the four meteorological stations of the National Capital Region for 1968–2005. The analysis revealed that the annual mean maximum temperature did not show any specific trend; however, the annual mean minimum temperature indicates a warming trend in general over the National Capital Region indicating significant urbanization process in the past few decades.

Table 11.1 Canopy layer heat island studies in India.

Study area	Assessment basis	Salient features
Based on measurements		
Chennai (Rajan and Amirtham, 2021)	Traverse Survey	• Observations through traverse survey (1 summer day, 1 winter day)
		• Maximum air temperature difference of 4.5°C in winter and 2.5°C in summer between the city center and suburban/fringe areas
Angul-Talcher Area, Odisha (Mohan et al., 2020a)	Field Campaign	• In-situ observations through 3 months long field campaign (April–July2016)
		• Industrial and mining sites were the most frequent nighttime canopy-layer heat island intensity (HIN) hotspots and thereby it was termed as "industrial heat island"
		• During the daytime, croplands experienced the most frequent canopy-layer HIN hotspots
		• Hourly maximum heat island intensities observed in the range of 7–9°C
Delhi NCR (Budhiraja et al., 2020)	AWS	• Based on fixed AWS data of year 2018 of four subcities in Delhi NCR
		• Highest nighttime UHI in the order of 7.52°C
		• Weak daytime inverted UHI with a magnitude 2–3°C
Chennai (Swamy et al., 2020)	Field Campaign	• Field measurements carried out for summer (May–June) and winter (Nov–Dec) seasons at three locations
		• Ambient air temperatures at urban locations were found to be more than 3°C in summer

Table 11.1 Canopy layer heat island studies in India.—cont'd

Study area	Assessment basis	Salient features
Nagpur (Kotharkar et al., 2019)	Mobile Survey	• Fewer and weaker variations of air temperature between the study regions for winter • mobile survey to collect nocturnal air-temperature data during two consecutive summers (2016 and 2017) at various sites classified using LCZ and city specific built parameters • Maximum UHI:4.05°C
Bhopal (Jain and Pathak, 2019)	Field Campaign	• Field measurements at nine sites during winter (December 2016−January 2017) and summer (May−June 2017) • Highest intraurban temperature difference: 6°C • Intersite temperature difference greater in summer than winter
Delhi (Yadav and Sharma, 2018)	Traverse Survey	• Intracity UHI studied by mobile transverse technique for selected days in July (Monsoon season) and November 2014 (Winter) • Least variation in UHII (0−2°C) during the afternoon period, highest values of UHII found during night time up to 8°C • Low UHII values obtained in the monsoon season and high UHII values in winter season
Nagpur (Kotharkar and Bagade, 2018b)	Field Campaign and Mobile Survey	• UHI evaluation based on local climate zone (LCZ) using fixed station points and mobile traverse survey conducted during the month of December 2015 and February 2016 of winter season • UHI intensity within built LCZ ranges from 1.76 to 4.09°C

Continued

Table 11.1 Canopy layer heat island studies in India.—cont'd

Study area	Assessment basis	Salient features
Delhi (Yadav et al., 2017)	AWS	• UHII determined as difference in air temperatures between two locations representing urban and suburban areas based on hourly daily temperature values for the period 2010–13 • High UHI obtained in morning hours (0700–0900) as compared to day and night times • Highest UHII magnitude ranging from 2.8 to 3°C observed in spring while Monsoon season showed least UHII values
Kanpur (Chakraborty et al., 2017)	Mobile Survey	• Mobile observations carried out in the months of May (premonsoon), June (premonsoon) and September (monsoon-cloudy) for examining urban–rural temperature difference (ΔTc) • Nighttime ΔTc values dominate during both the premonsoon (maximum of 3.6°C) and the monsoon (maximum of 2.0°C).
Nagpur (Kotharkar and Surawar, 2016)	Traverse Survey	• Traverse surveys carried out during the summer and winter seasons, 2012–14, to measure nocturnal mean canopy UHI intensity • Mean nocturnal UHII 2.14°C during summer and 2.36°C during winter • Negative impact of vegetation on UHI, positive impact of population density
Chennai Metropolitan Area (CMA) (Jeganathan et al., 2016)	Mobile measurements	• UHI temperature differences were seen in the range of 3–4.5°C within the city in the month of May 2012 • The maximum intensity of temperature noticed in the central core city and north Chennai

Table 11.1 Canopy layer heat island studies in India.—cont'd

Study area	Assessment basis	Salient features
Chennai Metropolitan Area (CMA) (Amirtham, 2016)	Field Campaign	• In situ field measurements at 30 locations from May 2008 to January 2009
		• Existence of a cool island in the urban core of CMA during daytime (1400 h) with a temperature difference of 10.4°C in summer and 3.7°C in winter
		• Significant positive UHI ranging from 3.6°C in summer to 4.1°C in winter at nighttime (0600 h)
Mumbai Metropolitan Region (Maral and Mukhopadhyay, 2015)	AWS	• Study of maximum and minimum temperatures of 32 years (1976–2007) at four meteorological stations
		• Maximum difference of mean temperatures in winter (2.4–2.6°C)
		• Negative UHI during monsoon nights
Guwahati (Borbora and Das, 2014)	Field Campaign and Mobile Survey	• Temperature data measured at four fixed observation sites representing urban core and periphery (May to October 2009)
		• Highest nighttime and daytime UHII values: 2.29 and 2.12°C
		• Higher DTR experienced in the month of May; variation in the average monthly DTR is lower in urban stations compared to rural ones
		• Mobile measurements also carried out during the months of June, July and August 2013. UHII recorded in the mobile runs, ranged from 1.23 to 0.78°C.
Delhi (Mohan et al., 2013)	Field Campaign	• UHIIs assessed based on in situ measurements at 30 sites during a selected period in March 2010

Continued

Table 11.1 Canopy layer heat island studies in India.—cont'd

Study area	Assessment basis	Salient features
Delhi (Roy et al., 2011)	Field Campaign	• Dense urban areas and highly commercial areas were observed to have highest UHI with maximum hourly magnitude peaking up to 10.7°C and average daily maximum UHI reaching 8.3°C • Built-up canopies reported largest gradient between air and skin temperature. • Comparison of intracity spatial temperature variations based UHI vis-à-vis a reference rural site temperature-based UHI indicated that intracity UHI can be assessed in place of urban-rural UHII area in the absence of rural reference station • automated weather sensors installed at 13 sites for a 1-year period from May 2007 to June 2008 • Largest spatial variations in temperatures observed during the cloud-free summer season; lowest during the cloud-covered monsoon season • Maximum UHIIs observed during late afternoon hours, minimal in the early morning hours before sunrise
Delhi (Mohan et al., 2009, 2012)	Field Campaign	• UHIIs assessed based on in situ measurements at 30 sites during a selected period in May 2008 • UHI effect found to be most dominant in areas of dense built-up infrastructure and at commercial centers • UHIIs observed to be higher in magnitude both during afternoon hours and night hours (maximum up to 8.3°C)

Table 11.1 Canopy layer heat island studies in India.—cont'd

Study area	Assessment basis	Salient features
Based on numerical models		
Northwest India (8 cities) (Kedia et al., 2021)	WRF Model	• WRF-based simulated UHII • Average nighttime UHI intensity: 2.4−5.0°C and during winter (Jan 2016) 0.6−2.0°C during summer over the eight selected city regions. • For all eight urban cities, the UHI intensity is higher during winter than in summer
Delhi (Sharma et al., 2019)	UrbClim Model	• Urban climate model run for base year 2014 for climate projections RCP8.5 using an ensemble of 11 GCM model outputs • Nighttime UHI intensity of 4.1°C and exhibits negligible change over time
Delhi (Bhati and Mohan, 2016, 2018)	WRF Model and Observations (Field Campaign)	• Urban heat island effect has been assessed using weather research and forecasting model (WRF v3.5) • Four simulations have been carried out with different types of LULC data viz. (1) USGS, (2) MODIS, (3) user-modified USGS and (4) user-modified land use data coupled with urban canopy model (UCM) for incorporation of canopy features • There is a significant improvement in model performance with modification of LULC and inclusion of UCM. Index of agreement for mean urban heat island intensities (UHI) improved from 0.4 to 0.7 with modified land use coupled with UCM • Model is able to capture the magnitude of UHI as well as high UHI zones well

Continued

Table 11.1 Canopy layer heat island studies in India.—cont'd

Study area	Assessment basis	Salient features
Bangalore (Gopinath and Thippesh, 2018)	Statistical Modeling	• Determination of UHII using Artificial Neural Network technique • Air temperature values collected over a period of 3 years (2010−13) at 12 stations were used for training • Knowledge based upon training tested and validated with the real-time data for forecasting with a good coefficient of correlation of 0.93 between the predicted and actual values

Table 11.2 Surface heat island studies in India.

Study area	Satellite	Salient features
Hyderabad (Badarinath et al., 2005)	ENVISAT-AATSR	• Day and nighttime datasets over urban areas of Hyderabad analyzed with a view to study UHI • Satellite derived surface temperature values are within $\pm 1°C$ from ground measured values. • Heat island formations in urban regions of Hyderabad and environs seen in the nighttime data with core urban regions showing high temperatures • Temperature variations during day and nighttime correlated well with the density patterns of urban areas • Spatial variation in apparent thermal inertia estimated from the AATSR data showed positive correlation with variability in land use/land cover in urban areas
Greater Bangalore (Ramachandra and Kumar, 2009)	Landsat MSS, TM, IRS LISS-III MSS, Landsat ETM+, IRS LISS-III, MODIS	• Changes in land surface temperature (LST) analyzed with respect to land cover changes during 1973−2007 • Positive correlation with the increase in paved surfaces and LST.

Table 11.2 Surface heat island studies in India.—cont'd

Study area	Satellite	Salient features
Delhi (Kant et al., 2009)	ASTER	• 466% increase in paved surfaces (buildings, roads, etc.) has led to the increase in LST by about 2°C, confirming UHI phenomenon • Minimum noise fraction (MNF) components used for LU/LC classification • Satellite-derived emissivity values found to be in good agreement with literature and field measured values
Chennai (Faris and Sudhakar Reddy, 2010)	Landsat-7 ETM+	• Fallow land, waste land/bare soil, commercial/industrial and high dense built-up area have high surface temperature values during daytime; during nighttime high surface temperature values are found over high dense built-up, water bodies, commercial/industrial and low dense built-up • Strong negative correlation between surface temperature and NDVI over dense vegetation, sparse vegetation, and low dense built-up area indicating that the relationship between the spatial distribution of LU/LC and vegetation density is closely related to the development of urban heat islands • Maximum LST difference between the urban and the surrounding area: 12°C. • Maximum LST observed for the Central Business District (CBD) and some impervious surfaces and industrial locations
Delhi (Pandey et al., 2012)	MODIS	• Daytime cool island over central parts of Delhi in winter months • Maximum Cool Island intensity: 4−6°C; Maximum nighttime UHII: 4−7°C • Significant negative correlations between daytime surface temperatures and AOD levels

Continued

Table 11.2 Surface heat island studies in India.—cont'd

Study area	Satellite	Salient features
Delhi (Mallick et al., 2012)	LANDSAT TM	• Emissivity derived by using normalized difference moisture index (NDMI) • A strong correlation is observed between surface temperatures with NDMI over different LULC classes, indicating that surface temperatures can be predicted if NDMI values are known.
Delhi (Mohan et al., 2013)	MODIS-TERRA	• UHI based on in situ ambient temperatures and satellite-derived land surface temperatures show reasonable comparison during nighttime in terms of UHI magnitude and hotspots but poor during daytime • MODIS-derived LSTs showed overestimation during daytime and underestimation during nighttime when compared with in situ skin temperature measurements
Delhi (Mallick et al., 2013)	ASTER and Landsat 7 ETM+ in the thermal infrared region 3–14 μm.	• LST estimation using night-time satellite data. • Central Business District (CBD) of Delhi, (Connaught Place, a high-density built-up area), and commercial/industrial areas display heat islands condition with a temperature greater than 4°C compared to the suburbs • Highly significant correlation between relative surface temperature and impervious surface area (ISA)
Delhi (Pandey et al., 2014)	MODIS-TERRA monthly LST product MOD11C3.005 at 5.6 km resolution	• Nocturnal heat island intensity is minimum (0–2 K) during the monsoon months and maximum during the month of March (4–6 K) • Day-time cool island forms over Delhi twice during the year in the months of May–June and October–December • Significant negative correlation between UHII and aerosol optical depth (AOD)

Table 11.2 Surface heat island studies in India.—cont'd

Study area	Satellite	Salient features
Delhi (Sharma and Joshi, 2014)	Landsat TM	• Maximum and minimum seasonal UHI intensities were observed in summer (intensity = 16.7°C) and winter (intensity = 7.4°C), respectively. (Data: 2010−11) • Major commercial and industrial sites across the city, and the airport area in south experienced higher UHI effects
Delhi (Chakraborty et al., 2015)	Landsat and MODIS	• During 2000 and 2010, the average change in surface temperature using Landsat over settlement and industrial areas is 1.4°C and for MODIS data is 3.7°C • The seasonal average change in anthropogenic heat flux estimated using Landsat and MODIS is up by around 38 Wm^{-2} and 62 Wm^{-2} respectively while higher change is observed over settlement and concrete structures
Delhi and Mumbai (Grover and Singh, 2015)	Landsat5 TM	• Validation of the heat island is done in relation to the Normalized Difference Vegetation Index (NDVI) patterns • Stronger UHI in Mumbai compared to Delhi
Gulbarga City (Kumar and Shekhar, 2015)	Landsat TM thermal bands data	• UHI in Kalaburagi (formerly Gulbarga) city is mainly located in the South-Eastern and North-Western part of the city • Negative correlation between LST and NDVI, positive correlation between LST and NDBI
Madurai (Subhashini et al., 2016)	Landsat 7 and Landsat 8	• LST estimated by using Single Channel (SC) algorithm and Split-Window (SW) algorithm; lower errors observed for SW algorithm • Variance of 5−6°C observed between urban areas, barren lands and vegetation covers thus indicating the presence of UHI

Continued

Table 11.2 Surface heat island studies in India.—cont'd

Study area	Satellite	Salient features
Mumbai (Grover and Singh, 2016)	Landsat 5 TM	• Study Period: Oct 2010 • Highest temperature in urban areas, ranging from 28°C for low built-up density and 34°C for high built-up and high-rise urban areas • High vegetation density is related with low temperature (23°C) and low density with high temperature (26°C) • The central and southern parts of the city have the highest temperature (34°C) whereas the city outskirts have lower temperatures (23°C)
Noida (Kikon et al., 2016)	Landsat ETM and Landsat 8	• Study Period: May 2000 and May 2013 • Mono-window algorithm model was used for the estimation of LST • Escalating trend of LST was observed in major parts of Noida city where built up area increased; mean LST increased from 40.14°C in 2000 to 40.95°C in 2013 • Positive relation of LST with NDBI and Albedo, negative with NDVI and emissivity
Kolkata (Khan and Chatterjee, 2016)	—	• UHII in Kolkata has been assessed using simplified numerical model for vertical temperature measurement in tropical monsoon summer month (June 2015) • Approximated temperature trapeziums determined by high and lower air temperatures and used to simulate the vertical surface temperature fluctuation or variation • The average temperature under urban concrete surface greater than that of suburban open surface by 3.54°C

Table 11.2 Surface heat island studies in India.—cont'd

Study area	Satellite	Salient features
Ahmedabad (Mathew et al., 2016b)	MODIS and ASTER	• Linear time series (LTS) model developed from LST values of 10 years along with enhanced vegetation index (EVI), road density (RD) and elevation to predict LST • Comparison of the model predicted LST and observed LST showed mean absolute error (MAE) and mean absolute percentage error (MAPE) varying between 0.23 and 0.31 K and 0.08%−0.10%, respectively for year 2014
Chandigarh (Mathew et al., 2016c)	MODIS	• Central part of the Chandigarh city is hotter compared to other part of the city based on LST data of years 2009−2013 • Average UHI intensity during monsoon, summer and winter seasons is 4.65 K, 5.92 K, and 5.03 K, respectively
Saranda forest, Jharkhand (Kayet et al., 2016)	Landsat 7 ETM+	• Relationship explored between LST, Normalized difference built-up index (NDBI), normalized difference vegetation index (NDVI), soil-adjusted vegetation index (SAVI) and ratio vegetation index (RVI) [May 2015] • Growth of the active mining and industrial areas significantly increased surface temperature
Various cities (Shastri et al., 2017)	MODIS-Aqua	• Study of the diurnal and seasonal characteristics of SUHII in India during 2003−13 • Negative SUHII over most urban areas during daytime in pre-monsoon summer, due to low vegetation in nonurban regions during dry premonsoon summers • Positive nighttime SUHII occurs when urban impacts are prominent. • Positive winter daytime SUHII in Indo-Gangetic plain

Continued

Table 11.2 Surface heat island studies in India.—cont'd

Study area	Satellite	Salient features
Kanpur (Chakraborty et al., 2017)	MODIS-Terra	• Diurnality and interseasonality in the urban–rural differences in surface temperature (ΔTs) investigated for premonsoon (April to June) and the monsoon (July to September) seasons in 2014. • ΔTs greater during the monsoon (5°C) versus premonsoon (3.4°C) • Strong association of ΔTs magnitude of urban–rural surface energy flux differences but weak during daytime
Hyderabad (Sannigrahi et al., 2017)	Landsat and MODIS	• Effects of urbanization and biophysical changes on UHI investigated in Hyderabad city for years 2002–15 • LST negatively correlated with NDVI for all LULC classes with highest negative association over the areas occupied by aquatic vegetation class followed by urban green space, urban built-up, farmland) and follow land
English Bazar, West Bengal (Pal and Ziaul, 2017)	LANDSAT TM and LANDSAT 8 OLI	• Seasonal and temporal LST is extracted in three phases: 1991, 2010, and 2014 • LST found to increase at 0.070°C/year and 0.114°C/year during winter and summer periods respectively • Built-up area retains maximum LST in all selected phases
Raipur (Guha et al., 2017)	Landsat	• During 1995 to 2016, the study area experienced a gradual increasing rate in mean LST (<1% per annum) • The UHI developed especially along the north-western industrial area and south-eastern bare land of the city. Mean UHI consistently increased from 2.6°C in 1995 to 3.63°C in 2016 • The urban thermal field variance index (UTFVI) applied to measure the thermal comfort level of the city; inner parts of the city ecologically more comfortable than the outer peripheries

Table 11.2 Surface heat island studies in India.—cont'd

Study area	Satellite	Salient features
Lucknow (Singh et al., 2017)	Landsat	• Spatio-temporal analysis of LST performed for May 2002 and 2014; LST estimated using Mono-window algorithm model • Mean LST in the central portion of Lucknow found to have increased from 2002 to 2014 by 0.75°C
Punjab State (12 districts) (Mukherjee et al., 2017)	MODIS	• MODIS (1000 m resolution)-derived LST downscaled to 250 m resolution using NDVI as proxy data • Mean temperature in urban built-up core higher (38.87°C) as compared to suburban (35.85°C) and rural (32.41°C) areas
Jaipur (Mathew et al., 2017)	MODIS, Landsat-TM/OLI, ASTER Terra	• Average maximum UHI intensity from 2003 to 2015 varies from 5.12 to 10.37 K, and overall average maximum UHI intensity is 7.86 K • Percent impervious surface area (% ISA) better urbanization parameter for SUHI studies than NDBI
Ranchi (Mohanta and Sharma, 2017)	Landsat	• With the urban built up growth of 251.89% in between 1992 and 2013, the increase in UHII is 1.42 K
Bhubaneswar (Swain et al., 2017)	MODIS	• MODIS LST at 1 km spatial resolution analyzed for a period of 15 years (2000–14). • Surface temperature on an average ∼1.75 K greater than that of the surrounding "pervious" surfaces and further recording a maximum difference greater than 19 K
Ahmedabad and Jaipur (Mathew et al., 2018a)	MODIS	• Inverse or negative surface UHI over Jaipur whereas moderate or very weak SUHI over Ahmedabad during daytime • Strong UHI during night time over both cities

Continued

Table 11.2 Surface heat island studies in India.—cont'd

Study area	Satellite	Salient features
Haridwar and Kanpur (Rani et al., 2018)	LANDSAT ETM+	• Higher LSTs during daytime but UHI effect prevalent only during nighttime • Time of observation important factor for analyzing the efficacy of remote sensing data for UHI • High LST areas of Haridwar sited mainly in the central part in 1989; in 2000 and 2006, the inner center of the downtown and the outer circular periphery of the town becomes high-temperature packet. due to fast progress in construction in Haridwar • Temperature difference between urban area and the suburbs as high as 6°C
5 cities of the state of Bihar (Barat et al., 2018)	MODIS	• LST data of 2001—14 assessed for five major towns/cities of Bihar classified into Urban, Suburban and Rural zones as per LULC • Most intense UHI during winter months (January, February, November, and December) over all towns/cities • Mann—Kendall applied on surface UHI shows significant increasing trend
Delhi (Panwar et al., 2018)	MODIS	• Nonparametric Mann—Kendall and Theil—Sen Slope tests are used to analyze pixel-wise LST trends from 2001 to 2015 • Positive temperature trend throughout the study period especially in night time in Delhi • LST trends varies for daytime, and the strength of trend diminishes with increase in significance level
Jaipur (Mathew et al., 2018b)	MODIS	• A criterion based on UHIindex and transect methods proposed to estimate the spatiotemporal surface UHI growth • Significant increase of up to 230% in the area of hotspots (UHIindex > 0.9) observed between 2003 and 2015

Table 11.2 Surface heat island studies in India.—cont'd

Study area	Satellite	Salient features
6 Indian metropolitan cities (Sultana and Satyanarayana, 2019)	Landsat 7 ETM+	• Spatial relationship of the changes in the land cover types and LST is analyzed for six metropolitan cities of India during summer season
		• The intensities of UHIs over these cities during summer season are noticed to be in the range of 10.5–14°C
		• Delhi possesses the highest UHI intensity in the range of 13.4–14.0°C, and Kolkata possessed the lowest UHI intensity in the range of 10.5–11.7°C
Ahmedabad, Gujrat (Mohammed et al., 2019)	MODIS	• This study examines the behavior of LST and SUHI over Ahmedabad from 2003 to 2018
		• During summer daytime, the rural zone exhibits a higher average LST than the urban area, while a slight positive SUHI (mean intensity of 0.4°C) during winter daytime
Bengaluru (Sussman et al., 2019)	MODIS	• The amount of urbanized land in Bengaluru has increased by 15% from 2003 to 2018
		• The nighttime, dry season (Dec–Feb) urban heat island (UHI) effect is most intense
		• An increase in aerosols reduces the UHI effect in the dry season during daytime
		• The UHI intensity exhibited an increasing trend in the dry season nighttime and wet season daytime and nighttime
Ludhiana (Singh and Kalota, 2019)	Landsat	• Study the problem of urban sprawl in Ludhiana city with the application of remote sensing and GIS techniques from 1955 to 2015 periods
		• The results show rise in the intensity and areal expansion of the area under high land surface temperature

Continued

Table 11.2 Surface heat island studies in India.—cont'd

Study area	Satellite	Salient features
Noida (Suhail et al., 2019)	Landsat-8 OLI−TIRS	• Spatial distribution of UHIs and their relationship with land use over NOIDA city is reported. • The results show that two clusters were developed in north and mid-east part of the city due to concentration of high-density building and industrial units
Tirunelveli, Tamilnadu (Padmanabhan et al., 2019)	Landsat 7 ETM+	• Surface permeability and temperature quantified using Soil-Adjusted Vegetation Index (SAVI) and Land Surface Temperature (LST) index, respectively • Southeastern built-up areas in Tirunelveli were depicted as a potential UHI hotspot, with a caution for the Western riparian zone for UHI emergence in 2017
44 cities in India (Raj et al., 2020)	MODIS	• Long-term (18 years) analysis of SUHII for 44 major Indian cities • Positive SUHII observed during day (up to 2°C) and night for most cities • Vegetation plays a key role in determining the daytime SUHII • The increasing nighttime SUHII in all seasons for most cities suggest increasing trend in temperature in cities due to the impact of the rapid urbanization
Chandigarh (Sultana and Satyanarayana, 2020)	Landsat 7 and Landsat 8	• Rapid increase (10%) in built-up area is noticed over the Chandigarh during 2000−18 • Dry Built-up Index (DBI) and Dry Bare-Soil Index (DBSI) are employed to differentiate the built-up areas from the drylands effectively • Identified an increase in UHI intensity of range 10.8−12.8°C (6.3−7.5°C) for summer (winter) season

Table 11.2 Surface heat island studies in India.—cont'd

Study area	Satellite	Salient features
Kolkata (Das et al., 2020)	MODIS and ERA-Interim remote sensing data	• The surface SUHI during the summer months reveals an average heat island effect of 1.5 K during the daytime and 0.4 K in the nighttime
Malda, West Bengal (Dutta and Das, 2020)	Landsat 5 TM and Landsat 8	• Regional Heat Island (RHI) aggregated in the main urban center as well as in its periurban areas • RHI is not only found in the main urban center but also its impact can be seen in its peri-urban areas • RHI class $2 < RLST \leq 4$ is identified as high-risk areas
Mansa, Punjab (Kaur and Pandey, 2020)	Landsat 8 OLI/TIRS	• Influence of LULC patterns on UHI effect was analyzed using normalized built-up and vegetation indices (NDBI, NDVI)
3 cities in Punjab (Majumdar et al., 2021)	MODIS Landsat 5, 7 and 8	• Spatial patterns of LST, SUHI, surface urban cold island (SUCI), and their seasonal variations during January (winter) and September (summer) were analyzed over the three cities of Indian Punjab (Balachaur, Ludhiana and Bathinda) • The SUHI was higher during September than January, and it was higher in Ludhiana followed by Bathinda and Balachaur, irrespective of the season • The SUCIs were formed in the center of Bathinda city during 1991 and in Ludhiana and Balachaur cities during 2011
Agra (Pathak et al., 2021)	Landsat 5 TM and Landsat 8	• The focus was on spatial pattern of LST and land indices (i.e., NDVI, NDBI and EBBI) and their interrelationship dynamics over the city landscape in directional profiling • The results of SUHI reveal that city center had experienced 0.5−3.5°C higher LST than urban periphery

Continued

Table 11.2 Surface heat island studies in India.—cont'd

Study area	Satellite	Salient features
Chennai (Kesavan et al., 2021)	Landsat 7 and 8	• Remote sensing techniques have been used for the estimation and forecasting of LST and identification of UHI using Autoregressive Integrated Moving Average (ARIMA) model • LST maps developed from the model study depicted growing UHI hotspots in the southeastern and western parts of the city where the development of the city is fast
Delhi (Kumari et al., 2021)	MODIS Terra	• Impact of UHI on electricity consumption in Delhi • UHI formation caused an increased electricity consumption of 2600 GWh (i.e., 11.4%) annually on an average over eight districts of Delhi during the period from April 2012 to March 2017
Hyderabad (Puppala and Singh, 2021)	Landsat 8 OLI/TIRS	• The temperature is increasing with time, and this phenomenon is more intense in the regions with the more built-up area and vegetative cover • To trade-off between UHI effect and development, it is recommended to plan green spaces for each of the existing and upcoming buildings
Kolkata (Dutta et al., 2021a)	Landsat 5 TM and Landsat 8	• The parameters (LULC) affecting the UHI intensity were rigorously investigated • The vegetation index dropped in each decade by −0.267 whereas rise in impervious surface index was 0.097 on an average at new UHI locations • Substantial cooling by 0.938°C was noted during daytime, from urban built-up at a 50-m distance to the green parks
Lucknow (Shukla and Jain, 2021)	Landsat 5,6 and 8	• Impact of various types of sprawl expansion and drivers in developing UHI phenomenon in Lucknow city, India assessed from 2005 to 2016.

Table 11.2 Surface heat island studies in India.—cont'd

Study area	Satellite	Salient features
NOIDA (Sharma et al., 2021)	Landsat 5 TM and Landsat 8	• The mean LST of impervious surface is found to be 4°C higher than that of vegetation area in 2005, which further increased to 6°C in the year 2016 • The study demonstrates a significant impact of landscape pattern on developments of UHI in Lucknow city • Increase of 6.42°C in overall LST of Noida from 2011 to 2019 • Drastic increase in the hotspots between 2011 and 2019 in the study
Varanasi (Bala et al., 2021)	Landsat 5 TM and Landsat 8	• The NDVI values have increased from 0.06 to 0.14 during these years, suggesting increase in the total urban greenness in the city • 259.11 km^2 of natural land cover was converted into urban built ups between years 1989 and 2018 • Urban Heat Intensity Ratio Index (UHIRI) was proposed to quantify the urban heat intensity from 1989 to 2018, which was found to increase from 0.36 in year 1989 to 0.87 in year 2018 • Bare land to urban pixels was observed to show small decrease in normalized LST, whereas vegetation to urban pixels showed significant increase in normalized LST

Mohan and Kandya (2015) studied the effect of urbanization on the LST-based DTR for Delhi for a period of 11 years during 2001–11. There was a consistent increase in the areas experiencing DTR below 11°C, which typically resembled the "urban class," namely from 26.4% in the year 2001% to 65.3% in the year 2011 and subsequently the DTR of entire Delhi, which was 12.48°C in the year 2001 gradually reduced to 10.34°C in the year 2011, exhibiting a significant decreasing trend. A decrease of about 5 K in DTR with increasing urbanization was also observed by Sati and Mohan (2018), who used WRF model to study the impact of LULC changes on spatial and temporal variations of meteorological parameters over Delhi for a span of about five decades (1972–2014). Similar decreasing trends of DTR with increasing urbanization have been observed in places such as Vadodara district in Gujrat with annual DTR showing a decreasing trend at the rate of 0.29°C per year (Nandkeolyar and Kiran, 2019). Linear trend analysis for the 15-year period of mean annual LST carried out by Prakash and Norouzi (2020) showed a decrease in diurnal temperature range over most parts of India (2003–17) due to rather rapid increase in nighttime LST than daytime LST, similar as changes in near-surface air temperature across the country. Pramanik and Punia (2020) observed that areas with high population growth and built-up densification in subdistricts of North-East, South-West, and Central Delhi fall under the low DTR categories indicating that UHI is getting concentrated in these regions.

4. Evolution of UHI with urbanization and development: case studies

An estimated 34% of the Indian population lives in the urban areas, and this percentage is projected to reach around 41% by the year 2030 (World Bank, 2017). In recent decades, we have seen an unprecedented expansion of various cities to urban agglomerates. The Intergovernmental Panel on Climate Change (IPCC) has recognized connections between urbanization and the development of UHI in several cities of the world including Indian cities (Revi et al., 2014). Further, it states that for cities in India, the implications of future climate for connections between urbanization and the development of UHI have been defined (Mohan et al., 2011a, b, 2012). Several studies relate increased urbanization to increase in LST and UHI over Indian cities (Table 11.3).

Most of these studies are based on the satellite imageries obtained from Landsat. Mohan et al. (2020b) explored the change in land use/land cover due to the evolution of urban sprawl during a five decadal period (1972–2014) over the central national capital region (CNCR) of India vis-à-vis impacts on heat island intensities using WRF model.

Table 11.4 shows changes in urbanization, temperature, and area with different CLHI with respect to D1972 for Delhi. From the 1970 to 2010s, the near-surface temperature in Delhi has increased by 1.02°C due to LULC changes of which the major changes are contributed from an increase in urban areas. An increase in nighttime CLHI of 2–3°C in 787 km^2 area and an increase of 3–4°C in 573 km^2 area between the decades of 1970 and 2010s have been estimated. Further, an area of 23 km^2 has emerged only in the last decade with CLHI greater than 5°C.

Mathew et al. (2016c) explored percent impervious surface area (%ISA) as an indicator of UHI effects in Chandigarh city, which showed that central part of the Chandigarh city (which is densely concretized) is hotter compared to other parts of the city because of large number of roads, complex infrastructure, and high-rise buildings. The study by Mohan et al. (2012) also indicated that dense urban areas/commercial centers were hotter than rest of the city and average daily maximum UHI reached 8.3°C.

There are few studies that indicate that industrialization has also led to formation of industrial heat Island (IHI) even with relatively low population density and lower built-up area (Mohan et al., 2020a). The Bhubaneswar airport has shown an increase in mean summer LST by 8% over the study period of 15 years, and 9.84% in LST in the last 5 years from 2013 to 2017 alone (Anasuya et al., 2020). Such changes around urban agglomerates can create their own microclimate and eventually effect the human–nature interactions on a regional scale.

Urbanization also alters the exchange of momentum, moisture, and energy fluxes subsequently affecting regional meteorology and global climate. These impacts are discussed in detail in the next subsections.

Table 11.3 Increase of urbanization vis à vis LST and UHI in Indian cities.

S. No.	City/Region	Time span	Urban extent vis à vis LST/ UHI	Source
1	Central NCR	1972−2014	Rise in built-up area: 1700% Rise in mean LST: 4−5°C Rise in mean UHI: 4−6°C	Mohan et al. (2020b); Sati and Mohan (2018)
2	Pune	1995−2006	Rise in built-up area: 32.7% Rise in mean LST: 2−4°C	Patki and Raykar-Alange (2012)
3	Jaipur	2000−11	Rise in built-up area: 41.09% Rise in mean LST: 3°C	Jalan and Sharma (2014)
4	NOIDA	2000−13	Rise in built-up area: 26.9% Rise in mean LST: 0.8°C	Kikon et al. (2016)
5	Bhubaneshwar	2000−14	Rise in built-up area: 83% Rise in mean LST: 1.5°C	Swain et al. (2017)
6	Chandigarh	2000−18	Rise in built-up area: 10% Rise in UHI: 1.2°C (Winter), 2°C (Summer)	Sultana and Satyanarayana (2020)
7	Lucknow	2002−14	Rise in built-up area: 38.7% Rise in mean LST: 0.75°C	Singh et al. (2017a)
8	Bengaluru	2003−18	Rise in built-up area: 15% Rise in mean LST: 1°C	Sussman et al. (2019)
9	Visakhapatnam	2014−19	Rise in built-up area: 63% Rise in mean LST: 4.8°C	Puppala and Singh (2021)

Table 11.4 Urbanization and associated changes in CLHI and decadal warming based on WRF model simulations in Delhi during 1970−2010s.

Decade →	1970s	1980s	1990s	2000s	2010s
Urban area [Total area of Delhi: 1435 km^2]	40 km^2	144 km^2	343 km^2	536 km^2	840 km^2
Decadal Warming wrt D1972	−	+0.16°C	+0.28°C	+0.63°C	+1.02°C
Area with CLHI intensity 3−4°C	33 km^2	92 km^2	193 km^2	236 km^2	355 km^2
Area with CLHI intensity 4−5°C	0 km^2	42 km^2	79 km^2	245 km^2	475 km^2
Area with CLHI intensity > 5°C	0 km^2	0 km^2	0 km^2	0 km^2	23 km^2

    The local-scale response to larger-scale meteorological forcing is determined in large part by surface characteristics such as albedo, emissivity, thermal capacity, available moisture, and surface roughness; all influencing the energy, mass, and momentum exchange between the surface and the atmosphere (Grossman-Clarke et al., 2010). Urbanization significantly impacts regional near-surface air temperatures, wind fields, the evolution of the planetary boundary layer (PBL), and precipitation; subsequently influencing air quality, human comfort, and health.

There are numerous studies that have correlated the impact of urbanization and urban temperatures. Sati and Mohan (2018) examined the impact of increase in urbanization in NCR (between 1972 and 2014) estimated to be 17-fold during this period and based on WRF model predictions reported noticeable increase of 3−5 K and 2−3 K in LST and ambient temperature, respectively. Furthermore, this study also reported decrease in the magnitude of surface winds up to 2 m s^{-1}, and about 7%−8% in the relative humidity was observed over the areas converted to urban form over the five decades. Studies carried out in several cities have shown urban built area leading to changes in convective activity and consequently modification in precipitation events (Chen and Dirmeyer, 2017; Niyogi et al., 2017; Shem and Shepherd, 2009). The presence of the UHI causes increased thermal internal boundary layer height (Wang et al., 2012). Larger urban width causes larger vertical velocity and higher thermal internal boundary layer. Stronger convergence and higher thermal internal boundary layer are also obtained in case of larger heat island intensity (Sarkar et al., 1998). Sati and Mohan (2021b) studied the impacts of increasing urban sprawls over the central-NCR region and have found significant impacts of urbanization on convective parameters such as convective available potential energy (CAPE) and convective inhibition (CIN.) Furthermore, it was seen that increasing urbanization over five decadal period led to increase in rainfall intensity mainly in the downwind region of the urban region.

Urban effects are shown to increase the near-surface air temperature over Chennai by 3.0 K during the early morning hours. The larger surface temperature gradient along the coast due to urban effects increased onshore flow by 4.0 m s^{-1}. Model sensitivity study revealed that precipitation totals were enhanced by 25 mm over a large region 150 km west of Chennai due to urban effects (Simpson et al., 2008).

5. Impacts of urban heat island effect
5.1 Thermal stress and consequent health impacts

A direct relationship has been found between UHI peaks and heat-related illness and fatalities, due to the incidence of thermal discomfort on the human cardiovascular and respiratory systems. During extreme weather events such as heat waves, the UHI has the potential to prevent the city from cooling down, maintaining higher nighttime temperatures and consequently lower DTR, which affects human health and comfort (Tan et al., 2010; Lo et al., 2003; Tomlinson et al., 2011; Mavrogianni et al., 2011). Heatstroke, heat exhaustion, heat syncope, and heat cramps are some of the main stress events, while a wide number of diseases may become worse, particularly in the elderly and children (Laaidi, 2012). Thermal stress is most relevant to people who spend a substantial time outdoors during a day. These include pedestrians, cyclists, vendors, shopkeepers near roadside, and most people from the lower strata of society who live in makeshift houses, which can form a significant proportion of population in developing countries (Mohan et al., 2014).

Urban areas have been found to experience 2.3 more number of heat wave days (NHWD) than rural areas per summer season as per urban climate simulations by Sharma et al. (2019). Kotharkar et al. (2021) evaluated summertime heat stress using heat index and humidex in Nagpur undertaking predictive modeling for probability of heat stress in different LCZs. Daytime heat stress was maximum in LCZ 9 (sparsely built low rise) as these areas have maximum exposure to heat during the hours of daylight. Compact low-rise zones (LCZ 3) exhibited higher heat stress during nighttime than other zones. Chaudhuri and Kumar (2021) noted drastic rise in area under thermally highly uncomfortable zone (35–40°C) from 0.005 to 56.68 km^2 and a decrease in area of thermally comfortable zone (≤26°C) from 0.46 km^2 to zero during 1992–2016, exhibiting deteriorating natural urban living condition in Bhubaneswar city. In Delhi, Mohan et al. (2020b) explored the change in land use/land cover due to the evolution of urban sprawl during a five decadal period (1972–2014) over the CNCR of India and found that thermally extremely uncomfortable hours have increased from an average of 10–13 h a day. Jacobs et al. (2019) explored associations between LCZ, socioeconomic status, and thermal stress for three south Asian cities, namely Delhi (India), Dhaka (Bangladesh), and Faisalabad (Pakistan) for thermal indices such as Heat Index (HI), Wet Bulb Globe Temperature (WBGT), and Universal Thermal Climate Index (UTCI) at walking level. The study further noted that the low-income neighborhoods in Delhi, a majority of which belonged to compact classes, LCZ 1–3 and LCZ 7, are always warmer during the night and the differences nearly always represent the maximum intraurban temperature difference unlike other two cities.

Rajan and Amirtham (2021) simulated physiological equivalent temperature (PET) using ENVI-met over different locations in Chennai as an indicator of thermal comfort. The study revealed a maximum PET difference of 22°C between the locations. Deevi and Chundeli (2020) assessed correlations between the PET and urban design control parameters and observed that SVF and mean radiant temperature (MRT) are major influencing factors in outdoor thermal conditions. Similar observations were noted by Mehrotra et al. (2020a), who assessed thermal stress using PET in Mumbai and observed that SVF has strong influence on thermal profile during the night hours compared to day hours. Both compact mid-rise and compact low-rise urban built forms experienced high heat stress than open high-rise/mid-rise/low-rise urban built forms.

Conventional thermal comfort rankings are usually based on prevalence and frequency of occurrence of comfortable hours. However, Mohan et al. (2014) noted that assessment of thermal comfort for a place using the approach based on the percentage of comfortable hours alone may be erroneous and misleading as this approach does not consider the percentages of uncomfortable classes, which could often be substantially high. Mohan et al. (2014) proposed a modified approach for thermal comfort classification demonstrating cumulative representation of all classes of thermal comfort including uncomfortability and provided relative ranking of five Indian cities as a case study. When the cities were compared only on the basis of comfortable hours, the decreasing order of comfortability was Hyderabad > Kolkata > Delhi > Chennai > Mumbai. However, considering the second methodology, they found that the contribution of uncomfortable hours is greater in Kolkata and Chennai in comparison to Mumbai. Hence, taking into account effective uncomfortability, the cities were relatively ranked as Hyderabad > Mumbai > Delhi > Chennai > Kolkata in decreasing order of comfort.

Diseases such as Dengue are strongly seasonal in Indian cities and associated with the increased temperatures and rainfall in monsoon season. Telle et al. (2021) observed that wintertime UHI extended the transmission period of dengue virus by the urban mosquito vector, *Aedes aegypti,* offering the potential for dengue transmission at a very local level and persistence of vectors in these areas with higher temperature owing to UHI effect. Misslin et al. (2016) compared the dengue case distribution within Delhi with the temperature maps and observed overlap between lower DTR areas and reported dengue incidences for years for the subepidemic years of 2008 and 2009, which suggested that local temperature and DTR may be important factors in dengue epidemic potential.

Kakkad et al. (2014) compared neonatal intensive care unit (NICU) admissions in a non-air-conditioned hospital during the 2010 heat wave in Ahmedabad with that of heat morbidity admissions in the prior (2009) and subsequent years (2011). During the summer months of year 2010 (April, May, and June), there were 24 NICU admissions for heat-related illnesses compared to eight admissions in year 2009 and four in 2011. Above 42°C, each daily maximum temperature increase of a degree was associated with 43% increase in heat-related admissions.

5.2 Impact on air quality

Urban areas are associated with sources of a variety of air pollutants and regional pollution problems such as acid rain and photochemical smog. The impact of UHI on air quality is expected to vary based on how both meteorology and atmospheric chemistry would respond to urbanization taking place in the region. UHIs promote high air temperatures that contribute to formation of ozone precursors, which undergo photochemical reactions to produce ground-level ozone. There are few studies that examine the impact of UHI in the Indian region.

Sati and Mohan (2021a) applied WRF-Chem model to study impact of increase in urban sprawls representing five decades (1972–2014) on summer-time air quality based on WRF-Chem model simulations over central-National Capital Region. In the various decades, where considerable area got urbanized, the model simulated a decrease of surface sulfur dioxide (SO_2) and particulate matter (PM_{10}) values of about 20% and 40%, respectively, during both, night and daytime. In contrast, the ozone (O_3) surface values show an increase of about 40% and 10% during nighttime and daytime, respectively. At higher levels, a significant increase in O_3 and PM_{10} values is observed attributed to redistribution from changing wind speed and temperature pattern, which alters atmospheric mixing and the boundary layer. It is inferred that the aerodynamic impacts of urban sprawls influence the dispersal behavior of pollutants.

The study by Devara et al. (2002) revealed higher pollution potential during late evenings in the winter and a total increase of about 3% in the aerosol loading over the 12 year observational period at Indian Institute of Tropical Meteorology, Pune. This increase was attributed partly due to the urban heat island effect and due to growing urbanization and industrialization. Aslam et al. (2017) studied the seasonal variation of UHI and its impact on air quality using SAFAR (System of Air Quality and Weather Forecasting and Research) observations at Delhi, India. It was found that UHI magnitudes $\sim 2.2°C$ and $\sim 1.5°C$ are formed at the evening traffic hours during May and December, respectively, which coincide with the $PM_{2.5}$ concentration peak during evening traffic hours.

Agarwal and Tandon (2010) developed a steady state two-dimensional mathematical model to study the dispersion of air pollutants under the effect of UHI, when the pollutants are assumed to be emitted from the ground-based area source. The results showed that the mesoscale wind produced by UHI helps the pollutants to circulate and move in upward direction, thus making the problem of air pollution more severe in urban areas.

5.3 Energy consumption and economic concerns

UHI increases significantly the ambient temperature. Higher temperatures have a serious impact on the electricity consumption of the building sector increasing considerably the peak and the total electricity demand. The increased energy demand means more costs to citizens and governments, which in large metropolitan areas may induce significant economic impacts (Taha, 1988; Santamouris, 2001; Kikegawa et al., 2006; Kolokotroni et al., 2012). Santamouris et al. (2015) analyzed several past studies dealing with the impact of the ambient temperature on the peak electricity demand and found out that for each degree of temperature increase, the increase of the peak electricity load varies between 0.45% and 4.6%. This corresponds to an additional electricity penalty of about 21 ($\pm$10.4) W per degree of temperature increase per person. Kumari et al. (2020) performed energy simulations on a calibrated building model placed at three different sites in Delhi, identified on the basis of land use and land cover percentage and annual LST. Simulation results showed that the site located in the central part of Delhi displayed higher annual energy consumption (255.21 MWh/y) compared to the site located in the rural periphery (235.69 MWh/y). Although in wintertime, the UHIs can result in energy savings, there is a great consent among researchers that this benefit is outweighed by the detrimental effects that occur in summertime. Kumari et al. (2021) noted that the increased electricity consumption in summer months in Delhi far outweighs the reduced consumption in winter months. They assessed SUHI in eight districts of Delhi and observed that all eight districts showed strong association between per-capita net electricity consumption (NEC) and nighttime LST. The UHI effect in Delhi was assessed to have caused an increased NEC of 2600 GWh annually based on the average of 5-year data (from April 2012 to March 2017). Further, they estimated that a UHI mitigation scenario of 1°C reduction in SUHII in Delhi would have saved electricity worth $\sim$ INR 11.9 billion and a 2°C reduction in SUHII would have saved $\sim$ INR 17 billion in the year 2016–17. Yadav et al. (2017) also estimated that UHI of magnitude 0.2–3°C would be capable of rising electricity demand in range of 37.87–1856 GWh over the base electricity requirement of Delhi city with corresponding increase in CO_2 emissions by 0.031–1.52 million ton. Positive correlations between surface LST and per capita electricity consumption have also been observed for Nagpur city both during summer and autumn/spring season (Jain et al., 2020).

5.4 UHI impact on other phenomena

- **Precipitation:** The analysis of daily maximum and minimum temperatures over Mumbai region confirmed the UHI effect during exceptionally heavy rainfall event of 25–26 July 2005 (Mohapatra et al., 2009). Similarly in Bangalore, UHI effect was found to lead to moisture convergence and pollutants, which may have worked as hygroscopic nuclei over the region to enhance rainfall near the urban center of Bangalore to produce unusually heavy rain in October 2005 (Mohapatra et al., 2010).
- **Fog:** Gautam and Singh (2018) reported a striking observation of holes in fog over urban areas in satellite imagery over the Indo-Gangetic Plains, based on 17 years of satellite data (2000–16). which was attributed to UHI effect.
- **Depletion of groundwater** is concomitant with increasing UHI effect because of conversion of permeable green cover to impermeable paved surfaces, which increases a city's surface runoff and reduces the infiltration processes that invariably affects the city's groundwater level (Sundaram, 2011). In Chennai city, groundwater level was observed to have lowered up to 10 m from the year 1997 to 2001 due to raised surface runoff and reduced retention capacity of the land cover, which almost stopped the groundwater recharging processes in the city. Mohammad et al. (2019) analyzed land cover maps across 16 years (2003–18) for SUHI footprints and other parameters,

which included groundwater level for Ahmedabad city. A clear sinking of groundwater table was observed from about 65 m in 2003 to below 140 m in 2018 against the mean nighttime SUHI magnitude of 1.84°C in summer and 3.19°C in winter over the 16 years.

- **Impact on aquatic life:** Urban streams are typically hotter than their nonurban counterpoints at base flow, due to convection with air warmed within UHIs as well as increased direct radiation resulting from decreased canopy cover. A large proportion of the heat absorbed by impervious surfaces in urban areas is transported into stream channels via stormwaters runoff, which raises temperatures of the water bodies it is released into, thereby negatively affecting aquatic life (Somers et al., 2016). Though impacts of warm wastewater from industrial processes including thermal power stations and nuclear reactors on various aspects of aquatic flora and fauna have been explored in India, such effects are yet to be investigated in context of UHI scenario in India.

6. Mitigation studies

Main causative factors of heat island effect are heat released by built-up structures and anthropogenic emissions. Mitigation measures of UHI effect are therefore centered on reducing heat due to these two factors. Using high-albedo materials and pavements, increasing green vegetation and green roofs, urban planning, pervious pavements, shade trees, and existence of water bodies in city areas are some of the potential UHI mitigation strategies proposed (Nuruzzaman, 2015).

Fig. 11.4 displays the common measure that are employed for UHI mitigation. These can either be done at building level (microenvironment) or on a street/larger scale (macroenvironment) as discussed below.

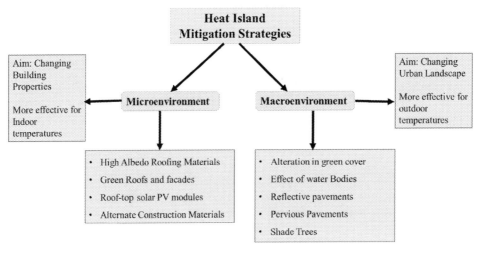

FIGURE 11.4

UHI mitigation measures.

6.1 Microenvironment

With increasing the solar reflectance of urban surfaces, the outflow of short-wave solar radiation increases, less solar heat energy is absorbed leading to lower surface temperatures and reduced outflow of thermal radiation into the atmosphere. This process of negative radiative forcing effectively counters warming (Akbari and Mathhews, 2012). Few strategies are as follows:

(I) **High-albedo roofing materials:** Dark roofs absorb heat from the sunlight making houses warm while light-colored roofs with similar insulation properties do not get warmed significantly by reflecting solar radiation (Akbari et al., 2001). So, one of the mitigation strategies is to use high-albedo roofing materials. For buildings monitored in the Metropolitan Hyderabad region, the measured annual energy savings from roof whitening of previously black roofs ranged from 20 to 22 kWh/m^2 of roof area, corresponding to a cooling energy use reduction of 14%−26% (Xu et al., 2012). Application of cool roof in Nagpur city showed significant reductions in air temperature in the older unplanned settlement with dense urban agglomeration (Kotharkar et al., 2020). Arumugam et al. (2014) performed monitoring for a building located in Pantnagar, Uttarakhand, for a period of 6 months (from January to June 2012) on two adjacent sections of continuous concrete roof surface, one of which had been previously coated with a white paint coating. The increased reflectivity reduced the seasonal average indoor air temperature by 1.07°C, thereby increasing the number of adaptive human comfort hours by about 8%.

(II) **Green roofs and facades:** Another method is greening of roofs and the facades (walls). A green roof is a vegetative layer grown on a rooftop while the vertical plantation around the walls and facades is used for greening walls. Green roofs provide shade and remove heat from the air through evapotranspiration, reducing temperatures of the roof surface and the surrounding air (USEPA, 2008). For English bazaar Town (West Bengal), Ziaul and Paul (2020) reported that 100% greening of roof and walls was the best mitigation strategy for open mid and compact low-rise area while 50% greening of roof and walls was found best for open low-rise buildings. Similarly, a study in Mumbai suggests that the combination of 50% concrete and 50% vegetation and green roofs can reduce around 25% heat in the area (Dwivedi and Mohan, 2018).

(III) **Roof-top solar PV modules:** Energy required for roof-induced cooling load decreased between 73% and 90% after installation of the PV system (Kotak et al., 2014).

(IV) **Alternate construction materials:** Kandya and Mohan (2018) investigated the thermal performance (in terms of energy consumption for space cooling) of composite materials such as Bamcrete (bamboo−concrete composite) and natural materials such as Rammed Earth. Bamboo−concrete wall was found to reduce the annual cooling load by around 7.5% when compared to the conventional brick wall. Anupam et al. (2021) noted that 20% replacement of fine aggregate with PVC−glass mix can be incorporated in concrete pavements with a consequent peak reduction of 7.3°C in the pavement surface temperature.

(V) **H/W ratio:** The ratio between the height of the buildings (H) and the width of the adjacent street (W) is a prominent factor in thermal comfort, especially in tropical climates. Taslim et al. (2015) suggested that building a combination of streets with diverse H/W ratios is advised for hot and dry climates. Preferably, the north-south canyons, where the thermal situation is comparatively better, should have an H/W ratio of equal or greater than 2. Deeper canyons with H/W ratios higher than four are desirable for east-west-oriented streets. Increasing the heights of buildings and making the streets narrower are two important ways of growing the H/W ratios.

6.2 Macroenvironment

Proper urban planning can also play a vital role in the mitigation of the UHI effect. At macro scale, there are few strategies that have been utilized across the globe as well as over Indian cities:

1. **Alteration in green cover:** Increase in vegetation has long been known to weaken heat island effect. It increases evapotranspiration and consequently reduces sensible heat flux. The NDVI analysis of Nagpur metropolitan also indicated that the temperature is lower in the areas where vegetation is high (Jain et al., 2020). In Bangalore, street segments with trees were found to have lower temperature with afternoon ambient air temperatures lower by as much as 5.6°C and road surface temperatures lower by as much as 27.5°C (Vailshery et al., 2013). In another case study in Bangalore (Shah et al., 2021), urban green spaces were found to be 2.23°C cooler and provided cooling till 347 m beyond their boundaries. The study over Delhi showed that right from open parks to inclusion of dense vegetation and trees showed reduction in the LST of the region (Pramanik and Punia, 2019). In Kolkata, an addition of around 5%–15% in the vegetation coverage resulted in an average reduction of around 0.8°C in the nocturnal air temperature in all the building environments (Chatterjee et al., 2019). Ghosh and Das (2018) noted that green space can control 1°C temperature minimization for a 150–180 m distance from green space boundary for a case study in Kolkata city. Similar cooling of 0.938°C was observed during daytime for urban built-up at a 50-m distance to the green parks in another case study in Kolkata (Dutta et al., 2021a). A parametric study in Madurai showed that a green plot ratio of 0.6 in high density built-up spaces could bring down the air temperature by around 1.2°C (Chandramathy and Kitchley, 2018). The design and development of urban forestry systems to assist urban microclimate management provide scope to reduce the thermal stress from pavements during the day. The successful implementation of urban forestry in UHI mitigation, however, also requires an understanding of climatic conditions, native tree species selection, tree planting density, and urban geometry based on the required geographic location (Cheela et al., 2021). Upcoming urban forestry techniques such as Miyawaki forests enable quicker development of natural vegetation or native forests in an urban area sustained by existing conditions of the location in the absence of any human support (Kurian, 2020).
2. **Effect of water bodies:** In addition, water body is another land use type with negative influence on heat island as the water bodies achieve cooling effect by transpiration and heat exchange with the surrounding environment (Robitu et al., 2006; Manteghi et al., 2015). For example: An appreciable average temperature dip of 7.51 and 3.12°C was observed during summer and winter, respectively, near the Sukhna Lake in Chandigarh city. Similarly, dip of about 1.57 and 1.71°C was observed during summer and winter, respectively, near Sabarmati river (Gupta et al., 2019). In a modeling-based impact analysis case study for Angul-Talcher industrial area in Odisha, introduction of water bodies was found to decrease ambient temperature in immediate vicinity of the water body by 5°C (OSPCB, 2018).

3. **Reflective pavements:** As in case of roofs and walls, road surfaces can also be painted with reflective paints. In Kolkata, in the cool pavement model, the materials of the road pavement were changed from asphalt to concrete (Chatterjee et al., 2019). The study reported that the median air temperature decreased by 0.2°C in the open low-rise, 0.5°C in the compact low-rise, and 0.8°C in mid-rise building environments.

4. **Pervious pavements:** Impervious pavements do not allow water to infiltrate and cooling effect by evapotranspiration is not significant in this case (Sailor, 2006). If the impermeable pavements are replaced with pervious pavements, which will allow water to infiltrate, it can be expected that it will be able to reduce the temperature to a reasonable extent. In recent years, pervious concrete pavement (PCP) is emerging as a novel pavement technology that is gaining attention due to its storm water runoff capabilities and hence UHI mitigation (Kant Sahdeo et al., 2020). Infiltrated water will help keep the pavement cool and directly affect the temperature.

5. **Shade trees:** Shade trees are those with a huge canopy and can provide protection to houses and pedestrians from direct sunlight keeping them comparatively cool. In addition to the shading effect, trees release vapor to the atmosphere through evapotranspiration when exposed to direct solar radiation, thus increasing the relative humidity and reducing the air temperature around them; this in turn can lead to a local increase in thermal comfort (Sailor, 2006).

7. Conclusions

UHI studies in India have picked up actual momentum only in past decade. In past five years, studies are now exploring multifaceted aspects of urban microclimate with increasing focus on mitigation. Grimmond et al. (2010) reviewed capabilities to observe and predict urban atmospheric processes across a range of spatial scales and identified key strategic areas where focus needs to be increased. These areas include observations, data, understanding, modeling, tools, and education. In context of this, following points have been noted in this review for UHI studies in India.

(i) Observations and data
- Maximum UHI studies in India are based on SUHI, which use satellite-derived temperatures. This could be due to the advantage of satellite data offering a spatial continuity and convenience of not carrying out instrument maintenance for field campaigns as in canopy layer heat island studies. However, with further advancement of automatic weather stations (AWS) network in India, canopy layer heat island studies could be given a boost.
- The national capital region of India (Delhi) remains a popular area of interest in numerous studies. There needs to be further research in small and upcoming cites of India as the future will see migration of substantial population from megacities to such cities.

(ii) Modeling and tools
- The need of the future is to incorporate numerical modeling for analysis of UHI as it can complement satellite observations and in situ surface and canopy layer observations of field campaigns. Most importantly, numerical modeling can help in analysis of effectiveness of mitigation strategies as well as future planning. An integral part of the modeling framework will be urban canopy model to represent surface processes and energy exchanges in urban

canopy layer. Inclusion of sophisticated UCMs will also require availability of urban geometry and LULC data at finer resolution.

* Another important factor is estimation of anthropogenic heat emissions. In India, the built-up structures are still not of scale of megacities of developed cities. Yet the UHI effect is being observed in smaller cities also, which can be attributed to heat generated by anthropogenic heat. An inventory of anthropogenic heat emissions, constructed for both spatial and temporal variations, is crucial for Indian cities for better performance of UHI modeling framework and consequently designing UHI mitigation measures.

(iii) Understanding

* There are still very few studies exploring interlinkages of UHI effect and air quality in India.
* Efforts need to be directed toward studying boundary layer UHI. This shall facilitate greater understanding of urban canopy exchange processes in boundary layer.
* UHI mitigation aspects are now being studied in India with greater focus. While mitigation strategies are easier to apply to upcoming towns and cities, challenge remains to alleviate UHI impacts in densely built established cities. Measures such as high-albedo roof, wall, and pavements, green facades, urban forests, and street plantations are increasingly being studied as well as adopted for UHI mitigation. Avenues of increasing green clover and water bodies are being explored too.

(iv) Education

Most of the recent policies adopted by government in India such as are driven by climate change mitigation or air quality improvement benefits. Government of India has initiated many plans and policies such as National Clean Air Program (NCAP), India Cooling Action Plan, National Electric Mobility Mission Plan (for electric vehicles), Smart Cities Mission, and upscaling of renewable power applications. These measures consequently help in heat island mitigation too as urban microclimate, air quality, and global climate change are intricately linked. However, such efforts need to percolate to the local levels at grassroot-level administration and more so among the citizens. Hence, it is imperative that discussions on UHI effect in India take place at all levels starting from citizens to decision-making administrators at the local level. This shall entail use of all possible mass communication platforms to generate awareness and education about UHI effect. Ultimately, the purpose of scientific research should be to aid and guide the regulatory bodies to understand current scenario and determine future research focus and action plans with regard to UHI effect in India.

References

Agarwal, M., Tandon, A., 2010. Modeling of the urban heat island in the form of mesoscale wind and of its effect on air pollution dispersal. Appl. Math. Model. 34 (9), 2520–2530. https://doi.org/10.1016/j.apm.2009.11.016.

Akbari, H., Matthews, H.D., 2012. Global cooling updates: reflective roofs and pavements. Energy Build. 55, 2–6. https://doi.org/10.1016/j.enbuild.2012.02.055.

Akbari, H., Pomerantz, M., Taha, H., 2001. Cool surfaces and shade trees to reduce energy use and improve air quality in urban areas. Sol. Energy 70 (3), 295–310. https://doi.org/10.1016/S0038-092X(00)00089-X.

Amirtham, L.R., 2016. Urbanization and its impact on urban heat Island intensity in Chennai Metropolitan Area, India. Indian J. Sci. Technol. 9 (5). https://doi.org/10.17485/ijst/2016/v9i5/87201.

Anasuya, B., Swain, D., Vinoj, V., 2020. Rapid urbanization and associated impacts on land surface temperature changes over Bhubaneswar Urban District, India. Environ. Monit. Assess. 191 (3), 790. https://doi.org/10.1007/s10661-019-7699-2.

Anupam, B.R., Anjali Balan, L., Sharma, S., 2021. Thermal and mechanical performance of cement concrete pavements containing PVC-glass mix. Road Mater. Pavement Des. https://doi.org/10.1080/14680629.2020.186832.

Arumugam, R., Garg, V., Mathur, J., Reddy, N., Gandhi, J., Fischer, M.L., 2014. Experimental determination of comfort benefits from cool-roof application to an un-conditioned building in India. Adv. Build. Energy Res. 8 (1), 14−27. https://doi.org/10.1080/17512549.2014.890540.

Aslam, M.Y., Krishna, K.R., Beig, G., Tinmaker, M.I.R., Chate, D.M., 2017. Seasonal variation of urban heat island and its impact on air-quality using SAFAR observations at Delhi, India. Am. J. Clim. Change 6, 294−305. https://doi.org/10.4236/ajcc.2017.62015.

Badarinath, K.V.S., Kiran Chand, T.R., Madhavi Latha, K., Raghavaswamy, V., 2005. Studies on urban heat islands using ENVISAT AATSR data. J. Indian Soc. Remote Sens. 33 (4), 495−501. https://doi.org/10.1007/BF02990734.

Bahl, H.D., Padmanabhamurty, B., 1979. Heat island studies at Delhi. Mausam 30 (1), 119−122.

Bala, R., Prasad, R., Yadav, V.P., 2021. Quantification of urban heat intensity with land use/land cover changes using Landsat satellite data over urban landscapes. Theor. Appl. Climatol. 145 (1), 1−12. https://doi.org/10.1007/s00704-021-03610-3.

Barat, A., Kumar, S., Kumar, P., Parth Sarthi, P., 2018. Characteristics of surface urban heat island (SUHI) over the Gangetic Plain of Bihar, India. Asia Pac. J. Atmos. Sci. 54 (2), 205−214. https://doi.org/10.1007/s13143-018-0004-4.

Bhati, S., Mohan, M., 2016. WRF model evaluation for the urban heat island assessment under varying land use/land cover and reference site conditions. Theor. Appl. Climatol. 126 (1−2), 385−400. https://doi.org/10.1007/s00704-015-1589-5.

Bhati, S., Mohan, M., 2018. WRF-urban canopy model evaluation for the assessment of heat island and thermal comfort over an urban airshed in India under varying land use/land cover conditions. Geosci. Lett. 5 (1). https://doi.org/10.1186/s40562-018-0126-7.

Borbora, J., Das, A.K., 2014. Summertime urban heat island study for Guwahati city, India. Sustain. Cities Soc. 11, 61−66. https://doi.org/10.1016/j.scs.2013.12.001.

Budhiraja, B., Gawuc, L., Agrawal, G., 2019. Seasonality of surface urban heat island in Delhi city region measured by local climate zones and conventional indicators. IEEE J. Sel. Top. Appl. Earth Obs. Remote Sens. 12 (12), 5223−5232. https://doi.org/10.1109/JSTARS.2019.2955133.

Budhiraja, B., Agrawal, G., Pathak, P., 2020. Urban heat island effect of a polynuclear megacity Delhi − compactness and thermal evaluation of four sub-cities. Urban Clim. 32. https://doi.org/10.1016/j.uclim.2020.100634.

Chakraborty, S.D., Kant, Y., Mitra, D., 2015. Assessment of land surface temperature and heat fluxes over Delhi using remote sensing data. J. Environ. Manag. 148, 143−152. https://doi.org/10.1016/j.jenvman.2013.11.034.

Chakraborty, T., Sarangi, C., Tripathi, S.N., 2017. Understanding diurnality and inter-seasonality of a sub-tropical urban heat island. Boundary-Layer Meteorol. 163 (2), 287−309. https://doi.org/10.1007/s10546-016-0223-0.

Chandler, T.J., 1962. London's urban climate. Geogr. J. 128 (3), 279−298.

Chandler, T., 1987. Four Thousand Years of Urban Growth: An Historical Census. David's University Press, St.

Chandramathy, I., Kitchley, J.L., 2018. Study and analysis of efficient green cover types for mitigating the air temperature and urban heat island effect. Int. J. Glob. Warming 14 (2), 238−259. https://doi.org/10.1504/IJGW.2018.090182.

Chatterjee, S., Khan, A., Dinda, A., Mithun, S., Khatun, R., Akbari, H., Wang, Y., 2019. Simulating micro-scale thermal interactions in different building environments for mitigating urban heat islands. Sci. Total Environ. 663, 610–631. https://doi.org/10.1016/j.scitotenv.2019.01.299.

Chaudhuri, S., Kumar, A., 2021. Evaluating the contribution of urban ecosystem services in regulating thermal comfort. Spat. Inf. Res. 29 (1), 71–82. https://doi.org/10.1007/s41324-020-00336-8.

Cheela, V.R.S., John, M., Biswas, W., Sarker, P., 2021. Combating urban heat island effect—a review of reflective pavements and tree shading strategies. Buildings 11 (3), 93.

Chen, L., Dirmeyer, P.A., 2017. Impacts of land-use/land-cover change on afternoon precipitation over north America. J. Clim. (30), 2121–2140. https://doi.org/10.1175/JCLI-D-16-0589.1.

Ching, J., Mills, G., Bechtel, B., See, L., Feddema, J., Wang, X., Theeuwes, N., 2018. WUDAPT: an urban weather, climate, and environmental modeling infrastructure for the anthropocene. Bull. Am. Meteorol. Soc. 99 (9), 1907–1924. https://doi.org/10.1175/bams-d-16-0236.1.

Choudhury, D., Das, A., Das, M., 2021. Investigating thermal behavior pattern (TBP) of local climatic zones (LCZs): a study on industrial cities of Asansol-Durgapur development area (ADDA), eastern India. Urban Clim. 35. https://doi.org/10.1016/j.uclim.2020.100727.

Daniel, C.E.J., Krishnamurty, K., 1973. Urban temperature fields at Pune and Bombay. Indian J. Meteorol. Geophys. 24, 407–412.

Das, Y., Padmanabhamurty, B., 2007. Aspects of thermal discomfort during summer over a Tropical City - Delhi (India). J. Environ. Sci. Eng. 49 (3), 170–177.

Das, P., Vamsi, K.S., Zhenke, Z., 2020. Decadal variation of the land surface temperatures (LST) and urban heat island (UHI) over Kolkata city projected using MODIS and ERA-interim DataSets. Aerosol Sci. Eng. 4 (3), 200–209. https://doi.org/10.1007/s41810-020-00067-1.

Davis, K., 1955. The origin and growth of urbanization in the world. Am. J. Sociol. 60 (5), 429–437. https://doi.org/10.1086/221602.

Deevi, B., Chundeli, F.A., 2020. Quantitative outdoor thermal comfort assessment of street: a case in a warm and humid climate of India. Urban Clim. 34. https://doi.org/10.1016/j.uclim.2020.100718.

Deosthali, V., 2000. Impact of rapid urban growth on heat and moisture islands in Pune City, India. Atmos. Environ. 34 (17), 2745–2754. https://doi.org/10.1016/S1352-2310(99)00370-2.

Devara, P.C.S., Maheskumar, R.S., Raj, P.E., Pandithurai, G., Dani, K.K., 2002. Recent trends in aerosol climatology and air pollution as inferred from multi-year lidar observations over a tropical urban station. Int. J. Climatol. 22 (4), 435–449. https://doi.org/10.1002/joc.745.

Dutta, I., Das, A., 2020. Exploring the Spatio-temporal pattern of regional heat island (RHI) in an urban agglomeration of secondary cities in Eastern India. Urban Clim. 34. https://doi.org/10.1016/j.uclim.2020.100679.

Dutta, K., Basu, D., Agrawal, S., 2021a. Synergetic interaction between spatial land cover dynamics and expanding urban heat islands. Environ. Monit. Assess. 193 (4). https://doi.org/10.1007/s10661-021-08969-4.

Dutta, D., Rahman, A., Paul, S.K., Kundu, A., 2021b. Impervious surface growth and its inter-relationship with vegetation cover and land surface temperature in peri-urban areas of Delhi. Urban Clim. 37. https://doi.org/10.1016/j.uclim.2021.100799.

Dwivedi, A., Mohan, B.K., 2018. Impact of green roof on micro climate to reduce Urban Heat Island. Remote Sens. Appl. Soc. Environ. 10, 56–69. https://doi.org/10.1016/j.rsase.2018.01.003.

Faris, A.A., Sudhakar Reddy, Y., 2010. Estimation of urban heat Island using Landsat ETM+ imagery at Chennai city-A case study. Int. J. Earth Sci. Eng. 3 (3), 332–340.

Gadgil, A., Deosthali, V., 1994. Temperature fields of Pune city. Curr. Sci. 66 (4), 297–299.

Gautam, R., Singh, M.K., 2018. Urban heat island over Delhi punches holes in widespread fog in the Indo-Gangetic Plains. Geophys. Res. Lett. 45 (2), 1114–1121. https://doi.org/10.1002/2017GL076794.

Ghosh, S., Das, A., 2018. Modelling urban cooling island impact of green space and water bodies on surface urban heat island in a continuously developing urban area. Model. Earth Syst. Environ. 4 (2), 501−515. https://doi.org/10.1007/s40808-018-0456-7.

Gopinath, R., Thippesh, V., 2018. Artificial neural network trained 'simultaneous extent analysis' as a logical tool in computation of urban heat island intensity. Sci. Technol. Aliment. 23 (4), 18−22. https://doi.org/10.14456/scitechasia.2018.28.

Grimmond, C.S.B., Roth, M., Oke, T.R., Au, Y.C., Best, M., Betts, R., Voogt, J., 2010. Climate and more sustainable cities: climate information for improved planning and management of cities (Producers/Capabilities perspective). Procedia Environ. Sci. 1, 247−274. https://doi.org/10.1016/j.proenv.2010.09.016.

Grossman-Clarke, S., Zehnder, J.A., Loridan, T., Grimmond, C.S.B., 2010. Contribution of land use changes to near-surface air temperatures during recent summer extreme heat events in the phoenix metropolitan area. J. Appl. Meteorol. Climatol. 49 (8), 1649−1664. https://doi.org/10.1175/2010jamc2362.1.

Grover, A., Singh, R.B., 2015. Analysis of urban heat island (UHI) in relation to normalized difference vegetation index (NDVI): a comparative study of Delhi and Mumbai. Environments 2 (2), 125−138. https://doi.org/10.3390/environments2020125.

Grover, A., Singh, R.B., 2016. Monitoring Spatial patterns of land surface temperature and urban heat island for sustainable megacity: a case study of Mumbai, India, using landsat TM data. Environ. Urban. ASIA 7 (1), 38−54. https://doi.org/10.1177/0975425315619722.

Guha, S., Govil, H., Mukherjee, S., 2017. Dynamic analysis and ecological evaluation of urban heat islands in Raipur city, India. J. Appl. Remote Sens. 11 (3). https://doi.org/10.1117/1.JRS.11.036020.

Gunwani, P., Mohan, M., 2017. Sensitivity of WRF model estimates to various PBL parameterizations in different climatic zones over India. Atmos. Res. 194, 43−65. https://doi.org/10.1016/j.atmosres.2017.04.026.

Gunwani, P., Sati, A.P., Mohan, M., Gupta, M., 2021. Assessment of physical parameterization schemes in WRF over national capital region of India. Meteorol. Atmos. Phys. 133 (2), 399−418. https://doi.org/10.1007/s00703-020-00757-y.

Gupta, M., Mohan, M., 2013. Assessment of contribution to PM10 concentrations from long range transport of pollutants using WRF/Chem over a subtropical urban airshed. Atmos. Pollut. Res. 4 (4), 405−410. https://doi.org/10.5094/APR.2013.046.

Gupta, M., Mohan, M., 2015. Validation of WRF/Chem model and sensitivity of chemical mechanisms to ozone simulation over megacity Delhi. Atmos. Environ. 122, 220−229. https://doi.org/10.1016/j.atmosenv.2015.09.039.

Gupta, N., Mathew, A., Khandelwal, S., 2019. Analysis of cooling effect of water bodies on land surface temperature in nearby region: a case study of Ahmedabad and Chandigarh cities in India. Egypt. J. Remote Sens. Space Sci. 22 (1), 81−93. https://doi.org/10.1016/j.ejrs.2018.03.007.

Gupta, K., Pushplata Lalitha, A., Ghosh Dastidar, P., Malleswara Rao, J., Thakur, P., … Senthil Kumar, A., 2021. Modeling seasonal variation in urban weather in sub-tropical region of Delhi. J. Indian Soc. Remote Sens. 49 (2), 193−213. https://doi.org/10.1007/s12524-020-01198-1.

Howard, L., 1818. The climate of London: deduced from meteorological observations, made at different places. In: The Neighbourhood of the Metropolis: W. Phillips, George Yard, Lombard Street, Sold Also by J. and A. Arch, Cornhill; Baldwin, C., and Joy, and W. Bent, Paternoster Row; and J. Hatchard, Picadilly.

IPCC, 2001. In: Houghton, J.T., Ding, Y., Griggs, D.J., Noguer, M., van der Linden, P.J., Dai, X., Maskell, K., Johnson, C.A. (Eds.), Climate Change 2001: The Scientific Basis. Contribution of Working Group I to the Third Assessment Report of the Intergovernmental Panel on Climate Change. Cambridge University Press, Cambridge, United Kingdom and New York, NY, USA, p. 881pp.

Jacobs, C., Singh, T., Gorti, G., Iftikhar, U., Saeed, S., Syed, A., Siderius, C., 2019. Patterns of outdoor exposure to heat in three South Asian cities. Sci. Total Environ. 674, 264−278. https://doi.org/10.1016/j.scitotenv.2019.04.087.

Jain, M., Pathak, K.K., 2019. Effect of urban morphology on subtropical humid microclimate: the case of Bhopal, India. Int. J. Recent Technol. Eng. 8 (3), 2376–2382. https://doi.org/10.35940/ijrte.C4661.098319.

Jain, S., Sannigrahi, S., Sen, S., Bhatt, S., Chakraborti, S., Rahmat, S., 2020. Urban heat island intensity and its mitigation strategies in the fast-growing urban area. J. Urban Manag. 9 (1), 54–66. https://doi.org/10.1016/j.jum.2019.09.004.

Jalan, S., Sharma, K., 2014. Spatio-temporal assessment of land use/land cover dynamics and urban heat island of Jaipur city using satellite data. ISPRS - Int. Arch. Photogramm. Remote Sens. Spat. Inf. Sci. XL-8, 767–772. https://doi.org/10.5194/isprsarchives-XL-8-767-2014.

Jeganathan, A., Andimuthu, R., Prasannavenkatesh, R., Kumar, D.S., 2016. Spatial variation of temperature and indicative of the urban heat island in Chennai Metropolitan Area, India. Theor. Appl. Climatol. 123 (1–2), 83–95. https://doi.org/10.1007/s00704-014-1331-8.

Joshi, R., Raval, H., Pathak, M., Prajapati, S., Patel, A., Singh, V., Kalubarme, M.H., 2015. Urban heat island characterization and isotherm mapping using geo-informatics technology in Ahmedabad city, Gujarat state, India. Int. J. Geosci. 6 (03), 274.

Kakkad, K., Barzaga, M.L., Wallenstein, S., Azhar, G.S., Sheffield, P.E., 2014. Neonates in Ahmedabad, India, during the 2010 Heat Wave: a climate change adaptation study. J. Environ. Public Health. https://doi.org/10.1155/2014/946875, 2014.

Kandya, A., Mohan, M., 2018. Mitigating the Urban Heat Island effect through building envelope modifications. Energy Build. 164, 266–277. https://doi.org/10.1016/j.enbuild.2018.01.014.

Kant, Y., Bharath, B.D., Mallick, J., Atzberger, C., Kerle, N., 2009. Satellite-based analysis of the role of land use/land cover and vegetation density on surface temperature regime of Delhi, India. J. Indian Soc. Remote Sens. 37 (2), 201–214. https://doi.org/10.1007/s12524-009-0030-x.

Kant Sahdeo, S., Ransinchung, G.D., Rahul, K.L., Debbarma, S., 2020. Effect of mix proportion on the structural and functional properties of pervious concrete paving mixtures. Construct. Build. Mater. 255. https://doi.org/10.1016/j.conbuildmat.2020.119260.

Karl, T.R., Kukla, G., Gavin, J., 1984. Decreasing diurnal temperature range in the United States and Canada from 1941 through 1980. J. Clim. Appl. Meteorol. 23 (11), 1489–1504. https://doi.org/10.1175/1520-0450(1984)023<1489:DDTRIT>2.0.CO;2.

Katpatal, Y.B., Kute, A., Satapathy, D.R., 2008. Surface- and air-temperature studies in relation to land use/land cover of Nagpur urban area using landsat 5 TM data. J. Urban Plann. Dev. 134 (3), 110–118. https://doi.org/10.1061/(ASCE)0733-9488, 2008)134:3(110.

Kaur, R., Pandey, P., 2020. Monitoring and spatio-temporal analysis of UHI effect for Mansa district of Punjab, India. Adv. Environ. Res. 9 (1), 19–39. https://doi.org/10.12989/AER.2020.9.1.019.

Kayet, N., Pathak, K., Chakrabarty, A., Sahoo, S., 2016. Urban heat island explored by co-relationship between land surface temperature vs multiple vegetation indices. Spat. Inf. Res. 24 (5), 515–529. https://doi.org/10.1007/s41324-016-0049-3.

Kedia, S., Bhakare, S.P., Dwivedi, A.K., Islam, S., Kaginalkar, A., 2021. Estimates of change in surface meteorology and urban heat island over northwest India: impact of urbanization. Urban Clim. 36. https://doi.org/10.1016/j.uclim.2021.100782.

Kesavan, R., Muthian, M., Sudalaimuthu, K., Sundarsingh, S., Krishnan, S., 2021. ARIMA modeling for forecasting land surface temperature and determination of urban heat island using remote sensing techniques for Chennai city, India. Arabian J. Geosci. 14, 1016. https://doi.org/10.1007/s12517-021-07351-5.

Khan, A., Chatterjee, S., 2016. Numerical simulation of urban heat island intensity under urban–suburban surface and reference site in Kolkata, India. Model. Earth Syst. Environ. 2 (2). https://doi.org/10.1007/s40808-016-0119-5.

Kikegawa, Y., Genchi, Y., Yoshikado, H., Kondo, H., 2003. Development of a numerical simulation system toward comprehensive assessments of urban warming countermeasures including their impacts upon the urban buildings' energy-demands. Appl. Energy 76 (4), 449−466.

Kikegawa, Y., Genchi, Y., Kondo, H., Hanaki, K., 2006. Impacts of city-block-scale countermeasures against urban heat-island phenomena upon a building's energy-consumption for air-conditioning. Appl. Energy 83 (6), 649−668. https://doi.org/10.1016/j.apenergy.2005.06.001.

Kikon, N., Singh, P., Singh, S.K., Vyas, A., 2016. Assessment of urban heat islands (UHI) of Noida City, India using multi-temporal satellite data. Sustain. Cities Soc. 22, 19−28. https://doi.org/10.1016/j.scs.2016.01.005.

Kim, S.W., Brown, R.D., 2021. Urban heat island (UHI) intensity and magnitude estimations: a systematic literature review. Sci. Total Environ. 779, 146389. https://doi.org/10.1016/j.scitotenv.2021.146389.

Kolokotroni, M., Ren, X., Davies, M., Mavrogianni, A., 2012. London's urban heat island: impact on current and future energy consumption in office buildings. Energy Build. 47, 302−311. https://doi.org/10.1016/j.enbuild.2011.12.019.

Kotak, Y., Gago, E.J., Mohanty, P., Muneer, T., 2014. Installation of roof-top solar PV modules and their impact on building cooling load. Build. Serv. Eng. Technol. 35 (6), 613−633. https://doi.org/10.1177/0143624414527098.

Kotharkar, R., Bagade, A., 2018a. Evaluating urban heat island in the critical local climate zones of an Indian city. Landsc. Urban Plann. 169, 92−104. https://doi.org/10.1016/j.landurbplan.2017.08.009.

Kotharkar, R., Bagade, A., 2018b. Local Climate Zone classification for Indian cities: a case study of Nagpur. Urban Clim. 24, 369−392. https://doi.org/10.1016/j.uclim.2017.03.003.

Kotharkar, R., Surawar, M., 2016. Land use, land cover, and population density impact on the formation of canopy urban heat islands through traverse survey in the Nagpur urban area, India. J. Urban Plann. Dev. 142 (1). https://doi.org/10.1061/(ASCE)UP.1943-5444.0000277.

Kotharkar, R., Bagade, A., Ramesh, A., 2019. Assessing urban drivers of canopy layer urban heat island: a numerical modeling approach. Landsc. Urban Plann. 190. https://doi.org/10.1016/j.landurbplan.2019.05.017.

Kotharkar, R., Bagade, A., Singh, P.R., 2020. A systematic approach for urban heat island mitigation strategies in critical local climate zones of an Indian city. Urban Clim. 34. https://doi.org/10.1016/j.uclim.2020.100701.

Kotharkar, R., Ghosh, A., Kotharkar, V., 2021. Estimating summertime heat stress in a tropical Indian city using Local Climate Zone (LCZ) framework. Urban Clim. 36, 100784. https://doi.org/10.1016/j.uclim.2021.100784.

Kumar, D., Shekhar, S., 2015. Statistical analysis of land surface temperature-vegetation indexes relationship through thermal remote sensing. Ecotoxicol. Environ. Saf. 121, 39−44. https://doi.org/10.1016/j.ecoenv.2015.07.004.

Kumari, P., Kapur, S., Garg, V., Kumar, K., 2020. Effect of surface temperature on energy consumption in a calibrated building: a case study of Delhi. Climate 8 (6). https://doi.org/10.3390/CLI8060071.

Kumari, P., Garg, V., Kumar, R., Kumar, K., 2021. Impact of urban heat island formation on energy consumption in Delhi. Urban Clim. 36. https://doi.org/10.1016/j.uclim.2020.100763.

Kurian, A.L., 2020. Urban heat island mitigation and Miyawaki forests: an analysis. Pollut. Res. 39, 6.

Kusaka, H., Kimura, F., 2004. Thermal effects of urban canyon structure on the nocturnal heat island: numerical experiment using a mesoscale model coupled with an urban canopy model. J. Appl. Meteorol. 43 (12), 1899−1910. https://doi.org/10.1175/jam2169.1.

Laaidi, K., Zeghnoun, A., Dousset, B., Bretin, P., Vandentorren, S., Giraudet, E., Beaudeau, P., 2012. The impact of heat islands on mortality in Paris during the august 2003 heat wave. Environ. Health Perspect. 120 (2), 254−259. https://doi.org/10.1289/ehp.1103532.

Lo, C.P., Quattrochi, D.A., 2003. Land-use and land-cover change, urban heat island phenomenon, and health implications. Photogramm. Eng. Remote Sens. 69 (9), 1053−1063. https://doi.org/10.14358/PERS.69.9.1053.

Majumder, A., Setia, R., Kingra, P.K., Sembhi, H., Singh, S.P., Pateriya, B., 2021. Estimation of land surface temperature using different retrieval methods for studying the spatiotemporal variations of surface urban heat and cold islands in Indian Punjab. Environ. Dev. Sustain. https://doi.org/10.1007/s10668-021-01321-3.

Mallick, J., Singh, C.K., Shashtri, S., Rahman, A., Mukherjee, S., 2012. Land surface emissivity retrieval based on moisture index from LANDSAT TM satellite data over heterogeneous surfaces of Delhi city. Int. J. Appl. Earth Obs. Geoinf. 19 (1), 348−358. https://doi.org/10.1016/j.jag.2012.06.002.

Mallick, J., Rahman, A., Singh, C.K., 2013. Modeling urban heat islands in heterogeneous land surface and its correlation with impervious surface area by using night-time ASTER satellite data in highly urbanizing city, Delhi-India. Adv. Space Res. 52 (4), 639−655. https://doi.org/10.1016/j.asr.2013.04.025.

Manley, G., 1958. On the frequency of snowfall in metropolitan England. Q. J. R. Meteorol. Soc. 84 (359), 70−72. https://doi.org/10.1002/qj.49708435910.

Manteghi, G., Bin Limit, H., Remaz, D., 2015. Water bodies an urban microclimate: a review. Mod. Appl. Sci. 9 (6), 1−12. https://doi.org/10.5539/mas.v9n6p1.

Maral, S.G., Mukhopadhyay, T., 2015. Signal of urban heat island (UHI) effect: a case study of Mumbai metropolitan region. Mausam 66 (4), 729−740.

Martin, P., Baudouin, Y., Gachon, P., 2015. An alternative method to characterize the surface urban heat island. Int. J. Biometeorol. 59 (7), 849−861. https://doi.org/10.1007/s00484-014-0902-9.

Maske, S.J., Krishna, N., Behere, P.G., Kachare, S.D., 1978. Characteristics of Heat Island at Pune. Prepublished Scientific Report No. 78112. India Meteorological Deptartment, Pune.

Mathew, A., Sreekumar, S., Khandelwal, S., Kaul, N., Kumar, R., 2016b. Prediction of surface temperatures for the assessment of urban heat island effect over Ahmedabad city using linear time series model. Energy Build. 128, 605−616. https://doi.org/10.1016/j.enbuild.2016.07.004.

Mathew, A., Khandelwal, S., Kaul, N., 2016c. Spatial and temporal variations of urban heat island effect and the effect of percentage impervious surface area and elevation on land surface temperature: study of Chandigarh city, India. Sustain. Cities Soc. 26, 264−277. https://doi.org/10.1016/j.scs.2016.06.018.

Mathew, A., Khandelwal, S., Kaul, N., 2017. Investigating spatial and seasonal variations of urban heat island effect over Jaipur city and its relationship with vegetation, urbanization and elevation parameters. Sustain. Cities Soc. 35, 157−177. https://doi.org/10.1016/j.scs.2017.07.013.

Mathew, A., Khandelwal, S., Kaul, N., 2018a. Analysis of diurnal surface temperature variations for the assessment of surface urban heat island effect over Indian cities. Energy Build. 159, 271−295. https://doi.org/10.1016/j.enbuild.2017.10.062.

Mathew, A., Khandelwal, S., Kaul, N., 2018b. Investigating spatio-temporal surface urban heat island growth over Jaipur city using geospatial techniques. Sustain. Cities Soc. 40, 484−500. https://doi.org/10.1016/j.scs.2018.04.018.

Mavrogianni, A., Davies, M., Batty, M., Belcher, S.E., Bohnenstengel, S.I., Carruthers, D., Ye, Z., 2011. The comfort, energy and health implications of London's urban heat island. Build. Serv. Eng. Technol. 32 (1), 35−52. https://doi.org/10.1177/0143624410394530.

Mehrotra, S., Bardhan, R., Ramamritham, K., 2020a. Diurnal thermal diversity in heterogeneous built area: Mumbai, India. Urban Clim. 32. https://doi.org/10.1016/j.uclim.2020.100627.

Mehrotra, S., Bardhan, R., Ramamritham, K., 2020b. Urban form as policy variable for climate-sensitive area planning under heterogeneity: a geographically weighted regression approach. Area Dev. Policy 5 (2), 167−188. https://doi.org/10.1080/23792949.2019.1609368.

Misslin, R., Telle, O., Daudé, E., Vaguet, A., Paul, R.E., 2016. Urban climate versus global climate change—what makes the difference for dengue? In: Annals of the New York Academy of Sciences, vol. 1382, pp. 56−72.

Mohammad, P., Goswami, A., 2021a. A spatio-temporal assessment and prediction of surface urban heat island intensity using multiple linear regression techniques over Ahmedabad city, Gujarat. J. Indian Soc. Remote Sens. https://doi.org/10.1007/s12524-020-01299-x.

Mohammad, P., Goswami, A., 2021b. Spatial variation of surface urban heat island magnitude along the urban-rural gradient of four rapidly growing Indian cities. Geocarto Int. https://doi.org/10.1080/10106049.2021.1886338.

Mohammad, P., Goswami, A., Bonafoni, S., 2019. The impact of the land cover dynamics on surface urban heat island variations in semi-arid cities: a case study in Ahmedabad City, India, using multi-sensor/source data. Sensors 19 (17). https://doi.org/10.3390/s19173701.

Mohan, M., 1985. Diurnal variation of mean mixing depths in different months at Delhi. Mausam 36, 71–74.

Mohan, M., Bhati, S., 2011. Analysis of WRF model performance over subtropical region of Delhi, India. Adv. Meteorol. 621235. https://doi.org/10.1155/2011/621235, 2011.

Mohan, M., Gupta, M., 2018. Sensitivity of PBL parameterizations on PM10 and ozone simulation using chemical transport model WRF-Chem over a sub-tropical urban airshed in India. Atmos. Environ. 185, 53–63. https://doi.org/10.1016/j.atmosenv.2018.04.054.

Mohan, M., Kandya, A., 2015. Impact of urbanization and land-use/land-cover change on diurnal temperature range: a case study of tropical urban airshed of India using remote sensing data. Sci. Total Environ. 506–507, 453–465. https://doi.org/10.1016/j.scitotenv.2014.11.006.

Mohan, M., Sati, A.P., 2016. WRF model performance analysis for a suite of simulation design. Atmos. Res. 169, 280–291. https://doi.org/10.1016/j.atmosres.2015.10.013.

Mohan, M., Kikegawa, Y., Gurjar, B., Bhati, S., Kandya, A., Ogawa, K., 2009. Assessment of Urban Heat Island Intensities over Delhi. Paper presented at the Seventh International Conference on Urban Climate (ICUC-7), Yokohama, Japan. http://www.ide.titech.ac.jp/~icuc7/extended_abstracts/pdf/375621-2-090515211144-004.pdf.

Mohan, M., Kandya, A., Battiprolu, A., 2011a. Urban heat island effect over national capital region of India: a study using the temperature trends. J. Environ. Protect. 04, 8. https://doi.org/10.4236/jep.2011.24054.

Mohan, M., Pathan, S.K., Narendrareddy, K., Kandya, A., Pandey, S., 2011b. Dynamics of urbanization and its impact on land-use/land-cover: a case study of megacity Delhi. J. Environ. Protect. 09, 10. https://doi.org/10.4236/jep.2011.29147.

Mohan, M., Kikegawa, K., Gurjar, B.R., Bhati, S., Kandya, A., Ogawa, K., 2012. Urban heat island assessment for a tropical urban airshed in India. Atmos. Clim. Sci. 2 (2), 12. https://doi.org/10.4236/acs.2012.22014.

Mohan, M., Kikegawa, Y., Gurjar, B.R., Bhati, S., Kolli, N.R., 2013. Assessment of urban heat island effect for different land use-land cover from micrometeorological measurements and remote sensing data for megacity Delhi. Theor. Appl. Climatol. 112 (3–4), 647–658. https://doi.org/10.1007/s00704-012-0758-z.

Mohan, M., Gupta, A., Bhati, S., 2014. A modified approach to analyze thermal comfort classification. Atmos. Clim. Sci. 01, 13. https://doi.org/10.4236/acs.2014.41002.

Mohan, M., Singh, V.K., Bhati, S., Lodhi, N., Sati, A.P., Sahoo, N.R., Dey, S., 2020a. Industrial heat island: a case study of Angul-Talcher region in India. Theor. Appl. Climatol. 141 (1–2), 229–246. https://doi.org/10.1007/s00704-020-03181-9.

Mohan, M., Sati, A.P., Bhati, S., 2020b. Urban sprawl during five decadal period over National Capital Region of India: impact on urban heat island and thermal comfort. Urban Clim. 33, 100647. https://doi.org/10.1016/j.uclim.2020.100647.

Mohanta, K., Sharma, L.K., 2017. Assessing the impacts of urbanization on the thermal environment of Ranchi City (India) using geospatial technology. Remote Sens. Appl. Soc. Environ. 8, 54–63. https://doi.org/10.1016/j.rsase.2017.07.008.

Mohapatra, M., Kumar, N., Bandyopadhyay, B.K., 2009. Role of mesoscale low and urbanization on exceptionally heavy rainfall event of 26th July 2005 over Mumbai: some observational evidences. Mausam 60 (3), 317–324.

Mohapatra, M., Kumar, N., Bandyopadhyay, B.K., 2010. Unprecedented rainfall over Bangalore city during october, 2005. Mausam 61 (1), 105–112.

Mohapatra, G.N., Rakesh, V., Ramesh, K.V., 2017. Urban extreme rainfall events: categorical skill of WRF model simulations for localized and non-localized events. Q. J. R. Meteorol. Soc. 143 (707), 2340—2351. https://doi.org/10.1002/qj.3087.

Mukherjee, A.K., Daniel, C.E.J., 1976. Temperature distribution over Bombay during a cold night. Indian J. Met. Geophys 27 (1), 37—41.

Mukherjee, A.K., Mukhopadhyay, B., Krishna, N., 1987. Influence of urbanization on local temperature and humidity fields in a few major cities in India. In: Selvamurthy (Ed.), Contributions to Human Biometeorology. SPB Academic Publishing, The Netherlands, 3—1.

Mukherjee, S., Joshi, P.K., Garg, R.D., 2017. Analysis of urban built-up areas and surface urban heat island using downscaled MODIS derived land surface temperature data. Geocarto Int. 32 (8), 900—918. https://doi.org/10.1080/10106049.2016.1222634.

Nandkeolyar, N., Sandhya Kiran, G., 2019. A climatological study of the spatio-temporal variability of land surface temperature and vegetation cover of Vadodara district of Gujarat using satellite data. Int. J. Remote Sens. 40 (1), 218—236. https://doi.org/10.1080/01431161.2018.1512766.

Neog, R., Lahkar, B., Baruah, J., Acharjee, S., Gogoi, B.S., Sonowal, B., Das, T., 2020. An infrared thermography-based study on the variation in diurnal and seasonal land surface temperature at Dibrugarh city, India. Model. Earth Syst. Environ. 6 (4), 2047—2061. https://doi.org/10.1007/s40808-020-00772-3.

Nimish, G., Bharath, H.A., Lalitha, A., 2020. Exploring temperature indices by deriving relationship between land surface temperature and urban landscape. Remote Sens. Appl. Soc. Environ. 18. https://doi.org/10.1016/j.rsase.2020.100299.

Niyogi, D., Lei, M., Kishtawal, C., Schmid, P., Shepherd, M., 2017. Urbanization impacts on the summer heavy rainfall climatology over the eastern United States. Earth Interact. 21 (5), 1—17.

Niyogi, D., Osuri, K.K., Busireddy, N.K.R., Nadimpalli, R., 2020. Timing of rainfall occurrence altered by urban sprawl. Urban Clim. 33, 100643. https://doi.org/10.1016/j.uclim.2020.100643.

Nuruzzaman, M., 2015. Urban heat island: causes, effects and mitigation measures - a review. Int. J. Environ. Monit. Anal. 3 (2). https://doi.org/10.11648/j.ijema.20150302.15.

Oke, T.R., 1973. City size and the urban heat island. Atmos. Environ. 7, 769—779.

OSPCB (State Pollution Control Board, Odisha), 2018. Proposed Mitigation Strategies for the Angul—Talcher Industrial Area in the State of Odisha. Retrieved from. http://ospcboard.org/wp-content/plugins/publication//uploads/files_1558748737_26031.pdf.

Padmanaban, R., Bhowmik, A., Cabral, P., 2019. Satellite image fusion to detect changing surface permeability and emerging urban heat islands in a fast-growing city. PLoS One 14. https://doi.org/10.1371/journal.pone.0208949.

Padmanabhamurty, B., 1979. Isotherms and isohumes in Pune on clear winter nights: a Mesometeorological study. Mausam 80 (1), 134—138.

Padmanabhamurty, B., 1990. Microclimates in tropical urban complexes. Energy Build. 15 (1—2), 83—92. https://doi.org/10.1016/0378-7788(90)90119-4.

Padmanabhamurty, B., Bahl, H.D., 1984. Isothermal and isohyetal patterns of Delhi as a sequel of urbanization. Mausam 35 (4), 539—540.

Padmanabhmurty, B., Bahl, H.D., 1982. Some physical features of heat and humidity islands at Delhi. Mausam 33, 211—221.

Pal, S., Ziaul, S., 2017. Detection of land use and land cover change and land surface temperature in English Bazar urban centre. Egypt. J. Remote Sens. Space Sci. 20 (1), 125—145. https://doi.org/10.1016/j.ejrs.2016.11.003.

Pandey, P., Kumar, D., Prakash, A., Masih, J., Singh, M., Kumar, S., Kumar, K., 2012. A study of urban heat island and its association with particulate matter during winter months over Delhi. Sci. Total Environ. 414, 494—507. https://doi.org/10.1016/j.scitotenv.2011.10.043.

Pandey, A.K., Singh, S., Berwal, S., Kumar, D., Pandey, P., Prakash, A., Kumar, K., 2014. Spatio−temporal variations of urban heat island over Delhi. Urban Clim. 10 (P1), 119−133. https://doi.org/10.1016/j.uclim.2014.10.005.

Panwar, M., Agarwal, A., Devadas, V., 2018. Analyzing land surface temperature trends using non-parametric approach: a case of Delhi, India. Urban Clim. 24, 19−25. https://doi.org/10.1016/j.uclim.2018.01.003.

Parry, M., 1950. The climates of towns. Weather 5 (10), 351−356. https://doi.org/10.1002/j.1477-8696.1950.tb01100.x.

Patel, P., Ghosh, S., Kaginalkar, A., Islam, S., Karmakar, S., 2019. Performance evaluation of WRF for extreme flood forecasts in a coastal urban environment. Atmos. Res. 223, 39−48. https://doi.org/10.1016/j.atmosres.2019.03.005.

Patel, P., Karmakar, S., Ghosh, S., Niyogi, D., 2020. Improved simulation of very heavy rainfall events by incorporating WUDAPT urban land use/land cover in WRF. Urban Clim. 32. https://doi.org/10.1016/j.uclim.2020.100616.

Pathak, C., Chandra, S., Maurya, G., Rathore, A., Sarif, M.O., Gupta, R.D., 2021. The effects of land indices on thermal state in surface urban heat island formation: a case study on Agra city in India using remote sensing data (1992−2019). Earth Syst. Environ. 5 (1), 135−154. https://doi.org/10.1007/s41748-020-00172-8.

Patki, P., Raykar-Alange, P., 2012. Study of influence of land cover on urban heat islands in pune using remote sensing. J. Mech. Civil Eng. 3, 39−43.

Pattnaik, S., 2019. Weather forecasting in India: recent developments. Mausam 70 (3), 453−464.

Paul, S., Ghosh, S., Mathew, M., Devanand, A., Karmakar, S., Niyogi, D., 2018. Increased spatial variability and intensification of extreme monsoon rainfall due to urbanization. Sci. Rep. 8 (1), 3918. https://doi.org/10.1038/s41598-018-22322-9.

Payra, S., Mohan, M., 2014. Multirule based diagnostic approach for the fog predictions using WRF modelling tool. Adv. Meteorol. 456065. https://doi.org/10.1155/2014/456065, 2014.

Powers, J.G., Klemp, J.B., Skamarock, W.C., Davis, C.A., Dudhia, J., Gill, D.O., Duda, M.G., 2017. The weather research and forecasting model: overview, system efforts, and future directions. Bull. Am. Meteorol. Soc. 98 (8), 1717−1737. https://doi.org/10.1175/bams-d-15-00308.1.

Prakash, S., Norouzi, H., 2020. Land surface temperature variability across India: a remote sensing satellite perspective. Theor. Appl. Climatol. 139 (1−2), 773−784. https://doi.org/10.1007/s00704-019-03010-8.

Pramanik, S., Punia, M., 2019. Assessment of green space cooling effects in dense urban landscape: a case study of Delhi, India. Model. Earth Syst. Environ. 5 (3), 867−884. https://doi.org/10.1007/s40808-019-00573-3.

Pramanik, S., Punia, M., 2020. Land use/land cover change and surface urban heat island intensity: source−sink landscape-based study in Delhi, India. Environ. Dev. Sustain. 22 (8), 7331−7356. https://doi.org/10.1007/s10668-019-00515-0.

Przybylak, R., Uscka-Kowalkowska, J., Araźny, A., Kejna, M., Kunz, M., Maszewski, R., 2015. Spatial distribution of air temperature in Toruń (Central Poland) and its causes. Theor. Appl. Climatol. 1−23. https://doi.org/10.1007/s00704-015-1644-2.

Puppala, H., Singh, A.P., 2021. Analysis of urban heat island effect in Visakhapatnam, India, using multi-temporal satellite imagery: causes and possible remedies. Environ. Dev. Sustain. https://doi.org/10.1007/s10668-020-01122-0.

Raj, S., Paul, S.K., Chakraborty, A., Kuttippurath, J., 2020. Anthropogenic forcing exacerbating the urban heat islands in India. J. Environ. Manag. 257. https://doi.org/10.1016/j.jenvman.2019.110006.

Rajan, E.H.S., Amirtham, L.R., 2021. Urban Heat Island Intensity and Evaluation of Outdoor Thermal Comfort in Chennai. Environment, Development and Sustainability, India. https://doi.org/10.1007/s10668-021-01344-w.

Ramachandra, T.V., Kumar, U., 2009. Land surface temperature with land cover dynamics: multi-resolution, spatio-temporal data analysis of greater Bangalore, India. Int. J. Geoinformatics 5 (3), 43−53.

Rani, M., Kumar, P., Pandey, P.C., Srivastava, P.K., Chaudhary, B.S., Tomar, V., Mandal, V.P., 2018. Multi-temporal NDVI and surface temperature analysis for Urban Heat Island inbuilt surrounding of sub-humid region: a case study of two geographical regions. Remote Sens. Appl. Soc. Environ. 10, 163−172. https://doi.org/10.1016/j.rsase.2018.03.007.

Revi, A., Satterthwaite, D., Aragón-Durand, F., Corfee-Morlot, J., Kiunsi, R., Pelling, M., . . . Solecki, W. (2014). Urban areas climate change 2014: impacts, adaptation, and vulnerability. Part A: global and sectoral aspects. In Field, C.B., Barros, V.R., Dokken, D.J. et al. (Eds.), Contribution of Working Group II to the Fifth Assessment Report of the Intergovernmental Panel on Climate Change. pp. 535−612.

Robitu, M., Musy, M., Inard, C., Groleau, D., 2006. Modeling the influence of vegetation and water pond on urban microclimate. Sol. Energy 80 (4), 435−447. https://doi.org/10.1016/j.solener.2005.06.015.

Roy, S., Singh, R., Kumar, M., 2011. An analysis of local spatial temperature patterns in the Delhi Metropolitan Area. Phys. Geogr. 32 (2), 114−138. https://doi.org/10.2747/0272-3646.32.2.114.

Sahoo, S.K., Himesh, S., Gouda, K.C., 2020. Impact of urbanization on heavy rainfall events: a case study over the megacity of Bengaluru, India. Pure Appl. Geophys. 177 (12), 6029−6049. https://doi.org/10.1007/s00024-020-02624-8.

Sailor, D.J., 2006. Mitigation of Urban Heat Islands - Recent Progress and Future Prospects. Paper presented at the Sixth Symposium on the Urban Environment, Atlanta. https://ams.confex.com/ams/pdfpapers/105264.pdf.

Sannigrahi, S., Rahmat, S., Chakraborti, S., Bhatt, S., Jha, S., 2017. Changing dynamics of urban biophysical composition and its impact on urban heat island intensity and thermal characteristics: the case of Hyderabad City, India. Model. Earth Syst. Environ. 3 (2), 647−667. https://doi.org/10.1007/s40808-017-0324-x.

Santamouris, M., Papanikolaou, N., Livada, I., Koronakis, I., Georgakis, C., Argiriou, A., Assimakopoulos, D.N., 2001. On the impact of urban climate on the energy consumption of buildings. Sol. Energy 70 (3), 201−216. https://doi.org/10.1016/S0038-092X(00)00095-5.

Santamouris, M., Cartalis, C., Synnefa, A., Kolokotsa, D., 2015. On the impact of urban heat island and global warming on the power demand and electricity consumption of buildings—a review. Energy Build. 98, 119−124. https://doi.org/10.1016/j.enbuild.2014.09.052.

Sarkar, A., Saraswat, R.S., Chandrasekar, A., 1998. Numerical study of the effects of urban heat island on the characteristic features of the sea breeze circulation. Proc. Indian Acad. Sci. Earth Planet Sci. 107 (2), 127−137.

Sati, A.P., Mohan, M., 2018. The impact of urbanization during half a century on surface meteorology based on WRF model simulations over National Capital Region, India. Theor. Appl. Climatol. 134 (1−2), 309−323. https://doi.org/10.1007/s00704-017-2275-6.

Sati, A.P., Mohan, M., 2021a. Impact of increase in urban sprawls representing five decades on summer-time air quality based on WRF-Chem model simulations over central-National Capital Region, India. Atmos. Pollut. Res. 12 (2), 404−416. https://doi.org/10.1016/j.apr.2020.12.002.

Sati, A.P., Mohan, M., 2021b. Impact of urban sprawls on thunderstorm episodes: assessment using WRF model over central-national capital region of India. Urban Clim. 37, 100869. https://doi.org/10.1016/j.uclim.2021.100869.

Shah, A., Garg, A., Mishra, V., 2021. Quantifying the local cooling effects of urban green spaces: evidence from Bengaluru, India. Landsc. Urban Plann. 209. https://doi.org/10.1016/j.landurbplan.2021.104043.

Sharma, R., Joshi, P.K., 2014. Identifying seasonal heat islands in urban settings of Delhi (India) using remotely sensed data - an anomaly based approach. Urban Clim. 9, 19−34. https://doi.org/10.1016/j.uclim.2014.05.003.

Sharma, R., Hooyberghs, H., Lauwaet, D., De Ridder, K., 2019. Urban heat island and future climate change—implications for Delhi's heat. J. Urban Health 96 (2), 235−251. https://doi.org/10.1007/s11524-018-0322-y.

Sharma, R., Pradhan, L., Kumari, M., Bhattacharya, P., 2021. Assessing urban heat islands and thermal comfort in Noida City using geospatial technology. Urban Clim. 35, 100751. https://doi.org/10.1016/j.uclim.2020.100751.

Shastri, H., Paul, S., Ghosh, S., Karmakar, S., 2015. Impacts of urbanization on Indian summer monsoon rainfall extremes. J. Geophys. Res. Atmos. 120 (2), 496−516. https://doi.org/10.1002/2014JD022061.

Shastri, H., Barik, B., Ghosh, S., Venkataraman, C., Sadavarte, P., 2017. Flip flop of day-night and summer-winter surface urban heat island intensity in India. Sci. Rep. 7. https://doi.org/10.1038/srep40178.

Shastri, H., Ghosh, S., Paul, S., Shafizadeh-Moghadam, H., Helbich, M., Karmakar, S., 2019. Future urban rainfall projections considering the impacts of climate change and urbanization with statistical−dynamical integrated approach. Clim. Dynam. 52 (9), 6033−6051. https://doi.org/10.1007/s00382-018-4493-8.

Shem, W., Shepherd, M., 2009. On the impact of urbanization on summertime thunderstorms in Atlanta: two numerical model case studies. Atmos. Res. 92 (2), 172−189.

Shukla, A., Jain, K., 2021. Analyzing the impact of changing landscape pattern and dynamics on land surface temperature in Lucknow city, India. Urban For. Urban Green. 58. https://doi.org/10.1016/j.ufug.2020.126877.

Simpson, M., Raman, S., Suresh, R., Mohanty, U.C., 2008. Urban effects of Chennai on sea breeze induced convection and precipitation. J. Earth Syst. Sci. 117 (6), 897−909. https://doi.org/10.1007/s12040-008-0075-1.

Singh, R., Kalota, D., 2019. Urban sprawl and its impact on generation of urban heat island: a case study of Ludhiana city. J. Indian Soc. Remote Sens. 47 (9), 1567−1576. https://doi.org/10.1007/s12524-019-00994-8.

Singh, P., Kikon, N., Verma, P., 2017a. Impact of land use change and urbanization on urban heat island in Lucknow city, Central India. A remote sensing based estimate. Sustain. Cities Soc. 32, 100−114. https://doi.org/10.1016/j.scs.2017.02.018.

Singh, J., Sekharan, S., Karmakar, S., Ghosh, S., Zope, P.E., Eldho, T.I., 2017b. Spatio-temporal analysis of sub-hourly rainfall over Mumbai, India: is statistical forecasting futile? J. Earth Syst. Sci. 126 (3). https://doi.org/10.1007/s12040-017-0817-z.

Somers, K.A., Bernhardt, E.S., McGlynn, B.L., Urban, D.L., 2016. Downstream dissipation of storm flow heat pulses: a case study and its landscape-level implications. J. Am. Water Resour. Assoc. 52 (2), 281−297. https://doi.org/10.1111/1752-1688.12382.

Stewart, I., Oke, T., 2012. Local climate zones for urban temperature studies. Bull. Am. Meteorol. Soc. 93, 1879−1900. https://doi.org/10.1175/BAMS-D-11-00019.1.

Subhashini, S., Thirumaran, K., Saravanan, V., Alaguraja, R.A., 2016. A comparative analysis of land surface retrieval methods using landsat 7 and 8 data to study urban heat island effect in Madurai. Int. J. Earth Sci. Eng. 9 (4), 1397−1404.

Suhail, M., Khan, M.S., Faridi, R.A., 2019. Assessment of urban heat islands effect and land surface temperature of Noida, India by using landsat satellite data. MAPAN-J. Metrol. Soc. India 34 (4), 431−441. https://doi.org/10.1007/s12647-019-00309-9.

Sultana, S., Satyanarayana, A.N.V., 2019. Impact of urbanisation on urban heat island intensity during summer and winter over Indian metropolitan cities. Environ. Monit. Assess. 191. https://doi.org/10.1007/s10661-019-7692-9.

Sultana, S., Satyanarayana, A.N.V., 2020. Assessment of urbanisation and urban heat island intensities using landsat imageries during 2000−2018 over a sub-tropical Indian City. Sustain. Cities Soc. 52. https://doi.org/10.1016/j.scs.2019.101846.

Sundaram, A.M., 2011. Urban green-cover and the environmental performance of Chennai city. Environ. Dev. Sustain. 13 (1), 107−119. https://doi.org/10.1007/s10668-010-9251-y.

Sundersingh, S.,D., 1990. Effect of heat islands over urban madras and measures for its mitigation. Energy Build. 15 (1−2), 245−252. https://doi.org/10.1016/0378-7788(90)90136-7.

Surawar, M., Kotharkar, R., 2017. Assessment of urban heat island through remote sensing in Nagpur urban area using landsat 7 ETM+ satellite images. Int. J. Urban Civ. Eng. 11 (7), 868−874.

Sussman, H.S., Raghavendra, A., Zhou, L., 2019. Impacts of increased urbanization on surface temperature, vegetation, and aerosols over Bengaluru, India. Remote Sens. Appl. Soc. Environ. 16, 100261. https://doi.org/10.1016/j.rsase.2019.100261.

Swain, D., Roberts, G.J., Dash, J., Lekshmi, K., Vinoj, V., Tripathy, S., 2017. Impact of rapid urbanization on the city of Bhubaneswar, India. Proc. Natl. Acad. Sci. India Phys. Sci. 87 (4), 845−853. https://doi.org/10.1007/s40010-017-0453-7.

Swamy, G.S.N.V.K.S.N., Nagendra, S.M., Schlink, U., 2020. Impact of urban heat island on meteorology and air quality at microenvironments. J. Air Waste Manag. Assoc. 1−16. https://doi.org/10.1080/10962247.2020.1783390.

Taha, H., Akbari, H., Rosenfeld, A., Huang, J., 1988. Residential cooling loads and the urban heat island—the effects of albedo. Build. Environ. 23 (4), 271−283. https://doi.org/10.1016/0360-1323(88)90033-9.

Tan, J., Zheng, Y., Tang, X., Guo, C., Li, L., Song, G., Chen, H., 2010. The urban heat island and its impact on heat waves and human health in Shanghai. Int. J. Biometeorol. 54 (1), 75−84. https://doi.org/10.1007/s00484-009-0256-x.

Taslim, S., Monsefi Parapari, D., Shafaghat, A., 2015. Urban design guidelines to mitigate urban heat island (UHI) effects in hot- dry cities. J. Teknol. 74, 119−124. https://doi.org/10.11113/jt.v74.4619.

Telle, O., Nikolay, B., Kumar, V., Benkimoun, S., Pal, R., Nagpal, B.N., Paul, R.E., 2021. Social and environmental risk factors for dengue in Delhi city: a retrospective study. PLoS Negl. Trop. Dis. 15 (2), e0009024. https://doi.org/10.1371/journal.pntd.0009024.

Tewari, M., Chen, F., Kusaka, H., Miao, S., 2007. Coupled WRF/Unified Noah/urban-canopy modeling system. Ncar WRF Documentation, NCAR, Boulder 122, 1−22.

Tomlinson, C.J., Chapman, L., Thornes, J.E., Baker, C.J., 2011. Including the urban heat island in spatial heat health risk assessment strategies: a case study for Birmingham, UK. Int. J. Health Geogr. 10. https://doi.org/10.1186/1476-072X-10-42, 42-42.

U.S. Environmental Protection Agency (USEPA, 2008. Reducing Urban Heat Islands: Compendium of Strategies. Draft. https://www.epa.gov/heat-islands/heat-island-compendium.

Vailshery, L.S., Jaganmohan, M., Nagendra, H., 2013. Effect of street trees on microclimate and air pollution in a tropical city. Urban For. Urban Green. 12 (3), 408−415. https://doi.org/10.1016/j.ufug.2013.03.002.

Voogt, J., 2004. How Researchers Measure Urban Heat Islands. https://www.epa.gov/sites/default/files/2014-07/documents/epa_how_to_measure_a_uhi.pdf.

Wan, Z., Zhang, Y., Zhang, Q., Li, Z.-L., 2004. Quality assessment and validation of the MODIS global land surface temperature. Int. J. Remote Sens. 25 (1), 261−274. https://doi.org/10.1080/0143116031000116417.

Wang, J., Feng, J., Yan, Z., Hu, Y., Jia, G., 2012. Nested high-resolution modeling of the impact of urbanization on regional climate in three vast urban agglomerations in China. J. Geophys. Res. 117, D21103. https://doi.org/10.1029/2012JD018226.

World Bank, 2017. Urban Population (% of Total) | Data. data.worldbank.org. Retrieved 17 January 2019.

Wright, R.P., 2009. The Ancient Indus: Urbanism, Economy, and Society. Cambridge University Press.

Xu, T., Sathaye, J., Akbari, H., Garg, V., Tetali, S., 2012. Quantifying the direct benefits of cool roofs in an urban setting: reduced cooling energy use and lowered greenhouse gas emissions. Build. Environ. 48 (1), 1−6. https://doi.org/10.1016/j.buildenv.2011.08.011.

Yadav, N., Sharma, C., 2018. Spatial variations of intra-city urban heat island in megacity Delhi. Sustain. Cities Soc. 37, 298−306. https://doi.org/10.1016/j.scs.2017.11.026.

Yadav, N., Sharma, C., Peshin, S.K., Masiwal, R., 2017. Study of intra-city urban heat island intensity and its influence on atmospheric chemistry and energy consumption in Delhi. Sustain. Cities Soc. 32, 202−211. https://doi.org/10.1016/j.scs.2017.04.003.

Ziaul, S., Pal, S., 2020. Modeling the effects of green alternative on heat island mitigation of a meso level town, West Bengal, India. Adv. Space Res. 65 (7), 1789−1802. https://doi.org/10.1016/j.asr.2019.12.031.

Urban heat island in Latin American cities: a review of trends, impacts, and mitigation strategies

12

Massimo Palme[1,2] and Claudio Carrasco[3]

[1]*Universidad Católica del Norte, Escuela de Arquitectura, Antofagasta, Región de Antofagasta, Chile;* [2]*Universidad Católica del Norte, Centro de Investigación Tecnológica del Agua en el Desierto, Antofagasta, Región de Antofagasta, Chile;* [3]*Universidad de Valparaíso, Facultad de Ingeniería, Escuela de Ingeniería en Construcción, Valparaíso, Región de Valparaíso, Chile*

1. Introduction

Urban heat island (UHI), a phenomenon that is worsening the liveability of cities and increasing climate change associated risks worldwide, is one of the clearest results of human activities and a signal of the Anthropocene Epoch (Crutzen and Stoermer, 2000). UHI has been studied since the 19th century (Howard, 1833), and up to date, many studies are available, both theoretical and experimental, for many cities of the world, especially in Europe, North America, and Asia (Santamouris and Kolokotsa, 2016; Santamouris, 2020). Africa and Central—South America, however, are world regions with few academic developments in the field, nevertheless of being regions with high urban growth rates.

In the past years, however, most governments have focused the attention on climate change mitigation and adaptation (United Nations, 2011), as well as on the accomplishment of the Sustainable Development Goals of United Nations (United Nations, 2015). This implies taking concrete action against the impacts of climate change, and this has inevitable repercussion on UHI mitigation policies. For example, the orientations for policymakers of UN-Habitat include the building sector in both mitigation and adaptation strategies to fight against climate change, and the building sector is directly responsible of the UHI. Moreover, the orientations for policymakers (United Nations, 2011; OCDE, 2014) also recommend considering changes in transportation systems and in energy transformation and final use, which are other aspects directly related to UHI. Everything seems to be connected.

As a consequence of the implementation of general laws and plans of actions against climate change, some specific policies focused on UHI mitigations are under assessment in Latin-American countries. For example, the preparation of the COP 25 Conference, which should have taken place in Chile in November 2020 (moved to Madrid at last minute), motivated the public sector and the Academia of the country to prepare documents to be presented at the conference. Among these

Global Urban Heat Island Mitigation. https://doi.org/10.1016/B978-0-323-85539-6.00014-7

documents, the report "Cities and Climate Change in Chile" (Muñoz et al., 2019) focused on cities' energy policies, underlying the importance of urban climate and UHI mitigation for comfort and energy needs reduction of the building sector.

If general mitigation/adaptation plans are present in most Latin-American countries, the practical implementation of mitigation interventions in infrastructure is still insufficient to cope with the phenomenon. Among strategies, city greening and public mobility are the most implemented, as demonstrated by the best practice cases of Medellín in Colombia (Nuñez and Wang, 2020) and Curitiba in Brazil (Pérez and Ziede, 2020). However, actions taken until now are clearly not sufficient to achieve the ambitious goals. Some more specific action in counteracting UHI has been taken by local authorities in collaboration with universities and research institutes. For example, in Ecuador, the Municipality of Durán signed an agreement with the Polytechnical University (ESPOL) to assess the climatic vulnerability and implement mitigation actions for the city (RESCLIMA Durán Project, Cornejo et al., 2020). These kinds of preliminary actions are the base for the construction of a real mitigation and adaption public plan, which is still a sensible lack in this world region.

2. Cities and climate in Latin America

Latin America is one of the world regions with the highest rate of urban growth. Today there are at least nine megacities with more than 5,000,000 people and many cities with more than 1,000,000 people (United Nations, 2019). Table 12.1 resumes the biggest cities in Latin America and their climate following Köppen−Geiger classification (Peel et al., 2007, Fig. 12.1).

Cities are located in three macroclimates (following Köppen−Geiger): Temperate climate (21), Tropical (40), and Arid (13). More of the half are placed in hot tropical climates, as recently observed and discussed by Palme (2021). In such climates, UHI phenomenon can have strong negative impacts on buildings' energy performance and on liveability of outdoor environment. Studies conducted mostly in Asia show that, in these climates, the presence of UHI combined with the increased accessibility to air-conditioning could lead to the impressive increase of energy use of 300% in a couple of years (Santamouris, 2020). In Latin America, the social development has been rising during the last decades, and now almost all the countries of the region are placed in an acceptable range of human development with a reasonably low ecological footprint (Moran et al., 2008). So, this region of the world seems to stay at the corner of (un)sustainable development (Wackernagel et al., 2017). However, there are still many problems to be resolved, especially in terms of incomes distribution and environmental rights of the whole population.

On the other hand, urbanization rates of Latin-American countries are among the highest of the world, with cities border expansion and population constantly increasing for big cities (Inostroza et al., 2013) and for intermediate and small cities as well (Andrade-Nuñez and Aide, 2018). It should be considered that most of the new human settlements are placed in climate-sensitive risk zones, in many cases without the minimum habitability requirements (slums). It has been observed (Inostroza et al., 2016) that a symmetry exits in the distribution of exposition and sensitivity to risk: the more exposed the urban sector, the more sensitive the population (elderly and unemployed people, children, poor families). Adaptive capacity is almost always concentrated in sectors where it is less needed: the more the incomes of the inhabitants, the more the green areas, health services, etc. (De la Barrera et al., 2019).

Table 12.1 Cities over 1,000,000 inhabitants and climate classification for Latin America.

City	Country	Inhabitants	Climate	Classification
Sao Paulo	Brazil	22.043.028	Humid subtropical	Cfa
Mexico City	Mexico	21.782.378	Subtropical highland with dry winter	Cwb
Buenos Aires	Argentina	15.173.529	Humid subtropical	Cfa
Rio de Janeiro	Brazil	13.458.075	Tropical savanna with dry winter	Aw
Bogotá	Colombia	10.978.360	Subtropical highland with uniform rainfall	Cfb
Lima	Perù	10.719.188	Arid hot climate	Bwh
Santiago	Chile	6.767.223	Mediterranean hot summer	Csa
Belo Horizonte	Brazil	6.084.430	Humid subtropical	Cfa
Guadalajara	Mexico	5.179.479	Humid subtropical with dry winter	Cwa
Monterrey	Mexico	4.874.095	Semiarid hot climate	Bsh
Brasilia	Brazil	4.645.843	Tropical savanna with dry winter	Aw
Porto Alegre	Brazil	4.137.417	Humid subtropical	Cfa
Recife	Brazil	4.127.091	Tropical monsoon	Am
Fortaleza	Brazil	4.073.465	Tropical savanna with dry summer	As
Medellín	Colombia	4.000.263	Tropical rainforest	Af
Salvador de Bahia	Brazil	3.839.076	Tropical rainforest	Af
Curitiba	Brazil	3.678.732	Oceanic climate	Cfb
Asunción	Paraguay	3.336.562	Tropical savanna with dry winter	Aw
Santo Domingo	Rep. Dom.	3.317.784	Tropical monsoon	Am
Campinas	Brazil	3.300.794	Humid subtropical with dry winter	Cwa
Puebla	Mexico	3.184.948	Subtropical highland with uniform rainfall	Cfb
Guayaquil	Ecuador	2.994.218	Tropical savanna with dry winter	Aw
Caracas	Venezuela	2.938.992	Tropical savanna with dry winter	Aw
Guatemala City	Guatemala	2.934.841	Tropical savanna with dry winter	Aw
Cali	Colombia	2.781.980	Tropical savanna with dry summer	As
Port au Prince	Haiti	2.773.553	Tropical savanna with dry winter	Aw

(Continued)

Table 12.1 Cities over 1,000,000 inhabitants and climate classification for Latin America.—cont'd

City	Country	Inhabitants	Climate	Classification
Goiania	Brazil	2.690.011	Tropical savanna with dry winter	Aw
Toluca	Mexico	2.467.241	Subtropical highland with dry winter	Cwb
San Juan	Puerto Rico	2.448.417	Tropical savanna with dry winter	Aw
Belém	Brazil	2.334.462	Tropical rainforest	Af
Barranquilla	Colombia	2.272.914	Tropical savanna with dry winter	Aw
Manaus	Brazil	2.260.778	Tropical rainforest	Af
Maracaibo	Venezuela	2.257.999	Tropical savanna with dry winter	Aw
Havana	Cuba	2.140.423	Tropical savanna with dry winter	Aw
Tijuana	Mexico	2.140.398	Semiarid cold climate	Bsk
Grande Vitoria	Brazil	2.075.857	Tropical savanna with dry winter	Aw
Valencia	Venezuela	1.910.188	Tropical savanna with dry winter	Aw
Santos	Brazil	1.892.314	Tropical rainforest	Af
Quito	Ecuador	1.873.763	Subtropical highland with uniform rainfall	Cfb
Panama City	Panama	1.860.291	Tropical monsoon	Am
La Paz	Bolivia	1.857.787	Subtropical highland with dry winter	Cwb
Leon	Mexico	1.820.127	Semiarid hot climate	Bsh
Montevideo	Uruguay	1.752.788	Humid subtropical	Cfa
Santa Cruz	Bolivia	1.712.688	Tropical savanna with dry winter	Aw
La Laguna	Mexico	1.614.854	Arid cold climate	Bwk
Cordoba	Argentina	1.571.944	Dry-winter humid subtropical	Cwa
Rosario	Argentina	1.532.538	Humid subtropical	Cfa
Ciudad Juarez	Mexico	1.517.235	Arid hot climate	Bwk
Sao Luis	Brazil	1.485.763	Tropical savanna with dry winter	Aw
Natal	Brazil	1.456.844	Tropical savanna with dry summer	As
Tegucigalpa	Honduras	1.444.085	Humid subtropical	Cfa
San José	Costa Rica	1.399.629	Tropical monsoon	Am
Joao Pessoa	Brazil	1.378.249	Tropical savanna with dry winter	Aw

Table 12.1 Cities over 1,000,000 inhabitants and climate classification for Latin America.—cont'd

City	Country	Inhabitants	Climate	Classification
Queretaro	Mexico	1.339.103	Semiarid cold climate	Bsk
Bucaramanga	Colombia	1.331.453	Tropical monsoon	Am
Maceio	Brazil	1.323.039	Tropical monsoon	Am
Cochabamba	Bolivia	1.303.907	Subtropical highland with dry winter	Cwb
Joinville	Brazil	1.303.141	Humid subtropical	Cfa
Florianópolis	Brazil	1.239.331	Humid subtropical	Cfa
San Luis Potosí	Mexico	1.216.564	Semiarid cold climate	Bsk
Barquisimeto	Venezuela	1.214.362	Semiarid hot climate	Bsh
Macaray	Venezuela	1.203.227	Tropical savanna with dry winter	Aw
Mendoza	Argentina	1.172.619	Arid cold climate	Bwk
Merida	Mexico	1.161.475	Tropical savanna with dry winter	Aw
Mexicali	Mexico	1.120.872	Arid hot climate	Bwh
Aguascalientes	Mexico	1.106.453	Semiarid hot climate	Bsh
San Salvador	El Salvador	1.105.766	Tropical savanna with dry winter	Aw
Cuernavaca	Mexico	1.075.022	Tropical savanna with dry winter	Aw
Managua	Nicaragua	1.063.698	Tropical savanna with dry winter	Aw
Cartagena	Colombia	1.062.622	Tropical savanna with dry winter	Aw
Cihuahua	Mexico	1.054.766	Semiarid cold climate	Bsk
Teresina	Brazil	1.021.229	Tropical savanna with dry winter	Aw
Aracaju	Brazil	1.009.534	Tropical savanna with dry summer	As
Tampico	Mexico	1.001.278	Tropical savanna with dry winter	Aw

3. UHI studies in Latin America: a brief review

Despite the urbanization rate, urban climate studies are still few in the region. Pioneer work was done since the 1970 by Jáuregui in Mexico, and some recent study has been developed in Brazil, Chile, and Argentina. Only a very few research works are available in Ecuador, Peru, Colombia, and other countries (Fig. 12.2).

A recent review (Palme, 2021) identified around 30 studies published in the last 5 years and focused on tropical and subtropical cities. Other 15 studies focus on temperate climates, particularly in

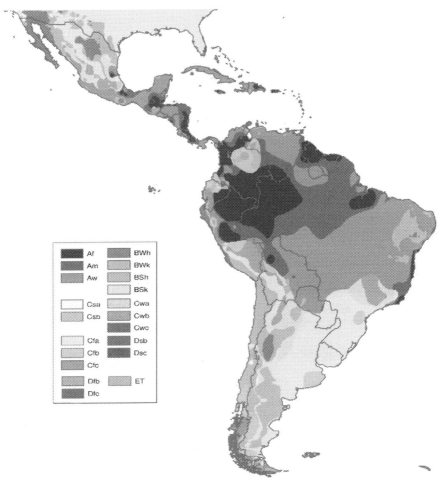

FIGURE 12.1

Köppen–Geiger classification for Latin America.

From Peel, M.C., Finlayson, B.L., McMahon, T.A., 2007. Updated world map of the Kö-ppen-Geiger climate classification. Hydrol. Earth Syst. Sci. 11, 1633–1644.

Argentina and Chile. Analyzed studies used different concepts and methods: some evaluate surface urban heat island (SUHI) by using remote sensing techniques (Wu et al., 2019), others evaluate the canopy layer (UHI by monitoring, fixed or mobile, or by simulation). Few studies analyze only the intensity of the phenomenon, most of them investigate also the impacts, trends, and driving factors.

Brazil is the country where almost the half of the studies concentrate, probably because most of the territory is placed in tropical hot climate, confirming the idea that the UHI phenomenon is especially important for such emplacements. UHI studies in Brazil focused on megacities (Sao Paulo, Rio de

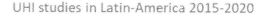

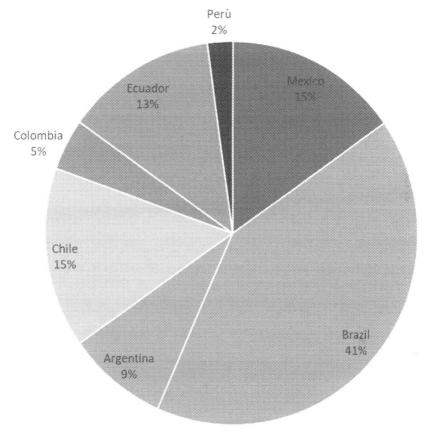

FIGURE 12.2

Academic papers (WoS, Scopus, and Scielo) for UHI studies in Latin America.

Janeiro, Belo Horizonte, Brasilia), big cities (Manaus, Curitiba, Campinas) as well as intermediate (Santos, Petrolina, Uberlandia, Rio Preto, Florianópolis) and small cities (Presidente Prudente, Penápolis, Rosana, Paranavai, Nova Adreatina).

In México, Mexico City and Guadalajara were the first cities to be assessed in terms of UHI, followed by few more (Queretaro, Tampico). In Chile, historical monitoring was conducted for the case of Santiago, and some recent work has been done for coastal (Antofagasta, Valparaíso, Concepción) and internal cities (Temuco, Rancagua). In Argentina, the most studied cases are Buenos Aires and Mendoza. In Colombia, recent studies started the assessment of Bogotá and Medellín. In Ecuador, only Guayaquil metropolitan area and Cuenca city have been studied. In Perú, studies are very few, basically conducted by simulation for the case of Lima, a city that hosts the third part of the country population.

All the studies detected UHI or SUHI with intensities mostly in the range 1−6 K and a strong dependence on urban morphology (Palme, 2021).

4. Trends and impacts

In general, UHIs have been recorded constantly over time only in about the 20%−30% of the cities listed in Table 12.1. Despite that, at least for the megacities, some information is available. Table 12.2 resumes the UHI intensity obtained for the nine megacities of the region.

With respect to interannual variability, a general trend of increase in UHI intensity has been detected in most of the studied cases. The main reason for this is the increase in population and extension of the cities' boundaries. Densification and vertical development are also causing the increase in urban temperatures, especially at night, as observed by Jauregui (1992).

Palme et al. (2016) suggest that for coastal cities on the Pacific Ocean, the most important driving factors are the anthropogenic heat release by vehicles and the changes in urban morphology of cities due to increased building density.

With respect to impacts, many studies indicate that changes in outdoor comfort and an increase in building energy needs are the most important. Only a little of research has been done, until now, on the impact on public health of the UHI intensity in this world region (Wong et al., 2013).

In terms of energy penalties introduced by UHI, some studies evidenced a global energy penalty in the range of 20%−200% for various cities of the region (Palme et al., 2016). These results are in line with many studies conducted worldwide (Santamouris, 2020).

5. Mitigation strategies: recent implementations, advances, and proposals

Among mitigation strategies normally considered to face UHI, we can account at least (Santamouris and Kolokotsa, 2016):

— Urban greening (roofs, streets, façades)
— Water-related urban design and evaporative cooling

Table 12.2 Studies on UHI intensity for the nine megacities over 5,000,000 inhabitants.

City	UHI intensity (K)	Season	References study
Sao Paulo	8.0	Summer	Barros and Lombardo (2016)
Mexico City	8.0	Winter	Jáuregui (2000)
Buenos Aires	4.6	Winter	Figuerola and Mazzeo (1998)
Rio de Janeiro	5.0	Fall	Marques Filho et al. (2009)
Bogotá	3.0	Year	Ángel et al. (2010)
Lima	2.4	Summer	Palme et al. (2019)
Santiago	4.8	Summer	Sarricolea and Martin-Vide (2013)
Belo Horizonte	4.7	Year	Magalhaes Filho (2006)
Guadalajara	4.0	Winter	Jáuregui et al. (1992)

- Cool materials for pavements, facades and roofs
- Reduction of anthropogenic heat release from buildings, vehicles, etc.
- Urban form: design with ventilation and shadows
- Geothermal solutions

These strategies do not perform equally well in all climates, nor at all scales. Depending on specific climatic location and on the dimensions of the site of intervention, some of these strategies should be preferred. Moreover, as a general rule, mitigative strategies that are also adaptive should be privileged (Stone, 2012).

6. Tropical climate

Tropical climates are characterized by high temperatures and precipitation across the whole year (Fig. 12.3). Depending on specific location (altitude, distance from the see), these climates can have a dry season. UHI in cities located in such climates can have pernicious effects on health and comfort indoor and outdoor, plus energy consumption impacts on building sector.

Cities in tropical climates include some of the biggest cities, such as Rio de Janeiro, Brasilia, and Medellín, and most of the other cities. In this kind of climate, mitigation strategies to be considered are urban ventilation, city greening, reduction of anthropogenic heat release, reduction of the thermal mass. Unfortunately, many times the locations in such climates have also low winds or no wind at all to be used to the scope. It is the case, for example, of Guayaquil, where counteract UHI is really difficult (Fig. 12.4). Simulation studies (Litardo et al., 2020) conducted by using the Urban Weather Generator tool (UWG) to obtain urban weather files and TRNSY tool to simulate building performance lead to the result of suggesting a reduction in building density combined with green areas increase as the main strategy to reduce UHI intensity. So, the importance of spatial planning and land use emerges as the key factor in controlling and mitigating UHI (Fig. 12.5).

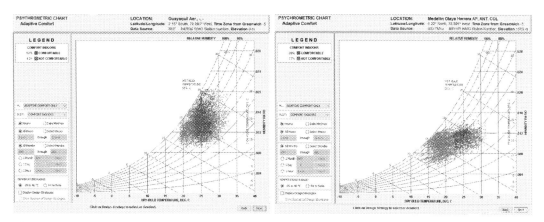

FIGURE 12.3

Psychrometric chart for tropical cities (Guayaquil, Aw and Medellín, Af).

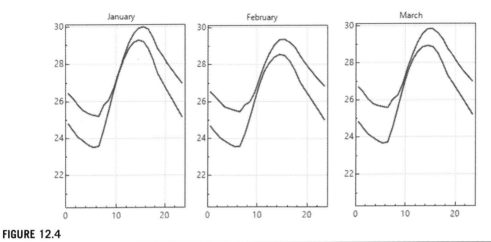

FIGURE 12.4

UHI intensity for average days of summer months, Guayaquil, Ecuador.

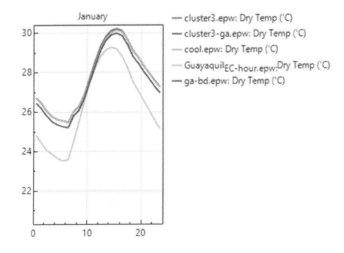

FIGURE 12.5

UHI intensity reduction, different mitigation strategies: rural temperature (orange (light gray in print)), urban as it is (blue (black in print)), cool pavements (green (gray in print)), urban vegetation (red (dark gray in print)), and building density reduction plus vegetation (gray (black in print)).

Some studies also suggest that the influence of big water bodies (e.g., the lagoons of Tampico in Mexico) can reduce urban temperatures as well as or even more than park areas (Rosas et al., 2016 and 2017). The combined use of green and blue strategies has reached good results for urban thermal comfort improvement, even in humid locations (Fig. 12.6).

FIGURE 12.6

Water and plants use to improve liveability of urban spaces in Medellín, Colombia.

Photography by Paula Kapstein.

7. Arid climate

In arid climates, we find the megacity of Lima and other big cities such as Monterrey, Tijuana, and most of Mexican big cities. Climate variability through the year depends on the Ocean influence: cities such as Lima present a stable climate, with mild temperatures and relatively high humidity values, while cities placed in central deserts present high thermal excursion and lower humidity (Fig. 12.7).

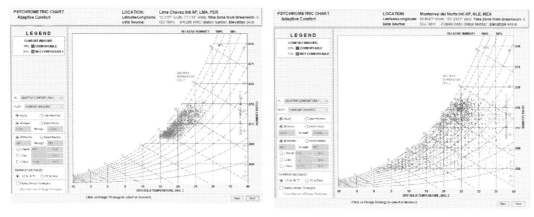

FIGURE 12.7

Psychrometric chart for arid cities (Lima, Bwh and Monterrey Bsh).

For coastal cities, most applicable mitigation strategy is natural ventilation (Yang et al., 2019; Takebayashi et al., 2018). Evaporative cooling that can be obtained with blue-infrastructure solutions can be very useful. Cool materials are also very much recommended because of the high levels of solar radiation (Santamouris, 2013; Álvarez and Sanchez, 2016). Geothermal solutions can be applied (Zoras and Dimoudi, 2016). Reduction in buildings' energy needs is also a very useful strategy (He, 2019).

A study conducted by Salvati et al. (2019) evidenced that in arid climates, one of the most influencing parameters on the global energy penalty for the building sector, introduced by urbanization-related aspects, is the height of buildings, favoring the generation of shadows and balancing the UHI intensity increase. So, in terms of urban design, cities in the desert should be compact, with high-rise buildings placed appropriately to obstruct the solar access in the hottest part of the day and protecting the outdoor public space, but taking care to not obstruct the air circulation (Fig. 12.8). In fact, another study (Palme et al., 2018) suggest the existence of a threshold value in the technomass (Inostroza, 2014) that should be deposed in a site to avoid exponential increase in cooling loads of buildings.

Shadow management is probably the easier way to assure comfort in the urban space. At the level of building design, the intermediate spaces should be privileged, as well as compact urban morphologies.

8. Temperate climates

Most of the megacities are placed in climates defined as temperate (Fig. 12.9). Some cases are in the highlands (Mexico City, Bogotá), others are placed at subtropical latitudes (Sao Paulo, Buenos Aires, Santiago de Chile).

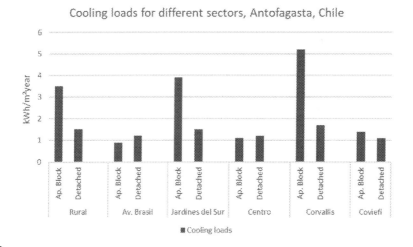

FIGURE 12.8

Cooling loads for two buildings typologies in different city sectors, arid climate. Some sector presents an increase in cooling loads while others present a decrease (depending mostly by the average building height).

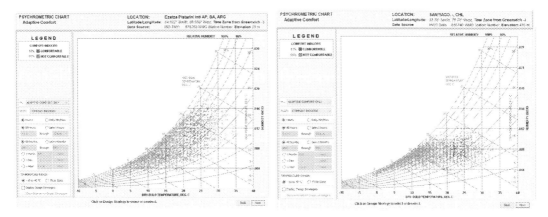

FIGURE 12.9

Psychrometric chart for temperate climates (Buenos Aires, Cfa and Santiago de Chile, Csa).

City greening is largely the most recommended mitigation strategy for temperate climates, followed by cool materials for building envelopes, as indicated studies conducted for Santiago de Chile (De la Barrera and Reyes, 2018), Mendoza (Alchapar and Correa, 2020), and Temuco (Moreno et al., 2020). Geothermal solutions and evaporative cooling can be applied.

A remarkably interesting study, done by Sosa et al. (2020), compares the use of green corridors and the increase of the albedos for the entire envelope (roofs, pavements, and walls) in the case of Mendoza (open structure, with streets width in the range of 16−30 m). They found that a combination of increased albedos and trees shadows is the best option for all the street orientations; however, the contribution of the envelope optical properties is determinant only in the widest case. So, green solutions in this case should be privileged. Another study in favor of the city greening is the research conducted by Alchapar et al. (2018) that evaluates green roofs and cool roofs for the case of Mendoza, showing that green roofs perform slightly better than cool roofs in all considered scenarios.

9. Increasing adaptive capacity

If mitigation of UHI intensity is in general a clear need, as mentioned before, there are some strategies that should be privileged, in particular the strategies that are also adaptive and contribute to increase resilience to UHI. This is a two-way principle: the adaptive actions should also be mitigative in order to have priority. Inostroza et al. (2016) performed a study on the heat vulnerability facing heat for the city of Santiago in Chile. Results show that the highest correlations with the heat vulnerability are achieved for water disposal and roofing material of dwellings. So, the adaptive actions to be taken are: extend water distribution to the city sectors where it is not available today; and replace the poor materials of dwellings in slums and other informal settlements. If these adaptive strategies can be taken also improving mitigation, much better will be the result. For example, replacing the roof of houses permits

Table 12.3 Recommended strategies by climatic emplacement.

Climate	Strategies	Type
Tropical	Urban ventilation	Adaptive/mitigative
	City greening	Adaptive/mitigative
	Open planning	Mitigative
	Water bodies	Adaptive
Arid	Urban ventilation	Adaptive/mitigative
	Evaporative cooling	Mitigative
	Cool materials	Mitigative
	Geothermal cooling	Mitigative
	Compact planning	Mitigative
Temperate	City greening	Adaptive/mitigative
	Cool materials	Mitigative
	Evaporative cooling	Mitigative
	Geothermal solution	Mitigative
All climates	Anthropogenic heat reduction	Mitigative

to use cool selective materials (if the cost is affordable) instead of simply insulating better the envelope. A new water distribution system could consider also evaporative cooling urban systems, possible recycling the gray water using specific recirculation systems for that. Table 12.3 resumes the recommended strategies for each climatic region.

10. Conclusion

This chapter analyzed the current knowledge on UHI phenomenon and related impacts in Latin-American cities. The first conclusion is that more research is needed for this world region, where the high urbanization rates, the global climate change impact, and the increased social development of the populations converge into key challenges. Analysis of existing academic research on UHI and more in general on urban climate for the region indicates that there is a general agreement on the increasing intensity of the UHI phenomenon, associated with land use change, uncontrolled urbanization, and more intense energy used for transport and buildings operation.

Researchers also agree on the urgent need for interventions that could help to mitigate the UHI impacts and to adapt to the new urban climate. However, at a policy level, there is still a lack of detailed recommendations and actions to be taken. Most of Latin-American countries have general principle statements for controlling climate change and achieve sustainable development, but still vague and difficult to be implemented. Among mitigation strategies, the most frequent action is the investment in green infrastructure, once again without specific indications that should conform an integrated urban planning perspective.

A third conclusion is that the mitigation strategies should be evaluated by specific considerations, as the impacts of these actions are climate-sensitive. We conducted a general analysis for the most important macroclimatic classification of the region: tropical hot, arid, and temperate climates. Most recommended strategies, according to this analysis and other previous results, are indeed: open city planning (wind sensitive) for tropical climates; compact city planning (sun and wind sensitive), cool materials and evaporative cooling techniques for arid climates; greening the city, cool materials, evaporative and geothermal systems for temperate climates. Reduction of anthropogenic heat, by vehicles and buildings, is always a good strategy.

References

Alchapar, N., Correa, E., Cantón, M.A., 2018. Techos reflectivos o verdes? Influencia sobre el microclima en ciudades de zonas áridas. Mendoza, Argentina. Cuad. Vivienda Urban. 11 (22).

Alchapar, N., Correa, E., 2020. Optothermal properties of façade coatings. Effects of environmental exposure over solar reflective index. J. Build. Eng.

Álvarez, S., Sanchez, F., 2016. Evaporative cooling techniques. In: Santamouris, M., Kolokotsa, D. (Eds.), Urban Climate Mitigation Techniques. Routledge.

Andrade-Nuñez, M.J., Aide, T.M., 2018. Built-up expansion between 2001 and 2011 in South America continues well beyond the cities. Environ. Res. Lett. 13.

Ángel, L., Ramírez, A., Dominguez, E., 2010. Isla de calor y cambios espacio-temporales de la temperatura en la ciudad de Bogotá. Revista de la Academia Colombiana de Ciencias Exactas, Físicas y Naturales 34 (131), 173−183.

Barros, H.R., Lombardo, M.A., 2016. A ihla de calor urbana e o uso e cobertura do solo em Sao Paulo. Geosup − Espaço e Tempo 20 (1), 160−177.

Cornejo-Rodriguez, M.P., Borbor-Cordova, M., Arias-Hidalgo, M., Matamoros-Camposano, D., Sanclemente, E., Soriano-Idrovo, G., Macias-Zambrano, J., Ochoa-Donoso, D., Dominguez-Bonini, F., Nolivos-Alvarez, I., Villafuerte-Arias, R., Menoscal-Aldas, L., Valdiviezo-Ajila, A., 2020. Diseñando Estrategias para la Resiliencia Climática en Ciudades: Informe de Políticas. CIP-RRD, Guayaquil, Ecuador.

Crutzen, P.J., Stoermer, E.F., 2000. The "Anthropocene. Global Change Newsl. 41, 17−18.

De la Barrera, F., Reyes, S., 2018. Urban green infrastructure in support of ecosystem services in a highly dynamic South American city. In: Atlas of Ecosystem Services. Springer.

De la Barrera, F., Henriquez, C., Ruiz, V., Inostroza, L., 2019. Urban Parks and Social Inequalities in the Acess to Ecosystem Services in Santiago de Chile. IOP Conf. Ser. Mater. Sci. Eng. 471.

Figuerola, P.I., Mazzeo, N.A., 1998. Urban-rural temperature differences in Buenos Aires. Int. J. Climatol. 18 (15), 1709−1723.

He, B.J., 2019. Towards the next generation of green building for urban heat island mitigation: Zero UHI impact building. Sustain. Cities Soc. 50, 101647.

Howard, L., 1833. The Climate of London. Reprinted by the International Association on Urban Climate. Available online: https://www.urban-climate.org/documents/LukeHoward_Climate-of-London-V1.pdf (Last accessed on February 2021).

Inostroza, L., 2014. Measuring urban ecosystem functions through 'Technomass'—a novel indicator to assess urban metabolism. Ecol. Indicat. 42, 2−19.

Inostroza, L., Baur, R., Csaplovics, E., 2013. Urban sprawl and fragmentation in Latin America: a dynamic quantification and characterization of spatial patterns. J. Environ. Manag. 115, 87−97.

Inostroza, L., Palme, M., De la Barrera, F., 2016. A Heat Vulnerability Index: spatial Patterns of Exposure, Sensitivity and Adaptive Capacity for Santiago de Chile. PLoS One 11 (9).

Jauregui, E., 1992. Aspects of heat-island development in Guadalajara, Mexico. Atmos. Environ. 26B (3), 391−396.

Jauregui, E., 2000. El clima de la ciudad de México. Plaza y Valdés vol. 1.

Litardo, J., Palme, M., Borbor, M., Caiza, R., Macias, J., Hidalgo, R., Soriano, G., 2020. Urban Heat Island intensity and buildings' energy needs in Durán, Ecuador: simulation studies and proposal of mitigation strategies. Sustain. Cities Soc. 62, 102387.

Magalhaes Filho, L. Ilha de Calor Urbana, Metodologia para Mesuraçao: Belo Horizonte, uma analise exploratoria. Tese de Doutoramiento — Programa de Pos-Graduaçao em Geografia, PUC-MG, Belo Horizonte.

Marques Filho, E., Karam, H., Miranda, A., França, J., 2009. Rio de Janeiro's tropical urban climate. In: Newsletter of the International Association of Urban Climate, 32, pp. 5—9.

Moran, D., Wackernagel, M., Kitzes Goldfinger, S., Boutaud, A., 2008. Measuring sustainable development — Nation by nation. Ecol. Econ. 64, 470—474.

Moreno, R., Ojeda, N., Azocar, J., 2020. Application of NDVI for Identify Potentiality of the Urban Forest for the Design of a Green Corridor System in Intermediate Cities of Latin-America: Case Study, Temuco, Chile.

Muñoz, J.C., Barton, J., Frías, D., Godoy, A., Bustamante, W., Cortés, S., Munizaga, M., Rojas, C., Wagemann, E., 2019. Ciudades y Cambio Climático en Chile: Recomendaciones desde la evidencia científica. Santiago de Chile, Ministerio de Ciencia, Tecnología, Conocimiento e Innovación.

Nuñez, J.R., Wang, H.H., 2020. Slum upgrading and climate change adaptation and mitigation: lessons form Latin America. Cities 104, 102791.

OCDE, 2014. Cities and Climate Change. Policy Perspectives. Available online: https://sustainabledevelopment. un.org/topics/sustainablecities (Last accessed on February 2021).

Palme, M., 2021. Urban heat island studies in hot and humid climates: a review of the state of art in Latin-America. In: Enteria, N., Santamouris, M., Eicker, U. (Eds.), Urban Heat Island Mitigation — Hot and Humid Regions. Springer Nature, Singapore.

Palme, M., Inostroza, L., Villacreses, G., Lobato, A., Carrasco, C., 2016. From urban climate to energy consumption. Enhancing building performance simulation by including the urban heat island effect. Energy Build. 145.

Palme, M., Inostroza, L., Salvati, A., 2018. Technomass and cooling demand in South America: a superlinear relationship? Build. Res. Inf. 46 (8), 864—880.

Palme, M., Inostroza, L., Villacreses, G., Lobato, A., Carrasco, C., 2019. Urban climate in the South American coastal cities of Guayaquil, Lima, Antofagasta and Valparaíso, and its impacts on the energy efficiency of buildings. In: Henriquez, C., Romero, H. (Eds.), Urban Climates in Latin America. Springer Nature, Basel.

Peel, M.C., Finlayson, B.L., McMahon, T.A., 2007. Updated world map of the Kö-ppen-Geiger climate classification. Hydrol. Earth Syst. Sci. 11, 1633—1644.

Pérez, G., Ziede, M., 2020. Shifting from a risk mitigation Project to an adaptation Project: the case of Curitiba's lagoon parks. IOP Conf. Ser. Mater. Sci. Eng. 960, 042072.

Rosas, M., Bartorila, M., 2017. Forestation contributions to urban sustainability in tropical cities. Nuevo Amanecer wetland, Ciudad Madero, Mexico. Nova Ciencia 9 (19), 528—550.

Rosas, M., Bartorila, M., Ocón, S., 2016. Laguna del Carpintero, regulador climático den el área urbana de Tampico. Revista Legado de Arquitectura y Diseño 11 (20), 113—124.

Salvati, A., Palme, M., Chiesa, G., Kolokotroni, M., 2019. Built form, urban climate and building energy modelling: case studies in Rome and Antofagasta. J. Build. Perform. Simul. 13 (2).

Santamouris, M., 2013. Using cool pavements as a mitigation strategy to tight urban heat island — a review of actual developments. Renew. Sustain. Energy Rev. 26, 224—240.

Santamouris, M., 2020. Recent progress on urban overheating and heat island research. Integrated assessment of the energy, environmental, vulnerability and health impact. Synergies with the global climate change. Energy Build. 207.

Santamouris, M., Kolokotsa, D., 2016. Urban Climate Mitigation Techniques. Routledge.

Sarricolea, P., Martin-Vide, J., 2013. La isla de calor urbana del área Metropolitana de Santiago de Chile a partir de diferencias térmicas de los observatorios de Talagante y Cerrillos. Perspect. Geogr. 18 (2), 239–256.

Sosa, B., Correa, E., Cantón, M.A., 2020. Eficacia de estrategias de disminución del calentamiento urbano. Estudio para una ciudad de clima árido. Inf. Construcción 72, 559.

Stone, B., 2012. The City and the Coming Climate. Cambridge University Press.

Takebayashi, H., Tanaka, T., Moriyama, M., Watanabe, H., Miyazaki, H., Kittaka, K., 2018. Relationship between city size, coastal land use, and summer daytime air temperature. Climate 6 (4), 84.

United Nations, 2011. Cities and Climate Change: Global Report on Human Settlements. Earthscan.

United Nations, 2015. Sustainable Development Goals. Available online: https://sdgs.un.org/goals (Last accessed on February 2021).

United Nations, 2019. World Population Prospects. Available online: https://population.un.org/wup/ (Last accessed on January 2021).

Wackernagel, M., Hanscom, L., Lin, D., 2017. Making the sustainable development Goals Consistent with sustainability. Front. Energy Res. 103389.

Wong, K., Paddon, A., Jimenez, A., 2013. Review of world urban heat islands: many linked to increased mortality. J. Energy Resour. Technol. 135 (2).

Wu, X., Wang, G., Yao, R., Wang, L., Yu, D., Gui, X., 2019. Investigating surface urban heat islands in South America based on MODIS data from 2003–2016. Rem. Sens. 11, 1212.

Yang, J., Jin, S., Xiao, X., Jin, C., Xia, J., Li, X., Wang, S., 2019. Local climate ventilation and urban land surface temperatures: towards a performance based and wind sensitive planning proposal in megacities. Sustain. Cities Soc. 47, 101487.

Zoras, S., Dimoudi, A., 2016. Exploring earth cooling to mitigate heat. In: Santamouris, M., Kolokotsa, D. (Eds.), Urban Climate Mitigation Techniques. Routledge.

Air quality and heat-related health impacts of increasing urban greenery cover

13

Mohamed Dardir and Umberto Berardi

Faculty of Engineering and Architectural Science, Ryerson University, Toronto, ON, Canada

1. Introduction

The combination of climate change, Urban Heat Island (UHI), and heat waves leads to higher daytime temperatures, causes excessive heat stress for urban dwellers, and increases the heat-related morbidity (illness) and mortality (death) (Fischer and Schär, 2010; Lee et al., 2014; Jandaghian and Akbari, 2018) mostly in vulnerable sections of the society such as elderly, homeless, and socially disadvantaged people (Benmarhnia et al., 2015; Declet-Barreto et al., 2016). The severe impacts of heat waves are associated with multiday heat stress, warm nights, and increased relative humidity. The characteristics of the heat waves are defined regionally according to the local climatic conditions.

According to Health Canada (2017), the local weather of the Greater Toronto Area (GTA) is considered as a heat wave when the daytime maximum temperature exceeds 31°C, and the nighttime minimum temperature exceeds 20°C for at least two consecutive days. Considering the ambient dew point temperature, Health Canada also reports heat warnings if the local heat stress index, temperature-humidity index (Humidex), reaches 40 or more for at least two consecutive days.

The Canadian Environmental Health Atlas (CEHA) and the Toronto Public Health Department estimated that 120 people die in the GTA annually because of high temperatures. The predictions indicate that heat-related mortality will be doubled by 2050 (Pengelly et al., 2007). Moreover, the correlations among temperature, humidity, poor air quality, mortality, and morbidity are proved in many studies (Azhar et al., 2014; Bae et al., 2020; Tsekeri et al., 2020). In a recent Spanish study, the effect of climate change increases the annual air pollution deaths by 129 cases and reduces the health benefits by 10% (Borge et al., 2019). Moreover, a significant correlation was found between extreme heat stress and poor air quality conditions with increased concentrations of O_3, NO_2, and SO_2 (Theoharatos et al., 2010). To support the association between health and air quality, the recent change in human activity due to the Covid-19 crisis led to reduced concentrations of particulate matter (PM) around the world. Based on WHO statistical data, the PM concentration was reduced in Canada in the first quarter of 2020 by 23% compared to the first quarter of 2019, a percentage associated with a reduction of 1497 air-pollution-related mortalities for the same period (Karkour and Itsubo, 2020). Given the large transformation and fast-growing population that the GTA is facing, it is crucial to investigate the urban climate influences on the well-being of city inhabitants. Therefore, applying heat

Global Urban Heat Island Mitigation. **https://doi.org/10.1016/B978-0-323-85539-6.00008-1**

and air pollution mitigation strategies that protect human health and improve the urban environment is essential in the strategic planning for new and existing urban settlements (Berardi and Wang, 2016; Wang et al., 2016). Increasing the urban green infrastructure, which includes vegetation, tree canopy, and building vegetation elements, influences the urban canyon thermal environment and the air quality (Berardi et al., 2020; Santamouris and Osmond, 2020). The associated influences on the urban environment are mainly claimed to reduce the air temperature. This chapter reflects the effects of adaptation and mitigation strategies on air quality and heat-related health and deaths. Results can be used by decision-makers to initiate policies to improve the living conditions for urban dwellers.

Regarding the heat-related health impacts, Rainham and Smoyer-Tomic (2003) reported a significant correlation between heat-related mortality for elderly people and hot ambient conditions during summer seasons for the period from 1980 to 1996 for the City of Toronto. Goldberg et al. (2003) posted a linear increase in daily mortality of elderly people due to air pollution associated with warm conditions in Montreal. Kolb et al. (2010) conducted a similar study due to the hot weather of Montreal; the authors reported a strong short-term relationship between hot weather (over 25°C) and elderly cardiac-related daily mortality with no significant associations with humidity levels. Anderson and Bell (2011) estimated an increment of death by 4.5% per degree Celsius during intensive heat waves. Gronlund et al. (2014) used mortality data across the United States and found that mortalities increase by 3.6% per degree Celsius increase in temperature. Berko et al. (2014) reported that around 31% of the weather-related mortality in various US regions was related to exposure to excessive heat. D'Ippoliti et al. (2010) reported an increase of up to 33.6% in elderly mortality rates due to exposure to European heat waves with a stronger association for respiratory-related fatalities. Tsekeri et al. (2020) proved the high probability of the deaths' occurrence due to extremely hot weather associated with high humidity. Elderly mortality is not only related to extreme heat stress and heat wave conditions. Some studies reported the increased mortality cases for elderly people regarding hot and warm conditions. The association between excess heat mortality and hot humid weather of Toronto was discussed by Smoyer-Tomic and Rainham (2001). They flagged increased mortality cases related to a Humidex range of 30−35, which does not meet the local heat wave conditions. With more intense and long hot summers in the future, the authors expected the heat fatalities to increase significantly. Paravantis et al. (2017) reported an average daily cardiorespiratory-related death of elderly people of 12.98 during heat waves. Whereas a daily average mortality value of 13.24 was associated with hot ambient temperatures, even when the heat waves conditions were not met. Lee et al. (2014) assured the importance of considering the effects of temperature variations, not only the extremes, on mortality rates as they found an increased causality between mortality cases and hot weather where the heat waves are less common.

Regarding the air-quality-based health impacts, based on the 2001 Canadian Census Health and Environment Cohort, Pinault et al. (2017) ensured the association between increased fine particulate matter ($PM_{2.5}$) concentration and mortalities. They reported an 18% increase in nonaccidental mortalities and up to 36% increase in cardiorespiratory mortalities for each increase of 10 μg/m^3 in $PM_{2.5}$ concentration. Various values of nonaccidental mortalities increase were reported in different countries: 8.4% (Di et al., 2017), 13% (Hart et al., 2015), and 7% (Turner et al., 2015) in the United States, 4% (Cesaroni et al., 2013) in Italy, and 9% (Yin et al., 2017) in China. For more accurate predictions of health risks of PM concentrations, Coffman et al. (2020) presented a quantitative approach to define uncertainty for the prediction method of health risks, especially at low PM annual mean concentrations. In a study for long-term exposure to $PM_{2.5}$ in Beijing, Zheng et al. (2015)

reported a monthly mean $PM_{2.5}$ concentration of around 100 $\mu g/m^3$. They related the change in cardiorespiratory mortality from the baseline rate to the relative health risk due to PM exposure during the period of the study. They claimed that an annual all-age mortality rate of 15 per 10,000 persons was detected due to exposure to $PM_{2.5}$. Moreover, the correlation between all-cause mortality and ozone concentration was confirmed, especially in high-density urban cities, such as London (Atkinson et al., 2012). In a relationship with climate change, Lee et al. (2017) estimated the increase in mortality in 2050 by up to 0.6% due to future increase in ozone concentration level. Turner et al. (2015) reported an increase of 2% in all-cause mortality and 12% in respiratory mortality for each increase of 10 ppb of ozone concentration. However, Bae et al. (2020) figured out that the effect of ozone exposure on mortality differs according to the daily mean ozone concentration. While the increase in mortalities was noticed with daily mean ozone concentration starting from 11.6 ppb.

The intensified green cover within urban areas is associated with enhancements in the urban environment. The increased tree canopy, green roofs, and urban vegetated areas achieved a reduction in ambient air temperature of up to 2.9°C in specific locations around New York City (Rosenzweig et al., 2006). Chapman et al. (2018) emphasized the vital role of the vegetation cover in a study within the subtropical climate of Australia. They reported an increase of 3.8°C in the ambient temperature associated with zero urban vegetation, which is claimed to increase heat-related illnesses and deaths. Žuvela-Aloise et al. (2016) reported a reduction in ambient air temperature of up to 1°C while increasing the vegetation and waterscape areas by 20% in Vienna. In Stuttgart, Fallmann et al. (2014) showed that increasing the green spaces and cool roofs within the urban texture reduced the ambient air temperature by up to 2.5°C. Although the effect of the increased green cover on the ambient air temperature and outdoor thermal indices has been widely discussed, most of the reviewed studies focus on the sensible cooling effect reporting some effects of humidity content on the urban environment due to evapotranspiration processes and increased latent fluxes. The cooling effect of intensifying the tree coverage on thermal comfort during a heat wave in the GTA was studied by Berardi et al. (2020). Increasing the tree canopy by 80% achieved a reduction up to 1.4°C in ambient air temperature; however, an increase in the thermal index was observed during the evening. Duarte et al. (2015) investigated the effect of increased tree canopy on the ambient air temperature of Sao Paulo during the summer season. The air temperature was reduced by up to 0.6°C for an increase of 11% of the street tree density. Although an enhancement in the thermal comfort index, Physiological Equivalent Temperature (PET), of up to 23% was observed, the effect of the increased humidity was not discussed. Jacobs et al. (2018) assured the increased cooling effect by up to 1.5°C of the ambient air temperature of an increased tree canopy (up to 40%) for low-density urban spaces in the city of Melbourne during a heatwave. They also claimed a possible increase in outdoor thermal stress due to the humidity ratio enlarged by intensified tree coverage. The cooling effect of increasing the vegetation areas was recorded by Li and Norford (2016) in the tropical climate of Singapore. With a reduction of up to 2.4°C in the ambient air temperature, they recorded an increase of 8% of relative humidity, which affected the outdoor thermal comfort. Arghavani et al. (2019) reported a warming effect (up to 2°C) due to lower air velocities and limited nighttime radiative cooling associated with lower sky view factors due to the intensified tree coverage. Moreover, the increased cooling effect of the green spaces was observed regarding the evapotranspiration process, especially during the nighttime (Gao et al., 2020; Qiu et al., 2017). Konarska et al. (2016) claimed that a transpiration rate of 0.1 $mmol/m^2/s$ has a cooling rate of 0.25°C/h for the surrounding air. They also valued nighttime transpiration by 7%−20%

of daytime transpiration. Hoelscher et al. (2016) reported that green façade systems promote indoor heat stress mitigation and outdoor thermal comfort. Hsieh et al. (2018) studied the effect of tree coverage on building energy use; they figured out that the combined impact of shading and transpiration reduced the indoor cooling consumption by up to 15.2%.

Regarding the effect of increasing the green infrastructure on the urban air quality, some studies stated that the effectiveness of capturing PM depends on the tree canopy density, the species of trees, and the shape and structure of the leaves (Beckett et al., 2000; Chen et al., 2017). Arghavani et al. (2019) argued that the increased urban green cover slows down the rate of pollutants' emissions. Nyelele et al. (2019) confirmed a removal ability of 5.1 tons/year of $PM_{2.5}$ for 2470 ha (22.7% of the cityscape) of tree cover (187.3 $kg/km^2/year$) in 2010 in the Bronx district, NY. With a predicted increase of up to 5% of well-maintained tree coverage in 2030, they expected the pollutant removal ability to reach 6.2 tons/year (216.9 $kg/km^2/year$) and the air temperature to reduce by 0.17°C. While the correlation between ozone level and green infrastructure is complicated, some studies stated that biogenic Volatile Organic Compounds (VOCs) produced by some tree species accelerate the formulation of ozone (Calfapietra et al., 2013; Simon et al., 2019). Wai et al. (2020) reported a reduced cooling potential of the tree cover due to increased ozone level. With high ambient ozone stress, they claimed a 25% reduction in cooling ability with a potential increase of 1°C in PET. Anav et al. (2011) and Hewitt (2015) referred this correlation to the increased negative effect of ozone level on photosynthesis of the green cover, growth of the plants, and the leaf area index of the coverage, with larger impacts during summer and hot periods. On the other hand, other studies confirmed that the increased tree coverage controls the ambient ozone concentration. Nowak et al. (2000) reported an average reduction of ozone concentration of 0.5 ppb with a peak reduction of 2.4 ppb in the daytime associated with an increase of the tree cover by 20%. Overall, the selection of the proper tree species with the optimum density is crucial to managing the levels of air pollutants.

The consequences of the UHI and the frequency and duration of the heat waves in the GTA are becoming more evident. Meanwhile, preserving and maintaining the green areas in Ontario's Greenbelt, the protected natural land, and river valleys help in decreasing the ambient temperature and biogenic emissions and the increase in the evapotranspiration and shadings. Mainly, increasing the green infrastructure and vegetation cover, as an evolutionary UHI mitigation, targets to reduce ambient temperature and to enhance air quality levels. In this chapter, a developed and integrated statistical-simulation approach is designed to explore whether protecting and increasing the green spaces of the GTA can be more useful to the urban microclimate, in terms of temperature and air quality and human health with the potential of the proximity to the Greenbelt and river valleys. Specifically, the chapter investigates the effects of enriching the urban greenery cover on the urban thermal environment, air quality, and heat-related health issues.

2. Method and results

The method combines the statistical approach with the microclimate simulations to investigate the impact of increasing the urban greenery cover on the air quality and heat-related health responses. Firstly, the study intends to correlate the behavior of the meteorological parameters with the concentration of air quality variables to investigate the heat-related impacts on air quality in the region of study. A statistical approach is introduced, including regression analyses and Bayesian causality networks for establishing a correlation between study parameters. Then, microclimate simulations are designed to assess the impacts of intensifying the green infrastructure on the urban microclimate. The outputs of the predictive regression analysis and the microclimatic simulations are linked to concluding the impacts of the thermal behavior on air quality and human health response in the GTA. The study parameters include *meteorological parameters* (air temperature, relative humidity, and wind speed), *air quality variables* (ground-level ozone and particulate matter concentrations), *heat stress indices* (Humidex), and *heat-related mortalities*.

2.1 Heat-related impacts on air quality

Applying regression analyses, this study assesses the effect of meteorological parameters' variation on air quality levels. Particularly, this study focuses on ground-level ozone (O_3) and Fine Particulate Matter ($PM_{2.5}$) to identify the air quality levels. According to the Canadian Council of Ministers of the Environment (CCME), the exposure to ozone and fine particulate matter causes respiratory symptoms and reduced lung and heart function, with an increased high risk of emergency cases of respiratory or cardiovascular issues for sensitive populations (children, elderly, and people suffering from chronic diseases) (Air Quality, 2017). The threshold of daily average concentrations for red flag required actions defined by Canadian Ambient Air Quality Standards (CAAQS) in 2012 is 63 ppb for O_3 and 28 $\mu g/m^3$ for $PM_{2.5}$. The study domain, shown in Fig. 13.1, includes the Peel region focusing on Mississauga and Brampton municipalities. *Mississauga* is featured by higher urban densities, and *Brampton* is more featured by river valleys dispersal.

The air quality data are obtained from the Ministry of the Environment, Conservation, and Parks, Ontario, for 12 years from 2006 to 2017. This study focuses on warm and hot seasons, which extend from May to September each year. Accordingly, 1836 daily values in total are included in the dataset. The historical hourly concentrations for O_3 and $PM_{2.5}$ are collected from Mississauga and Brampton air monitoring stations (43.55N −79.66W, and 43.70N −79.78W, respectively) at a height of 5 m from ground level. The daily average and maximum concentrations are calculated for the selected period.

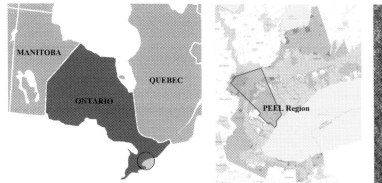

FIGURE 13.1

Brampton and Mississauga regarding Peel region (right), Greenbelt (Center), and Province of Ontario (left).

Besides, the dataset includes the daily weather parameters of ambient temperature (maximum, minimum, and mean values), relative humidity (maximum and mean values), and humidex (maximum and mean values). The weather data are obtained from the international airport weather station located in Mississauga. Both daily maximum and mean values are considered separately in two different models, **model-A** and **model-B**, respectively, to investigate if the correlation among extreme values follows the one among the average values. A statistical model is built in both Microsoft Excel and JASP software to analyze the provided dataset using multiple regression analyses. The selected software provides complete correlations, regression diagnostics, and predictive regression analyses. The designed model provides evidence-based correlations between the parameters promoting the predictive potential for future estimations. To validate the model's predictive abilities, a causality network is designed for the provided dataset using a Bayesian approach in BayesiaLab software. The software builds predictive probabilities among the model variables based on machine learning approaches that define the causality among variables. The causality network has the potential to predict the occurrence probabilities of an event, a discretized range of the dependent variable, regarding the observed occurrence of the other variables. This method is used to predict the values of air quality variables regarding the observation of weather parameters. The results of both statistical models are compared and a quantitative predictive model is formulated.

2.1.1 Preparation of statistical model variables

Initially, the dataset was cleared from all missing data; around 90 data entries were removed from the dataset. Before proceeding with regression analyses, critical regression assumptions diagnostics are conducted. Firstly, the regression assumes no collinearity among variables. The collinearity appears when there is a strong relationship between variables; thus, regression coefficients and predictive ability of the model become unreliable. For the latter case, removing one of the correlated variables fixes the collinearity issue. In the case of meteorological parameters, the correlation among specific variables may exist. Accordingly, the correlation analyses are performed among the variables of model-A considering the $PM_{2.5}$ and O_3 concentrations in both locations as distinguished dependent variables. With a threshold of around 0.9, the highly correlated variables are defined. The results of the correlation analyses presented in Table 13.1 show that there is a strong correlation between maximum humidex value and maximum temperature, which affects the reliability of the regression analysis.

Table 13.1 Correlations among meteorological variables in Mississauga and Brampton.

	Max Temp	Min Temp	RH_max	Hmdx_max	O₃_Mis_Max	O₃_Brm_Max	PM_Mis_Max	PM_Brm_Max
Max Temp	1							
Min Temp	0.817	1						
RH_max	-0.087	0.164	1					
Hmdx_max	0.953	0.883	0.110	1				
O₃_Mis_Max	0.588	0.349	-0.221	0.537	1			
O₃_Brm_Max	0.555	0.329	-0.216	0.515	-	1		
PM_Mis_Max	0.445	0.388	0.076	0.493	0.580	-	1	
PM_Brm_Max	0.373	0.338	0.106	0.430	-	0.557	-	1

Table 13.2 Collinearity (VIFs) among meteorological variables in Mississauga and Brampton.

	VIF values for model variables in Mississauga							
	Dependent variable: O_3_Mis_Max				Dependent variable: PM_Mis_Max			
	Case (1)	Case (2)	Case (3)	Case (4)	Case (1)	Case (2)	Case (3)	Case (4)
Max Temp	18.738	3.816	–	1.27	18.677	4.76	–	1.534
Min Temp	4.749	3.614	1.203	–	5.056	3.797	1.224	–
RH_max	1.713	1.228	1.028	1.025	1.773	1.225	1.13	1.054
Hmdx_max	25.434	–	–	–	24.551	–	–	–
O_3_Mis_Max	–	–	–	–	1.737	1.682	1.252	1.6
PM_Mis_Max	1.357	1.268	1.178	1.268	–	–	–	–
	VIF values for model variables in Brampton							
	Dependent variable: O_3_Brm_Max				Dependent variable: PM_Brm_Max			
	Case (1)	Case (2)	Case (3)	Case (4)	Case (1)	Case (2)	Case (3)	Case (4)
Max Temp	18.84	3.721	–	1.184	18.517	4.531	–	1.447
Min Temp	4.742	3.614	1.15	–	5.065	3.758	1.2	–
RH_max	1.712	1.234	1.031	1.031	1.795	1.225	1.122	1.051
Hmdx_max	25.403	–	–	–	25.054	–	–	–
O_3_Brm_Max	–	–	–	–	1.651	1.566	1.225	1.506
PM_Brm_Max	1.27	1.188	1.132	1.188	–	–	–	–

This means that the information provided by one variable is sufficient, while the other variable duplicates the learning process of the model. Moreover, there is a significant positive correlation between minimum temperature and both humidex value and maximum temperature.

Another more robust test for collinearity is the detection of the Variance Inflation Factor (VIF) for the model variables. The VIF test creates auxiliary regression analyses for each model variable against other model variables. A higher value of VIF is considered a sign of collinearity between a variable that works as a dependent variable in the auxiliary regression and other model variables. Better performance is obtained when VIF is close to 1. The test was performed for the previous model in both locations for four different cases: using all the variables (case-1), removing the highest correlated variable (humidex value) (case-2), and removing the higher two correlated variables, humidex value and maximum temperature (case-3) or minimum temperature (case-4). The results shown in Table 13.2 infer that for both locations considering all variables (case-1) affect the model reliability in terms of collinearity, especially with humidex value, which reflects the highest VIF value. This is justified by that humidex is ideally correlated with the other variables, as the temperature and humidity are variables themselves in the calculations of humidex. Removing the humidex value (case-2) enhances the model's reliability. However, the VIF values of maximum and minimum temperatures indicate a moderate collinearity effect due to the relationship between the two variables. Additional elimination of one of the latter two variables (case-3 and case-4) refers to better performance, as the information provided by each of the two cases is considered unique and significant to the model regression.

2.1.2 Effect of meteorological parameters variation

The main objective of the regression analysis is to figure out if the variance in meteorological parameters affects the pollutants' concentration in a specific location. Accordingly, the concentration of a pollutant in a specific location is considered a dependent variable. The model variables include the meteorological parameters and the concentration of other pollutants that can affect multiple predictive regression.

2.1.2.1 Regression analyses for model-A (maximum values)

In model-A, the maximum daily value of a pollutant's concentration in both Mississauga (*Mis*) and Brampton (*Brm*) is the dependent variable. The multiple regression analysis is conducted for case-3 (main variable of minimum temperature) and case-4 (main variable of maximum temperature) for both locations. Table 13.3 presents the results of the regression analysis for both cases (3 and 4) in Mississauga. It can be inferred that the O_3 level is more correlated with the variations in maximum temperature than minimum temperature, with a higher R^2 value of 0.519. Moreover, in case 4, the greater influencer in the model is the maximum temperature with a higher regression coefficient, while in case 3, $PM_{2.5}$ is the superior contributor. Overall, with a significant *P-value*, the model shows a strong positive correlation between O_3 maximum concentration and maximum, minimum temperatures, and $PM_{2.5}$ maximum concentration. Meanwhile, a strong negative correlation is observed between O_3 maximum concentration and RH maximum value. Generally, the two models show a high degree of autocorrelation, represented by the Durbin–Watson test, caused by the internal time-series relationship of data points for each variable. This is caused by the correlations among time-series values of the same variable where relationships can be anticipated with the value at a specific day and the values of the day after and the day before. This happens regularly in climatic datasets where the temperature, for example, in a day is correlated with values of temperature for the day after and the day before. It can be noticed that Root Mean Square Error (RMSE) values are quite significant; however, with very low outliers, represented by Cook's distance (with a threshold of 0.1) and studentized residuals (with a threshold of 3), and fitted model behavior (significant R^2 values), the predictive

Table 13.3 Regression analyses for maximum ozone concentration in Mississauga.

Model	Adjusted R^2	RMSE	df	Outliers (>3)	Cook's D (>0.1)	Durbin–Watson Autocorr.	Durbin–Watson Statistic	Durbin–Watson P-value
Case 3	0.436	9.944	1744	7	1	0.285	1.430	<0.001
Case 4	0.519	9.189	1744	6	1	0.354	1.292	<0.001

Case 3				Case 4			
Model	Coef.	T	P-value	Model	Coef.	T	P-value
(Intercept)	59.441	28.459	<0.001	(Intercept)	37.609	16.583	<0.001
RH_max	−0.391	−16.058	<0.001	RH_max	−0.295	−13.110	<0.001
PM_Mis_Max	0.831	27.052	<0.001	PM_Mis_Max	0.674	22.895	<0.001
Min Temp	0.550	9.758	<0.001	Max Temp	0.972	20.240	<0.001

regression can be reliable. The predictive regression equations can be expressed by Eqs. (13.1) and (13.2) for variables of minimum and maximum temperatures, respectively. It can be concluded that for every 1°C increase in the maximum temperature, the O_3 maximum concentration is expected to increase by 0.97 ppb on average. Similarly, for every 1°C increase in the minimum temperature, the O_3 maximum concentration is expected to increase by 0.55 ppb on average.

$$O_3 \text{ max. conc.} = 0.55\ T_{min} + 0.831\ PM_{2.5} - 0.391\ RH + 59.441 \tag{13.1}$$

$$O_3 \text{ max. conc.} = 0.972\ T_{max} + 0.674\ PM_{2.5} - 0.295\ RH + 37.609 \tag{13.2}$$

Fig. 13.2 shows the correlations between maximum and minimum temperatures and the predicted values of O_3 maximum concentration. Two months (August and September 2016) are selected randomly to establish the relationship between the daily predicted O_3 maximum concentration (the outcome of the predictive regression) and the daily minimum temperature (shown in Fig. 13.3) and maximum temperature (shown in Fig. 13.4). A higher correlation is noticed with the maximum temperature, as implied by the regression results.

The previous analysis is repeated for $PM_{2.5}$ maximum concentration in Mississauga. Based on R^2, RMSE, outliers, and coefficient values, shown in Table 13.4, the model is less fitted than the ozone model, which implies that the ozone concentration model is more robust and reliable. Fig. 13.5 shows the correlations among $PM_{2.5}$ maximum concentration and model variables. It can be noticed that in both cases (3 and 4), the most robust and influencing variable for predicting particulate matter concentration is the ozone concentration, with a higher coefficient and t value. Meanwhile, the correlations between predicted $PM_{2.5}$ maximum concentration and minimum and maximum temperatures during August and September 2016, shown in Figs. 13.6 and 13.7, confirm some discrepancies in prediction behavior. However, the general correlation trend remains significant. The model shows a strong positive correlation between $PM_{2.5}$ maximum concentration and O_3 maximum concentration, maximum, minimum temperatures, and RH maximum value. It can be inferred that for every 1°C increase in the maximum and minimum temperatures, the $PM_{2.5}$ maximum concentration is expected

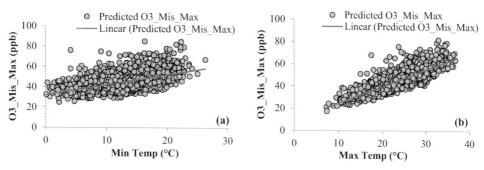

FIGURE 13.2

Correlations between maximum ozone concentration and minimum temperature (A) and maximum temperature (B).

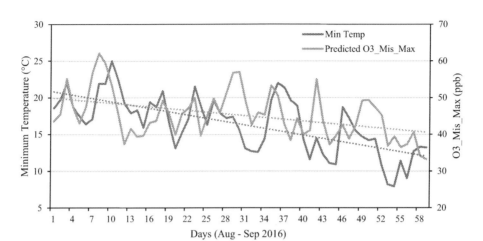

FIGURE 13.3

Predictions of ozone maximum concentration based on minimum temperature.

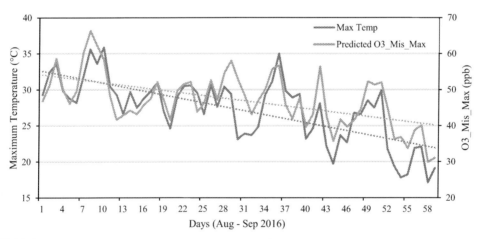

FIGURE 13.4

Predictions of ozone maximum concentration based on maximum temperature.

to increase by 0.24 and 0.3 µg/m³ on average, respectively. Eqs. (13.3) and (13.4) express the predicted regression of the $PM_{2.5}$ maximum concentration.

$$PM_{2.5} \text{ max. conc.} = 0.298 \, T_{min} + 0.356 \, O_3 + 0.147 \, RH - 18.361 \tag{13.3}$$

$$PM_{2.5} \text{ max. conc.} = 0.237 \, T_{max} + 0.343 \, O_3 + 0.177 \, RH - 21.933 \tag{13.4}$$

Table 13.4 Regression analyses for PM maximum concentration in Mississauga.

Model	Adjusted R²	RMSE	Df	Outliers (>3)	Cook's D (>0.1)	Durbin–watson Autocorr.	Durbin–watson Statistic	Durbin–watson P-value
Case 3	0.401	6.509	1744	29	0	0.337	1.326	<0.001
Case 4	0.393	6.553	1744	28	0	0.327	1.345	<0.001

Case 3 Model	Case 3 Coef.	Case 3 T	Case 3 P-value	Case 4 Model	Case 4 Coef.	Case 4 T	Case 4 P-value
(Intercept)	−18.361	−11.512	<0.001	(Intercept)	−21.933	−13.220	<0.001
RH_max	0.147	8.779	<0.001	RH_max	0.177	10.857	<0.001
O₃_Mis_Max	0.356	27.052	<0.001	O₃_Mis_Max	0.343	22.895	<0.001
Min Temp	0.298	8.016	<0.001	Max temp	0.237	6.299	<0.001

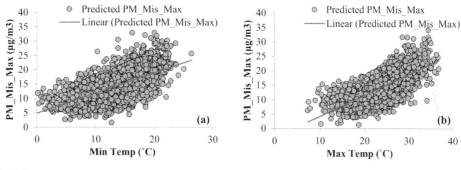

FIGURE 13.5

Correlations between fine particulate matters maximum concentration and minimum temperature (A) and maximum temperature (B).

The results of O_3 and $PM_{2.5}$ maximum concentration in Brampton are presented in Tables 13.5 and 13.6, respectively. Comparing the results with those of the municipality of Mississauga, it can be inferred that the correlation between air pollutants and weather parameters is identical in Mississauga and Brampton. Regarding O_3 maximum concentration, the effect of relative humidity in predicting the O_3 levels is greater in Brampton. Moreover, the robust correlation between O_3 maximum concentration and maximum temperature is maintained in Brampton. However, referring to the intercept values in both municipalities, it can be noticed that the absolute value of the ozone maximum concentration is higher in Brampton, with a maximum value of 106 ppb, compared to 95 ppb in Mississauga with a difference of mean maximum values of 1.6 ppb. Regarding $PM_{2.5}$ maximum concentration, the correlations among model variables remain identical. The ozone concentration remains a dominant variable in predicting the $PM_{2.5}$ concentration with less effect of maximum and minimum

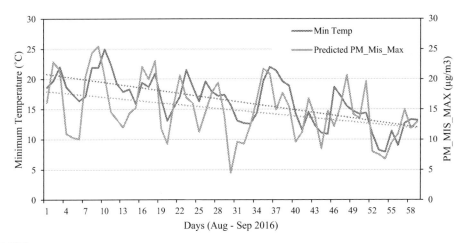

FIGURE 13.6

Predictions of $PM_{2.5}$ maximum concentration based on minimum temperature.

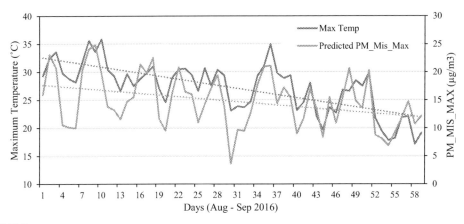

FIGURE 13.7

Predictions of $PM_{2.5}$ maximum concentration based on maximum temperature.

temperatures. Moreover, the absolute values of $PM_{2.5}$ maximum concentration in Brampton are higher, with a maximum value of 65 $\mu g/m^3$, compared to 55 $\mu g/m^3$ in Mississauga with a difference of mean maximum values of 0.8 $\mu g/m^3$.

It can be concluded that with less building density and larger green cover (municipality of Brampton), the ozone and particulate matter concentrations report higher levels in terms of the maximum values. However, the humidity positively affects more the concentration level of ozone with larger reduction factors. In general, referring to correlation results, the predictive regression equations can be applied for pollutants' maximum concentration predictions in the GTA.

Table 13.5 Regression analyses for ozone maximum concentration in Brampton.

Model	Adjusted R²	RMSE	df	Outliers (>3)	Cook's D (>0.1)	Durbin–Watson Autocorr.	Durbin–Watson Statistic	Durbin–Watson P-value
Case 3	0.422	10.345	1744	8	0	0.266	1.467	<0.001
Case 4	0.501	9.613	1744	8	0	0.320	1.359	<0.001

Case 3				Case 4			
Model	Coef.	T	P-value	Model	Coef.	T	P-value
(Intercept)	62.895	28.979	<0.001	(Intercept)	40.778	17.219	<0.001
RH_max	−0.419	−16.505	<0.001	RH_max	−0.317	−13.465	<0.001
PM_Brm_Max	0.776	26.894	<0.001	PM_Brm_Max	0.662	24.085	<0.001
Min temp	0.598	10.437	<0.001	Max temp	0.972	20.053	<0.001

Table 13.6 Regression analyses for $PM_{2.5}$ maximum concentration in Brampton.

Model	Adjusted R²	RMSE	df	Outliers (>3)	Cook's D (>0.1)	Durbin–Watson Autocorr.	Durbin–Watson Statistic	Durbin–Watson P-value
Case 3	0.374	7.216	1744	31	0	0.329	1.342	<0.001
Case 4	0.367	7.256	1744	31	0	0.319	1.362	<0.001

Case 3				Case 4			
Model	Coef.	T	P-value	Model	Coef.	T	P-value
(Intercept)	−22.130	−12.541	<0.001	(Intercept)	−24.468	−13.279	<0.001
RH_max	0.192	10.404	<0.001	RH_max	0.216	12.038	<0.001
O₃_Brm_Max	0.378	26.894	<0.001	O₃_Brm_Max	0.377	24.085	<0.001
Min temp	0.232	5.687	<0.001	Max temp	0.144	3.569	<0.001

2.1.2.2 Regression analyses for model-B (mean values)

The correlation analyses among model variables are repeated for model-B investigating the collinearity among mean values. A significant positive correlation of 0.977 is observed between daily humidex mean values and daily mean temperature. Eliminating the humidex variable results in a model that contains the pollutant's daily mean concentration as a dependent variable and mean temperature, relative humidity, and the other pollutant's mean concentration as model variables. The conducted multiple regression analyses for both pollutants in Mississauga are presented in Table 13.7 and Fig. 13.8. In both models, the correlations between both pollutants' mean concentrations and model variables in terms of significance meet those of model-A (with maximum values). However, unlike model-A, the most influencing variable in predicting the O_3 mean concentration is the $PM_{2.5}$

Table 13.7 Regression analyses for pollutants' average concentration in Mississauga.

Dep. Variable	Adjusted R²	RMSE	df	Outliers (>3)	Cook's D (>0.1)	Durbin–watson		
						Autocorr.	Statistic	P-value
Ozone	0.377	7.232	1735	5	0	0.476	1.047	<0.001
PM	0.416	4.076	1735	30	0	0.466	1.068	<0.001

Dependent variable: O3_MIS_AVR

Model	Coef.	T	P-value	VIF
(Intercept)	32.411	26.356	<0.001	
RH_avr	−0.255	−17.294	<0.001	1.007
PM_Mis_avr	0.736	19.004	<0.001	1.419
Mean temp	0.338	7.670	<0.001	1.411

Dependent variable: PM_MIS_AVR

Model	Coef.	T	P-value	VIF
(Intercept)	−12.320	−16.104	<0.001	
RH_avr	0.086	9.826	<0.001	1.119
O3_Mis_avr	0.234	19.004	<0.001	1.330
Mean temp	0.429	18.584	<0.001	1.216

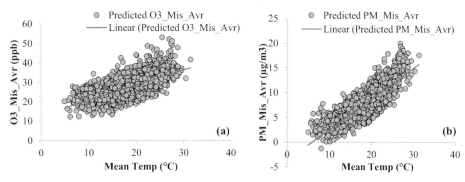

FIGURE 13.8

Correlations between ozone (A) and fine particulate matters (B) mean concentrations and mean temperature.

mean concentration, then the mean temperature is in the second place. While the most effective variable in predicting the PM$_{2.5}$ mean concentration is the mean temperature. In both models, the least effective variable remains the relative humidity, with the least robust relationship. Figs. 13.9 and 13.10 represent the correlation between mean temperature and O$_3$ and PM$_{2.5}$ mean concentrations respectively during August and September 2016. It can be inferred that a more significant correlation with the mean temperature is achieved by the PM$_{2.5}$ mean concentration. The predictive regression equations can be expressed by Eqs. (13.5) and (13.6) for predicting O$_3$ and PM$_{2.5}$ mean concentrations, respectively. It can be concluded that for every 1°C increase in the mean temperature, the O$_3$ and PM$_{2.5}$ mean concentrations are expected to increase by 0.34 ppb and 0.43 μg/m^3 on average, respectively.

$$O_3 \text{ mean. conc.} = 0.338\ T_{avr} + 0.736\ \text{p.m.}_{2.5} - 0.255\ RH + 32.411 \tag{13.5}$$

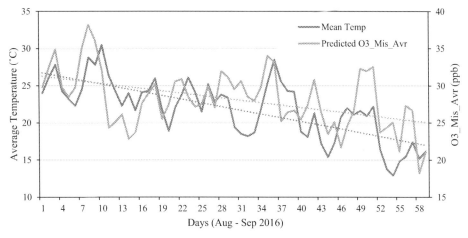

FIGURE 13.9

Predictions of ozone mean concentration based on mean temperature.

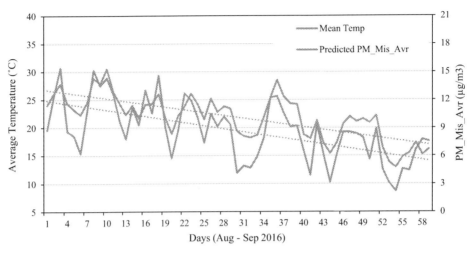

FIGURE 13.10

Predictions of PM$_{2.5}$ mean concentration based on mean temperature.

$$PM_{2.5} \text{ mean. conc.} = 0.429 \, T_{avr} + 0.234 \, O_3 + 0.086 \, RH - 12.32 \qquad (13.6)$$

Comparing the results of both pollutants' average concentration in Brampton, presented in Table 13.8, with those of the municipality of Mississauga, it is confirmed that correlations and effective variables are identical in both municipalities. As reported in Mississauga, the correlation is more significant between the mean temperature and the PM$_{2.5}$ mean concentrations. Overall, the predictive regression results are close to the predictive regression equations for Mississauga, which can be verified to predict pollutants' mean concentrations in the GTA. Regarding absolute values, although the intercept values in the Brampton model are slightly higher, the absolute values of O$_3$ and PM$_{2.5}$ mean concentrations report different conclusions. For O$_3$, the average daily mean concentration in Brampton (30.4 ppb) is higher by 2.7 ppb than this of Mississauga. On the contrary, the average of the daily mean concentrations of PM$_{2.5}$ in Brampton (7.7 µg/m^3) is lower by 0.3 µg/m^3 than this of Mississauga.

2.1.3 Validation of regression analyses

To verify the results of the predictive regression, causality networks are built following the Bayesian approach using BayesiaLab software. Due to the maximum allowed data entry points of BayesiaLab (1000 entries), the dataset is reduced by excluding the months of May and September from the dataset and focused on the summer season months during the 12 years. The probabilistic approach of the Bayesian network requires the discretization of the entered continuous data. The data entries of each variable are grouped into five discretized intervals using the density approximation method, which ensures weighted density periods based on the capacity of the data values in each group regardless of the distance between values. The ozone concentration is selected to be the target (dependent) variable.

Table 13.8 Regression analyses for pollutants' average concentration in Brampton.

Dep. Variable	Adjusted R²	RMSE	df	Outliers (>3)	Cook's D (>0.1)	Durbin—Watson		
						Autocorr.	Statistic	P-value
Ozone	0.433	7.042	1735	3	0	0.470	1.059	<0.001
PM	0.380	4.193	1735	29	0	0.442	1.113	<0.001

Dependent variable: O3_BRM_AVR

Model	Coef.	T	P-value	VIF
(Intercept)	34.036	28.474	<0.001	
RH_avr	−0.285	−19.842	<0.001	1.014
PM_Brm_avr	0.724	19.911	<0.001	1.315
Mean temp	0.518	12.561	<0.001	1.300

Dependent variable: PM_BRM_AVR

Model	Coef.	T	P-value	VIF
(Intercept)	−13.298	−16.604	<0.001	
RH_avr	0.111	12.133	<0.001	1.147
O3_Brm_avr	0.257	19.911	<0.001	1.439
Mean temp	0.310	12.637	<0.001	1.299

The supervised learning utilizing an Augmented Naive Bayes approach is applied to enforce connections between target node and model variables. The selected learning approach is applied to ensure complete network connections regardless of their significance to the target value to replicate the condition of the predictive regression analysis. For example, as it can be noticed in Table 13.9, the mutual information provided by the relative humidity is low; however, the variable is considered in the network. It is worth emphasizing that the objective of the Bayesian approach is to verify the regression results and not to reach the optimum probabilistic predictions for the model.

Model-A and model-B are considered for predicting ozone maximum and mean concentrations in Mississauga. For model-A, maximum values for temperature, relative humidity, and $PM_{2.5}$ concentration are considered as variables. The results of the probabilistic correlations for model-A, shown in Table 13.9, confirm the correlation between O_3 maximum concentration and model variables with more than 99% confidence level. In the table, the regression coefficients for the same model are added for comparison purposes. Regarding the mutual information, which represents the information with interpretative abilities between variables, and Pearson's correlation values, it can be inferred that the results of the Bayesian network meet exactly the regression analysis correlation in terms of weight and direction. Similar to the regression model, the maximum temperature represents the most significant variable in predicting the O_3 maximum concentration. Both Bayesian and regression models are used to predict the O_3 maximum concentration during August and September 2016, with a reference to the original (measured) data for the pollutant's concentrations. To quantify the results shown in Fig. 13.11, two comparison criteria, RMSE and Mean Bias Error (MBE), are used to compare the model results with the measured data. It is inferred that the regression model achieves better RMSE and MBE values. However, it can be noticed that the regression model underestimates the peak values, while the Bayesian model respects the latitude of values, but occasionally misses the behavior trend.

Regarding model-B, Table 13.10 shows the probabilistic correlations for the mean values of temperature, relative humidity, and $PM_{2.5}$ concentration with the target value, O_3 mean concentration. The results confirm the correlations between the target and model variables with more than 99% confidence level. Again, it can be inferred from the results that the Bayesian correlations meet exactly the regression analysis correlation in terms of weight and direction. Similar to the regression model, the $PM_{2.5}$ mean concentration represents the most significant variable in predicting the O_3 mean concentration. However, the mean temperature almost shares the model mutual information with the $PM_{2.5}$ mean concentration, which ensures the significance of the mean temperature in predicting the ozone mean concentration. Regarding the comparison between Bayesian and regression models in predicting the O_3 mean concentration, it is inferred from Fig. 13.12 that the regression predictions are enhanced better than the Bayesian predictions in terms of MBE values. While RMSE values remain close between the two models. Once more, the regression model is noticed to underestimate the latitude peaks, especially the low values. Overall, the performance of the regression model against the

Table 13.9 Probabilistic correlations of ozone maximum concentration in Mississauga.

Target	Variables	Mutual info.	P-value	Pearson's Corr.	Regression Coef.
O₃_Mis_Max	Max temp	0.3839	0.00%	0.6359	*0.972*
	PM_Mis_Max	0.3123	0.00%	0.5775	*0.674*
	Max RH	0.0279	0.42%	−0.1292	*−0.295*

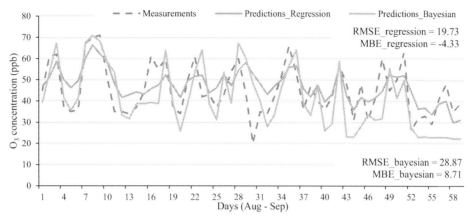

FIGURE 13.11

Bayesian and regression-based predictions of ozone maximum concentration.

Table 13.10 Probabilistic correlations of ozone mean concentration in Mississauga.

Target	Variables	Mutual info.	P-value (%)	Pearson's corr.	Regression Coef.	P-value
O$_3$_Mis_Avr	Mean temp	0.2445	.00	0.4964	0.338	<.001
	PM_Mis_Mean	0.2277	.00	0.538	0.736	<.001
	Mean RH	0.0708	.00	−0.1614	−0.255	<.001

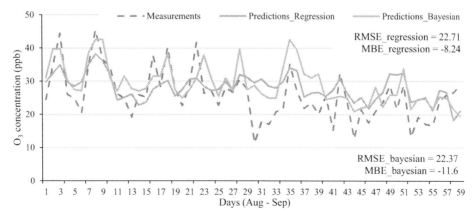

FIGURE 13.12

Bayesian and regression-based predictions of ozone mean concentration.

Bayesian model proves the improved ability of the designed regression model to predict the pollutant's concentration, for both mean and maximum values, based on the weather parameters and the available air quality variables.

2.2 Effect of increasing urban greenery cover

The major cooling effect of the urban green infrastructure is due to the fraction of the blocked solar radiation that reaches the urban surfaces. Accordingly, the selection of the trees species should be carefully considered as the leaf density and branching structure significantly influence the shading ability of the tree (Shahidan et al., 2006). The impermeable urban surfaces such as asphalt and concrete promote heat storage during the daytime and increase the sensible heat emissions to the urban climate. When those materials are replaced by vegetation areas, the stored heat emissions are reduced (Santamouris and Osmond, 2020). Meanwhile, the blocked thermal radiation to the night sky and the longwave emissions from tree coverage itself should also be considered (Dardir et al., 2019). Along with the shading effect, the cooling effect of the green cover includes the evapotranspiration of plants and soil of vegetation and tree coverage, where the required energy for the evaporation process of the plants is absorbed from the energy of the urban air volume. which reduces the air temperature (Erickson et al., 2010). Chen et al. (2019) assured that the tree canopy cooling effect by transpiration is positively associated with ambient temperature and solar radiation. While the transpiration rate increases proportionally to the ambient temperature, it is also stimulated by solar radiation. Moreover, some studies indicated that nighttime transpiration reaches up to 30% of the daytime transpiration with a typical range of 5%–15% (Fricke, 2019; Howard et al., 2009). Imran et al. (2019) tested the effect of an increase of up to 50% of mixed tree and vegetation covers for urban spaces of Melbourne during a heat wave. They reported a reduction of the ambient air temperature of up to 3.7°C and a reduction of the thermal comfort index, Universal Thermal Comfort Index (UTCI), of up to 5°C. The claimed cooling effect was due to the increased shading effect and latent fluxes, especially during nighttime and early mornings. Tan et al. (2020) recommended further investigations on urban cooling due to the combined effect on tree canopy that considers evaporative cooling, shading, mean radiant temperature, wind velocity, and relative humidity.

Most of the reviewed studies utilized numerical simulations applying WRF or Envi-met engines to predict the effect of increasing the green infrastructure (Berardi et al., 2020; Jandaghian and Berardi, 2020). Using these simulation platforms is associated with some limitations of prediction of cooling effect due to evapotranspiration, especially during nighttime. While the increased humidity levels due to evaporation can affect the thermal comfort causing a counter warming effect, an accurate representation of the energy and mass balance for the urban air volume is required. However, the prediction of the warming effect and increased relative humidity due to evaporation of the increased green cover is limitedly discussed or operated using these simulation engines. This ensures the importance of developing a simulation tool that well estimates the cooling effect of the green cover while considering the sequences of the warming effect on the urban climate.

2.2.1 Microclimate simulations

To holistically investigate the cooling and warming effects associated with the increase of urban green cover, the Urban Weather Generator (UWG) code is utilized. The model was initially created by Bueno et al. (2013) and Joseph Yang (2016). The UWG predicts the microclimate changes of a selected urban environment compared to the weather data from a nearby rural/airport weather station to assess the effects of the UHI on a local neighborhood scale. The multilayered three-dimensional code considers dynamic surface temperature, shortwave and longwave radiation fluxes, and sensible heat fluxes from roofs, walls, and roads. The model aggregates the fluxes into the exchange of momentum and energy between the urban surface and atmosphere. Detailed descriptions of the updated model components, theoretical approaches, and model validation procedures are published in (Dardir and Berardi, 2021). The model is used to assess the mitigation scenarios associated with the urban green strategies, which include tree canopy, vertical vegetation façades, and green roofs.

The microclimate simulations are designed to study the effect of the current preserved natural infrastructure around the river valleys within the greenbelt perimeter and to assess the effects of increasing the green and vegetation infrastructure on the urban canyon thermal behavior and building energy performance. Specifically, the study investigates the effects of preserving and developing the natural content of the river valleys region in Brampton, ON. A typical urban typology adjacent to a river valley is selected representing the Brampton residential neighborhood. The weather data for Guelph town, ON, are used as the rural weather station for simulation. The simulation is extended for 10 days (from June 27, 2018, to July 06, 2018). Details of location, urban features, and assumptions are provided in Table 13.11.

The study mainly focuses on the following simulation outputs: air temperature, relative humidity, and air velocity. It also monitors the energy consumption of the buildings, which includes lighting power, energy for heating and cooling, and electric equipment. The comparisons between the current condition of the Brampton neighborhood and the rural site at Guelph are represented in terms of air temperature and UHI (Fig. 13.13). The results infer that the 10-day average air temperature of the neighborhood is lower than the 10-day average air temperature of the rural site by 1.48°C, which is the average reduction in UHI. This ensures the cooling effect of the river valley to its surroundings. The reported energy consumption of the neighborhood for 10 days is 6.05 kWh/m^2, which equals 1573.4 MW for the whole neighborhood. This is influenced by the high cooling demand during the heat event.

To assess the effects of increasing the greenery cover on the local urban climate of Brampton neighborhood, three levels of investigation are designed: increasing the tree canopy by 10% for three scenarios, integrating vertical vegetation façade systems that increase by 20% for three scenarios associated with larger tree canopy area, and proposing green roofs coverage that increases by 20% for three scenarios associated with the maximum tree canopy and the vegetated façade system. The green roofs involve integrated vegetated areas and plantation to building roofs, which provide both insulation and shading. The results of the mitigation scenarios are compared with the current condition that is considered as a reference case. The reference conditions present 20% urban tree canopy, 0% green façade systems, and 0% green roof installations. All the results of the proposed scenarios for all mitigation strategies are presented in Table 13.12.

Referring to the comparisons between the reference case and the scenario of maximum enhancements (50% of the tree canopy, 60% of green façade coverage, and 60% of green roofs), it is inferred from Fig. 13.14 that the 10-day average air temperature is reduced by around 2°C. The maximum reduction in peak air temperature is calculated by 3.7°C, from 30.9 to 27.2°C. Fig. 13.15 shows how far the mitigation strategies contribute to the evolution of canyon air temperature. As noticed, the vegetated facade systems are the least effective on canyon air temperature with a reduction of 0.08°C for each 10% increase of the green façade system, as derived from graph slope. Meanwhile,

Table 13.11 Specifications of the urban microclimate parameters.

Location	Brampton, ON
Coordinates	43 degrees 41′31″ N 79 degrees 49′23″ W
Distance from rural	35.5 km
Site area	528,000 m²
Building density	24.6% (130,000 m²)
Avr. building height	6 m
V-*to*-H ratio	0.25
Roads urban area	33.5% (133,500 m²)
Water surface area	5.7% (22,500 m²)
Tree canopy	20%
Vegetation cover	60%
Building types	100% residential

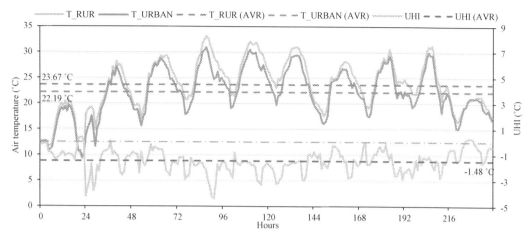

FIGURE 13.13

Canyon and rural air temperatures.

Table 13.12 Ten-day average values for the simulation parameters.

		Air temp (°C)	RH (%)	Velocity (m/s)	E (kWh/m²)
Reference case		22.19	71.88	3.42	6.05
Increasing tree canopy	30%	21.95	72.76	3.41	5.84
	40%	21.74	73.6	3.41	5.74
	50%	21.5	74.45	3.41	5.68
Increasing green façade system[a]	20%	21.37	74.98	3.41	5.36
	40%	21.22	75.53	3.41	5.14
	60%	21.07	76.09	3.41	4.77
Increasing green roofs[b]	20%	20.76	77.2	3.44	4.66
	40%	20.47	78.17	3.45	4.57
	60%	20.2	79.06	3.45	4.5

[a]Applying 50% of tree canopy.
[b]Applying 50% of the tree canopy, and 60% of green façade coverage.

reductions of 0.23 and 0.14°C are associated with each 10% increase of tree canopy and green roofs, respectively.

Fig. 13.16 shows that the intensively enhanced scenario achieved an increase of 7.2% of the 10-day average relative humidity more than the reference case. This increase should be considered in calculations of the heat stress index to assess its effect on outdoor thermal comfort. Regarding the energy consumption of the buildings, it can be implied from Fig. 13.17 that applying the intensively enhanced scenario benefits the buildings' cooling consumption, where all the changes are noticed due to HVAC operation. Most importantly, the operation hours of the HVAC arc reduced during 3 days of the heat wave. Also, for all other days, except for the first day where no cooling demand is required, the cooling

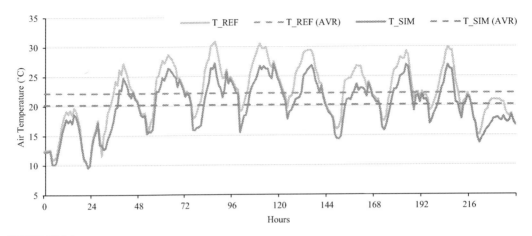

FIGURE 13.14

Air temperature of reference case and enhanced urban canyon.

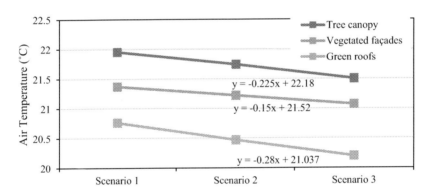

FIGURE 13.15

Effect of mitigation strategies on canyon air temperature.

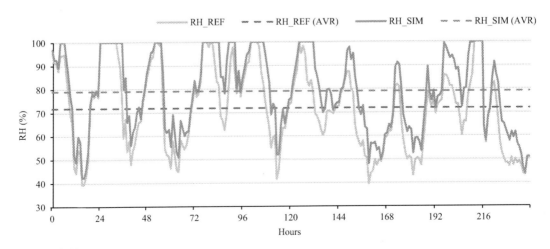

FIGURE 13.16

Relative humidity of reference case and enhanced urban canyon.

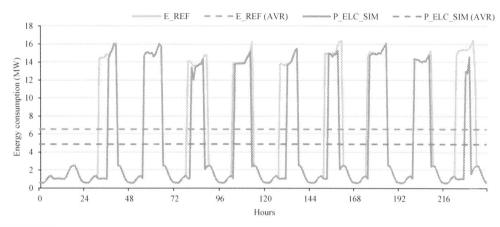

FIGURE 13.17

Buildings' energy consumption of reference case and enhanced urban canyon.

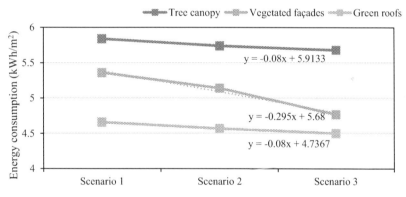

FIGURE 13.18

Effect of mitigation strategies on buildings' energy consumption.

consumption is reduced and occasionally intensively reduced (the case of the last day of the simulation). In general, applying the enhanced scenario saves an amount of 1.55 kWh/m^2 of energy consumption, which represents 25.6% of the energy consumption during 10 days of operation. Referring to Fig. 13.18, it can be concluded that the green façade systems are the most contributor to energy savings with an amount of 0.15 kWh/m^2 for each 10% increase of façade vegetation. Moreover, each increase of 10% of the tree canopy and green roofs contributes to the buildings' energy savings by 0.08 kWh/m^2 and 0.04 kWh/m^2, respectively.

3. Air quality and health responses

Based on statistics Canada (Government of Canada, 2020) and Region of Peel (Peel Data Center - Region of Peel, 2016), the annual all-cause mortality cases in Mississauga and Brampton are estimated to reach 3530 and 3290 persons in 2030, respectively. Also, cardiorespiratory-related mortalities are expected to reach 24.6% of all-cause mortalities in Canada in 2030. Based on the correlations between all-cause mortalities and ambient temperature conducted by Anderson and Bell (2011) and Gronlund et al. (2014), the increase in mortality cases is estimated by 3.6%–4.5% for each degree Celsius increase in ambient temperature. Utilizing these rates, the annual all-cause mortalities cases are expected to increase by 127–159 persons in Mississauga, and by 118–148 in Brampton for each degree Celsius increase in ambient temperature. Referring to the simulation results of the maximum enhancements for increasing green infrastructure, it can be inferred that, by reducing the peak ambient air temperature by 3.7°C, the average reduction in all-cause mortalities in 2030 can reach 500 persons in Mississauga and 466 persons in Brampton. This could reduce the total mortality cases by 14% in both Mississauga and Brampton. Assuming that all the mortality reductions fall into the cardiorespiratory-related mortalities, it can be claimed that cardiorespiratory-related mortalities could reduce by 57.5% in both Mississauga and Brampton.

Regarding the effect of the urban green cover on the air quality level, based on the study conducted by Nyelele et al. (2019), the $PM_{2.5}$ removal ability of well-maintained tree coverage is estimated by 216.9 kg/km^2/year. Referring to the simulation results of the scenario with maximum enhancements, considering only the increase of tree coverage from 20% to 50% of the urban area, the expected daily removed $PM_{2.5}$ by the tree coverage is increased from 19.8 µg/m^3 to 49.5 µg/m^3. Referring to the correlation between $PM_{2.5}$ concentration and mortalities conducted by Pinault et al. (2017), they reported an increase of 36% in cardiorespiratory mortalities for each increase of 10 µg/m^3 in $PM_{2.5}$ concentration. Thus, considering the PM removal ability by the increased tree coverage can reduce the mortalities related to cardiac and respiratory causes. While the annual cardiorespiratory-related mortalities in Brampton are expected to be 809 persons in 2030, then, the expected cardiorespiratory mortalities would decrease to 216 persons in 2030, with an enhancement percentage of 73%, due to both heat resilience and PM removal ability. These assumptions are repeated for Mississauga assuming a similar site area, the results showed the same enhancement percentage in the cardiorespiratory mortalities in 2030.

Regarding the effect of increasing the green coverage on the ambient ozone concentrations, Nowak et al. (2000) reported an 8-hour average reduction of ozone concentration of 0.5 ppb for 25.2 ha (29.8 ppb/km^2/day) for each 20% increase of the tree cover. Referring to the Brampton site area and the simulation scenario with a maximum tree coverage increase of 30%, the daily reduction in ozone concentration due to increased tree coverage is expected to be 17.8 ppb per site area. According to Turner et al. (2015), an increase of 2% in all-cause mortality and 12% in respiratory mortality is associated with each increase of 10 ppb of ozone concentration. Accordingly, applying the increased tree coverage scenario in Brampton in 2030 can reduce the all-cause mortalities by 3.6% (118 persons) and the cardiorespiratory mortalities by 21.4% (173 persons). However, further investigations are required to better estimate the ozone removal ability and formation possibility due to the tree coverage.

Overall, based on the proposed increased area of the tree coverage, assuming the plantation of mature trees of around 8 m in radius (crown area of 220 m^2), 542 new trees are promoted to be planted in the Brampton site area. This means that almost every tree can save one person in terms of heat-related mortalities and fine particulate matter–based respiratory-related mortality, and almost every three trees can save one person in terms of ozone-based respiratory-related mortality.

4. Conclusions

An integrated statistical-simulation approach is designed to figure out the influences of the adaptation of urban green infrastructure on air quality and heat-related health and deaths, with the main objective of exploring whether protecting and increasing the green spaces can enhance the urban microclimate. The UWG is used to assess the effects of the UHI on a local neighborhood scale. Then, the model is used to assess the UHI mitigation scenarios including increasing the tree canopy, integrating vertical vegetation façade systems, and incorporating a moderate-to-intense leaf area index for green roofs. The effect of intensifying the urban greenery cover is then assessed on outdoor air quality and health responses. The proposed application ensured the increased cooling effect of magnifying the urban green infrastructure, with significant benefits for ambient air temperature and district energy consumption. The results prove that increasing the tree canopy is the most effective mitigation strategy for the reduction of canyon air temperature, while ensured that the green façade vegetation is the most effective mitigation strategy for minimizing the energy consumption during the period of operation.

A statistical approach is introduced including regression analyses validated by Bayesian causality networks for establishing correlations between meteorological parameters and air quality variables. The regression analyses ensure a strong positive correlation between ozone and fine particulate matter concentrations and the ambient temperature. Accordingly, referring to the simulation results, due to the reduction in the ambient temperature achieved by increasing the green infrastructure, the ozone and fine particulate matters daily mean concentrations are expected to decrease significantly. Regarding absolute values, it can be concluded that with less building density and larger green cover (the case of municipality of Brampton), the ground-level ozone can be formulated faster, which leads to higher concentrations, while the particulate matter concentrations remain lower than other regions with higher building densities regarding reduced anthropological activities.

The results also discussed the air quality and health responses due to the proposed enhancements in the urban microclimates. Based on the reported correlations between ambient temperature and mortality rates, the research posted a possible reduction of all-casue mortality cases by 14% and cardiorespiratory-related mortalities by 57.5% as a result of applying the proposed heat mitigation strategy. Additionally, when counting the pollutants' removal ability of the enhanced greenery cover, an additional reduction in cardiorespiratory mortalities is expected to reach 73% due to both heat resilience and improved air quality levels. Overall, the research ensures the potential of the urban green infrastructure as an effective heat and pollution mitigation strategy, and its direct impact on population health.

References

Air Quality, 2017 [WWW Document]. http://airquality-qualitedelair.ccme.ca/en/ (Accessed 1.29.21).

Anav, A., Menut, L., Khvorostyanov, D., Viovy, N., 2011. Impact of tropospheric ozone on the Euro-Mediterranean vegetation. Global Change Biol. 17, 2342–2359. https://doi.org/10.1111/j.1365-2486.2010.02387.x.

Anderson, G.B., Bell, M.L., 2011. Heat waves in the United States: mortality risk during heat waves and effect modification by heat wave characteristics in 43 U.S. Communities. Environ. Health Perspect. 119, 210–218. https://doi.org/10.1289/ehp.1002313.

Arghavani, S., Malakooti, H., Bidokhti, A.A., 2019. Numerical evaluation of urban green space scenarios effects on gaseous air pollutants in Tehran Metropolis based on WRF-Chem model. Atmos. Environ. 214, 116832. https://doi.org/10.1016/j.atmosenv.2019.116832.

Atkinson, R.W., Yu, D., Armstrong, B.G., Pattenden, S., Wilkinson, P., Doherty, R.M., Heal, M.R., Anderson, H.R., 2012. Concentration–response function for ozone and daily mortality: results from five urban and five rural U.K. populations. Environ. Health Perspect. 120, 1411–1417. https://doi.org/10.1289/ehp.1104108.

Azhar, G.S., Mavalankar, D., Nori-Sarma, A., Rajiva, A., Dutta, P., Jaiswal, A., Sheffield, P., Knowlton, K., Hess, J.J., Ahmedabad Heat Climate Study Group, 2014. Heat-related mortality in India: excess all-cause mortality associated with the 2010 Ahmedabad heat wave. PLoS One 9, e91831. https://doi.org/10.1371/journal.pone.0091831.

Bae, S., Lim, Y.-H., Hong, Y.-C., 2020. Causal association between ambient ozone concentration and mortality in Seoul, Korea. Environ. Res. 182, 109098. https://doi.org/10.1016/j.envres.2019.109098.

Beckett, K.P., Freer-Smith, P.H., Taylor, G., 2000. The capture of particulate pollution BY trees at five contrasting urban sites. Arboric. J. 24, 209–230. https://doi.org/10.1080/03071375.2000.9747273.

Benmarhnia, T., Deguen, S., Kaufman, J.S., Smargiassi, A., 2015. Review article: vulnerability to heat-related mortality: a systematic review, meta-analysis, and meta-regression analysis. Epidemiology 26, 781–793. https://doi.org/10.1097/EDE.0000000000000375.

Berardi, U., Jandaghian, Z., Graham, J., 2020. Effects of greenery enhancements for the resilience to heat waves: a comparison of analysis performed through mesoscale (WRF) and microscale (Envi-met) modeling. Sci. Total Environ. 747. https://doi.org/10.1016/j.scitotenv.2020.141300.

Berardi, U., Wang, Y., 2016. The effect of a denser city over the urban microclimate: the case of Toronto. Sustainability 8, 822. https://doi.org/10.3390/su8080822.

Berko, J., Ingram, D.D., Saha, S., Parker, J.D., 2014. Deaths Attributed to Heat, Cold, and Other Weather Events in the United States, 2006–2010. Natl Health Stat Report 1–15.

Borge, R., Requia, W.J., Yagüe, C., Jhun, I., Koutrakis, P., 2019. Impact of weather changes on air quality and related mortality in Spain over a 25 year period [1993–2017]. Environ. Int. 133, 105272. https://doi.org/10.1016/j.envint.2019.105272.

Bueno, B., Norford, L., Hidalgo, J., Pigeon, G., 2013. The urban weather generator. J. Build. Perf. Simul. 6, 269–281. https://doi.org/10.1080/19401493.2012.718797.

Calfapietra, C., Fares, S., Manes, F., Morani, A., Sgrigna, G., Loreto, F., 2013. Role of Biogenic Volatile Organic Compounds (BVOC) emitted by urban trees on ozone concentration in cities: a review. Environ. Pollut. 183, 71–80. https://doi.org/10.1016/j.envpol.2013.03.012.

Cesaroni, G., Chiara, B., Claudio, G., Massimo, S., Roberto, S., Marina, D., Francesco, F., 2013. Long-term exposure to urban air pollution and mortality in a Cohort of more than a million adults in rome. Environ. Health Perspect. 121, 324–331. https://doi.org/10.1289/ehp.1205862.

Chapman, S., Thatcher, M., Salazar, A., Watson, J.E.M., McAlpine, C.A., 2018. The effect of urban density and vegetation cover on the heat island of a subtropical city. J. Appl. Meteorol. Climatol. 57, 2531–2550. https://doi.org/10.1175/JAMC-D-17-0316.1.

Chen, L., Liu, C., Zhang, L., Zou, R., Zhang, Z., 2017. Variation in tree species ability to capture and retain airborne fine particulate matter (PM2.5). Sci. Rep. 7, 1–11. https://doi.org/10.1038/s41598-017-03360-1.

Chen, X., Zhao, P., Hu, Y., Ouyang, L., Zhu, L., Ni, G., 2019. Canopy transpiration and its cooling effect of three urban tree species in a subtropical city- Guangzhou, China. Urban For. Urban Green. 43, 126368. https://doi.org/10.1016/j.ufug.2019.126368.

Coffman, E., Burnett, R.T., Sacks, J.D., 2020. Quantitative characterization of uncertainty in the concentration–response relationship between long-term PM2.5 exposure and mortality at low concentrations. Environ. Sci. Technol. 54, 10191–10200. https://doi.org/10.1021/acs.est.0c02770.

Dardir, M., Berardi, U., 2021. Development of microclimate modeling for enhancing neighborhood thermal performance through urban greenery cover. Energy Build. 252. https://doi.org/10.1016/j.enbuild.2021.111428.

Dardir, M., Mankibi, M.E., Haghighat, F., Klimes, L., 2019. Development of PCM-to-air heat exchanger for integration in building envelope—modeling and validation. Sol. Energy 190, 367—385. https://doi.org/10.1016/j.solener.2019.08.003.

Declet-Barreto, J., Knowlton, K., Jenerette, G.D., Buyantuev, A., 2016. Effects of urban vegetation on mitigating exposure of vulnerable populations to excessive heat in cleveland, Ohio. Weather Clim. & Soc. 8, 507—524. https://doi.org/10.1175/WCAS-D-15-0026.1.

Di, Q., Wang, Y., Zanobetti, A., Wang, Y., Koutrakis, P., Choirat, C., Dominici, F., Schwartz, J.D., 2017. Air Pollution and Mortality in the Medicare Population. https://doi.org/10.1056/NEJMoa1702747 [WWW Document].

D'Ippoliti, D., Michelozzi, P., Marino, C., de'Donato, F., Menne, B., Katsouyanni, K., Kirchmayer, U., Analitis, A., Medina-Ramón, M., Paldy, A., Atkinson, R., Kovats, S., Bisanti, L., Schneider, A., Lefranc, A., Iñiguez, C., Perucci, C.A., 2010. The impact of heat waves on mortality in 9 European cities: results from the EuroHEAT project. Environ. Health 9, 37. https://doi.org/10.1186/1476-069X-9-37.

Duarte, D.H.S., Shinzato, P., dos Santos Gusson, C., Alves, C.A., 2015. The impact of vegetation on urban microclimate to counterbalance built density in a subtropical changing climate. Urban Clim. 14, 224—239. https://doi.org/10.1016/j.uclim.2015.09.006.

Erickson, A.J., Gulliver, J.S., Hozalski, R.M., Mohseni, O., Nieber, J.L., Wilson, B.N., Weiss, P.T., 2010. Evaporation and Evapotranspiration [WWW Document]. http://stormwaterbook.safl.umn.edu/water-budget-measurement/evaporation-and-evapotranspiration (Accessed 12.5.20).

Fallmann, J., Emeis, S., Suppan, P., 2014. Mitigation of urban heat stress - a modeling case study for the area of Stuttgart. Die Erde. Z. Ges. Erdkd. Berl. 144, 202—216.

Fischer, E.M., Schär, C., 2010. Consistent geographical patterns of changes in high-impact European heatwaves. Nat. Geosci. 3, 398—403. https://doi.org/10.1038/ngeo866.

Fricke, W., 2019. Night-time transpiration — favouring growth? Trends Plant Sci. 24, 311—317. https://doi.org/10.1016/j.tplants.2019.01.007.

Gao, K., Santamouris, M., Feng, J., 2020. On the efficiency of using transpiration cooling to mitigate urban heat [WWW document]. Climate. https://doi.org/10.3390/cli8060069.

Goldberg, M.S., Burnett, R.T., Valois, M.-F., Flegel, K., Bailar, J.C., Brook, J., Vincent, R., Radon, K., 2003. Associations between ambient air pollution and daily mortality among persons with congestive heart failure. Environ. Res. 91, 8—20. https://doi.org/10.1016/s0013-9351(02)00022-1.

Government of Canada, 2020. Mortality Rates, by Age Group [WWW Document]. https://www150.statcan.gc.ca/t1/tbl1/en/tv.action?pid=1310071001 (Accessed 1.25.21).

Gronlund, C.J., Zanobetti, A., Schwartz, J.D., Wellenius, G.A., O'Neill, M.S., 2014. Heat, heat waves, and hospital admissions among the elderly in the United States, 1992—2006. Environ. Health Perspect. 122, 1187—1192. https://doi.org/10.1289/ehp.1206132.

Hart, J.E., Liao, X., Hong, B., Puett, R.C., Yanosky, J.D., Suh, H., Kioumourtzoglou, M.-A., Spiegelman, D., Laden, F., 2015. The association of long-term exposure to PM2.5 on all-cause mortality in the Nurses' Health Study and the impact of measurement-error correction. Environ. Health 14, 38. https://doi.org/10.1186/s12940-015-0027-6.

Health Canada, 2017. Health [WWW Document]. AEM. https://www.canada.ca/en/services/health.html (Accessed 6.11.20).

Hewitt, D., 2015. Quantifying the Impacts of Ozone Pollution on the Sustainability of Pasture (PhD). Lancaster University.

Hoelscher, M.-T., Nehls, T., Jänicke, B., Wessolek, G., 2016. Quantifying cooling effects of facade greening: shading, transpiration and insulation. Energy Build. 114, 283–290. https://doi.org/10.1016/j.enbuild.2015.06.047.

Howard, A.R., Iersel, M.W.V., Richards, J.H., Donovan, L.A., 2009. Night-time transpiration can decrease hydraulic redistribution. Plant Cell Environ. 32, 1060–1070. https://doi.org/10.1111/j.1365-3040.2009.01988.x.

Hsieh, C.-M., Li, J.-J., Zhang, L., Schwegler, B., 2018. Effects of tree shading and transpiration on building cooling energy use. Energy Build. 159, 382–397. https://doi.org/10.1016/j.enbuild.2017.10.045.

Imran, H.M., Kala, J., Ng, A.W.M., Muthukumaran, S., 2019. Effectiveness of vegetated patches as Green Infrastructure in mitigating Urban Heat Island effects during a heatwave event in the city of Melbourne. Weather & Clim. Extre. 25, 100217. https://doi.org/10.1016/j.wace.2019.100217.

Jacobs, S.J., Gallant, A.J.E., Tapper, N.J., Li, D., 2018. Use of cool roofs and vegetation to mitigate urban heat and improve human thermal stress in Melbourne, Australia. J. Appl. Meteorol. Climatol. 57, 1747–1764. https://doi.org/10.1175/JAMC-D-17-0243.1.

Jandaghian, Z., Akbari, H., 2018. The effects of increasing surface reflectivity on heat-related mortality in Greater Montreal Area, Canada. Urban Clim. 25. https://doi.org/10.1016/j.uclim.2018.06.002.

Jandaghian, Z., Berardi, U., 2020. Comparing urban canopy models for microclimate simulations in Weather Research and Forecasting Models. Sustain. Cities Soc. 55, 102025. https://doi.org/10.1016/j.scs.2020.102025.

Joseph, Y., 2016. The Curious Case of Urban Heat Island: A Systems Analysis (Master of Science in Engineering). Massachusetts Institute of Technology, Massachusetts, US.

Karkour, S., Itsubo, N., 2020. Influence of the Covid-19 crisis on global $PM_{2.5}$ concentration and related health impacts. Sustainability. https://doi.org/10.3390/su12135297 [WWW Document].

Kolb, S., Radon, K., Valois, M.-F., Héguy, L., Goldberg, M.S., 2010. The short-term influence of weather on daily mortality in congestive heart failure. Arch. Environ. Occup. Health. https://doi.org/10.3200/AEOH.62.4.169-176.

Konarska, J., Uddling, J., Holmer, B., Lutz, M., Lindberg, F., Pleijel, H., Thorsson, S., 2016. Transpiration of urban trees and its cooling effect in a high latitude city. Int. J. Biometeorol. 60, 159–172. https://doi.org/10.1007/s00484-015-1014-x.

Lee, J.Y., Lee, S.H., Hong, S.-C., Kim, H., 2017. Projecting future summer mortality due to ambient ozone concentration and temperature changes. Atmos. Environ. 156, 88–94. https://doi.org/10.1016/j.atmosenv.2017.02.034.

Lee, M., Nordio, F., Zanobetti, A., Kinney, P., Vautard, R., Schwartz, J., 2014. Acclimatization across space and time in the effects of temperature on mortality: a time-series analysis. Environ. Health 13, 89. https://doi.org/10.1186/1476-069X-13-89.

Li, X.-X., Norford, L.K., 2016. Evaluation of cool roof and vegetations in mitigating urban heat island in a tropical city, Singapore. Urban Clim. 16, 59–74. https://doi.org/10.1016/j.uclim.2015.12.002.

Nowak, D.J., Civerolo, K.L., Trivikrama Rao, S., Gopal, S., Luley, C.J., Crane, D.E., 2000. A modeling study of the impact of urban trees on ozone. Atmos. Environ. 34, 1601–1613. https://doi.org/10.1016/S1352-2310(99)00394-5.

Nyelele, C., Kroll, C.N., Nowak, D.J., 2019. Present and future ecosystem services of trees in the Bronx, NY. Urban For. Urban Green. 42, 10–20. https://doi.org/10.1016/j.ufug.2019.04.018.

Paravantis, J., Santamouris, M., Cartalis, C., Efthymiou, C., Kontoulis, N., 2017. Mortality associated with high ambient temperatures, heatwaves, and the urban heat island in Athens, Greece. Sustainability 9, 1–22.

Peel Data Centre - Region of Peel. [WWW Document]. https://www.peelregion.ca/planning/pdc/data/health/mortality-rates.htm (Accessed 1.24.21).

Pengelly, L.D., Campbell, M.E., Cheng, C.S., Fu, C., Gingrich, S.E., Macfarlane, R., 2007. Anatomy of heat waves and mortality in Toronto: lessons for public health protection. Can. J. Public Health/Revue Canadienne de Sante'e Publique 98, 364–368.

Pinault, L.L., Weichenthal, S., Crouse, D.L., Brauer, M., Erickson, A., Van Donkelaar, A., Martin, R.V., Hystad, P., Chen, H., Finès, P., Brook, J.R., Tjepkema, M., Burnett, R.T., 2017. Associations between fine particulate matter and mortality in the 2001 Canadian Census Health and Environment Cohort. Environ. Res. 159, 406–415. https://doi.org/10.1016/j.envres.2017.08.037.

Qiu, G.Y., Zou, Z., Li, X., Li, H., Guo, Q., Yan, C., Tan, S., 2017. Experimental studies on the effects of green space and evapotranspiration on urban heat island in a subtropical megacity in China. Habitat Int. Smart Devel. Spat. Sustain. & Environ. Qual. 68, 30–42. https://doi.org/10.1016/j.habitatint.2017.07.009.

Rainham, D.G.C., Smoyer-Tomic, K.E., 2003. The role of air pollution in the relationship between a heat stress index and human mortality in Toronto. Environ. Res. 93, 9–19. https://doi.org/10.1016/S0013-9351(03)00060-4.

Rosenzweig, C., Solecki, W., Parshall, L., Gaffin, S., Lynn, B., Goldberg, R., Cox, J., Hodges, S., 2006. Mitigating New York City's heat island with urban forestry, living roofs, and light surfaces. In: 86th AMS Annual Meeting.

Santamouris, M., Osmond, P., 2020. Increasing green infrastructure in cities: impact on ambient temperature, air quality and heat-related mortality and morbidity. Buildings 10, 233. https://doi.org/10.3390/buildings10120233.

Shahidan, M., Salleh, H., Shariff, M., 2006. The Influence of Tree Canopy on Thermal Environment in a Tropical Climate.

Simon, H., Fallmann, J., Kropp, T., Tost, H., Bruse, M., 2019. Urban trees and their impact on local ozone concentration—a microclimate modeling study. Atmosphere. https://doi.org/10.3390/atmos10030154 [WWW Document].

Smoyer-Tomic, K.E., Rainham, D.G., 2001. Beating the heat: development and evaluation of a Canadian hot weather health-response plan. Environ. Health Perspect. 109, 1241–1248. https://doi.org/10.1289/ehp.011091241.

Tan, P.Y., Wong, N.H., Tan, C.L., Jusuf, S.K., Schmiele, K., Chiam, Z.Q., 2020. Transpiration and cooling potential of tropical urban trees from different native habitats. Sci. Total Environ. 705. https://doi.org/10.1016/j.scitotenv.2019.135764.

Theoharatos, G., Pantavou, K., Mavrakis, A., Spanou, A., Katavoutas, G., Efstathiou, P., Mpekas, P., Asimakopoulos, D., 2010. Heat waves observed in 2007 in Athens, Greece: synoptic conditions, bioclimatological assessment, air quality levels and health effects. Environ. Res. 110, 152–161. https://doi.org/10.1016/j.envres.2009.12.002.

Tsekeri, E., Kolokotsa, D., Santamouris, M., 2020. On the association of ambient temperature and elderly mortality in a Mediterranean island - Crete. Sci. Total Environ. 738, 139843. https://doi.org/10.1016/j.scitotenv.2020.139843.

Turner, M.C., Jerrett, M., Pope, C.A., Krewski, D., Gapstur, S.M., Diver, W.R., Beckerman, B.S., Marshall, J.D., Su, J., Crouse, D.L., Burnett, R.T., 2015. Long-term ozone exposure and mortality in a large prospective study. Am. J. Respir. Crit. Care Med. 193, 1134–1142. https://doi.org/10.1164/rccm.201508-1633OC.

Wai, K.-M., Tan, T.Z., Morakinyo, T.E., Chan, T.-C., Lai, A., 2020. Reduced effectiveness of tree planting on micro-climate cooling due to ozone pollution—a modeling study. Sustain. Cities Soc. 52, 101803. https://doi.org/10.1016/j.scs.2019.101803.

Wang, Y., Berardi, U., Akbari, H., 2016. Comparing the effects of urban heat island mitigation strategies for Toronto, Canada. Energy & Build. SI: Countermeasur. Urban Heat Island 114, 2–19. https://doi.org/10.1016/j.enbuild.2015.06.046.

Yin, P., Brauer, M., Cohen, A., Burnett Richard, T., Liu, J., Liu, Y., Liang, R., Wang, W., Qi, J., Wang, L., Zhou, M., 2017. Long-term fine particulate matter exposure and nonaccidental and cause-specific mortality in a large national Cohort of Chinese men. Environ. Health Perspect. 125, 117002. https://doi.org/10.1289/EHP1673.

Zheng, S., Pozzer, A., Cao, C.X., Lelieveld, J., 2015. Long-term (2001—2012) concentrations of fine particulate matter (PM2.5) and the impact on human health in Beijing, China. Atmos. Chem. Phys. https://doi.org/10.5194/acp-15-5715-2015 [WWW Document].

Žuvela-Aloise, M., Koch, R., Buchholz, S., Früh, B., 2016. Modelling the potential of green and blue infrastructure to reduce urban heat load in the city of Vienna. Clim. Chang. 135, 425—438. https://doi.org/10.1007/s10584-016-1596-2.

Visualization of landuse change pattern and its impact on Urban Heat Islands

14

G. Nimish[1], H.A. Bharath[1] and T.V. Ramachandra[2]

[1]*Ranbir and Chitra Gupta School of Infrastructure Design and Management, Indian Institute of Technology Kharagpur, Kharagpur, West Bengal, India;* [2]*Centre for Ecological Science, Indian Institute of Science, Bangalore, Karnataka, India*

1. Introduction

It has been witnessed since the beginning of history, that humans have a tendency to prove themselves to be superior to all other living organisms. It is now truthful to state that there exists an ego among the human breed to dominate the available resources for their immediate benefits. Previously, this was just altering the local climate which was almost negligible as nature has a self-cleansing and maintaining property, but from past few decades, due to extreme pressure on nature, the climate across the globe is being affected due to anthropogenic activities. Initially, climate change was considered essential only on academic basis, but over the past few years, due to increased awareness among people, it has become one of the most concerned and researched topics, also being one of the most significant developmental challenges for humans (Lal, 2017). One of the most critical factors of changing climate can be inferred as unplanned and hap-hazardous urban areas development. Urbanization has conveniently brought numerous positive changes such as making cities economically sustainable, increasing the GDP per capita, providing a better standard of living and quality of life, improved medical facilities, increased occupational opportunities, and better education (Keeling, 1997; Karoly et al., 2003; Stott et al., 2006). However, due to increased demographic pressure on the cities due to large movement of population from rural to urban areas, rapid and unorganized developments have started to come-up in cities for satisfying the needs of incoming residents. These changes gradually collapse the balance, creating problems such as unavailability of basic housing, lack of fresh and treated water supply, inadequate infrastructure, and rise in greenhouse gases as well as pollution levels (Ramachandra et al., 2012). Scientific communications have found that these alterations in urban areas can be understood by deriving land use/land cover maps, and these maps can be used to demonstrate the phenomenon of urbanization. These changes in LULC includes the development of urban pockets (pervious surface) on the cost of areas that serves important feeders for human life such as vegetation, open/bare fields, agricultural fields, etc. (Kandlikar and Sagar, 1999; Mallick et al., 2008; Ramachandra et al., 2016). In today's scenario, there have been numerous cases where urban areas have come-up by encroaching water bodies such as lakes, ponds, and catchment areas, leading to a rise in urban floods. These unprecedented alterations in LULC affect evapotranspiration rates, surface albedo, storage of heat and moisture content of the surfaces, pollution displacement, and surface temperature (Pal and Ziaul, 2017). Due to such changes, the phenomenon of global warming has been intensifying over the years, and it creates a massive threat for sensitive species in nature as most of the flora and fauna are sensitive to temperature.

Researchers across the globe have found a strong relationship between alteration in LULC and climate change in terms of Land Surface Temperature (LST) (Aggarwal et al., 2012; Mutiibwa et al., 2014). LST is an important parameter that accounts for the upward thermal radiation and can be defined as the radiative skin temperature of the earth's surface. It is a crucial parameter to describe the thermal comfortability of the residents (Bento et al., 2017). LST not only affects human but also disturbs rainfall patterns, wind turbulence and speed, crop patterns, ecology of the region, and earth's natural cycles including biogeochemical cycle, water cycle, and carbon cycle. It is one of the key input parameters in numerous applications such as urban climatology, greenhouse gas quantification, crop monitoring, studies related to global warming and also defines the phenomena of Urban Heat Island (UHI) (Schmugge and Becker, 1991; Li and Becker, 1993; Running et al., 1994; Anderson et al., 2008; Li et al., 2013; Ramachandra et al., 2017; Khandelwal et al., 2018). UHI is a phenomenon that is being observed in many cities across the globe as a result of higher temperatures in urban areas when compared to nearby rural areas due to increased impervious surfaces in urban areas. UHI is an issue of serious concern as it is responsible for a large number of health-related issues and deaths across the globe. Thus, it is a need-of-hour to study the dreadful effects of rising LST on the inhabitants and suggest some mitigation measures.

Remote Sensing (RS) and Geographic Information System (GIS) have developed across the years and are now considered as a state-of-the-art technology for any climate and urban-related studies. Thus, the case study presented in this chapter uses remote sensing data and open source GIS software for complete analysis. This book chapter deals with the understanding of how changes in landscape due to increased anthropogenic activities affect climate in terms of land surface temperature. The chapter also deals with explaining how a rise in LST causes an increase in UHI effect, that further affects the health and welfare of inhabitants in an urban area with a case study. Also, few mitigation measures were suggested to reduce the overall rise and eliminate the ill-effects of LST. The chapter is divided into sections as mentioned below:

1. **Introduction:** This section gives a brief idea about the overall research work presented in this chapter.
2. **Understanding LST:** This section provides basic information about Land Surface Temperature.
3. **Urban Heat Islands**: This section deals with understanding the phenomenon of UHI.
4. **Significance of studying LST and UHI:** As the name suggests this chapter highlights the need and motivation behind studying LST and understanding the phenomenon of UHI in an urban area.
5. **Theoretical Background:** This section gives a brief introduction to the principles on which thermal remote sensing works.
6. **Practical example:** This section provides a case study showing a relationship between growing urban area and rise in LST, followed by the UHI index for Kolkata Metropolitan Area in India.
7. **Mitigation measures:** The section suggests a few mitigation measures that can be implemented for reducing the overall regional scale LST.
8. **Conclusion:** This section includes the takeaway points from this chapter.

2. Understanding LST

Land Surface Temperature is a direction-based radiometric temperature of the collective surfaces on the earth as observed from the thermal region of the sensor onboard (Sismanidis et al., 2016). It is a basic element of earth's thermal behavior and is an important index that determines the earth's energy balance and climate change (AATSR and SLSTR, 2018). It is an important indicator of global warming and greenhouse effect (Jia et al., 2007) and is directly linked with the sensible and latent heat fluxes, thus, playing a pivotal role in defining local, regional, as well as global processes over the surface of the earth (Mannstein, 1987). One of the main advantages of estimating LST is that it provides the value of temperature at a pixel level, thus making it possible to capture and map even a very minute change in temperature which is not possible with measurements collected from meteorological stations especially in case of developing countries as they have only one meteorological station installed for a large area. Changes in landscape affect the overall evaporation and transpiration rates that alter the latent and sensible heat fluxes (Mojolaoluwa et al., 2018). Scientific community across the globe have predicted that there would be higher climatic variation and increased thermal discomfort to the urban residents as a result of continuous rise in urban population because this will lead to increase in construction activities, rise in traffic congestions, and higher production of power supply. Fulfilling these needs would hamper the environment critically as they will lead to an increment in the concentration of pollutants in the air (PM_{10}, $PM_{2.5}$, PM_1, and Suspended PM) as well as water (chemicals, leakages, discharges), and would also lead to a rise in GHGs (CO_2, CO, NO_X, SO_X, O_3, CH_4) that further instigates increment in LST (Ministry of Statistic and Programme Implementation, 2015). Quantification of LST largely depends upon atmospheric parameters including atmospheric transmittance, upwelling and downwelling radiance, atmospheric water vapor content; sensor parameters such as viewing angle, sensor calibration, spectral range; surface parameters (surface albedo, land surface emissivity); and condition of the atmosphere (cloud cover) when the data are captured. Some of the selected (latest) studies performed by various researchers that relate LST and LULC (for reference) are as shown in Table 14.1.

A rise in LST not only critically affects the health and welfare of urban dwellers but also of the ones residing in rural as well as suburban areas. Elevated LST can affect us in multiple ways such as causing power outages, deteriorating the quality of air and water, causing severe health issues, affecting the thermal comfort, leading to food and water crisis, rising intensity and frequency of extreme weather events, and increasing mortality rates. Rise in LST also gives rise to a phenomenon of UHI that is an issue of serious concern these days.

3. Urban Heat Island

As a result of increased demographic pressure and in turn alteration in landscape toward increasing urban areas, cities these days are more susceptible to heatwaves and UHI phenomenon. This has now extended to such levels that the UHI effect is becoming a common phenomenon, is getting stronger, and is continuing for longer durations, which further aggravates thermal risk for the inhabitants (Founda and Santamouris, 2017). UHI is a phenomenon observed in cities, where the city's temperature becomes higher compared to the nearby suburban or rural areas (Liang and Shi, 2009).

Table 14.1 Literature—relationship between land surface temperature and urban landscape.

Author	Inference
Qian et al. (2020)	Retrieved LST and emissivity from ground-based time-series thermal infrared data
Nimish et al. (2020)	Explored temperature indices by deriving a relationship between LST and urban landscape
Guha et al. (2020)	Performed long-term analysis on relationship between LST and built-up index (NDBI)
Wang and Murayama (2020)	Performed geosimulation of LULC scenarios and identified their impacts on LST for Sapporo, Japan
Mustafa et al. (2020)	Compared four algorithms to predict LST using Landsat data
Daramola et al. (2018)	Assessed thermal response of variations in the landscape of an urban area
Chandra et al. (2018)	Performed geospatial analysis on the city of Jaipur, India, to demonstrate a linkage between urban expansion and LST
Tran et al. (2017)	Characterized relationship between changes in LULC and LST
Pal and Ziaul (2017)	Detected LULC changes and LST for pre-monsoon, monsoon, and post-monsoon over English Bazar urban center
Youneszadeh et al. (2015)	Studied the effect of LU changes on LST over the Netherlands
Yu et al. (2014)	Compared various LST retrieval methods/algorithms
Bharath et al. (2013)	Studied LST responses to landscape dynamics over central Western Ghats in India
Sobrino et al. (2006)	Derived LST using an airborne hyperspectral thermal infrared scanner

These can be inferred to the difference in the percentage of vegetation, water, and impervious surface. UHIs can be divided into two categories:

1. Atmospheric UHI (AUHI): As a result of absorption of heat in the air due to the presence of particles, air temperature increases causing AUHI effect. It is further classified into two categories based on height: canopy layer UHI (heat islands present in air layer from surface level to the top of buildings or vegetation), and boundary layer UHI (heat islands present in the region above rooftops and vegetation).
2. Surface UHI (SUHI): This occurs as a result of higher surface temperatures in urban areas due to the presence of large region covered with impervious surfaces.

Some of the causal factors of UHI are multiple internal reflections, higher absorption of shortwave radiations, rise in anthropogenic heat sources, hindrance in the transmission of longwave radiations, lower evapotranspiration rates, changes in wind gust and turbulence, reduction in radiative cooling, etc. (Dash et al., 2002). The main reasons behind these factors are the difference in the thermal properties of materials used for construction in urban areas when compared to the naturally occurring and imbalance in the composition of the landscape over a region. As a result of the difference in heat storage capacity of materials, the latent and sensible heat budget varies, leading to changes in the convective and advective energy flow (Oke, 1982; Roth, 2012). Fig. 14.1 shows a schematic representation of surface temperatures in urban, suburban, and rural areas.

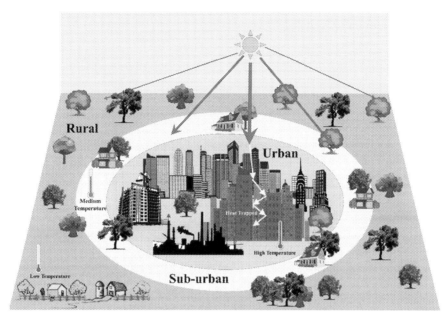

FIGURE 14.1

Temperature distribution in urban, suburban, and rural areas signifying UHI.

Understanding UHI phenomena is one of the biggest challenges for the scientific community as it is directly related to providing apt infrastructure and a suitable environment for the residents (Stewart, 2011). Interpretation of UHI was first studied in 1833 by Luke Howard over London, where he noticed the city center being warmer when compared to the countryside (Mills, 2008). His annotation was then noticed and motivated many researchers raising concern regarding the exclusion of meteorology in the field of science. This triggered a need to perform UHI and LST studies over the cities as shown in Table 14.2.

The continual rise in surface temperature leads to discomfort that further increases energy consumption due to the increased usage of various electronic devices such as air conditioning and water coolers. This leads to increment in concentration of GHGs in the atmosphere leading to rising air temperatures that further instigates UHI. Rise in UHI is one of the most critical parameters to increase surface temperature. Thus this vicious cycle continues, further damaging human health and welfare. UHI not only affects human health but also disrupts complete urban ecological system. It affects the microclimate of the region and exerts tremendous pressure on the floral and faunal diversity especially on the ones that are sensitive to alteration in temperature. UHI also affects the evapotranspiration rates, that alters the moisture content in the atmosphere and earth's surface. Increased frequency and intensity of UHI can have numerous impacts on human health and welfare that includes cramps due to heat, difficulty in breathing and other pulmonary diseases, thermal discomfort, lethal and nonlethal heat strokes, exhaustion, etc. (EPA, 2019). UHI is one of the key factors that lead to the generation of heatwaves and is solely responsible for many deaths.

Table 14.2 Literature—LST and UHI studies over cities.

Author	Inference
Sarif et al. (2020)	Assessed alterations in LULC and LST, further identified their impact on SUHI over Kathmandu Valley for a period of 30 years
Oh et al. (2020)	Used deep learning algorithm for forecasting the magnitude of UHI in Seoul and introduced a new index for determining the same
Kimuku and Ngigi (2017)	Studied urban heat island trends and simulated LST for 2025 across Nakuru county in Kenya for aiding in urban planning
Mathew et al. (2016)	Estimated UHI over the city of Chandigarh over a period of 4 years
Grover and Singh (2015)	Performed UHI analysis on Mumbai and identified the major sectors behind the rise of UHI
More et al. (2015)	Compared estimation of UHI using LST and ambient air temperature
Murata et al. (2013)	Calculated UHI by simulating biases in surface air temperature using regional climatic model for Japan
Wolters and Brandsma (2012)	Estimated UHI in residential areas of Netherlands using weather amateurs
Gedzlman et al. (2003)	Performed UHI analysis over New York City and identified the intensity throughout the day
Yamashita (1996)	Estimated and compared UHI intensity over seasonal basis for Tokyo

4. Significance of studying LST and UHI

As per a review paper published in *Environmental Research Letters*, 97% of the studies established that human-induced changes are the key source of rising global warming and climate change (NASA, 2018). As per Jordon (2007), there are sufficient studies to prove and infer that the surface temperature of the earth is changing significantly at an alarming pace and is an issue of serious concern. As per a report by UN DESA (2018), 54% of the global population already reside in urban areas which are predicted to increase at a faster rate in the near future, majorly being concentrated in developing countries (Chen et al., 2014). Exceptional rise is LST, and the phenomenon of UHI, affects almost all the sectors on which our life depends. These sectors include

- Energy: Higher energy consumption due to increased usage of air conditioning, irrigation, and rise in fuel requirement in the transportation sector (Scott et al., 1990).
- Agriculture: Crop failure can affect food security.
- Water resources: Changes in the natural water cycle as a result of alteration in the rate of evaporation and precipitation. Melting of ice caps can also result in the rise of sea level causing huge concern for the coastal cites (Bolin et al., 1986).
- Forest: Rising temperatures can exert stress on few species, thus making them vulnerable for fire, disease, and pest infection.
- Ecosystem biodiversity: Not every flora and fauna can sustain large-scale changes in temperatures, thus, can gradually become endangered or even extinct (Davis, 1989).
- Air quality: Air pollution levels and temperature are interdependent and rise in one can lead to an increment in the other.

- Infrastructure: Rising LST can affect the construction material of the available infrastructure and can lead to bending or breaking of some critical joints. Damage can be in the form of material as well as life.
- Marine life: Alteration in temperature affects marine biodiversity as a result of migration of few species from one area to other (as they are unable to acclimatize to higher temperatures) or can even lead to mass extinction (Science for Environmental Policy, 2007).
- Human health: The increasing temperature can lead to increased skin diseases, asthma, migraine, stress, hay fever, and vector-borne diseases (Raloff, 1989).

5. Theoretical background

Electromagnetic spectrum can be divided into various segments based on wavelength range, and their intensity varies with the transmission allowed by the atmospheric windows. One of the regions is dedicated to thermal remote sensing that can be defined between the wavelength range of 3−35 μm. Within this range, an excellent atmospheric window lies between 10 and 12 μm and thus, this region is used for various applications. The surface energy budget is a combination of radiative and nonradiative elements (Santra, 2019). Radiative elements include incoming shortwave and outgoing longwave radiations, while latent heat and sensible heat form nonradiative components. Net energy is the summation of downward (heating of earth's surface) and upward (summation of reradiated energy and reflected radiation of the earth's surface) radiation. Two of the primary parameters that influence thermal remote sensing are albedo and land surface emissivity. Albedo can be defined as the fraction of the total energy incident on a surface that gets reflected (Oke and Cleugh, 1987). Albedo varies with surface properties (type, shape, color, and size of the surface), angle of incidence, amount of aerosols and water vapor content in the atmosphere, and distribution of solar energy. Land surface emissivity can be elaborated as the ratio of energy radiated by any material to the energy emitted by a blackbody at the same wavelength and viewing angle under similar atmospheric conditions. This depends upon the composition of the material, surface roughness, and viewing angle (Li et al., 2013). Application of thermal remote sensing can be explained via three basic laws as mentioned below:

- **Stephan−Boltzmann law:** explains the relationship between energy radiated and the temperature of an object as shown in Eq. (14.1). The law signifies that any object above 0K emits energy equivalent to the fourth power of its absolute temperature.

$$E = \sigma T^4 \tag{14.1}$$

Here, E = Energy emitted; σ = Stephan−Boltzmann constant; T = Temperature in Kelvin.

- **Wein's displacement law:** states that radiation by blackbody will reach its peak at different temperatures depending on its wavelength. Higher the temperature, it will have peak radiation at lower wavelengths. Mathematically it can be expressed as Eq. (14.2).

$$\lambda_m \times T = 2897 \ \mu mK \tag{14.2}$$

Here, T = Temperature in Kelvin; λ_m = Wavelength at which maximum radiation is achieved.

This law also explains how thermal range for the earth's surface is obtained. Considering average temperature of earth's surface as 300K (27°C), then as per Eq. (14.2), the wavelength at which peak radiation is obtained comes out to be 9.66 μm.

- **Planck's law/function:** relates spectral radiance of a blackbody or nonblackbody with its temperature and is the basis of deriving LST using thermal remote sensing. Since there is no blackbody, emissivity is used with blackbody radiance to derive nonblackbody radiance (Eq. 14.3) and further temperature.

$$R_{\lambda,\,T} = \varepsilon_\lambda \times B_{\lambda,T} = \varepsilon_\lambda \times \frac{C_1 \times \lambda^{-5}}{\pi \left[e^{\frac{C_2}{\lambda T}} - 1 \right]} \tag{14.3}$$

Here, $R_{\lambda,T}$ = Spectral radiance of nonblack body at wavelength λ and temperature T (in $Wm^{-2}\mu m^{-1}sr^{-1}$); $B_{\lambda,T}$ = Spectral radiance of black body at wavelength λ and temperature T (in $Wm^{-2}\mu m^{-1}sr^{-1}$) [Planck's radiation law]; λ = Wavelength (μm); T = Temperature (K); ε_λ = emissivity of the body at wavelength λ; C_1 and C_2 are radiation constants.

The surface temperature of objects with a Lambertian surface with known emissivity can be determined as shown in Eq. (14.4).

$$T = \frac{C_2}{\lambda \ln \left(\frac{\varepsilon_\lambda C_1}{\pi \lambda^5 R_{\lambda,T}} + 1 \right)} \tag{14.4}$$

6. Practical example

This section of the chapter provides a case study to understand the effect of increasing urbanization on the land surface temperature. Further, it deals with the estimation of UHI index and concluded with the suggestion of mitigation measures for minimizing the discomfort of the residents. The following subsection provides detailed information about the study area, method used, and observed results.

6.1 Introduction and study area

Kolkata Metropolitan Area (KMA), also termed as Greater Kolkata, was chosen for the analysis as shown in Fig. 14.2. A buffer of 10 km was also considered around the boundary to understand UHI's phenomenon over the metropolitan. The city of Kolkata holds a significant position in Indian history as it was the first capital of British India and is one of the oldest metropolitan cities in India. It serves as a capital city for the Indian state of West Bengal and is located on the bank of river Hooghly. The metropolitan shares its boundary with the Indian state of Assam and Sikkim, along with an international boundary with Bangladesh. The metropolitan serves as a domineering center for Indian art, literature and is home to several architecture heritages. Earlier most of the metropolitan region was a wetland but as a result of increased movement of people and rising urbanization, it was converted into urban settlements. Later in August 2002, the undeveloped and the remaining part of wetlands were designated as Ramsar site, thus providing it with an environmental value.

The metropolitan is spread across an area of 1886.67 km^2 and has an elevation of 1.5–9 m above MSL (mean sea level). As per Köppen climate classification, it has a tropical wet and dry climate. The mean annual temperature and rainfall over the city estimate to 26.8°C and 1850 mm, respectively.

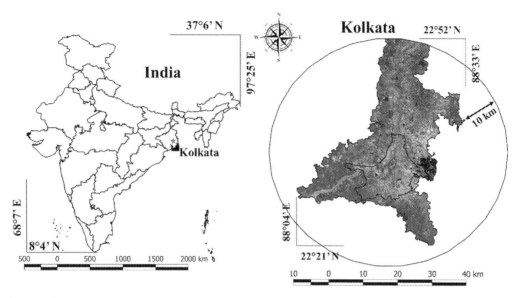

FIGURE 14.2

Study area depicting KMA and its location in India.

The region experiences four seasons—summer (March to June), monsoon (June to September), post-monsoon autumn transition (September to November), and winter (December to February). The minimum winter temperatures range from 9 to 11°C, while the maximum summer temperature often exceeds >40°C. The population curve of the metropolitan is as shown in Fig. 14.3.

The metropolitan is home for several esteemed historical, cultural, and academic institutions of great national importance. It has many public and private sector industrial units including steel, minerals, heavy engineering, mining, electronics, textile, tobacco, food processing, and jute.

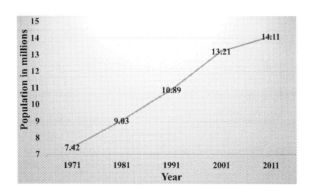

FIGURE 14.3

Demographic information of Kolkata Metropolitan Area.

The region also houses the headquarters of various companies such as ITC Limited, Coal India Limited, Exide Industries, Britannia, etc. The city is connected via a good transportation system (road, rail, and air) with other parts of India as well as internationally. All this has contributed to the large-scale migration that has led to the development of the city with enormous landscape changes. The infrastructure of the region is highly diverse where few parts of the city have congested growth, old architecture, overpopulated slums, heavily crowded markets places, ramshackle buildings and narrow alleyway. In contrast, the other has a completely planned architecture with ample open and vegetated space. As a result of enormous growth and changes in urban pattern and structure of the metropolitan, numerous problems are being faced by the residents including a rise in pollution levels, increased level of discomfort, heat stress, and rise in the level of RSPM (respirable suspended particulate matter) that has led to increased cases of people with pulmonary related diseases. The city is facing various environmental problems that have affected the microclimate of the region in terms of surface temperature that has further led to increased intensity and days of UHI.

6.1.1 Method used

A five-step process as shown in Fig. 14.4 was involved in the research work to fulfill the main objective. It includes: (1) Data acquisition and preprocessing, (2) Land use analysis, (3) Quantification of emissivity and Land Surface Temperature, 4) Estimation of Normalized Urban Heat Island Index (NUHII), (5) Derivation of relationship between LU and LST

- Data acquisition and preprocessing: Primary and secondary data used for the analysis include Landsat series (5 = thematic mapper and 8 = operational land imager/thermal infrared), city development plan, survey of India toposheets (1:50,000 scale), ground truth/collected data, data obtained from Google Earth pro and Bhuvan. CDP was georegistered using GCPs (ground control points) obtained from Google Earth and ground collected data. Toposheets, CDP, and maps from Bhuvan were used to delineate the boundary of Kolkata Metropolitan Area (KMA). All the remote sensing data were then corrected for any geometric errors and was resampled with the help of ancillary data. All the required bands were then cropped pertaining to the study area.
- Land use analysis: Land use analysis was performed using a supervised classification technique and was estimated using four steps. At first, False Color Composite (FCC) was generated, which involves assigning blue color to green band, green color to red band, and red color to near-infrared (NIR) band. FCC is useful as it can help in easy identification of certain features due to the presence of heterogeneity among various classes in urban areas. In the second step, representative training polygons for each class were digitized taking into account the heterogeneity and interclass variations using FCC. These polygons were then converted into signature by using mean and covariance matrix (obtained from overlapping polygons and FCC). In the third step, classification was performed using Gaussian maximum likelihood classifier that takes into account the probability density function for assigning the class to each pixel. Four classes, namely, urban, vegetation, water, and others, were considered for this analysis. Mathematically the algorithm can be defined as shown in Eq. (14.5).

$$X \, \varepsilon \, Cj, \text{ if } p(Cj / X) = \max[p(C1 / X), \; p(C2 / X), ..., p(Cm / X)] \qquad (14.5)$$

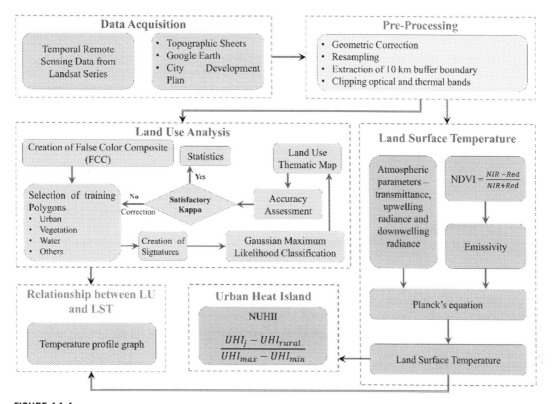

FIGURE 14.4

Method.

Here, p(Cj/X) denotes the conditional probability of pixel X being a member of the class; max [p(C1/X), p(C2/X), …, p(Cm/X)] is a function that returns the largest probability among four categories.

The last step of land use analysis was accuracy assessment which was performed by comparing the classified map obtained from GMLC algorithm and validation map obtained from Google Earth and ground truth data for 2019. For historical years, the classified map was created using 70% of the signatures and validation map was created from the remaining ones. These maps, when compared to each other, generated a confusion matrix that was further used to estimate overall accuracy and kappa coefficient (measures of accuracy).

- Quantification of emissivity and LST: Emissivity was estimated using NDVI threshold method. This method considers mixed pixels of soil and vegetation and assigns values to them based on the proportion of vegetation. A thorough literature review was conducted to obtain the emissivity values of pure water, soil, and vegetation class ($\varepsilon_{water} = 0.9910$, $\varepsilon_S = 0.9668$, $\varepsilon_V = 0.9863$). The formulas used for estimation of emissivity are as shown in Eqs. (14.6)-(14.8).

$$\varepsilon_{SV} = \varepsilon_V P_V + \varepsilon_S (1 - P_V) + C \tag{14.6}$$

Here,

$\varepsilon_{SV} \rightarrow$ emissivity of soil + vegetation

$\varepsilon_V \rightarrow$ emissivity of vegetation

$\varepsilon_S \rightarrow$ emissivity of soil

$$P_V = \left(\frac{NDVI_i - NDVI_S}{NDVI_V - NDVI_S}\right)^2 \tag{14.7}$$

Here,

$P_V \rightarrow$ proportion of vegetation

$NDVI_i \rightarrow$ Normalized Difference Vegetation Index of the pixel under consideration

$NDVI_S \rightarrow$ NDVI of pure soil

$NDVI_V \rightarrow$ NDVI of pure vegetation

$$C = (1 - \varepsilon_S)\varepsilon_V F(1 - P_V) \tag{14.8}$$

Here,

$C \rightarrow$ constant defining surface characteristics

$F \rightarrow$ geometrical factor (depends on surface geometry, usually considered 0.55)

Postestimation of emissivity, LST was quantified using Radiative Transfer Equation (RTE) that takes surface (emissivity) and atmospheric parameters (atmospheric transmittance, upwelling radiance, and downwelling radiance) into account. A simplified RTE can be expressed as shown in Eq. (14.9).

$$B_i(T_i) = \tau_i \left[\varepsilon_i B_i(T_s) + (1 - \varepsilon_i)I_i^{\downarrow}\right] + I_i^{\uparrow} \tag{14.9}$$

Here,

$B_i(T_i) \rightarrow$ top-of-atmosphere radiance received at the sensor for channel i having T_i at-satellite brightness temperature; it can be obtained by using gain and offset value

$\tau_i \rightarrow$ atmospheric transmittance for channel i

$\varepsilon_i \rightarrow$ emissivity for channel i

$I_i^{\downarrow} \rightarrow$ downwelling radiance

$I_i^{\uparrow} \rightarrow$ upwelling radiance

Planck's equation can be further expressed as shown in Eq. (14.10).

$$B_i(T_s) = \frac{2hc^2}{\lambda_i^5 \times \left(e^{\frac{hc}{\lambda_i kT_s}} - 1\right)} \tag{14.10}$$

Here,

$h \rightarrow$ Planck's constant $= 6.626 \times 10^{-34}$ J s

$c \rightarrow$ speed of light $= 2.98 \times 10^8$ m/s

$\lambda_i \rightarrow$ effective wavelength for channel i

$k \rightarrow$ Boltzmann constant $= 1.3806 \times 10^{-23}$ J/K

$T_s \rightarrow$ Land Surface Temperature

Eqs. (14.9) and (14.10) were then rearranged to get Eq. (14.11) which was utilized for estimating LST:

$$T_s = \cfrac{C_1}{\lambda_i \times \ln\left(\cfrac{C_2}{\lambda_i^5\left(\cfrac{B_i(T_i)-I_i^\uparrow-\tau_i(1-\varepsilon_i)I_i^\downarrow}{\tau_i\varepsilon_i}\right)}\right)} \tag{14.11}$$

Here,

$C_1 \rightarrow 14{,}387.7$ μm K.

$C_2 \rightarrow 1.19104 \times 10^8$ W μm^4 m^{-2} sr^{-1}

Atmospheric parameters including transmittance, upwelling, and downwelling radiance were estimated by using an online calculator as provided by NASA (https://atmcorr.gsfc.nasa.gov/). The calculator considers geographic coordinates; information about the type of sensor; year, month, date, and time of image captured and surface meteorological parameters (temperature, the altitude of mounted sensor, pressure, and relative humidity). These parameters along with emissivity values were provided in Eq. (14.11) to obtain LST. Further, interclass variability was assessed using the Coefficient of Variation (CoV) as shown in Eq. (14.12). CoV is a statistical parameter that defines how distributed the surface temperature is within the same land use class.

$$\text{CoV} = \frac{\sigma}{\mu} \times 100 \tag{14.12}$$

Here, CoV = Coefficient of Variation (%), σ = Standard deviation, μ = mean.

- Estimation of Normalized Urban Heat Island Index (NUHII): NUHII is an index that can define the intensity of heat islands across the area of interest. This index was evaluated by estimating LST for only urban area (extracted using land use classification map and LST map obtained in previous subsections) for 2019. LST for few areas with low-density urban and very small urban pockets in the study area's buffer region was averaged out to get the LST of rural area. NUHII was then estimated using 13.

$$\text{NUHII} = \frac{(\text{LST}_i - \text{LST}_{\text{Rural}})}{(\text{LST}_{\text{max}} - \text{LST}_{\text{min}})} \tag{14.13}$$

- Derivation of relationship between LU and LST: This was performed by overlaying land use maps and LST maps on each other. A transact "A-B" was then considered over LU map such that it covered all the classes. LST values corresponding to this transact were considered to create a temperature profile graph. This graph represented the LST values for each LU class over the transact, and variations were estimated.

6.1.2 Results and discussion

- Land use analysis: Temporal analysis was performed over the KMA region with 10 km buffer for 2000, 2004, 2009, 2014, and 2019. Figs. 14.5 and 14.6 depict the land use map and percentage coverage of each land use class over the study region. A three-fold rise in urban class was observed across the study area with an infill type of development in the core of the metropolitan and development or swelling of urban pockets in the buffer especially in the North direction. It was observed that the alterations were at the cost of vegetation and others category. Over the years, vegetation and others category have reduced drastically by 18% and 13.82%. However, the water classes have increased slightly due to the complete utilization of available landscape that is dedicated to the Eastern wetlands (Ramsar site).

- Land Surface Temperature: Land Surface Temperature for the metropolitan with 10 km buffer was quantified, as shown in Fig. 14.7. It was observed that the mean LST of the region has increased from 19.15 to 29.74°C. The minimum and maximum surface temperature of the study area has also experienced a significant rise. Post this, a classwise analysis was performed wherein each land use class was extracted, and LST corresponding to them was calculated. Fig. 14.8 illustrates the minimum, maximum, and mean values of surface temperature and estimated CoV for understanding variation due to each land use class and within each of the class. It was observed that the highest surface temperature corresponds to urban class, followed by others and vegetation category. Water class including ponds, lakes, wetlands, aquaculture, and river

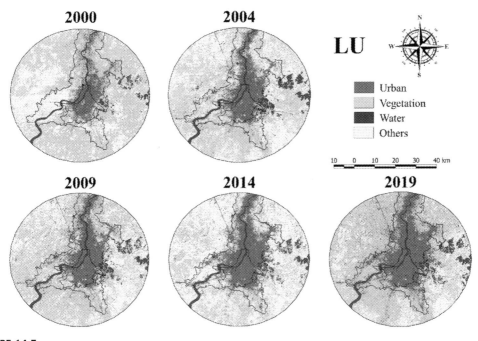

FIGURE 14.5

Land use maps for KMA with 10 km buffer.

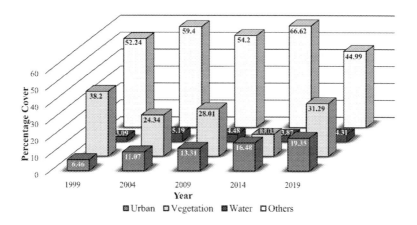

FIGURE 14.6

Classwise statistical analysis of LST from the study area.

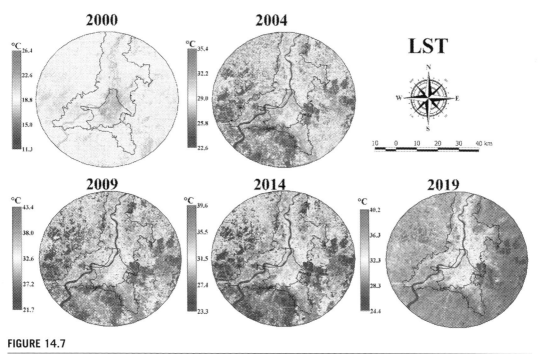

FIGURE 14.7

Temporal land surface temperature maps for KMA with 10 km Buffer.

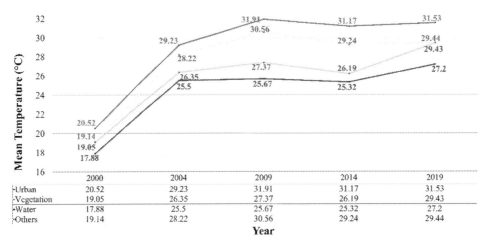

Year	2000	2004	2009	2014	2019
Urban	20.52	29.23	31.91	31.17	31.53
Vegetation	19.05	26.35	27.37	26.19	29.43
Water	17.88	25.5	25.67	25.32	27.2
Others	19.14	28.22	30.56	29.24	29.44

FIGURE 14.8

Classwise statistical analysis of LST from the study area.

corresponded to minimum surface temperature. It was visible from the results that each land use class has experienced a rise in minimum, maximum, and mean surface temperature. Rise in LST for urban class can be explained with the changes in the land use where there has been a significant rise observed in urban area, and these areas have high heat storage capacity. Rise in LST of vegetation and other class can be explained by the reduction in density of vegetation and breathing spaces. The rise in LST of water bodies can be inferred to the increased area of wetlands because these have higher surface temperature than other deeper water bodies.

• Normalized Urban Heat Island Index (NUHII): NUHII obtained was then reclassified into six classes wherein first class represented negative heat islands and rest of them with the increasing class value corresponded to increased positive UHI. The reclassified NUHII for the study area is shown in Fig. 14.9 and it was found that most of the anthropogenic constructions exhibit positive UHIs. The highest values were observed in the core region and few urban pockets toward the western part due to increased developments. More than half of the urban area has NUHII value of 0.1–0.3 that affects more than 70% of the residents. One-tenth of the study region was observed to experience very high positive heat islands. Approximately 80% of the core part of metropolitan was observed to have a positive UHI that can be inferred to the domination of urban surface over any other class. Percentage area cover under each class is as shown in Table 14.3.

• Derivation of relationship between LU and LST: The LU and LST maps obtained in the study for 2019 were examined to comprehend surface temperatures corresponding to each LU class. A transact A-B was considered across LU map, and temperature profile graph was created as illustrated in Fig. 14.10. It was observed that high value or the crest signifies the presence of urban or others category while moderate/low values or dips correspond to the presence of vegetation and water bodies, respectively. It can be inferred that presence of vegetation and water bodies in the region can help in regulating the microclimate of the region, while construction of impervious surfaces or leaving surface bare can lead to a rise in the surface temperatures.

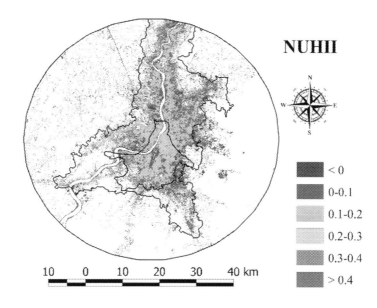

NUHII

<0

0-0.1

0.1-0.2

0.2-0.3

0.3-0.4

> 0.4

10   0   10   20   30   40 km

FIGURE 14.9

NUHII for KMA region with 10 km buffer for 2019.

Table 14.3 UHI type and percentage cover.

Category	Range	UHI type	Percentage coverage
1	<0	Negative	19.18
2	0–0.1	Weak	39.45
3	0.1–0.2	Low	30.78
4	0.2–0.3	Moderate	8.55
5	0.3–0.4	High	1.64
6	>0.4	Extreme	0.40

7. Mitigation measures

There are several criteria at the building level, neighborhood level, community level, building design level, and meso-town level that can help in reducing the overall UHI effect by reducing the surface temperatures. Few of them includes understanding the ratio of building height to width of the street, the orientation of the building, reflectivity of the surface, conductivity of materials, and the presence of urban cooling spaces. Some necessary mitigation measures that can be considered for reducing the overall LST and UHI in the city are as follows:

- Shading: Providing provision of shading on building entries, streets, and public ventures with the help of artificial structures or greenery.

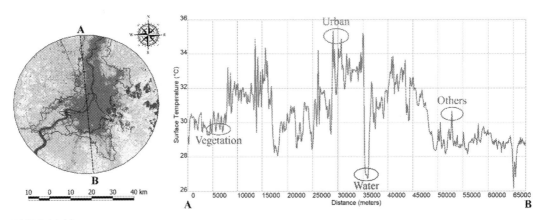

FIGURE 14.10

Temperature profile graph for KMA considering 10 km buffer.

- Mini forest: Dedicating a small area for vegetation and planting native species of trees in every locality.
- Development of gardens: Considering that the free space available is small, then it can be converted into parks or community gardens.
- Water-sensitive urban design: Developing ponds, pools, and fountains in every locality or installation of hybrid systems such as wind towers and sprinklers. Another advantage associated with this measure is that it improves the aesthetics and beauty of the locality.
- Building design and planning: Introduction of cool roofs and green roof can reduce the overall heat storage. Avoiding dark color paints and using high reflectivity materials for building exteriors can be implemented as a part of the design. Another design intervention can be construction of vertical gardens on the external surface of building walls.
- Road infrastructure: Constructing road with cooler material instead of asphalt or painting roads with white color can increase the reflectivity and reduce the overall heat storage capacity.
- Creation of pollution-free zones: Few areas and the city's main markets can have no vehicle policy, i.e., a complete ban on vehicles throughout the day or for a few hours.
- Green power generation: Government can introduce some incentives for green power generation at the individual level or can even set up a few power generation plants that use a cleaner source of energy.
- Behavior change: Outreach program and other strategies can be created to make people environmentally educated. These programs can be associated with
  - ➢ Reduction in the usage of private cars along with promoting carpooling and public transport
  - ➢ Teaching residents to avoid misuse of electricity/power and other available resources
  - ➢ Installation of a cleaner source of energy at individual, community, or city level

8. Conclusion

This chapter provided insight into how unplanned and rapid urbanization can affect a region's surface temperature. The study sets out to understand how LST leads to the development of UHI and further affects the residents' health and welfare. The research also provided a practical example of how the study of UHI can be performed supplemented with an estimation of LST and development of LU. The key purpose of this study was to provide the effects of UHI and suggest mitigation measures for reducing them. One of the most important take away points from this chapter is that a rise in impervious surfaces can significantly alter the microclimate of a region in terms of LST that further instigates or increases the intensity and frequency of positive UHIs. Altogether, unplanned and unregulated urbanization with lesser vegetation, open spaces, and water bodies can lead to a rise in warming throughout the urban area and increases heat-related issues among the residents. Therefore, it can be concluded that plantation of dense vegetation rather than fragmented ones and the presence of water bodies throughout the urban area can solve the problem of high surface temperature and ill-effects of UHIs. Open spaces in the city serve as regions where high pollutants and other dust particles can be displaced properly and avoid them being blocked within the localities in a city, thus creating breathing spaces. The study was complemented by practical example performed for KMA with 10 km buffer, and it was observed that the study area has experienced tremendous growth in terms of impervious surface on the cost of vegetation and others category that has led to an average rise of 10.6°C in surface temperature.

Further, the relationship between LU and LST was derived, and it was inferred that urban areas and barren grounds contribute to high, vegetation corresponds to moderate, and water bodies corresponds to low surface temperatures. The final part of this chapter deals with the suggestion of a few mitigation measures to tackle the rising issue of UHI. The information provided in this chapter and other research findings can act as background data and suggestions to the urban planners, stakeholders, and decision-makers to reformulate the older and develop new policies for achieving sustenance.

References

AATSR and SLSTR, 2018. LST Portal: Welcome to the AATSR/SLSTR Land Surface Temperature Portal. Retrieved from: http://lst.nilu.no/ (Accessed 10 March 2018).

Aggarwal, S.P., Garg, V., Gupta, P.K., Nikam, B.R., Thakur, P.K., 2012. Climate and Lulc change scenarios to study its impact on hydrological regime. In: ISPRS - International Archives of the Photogrammetry, Remote Sensing and Spatial Information Sciences, vol. 34, pp. 147–152.

Anderson, M.C., Norman, J.M., Kustas, W.P., Houborg, R., Starks, P.J., Agam, N., 2008. A thermal-based remote sensing technique for routine mapping of land-surface carbon, water and energy fluxes from field to regional scales. Remote Sens. Environ. 112, 4227–4241.

Bento, V.A., DaCamara, C.C., Trigo, I.F., Martins, J.P.A., Duguay-Tetzlaff, A., 2017. Improving land surface temperature retrievals over mountainous regions. Remote Sens. 9 (1), 38–50.

Bharath, S., Rajan, K.S., Ramachandra, T.V., 2013. Land surface temperature responses to land use land cover dynamics. Geoinfor. Geostat. 1 (4), 1–10.

Bolin, B., Doos, B.R., Jaeger, J., Warrick, R.A. (Eds.), 1986. The Greenhouse Effect, Climatic Change, and Ecosystems, Scope 29. Wiley, Chichester, West Sussex.

Chandra, S., Sharma, D., Dubey, S.K., 2018. Linkage of urban expansion and land surface temperature using geospatial techniques for Jaipur City, India. Arabian J. Geosci. 11 (2), 1−12.

Chen, M., Zhang, H., Liu, W., Zhang, W., 2014. The global pattern of urbanization and economic growth: evidence from the last three decades. PLoS One 9 (8), 1−15.

Daramola, M.T., Eresanya, E.O., Ishola, K.A., 2018. Assessment of the thermal response of variations in land surface around an urban area. Model. Earth Syst. Environ. 4 (2), 535−553.

Dash, P., Göttsche, F.M., Olesen, F.S., Fischer, H., 2002. Land surface temperature and emissivity estimation from passive sensor data: theory and practice-current trends. Int. J. Remote Sens. 23 (13), 2563−2594.

Davis, M.B., 1989. Address of the past president: Toronto, Canada, August 1989: insights from paleoecology on global change. Bull. Ecol. Soc. Am. 70 (4), 222−228.

EPA, 2019. Heat Island Impacts. Retrieved from: https://www.epa.gov/heat-islands/heat-island-impacts (Accessed 11 January 2021).

Founda, D., Santamouris, M., 2017. Synergies between urban heat island and heat waves in Athens (Greece), during an extremely hot summer (2012). Sci. Rep. 7 (1), 1−11 (Article number: 10973).

Gedzelman, S.D., Austin, S., Cermak, R., Stefano, N., Partridge, S., Quesenberry, S., Robinson, D.A., 2003. Mesoscale aspects of the urban heat island around New York City. Theor. Appl. Climatol. 75 (1−2), 29−42.

Grover, A., Singh, R., 2015. Analysis of urban heat island (UHI) in relation to normalized difference vegetation index (NDVI): a comparative study of Delhi and Mumbai. Environments 2 (2), 125−138.

Guha, S., Govil, H., Gill, N., Dey, A., 2020. A long-term seasonal analysis on the relationship between LST and NDBI using Landsat data. Quat. Res. (Pre-proof).

Jia, Y.Y., Tang, B., Zhang, X., Li, Z.L., July 23−27, 2007. Estimation of Land Surface Temperature and Emissivity from AMSR-E Data. Paper Presented at the Conference of Geoscience and Remote Sensing Symposium (IGARSS). Barcelona, Spain. Retrieved from: https://ieeexplore.ieee.org/stamp/stamp.jsp?tp=&arnumber=4423183.

Jordon, S.D., 2007. Global climate change triggered by global warming. Skeptical Inq. 31 (3), 32−39.

Kandlikar, M., Sagar, A., 1999. Climate change research and analysis in India: an integrated assessment of a South-North divide. Global Environ. Change 9 (2), 119−138.

Karoly, D.J., Braganza, K., Stott, P.A., Arblaster, J.M., Meehl, G.A., Broccoli, A.J., Dixon, K.W., 2003. Detection of a human influence on North American climate. Science 302 (5648), 1200−1203.

Keeling, C.D., 1997. Climate change and carbon dioxide: an introduction. Proc. Natl. Acad. Sci. USA 94 (16), 8273−8274.

Khandelwal, S., Goyal, R., Kaul, N., Mathew, A., 2018. Assessment of land surface temperature variation due to change in elevation of area surrounding Jaipur, India. Egypt. J. Remote Sens. Space Sci. 21 (1), 87−94.

Kimuku, C.W., Ngigi, M.M., 2017. Study of Urban heat island trends to aid in urban planning in Nakuru County-Kenya. J. Geogr. Inf. Syst. 9, 309−325.

Lal, D.S., 2017. Climatology (Revised Edition: 2017). Allahabad: Sharda Pustak Bhawan.

Li, Z.L., Becker, F., 1993. Feasibility of land surface temperature and emissivity determination from AVHRR data. Remote Sens. Environ. 43 (1), 67−85.

Li, Z.-L., Tang, B.-H., Wu, H., Ren, H., Yan, G., Wan, Z., et al., 2013. Satellite-derived land surface temperature: current status and perspectives. Remote Sens. Environ. 131, 14−37.

Liang, S., Shi, P., May 20−22, 2009. Analysis of the Relationship between Urban Heat Island and Vegetation Cover through Landsat ETM+: A Case Study of Shenyang. Paper Presented at 2009 Joint Urban Remote Sensing Event. Shanghai, China.

Mallick, J., Kant, Y., Bharath, B.D., 2008. Estimation of land surface temperature over Delhi using Landsat-7 ETM+. J. Ind. Geophys. Union 12 (3), 131−140.

Mannstein, H., 1987. Remote Sensing Applications in Meteorology and Climatology: Surface Energy Budget, Surface Temperature and Thermal Inertia. Springer, Dordrecht, pp. 391−410.

Mathew, A., Khandelwal, S., Kaul, N., 2016. Spatial and temporal variations of urban heat island effect and the effect of percentage impervious surface area and elevation on land surface temperature: study of Chandigarh city, India. Sustain. Cities Soc. 26, 264−277.

Mills, G., 2008. Luke howard and the climate of London. Weather 63 (6), 153−157.

Ministry of Statistics and Programme Implementation, Government of India, 2015. Statistics Related to Climate Change - India 2015. Retrieved from: http://www.mospi.gov.in/sites/default/files/publication_reports/climateChangeStat2015.pdf.

Mojolaoluwa, T.D., Emmanuel, O.E., Kazeem, A.I., 2018. Assessment of thermal response of variation in land surface around an urban area. Model. Earth Syst. Environ. 4 (2), 535−553.

More, R., Kale, N., Kataria, G., Rane, R.A., Deshpande, S., 2015. Study of the different approaches used to estimate the urban heat island effect in India. Int. J. Adv. Multidiscip. Sci. Emerg. Res. 4 (2).

Murata, A., Sasaki, H., Hanafusa, M., Kurihara, K., 2013. Estimation of urban heat island intensity using biases in surface air temperature simulated by a nonhydrostatic regional climate model. Theor. Appl. Climatol. 112 (1−2), 351−361.

Mustafa, E.K., Co, Y., Liu, G., Kaloop, M.R., Beshr, A.A., Zarzoura, F., Sadek, M., 2020. Study for predicting land surface temperature (LST) using landsat data: a comparison of four algorithms. Adv. Civ. Eng. 2020.

Mutiibwa, D., Kilic, A., Irmak, S., 2014. The effect of land cover/land use changes on the regional climate of the USA high plains. Climate 2 (3), 153−167.

NASA, 2018. Global Climate Change − Vital Signs of the Planet. Retrieved from: https://climate.nasa.gov/scientific-consensus/ (Accessed May 15, 2018).

Nimish, G., Bharath, H.A., Lalitha, A., 2020. Exploring temperature indices by deriving relationship between land surface temperature and urban landscape. Remote Sens. Appl. 18, 100299.

Oh, J.W., Ngarambe, J., Duhirwe, P.N., Yun, G.Y., Santamouris, M., 2020. Using deep-learning to forecast the magnitude and characteristics of urban heat island in Seoul Korea. Sci. Rep. 10 (1), 1−13.

Oke, T.R., 1982. The energetic basis of the urban heat island. Q. J. R. Meteorol. Soc. 108 (455), 1−24.

Oke, T.R., Cleugh, H.A., 1987. Urban heat storage derived as energy balance residuals. Boundary-Layer Meteorol. 39 (3), 233−245.

Pal, S., Ziaul, S., 2017. Detection of land use and land cover change and land surface temperature in English Bazar urban centre. Egypt. J. Remote Sen. Space Sci. 20 (1), 125−145.

Qian, Y., Wang, N., Li, K., Wu, H., Duan, S., Liu, Y., Li, C., 2020. Retrieval of surface temperature and emissivity from ground-based time-series thermal infrared data. IEEE J. Sel. Top. Appl. Earth Obs. Remote Sens. 13, 284−292.

Raloff, J., April 29, 1989. Global Smog: Newest Greenhouse Projection. Science News, pp. 262−263. Retrieved from. https://www.sciencenews.org/author/janet-raloff?sort_by=published_at&page=76 (Accessed 22 May 2019).

Ramachandra, T.V., Aithal, B.H., Sreekantha, S., 2012. Spatial metrics based landscape structure and dynamics assessment for an emerging Indian megalopolis. Int. J. Adv. Res. Artif. Intell. 1 (1), 48−57.

Ramachandra, T.V., Bharath, H.A., Vinay, S., Kumar, U., Venugopal, K.R., Joshi, N.V., 2016. Modelling and Visualization of Urban Trajectory in 4 Cities of India. Paper Presented at IISc-ISRO STC, Bangalore, India. Retrieved from: https://www.researchgate.net/publication/289687302_Modelling_and_Visualization_of_Urban_Trajectory_in_4_cities_of_India.

Ramachandra, T.V., Setturu, B., Nimish, G., Bhargavi, R.S., 2017. Monitoring Forest Dynamics within and Buffer Regions of Protected Areas in Karnataka, India (Sahyadri Conservation Series 63, ENVIS Technical Report 117. CES, Indian Institute of Science, Bangalore 560012. Retrieved from: http://wgbis.ces.iisc.ernet.in/biodiversity/sahyadri_enews/newsletter/Issue58/article1/SCR63_ETR117_National%20Parks_Karnataka.pdf.

Roth, M., 2012. Urban heat islands. In: Fernando, H.J.S. (Ed.), Handbook of Environmental Fluid Dynamics. Taylor and Francis, London, pp. 143−162.

Running, S.W., Justice, C.O., Salomonson, V., Hall, D., Barker, J., Carneggie, D., 1994. Terrestrial remote sensing science and algorithms planned for EOS/MODIS. Int. J. Remote Sens. 15 (17), 3587−3620.

Santra, A., 2019. Land surface temperature estimation and urban heat island detection: a remote sensing perspective. In: Santra, A., Mitra, S.S. (Eds.), Environmental Information Systems: Concepts, Methodologies, Tools, and Applications. IGI Global, USA, pp. 1538−1560.

Sarif, M., Rimal, B., Stork, N.E., 2020. Assessment of changes in land use/land cover and land surface temperatures and their impact on surface urban heat island phenomena in the Kathmandu valley (1988-2018). ISPRS Int. J. Geo-Inf. 9 (12), 726.

Schmugge, T.J., Becker, F., 1991. Remote sensing observations for the monitoring of land-surface fluxes and water budgets. In: Schmugge, T.J., André, J.C. (Eds.), Land Surface Evaporation. Springer, New York, USA, pp. 337−347.

Science for Environmental Policy, 2007. How Do Changes in Ocean Temperature Affect Marine Ecosystems? Retrieved from: http://ec.europa.eu/environment/integration/research/newsalert/pdf/52na2_en.pdf (Accessed 22 May 2019).

Scott, M.J., Rosenberg, N.J., Edmonds, J.A., Cushman, R.M., Darwin, R.F., et al., 1990. Consequences of climatic change for the human environment. Clim. Res. 1, 63−79.

Sismanidis, P., Keramitsoglou, I., Bechtel, B., Kiranoudis, C.T., 2016. Improving the downscaling of diurnal land surface temperatures using the annual cycle parameters as disaggregation kernels. Remote Sens. 9 (1), 23−42.

Sobrino, J.A., Jiménez-Muñoz, J.C., Zarco-Tejada, P.J., Sepulcre-Cantó, G., de Miguel, E., 2006. Land surface temperature derived from airborne hyperspectral scanner thermal infrared data. Remote Sens. Environ. 102 (1−2), 99−115.

Stewart, I.D., 2011. A systematic review and scientific critique of methodology in modern urban heat island literature. Int. J. Climatol. 31 (2), 200−217.

Stott, P.A., Mitchell, J.F., Allen, M.R., Delworth, T.L., Gregory, J.M., Meehl, G.A., Santer, B.D., 2006. Observational constraints on past attributable warming and predictions of future global warming. J. Clim. 19 (13), 3055−3069.

Tran, D.X., Pla, F., Latorre-Carmona, P., Myint, S.W., Caetano, M., Kieu, H.V., 2017. Characterizing the relationship between land use land cover change and land surface temperature. ISPRS J. Photogrammetry Remote Sens. 124, 119−132.

UN DESA, 2018. 2018 Revision of World Urbanization Prospects. Retrieved from: https://www.un.org/development/desa/publications/2018-revision-of-world-urbanization-prospects.html (Accessed 27 September 2018).

Wang, R., Murayama, Y., 2020. Geo-simulation of Land Use/cover Scenarios and Impacts on Land Surface Temperature in Sapporo, Japan. Sustain. Cities Soc. (Pre-proof).

Wolters, D., Brandsma, T., 2012. Estimating the urban heat island in residential areas in The Netherlands using observations by weather amateurs. J. Appl. Meteorol. Climatol. 51 (4), 711−721.

Yamashita, S., 1996. Detailed structure of heat island phenomena from moving observations from electric tramcars in metropolitan Tokyo. Atmos. Environ. 30 (3), 429−435.

Youneszadeh, S., Amiri, N., Pilesjo, P., 2015. The effect of land use change on land surface temperature in The Netherlands. Int. Arch. Photogram. Remote Sens. Spatial Inf. Sci. 40 (1), 745. https://dx.doi.org/10.5194/isprsarchives-XL-1-W5-745-2015.

Yu, X., Guo, X., Wu, Z., 2014. Land surface temperature retrieval from landsat 8 TIRS-comparison between radiative transfer equation-based method, split window algorithm and single channel method. Remote Sens. 6 (10), 9829−9852.

Surface urban heat islands in 33 medium-sized cities across different climates in Chile

G. Pamela Smith, E. Pablo Sarricolea, T. Orlando Peralta and Catalina Toro
Department of Geography, University of Chile, Center for Climate and Resilience Research (CR)²,
Santiago, Chile

1. Introduction

An accelerated process of urbanization has been experienced worldwide in recent decades. Currently, Latin America is one of the most urbanized developing regions, reaching a level of 75%. In the specific case of Chile, 87.8% of the population live in cities. Constant urban growth has entailed a series of challenges that include the production of new residential infrastructures, thereby transforming the urban morphology (Santamouris et al., 2001), which in turn has an impact on the social, environmental, and climatic conditions of the city (Cuadrat et al., 2005). Cities are also responsible for more than 70% of global greenhouse gas (GHG) emissions (World Bank, 2016), with the urban construction industry accounting for 39% of GHG emissions (United Nations Environment and International Energy Agency, 2018). In addition, climate change is expected to cause an intensification of extremes, such as an increase in heatwaves that affect cities in the summer.

Urban growth is characterized by a replacement of natural and seminatural land by highly artificial land uses that—among other things—trigger the formation of a different climate, known as an urban climate, which is defined by the difference in temperature between the city and its surroundings. The difference in temperatures is chiefly due to three factors: (1) the direct production of heat by combustion, (2) the gradual release of the heat stored by urban buildings during the day, and (3) the radiation returned to the earth's surface by reflection of the atmospheric pollution layer (Moreno and Serra, 2016).

The surface urban heat island (SUHI) refers to the difference in temperatures between typically urban surfaces, such as pavements, buildings, etc., and the natural surfaces of rural areas, which include farmland, native forests, deserts, or rocky areas (Moreno and Serra, 2016). The larger the built-up area, the greater the alteration of the climatic parameters that regulate the local climate, leading to a decrease in factors such as the contribution of humidity by artificial evapotranspiration and shade provided by vegetation, which in turn increase the impact of solar radiation, warming, and the emissivity of heat during the first few hours of the night (Sarricolea and Martín-Vide, 2014). SUHIs occur both during the day and at night, but they are much more intense during the day and in the

Global Urban Heat Island Mitigation. https://doi.org/10.1016/B978-0-323-85539-6.00004-4

summer (Tamini, 2010). According to studies carried out in cities with a Mediterranean climate, the intensity of SUHIs may vary between 10 and 15°C during the day and between 5 and 10°C at night (Moreno and Serra, 2016). Remote sensing is the identification method for this type of heat island, with its representation being a thermal image that shows how the temperatures in the image vary (Moreno and Serra, 2016).

The characteristic urban climate and heat islands have effects on the population's health, thermal comfort, and energy demand for air conditioning, among other factors. According to research findings, a significant increase has been observed in hospital admissions due to thermal extremes (Moreno and Fernández, 2003), while heat-generated stress is related to an increase in energy demand for cooling between 2% and 4% for every 1°C increase in the maximum daily temperature, above a threshold between 15 and 20°C (Akbari et al., 2001). Meanwhile, according to estimates by the US Department of Energy, the United States spends close to 10 billion dollars annually to reduce the urban heat island effect (Rosenfeld et al., 1998). Moreover, the use of fans or air conditioning releases more heat and greenhouse gases into the air, which further degrades the city's air quality (Voogt, 2008).

This paper studies the average daytime and nighttime SUHI during the summer and the winter in 33 medium-sized Chilean cities. Based on the categorization of each of the cities, clusters were identified, their climatic, geographical, environmental, urban, and social behavior was classified, and explanatory factors of local SUHIs were identified. All these inputs provide a deeper insight into the city's climate behavior and make it possible to identify ways of adapting to climate variability and change, while also detecting strategies associated with factors that can increase or decrease its intensity by mitigating its effect in the summer and leveraging it in the winter.

2. Method

This paper studied urban climates in Chilean cities by integrating climate parameters with environmental and urban characteristics on a local scale, which coincides with the Urban Boundary Layer (UBL) defined by Oke (1988), thereby providing the climate categorization of the city in relation to its surroundings. All major medium-sized cities (between 100,000 and 299,999 inhabitants) were included according to the classification drawn up by the Ministry of Housing and Urban Planning and the National Institute of Statistics (2019). Meanwhile, the smaller city of Coyhaique was also included so that all regional capitals were represented. This was because studies on the urbanization process and its effects have focused on metropolises and large urban agglomerations (Bellet and Llop, 2004), despite the fact that most of the urban population (65%, UN, 2002) lives in medium-sized and small cities. Medium-sized cities. including those in Chile, are gradually mirroring the structure and functioning of large cities, showing key features of metropolization that are expressed, for example, in the emergence of environmental problems, spatial segregation, and periurbanization processes (Maturana, 2015).

The study area of each city was delimited, considering the urban area as of 2019 and its nonurban hinterland, defined as an area of influence of 25 km, in order to identify the monitoring points of the surface urban and rural heat island within this radius (See Fig. 15.1) and to calculate the average values of each variable considered in the study. The urban limit for the year 2019 was defined through the photo interpretation of Google Earth images, taking the urban area prepared by the Ministry of Housing and Urban Planning (MINVU, 2018) in 2017 as a starting point.

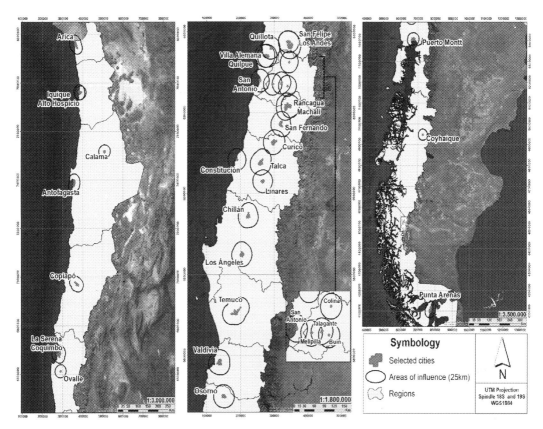

FIGURE 15.1

Chilean cities considered in the study and their areas of influence.

Compiled by author based on shapefiles from the Office for National Statistics (2017).

2.1 Calculation of the surface urban heat island (SUHI)

The average daytime and nighttime surface temperatures were obtained from MODIS satellite images available for the summer (Jan–Feb) and the winter (Jul–Aug) seasons between 2008 and 2018. They were processed using a code on Google Earth Engine (GEE).[1] The MODIS images have a spatial resolution of 1000 m, but were rescaled to a resolution of 200 m.

These images were also used to define the points in the rural and urban areas in order to calculate the SUHI intensity for each of the 33 cities.

The urban point was defined according to the area with the highest average temperature for each period, generally coinciding with the city center. The rural points were selected when they fulfilled certain conditions for their definition, which corresponded to:

---

[1]https://code.earthengine.google.com/6232cc53a24441d0601dab4199c930f3.

- Distance from water courses and bodies (including the sea for coastal cities) equivalent to the point defined in the urban area
- Same climate zone as the point defined in the urban area
- Altitude difference no greater than 300 m between the urban point and the rural point
- Conformity with the rural context surrounding the city
- Not at the bottom of a stream or wetland

The SUHI intensity was obtained in each city from the difference between temperature at urban point and temperature at rural point.

2.2 SUHI relationship with social, urban, and environmental factors

Existing climatic, social, urban, and environmental information was collected for each city, or each indicator defined in Table 15.1 was calculated. The average values for each city considered the predefined urban limit.

To evaluate the relationship between the SUHI and the characteristic variables of each city, a multiple linear regression model was constructed corresponding to a statistical method characterized by the existence of a dependent variable "Y", whose behavior is explained as a linear function of different independent variables (Aguayo and Lora, 2005). This model established the extent to which a dependent variable, in this case the SUHI, is influenced by one or more independent variables. The multiple regression equation was obtained in the SPSS Statistics 25 program using the backward method.

Table 15.1 Variables calculated for each city.

Dimension	Variable	Method description/data source	Model	Cluster
Geographical	Position (lat)	Latitude (in decimal degrees), calculated according to the central point of the city		x
	Distance to the sea (Dis_sea)	Calculation of the average Euclidean distance to the sea (in meters) of each city's urban area, according to the coastline vector	x	x
	Elevation (elev)	Average elevation of each city's urban area according to SRTM digital Elevation Data 30m, NASA/USGS, available on GEE	x	x
	Climate	The average values of the summer season (DEF) calculated by the 2020 ARCLIM project were considered. The parameters included were: **a.** Mean air temperature (T_mean) **b.** Maximum temperature (T_max) **c.** Number of hot days/T_max equal to or greater than 30°C (hot day) **d.** Mean air humidity (Humi_mean) **e.** Mean solar radiation (Rad_mean)		x

Table 15.1 Variables calculated for each city.—cont'd

Dimension	Variable	Method description/data source	Model	Cluster
Environmental	NDVI (dif_ndvi)	The difference of the average value of the NDVI between urban and rural areas was included. The normalized Difference Vegetation Index was calculated according to sentinel images available between 2016 and 2019. NDVI = (NIR-RED)/NIR + RED NIR: Band 8 Red: Band 4	x	x
	GP/hab (Green_pop)	Square meters per inhabitant, considering parks and squares (SIEDU, 2021)	x	x
	Thermal comfort (THI_max)	Calculation of environmental thermal comfort in summer based on Thom's THI index (1959), considering the average of the maximum daily temperatures of the warmest month/January (ARCLIM, 2021)		x
Social	Population (Popul)	Number of urban inhabitants for the year 2017, and the difference in inhabitants between 2002 and 2017 (Census, 2002, 2017)	x	x
	Poverty (poverty)	The multidimensional poverty indicator that integrates education, health, work, social security, living place and social networks was used. The value used corresponds to estimates from the Ministry for social development (CASEN, 2015).	x	x
Urban	Urban surface (area)	Total area of urban surface in 2017 (hectares).	x	x
	NDBI (dif_Ndbi)	Difference of the average value of the NDBI between urban and rural areas. Normalized difference built-up index, average value) calculated on sentinel images (Bands 8 and 11) on google earth engine. NDBI = (MIR − NIR)/(MIR + NIR) NIR: Band 8 MIR: Band 11	x	x

This paper considered the equation established by McGrath (1975):

$$Y = \beta_1 X_1 + \beta_2 X_2 + \beta_3 X_3 + \varepsilon$$

Where,

Y is the dependent variable;

X_1, X_2, and X_3 are the independent variables;

β1, β2, and β3 are the Beta coefficients or constant partial regression coefficients, which represent the magnitude of the change in the dependent variable resulting from transformations of the independent variables, or—in other words—the unique contribution of each independent variable (McGrath, 1975; Bryman and Cramer, 1994);

and ε is the proportion of the variance not explained by the independent variables included in the equation.

2.3 Cluster analysis

The K-Medoids technique in the ArcGIS Pro 2.7 software was chosen for the cluster analysis. K-Medoids has an advantage over other techniques as it is less sensitive to noise and the effect of outliers. The K-Medoids algorithm used was Partitioning Around Medoids (PAM), which has been applied in urban climate studies both for time (Acero et al., 2020) and typical urban features (Wang et al., 2020). Table 15.1 shows the variables used in the cluster.

3. Results

3.1 Daytime and nighttime surface urban heat island

The results of the SUHI show significant heterogeneity. The highest intensities are observed with the daytime data of the summer season, reaching an average of 3.1°C, while the lowest average value occurs at the same time in the winter, with only 0.4°C. The values of the nighttime SUHI for both stations show a smaller difference in their average values, with 2.0°C and 1.4°C, respectively, for the summer and winter seasons (Table 15.2). In general, the highest intensities are observed in cities located in the temperate domain and inland, whereas coastal cities have less intense or negative heat islands.

For each season of the year, it is possible to observe differences between cities. For example, the summer nighttime SUHI shows values ranging from 0.8 to 3.4°C. The highest intensities at this time were registered in the cities of San Felipe and Calama, the latter located at more than 2200 m above sea level. Only one negative value is observed, in the city of Copiapó, which means that the urban area has a lower temperature than its rural hinterland. Copiapó is a city located in a semidesert environment, which could explain its behavior as a cold island, which is also observed on summer days, with less intensity.

Meanwhile, the winter nighttime SUHI values are mainly between 0 and 2°C, which, in this case, although not significantly high, could be considered as favorable, as they could mitigate the low temperatures. The winter daytime SUHI shows largely negative intensities, in relation to the temperature of the rural area, with Alto Hospicio having the highest negative intensity value, showing a 6.2°C difference between the urban temperature and the rural temperature.

However, it is the summer daytime SUHI that shows the most significant differences across the country. Cities with a higher intensity tend to be clustered in the central zone of Chile, in the regions of Valparaíso, O'Higgins, and Maule, with other cities across Chile also recording high differences, with intensities above 5°C. The most noteworthy cities in this regard are Iquique (7.5°C), San Felipe (8.4°C), Los Andes (7.3°C), Quilpué (6.5°C), Rancagua (7.5°C), Curicó (5.9°C), and Los Angeles (5.9°C).

Table 15.2 Daytime and nighttime SUHI values in the summer and the winter for each selected city.

Region	city	Lat	Elevation (m)	Climatic Zones	Population 2017	Area (has)	S_D	S_N	W_D	W_N
Arica y Parinacota	Arica	18° 35	66,0	BWh	205079	2906,5	-0,6	1,5	-1,6	1,7
Tarapacá	Iquique	20° 74	40,0	BWh	189065	2171,4	7,5	2,2	0,4	1,1
	Alto Hospicio	20° 15	339,0	BWk	105884	1555,8	-4,8	2,3	-6,2	1,6
Antofagasta	Antofagasta	23° 26	60,6	BWh	354104	3636,7	-2,1	2,8	-1,3	3,4
	Calama	22° 27	2274,8	BWk	158487	2408,1	-2,1	3,1	-2,4	2,3
Atacama	Copiapó	27° 22	412,1	BWk(s)	150962	2328,9	-0,3	-1,1	2,2	2,4
	La Serena	29° 54	68,9	BSk'(s)	200640	4636,2	-5,1	2,1	-1,6	3,2
Coquimbo	Coquimbo	30° 45	68,9	BSk'(s)	214550	4565,3	2,5	3,6	0,9	-0,1
	Ovalle	36° 00	222,0	BSk(s)	87539	946,4	2,2	1,7	2,7	2,0
	San Felipe	32° 44	666,4	BSk(s)	69617	1070,8	8,4	3,2	1,2	4,2
	Los Andes	32° 57	797,6	BSk(s)	61017	1331,7	7,3	2,6	0,5	2,5
Valparaíso	Quilpué	33° 03	149,0	Csb	149596	3805,9	6,5	1,9	3,4	0,1
	Villa Alemana	33° 02	143,0	Csb	125327	2932,7	3,1	1,8	3,7	0,0
	Quillota	32° 54	248,0	Csb	78331	1581,2	5,2	2,2	2,1	1,5
	San Antonio	33° 35	4,0	Csb'	86569	2356,8	2,8	2,7	1,4	1,9
	Colina	33° 12	596,0	BWk(s)	118.018	787,4	-1,2	1,7	-0,2	2,2
Metropolitana	Buin	33° 43	480,0	Csb	82911	2963,4	5,3	2,2	0,3	1,0
	Melipilla	33° 41	175,0	Csb	84724	1002,4	5,5	1,4	2,2	1,5
	Talagante	33° 39	344,0	Csb	59209	1048,6	5,2	1,8	1,5	1,3
Libertador Gral Bdo O'higgins	Rancagua	34° 42	505,6	Csb	234183	4954,2	7,5	2,5	0,9	0,9
	Machalí	34° 10	568,0	Csb	51504	1648,5	3,7	1,3	-0,3	1,4
	San Fernando	34° 44	339,1	Csb	63712	1147,6	4,8	1,5	0,9	0,5
	Curicó	34° 58	226,6	Csb	132569	2592,0	5,9	2,2	1,3	0,8
Maule	Talca	35° 43	110,2	Csb	210916	4064,7	5,2	2,4	-0,1	1,8
	Linares	35° 50	161,1	Cfb	77762	1305,2	3,6	1,6	0,1	0,8
Ñuble	Chillán	36° 34	126,0	Csb	196056	3118,4	3,7	1,4	-0,4	0,7
Biobío	Los Ángeles	34° 03	146,3	Csb	151087	4188,1	5,9	1,2	-0,7	1,1
La Araucanía	Temuco	38° 45	114,5	Csb	308608	4449,3	2,9	2,3	0,4	1,0
Los Lagos	Osorno	40° 34	52,7	Cfb(s)	147826	2608,7	3,5	2,5	0,0	1,5
	Puerto Montt	41° 43	84,8	Cfb'	220143	3193,5	3,5	0,8	-0,7	-0,8
Los Ríos	Valdivia	39° 65	12,8	Cfb'(s)	154716	2552,3	4,3	2,8	1,5	1,2
Aysén	Coihaique	45° 59	345,1	Cfb	49968	931,1	1,6	1,7	0,0	0,5
Magallanes	Punta Arenas	53° 00	43,6	Csc	125932	2608,5	1,5	1,2	0,3	0,1

Öppen Climatic Zonaes (Sarricolea et al, 2017)		SUHI Intensity
BWh	Hot Desert climate	
BWk	Cold Desert climate	(+) (-)
BWk(s)	Cold Desert climate with dry summer	
BSk	Cold Semi-arid climate	
BSk(s)	Cold Semi-arid climate with dry summer	
BSk'(s)	BSk'(s) Cold Semi-arid climate with dry summer and oceanic influence	
Csb	Mediterranean climate (warm summer)	
Csb'	Mediterranean climate (warm summer) with oceanic influence	
Cfb	Marine West Coast climate (warm summer)	
Cfb(s)	Marine West Coast climate (warm and dry summer)	
Cfb'(s)	Marine West Coast climate (warm and dry summer) with oceanic inf	
Csc	Mediterranean climate (mild summer)	

Notes: S_D, Summer diary; S_N, Summer night; W_D, Winter diary; W_N, Winter night.

3.2 SUHI relationship with urban-environmental factors

Taking into account the previous results, which indicate that the highest intensity is observed in the summer daytime SUHI, this period of time was chosen to evaluate the relationship with geographical, environmental, urban, and social variables in order to identify how they affect its behavior on a local scale. The incorporation of the climate variables indicated in Table 15.1 was ruled out, because their relationship with the SUHI is very high, which could affect the results of the model.

With the backward method, six linear regression models were tested: Model 1 included all variables as predictors, and Model 6 included only three of them. All the models have R-squared close to 0.5 (Table 15.3).

Of the models obtained, number 3 was chosen, which includes variables of all the dimensions considered, without significantly reducing the value of the R-squared. As can be seen in Table 15.4 and from the Beta (B) values, the distance to the sea and the NDBI play a role in increasing the value of the SUHI for an average midday in the summer season. All the remaining variables (elevation, population growth, green areas per capita, and multidimensional poverty) will mean a decrease in the difference

Table 15.3 Linear regression models obtained.

Predictors	Mod1	Mod2	Mod3	Mod4	Mod5	Mod6
Dis_sea	X	x	X	x		
Elev	X	x	X	x	X	x
Popul	X	x	X	x	X	x
Poverty	X	x	X	x	X	
Area	x	x				
Dif_Ndbi	x	x	X	x	X	x
Dif_ndvi	x					
Green_pop	x	x	X			
R-squared	0.486	0.483	0.480	0.471	0.457	0.439

Compiled by author.

Table 15.4 Selection of variables to calculate the value of SUHI intensity.

	B	Dev. error	T	Sig.	Correlation coefficient
(Constant)	5.476	4.087	1.340	0.192	
Dis_sea	0.032	0.030	1.068	0.295	0.255
Elev	−0.003	0.002	−1.794	0.084	−0.126
Popul	−0.001	0.0.01	−1.53	0.138	−0.481
Poverty	−0.146	0.110	−1.33	0.196	−0.310
Dif_Ndbi	3.267	3.829	0.853	0.401	0.559
Green/pop	−0.130	0.198	−0.657	0.517	−0.053

Compiled by author.

between the urban and the rural surface temperature. This means, for example, that a difference of 1 between the value of the urban and the rural NDBI accounts for a 3.267°C increase in the SUHI intensity, while a 1 m² increase in green areas per capita accounts for a 0.13°C decrease.

3.3 City cluster analysis

According to the climatic, geographical, environmental, urban, and social behavior of the cities, these are grouped into eight clusters, two of which, number 3 and number 5, display peculiarities. As can be seen in Fig. 15.2, cluster number 3 has a peculiar behavior in the variables of elevation and relative air humidity, while cluster number 5 has a peculiar behavior in the summer nighttime intensity of the surface urban heat surface.

In general, the cities in each of the clusters have similarities with regard to their location, i.e., located in similar climate domains and, on the whole, inland or on the coast. Some cities such as Osorno stand out, which is part of cluster number 1 together with three coastal cities, Puerto Montt, Coyhaique, and Punta Arenas. Cluster number 8 has the highest number of cities (eight in total) and the greatest diversity, with six inland cities and two coastal cities, located between regions IV and X. Cluster number 7 includes seven cities, all of them located in the central valleys of the Mediterranean area. Meanwhile, cluster number 4 includes cities that are also located inland, but they are smaller in area and number of inhabitants. Finally, in cluster number 2 there are only two cities, San Felipe and Los Andes, both of which are neighbors located north of the city of Santiago in the piedmont of the Valparaíso region (Fig. 15.3).

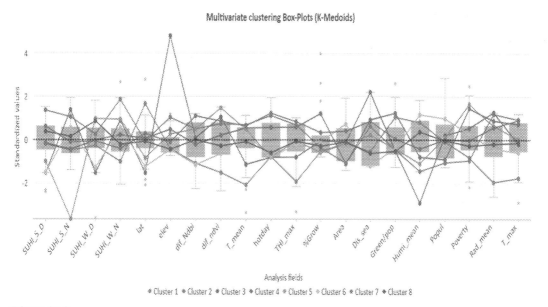

FIGURE 15.2

Multivariate clustering diagram of the selected cities.

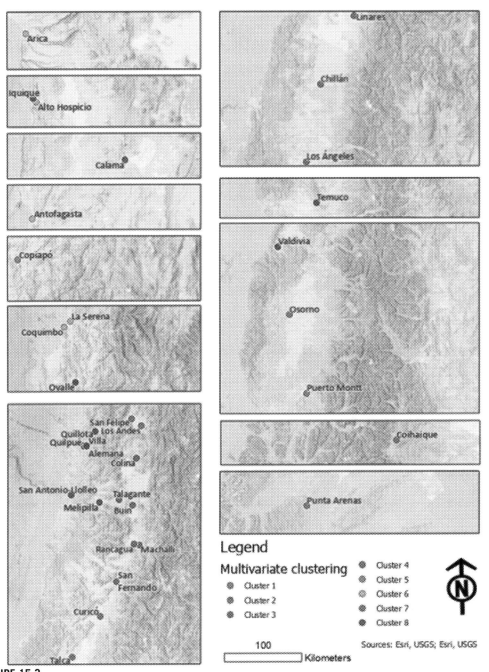

FIGURE 15.3

Geographical location of the multivariate clustering of the selected cities.

Compiled by author.

4. Final considerations

Although the existence of a daytime and nighttime summer SUHI can be seen, differences in intensity are recognized, explained in principle by the latitude and distance from the coast of the cities.

It is clear that the existence and intensity of an SUHI is explained by geographical factors, just as the relationship with other environmental and urban factors is apparent. Building density, represented by the NDBI, plays an important role in increasing the intensity of the heat island, as does the city's green area surface in decreasing it. In turn, and as can be seen in the cluster results, the city's population density and size are also determining factors in the form and intensity of the SUHI.

The findings above provide information that could be used for conducting studies and preparing plans to mitigate this phenomenon according to the different dimensions and factors that affect each city, considering annual and daily differences. Likewise, there is a focus on factors that may be showing intraurban differences and generating differential impacts between different neighbourhoods, which may require access to cooling appliances to mitigate daytime or nighttime heat in the city, with a view to improving well-being and quality of life.

Acknowledgments

This research had the support of National Research and Development Agency (ANID) of Chile through its FONDECYT Project N° 11180990.

References

Acero, J.A., Koh, E.J., Pignatta, G., Norford, L.K., 2020. Clustering weather types for urban outdoor thermal comfort evaluation in a tropical area. Theor. Appl. Climatol. 139 (1), 659−675.

Aguayo, M., Lora, E., 2005. Como hacer una regresión logística binaria "paso a paso" (II): Análisis multivariante. Fundación Andaluza Beturia Para La Investigación En Salud, pp. 1−35. https://www.scribd.com/document/110941732/Como-Hacer-Un-Regresion-Logistica-Paso-a-Paso.

Akbari, H., Pomerantz, M., Taha, H., 2001. Cool surfaces and shade trees to reduce energy use and improve air quality in urban areas. Sol. Energy 70 (3), 295−310.

ARCLIM, 2021. Amenaza Climática: Promedio de la temperatura máxima diaria enero. Atlas de Riesgos Climáticos. https://arclim.mma.gob.cl/amenazas.

Bellet, C., Llop Torné, J.M., 2004. Miradas a otros espacios urbanos: las ciudades intermedias. Scr. Nova Rev. Electrón. Geogr. Ciencias Soc. 8 (165), 1−28.

Bryman, A., Cramer, D., 1994. Quantitative Data Analysis for Social Scientists. Routledge, New York: NY.

Cuadrat, J., Vicente-Serrano, S., Saz, M., 2005. Los efectos de la urbanización en el clima de Zaragoza (España): la isla de calor y sus factores condicionantes. Boletín de la A.G.E. N°40, pp. 311−327.

Instituto Nacional de Estadísticas, 2017. Síntesis de Resultados del Censo 2017. https://www.censo2017.cl/descargas/home/sintesis-de-resultados-censo2017.pdf.

Maturana, F., 2015. ¿Ciudad media o ciudad intermedia? Evolución conceptual y estudio en Chile. In: Maturana, E.F., Rojas, R. (Eds.), Ciudades intermedias en Chile: Territorios olvidados. RIL Editores, Santiago, Chile, pp. 21−42.

Moreno, C. y, Serra, J.A., 2016. El estudio de la isla de calor urbana en el ámbito mediterráneo: una revisión bibliográfica. Rev. Biblio XXI (1), 179, 3W.

Moreno Jiménez, A., Fernández García, F., 2003. El confort climático en los entornos residenciales de las capas altas, medias y bajas de la Comunidad de Madrid: otra forma de desigualdad socioespacial. La distribución espacial de la renta en la Comunidad de Madrid. Análisis y aplicaciones. Instituto de Estadística, Consejería de Economía e Innovación Tecnológica, Madrid, pp. 153–175.

Oke, T.R., 1988. Boundary Layer Climates. Routledge.

Rosenfeld, A.H., Akbari, H., Romm, J.J., Pomerantz, M., 1998. Cool communities: strategies for heat island mitigation and smog reduction. Energy Build. 28 (1), 51–62.

Santamouris, M., Papanikolaou, N., Livada, I., Koronakis, I., Georgakis, C., Argiriou, A., Assimakopoulos, D., 2001. On the impact of urban climate on the energy consumption of buildings. Pergamon 70 (3), 201–2016.

Sarricolea Espinoza, P., Martín-Vide, J., 2014. El estudio de la Isla de Calor Urbana de Superficie del Área Metropolitana de Santiago de Chile con imágenes Terra-MODIS y Análisis de Componentes Principales. Rev. Geogr. Norte Gd. 57, 123–141.

Tamini, I., 2010. Estrategias para reducción del efecto isla de calor en los espacios urbanos. Estudio aplicado al caso de Madrid. In: Sustainable Building Conference. Madrid, España.

Thom, E.C., 1959. The discomfort index. Weatherwise 12, 57–60.

United Nations Environment and International Energy Agency, 2018. Global Status Report 2018. Global Aliance for Buildings and Construction. https://wedocs.unep.org/bitstream/handle/20.500.11822/27140/Global_Status_2018.pdf?sequence=1&isAllowed=y.

Voogt, J., 2008. Islas de Calor Urbana: Ciudades más calientes. ActionBioscience.org. Obtenido en. http://www.actionbioscience.org/esp/ambiente/voogt.html.

Wang, C., Wang, Z.H., Li, Q., 2020. Emergence of urban clustering among US cities under environmental stressors. Sustain. Cities Soc. 63, 102481.

World Bank, 2016. Climate Hotspots: World Bank Climate Action Plan Supports Cities, Urban Poor. www.worldbank.org/en/news/feature/2016/05/13/climate-hotspots-world-bank-climate-action-plan-supports-cities-urban-poor#:%7E:text=%E2%80%9CCities%20are%20responsible%20for%20more,cities%20for%20growing%20urban%20populations.%E2%80%9D.

Investigating the intra-urban urban heat island effect for two subtropical mega-urban regions in China by adopting local climate zone

16

Meng Cai[1], Ran Wang[2], Chao Ren[3] and Edward Ng[1]

[1]*School of Architecture, The Chinese University of Hong Kong, Hong Kong, PR China;* [2]*College of Economic and Social Development, Nankai University, Tianjin, PR China;* [3]*Division of Landscape Architecture, Department of Architecture, Faculty of Architecture, The University of Hong Kong, Pokfulam, Hong Kong, PR China*

1. Introduction

The phenomenon that urban temperature is higher than that of its surrounding rural areas, which is called Urban Heat Island (UHI), has been observed and documented worldwide (Clinton and Gong, 2013; Heinl et al., 2015; McCarthy et al., 2010; Oke, 1973; Peng et al., 2011; Santamouris et al., 2015; Zhao et al., 2014). An intensifying UHI effect, which is closely related to surface changes, is seen as an inevitable problem (Mallick et al., 2008). Given the significant urbanization around the world, the surface temperature is expected to keep rising, and an increasing proportion of the worldwide population will be exposed to the rising temperature in urban areas (Allen et al., 2014). Generally, the UHI comprises both air temperature UHI and surface UHI (SUHI), which are defined by (canopy or boundary layer) air temperature and LST differences between urban and rural areas, respectively. Air temperature is measured in situ using station networks. However, the coverage of ground-level observational meteorological stations is limited in China, and air temperature is difficult to acquire in high temporal and spatial resolution. Land surface temperature (LST) measured by thermal infrared radiometers carried by aircraft or satellites can provide continuous coverage, high integrity, and real-time data acquisition over large areas (Voogt and Oke, 2003).

Scholars have investigated the changes of land covers, LST, and SUHI effect as well as their relationship (Qian and Ding, 2005; Weng, 2001). However, most studies adopt a rough urban classification scheme with commonly one urban category (Tian et al., 2017). Such a single urban classification system ignores the complexity and spatial heterogeneity of urban structure. Detailed urban categories will help develop an in-depth understanding of the spatial variations of the local climate, as well as the relationship between land cover and the magnitude of the SUHI. To ensure effective and coherent development of adaptation strategies aimed at improving the urban thermal environment, it is necessary to utilize a uniform urban classification scheme for the understanding of the intraurban UHI and the impact of urban land cover.

The World Urban Database and Access Portal Tools (WUDAPT) was developed as a new global initiative to produce standardized data on urban form and function for different applications and in different levels of detail (Bechtel et al., 2015; Ching et al., 2018). This most basic description of urban landscapes in WUDAPT (= level zero) (Bechtel et al., 2019) discretizes urban landscapes into Local Climate Zones (LCZs), a scheme that comprises 10 built types and seven land cover types (Table 16.1) (Stewart and Oke, 2012). With the 10 built types, the intraurban structure can be investigated in sufficient detail for many climatic applications. Moreover, LCZ links land cover types and urban morphology with corresponding thermal properties, which is particularly suitable as a standardized method for intraurban UHI investigations across different cities and regions (Stewart and Oke, 2012).

WUDAPT suggests a standardized workflow to generate LCZ maps representing different built and natural land cover types (Bechtel et al., 2015). It contains three major steps: Firstly, the preprocessing of Landsat images: Landsat images were mosaicked into one image to cover the study area. Next, this image was resampled from 30 to 100 m resolution and clipped to fit the range of the region. Secondly, selection of training samples: polygons, representing training samples for all LCZ types present, were digitized from Google Earth based on local knowledge. Thirdly, LCZ classification by the random forest classifier: the preprocessed Landsat images and selected training samples were used to train a random forest classifier (Breiman, 2001). Taking advantage of spectral features contained in each training sample, the random forest classifier generated the classification rule and applied it to identify each pixel. The random classifier was selected as an ideal compromise between the achieved accuracy and computational performance among the previously tested classifiers (Bechtel and Daneke, 2012).

As a consequence of the opening and reform policy since 1978, China is experiencing rapid growth in both the number of megaurban regions and their population (Tan, 20107). The central government of China regards megaurban region development strategy as a principal urbanization platform in 2014 (CCCPC and SC, 2014). Yangtze River Delta (YRD) and Pearl River Delta (PRD) regions are two leading subtropical megaurban regions experiencing rapid urban expansion and warming land surface. In this context, it is imperative to understand the spatial patterns of the UHI and propose UHI mitigation strategies for the two regions. Thus, this study applied the LCZ-based WUDAPT data and LST to analyze the intraurban UHI in the YRD and PRD regions.

2. Case study: Pearl River Delta region

2.1 Location and urbanization of the PRD

The PRD region is located in the Guangdong province, in the southeast of China, close to the South China Sea (Fig. 16.1). The PRD region covers an area of 55,000 km^2. It used to be a major agricultural production area before the implementation of the opening and reform policy in 1978. In the 1980s, the name "Pearl River Delta (PRD) region" was put forward as an economic and industrial region. After the putting forward of the opening and reform policy, with the increasing prosperity of different industries, a large population of workers and new immigrants moved into this region. Correspondingly, a large amount of agricultural land was converted into construction land to support economic growth and building construction for urban dwellers. From 2000 to 2010, the urban area in the PRD region grew by 2615 km^2 (Statistics Bureau of Guangdong Province, 2001, 2011). In 2008, the urbanization rate of the

Table 16.1 Snapshots of different LCZ classes in the YRD megaurban region from Google Earth.

LCZ 1: Compact high-rise

- Tightly packed buildings with more than 10 stories

- Little or no green space

- Built by concrete, steel, stone, and glass

LCZ 2: Compact mid-rise

- Tightly packed buildings with three to nine stories

- Little or no green space

- Built by stone, brick, tile, and concrete

LCZ 3: Compact low-rise

- Tightly packed buildings with one to three stories

- Little or no green space

- Built by concrete, steel, stone, and glass

LCZ 4: Open high-rise

- Openly arranged buildings with more than 10 stories

- Abundance green space

- Built by concrete, steel, stone, and glass

LCZ 5: Open mid-rise

- Openly arranged buildings with three to nine stories

- An abundance of green space

- Built by concrete, steel, and glass

LCZ 6: Open low-rise

- Openly arranged buildings with one to three stories

- An abundance of green space

- Built by wood, brick, tile, and concrete

LCZ 7: Lightweight low-rise

- Lightweight building materials with one to two stories

- Few or no trees

- Land cover is hard-packed

LCZ 8: Large low-rise

- Large, openly arranged buildings with one to three stories

- Few green spaces

- Land cover is mostly paved

LCZ 9: Sparsely built

- Sparse arrangement of small or medium-sized buildings in a natural setting

- An abundance of pervious cover

Continued

Table 16.1 Snapshots of different LCZ classes in the YRD megaurban region from Google Earth.—cont'd

LCZ 10: Heavy industry

- Low-rise and mid-rise industrial structures (towers, tanks, stacks)
- Few or no trees

LCZ A: Dense trees

- The heavily wooded landscape of deciduous and/or evergreen trees

LCZ B: Scattered trees

- The lightly wooded landscape of deciduous and/or evergreen trees

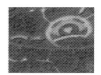

LCZ C: Bush, scrub

- Open arrangement of bushes, shrubs, and short, woody trees

LCZ D: Low plants

- Grass or herbaceous plants/crops

LCZ E: Bare rock or paved

- Rock or paved cover

LCZ F: Bare soil or sand

- Soil or sand cover

LCZ G: Water

- Large, open water bodies

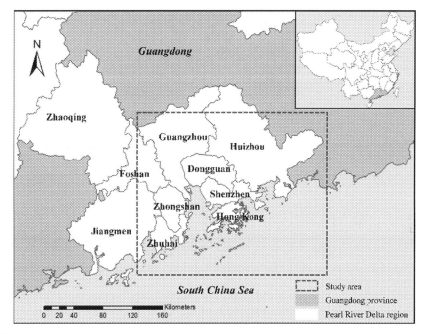

FIGURE 16.1

Location and main cities of the Pearl River Delta (PRD) region.

PRD region was up to 80.5%, and the built-up areas took up around 16% of the whole area of the PRD region (Government of Guangdong Province, 2010). This leads to rapid land cover change with urban development, a problem that is not unique to the PRD region, since many cities or regions within fast urban development in China. And other fast-developing countries are facing similar problems (Lambin, 1997; Murdiyarso, 2000).

2.2 Land cover change in the PRD

The LCZ maps of the PRD region for 1999, 2009, and 2014 are shown in Fig. 16.2. Accuracy assessment is conducted based on three sets of independent validation samples, which were depicted using Google Earth. The overall accuracies for the LCZ maps of 1999, 2009, and 2014 are 73%, 71%, 76% and the Kappa coefficients for the three maps are 0.70, 0.68, and 0.73. Qualitatively, it is found that the built-up areas in the PRD region kept on enlarging from 1999 to 2014.

Table 16.2 illustrates the quantitative change of each LCZ type in the PRD region from 1999 to 2014. The results show that the percentage of compact LCZs (LCZ 1−3) keeps rising; while the percentage of open LCZs (LCZ 4−6) decreases slightly between 1999 and 2014. The area of LCZ 7 (lightweight low-rise), most of which are rural villages, reduced over the entire period. The extent of the most natural land cover types, namely LCZ A-G, was reduced during the study period.

As shown in Tables 16.3 and 16.4, the areas of LCZ built types (LCZ 1−10) increased with a faster increasing rate during subperiod 1 (1999−2009). The area of compact LCZ types (LCZ 1−3)

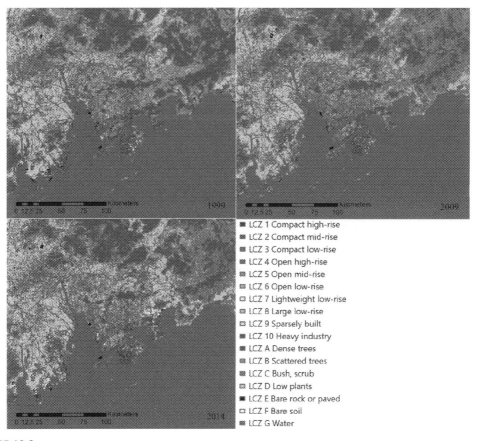

FIGURE 16.2

LCZ maps of the PRD region in the year of 1999, 2009, and 2014.

increased mainly due to the transformation from other built types (e.g., open LCZs) and transformation from natural LCZ types, especially LCZ B (scattered trees) and LCZ D (low plants), illustrating both densification and vertical enhancement in the PRD region.

For natural LCZ types, transformations mainly occurred between different land covers and from land cover types to built types. LCZ A (dense trees), LCZ B (scattered trees), LCZ C (bush, scrub), and LCZ D (low plants) converted to each other. Noticeably, the area of LCZ A (dense trees) decreased by 2386 km² with nearly no incoming sources from other LCZ classes during subperiod 1. While LCZ A and LCZ D both gained areas from LCZ B and LCZ C during subperiod 2 (2009−14). For LCZ E (bare rock/paved) and LCZ F (bare soil), both areas decreased during subperiod 1, respectively; but increased during subperiod 2. While the area of LCZ G (water bodies) remained stable with mere changes of 2 km².

Table 16.2 Share of the LCZ types in the PRD region from 1999 to 2014 (%).

Year	1	2	3	4	5	6	7	8	9	10	A	B	C	D	E	F	G
1999	0.21	0.41	1.78	4.87	0.23	2.30	0.52	0.49	0.05	0.12	17.54	11.58	3.23	10.26	0.86	0.57	45.00
2009	0.48	0.32	2.51	6.42	0.16	2.08	0.28	1.92	0.12	0.15	13.38	8.79	8.55	9.41	0.31	0.14	45.00
2014	0.51	0.76	2.70	4.80	0.10	2.06	0.38	2.07	0.22	0.13	14.30	6.51	8.45	9.96	0.43	1.61	45.00

Table 16.3 Land cover transformation matrix of the PRD region from 1999 to 2009 (km^2).

LCZ class[a] 1999	2009 1	2	3	4	5	6	7	8	9	10	A	B	C	D	E	F	G	Sum (1999)
1	50	2	13	22	0	8	0	10	1	1	0	1	1	7	1	1	0	120
2	47	55	85	21	4	2	2	17	0	1	0	0	0	1	1	0	0	237
3	28	76	599	67	5	44	30	132	1	7	0	1	3	25	5	0	0	1024
4	40	26	354	1505	27	190	31	322	4	22	7	14	13	216	17	6	0	2795
5	15	8	14	36	43	4	2	4	0	0	1	0	0	3	0	0	0	130
6	9	5	136	451	2	210	8	175	18	5	5	51	72	135	26	14	0	1320
7	2	2	72	39	2	32	68	12	0	0	6	13	7	44	1	0	0	300
8	2	0	11	43	1	5	1	160	0	0	0	1	2	36	1	0	16	279
9	0	0	0	4	0	3	0	0	6	0	5	3	4	2	0	0	0	28
10	1	0	3	18	0	9	0	6	0	19	0	0	1	4	4	0	1	67
A	3	0	2	94	4	30	0	6	11	1	6701	2058	990	155	7	4	3	10,068
B	19	1	37	421	1	191	3	85	15	3	491	2392	2318	620	25	22	0	6645
C	1	0	1	31	0	12	0	3	5	1	362	320	1062	48	2	3	0	1853
D	47	6	99	742	3	420	12	128	4	10	44	114	342	3881	22	11	1	5888
E	6	2	12	132	1	24	1	34	0	5	9	11	26	173	56	4	0	496
F	2	0	2	57	0	11	0	7	1	0	49	63	67	47	5	15	0	326
G	0	0	0	0	0	0	0	0	0	10	0	1	1	5	3	0	25,811	25,832
Sum (2009)	273	186	1440	3684	92	1196	158	1100	66	86	7682	5044	4908	5403	175	80	25,834	25,832

[a]Rows indicate LCZ types in 1999; columns indicate LCZ types in 2009.

Table 16.4 Land cover transformation matrix of the PRD region from 2009 to 2014 (km^2).

LCZ class[a] 2009		1	2	3	4	5	6	7	8	9	10	A	B	C	D	E	F	G	Sum (2009)
	1	75	19	16	86	1	5	1	12	0	1	0	1	2	24	4	25	0	273
	2	5	80	54	17	2	3	1	14	0	2	0	0	0	0	6	1	0	186
	3	16	186	841	81	4	46	50	168	2	7	1	5	1	12	13	8	0	1440
	4	110	78	226	1653	18	352	26	195	19	19	37	214	42	466	39	190	0	3684
	5	1	8	5	35	17	15	1	1	0	0	1	2	2	2	1	0	0	92
	6	11	20	112	103	6	289	38	34	13	3	9	57	54	297	31	118	0	1196
	7	1	8	45	10	2	16	62	4	0	0	0	1	1	5	2	2	0	158
	8	12	25	190	80	2	36	3	653	2	9	3	11	3	25	23	21	0	1100
	9	0	0	1	7	0	9	0	1	15	0	5	17	5	4	0	1	0	66
	10	5	2	5	4	0	2	0	18	0	21	0	1	1	1	16	6	4	86
	A	1	0	1	52	0	10	0	2	10	0	6163	591	679	141	2	30	0	7682
	B	1	1	5	78	1	34	2	6	18	1	1143	1538	1567	539	5	105	1	5044
	C	2	1	5	80	0	45	2	7	21	1	757	992	2248	607	4	136	1	4908
	D	42	9	34	451	5	305	26	51	24	6	82	302	237	3572	31	221	5	5403
	E	3	3	8	11	0	8	1	19	0	3	3	2	5	14	64	29	1	175
	F	2	1	2	8	0	5	0	5	0	1	1	7	4	10	4	31	0	80
	G	2	0	0	1	0	0	0	0	0	0	4	0	1	0	4	1	25,821	25,821
	Sum (2014)	290	439	1549	2757	59	1181	216	1190	125	75	8210	3739	4851	5718	249	926	25,834	25,834

[a]Rows indicate LCZ types in 2009; columns indicate LCZ types in 2014.

From the above two tables, the urbanization in the PRD region showed a continuous conversion from natural to urban LCZ types, but also densification as well as vertical enhancement of existing urban structures. All three processes can be seen in the multitemporal LCZ mapping.

2.3 Land surface temperature analysis in the PRD

LST of the PRD region during both the day and night from June to September was retrieved from MODIS image in 2000, 2009, and 2015. Table 16.5 shows the patterns of LST in the PRD region in 2000, 2009, and 2015, respectively. In general, the higher LST is located in the built-up areas, mainly compromised of the downtown areas of Guangzhou, Dongguan, Foshan, Shenzhen, Hong Kong, Zhuhai, and Macao. Besides, there is no apparent gap of the warmer surface (identified as red in the images) among different cities, indicating that the urbanization has led to the built-up areas in different cities merged into one large area.

For the daytime images, there is a significant expansion of areas of high LST value along the coast of Guangzhou, Hong Kong, Macao, Shenzhen, and Zhuhai. Furthermore, significant growth of LST heat intensity is captured from the LST images, and the urban areas in 2015 has reached the highest LST in comparison to 2000 and 2009, which may indicate a poor thermal environment in the red areas.

For the nighttime situation, the areas with high LST value are not noticeably detected in 2000. However, the nighttime image in 2009 identified an obvious increase of LST magnitude in the whole region. The area of high LST value also has a large expansion in comparison with the LST in 2000. Also, the nighttime LST pattern is different from that of daytime. Higher LST is more significant in the west of the urban areas such as Guangzhou, Foshan, and Zhuhai. The nighttime LST pattern in 2015 is similar to that of 2009 during the second period.

Here, hot days are defined as days with a maximum temperature of 33°C or above (Hong Kong Observatory, 2015). Hot nights are not detected based on the LST maps of the region. Only several isolated very hot day spots are identified in 2000 while the expansion of extremely hot weather grows significantly in the region, especially in the downtown areas of the PRD region. The northeast of the PRD region with less urbanization is also under the great potential of extreme heat according to the map. The excessive hot weather may lead to serious health-related impacts to the public in the identified areas.

The mean and standard deviation (SD) of LST for 2000, 2009, and 2015 and the corresponding LST differences are listed in Table 16.6. The average summer LST and SD kept growing during the two subperiods. From 2000 to 2009, the average LST increased by 1.39 and 1.28°C for daytime and nighttime. The SD increased from 1.74 to 1.99 during daytime and from 1.39 to 1.56 in the nighttime. During the second subperiod of 2000−2015, the mean summer LST growth was 0.73 and 0.15°C for daytime and nighttime, respectively. The SD also rose from 1.99 to 2.44 in the daytime and from 1.56 to 1.63 during nighttime during the second subperiod. LST in the daytime situation has a larger increase in LST and LST variations in comparison with nighttime LST.

However, the changes reported in Table 16.6 represent only discrete points in time, and analysis of the LST data each year during the whole period showed that there is substantial interannual variation in summer LST. Therefore, trends for the full period were computed as well.

2.4 Relation of surface warming trend to land cover changes

The land cover changes over the period from 1999 to 2014 in the PRD region were compared to LST trends. First, these trends were calculated based on the summer average (using all valid acquisitions from June to September) of the daily MODIS data for each year from 2000 to 2017. Then linear trends were derived from the time series of annual summer means. Fig. 16.3 indicates significant LST warming with positive trends of up to >0.3 K/year for some parts of the PRD region. Only for a few small parts, negative trends are found, gray areas indicate no significant trends at $P < .05$. Second, the land cover changes in the PRD region based on historical LCZ maps were reclassified as urbanization (natural turning to built LCZ type), deconstruction (vice versa), statically built (same built class in 1999 and 2014), conversion (change within built type), and natural/water (natural class without conversion). Fig. 16.4 shows the land cover changes in the PRD region from 1999 to 2014. Finally, a visual comparison was conducted between the LST trends and land cover changes of the PRD region. Both maps match closely, revealing great spatial accordance between the urbanization and conversion (often related to densification or height enhancement) in Fig. 16.4 and the great LST warming in Fig. 16.3. Thus, qualitatively, the LST changes echo the land cover changes in the PRD region during the study period and most likely dominantly result from the land cover change.

2.5 Thermal characteristic of LCZ type

To analyze the influence of land cover change on LST, the LST in each LCZ was calculated for daytime and nighttime (Fig. 16.5). It is noted that the mean LST of built types is higher than that of natural LCZ types. Among built types, LCZ 2 (compact mid-rise), 8 (large low-rise), and 10 (heavy industry) have the highest LST values at both daytime and nighttime. For natural cover types, LCZ A (dense trees), LCZ B (scattered trees), and LCZ C (bush, scrub) show relatively low mean LST values among all 17 LCZ classes. In addition, variations within the same LCZ class are higher in the daytime than at nighttime.

LSTs of the majority of the LCZ classes have increased during the two periods, indicating an overall trend of surface warming across the study area. However, it also could be related to conversion within one LCZ class or of adjacent patches, since the coarser MODIS data necessarily integrate over somewhat larger areas. In particular, the transformation between different LCZ types (especially urban expansion) has intensified the UHI effect by increasing the LST in the built-up LCZ classes (see Fig. 16.3). The only LST decrease is identified in LCZ B (scattered trees) from 2000 to 2009. Also, there is a greater increase in the first period than that in the second period.

2.6 Dominant LCZ type in SUHI zones

The LSTs have been categorized into SUHI zones, and the dominant LCZ type in the SUHI zone has been identified and summarized in Table 16.7. The low and medium SUHI zones with lower LST are dominated by vegetation and water, i.e., LCZ A (dense trees), LCZ D (low plants). These LCZ types with medium and low SUHI were constant during the 15 years in general, which can result from the low LST and the large areas of these classes.

The high SUHI zone caused by the urbanization process is mainly comprised of two built LCZ types, LCZ 4 (open high-rise) and LCZ 8 (large low-rise), which have large coverage and relatively

Table 16.5 LST in the PRD region in 2000, 2009, and 2015.

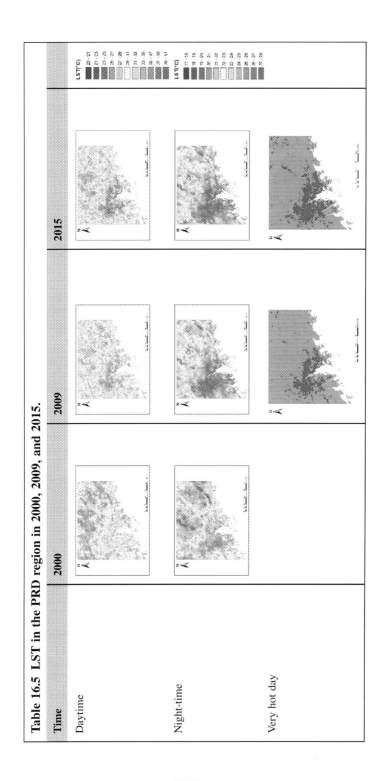

Time	2000	2009	2015
Daytime			
Night-time			
Very hot day			

Table 16.6 Mean LST, the LST difference, and standard deviation of LST in 2000, 2009, and 2015 in the PRD region (°C).

	2000	2009	2015
Average daytime summer LST	29.31	30.70 +1.39	31.43 +0.73
Average night summer LST	22.94	24.22 +1.28	24.37 +0.15
The standard deviation of daytime summer LST	1.74	1.99	2.44
The standard deviation of night summer LST	1.39	1.56	1.63

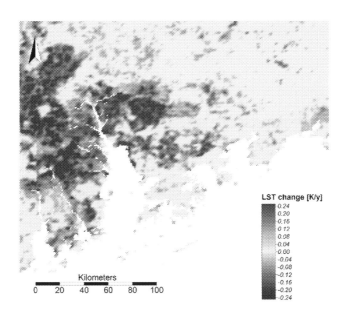

FIGURE 16.3

LST changes from 2000 to 2017 in the PRD region. Gray areas have no significant trends at $P < .05$ confidence level.

higher LST among the built types. LCZ 4 (open high-rise) is the principal LCZ type in high SUHI zones in the daytime. The prevailing LCZ type in high SUHI zones in the night has been changed from LCZ 4 (open high-rise) to LCZ 8 (large low-rise) in 2009. The increase of the area of LCZ 8 (large low-rise), which mainly belongs to manufacturing buildings, can lead to the increase of the LCZ type in the high SUHI zone. The rapid industrial and urbanization process, which can transform land cover types to manufacturing buildings, can aggravate the SUHI effect in the PRD region in the future. In addition, the construction of increasing LCZ 4 (open high-rise) can also intensify the SUHI effect in the PRD region.

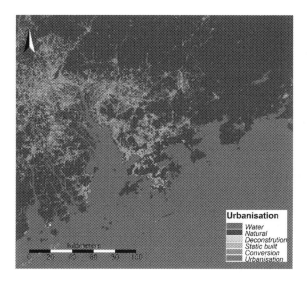

FIGURE 16.4

Land cover changes from 1999 to 2014 in the PRD region.

2.7 Implications for urban planning

LCZ data produced by WUDAPT are further shown to be effectively and efficiently integrated with land cover change and LST analysis in this study. The spatiotemporal distribution of LCZ can be used for land cover change analysis and LST studies, which are beneficial for understanding urban development, land use planning as well as the thermal environment to minimize the negative impact of urbanization. Rapid urban construction has led to the deterioration of the urban thermal environment; hot spots expanded from several cities into merging city groups. Apart from the positive influence of city group mode on urban development, its adverse impact on the urban thermal environment should also be taken into account, especially for regional planning, such as "The PRD Reform and Development Plan (2008–20)." This plan aims to improve the quality of town planning and the management of local urban development through three key aspects: "optimizing spatial plan via making appropriate land use zonings," "making intensive land use development," and also "conducting environment protection for sustainable development" (National Development and Reform Commission, 2016). Regarding LCZ classes, in the study period, compact LCZs (LCZ 1–3) were mainly converted from open LCZ types and natural cover types. LCZs with low building height tend to rebuild as LCZ classes with higher heights during the urbanization process. When looking into the thermal environment, LCZ 8 (large low-rise) has the largest increase of LST at daytime, and LCZ 1 (compact high-rise) and LCZ 6 (open low-rise) are the two with the largest increase at nighttime (Appendix.4). LCZ 4 (open high-rise) and LCZ 8 (large low-rise) also contributed largely to the SUHI in the PRD region. The areas of LCZ 1 (compact high-rise) LCZ 4 (open high-rise), and LCZ 8 (large low-rise) also rose dramatically during

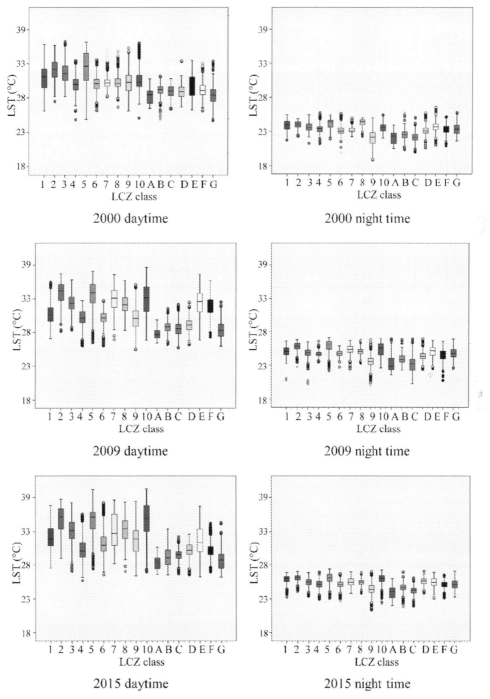

FIGURE 16.5

LST of each LCZ class during daytime and nighttime in 2000, 2009, and 2015.

Table 16.7 Dominant LCZ type in SUHI.

Year	Time	Low SUHI	Medium SUHI	High SUHI
2000	Daytime	LCZ D (low plants)	LCZ G (water)	LCZ 4 (open high-rise)
	Nighttime	LCZ A (dense trees)	LCZ A (dense trees)	LCZ 4 (open high-rise)
2009	Daytime	LCZ A (dense trees)	LCZ A (dense trees)	LCZ 4 (open high-rise)
	Nighttime	LCZ A (dense trees)	LCZ A (dense trees)	LCZ 8 (large low-rise)
2015	Daytime	LCZ A (dense trees)	LCZ A (dense trees)	LCZ 4 (open high-rise)
	Nighttime	LCZ A (dense trees)	LCZ A (dense trees)	LCZ 8 (large low-rise)

this period. Thus, when implementing urban planning for central areas of this megaurban region, compact LCZ types, particularly compact high-rise types, should be paid more attention, since this type has more impact on the thermal environment. The areas of LCZ 4 (open high-rise) and LCZ 8 (large low-rise) should also be restricted with a proper greenery plan in between.

3. Case study: Yangtze River Delta
3.1 Location and urbanization of the YRD

The YRD region is composed of the territory of Shanghai, southern Jiangsu Province, and northern Zhejiang Province (Fig. 16.6). The terrain of this region is generally flat and low-lying floodplain with some hilly areas located in the south of Hangzhou. The YRD region has a subtropical monsoon climate with an annual mean temperature of 15−16°C and annual precipitation of 1000−1,400 mm. Rapid urbanization in this region has given rise to one of the largest megalopolis in the world, covering an area of 99,600 km^2 and home to over the 83 million urban population (National Development and Reform Commission, 2016). This region is selected in the present paper due to the similar geographic characteristics and urban morphology of the YRD cities.

Two typical cities in the YRD megaurban region under rapid urban development were selected as case studies, namely Shanghai and Hangzhou. Shanghai is located in the center of the alluvial terrace of the Yangtze River delta. It has the highest population density in China and is one of the most vigorous economic zones in the world (Shanghai Municipal Statistics Bureau, 2011). It is divided into 18 county-level divisions with nine districts in the city core collectively identified as urban areas. Hangzhou is the capital of the Zhejiang Province and has the highest population in the province. It is located in the southern part of the YRD and now one of China's most prosperous major cities. Hangzhou municipality area includes nine urban districts, two county-level cities, and two counties.

Previous studies showed that there is a significant UHI phenomenon in the YRD region, characterized by more hot days, higher maximum air temperature, and longer duration of high temperature in urban areas than outer suburbs and periurban areas (Wang and Zheng, 2013; Zhang et al., 2013). UHI intensity in the YRD region reaches 4.7°C (Dong et al., 2014), and the areas experiencing intense UHI have rapidly expanded. In particular, the average UHI intensity in Shanghai reaches 2.4°C in summer (Ding et al., 2014) while the maximum UHI intensity reaches 5.6°C in Hangzhou (Wang and Liu, 1982).

FIGURE 16.6

Location of the study area.

3.2 LCZ maps of the YRD region

Fig. 16.7 is the LCZ map of the YRD megaurban region produced by the improved WUDAPT method. It captures the morphological characteristics of both rural and urban areas and detects the spatial pattern of the potential UHI phenomenon. As shown in Fig. 16.7, the vegetation in the central and northern YRD is dominated by farmland (LCZ D) while the southern and southwestern parts of the

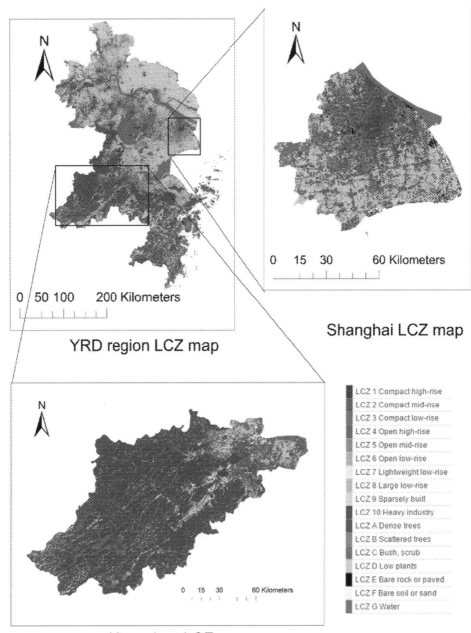

YRD region LCZ map

Shanghai LCZ map

Hangzhou LCZ map

LCZ 1 Compact high-rise
LCZ 2 Compact mid-rise
LCZ 3 Compact low-rise
LCZ 4 Open high-rise
LCZ 5 Open mid-rise
LCZ 6 Open low-rise
LCZ 7 Lightweight low-rise
LCZ 8 Large low-rise
LCZ 9 Sparsely built
LCZ 10 Heavy industry
LCZ A Dense trees
LCZ B Scattered trees
LCZ C Bush, scrub
LCZ D Low plants
LCZ E Bare rock or paved
LCZ F Bare soil or sand
LCZ G Water

FIGURE 16.7

LCZ maps in the YRD megaurban region.

YRD megaurban region are mainly mixed forestland. The vegetation pattern is consistent with the geographic characteristics of the YRD with a low-lying alluvial floodplain in the northern half of the YRD and mountainous terrain in the southwest.

Shanghai has the largest urban areas among all the YRD cities according to the LCZ map. The urban areas have expanded to adjacent cities, namely Suzhou, Wuxi, and Changzhou. These four cities have been integrated into a large city group with no obvious nonurban areas between the cities. Large urban areas are also identified in the two subprovincial-level cities, Hangzhou and Nanjing. There are also many isolated urban settlements in the northern part of YRD, which are mainly suburbs and prefecture-level cities that are possible heat sources of the YRD region.

Downtown areas of Shanghai Municipality, especially in the city center where the CBDs and commercial areas are situated, are extremely dense and compact so they are mainly classified into the LCZ 1–4, which are potential of high UHI intensity. Compact urban land cover is also found in the northern suburbs. Also, the LCZ map detects LCZ 10 (heavy industry) in Baoshan district in the north and Minhang district in the middle of Shanghai that are sources of anthropogenic heat.

The LCZ map of Hangzhou indicates that LCZ A (dense trees) occupies most of the rural areas in the mountain region. Urban settlements are concentrated in the northeastern downtown area. They are not as dense as Shanghai since mainly LCZ 2–5 are found in this region where the UHI phenomenon possibly occurs. In addition, the continuously connected downtown area and suburbs indicate potential aggregation of the UHI phenomenon in Hangzhou. The rest of the counties and county-level cities are mostly classified into LCZ 3 (compact low-rise).

In addition, there are misclassifications in vegetation covers such as LCZ B and C since it is difficult for the random forest classifier to distinguish vegetation with various heights and densities. It is also because the satellite imagery does not contain sufficient information about the height and density of vegetation. On the other hand, the misclassification results from the inconsistent dates of the images obtained from Google Earth and Landsat data since the density and height of vegetation may vary across different seasons. Therefore, multitemporal Landsat images are required to provide more accurate results.

3.3 SUHI intensity in the YRD

The SUHI of Shanghai and Hangzhou was classified according to (Zhang et al., 2013). Fig. 16.8 shows the spatial pattern of surface UHI classified in Shanghai and Hangzhou based on the LST acquired from night-time Aster thermal images. In Shanghai, the SUHI intensity reaches up to 4.2°C in downtown areas in the center and northern part of Shanghai. High LST was extensively found in the southern suburbs while scattered, extremely high LST values were observed outside the city center due to the presence of point sources such as the factories in the north of Baoshan and the south of Minhang. It is also notable that the distribution of high LST is dominant in the city.

SUHI is more prominent in Hangzhou with a large area of high LST found in the downtown area in the northwestern part of the city. The temperature difference between the downtown and surrounding rural areas reaches up to 12°C in LST. In particular, Hangzhou Bay in the southeast has a SUHI intensity of 10°C since it is an economic development zone surrounded by Hangzhou, Shanghai, and Ningbo, leading to such the prominence of SUHI in this area.

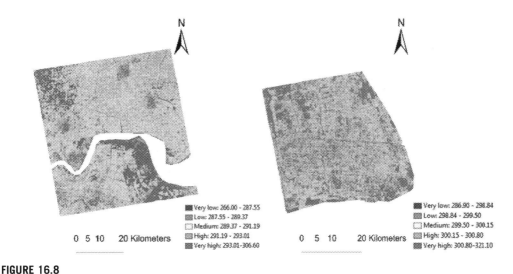

FIGURE 16.8

Spatial variation of surface UHI in Shanghai (left) and Hangzhou (right).

3.4 Relationship between surface temperature and LCZ classes

Fig. 16.9 shows the differences of LST from the mean value for each LCZ class. In general, there are large variations in LST across LCZ classes while the pattern is similar between the two cities despite the higher differences observed in Hangzhou. The LST of built-up LCZ classes is generally higher than that of the land cover classes, reiterating the high UHI intensity in urban areas. In particular, LCZ 1 (compact high-rise) has the highest LST among the built-up LCZ classes with mean values of 27.3 and 20.8°C for Shanghai and Hangzhou, respectively. LCZ 9 (sparsely built) shows an opposite trend in the two cities with 0.2°C above mean in Shanghai but 1.8°C below mean in Hangzhou. The complex and diverse urban morphology of this LCZ class in YRD is the predominant reason for such an opposite trend since most of the LCZ 9 areas in Hangzhou are located in mountain areas and villages surrounded by farmland and forest. In contrast, LCZ 9 in Shanghai is generally found in suburbs, which experienced rapid urbanization and extensive conversion of land cover.

Lower LST is generally observed in land cover LCZ classes due to the extensive pervious surface in natural land cover. LCZ A exhibits the lowest LST in both cities with mean values of 26.1 and 15.4°C observed in Shanghai and Hangzhou, respectively. However, there are certain inconsistencies in the LST of land cover classes due to the temporal difference in vegetation. Above-mean values were observed in LCZ E (bare rock or paved) in which some of them are concrete paved areas such as an airport and scattered settlements. LCZ G has the highest LST due to the highest heat capacity, which cools off slower than other LCZ classes during nighttime.

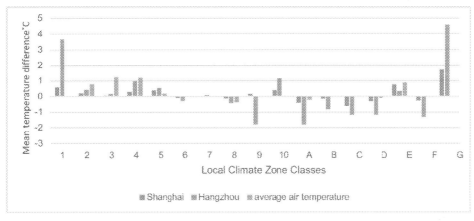

FIGURE 16.9

Temperature differences (C) from mean LST for each LCZ class.

3.5 Representation of urban morphology of the YRD cities

3.5.1 Regional level

The LCZ maps produced by using the improved WUDAPT methodology were found to be representative of the urban morphology at both city and regional scales. The urban areas in the YRD megaurban region can be classified into four urban agglomerations since the urban morphology is similar with no remarkable delineations among the cities within the agglomerations (Fig. 16.10). Region A is comprised of Shanghai municipality and the surrounding Kunshan in Suzhou and Nantong. The dominant land use in this area is urban and built-up areas with much commercial activity. The urban sprawl of the cities in the region has expanded beyond their administrative boundaries. It has the highest level of urbanization among the four regions, and the urban areas are extremely concentrated and compacted, merging into a large spatial agglomeration. Region B is the Suzhou—Wuxi—Changzhou urban agglomeration to the west of Shanghai. The built-up areas in this region are mainly industrial and commercial. A high level of urbanization is being experienced in this region, and they are likely to develop into a megalopolis in the future.

On the other hand, Region C, located in Hangzhou Bay including cities such as Hangzhou, Shaoxing, and Ningbo, has expanded closely to one another along the coast and contains most of the compact commercial areas. In the north of the YRD megaurban region, Region D consists of Nanjing, Zhenjiang, and Yangzhou, with Nanjing as the center of urban development. The urban area is relatively sparse and smaller than the previous three regions in terms of the size of the city. The urban sprawl of the cities in this region is relatively independent and has not spread together. Due to the rapid economic development in the YRD megaurban region, these four regions are expected to merge and form a megalopolis in the future.

3.5.2 City level

Despite the merging trend in the YRD megaurban region, cities exhibit their characteristics in urban morphology due to their corresponding rates and scenarios of urban development. In Shanghai

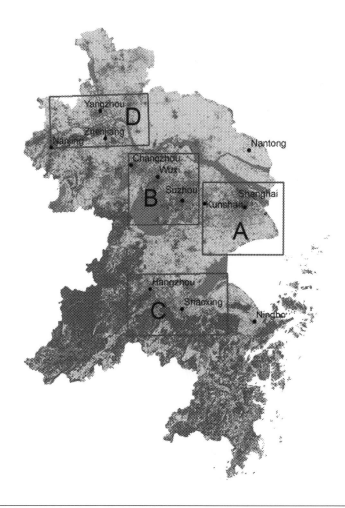

FIGURE 16.10

Urban agglomerations identified in the YRD megaurban region.

municipality, LCZ 1 dominates since buildings, especially those in commercial areas, are high-rise and the urban areas are merging into a larger metropolis. In contrast, newly developed districts such as Pudong and Baoshan are well regulated with homogeneous urban morphology. Downtown areas such as the Changning district are more irregular in size and urban form since they are at the early stage of urban development.

Cities at the subprovincial level such as Nanjing and Hangzhou have fewer built-up areas than Shanghai municipality. High-rise buildings and CBDs are generally sparsely located in the city center and often mixed with mid-rise buildings. The block size is usually around 300 m. For prefecture-level cities such as Wuxi and Yangzhou, residential areas dominate and are mostly classified into LCZ 4 and 5. The blocks in these cities are relatively small and disperse with a block size of less than 100 m. The land use is highly mixed in these cities, and the length of land with homogeneous urban morphology is only around 70−80 m.

Small building blocks mixed with dominant LCZ classes cause problems in selecting training samples from Google Earth, which affects the accuracy of LCZ mapping using the WUDAPT method. In this study, it was found that training samples with a size larger than 100 m^2 improved mapping results since they provide sufficient information for the classification. On the other hand, the sample with an area less than 100 m^2 cannot cover one pixel of the Landsat image so the chance of generating an erroneous classification is considerably increased. It is also likely to cause pixel mixing due to uncertainties about the location of the different physical landscapes. However, large samples of homogeneous urban morphology were absent in some cities such as Wuxi, leading to poor mapping results when they were applied to satellite images of 100 m resolution. To improve the mapping result, the small samples and the original Landsat data of 30 m resolution were used for classification. Thus, the Landsat data can better represent the spectral information of the samples and the classification accuracy has therefore been improved. Subclassification of the mix of LCZ types can also help improve the mapping result.

3.6 Implications for urban planning

As the LCZ classification scheme is based on the impact of urban morphology on temperature variation in the city, the LCZ maps can indicate the spatial distribution of the UHI phenomenon, which contributes to more climate-sensitive urban planning. The LCZ map visualizes the spatial characteristics so urban planners and architects can better understand the thermal environment in the decision-making process. Also, the LST characteristics of LCZ classes are helpful to minimize the impacts of urbanization by using urban vegetation and land use planning.

A more severe UHI phenomenon was found in the central and southern parts of the YRD megaurban region due to the higher level of urban development. Frequent communications between the cities in this part of the region facilitate the emergence of these cities into a megalopolis. Therefore, more careful planning strategies are required for future urban development concerning UHI mitigation. For the dense urban areas in Shanghai, Hangzhou, and Nanjing, further urban development should be avoided or carefully designed to alleviate the high temperature. Green patches with low UHI intensity can also be strategically used to effectively mitigate the UHI phenomenon. For areas with high UHI, it is also important to improve the thermal environment through measures such as efficient energy use, building materials, and other ecological measures.

The urban areas of prefecture-level cities such as Wuxi and Suzhou are sparsely distributed. Hotspots of the cities have sprawled from city center to urban fringe and suburban areas while local hotspots emerge in new towns where a large area of vegetation was converted to impervious surface cover. It suggests that urban development in these areas should be carefully planned and designed, for example, providing open space, preserving urban greenery, and enhancing ventilation. These measures are able to provide a cooling effect to mitigate the UHI intensity in these areas.

The extensive industrial zones in the YRD megaurban region such as Baoshan district in Shanghai and Hangzhou Bay also exhibit high LST and worsen the thermal environment. Further measures should be considered to not only limit the building density but also restrict the anthropogenic heat release of the industrial area. Natural land covers such as green space (LCZ A−D) and open space

(LCZ E and F) are beneficial to the surrounding areas. Low building density is therefore preferred to maximize the cooling effect and prevent any blockage of ventilation from these areas.

---

4. Discussions and implementations

Not only is the LCZ map suitable for formulating urban planning strategies to mitigate UHI by analyzing the intraurban UHIs, but it has also been proven helpful in improving the local climate via various applications, such as air pollution assessment, heatwave estimation, urbanization projection.

Our research team has already analyzed the impact of urban land cover on air pollution prediction, particularly the particulate matter that <2.5 μm in aerodynamic diameter (PM2.5) by adopting LCZ (Shi et al., 2019). PM2.5 is recognized as one of the major pollutants that reduce air quality and increase health burden. This study focused on identifying the influential landscape categories/types from LCZ that affect PM2.5 concentration levels in Hong Kong, a high-density city in the PRD region. The results show that a Geographically Weighted Regression (GWR) model, which only incorporates five land use/landscape categories from the LCZ map, can explain 62% of variations in PM2.5 without using any traffic-related variables or data in the emission inventory. The understanding of the impact of urban land cover on PM 2.5 can facilitate planning strategies in terms of mitigating air pollution. This finding can also be particularly useful to the urban air quality assessment in areas without detailed emission inventory or monitoring data since the LCZ map can be retrieved using open data. The method can also be applied to global cities with a globally standardized WUDAPT level 0 database, contributing to the global PM2.5 predictions.

The urban land cover properties from the LCZ maps have also been used to predict the distribution of heatwaves in the PRD region. Our research team estimated the spatial pattern of heatwaves in the PRD region at 100 m spatial resolution based on the LCZ maps, observational weather records, and a random forest classifier (Shi et al., 2021). The results show that the methodology can be used to estimate the spatial pattern of heatwaves using open data and provide a basis for policies and decision-making. The spatial pattern of heatwaves is essential for providing corresponding weather services, formulating strategies to adapt to climate change, and undertaking thermal sanitation actions.

Understanding future urbanization is essential for coping with the negative impacts of climate change. There are frequent transitions among different urban land covers and thus altering surface properties, especially for rapidly developing Chinese megaurban regions. To facilitate climate prediction with these changing attributes, the research team proposes a new framework that uses a cellular automata (CA) land use/land cover change (LCLUC) model to predict future LCZ maps of the PRD region (Huang et al., 2021). Unlike most existing LCLUC studies that treat urban areas as homogeneous, our work is the first attempt to simulate the complex conversion between low, medium, and high-rise urban land covers defined in the LCZ scheme. Based on the LCZ maps of the PRD region in 2009 and 2014 as well as the LCLUC rules discovered by data mining technology, we applied the 2014 forecast on the 2009 LCZ map of the CA model. The comparison between the LCZ prediction map and the observed map in 2014 yielded a kappa coefficient of 0.77, with a global accuracy of 82%. Our results show that the combination of the LCZ scheme and LCLUC modeling has the potential to capture changes in intraurban structure and provide the necessary input datasets for urban climate prediction.

5. Conclusions

The development of megaurban regions is a national strategy that focuses on future urban development in China. This study uses the LCZ scheme and LST to analyze the intraurban UHI effect of the YRD and PRD megaurban region. Although the concept of the LCZ classification scheme is based on measurements of air temperature, LST was found to be associated with LCZ classes and suitable for intraurban UHI analysis. In the PRD region, urbanization is found to comprise transformation from natural land covers to built types, densification, and vertical enhancement of existing urban structures. Second, the land surface was warming with a speed of up to >0.3 K/year, and the hot area expanded in accordance with urbanized areas in the PRD region during the study period. The expansion of LCZ built types has led to a significant LST increase. In particular, the large extension of LCZ 8 (large low-rise) and LCZ 6 (open low-rise) results in a high LST increase. LCZ 4 (open high-rise) and LCZ 8 (large low-rise) are the dominant LCZ types in the high SUHI zones. In the YRD region, built-up LCZ classes generally exhibit higher LST than land cover LCZ classes. LCZ 1 and 10 have the highest LST among the built-up classes in the two cities while vegetation (LCZ A-D) has the lowest among all classes. Inconsistencies in LST variations were found in LCZ 9, A, B, and C due to the highly variable urban morphology and the temporal variations in vegetation.

The findings can show researchers a new way of extracting the detailed urban and land use data from open-sourced satellite data. Owing to the diverse LCZ built types, this study can investigate the intraurban UHI difference in the two megaurban regions, instead of the rough one urban category or two to three urban classes (low/medium/high density) applied by previous studies. The findings can help urban planners and urban climate researchers better understand the influence of urban morphology (i.e., LCZ classes) on local climatic conditions. Thus, land use planning and management play a crucial role in SUHI reduction under climate change adaptation. Proper and reasonable distribution of LCZ with lower surface temperatures is advisable to mitigate the influence of UHI during the process of urban development. The findings of this study can also help researchers to better understand the influence of LCZ on local climate variations for other Chinese megaurban regions and global cities. Results also support air quality assessment, future urbanization projection, heatwave studies, and numerical models for climate change studies. However, limited by the resolution of freely available remote sensing images (tens of meters to hundreds of meters), the LCZ-based SUHI investigation focuses on the local scale, microscale exploration of the UHI effect needs to be conducted by other fine-scale numerical modeling or mobile measurement.

References

Allen, M.R., Barros, V.R., Broome, J., Cramer, W., Christ, R., Church, J.A., Edenhofer, O., 2014. IPCC Fifth Assessment Synthesis Report-Climate Change 2014 Synthesis Report.

Bechtel, B., Daneke, C., 2012. Classification of local climate zones based on multiple earth observation data. IEEE J. Sel. Top. Appl. Earth Obs. Rem. Sens. 5 (4), 1191.

Bechtel, B., Alexander, P.J., Böhner, J., Ching, J., Conrad, O., Feddema, J., Stewart, I., 2015. Mapping local climate zones for a worldwide database of the form and function of cities. ISPRS Int. J. Geo-Inf. 4 (1), 199–219.

Bechtel, B., Alexander, P.J., Beck, C., Böhner, J., Brousse, O., Ching, J., Xu, Y., 2019. Generating WUDAPT Level 0 data – current status of production and evaluation. Urban Climat. 27, 24–45. https://doi.org/10.1016/j.uclim.2018.10.001.

Breiman, L., 2001. Random forests. Mach. Learn. 45 (1), 5–32.

Ching, J., Mills, G., Bechtel, B., See, L., Feddema, J., Wang, X., Neophytou, M., 2018. World Urban Database and Access Portal Tools (WUDAPT), an Urban Weather, Climate and Environmental Modeling Infrastructure for the Anthropocene. Bulletin of the American Meteorological Society, 2018.

Clinton, N., Gong, P., 2013. MODIS detected surface urban heat islands and sinks: global locations and controls. Remote Sens. Environ. 134, 294–304. https://doi.org/10.1016/j.rse.2013.03.008.

Dong, L., Jiang, Z., Shen, S., 2014. Urban heat island change and its relationship with urbanization of urban agglomerations in Yangtze River Delta in past decade. Transact.Atmos. Sci. 37 (2), 146–154.

Government of Guangdong Province, 2010. Pearl River Delta Urban and Rural Integration Planning. Guangzhou: Government of Guangdong Province.

Heinl, M., Hammerle, A., Tappeiner, U., Leitinger, G., 2015. Determinants of urban–rural land surface temperature differences – a landscape scale perspective. Landsc. Urban Plann. 134, 33–42. https://doi.org/10.1016/j.landurbplan.2014.10.003.

Hong Kong Observatory, 2015. Hong Kong in a Warming World. Hong Kong Observatory, Hong Kong.

Huang, K., Leng, J., Xu, Y., Li, X., Cai, M., Wang, R., Ren, C., 2021. Facilitating urban climate forecasts in rapidly urbanizing regions with land-use change modeling. Urban Clim. 36, 100806.

Lambin, E.F., 1997. Modelling and monitoring land-cover change processes in tropical regions. Prog. Phys. Geogr. 21 (3), 375–393. https://doi.org/10.1177/030913339702100303.

Mallick, J., Kant, Y., Bharath, B.D., 2008. Estimation of land surface temperature over Delhi using Landsat-7 ETM+. J. Ind. Geophys. Union 12 (3), 131–140.

McCarthy, M.P., Best, M.J., Betts, R.A., 2010. Climate change in cities due to global warming and urban effects. Geophys. Res. Lett. 37 (9).

Murdiyarso, D., 2000. Adaptation to climatic variability and change: asian perspectives on agriculture and food security. Environ. Monit. Assess. 61 (1), 123–131. https://doi.org/10.1023/a:1006326404156.

National Development, Reform Commission, 2016. Regional Planning of Yangtze River Delta Beijing, China (Retrieved from).

Oke, T.R., 1973. City size and the urban heat island. Atmos. Environ. 7 (8), 769–779. https://doi.org/10.1016/0004-6981(73)90140-6.

Peng, S.S., Piao, S.L., Ciais, P., Friedlingstein, P., Ottle, C., Bréon, F.o.-M., Myneni, R.B., 2011. Surface urban heat island across 419 global big cities. Environ. Sci. Technol. 46 (2), 696–703.

Qian, L.X., Ding, S.Y., 2005. Impacts of land use and cover change on land surface temperature in the Zhujiang delta. Acta Geograph. Sin. 60 (5).

Santamouris, M., Cartalis, C., Synnefa, A., Kolokotsa, D., 2015. On the impact of urban heat island and global warming on the power demand and electricity consumption of buildings—a review. Energy Build. 98, 119–124. https://doi.org/10.1016/j.enbuild.2014.09.052.

Shanghai Municipal Statistics Bureau, 2011. Shanghai Statistical Yearbook 2000–2011. China Statistics Press, Beijing.

Shi, Y., Ren, C., Lau, K.K.L., Ng, E., 2019. Investigating the influence of urban land use and landscape pattern on PM2. 5 spatial variation using mobile monitoring and WUDAPT. Landsc. Urban Plann. 189, 15–26.

Shi, Y., Ren, C., Luo, M., Ching, J., Li, X., Bilal, M., Ren, Z., 2021. Utilizing world urban database and access portal tools (WUDAPT) and machine learning to facilitate spatial estimation of heatwave patterns. Urban Clim. 36, 100797.

Statistics Bureau of Guangdong Province, 2001. Guangdong Statistical Yearbook. China Statistics, Beijing.

Statistics Bureau of Guangdong Province, 2011. Guangdong Statistical Yearbook. China Statistics, Beijing.

Stewart, I.D., Oke, T.R., 2012. Local climate zones for urban temperature studies. Bull. Am. Meteorol. Soc. 93 (12), 1879−1900. https://doi.org/10.1175/bams-d-11-00019.1.

The Central Committee of the Communist Party of China and the State Council (CCCPC & SC), 2014. National Plan on New Urbanization 2014−2020. http://www.gov.cn/zhuanti/xxczh.

Tian, L., Li, Y., Yan, Y., Wang, B., 2017. Measuring urban sprawl and exploring the role planning plays: a shanghai case study. Land Use Pol. 67, 426−435.

Voogt, J.A., Oke, T.R., 2003. Thermal remote sensing of urban climates. Remote Sens. Environ. 86 (3), 370−384. https://doi.org/10.1016/S0034-4257(03)00079-8.

Wang, C., Liu, J., 1982. The climate of the city of Hangzhou. Acta Geograph. Sin. 37, 164−173.

Wang, W., Zheng, G., 2013. 2013 Green Book of Climate Change. Social Sciences and Academic Press.

Weng, Q., 2001. A remote sensing?GIS evaluation of urban expansion and its impact on surface temperature in the Zhujiang Delta, China. Int. J. Rem. Sens. 22 (10), 1999−2014. https://doi.org/10.1080/713860788.

Zhang, H., Qi, Z.F., Ye, X.Y., Cai, Y.B., Ma, W.C., Chen, M.N., 2013. Analysis of land use/land cover change, population shift, and their effects on spatiotemporal patterns of urban heat islands in metropolitan Shanghai, China. Appl. Geogr. 44, 121−133.

Zhao, L., Lee, X.H., Smith, R.B., Oleson, K., 2014. Strong contributions of local background climate to urban heat islands. Nature 511 (7508), 216.

Impact of urban cool strategies on energy performance of HVAC systems in a dense urban district of a Mediterranean city, Beirut, Lebanon

Jeff Fahed[1], Elias Kinab[2], Stephane Ginestet[1] and Luc Adolphe[3]

[1]*LMDC, Université de Toulouse, INSA, UPS, Toulouse, France;* [2]*Lebanese University, Beirut, Lebanon;* [3]*LRA, Université de Toulouse, ENSA, Toulouse, France*

1. Introduction

A large percentage of the total building energy consumption is used for cooling and ensure indoor thermal comfort. This concern has led to numerous studies conducted to improve building energy efficiency and to reduce energy consumption and greenhouses emission. The urban heat island "UHI" phenomenon, which is defined by a significant increase in the air temperature of urban locations as compared to the surrounding areas, has an important consequence on the building performance as well as the energy consumption. During winter, UHI can mitigate heating energy demand, while cooling energy demand is increased during summer due to the increase in the air temperature (Santamouris et al., 2001). Consequently, the additional use of air-conditioning systems releases additional thermal loads and increases urban anthropogenic heat. A self-amplification phenomenon is observed: the hotter it is, the more air conditioners are used, which generate thermal loads to the outdoor environment (Adnot et al., 2004). Multiple microclimate considerations and urban solutions were proposed to reduce UHI intensity and then to reduce cooling energy demand. For examples, urban morphology (Chen et al., 2008), surface albedo modification (Doya et al., 2012; Akbari et al., 1997), and implementation of green zones (Djedjig et al., 2015; Maleki and Mahdavi, 2016) can mitigate UHI and thus reduce cooling energy demand.

The effect of the urban microclimate and the climate change on the building performance has been the subject of several studies. Lu et al. (2010)work on the impact of temperature changes on the building energy consumption for heating and cooling in the western US grid. Lam et al. (2010) examined the case of Hong Kong while Wang et al. (2010) and Wilde and Tian (2010) studied respectively the cases of Australia and United Kingdom. In addition, the effect of UHI on the energy consumption for heating and cooling of office building in London was studied by Kolokotroni et al. (2012) taking into consideration the climate change projections.

Bozonnet (2006) used thermoaeraulic simulations to study the effect of UHI on the cooling demand of a building in the typical case of a canyon street. Bouyer et al. (2011) carried out the coupling of a thermoradiative code and the commercial computational fluid dynamics software "Fluent" to evaluate the energy demand of a building in an urban context. Yang et al. used the coupling between the microclimate model Envi-met and the BES software Energy plus (Crawley et al., 2000) to study the energy demand of an individual building in China (Yang et al., 2012). Likewise, Gros et al. (2016) used SOLENE microclimate and EnviBatE to study the effect of the local urban environment on a building energy simulation in the Atlantech district in La Rochelle France. The objective of this paper is to evaluate the energy interaction between the urban microclimate and the building for the case of a Mediterranean district in Beirut. This paper focuses on the cooling load reduction when using the method of UHI reductions.

2. Methodology

2.1 Simulation tools

Envi-met 4 was used in this study for the microclimatic simulations. Envi-met is a three-dimensional prognostic microclimate model (Huttner, 2012) with typical spatial resolution between 0.5 and 10 m and time steps between 1 and 10 s. Envi-met model is designed to simulate realistically the microclimate at the district scale. The model includes in the calculation the wind speed and direction, the flow around and between building, the turbulence, the radiative flux taken into consideration longwave and short-wave fluxes, the energy and mass exchanges between vegetation and its surrounding, air humidity, and soil wetness, as well as gas and particle dispersion. Envi-met 4 offers a new function called "meteorology forcing" allowing users to specify the meteorological conditions of the simulations by forcing the model with predefined weather profiles. This function is used in the simulations of this paper to force the air temperature and humidity profiles. Envi-met has been widely validated in different climate regions and verified with field measured data by several research studies (Huttner, 2012; Wang et al., 2016; Lahme and Bruse, 2002, 2003; Ghaffarianhoseini et al., 2015; Salata et al., 2016; Elnabawi et al., 2016). Or, Envi-met does not allow evaluating directly the air-conditioning demand, the extracted results must be coupled with another simulation tool allowing the calculation of air-conditioning loads such as Hourly Analysis Program (HAP), which is used in the study of this paper.

HAP, developed by Carrier (2015), is a computer tool for estimating load. HAP allows to calculate the air-conditioning and heating loads as well as the energy consumption of buildings, using the transfer function load method (TFM) validated by Ashrae (1997). The TFM method gives a precise estimation of the load calculation taking into account the transient evolution of heat exchanges in building.

2.2 Coupling method

The meteorological data of temperature and humidity extracted from the simulations carried out with ENVI-met define the meteorological inputs of HAP. Initially, an hourly profile of wet bulb and dry bulb temperatures for Beirut is defined in HAP for the 12 months of the year. This profile is set by default but could be modified as per the desired conditions. According to the files extracted from ENVI-met, the average values of temperature and relative humidity surrounding each floor of the studied building are deducted for each hour of the day. These values define the meteorological inputs for each simulation done by HAP instead of using the default values of the hourly profile initially integrated in HAP. The wet bulb temperature relative to each dry bulb temperature and relative humidity is deduced from the psychometric chart. Fig. 17.1 shows the hourly profile of wet bulb and dry bulb temperatures for the month of July manually modified in HAP, using the average values surrounding the studied floor of the building obtained from ENVI-met simulations.

In addition, the solar flux profile already defined in HAP could be adjustable by using the multiplier factor. This factor allows to take into account the decrease of the solar flux reaching the building caused by the shade created by an obstacle installed in front of the building such trees. The principle consists of multiplying the total flux by the multiplier factor in order to obtain an input of the solar fluxes in HAP similar to those extracted with ENVI-met. For example, if ENVI-met maps show 15% decrease of the maximum solar fluxes due shadow created by an obstacle, the multiplier factor will be 0.85. The use of this factor is very important to take into consideration the masking effect of obstacles on the building facades. The ground albedo is also adjustable in HAP, allowing the usage of the same albedo that is used in the ENVI-met simulations.

2.3 Description of urban district

The studied neighborhood is located in Dora, a high urban density region in the north east of Beirut. The selected zone is very compact as shown in Fig. 17.1, with very low percentage of vegetation zones,

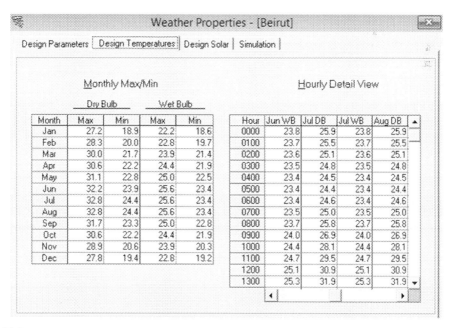

FIGURE 17.1

Hourly profile of dry bulb and wet bulb temperatures in HAP.

Table 17.1 Percentage of land surface coverage.

Case of study, district Dora	Buildings	Road asphalt	Concrete pavement	Vegetation coverage	Total
Surface (m²)	24,875	46,228	2175	222	73,500
Percentage (%)	33.84	62.9	2.96	0.3	100

Table 17.2 Characteristics of the roads, pavement, walls, and roof.

Surface	Exterior walls	Concrete roof	Road asphalt	Concrete pavement
Albedo	0.3	0.3	0.2	0.4
Emissivity	0.9	0.9	0.9	0.9

which need mitigation strategies to improve the effect of the UHI. The aim of this research is to study the effect of urban cooling strategies on the building cooling load in a compact district of Beirut, Lebanon. It is notable that very few studies on UHI phenomenon in Lebanon and its effects have been carried out. Recently, the effects of urbanization on the UHI in Beirut are studied by Kaloustian and Diab (2015). In addition, Kaloustian et al. (2018) proposed the use of the leftover spaces to mitigate the urban overheating in Municipal Beirut.

The dimensions of the selected district are 210 x 350m. It consists of 50 buildings; most of them having height between 15 and 36 m. Table 17.1 revealed the percentage of land surface coverage showing a very small percentage of vegetation coverage (0.3%). In the middle of the selected district, it is clear that the buildings are very close. The separating distance does not exceed 5 m in some cases. The albedo and the emissivity of the district's surfaces show the usage of low-albedo materials (Table 17.2).

3. Case study

3.1 Description of ENVI-met simulation cases

The domain grid created with ENVI-met used for this study is made up of $105 \times 40 \times 30$ pixels. Each pixel corresponds to a reduced resolution $2 \times 2.5 \times 2.5$ m (dx = 2 m, dy = 2.5 m, dz = 2.5 m). Fifteen receptors are installed in the model as shown in Fig. 17.2. We note that ENVI-met receptors are virtual sensors used to monitor atmospheric parameters in different locations of the model. Typical summer day was selected for the simulations and for a period of 24 h. The starting time chosen for the calculation is 7:00 a.m. of July 9th. As there are no meteorological stations installed in the Dora region, the choice of initial conditions is based on data available from Beirut Golf Station for the year 2015 and AUB (American University of Beirut) station for the consecutive years 1996 and 1997.

ENVI-met "forcing" function was used to force the model to a temperature and relative humidity boundary profiles for each hour of the simulation period. The graph of Fig. 17.3 reveals the boundary conditions of temperature and relative humidity forced for the 24 h of simulation. Since meteorological data for Dora district are not available, the forced values are extracted from a submodel

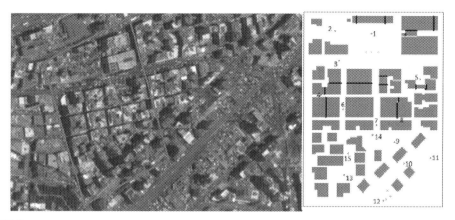

FIGURE 17.2

Satellite view of the selected district, Dora Beirut, Google Earth (left). Envi-met 2D model (right).

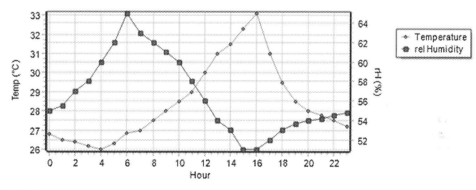

FIGURE 17.3

Profiles of forced temperature and relative humidity using "forcing" function of Envi-met.

simulated with ENVI-met as shown in Fig. 17.4. The initial temperature is 26.9°C and the relative humidity 65%, which corresponds to the average values of the Golf and AUB stations. In fact, the average values of air temperature and relative humidity around the buildings in the submodel represent the hourly boundary forced values into the big district model.

For the initial conditions in ENVI-met, we considered a low wind speed of 1 m/s at the height of 10 m, a constant wind direction of 245 degrees with the north direction, and the initial soil temperature was set to 20°C at a depth of 2 m.

A comparative analysis between initial case and various mitigation scenarios was performed:

1. Green scenario: Integration of trees and grass with a vegetation coverage ratio 7.4% higher than in the base case.

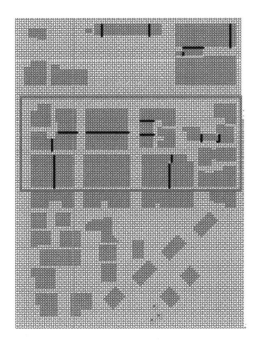

FIGURE 17.4

Submodel (part of the large model outlined in black) simulated to extract boundary conditions of air temperature and relative humidity.

2. Blue scenario: Integration of five water fountains with a continuous vertical emission with height of 4 m (Table 17.3). In addition, implementation of water sprays P1 and P2 with water jets at a height of 3.75 m from ground, Fig. 17.5. P1 corresponds to a continuous line of water jet, while in P2 jet type, the distance between two consecutives sources corresponds to a pixel dx or dy. The diameter of the particle is 10 μm with an hourly emission rate of 5 $\mu g/s$.

3. White scenario: Usage of higher-albedo materials for roads, pavements, and building's exterior surfaces. The albedo 0.2 of common asphalt used for roads has been replaced by 0.5 using red coating asphalt. The albedo 0.4 of the ordinary concrete used for pavements has been replaced by 0.8 using light concrete. The albedo 0.3 of facades in the base case has been replaced by 0.7 using PVC panels. The roof albedo (0.3) has been also modified by using terrazzo tiles with an albedo of 0.5.

4. White buildings scenario: the albedo of roofs and buildings façades is modified by using respectively PVC facades and Terracotta tiles. The roads and pavements are similar to the base model.

Table 17.3 Area of the fountains installed in the "blue scenario."

Fountain	F1	F2	F3	F4	F5
Area (m²)	60	30	20	60	120

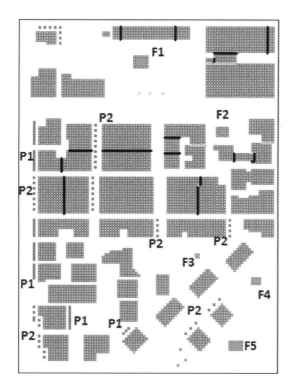

FIGURE 17.5

2D Blue model created by Envi-met.

3.2 Choice of the studied building

The influence of UHI reduction is not homogeneous throughout the district and varies according to the building position in the model and the location of the mitigation devices in each scenario. However, the impact of the proposed UHI mitigation scenarios on the air-conditioning loads differs from a building to another. The building (Fig. 17.6) used for the calculation of the cooling load, called "most sensitive building," is selected based on the following criteria: the microclimatic parameters surrounding this building are the most influenced at the same time by the UHI mitigation scenarios. ENVI-met results showed that the effect of the green, blue, and white models on the boundary conditions of the selected building is significant. Whereas for other buildings, we can notice that the attenuation effect of a scenario is clearly visible, while the impact of other scenarios is weak or almost negligible. This justifies the choice of the studied building, which is located close to a set of trees in the green model and near water sources in the blue model as shown in Fig. 17.7. The height of building is 28 m. The area of each floor is 225 m^2. The glass surfaces constitute 30% of each façade. All windows are single glazed with U value of 5 W/m^2.K. The shade coefficient of windows SHGC is 0.78. For infiltration rate, 1 air change per hour is assumed. The exteriors walls and floors comply with the data used in ENVI-met in terms of compositions and thermal properties. For internal gains, we assumed: 25 W/m^2 for lighting, 900 W as electrical equipment heat gain, and the number of occupants per floor is 20 persons with a sensible heat of 71.8 W/pers and a latent heat of 60.1 W/pers.

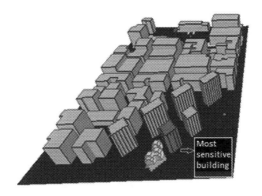

FIGURE 17.6

ENVI-met 3D model showing the "most sensitive building."

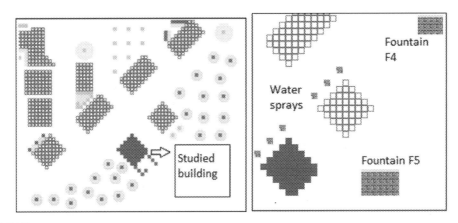

FIGURE 17.7

Studied building in the light black model (left). Studied building in the dark black model (right).

4. Results
4.1 Sensitive building cooling load

As there is a direct interaction between the urban heat island and the building energy performance, the effect of UHI mitigation scenarios on the building cooling load is presented in this section. Fig. 17.8 shows the hourly variation of the sensible load of the first floor. It was observed that the blue and green scenarios lead to a decrease in the sensible cooling load during the simulated 24 h compared to the initial case. While the white scenario caused an increase in the sensible load. For the white building scenario, where higher albedo is used only for the building envelope, the reduction in the sensible load is observed specially in the sunny hours.

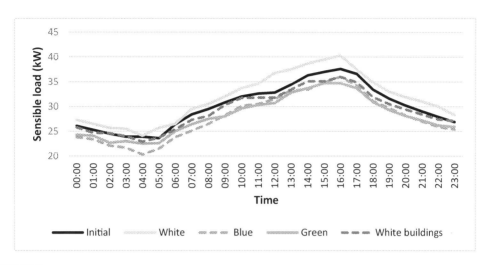

FIGURE 17.8

Hourly variation of sensible load.

At 16:00 when the sensible load is maximum, the green scenario produces a decrease of 2.9 kW (approximately 8%) compared to the base case. This reduction is mainly due to the shading effect created by the surrounding trees, which reduce the total solar radiation reaching the building. In the blue model, the sensible load at 16:00 is reduced by 4%. Indeed, the water sources decrease the ambient temperature by 1.2°C allowing the reduction of sensible load. This reduction is caused by the significant heat absorption required to evaporate the water droplets ejected by the fountains and the sprays in the air.

Conversely, the white scenario led to an increase of 7% in the sensible load at 16:00 (maximum load time in the base case). At noon, the maximum value of load increase is observed and reaches 4 kW (12%). The high-albedo materials used for ground and building facades contribute multireflections of the solar radiation causing the observed increased in the sensible load. By analyzing the load components, it is notable that windows transmission loads are essentially responsible of this increase; the radiations reflected by the high-albedo materials pass through the windows and then produce additional heat. Despite the freshness effect caused by the white model that led to a decrease in the ambient temperature, the use of high-albedo materials for all district's surfaces is not effective in term of cooling energy consumption. However, if the high-albedo materials are used only for the facades and roofs as described in the white buildings model, a reduction of the sensible load is observed due the reflecting effect of the light surfaces of the building. At 16:00, the load decrease is around 4%. The maximum reduction is observed at 15:00 and reaches 1.9 kW (5.2%).

For the latent load, as expected, the blue scenario leads to an increase in this load during the 24 h as shown in Fig. 17.9, due the rise in the relative humidity caused by the evaporation of the water droplets. The relative humidity in the blue model is higher than that in the base case and reaches an increase of 17% for some hours. At 16:00, water sources of the blue model contribute to 13% additional latent load. On the contrary, the effect of the other scenarios is small. Fig. 17.9 shows that the green model

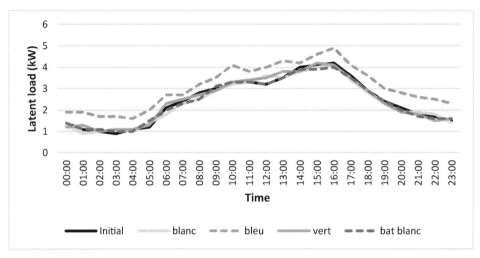

FIGURE 17.9

Hourly variation of latent load.

causes a slight increase in the latent load in some hours of the day, linked to the humidification effect of the evapotranspiration of the plants and trees.

Graphs of Fig. 17.10 revealed the variation of the total cooling load considered as the sum of latent and sensible loads. The green model seems the most efficient with a reduction of 7% at 16:00. Although the increase in the latent load is caused by the blue scenario, this variant still allows a 2% decrease in the total load at 16:00. For the white building scenario, the peak reduction in the total load

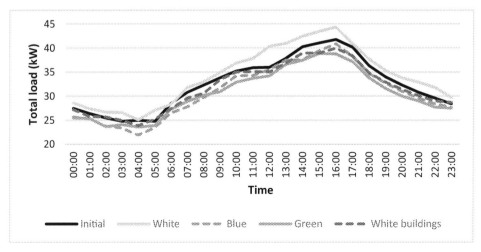

FIGURE 17.10

Hourly variation of total load.

Table 17.4 Cooling energy consumption integrated over the studied day.

Load	Initial model	White model	White buildings model	Blue model	Green model
Sensible (kWh)	720.7	761	701.3	667.5	673.9
Latent (kWh)	58.5	57.2	57.8	73.7	59
Total (kWh)	779.2	818.2	759.1	741.2	732.9

reach in some hours is 4%, while the white model contributes to an increase in the total load reaching of 6% at 16:00. The cooling energy consumption of each scenario over the whole day is shown in Table 17.4. The green model is the most efficient in terms of energy reduction with a difference of 46.2 kWh (6%). For the blue model where the water droplets evaporation is used as cooling process, the energy consumption related to the latent load is 15.2 kWh (26%) higher than the initial model. But in terms of total load, the freshness created by the water evaporation led to a 5% reduction of total energy consumption. On the other hand, the white building model mainly affects the sensible load and reduces the total energy consumption by 20 kWh (3%). Finally, the use of high-albedo surfaces for the buildings envelope and district soil in the white model allows an expected increase in the total energy consumption reaching 6%.

IHU reduction techniques do not only affect the cooling load of the first floor of the studied building, but also the other floors. The effect differs from one floor to another and depends also on the UHI reduction techniques used. Fig. 17.11 shows the sensible energy consumption of the entire building over the 24 h of the simulated day. The histogram shows that the blue scenario is the most efficient with a reduction of 297.7 kWh (5%). The water jets of the blue scenarios have reduced the average temperature surrounding the whole building. At the middle of the building, the maximum air temperature reduction is 1.4°C and is observed during the night. At the roof level, the air temperature is also reduced to reach a maximum value of 0.9°C. This decrease in the air temperature around each

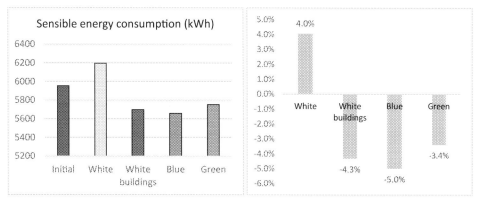

FIGURE 17.11

Sensible cooling energy consumption of the entire building throughout the studied day.

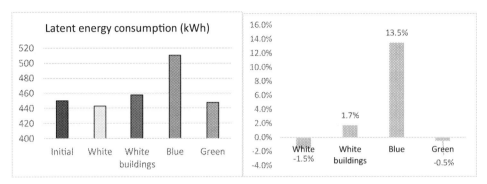

FIGURE 17.12

Latent cooling energy consumption of the entire building throughout the studied day.

floor of the building leads to the reduction in the sensible load. Concerning the latent load, it is quite clear that the energy consumption of the entire building related to the latent load is increased. The deviation from the initial case is around 13%. The first three floors of the buildings are the most affected by this rise of load, since the humidity surrounding these floors is significantly increased due the evaporation of phenomenon. The effect of the blue scenario on the latent loads of the top floors is almost negligible. For the other scenarios and as expected, the effect on the latent loads is small as shown in Fig. 17.12. Despite the increase in the latent load produced by the blue scenario, the total energy consumption is reduced by 237.1 kWh (3.7%) as indicated in Fig. 17.13.

Figs. 17.11 and 17.13 showed the potential of the green model in the reduction of sensible and total energy consumption, which reaches respectively 201.9 kWh and 204.1 kWh (a percentage of 4%). We recall that this reduction of energy is due to the decrease in ambient temperature and to the shading effect created by the trees. But this reduction is mainly observed in the first four floors since the trees height does not exceed 15 m. For the upper floors, the reduction is minor since the ambient temperature reduction is small and solar radiation is not masked.

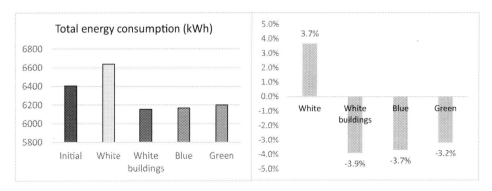

FIGURE 17.13

Total cooling energy consumption of the entire building throughout the studied day.

Unlike other models, the white model contributes to the increase in the cooling energy consumption (4%) showing that this scenario is not at all efficient in the energy saving. Hence, this variant should be optimized since the use of high-albedo materials in a random manner does not present an effective solution to limit the cooling loads, especially under the Lebanese climate and for an urban morphology such as "Dora."

Finally, Fig. 17.13 shows that white building model is the most efficient in the cooling energy saving. The reduction value is 250 kWh (4%). By observing the potential reduction at the top floor level, the reduction is important with a difference of 128 kWh (12%) between the white building model and the initial model. Consequently, this significant reduction at the top floor due the high-albedo material used for roof led the white building model to be the most efficient at the cooling energy saving level.

4.2 Reference building

In this section, we discuss the effect of UHI mitigation scenarios on the cooling effect of another building called "Reference building," which is located more in the center of the neighborhood. The aim is to highlight how the impact of the proposed scenarios on the cooling load varies from one building to another. Fig. 17.14 shows the position of the "reference building" in the neighborhood. The surface area of each floor is 1180 m², which is much larger than the sensitive building. The glass surfaces constitute 30% of each façade. The assumed number of occupants per floor is 85 persons. 4500 W is the electrical equipment heat gain. For the thermal properties, ventilation air flow rate, lighting load, and people heat emission, we considered the same conditions as used for the sensible building.

Figs. 17.15 and 17.16 show respectively the sensible and total energy consumption (kWh) of the first floor of the reference buildings. The results show that in this case, the blue model is the most efficient in the reduction of energy consumption with a difference of 246 kWh (8.7%) and 168.8 kWh

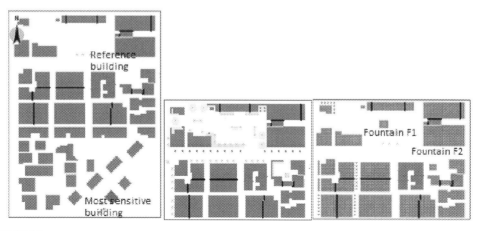

FIGURE 17.14

Location of the reference building in the initial model (left), in the green model (center) and in the blue model (right).

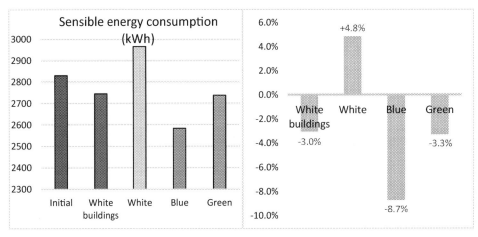

FIGURE 17.15

Sensible energy consumption for the air conditioning of the first floor of the reference building for the studied day for each model (left) and the percentage change from to the initial model (right).

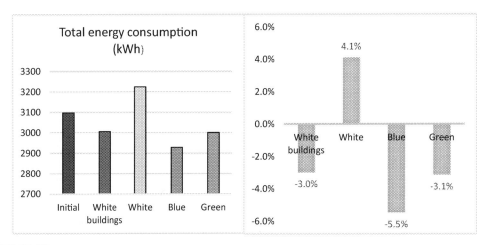

FIGURE 17.16

Total air conditioning energy consumption of the first floor of the reference building for the studied day for each model (left) and the percentage change from to the initial model (right).

(5.5%) for the total load. Regarding the latent loads, the blue variant leads always to an increase of 77.2 kWh (29%) compared to the initial case due the high humidity produced by the implemented water sources. For the other models, the effect on the latent loads is almost negligible. Unlike the sensitive building, the green model is not the most favorable and the reduction in the total energy consumption does not exceed 3.1%. This difference was around 6% in the sensitive building. In fact, the trees create shade on the half of the sensitive building facades, whereas in the case of the reference building the shadow effect is observed on approximately 25% of the exterior surfaces. Therefore, the difference in the vegetation impact on the cooling load is observed between the two studied building. In the case of the white building, the total energy saving is almost similar to the green scenario with a value of 3%. The reflective effect of the high-albedo material led to this decrease. Similarly to the case of the sensitive building, the white model led to an increase in the sensible and total loads and, thus, an increase in the energy consumption. The multiple solar radiations are caused by the high albedo of model surfaces (asphalt roads, pavements, building facades). The reflective radiations pass through the building windows and contribute to the increase in the cooling load.

5. Discussion

This study has presented computational simulations to assess the potential of UHI mitigation strategies on the building cooling load in a dense district of Lebanon. The above results led to some preliminary conclusions. First, the evaporative cooling effect of the water sources showed the highest potential in the reduction of sensible load despite the low wind speed in the studied case. In fact, the blue scenario is able to reduce the ambient temperature to reach punctually $5°C$ with a spatial extension of the freshness effect in the direction of the wind. But at the same time, the evaporation of water droplets ejected by water sprays and fountains contributes to a significant increase in the latent load caused by the increase of humidity. Therefore, for the type of buildings that require a high rate of fresh air, the implementation of water sources in the urban area will lead to a high energy consumption related to latent load. Second, cooling load of buildings is highly affected by the amount of solar radiations that reach building facades. The random use of high-albedo materials for district surfaces and buildings increases the air-conditioning energy consumption. The main cause is the multireflection phenomenon, which intensifies the amount of radiation passing through the buildings windows. Therefore, the adoption of high-albedo materials should be only limited to the buildings' facades and roofs in order to improve the cooling load in summer. Third, the results showed that the green model based on the implementation of trees creates a freshness effect during the warmer season, which contributes to a decrease in the cooling load. The potential of this scenario is directly related to the masking effect created by the trees to avoid solar radiation reaching building surfaces. Finally, the impact of UHI mitigation strategies on the building cooling load depends on the position of building in the studied area. The place of the implemented UHI mitigation devices in relation to the building strongly affects the potential of each scenario to save cooling energy consumption.

In addition, we should point out on the importance of the microclimatic simulations prior to building design and cooling load calculation. The integration of UHI limitation strategies could strongly affect the cooling load of a building by saving energy consumption and decrease of CO_2 emission.

6. Conclusion

This paper evaluates the impact of UHI mitigations on the air-conditioning load of buildings in the context of a dense district of Lebanon. The method relies on the coupling of the microclimatic model ENVI-met to the building energy simulation tool HAP. The proposed models used in the evaluation were based on the integration of green surfaces, water sources, and modification of albedo surfaces. The proposed method is capable to quantify the impact of the scenarios to reduce the cooling load. The analysis is not limited to the sensible loads, but also the latent loads are also evaluated. The impact on the latent load is highly observed in the blue scenario where the water sources are implemented. The results showed that blue scenario contributes to contradictory effect by increasing the latent load and decreasing the sensible load. Therefore, in terms of building energy performance, the adoption of the blue scenario is satisfactory in the type of building where the ventilation exchange rate is very low. In addition, the green areas could also improve the energy performance of building and lead to saving energy consumption. The potential of this scenario is highly related to the position of the trees in relation to the building facades. In contrary to the other scenarios, the white scenario is not a reliable solution for reducing cooling load. This scenario increases the amount of radiation entering the buildings windows, and this contributes to an increase in the sensible load. The proposed method in this paper could be useful for energy building designer and urban planning.

References

Adnot, J., Dominguez, S.A., Santamouris, M., 2004. Cooling the cities : rafraîchir les villes. Presse des Mines, p. 280.

Akbari, H., Bretz, S., Kurn, D.M., Hanford, J., 1997. Peak power and cooling energy savings of high-albedo roofs. Energy Build. 25 (2), 117−126.

Ashrae, 1997. ASHRAE Handbook 1997, Fundamentals.

Bouyer, J., Inard, C., Musy, M., 2011. Microclimatic coupling as a solution to improve building energy simulation in an urban context. Energy Build. 43, 1549−1559.

Bozonnet, E., 2006. Les microclimats urbains et la demande énergétique du bâti. In: XXIVemes Rencontres Universitaires de Génie Civil 2006 - Prix Jeunes Chercheurs.

Carrier, 2015. Hourly Analysis Program. Quick Reference Guide. Hap v4.91, ninth ed.

Chen, H., Ooka, R., Kato, S., 2008. Study on optimum design method for pleasant outdoor thermal environment using genetic algorithms (GA) and coupled simulation of convection, radiation and conduction. Build. Environ. 43 (1), 18−30.

Crawley, D., Lawrie, L., Pedersen, C., Winkelmann, F., 2000. EnergyPlus: energy simulation program. Ashrae J. 42 (4), 49−56.

Djedjig, R., Bozonnet, E., Belarbi, R., 2015. Experimental study of the urban microclimate mitigation potential of green roofs and green walls in street canyons. Int. J. Low Carbon Technol. 10 (1), 34−44.

Doya, M., Bozonnet, E., Allard, F., 2012. Experimental measurement of cool facades' performance in a dense urban environment. Energy Build. 55, 42−50.

Elnabawi, M.H., Hamza, N., Dudek, S., 2016. Thermal perception of outdoor urban spaces in the hot aridregion of Cairo, Egypt. Sustain. Cities Soc. 22, 136−145.

Ghaffarianhoseini, A., Berardi, U., Ghaffarianhoseini, A., 2015. Thermal performance Characteristics of unshaded courtyards in hot and humid climates. Build. Environ. 87, 154−168.

Gros, A., Bozonnet, E., Inard, C., Musy, M., 2016. Simulation tools to assess microclimate and building energy − a case study on the design of a new district. Energy Build. 114, 112−122.

Huttner, S., 2012. Further Development and Application of the 3D Microclimate Simulation ENVI-Met. Thèse de doctorat de l'université Johannes Gutenberg, Mainz.

Kaloustian, N., Diab, Y., 2015. Effects of urbanization on the urban heat island in Beirut. Urban Clim. 14, 154−165.

Kaloustian, N., Aouad, D., Battista, G., Zinzi, M., 2018. Leftover spaces for the mitigation of urban overheating in municipal Beirut. Climate 6 (3), 68–84.

Kolokotroni, M., Ren, X., Davies, M., Mavrogianni, A., 2012. London's urban heat island: impact on current and future energy consumption in office buildings. Energy Build. 47, 302–311.

Lahme, E., Bruse, M., 2002. Microclimatic effects of a small urban park in densely built–up areas: measurements and model simulations. In: The European Commission in the 5th Framework Program under the Contract EVK4-CT-2000-00041 (BUGS).

Lahme, E., Bruse, M., 2003. Microclimatic effects of a small urban park in densely built-up areas: measurements and model simulations. In: Fifth International Conference on Urban Climate, ICUC-5, Lodz, Poland.

Lam, T.N.T., Wan, K.K., Wong, S., Lam, J.C., 2010. Impact of climate change on commercial sector air conditioning energy consumption in subtropical Hong Kong. Appl. Energy 87 (7), 2321–2327.

Lu, N., Taylor, T., Jiang, W., Jin, C., James Correia, J., Leung, L.R., Wong, P.C., 2010. Climate change impacts on residential and commercial loads in the western U.S. Grid. IEEE Transact. Power Syst. 25 (1), 480–488.

Maleki, A., Mahdavi, A., 2016. Evaluation of urban heat islands mitigation strategies using 3-dimensional urban micro-climate model ENVI-met. As. J. Civil Eng. (BHRC) 17, 357–371.

Salata, F., Golasia, L., De Lieto Vollaro, R., De Lieto Vollaro, A., 2016. Urban microclimate and outdoor thermal comfort. A proper procedure to fit ENVI-met simulation outputs to experimental data. Sustain. Cities Soc. 26, 318–343.

Santamouris, M., Papanikolaou, N., Livada, I., Koronakis, I., Georgakis, A.A.C., Assimakopoulos, D., 2001. On the impact of urban climate on the energy consumption of buildings. Sol. Energy 70 (3), 201–2016.

Wang, X., Chen, D., Ren, Z., 2010. Assessment of climate change impact on residential building heating and cooling energy requirement in Australia. Build. Environ. 45 (7), 1663–1682.

Wang, Y., Beradi, U., Akbari, H., 2016. Comparing the effects of urban heat island mitigation strategies for Tornoto, Canada. Energy Build. 114, 2–19.

Wilde, P.d., Tian, W., 2010. Predicting the performance of an office under climate change: a study of metrics, sensitivity and zonal resolution. Energy Build. 42 (10), 1674–1684.

Yang, X., Zhao, L., Bruse, M., Meng, Q., 2012. An integrated simulation method for building energy performance assessment in urban environments. Energy Build. 54, 243–251.

Index

Note: 'Page numbers followed by 'f' indicate figures those followed by 't' indicate tables and 'b' indicate boxes.'

Printed in the United States
by Baker & Taylor Publisher Services